RODALE'S
ILLUSTRATED ENCYCLOPEDIA OF

GARDENING
AND
LANDSCAPING
TECHNIQUES

Barbara W. Ellis, Editor

Contributing writers:

Diane Bilderback
Steven Davis
Barbara W. Ellis
Sarah Fitz-Hugh
Judith Haraburda
Sandra F. Ladendorf

Rose Lounsbury
Lynn M. Lynch
Tovah Martin
Kristine S. Medic
Jerry A. Minnich
Margaret Parke

Barbara D. Pleasant
Sally Roth
Holly Shimazu
Susan Weaver

Rodale Press, Emmaus, Pennsylvania

Printed in the United States of America on acid-free, recycled paper

∞

Editor in Chief: William Gottlieb
Managing Editor: Margaret Lydic Balitas
Senior Editor: Barbara W. Ellis
Associate Editor: Fern Marshall Bradley
Research Associate: Heidi A. Stonehill
Editorial/Administrative Assistant: Stacy Brobst
Copy Editors: Sally Roth, Nancy Bailey
Book and Cover Design: Denise Mirabello
Book Layout: Greg Imhoff
Interior Illustrations: Robin Brickman
                         Ruth Bush
                         John Carlance
                         Jack Crane
                         Greg Imhoff
Front Cover Illustration: Robin Brickman
Back Cover Illustrations: Ruth Bush *(left)*,
                           Jack Crane *(right)*

If you have any questions or comments concerning this book, please
write:
   Rodale Press
   Book Reader Service
   33 East Minor Street
   Emmaus, PA 18098

Library of Congress Cataloging-in-Publication Data

Rodale's illustrated encyclopedia of gardening and landscaping
   techniques / Barbara W. Ellis : writers, Diane Bilderback . . . [et
al.].
        p.   cm.
   Includes bibliographical references.
   ISBN 0-87857-898-6 hardcover
   1. Organic gardening.   2. Gardening.   3. Landscape gardening.
I. Ellis, Barbara W.   II. Bilderback, Diane E.
SB453.5.R64   1990
635—dc20   90-31521
                                                  CIP

Distributed in the book trade by St. Martin's Press

2 4 6 8 10 9 7 5 3 1   hardcover

Contents

PART 1
The Basics

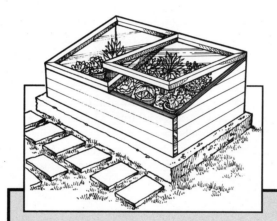

Working the Soil

Removing Sod

The first step in developing a new perennial island, vegetable garden, or rose bed is to remove the sod or other plants that are growing on the site you've selected. Of course, before you take shovel in hand, you'll need to consider how the new planting will fit into the overall design of your garden. The site you select may be dictated by the location of your house or other nearby structures, shade from a neighbor's tree, or the size of your lot. You'll need to consider factors like soil drainage, available light, air flow, soil type, orientation, existing trees, and the slope of the land. If you have a particular group of plants or type of planting in mind, you'll need to think about where they would be most likely to thrive. An herb garden, for example, is best off in a spot with full sun and well-drained soil. It's also a good idea to think about how the garden will look from inside your house. With a little planning, you can "paint" attractive views with perennial borders, ornamental shrubs, or annuals that you'll be able to enjoy whether you're outside or indoors. (For more information, see "Garden Design" on page 172.)

To carve a new garden out of an existing lawn, the first step is to outline the shape of the garden. The pattern for a traditional rectangular rose bed or vegetable garden can be marked out easily with small stakes and twine. Developing the attractive flowing curves essential to a free-form bed or a garden that hugs the shape of a walk or driveway takes a little more thought. The easiest way to visualize a free-form garden island or the curved front edge of a perennial bed is to experiment with a garden hose. Lay the hose on the ground to mark the outline of the bed, and then reposition it until you're pleased with the shape it forms. Then mark the pattern so you'll be able to follow the proper contour. Use a sprinkling of lime, a row of labels, or short pieces of orange surveyor's tape skewered on four-inch nails pushed into the ground for marking.

Dig, Don't Till

With the boundaries of your new garden defined, you can then remove the grass. Attempting to use a rotary tiller for this job is a mistake. Most tillers cannot tear through a healthy stand of lawn grass; thick matted roots and compacted soil are generally too much for them. Even if you do succeed in tilling the grass under, the tiller's action will leave tiny bits of grass rhizomes mixed with the soil. These will quickly sprout, and you'll end up with a new garden choked with weeds.

It's best to eliminate the grass completely from the start. A healthy stand of lawn grass is a thick, dense mat of leaves and roots. An easy way to dig it up is to cut it from below and roll it up, just as professional turf growers would handle it at a sod farm. Using a sharp edging tool or a straight-edged spade, cut along the outline of the garden you are planning. Then divide the area into strips that are easy to handle. Use an edging tool or spade to cut under the sod. Be sure to cut about two inches deep so that the grass crowns and runners will roll up easily.

This job moves quickly with two people working. One uses the sharp

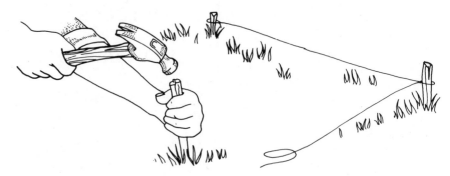

If you are removing sod from a square bed, use stakes and string to mark off the edges of the new garden.

A lawn edger or sharp spade cuts easily through lawn grass. Cutting and removing small pieces of sod one at a time is the best method for a gardener working alone.

If you have a helper, it's easy to roll up sod. Just cut the sod 2 inches below the surface and have a helper roll it up as you go.

SOD SENSE

Don't just throw away the sod you've dug to make your garden bed. Use it to repair any worn or unhealthy-looking spots on your lawn. All you need to do is remove the damaged turf, aerate and improve the soil, press the new sod in place, and water until it becomes established. Since sod you've dug is composed of the same grass or grasses as the rest of your lawn, it will match perfectly. Also, it will usually be fresher and healthier than sod you can buy.

If you don't have any spots in need of repair, you can also discard the sod you've dug by adding it to an existing compost heap or stacking it upside down to decompose in an out-of-the-way spot. Should any grass shoots appear, cover the stack with black plastic. Or you can turn the stack occasionally to make sure all the grass rhizomes decompose. When you're done, you'll have a pile of humus-rich soil to return to the garden.

tool, angled so its handle is near the ground, to shove under the sod and cut it. The other rolls it back. A gardener working alone will find it's easier to cut out small, manageable pieces, one at a time.

A Stitch in Time

Once you've cleared away the sod, work through the soil with a garden fork or shovel and remove any remaining grass rhizomes. It's also important to dig and discard the roots of other weeds such as dandelions. Weeds with taproots often will pull right through the sod when it's being rolled up. These roots will quickly sprout and start to grow if they're not removed, and you'll end up creating a weeding project rather than a flourishing garden. A little extra time spent sifting through the soil looking for weed roots will save you hours of work later. After you've taken out as many weeds as possible, it's time to prepare the bed by adding organic matter to the soil and tilling it to get it ready for planting.

Use a fork to work through the soil and remove weed roots and rhizomes.

Spread a layer of compost, well-rotted manure, or other organic matter over the newly cleared bed and work it in.

3

Making a Garden Bed

Whether you're making a new garden bed or renovating an old one, the first step is making the site the best it can be for the plants you want to grow. Most home gardeners rarely begin with an ideal site for their gardens. Instead, they pick the best place available and then modify it. Getting a bed ready for planting may be an easy process or a time-consuming one. You may need to cut away and remove sod or clear the area of brush, vines, large rocks, or debris. You also may want to consider adding a fence or a hedge to provide an attractive background and to act as a windbreak. Almost certainly, you'll need to improve the soil.

Start with the Soil

By the time you've cleared the new bed of grass or weeds, and you've worked the soil enough to remove the roots and rhizomes, you'll have started to get a feel for what type of soil you have. Whether it's predominantly clay, sand, or loam, it will be improved by digging or tilling and adding a generous amount of organic material. It's a good idea to get a soil test and learn more about the texture and structure of your soil before you till and plant. (For more information on these topics, see "Knowing Your Soil" on page 12.)

Before you start to dig, take a moment to test for soil moisture. Grab a handful of soil and clench it in your fist. If it forms a hard, wet ball that doesn't crumble easily, your soil is too wet to work. Working wet soil destroys its structure, so wait a few days and try again. On the other hand, hard, dry soil is difficult to dig. You'll make the job easier if you thoroughly moisten the bed with water and wait a day or two before digging.

The easiest way to prepare a new bed is to use a rotary tiller to break up the soil and work in organic matter. However, tillers can pack wet soil and destroy its structure. Be especially careful that your soil is dry enough to work before tilling.

To hand dig a bed, bring out your spade, garden fork, and a grading rake. Starting at one end, mark a strip across the new bed and dig a trench about the depth of a spade's blade. Toss the soil from this trench into a wheelbarrow. Use your garden fork to loosen the subsoil at the bottom of the trench. Then, place a layer of compost, leaf mold, or other organic material at the bottom of the trench and begin to dig an adjacent trench, tossing the soil from strip B into the empty strip A.

Thoroughly mix the soil and the compost with the fork and then repeat the process, strip by strip, for the entire length of the garden. Once you reach the end, use the soil from the first strip to fill in the final trench.

After you are finished digging, lightly rake the entire bed to level it out and remove any rocks, roots, or other debris that have worked to the surface.

Amend, Amend, Amend

Native topsoils differ tremendously throughout the country. And soil conditions can vary greatly from garden to garden. A gardener in Iowa may have several feet of rich loam, while one in Connecticut may have to sift each shovelful through mesh screen, losing almost 50 percent of the soil's volume to rock debris. A Californian may be dealing with adobe soil; a gardener in the Southeast may have impoverished red clay. Both may literally need pickaxes to break the surface of these compact materials. Coastal gardeners often have extremely sandy soils that do not hold water or nutrients. Gardeners in new housing developments may dig down only to find that all the topsoil has been carted away, leaving them with nothing but clayey subsoil.

If you've removed nearly as much rock as you have soil, or if you had nearly all clay to begin with, bringing in purchased topsoil may be the answer. In some cases, raised beds filled with purchased loam may be the best alternative. Whatever soil type or situation, to create a healthy garden bed, you'll need to amend the soil with plenty of organic matter—compost, rotted leaves, sawdust, or manure—both at planting time and regularly thereafter. Organic matter in the soil will improve the structure, drainage, and soil microorganism populations.

Seasonal Considerations

While it's possible to prepare a garden bed at any time of year, the best time to dig the soil and add organic matter is in the fall. Studies have shown that winter freezing and thawing actually improve soils, and spring tilling would eliminate this benefit. Fall preparation provides time for manure and other organic materials you have added to the bed to begin breaking down before planting time. Also, fall preparation means you'll be ready for early spring crops as soon as the soil can be worked in the spring, because the bed simply needs a raking and it is ready to plant.

BACK-SAVING ADVICE

Preparing garden beds can be hard work, and it's all too easy to end up on the couch with a hot-water bottle clutched to your back. You can minimize the strain on your back by learning to dig correctly. It's a simple, three-step process.

1. Drive the spade or shovel into the ground in an upright position, using the weight of your body to cut cleanly through the soil.

2. Bend at the knees—not just from the waist—as you slide one hand down on the shaft of shovel to get ready to lift the load of soil.

3. Each time you lift, straighten your knees to help raise the load and keep the strain off your back.

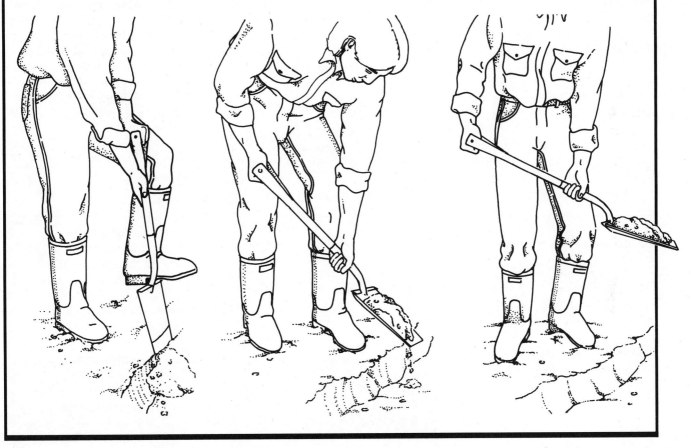

Making a Raised Bed

Raised beds are the perfect solution for gardeners with difficult soils such as poorly drained clay. With time and plenty of effort, you can turn a heavy clay or adobe into a friable loam rich in organic matter. But it's easier and quicker to build raised beds, filling them with humus-rich soil that drains well. With raised beds, you can in-stantly create the perfect environment for the plants you want to grow.

Raised beds offer an added plus for the older gardener. It is much easier to sit on the edge of a sturdy bed and weed than it is to get up and down to work a ground-level bed. Raised beds even can be designed to be accessible from a wheelchair. And carefully designed, multilayered beds can create a charming small garden for a town house.

Selecting Materials

The simplest way to make a raised bed is to build up a 6- to 8-inch mound of soil in the shape you desire. Mounded beds have sloping sides and are flat or slightly rounded on top, but they don't have a permanent frame to keep the mound from gradually washing away. More permanent raised beds are generally built with a frame of rocks, bricks, concrete blocks, railroad ties, or landscaping timbers. Frames can also be constructed with cedar or preservative-treated posts stuck vertically in the ground around the bed. A frame also serves to keep lawn grass and weeds from invading the bed.

If your raised beds will be near or beside the house, then it's important that the framework you select complement the material and style of the building. The beds become an architectural element of the building. For example, wooden railroad ties or landscape timbers work well with a house siding of cedar shakes, but a formal brick house calls for compatible brick beds.

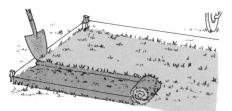

When building a raised bed, mark off the area and then remove any lawn grass or weeds.

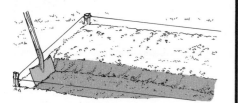

Loosen the soil and remove any remaining weed roots or rhizomes.

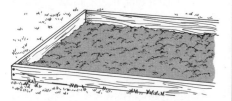

You can either build a frame with boards nailed together at the corners, as shown, or use landscape ties held in place with stakes or lengths of pipes driven in the ground.

For raised beds in out-of-the-way spots, concrete blocks or even broken-up pieces of concrete sidewalk make acceptable frames. Pressure-treated boards held in position with stakes driven in the ground is another easy and satisfactory way to frame a raised bed.

Cost is another important consideration. Hiring a skilled mason to lay a serpentine brick bed will be expensive; a bed constructed of landscape timbers can be a much less costly, do-it-yourself project. In the end, only you can determine what type of bed will be right for your ambitions, budget, health, and needs.

Matching Soil Mixes

Raised beds are essentially container gardening on a larger scale. The soil recipe you use to fill them can be matched to the specific needs of the plants you want to grow. For a raised bed designed for rhododendrons, azaleas, and other ericaceous plants, an acid mix of oak leaf compost, bark, topsoil, and just a little sand is ideal. For general gardening, you can select a commercial mix or a combination of topsoil, mushroom soil or peat humus with some sand, compost, and

well-rotted manure. The mix you select, and especially the organic materials you choose, will depend on what is available in your part of the country. After your bed is prepared, have the soil tested to see if you need to add any nutrients or lime to your mixture.

Rich, well-drained soil is the key to success with most plants. You can amend the soil you have with plenty of organic matter or bring in purchased topsoil.

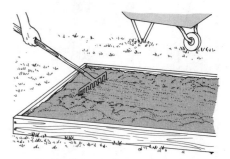

Once the bed has been filled, rake it smooth to get it ready for planting.

RAISED UP RIGHT

Many gardeners have turned to low raised beds as the optimum way to raise vegetables. This method saves space, is economical in its use of water and fertilizer, and is extremely productive. Best of all, the soil is never compacted by foot traffic because the beds are designed to be worked from either side. By building beds narrow enough so you can reach the center without stepping into the bed—from 3 to 5 feet wide, depending on how far you can reach—you can greatly reduce soil compaction and increase yields.

Once you've prepared the soil, you can space the plants evenly throughout the bed. You won't need to allow for conventional rows because you'll be tending the plants from the side. (Be sure to use proper spacing between plants, so they won't be overly crowded.)

In addition to increased yields, spacing plants in this way provides another benefit. By growing the vegetables closer together than suggested for typical row plantings, the leaves weave together and shade the ground. This keeps most weeds from germinating and also helps conserve soil moisture.

Double Digging

The best preparation for garden beds —especially those that won't be replanted every year—is double digging. Double digging involves digging up and incorporating soil amendments such as organic matter into two layers of the soil—generally to a depth of about 1½ feet, or twice the height of a shovel blade. It's a lot of work, but the results are well worth the effort.

Double digging is an excellent way to improve any area of the garden plagued with poor drainage. Beds that have been double-dug drain well, and deeply incorporating organic matter encourages plant roots to penetrate deeper in search of water and nutrients. The technique also improves soil aeration and provides plants with a deep, rich soil high in organic matter.

Although you can double-dig any garden bed, this technique is most often used when planting perennial borders, rose beds, or asparagus patches—any planting that is going to remain undisturbed for several years.

Start by marking off a 2-foot strip at one end of the bed. Then remove the topsoil from this strip to the depth of one spade—8 or 9 inches. Place the soil in a wheelbarrow or pile it at the opposite end of the bed on a piece of plastic. Loosen and turn over the soil at the bottom of the trench to the depth of another spade so that the trench is about 16 to 18 inches deep.

Mix a generous amount of compost, humus, manure, decomposed sawdust, or other organic material into the soil at the bottom of the trench. Then start a new trench next to the first by digging to the depth of one spade and dumping the first layer of topsoil on top of the first trench. As you fill in the first strip with soil from the top of the second, be sure to add organic matter here as well. Then dig and amend the bottom layer of the second trench. Slowly work your way down the entire length of the bed, and end by adding organic matter to the topsoil from the first strip you dug and using it to fill the top layer on the last strip.

An alternative method for working in organic matter is to amend only the soil in the bottom layer of each strip as you dig. Then, after you finish double-digging, cover the garden bed with a layer of compost or organic matter and dig it all in. This method is easy if you have a tiller and can simply till the compost into the soil. If you're double-digging a bed for annual vegetables, it's not necessary to add organic matter to the bottom layer, as most vegetable crop roots won't penetrate that deeply.

Either way, the end result will be a bed that has been thoroughly prepared to a depth of approximately 1½ feet and has a rich organic content.

To start double-digging a bed, dig an 8- to 9-inch-deep trench the length of one end of the garden. Place the soil you've removed in a wheelbarrow or at the other end of the bed.

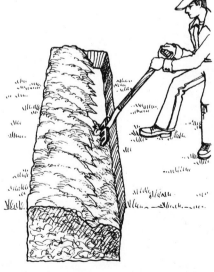

Next, use a spading fork or shovel to loosen the soil at the bottom of the trench to another spade's depth. Work in organic matter. Dig a second 8- to 9-inch trench next to the first, using the soil to fill the first. Loosen the soil at the bottom of the second trench.

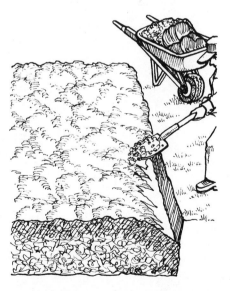

Continue digging trenches, using the soil to fill the previous trench, until you have dug the entire bed. Use the soil removed from the first trench to fill the last.

Terracing

Building terraces is an ancient method of turning a steep slope into flat, usable garden space. Terraces have festooned Himalayan mountainsides in Nepal for aeons, and Incas built elaborate terraces centuries ago in the mountains of Peru for potatoes and grain. But this gardening technique is as useful in contemporary American gardens as it was in ancient times. If you have a slope in your yard that is eroding and unattractive, consider building terraced beds to hold the soil, add beauty to your yard, and allow you to raise flowers and vegetables in an otherwise useless space.

One option for terracing is to hold landscape ties in place behind spikes or wooden posts driven into the ground.

Materials

The most noticeable component of any terrace is the material used to frame the beds. Several different materials can be used for the retaining walls of terraced garden beds. Native stone works well, as does broken concrete, which gives a natural appearance on the broken surfaces where the aggregate shows. You may have plenty of stone available on your land, and concrete may be obtained at no cost—any contractor tearing up old concrete sidewalks will likely be delighted to have it hauled away. However, pressure-treated, 6-by-6-inch landscape ties probably are the easiest material to work with. You can buy them at any lumber yard and they are reasonably priced. For a quick and casual terraced garden, you can sink posts and then stack landscaping ties against them.

While it is easy for amateur gardeners to build low walls successfully, any retaining wall must be sturdy enough to withstand the pressure of wet earth behind it. Stone should be laid with the largest rocks on the bottom, working to smaller, lighter ones at the top. A rock wall should also be built "on a batter"—it should have a receding upward slope. Dry wall construction, using no mortar, is particularly attractive when nooks and crannies are planted with campanulas, aubrietas, lewisias, thymes, and other attractive mat-forming plants as the wall is being constructed. (For detailed instructions on how to build a stone wall, see "Building a Stone Wall" on page 193.)

If you need to build any wall higher than 3 feet, consult a landscape architect or an expert stonemason, depending on the material you've chosen. A high wall is more of an engineering feat than a low one and must be able to withstand the considerable pressure from the earth behind it.

As you build your terrace, remember that you will need to leave an occasional weep hole at the base of each level of the terraced garden. It is helpful to put some coarse gravel or cinders in the bed just behind these drainage holes.

Laying Out the Terrace

Basically, there are two methods of constructing a terrace. You can *fill* or you can *cut and fill*. To make filled terraces, you bring in garden soil from some other location to create stepped beds. To make cut-and-filled terraces, you dig stepped beds into the slope. Dirt from the back half of each bed is used to fill the front of the bed. Although cut-and-filled terraces require

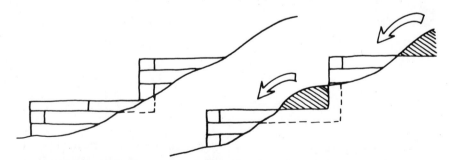

Filled terraces (left) are constructed by building the frames and then bringing in soil to fill them. Cut-and-filled terraces (right) are constructed by using the soil at the back of each terrace to fill the front.

more digging, you will need little or no additional soil to fill the beds.

The first step in building either type of terrace is to define the area. Pound a stake into the ground at each corner of the area you wish to terrace and then run string around the perimeter of the project at ground level. Then, in order to plan the series of beds you're going to construct, you need to determine the rise and run of the slope.

The rise is the difference in height between the top and bottom of the slope. To measure it, stand at the bottom of the terrace. Put a tape measure on the ground and pull the tape up until you can sight horizon-

tally past it to the string marking the top of the area. The measurement on the tape is the rise.

For slopes where the rise is greater than your height, measure the hillside in increments. Start at the top of the slope, and walk downhill along one of the layout strings. Watch the top corner stake as you descend: When it is about at eye level, stop and sight across a tape measure as before. Note the amount, and drive a stake at that point. Walk down the slope until the stake is at eye level, and measure again. Continue until you reach the bottom. Add all of the measurements together to determine the total rise.

To measure the run of the slope, ask a helper to hold the end of the tape at one of the top corner stakes. Walk down the slope along a layout string, and keep raising the tape measure so that the tape remains horizontal. Note where the tape crosses the bottom string. That measurement is your run. If you had to measure the rise of the slope in sections, then measure the run in sections, too.

Once you know the rise and run, you can determine how many terraced beds you will need. First, decide how long you want each bed to be, then divide the total run by the length of the beds to learn the number of beds. If your run is 100 feet, for example, and you want beds 20 feet long, you will need five beds (100 ÷ 20 = 5).

Once you have determined the dimensions of each bed, mark the front edge of each with stakes and string.

Building a Filled Terrace

The methods for building a filled terrace and a cut-and-filled terrace vary slightly. The cut-and-filled terrace is discussed later.

Before you can begin building, you'll need to know the rise of each bed in the terrace. The rise of a filled-terrace bed is simply the number of beds divided by the total rise of the terrace. In a five-bed terrace with a total rise of 5 feet, for example, the rise of each bed is 1 foot (5 ÷ 5 = 1).

A terrace begins with a series of trenches. The first layer of ties sits in these trenches, acting as a foundation for the rest of the ties. Dig a trench an inch deep for the front wall. The trench must be level; check it as you work with a long carpenter's level. Lay ties into the trench to form the first layer of the front wall.

Now dig trenches for the ties that will form the sides of the terrace. Begin at a front corner and dig a trench level with the bottom of the front trench. Dig your way uphill, creating another flat, level trench.

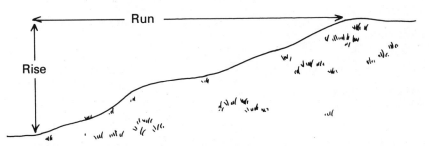

The rise of a slope is the height from the bottom of the hill to the crest. Run is the horizontal distance from the base to the crest.

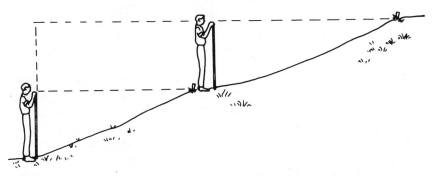

You can determine the rise, or height, of a slope by measuring up the hill in increments.

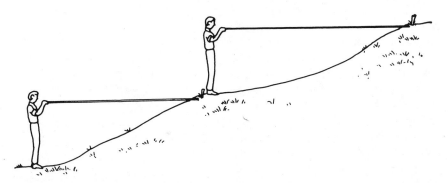

The run is measured in much the same way, by measuring the distance in increments and adding them together.

You've reached the uphill end of the trench when the trench is an inch deeper than the thickness of your landscaping ties. Cut a tie to the length of the trench, and put it in place.

Continue trenching up the hill. The bottom of each new trench is level with the top of the tie immediately downhill. Each trench ends when it is an inch deeper than the tie is thick.

After you've laid the first layer of ties, spike them into the ground with 10-inch galvanized spikes. To keep the ties from splitting and the spikes from bending, drill a $5/16$-inch pilot hole through the ties. Drive the spike into the pilot hole.

With the first layer of ties in, build the first bed. Building with ties is much like building with bricks: The side and front ties must overlap each other at the corners, as shown in the illustration below.

Start at the bottom of the hill and build one bed at a time. Measure from the outside of the front tie to the first step in the sidewall. Cut a tie or ties long enough to fit this dimension. Be sure each tie will overlap the tie downhill by at least 6 inches. Put the tie or ties in place so that the end of the side tie overlaps the front tie. Spike the ties in place at each point of overlap as before.

Fasten corners and seams between ties with 10-inch galvanized spikes. A tie across the back of the terrace forms the front of the next terrace.

Continue adding terraces up the hill until you've reached the top of the slope. Since these are filled terraces, they will be filled with soil brought in after construction is complete.

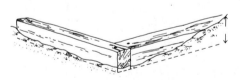

When laying the ties for the sides of each terrace, dig back into the slope until the trench is 1 inch deeper than the thickness of the ties.

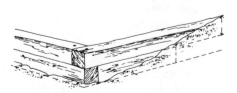

Lay the second layer of ties so the side tie overlaps the junction of the ties in the first layer.

Do the same on the other side of the bed; then cut a front tie (or ties) just long enough to nestle between the side ties. Spike it in place.

Install each successive layer of the first bed so that front and sides overlap each other at the corners. When the wall reaches its desired height, install the tie that forms the back of the bed. The back overlaps the side ties and sits in a shallow trench of its own. Spike it in place.

Build the next bed the same way you built the first. The back tie of the bed you just finished becomes the front tie of the bed you're building. Butt the side ties against it, and build the bed layer after layer.

If the back of a bed ever falls directly over the end of a side tie, there will be a weak link in the wall. If necessary, reposition the back by 6 inches or so to avoid this.

Continue building bed after bed until you reach the top of the hill. The back wall of the last bed is a single tie. When all the ties are in place, fill the beds with a mixture of

soil and organic matter such as compost. Then rake, plant, and enjoy.

Building a Cut-and-Filled Terrace

The major difference between a filled terrace and a cut-and-filled terrace is the height of the wall. A cut-and-filled bed is made by moving soil from the back to the front. Since it requires little, if any, new soil, the wall that holds the bed in place isn't as high.

In fact, on a given hillside, the walls of a cut-and-filled terrace are only half as high as those of a filled terrace. To determine the actual height of a cut-and-filled front wall, figure the height the filled bed would require, and divide by two.

Lay out and trench the first bed only. Begin putting the ties in place. Overlap them as before, and spike them together as you build. Before you install the final tier, however, stop: It's time to cut and fill. Move the soil from the back of the bed to the front of the bed. When you've created a level surface, finish laying the ties for the first bed, including the first layer of the bed's back wall.

Continue trenching and building bed by bed, up the hill. The back wall of the last bed will be the same height as the front wall of the first bed. Cut-and-filled beds may need a generous layer of compost dug into the soil.

Construction Options

You may want to try making half-lap corners for your terraces. This method makes an attractive and sturdy corner,

but requires more time to prepare than overlapping full ties. To make a half-lap corner, cut away a 6-by-6-inch square, 3 inches deep, from the bottom side of the top tie. Then cut away a square piece of the same dimensions from the top side of the bottom tie. The two lapped ends should fit together perfectly when laid in place. Be sure to spike them together for proper reinforcement.

To help the terrace walls withstand the pressure of the contained soil, strengthen the walls with upright stakes. Drive the stakes into the ground 3 or 4 feet apart, either outside or inside the terrace walls, and spike them to the ties.

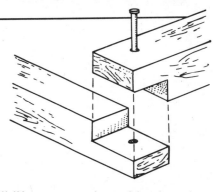

Half-lap corners require careful cutting and fitting, but provide a pleasing appearance and excellent strength for terrace corners.

Stakes driven in the ground either inside or outside the terrace walls can be used to strengthen the walls.

TERRACING OPTIONS

Although terraces are most commonly built with landscape ties, on a gentle slope, relatively flat, irregularly shaped stones can also be used to frame terraces. Stand the stones on edge, burying them about halfway in the soil. Be sure the edges fit snugly together so soil does not wash between them.

For terraces on steeper slopes, pile flat rocks into wide walls. Either way, be sure the beds slant slightly downhill to ensure proper drainage.

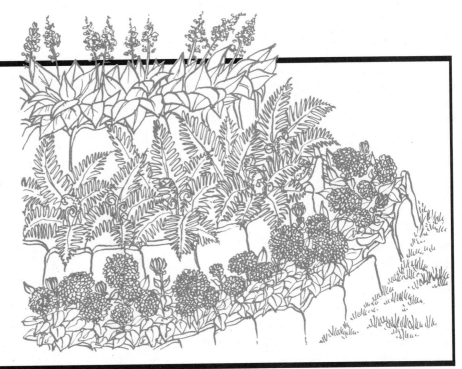

Knowing Your Soil

Testing the Soil

Gardeners who would like to become *good* gardeners can begin by learning as much as possible about their soil. Although you can garden successfully without knowing whether the soil is acid or alkaline and how much potassium or phosphorus is present, you will be more successful if you have these facts and know how to use them. Soil tests are an easy way to gather such useful information. In a sense, soil tests are like highway road signs: They help point your soil improvement and fertilization programs in the right direction.

Basically, soil tests reveal two things: They determine the acidity or alkalinity of the soil on the pH scale, and they indicate fertility by estimating how much of the major plant nutrients your soil contains.

Understanding pH

Madison Avenue exposed the world to pH. Advertisers ballyhooed its benefits in everything from foods to coffee and shampoo. But pH is particularly important to gardeners because it is an important factor governing plant growth. It not only determines the chemical availability of vital nutrients to plants, but also what plants will grow well in a given soil. For example, in very alkaline soils, iron and other vital minerals such as boron, copper, manganese, and zinc are chemically tied up and plants can't absorb them. As a result, acid-loving plants such as azaleas, which need

plenty of iron for growth, won't grow well in alkaline soil. Instead, they prefer acid soil, in which the nutrients they need are more readily available. On the other hand, phosphorus is the most important nutrient that is tied up in acid soil.

The pH scale ranges from 1.0 to 14.0. Neutral, a pH reading of 7.0, is in the center of the scale. All readings below 7.0 are acidic; readings above 7.0 are alkaline. Acidic soil is

sometimes referred to as sour; alkaline soil as either limey or sweet. A pH level that is slightly acid to neutral—between 6.0 and 7.0—is fine for most flower and vegetable gardens, because at that level the essential plant nutrients are most readily available. Most plants will tolerate a fairly wide pH range, especially if the soil is rich in organic matter.

It's important to remember that the pH scale is logarithmic; that is, a

Gardeners are most likely to find their soil pH falls somewhere between 4.5 and 7.5. The best range for most vegetables and flowers is between pH 6.0 and 7.0. Azaleas, rhododendrons, mountain laurel, and hydrangeas are among the plants that perform well in acid soils; lilacs, sweet William, peonies, and sweet peas prefer alkaline soil.

12

pH of 5.0 is 10 times as acid as a pH of 6.0, and 100 times more acid than a pH of 7.0. Changes in your soil's pH reading that seem small can result in major changes in actual acidity or alkalinity.

Types of Tests

The two most common methods to obtain a soil test are using a home soil test kit or sending a soil sample to the cooperative extension service or a commercial soil testing lab. While extension or commercial soil lab tests provide more accurate results, either method is adequate for determining pH and soil fertility levels. (Some commercial and cooperative extension labs will also test for the humus content of your soil.) In addition, soil pH can be tested with a specially designed pH meter that is used by sticking two metal probes in the soil, or with litmus paper and a corresponding color scale.

Home test kits are readily available, easy to use, and require no knowledge of chemistry or laboratory procedures. A big advantage is that they permit frequent, on-the-spot tests without the wait for results inherent in using a soil lab. Home soil tests are conducted by simply putting a small portion of the soil sample in a test tube and then adding one or more chemicals, called reagents. The reagent reacts with the nutrient being tested for and indicates the quantity of the nutrient by changing color. Color charts are provided with the kits, and the final analysis is made by comparing the color of the solution in the test tube to the proper color chart. Most kits provide solutions and guides for determining the approximate content of the three major soil nutrients: nitrogen (N), phosphorus (P), and potassium (K), as well as soil pH.

In addition to nitrogen, phosphorus, and potassium, soil samples can be tested for such minerals as calcium, magnesium, manganese, iron, copper, and zinc. City gardeners, as well as anyone who gardens near an old building or busy road should have the soil tested to make sure it hasn't been contaminated with heavy metals. Such tests are especially important if you are growing fruits or vegetables or if you have young children who might eat the soil. Lead, which leaches out of old paint, and cadmium are the most common heavy metals found in contaminated soil. Tests can also be performed to detect levels of sodium, mercury, chromium, and nickel.

For information on obtaining soil tests and equipment, see "Soil Test Sources" on page 16.

Taking Soil Samples

Regardless of the method used to test your own soil, the soil sample you take is all-important, because test results can be no better than the samples tested. In order to get an accurate picture of the soil in which you will be planting your garden, the sample must be as representative of the entire garden area as possible. (If you're using a pH meter, you won't need to take an actual soil sample, but it is important to take a series of readings to determine average soil pH.)

To take a soil sample, you'll need a digging or sampling tool such as a spade, trowel, narrow shovel with straight sides, or a soil auger or probe. For gathering samples, use a large bucket or similar container; coffee cans or small cardboard boxes that will hold about a pint of soil will serve to hold the final sample. Make sure the tools and containers are clean and free of foreign matter, especially fertilizer residue, which can throw the test results off completely.

Soil samples can be taken any time of year, but it is best if the soil is free of frost and fairly dry. Especially if you're planning to test a large area, you'll need to take a series of samples from several spots and mix them together to provide an overall representation of the soil. If you want to test two distinctly different areas, however, a combined sample would not suitably represent either one. In that case, take a series of samples from each area and keep them separate.

To take a composite or representative sample, start at one end of the plot, and cut straight down about 6 to 8 inches with the garden tool. Lift out a narrow slice, and lay it aside. Then take another thin slice, about ½ inch thick, from the same spot and put it in the collecting container. Shovel the first slice back in place. Now move about 6 feet in any direction and repeat

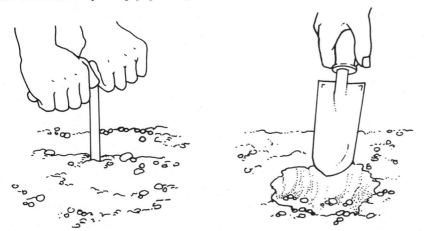

A sampling probe (on the left) is the best tool for getting soil samples for testing. All you do is plunge it into the ground and remove a core of soil. But a specialized tool isn't necessary. Just excavate a 6- to 8-inch-deep hole with a garden trowel, and then shave a ½-inch-thick slice from the side of the hole. Thoroughly mix several soil samples from other spots within the area to be tested. This technique will provide far more soil than is needed for testing, but it will provide a representative sample of the soil in your garden.

READING WEEDS

You can tell a great deal about soil by "reading" the plants growing in it, because they reflect the soil's structure, drainage, and pH. Our ancestors chose their cropland by the type of trees that grew there. They avoided the poor, sandy soils under pine forests and cleared the land where beech, maple, birch, and hemlock forests grew—indicators of fertile soil.

We can't clear a forest every time we plant a garden, but we can still find clues about our soil in the weeds that grow there. Creeping buttercup, chicory, coltsfoot, dandelion, broad-leaved dock, and mayweed are indicators of a heavy clay soil. A light sandy soil grows field bindweed, wild lettuce, goldenrod, sheep sorrel, and corn spurrey. Daisies, docks, hawkweed, horsetail, and knapweed are found in acidic soils. Areas with a hardpan (an impervious, crustlike layer 6 to 24 inches under the soil) often support chamomile, field mustard, horse nettle, morning glory, penny cress, and pineapple weed. Clovers, vetches, rape, and black medick indicate soils low in nitrogen. Poorly drained, waterlogged soils are characterized by coltsfoot, Joepye weed, sedges, smartweed, creeping buttercup, hedge nettle, horsetail, and silverweed.

If you're growing a healthy crop of chickweed, chicory, common groundsel, henbit, and lamb's-quarters, it's a good sign of a fertile, humus-rich soil. Pull your weeds and plant your garden.

Common sense must guide your soil evaluation. Get the whole picture—a single weed isn't reliable. But if you have several species that indicate heavy clay soil, for example, your conclusions will have more validity. Perennial weeds are better indicators than annuals, because they live in the same soil year after year. Annuals can just come up one season by chance.

Take time to look at your weeds before you pull them—they may be trying to tell you something.

---

the operation. Continue until you've taken samples from all over the plot. On a field of an acre or more, take samples several yards apart.

Mixing the Sample. Once you've covered the area to be tested, mix the soil you've collected thoroughly in the collecting container. Remove one pint of soil. Spread this "homogenized" sample out on newspapers or somewhere that it will dry. A dry sample is important, for damp or wet soil will give false test readings. Once the sample is completely dry, rub it through a screen or use a rolling pin to remove any remaining lumps before placing it in the sample container.

If you're using a home-test kit, use this sample to perform the required tests. If you're sending your soil sample out to a lab, label it, indicating where and when it was taken, the type of crop grown last season, and the type of crop to be planted this year.

Adjusting pH

The term pH, which stands for potential hydrogen, refers to the amount of free hydrogen in the soil. The two substances used to adjust free hydrogen in soil are lime and sulfur.

The type or texture of soil you have affects how easy or hard it is to alter the pH. The more organic matter in the soil, the more buffered—resistant to change—it is. That's why it takes much less lime to alter the pH of a very sandy soil than a loam soil. For major changes in pH, split the total quantity required and add it annually over two or more years.

If your soil is very acid, you'll need to add lime in the form of ground limestone or dolomite to adjust the pH upward. The following treatment will raise the pH by about one point:

● In very sandy soil, add 3 to 5½ pounds of ground limestone per 100 square feet.

● In sandy loam, add 5 to 7 pounds per 100 square feet.

● In loam, add 7 to 10 pounds per 100 square feet.

● In heavy clay, add 7 to 8 pounds per 100 square feet.

For alkaline soils, the following treatments will lower the pH one point:

● In sandy soil, add 1 pound of ground sulfur per 100 square feet.

● In heavy clay, add 2 pounds of ground sulfur per 100 square feet.

Organic Matter and pH

Organic matter in the soil is the great equalizer as far as pH is concerned. When added to any soil, organic mat-

---

Green Thumb Tip

QUICK LIME FIZZ

Here's a recipe for a quick soil test for lime: Put a tablespoonful of dry soil into a teacup and add an equal amount of white vinegar. As they mix, shake the cup and hold it to your ear. If you have very alkaline soil, you'll hear a strong fizzing as the acidic vinegar mixes with the alkaline lime. If you hear weak fizzing or none at all, you'll need to use a more sophisticated test, for your soil could range anywhere from slightly alkaline to acidic.

ter in the form of compost or humus will tend to bring the pH closer to neutral by lowering the pH of alkaline soils or raising the pH of acid soils. Organic matter such as sawdust, composted oak leaves, wood chips, leaf mold, cottonseed meal, and peat moss are especially effective in lowering the pH of alkaline soils. Wood ashes, especially those from slow-growing hardwoods such as oaks and hickories, as well as bone meal, crushed marble, and crushed oyster shells, are effective for raising the pH of acid soils.

Adding Nutrients

No matter which way you get your soil tested, the results can be of value only if you understand and use them. The soil test results on nitrogen, phosphorus, and potassium readings may be expressed in various ways—as percentages or using relative levels such as high, medium, and low, or abundant, adequate, and deficient, for each major nutrient. Some test kits and most extension service or laboratory reports make specific recommendations for improving weak or very deficient nutrient levels shown in the test. Some tests allow you to request either chemical or organic recommendations.

Packaged fertilizers—chemical or organic—carry a three-part number that indicates the percentages of nitrogen (N), phosphorus (P), and potassium (K) that they contain. For example, a fertilizer with the formulation 3-2-1 contains 3 percent nitrogen, 2 percent phosphorus, and 1 percent potassium.

If you depend on natural materials such as compost and manure for soil nutrients, keep in mind that the best way to maintain or build soil fertility is to do it slowly with annual applications.

If your soil test indicates a low nitrogen level, start applying one or more of the following materials: compost, manure, dried blood, cottonseed meal, cocoa bean or peanut shells, bonemeal, or sewage sludge.

A GUIDE TO NUTRIENT DEFICIENCIES

Just as a doctor can evaluate a patient's symptoms to reach a diagnosis, you, too, can "read" your plants. By evaluating their symptoms, you can determine whether they are deficient in essential nutrients. As a general rule, deficient plants are more susceptible to insect and disease attacks, grow more slowly, and have reduced yields. In many cases, these subtle signs are accompanied by more distinct symptoms. For example, tomatoes may be too bushy and have only small, dark leaves; cauliflower heads can be splotched with brown. The following guide isolates and exaggerates the visual symptoms of specific nutrient deficiencies.

Even though each nutrient deficiency has unique visual symptoms, analyzing them can be confusing. That's because the symptoms aren't always textbook-consistent, and they may be caused by a shortage of more than one element. Using a soil test can narrow down the possibilities, but bear in mind that test results are only approximations of what nutrients will be available to plants. Actual availability depends on a variety of factors, including pH, temperature, soil type, and the type of plants grown. Furthermore, most standard soil tests only measure nitrogen, phosphorus, and potassium. Tests for other nutrients such as magnesium and calcium are also available. Plant tissue analysis is another helpful test that measures the levels of macro- and micronutrients in plant leaves.

It's important to remember that nutrient availability is closely related to pH. For example, in alkaline soils, iron, manganese, and copper are less chemically available to plants than they are in slightly acid soils. Plants growing in alkaline soil may exhibit symptoms of iron chlorosis simply because the pH is too high and the iron in the soil is chemically unavailable. Thus, adjusting the pH of your soil can often make the difference between healthy and nutrient-deficient plants.

We've developed a handy key to help you determine what nutrient deficiencies may be affecting your plants. The eight deficiencies that are most likely to give you trouble are listed below along with characteristic symptoms. Molybdenum, copper, and manganese deficiencies occur in isolated pockets of the country; sulfur and chlorine are rarely deficient. If you get stuck between two descriptions detailing deficiencies, try correcting your soil for the more likely deficiency. If the symptoms disappear, you made the right choice. If they change, go through the list again—there might be a second deficiency. Also, ask your county extension agent if there are deficiencies common to your area.

Here's how to use the guide.

Step One: Pick the numbered statement in Section A that most closely matches the symptoms. Once you have done this, you will be directed to Section B or Section D.

Step Two: At Section B or Section D you must determine if the leaves on your plant are small or normal in size. Once you have made this choice, the deficiency either will be described, or you will be directed to a different section (or sections) that describes the symptoms your plants exhibit.

A 1. Symptoms affect entire plant. **Go to B.**

2. Symptoms principally evident on foliage. **Go to D.**

B 1. Leaves small. **Go to C.**

2. Leaves normal in size. New leaves and terminal branches deformed. Upper leaves may be dark green, but they curl upward, edges turn

(continued)

The best source for phosphorus is rock phosphate, ground to a meal or powder. It is most effective when used in combination with well-rotted manure. Apply the manure and work it into the surface of the soil, then apply the rock phosphate a month or two later. Other organic sources of phosphorus are dried blood, cotton-seed meal, and bonemeal.

There are two types of sources for potassium: plant residues and mineral sources. In addition to manures and compost, plant residue sources include wood ashes, seaweed extract, hay, and leaves. Granite dust, also called granite stone meal or ground rock potash, is the most common mineral source of potassium. However, greensand, a mineral-rich sediment deposited under the ocean, is another excellent source of potassium, along with a variety of other minerals, including silica, iron oxide, magnesium, lime, and phosphoric acid. It has been used as a soil builder for more than a hundred years. Since mineral sources take time to become available to plants, it's best to apply both organic and mineral sources of potassium.

A GUIDE TO NUTRIENT DEFICIENCIES—*Continued*

yellow, and they dry up and fall. Lower leaves normal. Stems fibrous and hard; roots short and brown. Plant wilts, becoming weak and flabby. Fruits have water-soaked lesions at the blossom end. Common on acidic, highly leached soils. **Calcium deficiency.**

C 1. Lower leaves turn pale green; chlorosis or yellowing follows, and older leaves drop. Eventually, all leaves may turn yellow. Undersides of leaves may become bluish purple. Plant grows slowly and becomes spindly and stunted. Individual branches may die. Fruit is small, pale green before ripening; highly colored when ripe. Common on highly leached soils or on soils high in organic matter at low temperatures. **Nitrogen deficiency.**

2. Chlorosis is not a dominant symptom. Undersides of leaves turn reddish purple. Color first appears in spots in the webs of leaves and then spreads to entire leaf. Stems slender, fibrous, and hard. Fruit sets and matures late, or drops prematurely. Plants and roots may be stunted. Common because of reduced availability in acid or alkaline soils and in cold, dry, or highly organic soils. **Phosphorus deficiency.**

3. Leaves turn dark purple to black while young. Terminal shoots curl inward, turn dark, and die. Lateral buds grow, then die, creating a bushy, witches'-broom effect. Leaf petioles and midribs become thickened, curled, and brittle. Fruit darkens and has dried or cracked areas. Symptoms vary widely from one vegetable to the next. Most likely on highly leached, acidic soils and highly organic, limey soils. **Boron deficiency.**

D 1. Leaves normal in size. **Go to E.**

2. Leaves small and/or mottled with yellow or necrotic areas of dead

SOIL TEST SOURCES

Materials for testing soil pH and nutrient levels are available at local garden centers, from many mail-order nurseries, and through the scientific supply companies listed below.

Scientific Supply Companies

Connecticut Valley Biological
82 Valley Road, P.O. Box 326
Southampton, MA 01073
Catalog free.

Edmund Scientific
101 E. Gloucester Pike
Barrington, NJ 08007
Catalog $5.

Nasco
901 Janesville Avenue
Fort Atkinson, WI 53538
Catalog free.

Soil Testing Labs

Write for information about the services and tests they can perform. You can have a number of tests done on your soil. Most cooperative extension service offices perform soil tests for a fee. Look in the telephone directory under the city or county government listings.

Camtronics Soil Testing Service
224 Nelson Lane, P.O. Box 1
Camus Valley, OR 97416

LaRamie Soils Service
P.O. Box 255
Laramie, WY 82070

Woods End Soil Labs
RFD 1, Box 4050
Old Rome Road
Mt. Vernon, ME 04352

tissue. Internodes are shortened. Some vegetables form "rosettes" of leaves. Common because of reduced availability in acidic, highly leached, sandy soils, and in alkaline and highly organic soils. **Zinc deficiency.**

E 1. Leaf margins of older leaves are tanned, scorched, or have black or brown necrotic spots. Margins become brown and cup downward. Leaves are mottled with yellow and may turn ashen gray-green, bronze or yellowish brown. Symptoms begin at the bottom of the plant and work upward. Young leaves crinkle and curl. Roots are poorly developed and brown. Stems slender, hard, and woody. Low crop yields are often the first symptom. Fruit ripens unevenly. Symptoms may be more severe late in the growing season due to translocation of potassium to developing fruit. Most common on highly leached, acidic soils, and on highly organic soils. **Potassium deficiency.**

2. Veins of lower leaves remain dark green while the area between veins turns yellow and then dark brown. Leaves are brittle and curl upward. Tissue breaks down. Maturity of fruit delayed. Symptoms usually occur late in the growing season. Most common on acidic, highly leached, sandy soils, or on soils with high potassium or calcium. **Magnesium deficiency.**

3. New leaves turn yellow, but chlorotic spots not usually followed by necrosis (dead tissue). Distinct yellow or white areas appear between veins; veins eventually become chlorotic. Symptoms are rare on older, mature leaves. Most common on alkaline soils. **Iron deficiency.**

Improving the Soil—Texture and Structure

The phrase "common as dirt" says it all. Too frequently, gardeners take soil for granted, viewing it simply as a medium for holding up plants. However, soil is a surprisingly complex biological system made up of inorganic minerals, organic matter, soil organisms, air, and water.

The term soil texture refers to the sizes of the individual mineral particles in a soil. Structure refers to the way the individual particles are arranged. Knowing the texture and structure of your soil is as important as knowing its pH. Why? Because together they play key roles in determining how well your soil absorbs and holds nutrients and water, how quickly or slowly it drains, and how easy or difficult it is to till. Indirect-ly, these factors also dictate the kinds of problems you may encounter.

Texture

The mineral portion of almost every soil contains sand, silt, and clay. The percentage of each of these particles determines the soil's texture. Sand particles, the largest and most irregular of the three, measure from $\frac{1}{50}$ to $\frac{1}{500}$ of an inch. Silt particles range from $\frac{1}{500}$ to $\frac{1}{12,500}$ of an inch. Clay particles, which are less than $\frac{1}{12,500}$ of an inch, are so small they can't be seen with an ordinary microscope.

Sand serves primarily as the soil's skeleton, helping to keep it permeable and well aerated, but playing only a small part in the soil's chemical activities. At the other end of the texture scale, clay particles (along with organic matter such as humus) are very active chemically. They are constantly taking on and giving up ions of other elements in the soil, and act as soil storage reservoirs for both water and nutrients. For this reason, clay soils tend to be more fertile than sandy ones, because sand particles lack the ability to hold nutrients and release them to plants.

Determining Texture

You don't have to be a scientist to determine the texture of the soil in your garden, but looking at it is not enough. You have got to get right down and feel it. To get a rough idea

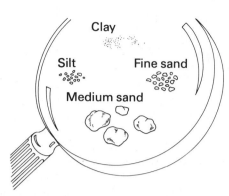

If you look at a soil sample under a magnifying glass, you'll see that it's composed of many sizes of particles. Clay particles are about $\frac{1}{12,500}$ inch across; silt particles range from $\frac{1}{12,500}$ to $\frac{1}{500}$ inch; fine sand from $\frac{1}{500}$ to $\frac{1}{250}$ inch; and medium sand from $\frac{1}{100}$ to $\frac{1}{50}$ inch. Coarse sand (not shown) can be as large as $\frac{1}{12}$ inch across.

of its texture, simply place a sample in the palm of your hand and wet it slightly. Then rub the mixture with your fingers. If it feels gritty, your soil is sandy; if it feel smooth, like cake flour or moist talcum powder, your soil is silty; if it feels harsh when dry, sticky or slippery when wet, or rubbery when moist, it is high in clay.

After you've done that, wet the soil and measure the plasticity, its ability to take and hold a new shape. Increasing plasticity is associated with increasing clay content. A moist clay soil (60 percent clay, 20 percent sand, and 20 percent silt) can readily be formed into a long, durable ribbon or wire about ⅛ inch thick. A clay loam (30 percent sand, 35 percent silt, and 35 percent clay) will form a ribbon or wire but not such a long or durable

one. Some loam soils (about 40 percent sand, 40 percent silt, and 20 percent clay) can be formed into short ribbons, but others will not form any ribbon. (For another way to determine the texture of your soil, see "Soil Fractional Analysis" below.

A soil that forms a moderately good ribbon is called a silty clay loam if it has a very smooth feel, a sandy clay loam if it has a very gritty feel, or simply a clay loam if the smooth and gritty particles are about equal.

Loam and silt loam soils are desirable because they have enough clay in them to store adequate amounts of water and plant nutrients, but not so much that the soil is poorly aerated or difficult to work.

Although textural comparisons usually apply only to topsoils, you can learn a lot about subsoil by mak-

SOIL FRACTIONAL ANALYSIS

Soil fractional analysis is an easy way to determine the texture of your soil. To perform your own at-home soil fractional analysis, you'll need a clear glass quart jar with a tight-fitting lid, 1 cup of dry, finely pulverized soil, 1 teaspoon of nonsudsing dishwasher detergent, a watch or clock, and a crayon or grease pencil. To get a soil sample that is representative of your entire garden, take tablespoon-size samples from several locations and depths, mix them, dry them thoroughly, and then pulverize them with a rolling pin or mallet.

Fill the jar two-thirds full of water, add the soil and detergent, and fasten the lid securely. Shake the jar vigorously for 10 to 15 minutes and let it sit undisturbed for several days.

The sand particles are largest and heaviest and will settle to the bottom within one minute. Mark the jar with a crayon or grease pencil at the end of one minute to indicate the level of sand. After two hours most of the silt will have settled, so make a second mark on the side of the jar to indicate level of silt. Clay particles are tiny and will require a few days to settle, but once the water is clear you'll know they've settled. Then mark the level of clay on the jar.

To determine the percentage of each type of particle, use the following formula: A equals the thickness of the sand; B equals the thickness of the silt; C equals the thickness of the clay; D equals the thickness of all three deposits. To calculate the percentage of sand, multiply A times 100 and divide by D; for the percentage of silt, multiply B times 100 and divide by D; for the percentage of clay, multiply C times 100 and divide by D.

To determine your exact soil type, compare the component percentages you arrived at with the texture triangle on the opposite page.

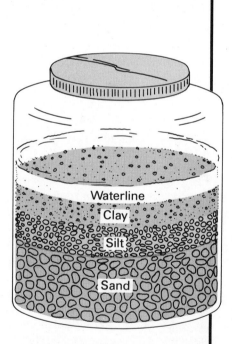

A soil fractional analysis test is easy to conduct at home and will help you identify the texture of your soil by determining percentages of sand, silt, and clay.

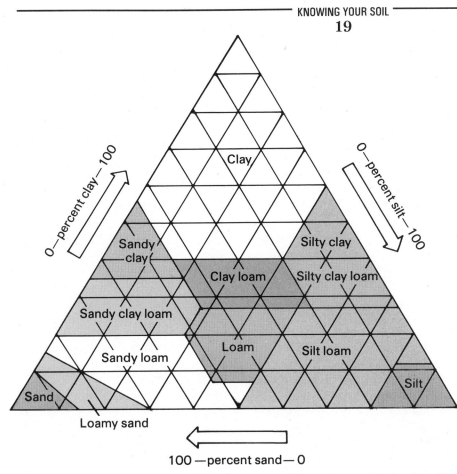

A texture triangle shows the limitless combinations of soil textures. A clay soil contains about 60 percent clay, 20 percent sand, and 20 percent silt. Loam, the most desirable texture for garden soil, contains 40 percent sand, 40 percent silt, and 20 percent clay.

ing the same tests. A subsoil with high clay content may seriously restrict air, water, and root penetration. Double-digging and working organic material in deeply is the answer for most tight subsoils.

Structure and Pore Space

Soil texture, structure, and pore space are closely related. Soil structure develops when sand, silt, and clay particles, along with organic matter, clump together. Ideally, they form a loose, crumbly mass. A variety of forces work together to create these clumps, called crumbs, including earthworms and other soil-dwelling organisms, plant roots, fungal hyphae, cycles of freezing and thawing, and other chemical reactions in the soil. Soils with good structure have plenty of both large and small pore space. For example, a good topsoil is only half solid. (The solid portion is made up

of about 5 percent organic matter and 95 percent minerals.) The other 50 percent is composed of pore space. Half of the pore space of a good loam soil is made up of large pores filled with air. The other half is small pores that can hold water in the soil.

Unfortunately, cultivation tends to destroy soil structure, breaking up the crumbs into smaller particles that pack together and form a crust or prevent drainage. A loss of soil structure usually means a loss of pore space, which in turn affects water and nutrient availability.

Sandy soils, because of the large particle size, have plenty of pore space, but the spaces are so large the water drains out very quickly. They also contain few particles (such as clay) that retain nutrients for plants. Clay soils, on the other hand, can hold plenty of water and nutrients, but the water is held very tightly in small pores, and plant roots have difficulty extracting it.

Soil Improvement

Unless you're willing to haul in truckloads of materials, or build raised beds and bring in new soil altogether, it is impractical to try to change your soil's texture. For example, to change a very clayey soil (60 percent clay, 20 percent silt, 20 percent sand) to a silty loam (10 percent clay, 70 percent silt, 20 percent sand) would require mixing in enough sand and silt to double the amount of soil already in the garden. Instead, the best strategy for improving any soil is to concentrate on building the organic content by working compost, manure, leaf mold, and other organic matter into the soil each year. Soil scientists have found that adding organic matter to clay soil is as beneficial as adding it to a sandy one, for it helps improve soil structure. In clay soils it improves drainage and aeration by helping to create large pores that can fill with air, and it helps sandy soils hold nutrients and water.

Sandy Soil

Because they don't have much clay or organic matter, sandy soils don't develop a loose, crumbly structure; even when wet, the soil particles don't stick together. As a result, sandy soils have large pore spaces and drain very quickly, often before plant roots can absorb the water flowing past them. For the same reason, sandy soils don't hold nutrients well either. Sandy soils are very well aerated, and the high oxygen content of the soil causes microbes to quickly burn up organic matter. Sandy soil is easy to work, though, when compared to soils with more clay content, so compost is easily incorporated into the soil. Also, compaction is never a problem.

The most important way to improve sandy soil is to add organic matter. In fact, you can hardly add too much organic matter to sandy soil, because it increases the soil's ability to retain water and nutrients. Start your soil improvement program by working 3 to 4 inches of organic matter such as manure, compost, or other rotted plant material, such as leaves, into the soil. Follow with a mulch of leaves, grass clippings, wood chips, bark, hay, or straw. Mulch helps retain water in the soil, and also keeps the soil cool, which will slow microbial activity and the resulting breakdown of soil organic matter. Mulch also slows down the flow of water through the soil, providing plants with a smaller, steadier trickle that they can absorb. On an annual basis, add another inch of organic matter, working it in deeply in the fall or winter. A green manure program also will improve the soil structure.

Clayey Soil

Soils dominated by clay (40 to 60 percent) become sticky and practically unworkable when wet; hard and cloddy when dry. They're called heavy soils for good reason—the pore spaces are so small that clay soils become completely waterlogged when wet. They drain slowly and generally can't be tilled until late spring, for working them when they are wet will destroy their fragile structure. Because of the small size of the clay particles, soil compaction is a problem with these soils. Plant roots can't penetrate clay soils readily because of the small pore space and poor aeration. Clay soils are generally low in organic matter, and poor aeration also causes a decrease in the activity of soil microorganisms.

Massive infusions of organic matter are needed to loosen up clay soil and develop a crumbly, friable structure that will promote good drainage and root zone aeration. It is also important to avoid walking on garden beds, since clay soils compact so easily.

Start your soil improvement program by working 2 to 3 inches of organic matter into the surface of the soil. (If your soil is a fine clay, start with 3 to 5 inches of organic matter.) Work in at least an inch of organic matter each year. Good materials to add are compost, manure, leaf mold, rice hulls, peat moss, coarse sand, sawdust, and wood chips. Work organic matter into the soil in fall and leave the soil surface in a rough condition over the winter to allow frost action to break up large clods. Don't always dig to the same depth, for this will encourage a hardpan layer to form, which will hinder drainage and cause salt concentrations to build up in the soil. Green manure crops, especially legumes, are very effective in improving clay soils.

Raised beds are a good solution for gardeners with extremely clayey soils. Till organic matter into the soil before constructing the beds. Once the beds are constructed, continue to add organic matter, but till it into the top 2 or 3 inches. This provides a surface soil that is very high in organic matter, greatly reduces the amount of tilling that is necessary, and prevents surface cracking and crusting characteristic of clay soils.

Loamy Soil

Generally speaking, a loam consists of 50 percent sand, 40 percent silt, and 10 percent clay. Soils with a higher proportion of clay are termed clay loams, and those with a higher proportion of sand are called sand loams. Loam soils are generally high in organic matter, very fertile, well drained and well aerated. They retain water well, too. If properly cared for, loamy soils are the ideal soil for gardening. Regular annual applications of organic matter such as compost, manure, or leaf mold will keep this ideal soil in top shape by maintaining fertility and structure.

Silty Soil

Like loamy soils, silty soils tend to be fertile. Silty soils have a large percentage of small particles, and, as a result, they are quite dense and have relatively small pore spaces and poor drainage. Add organic matter to the soil to improve soil structure and increase permeability. Working one inch of organic matter such as compost, manure, or leaf mold into the soil each year should be sufficient for silty soils. Incorporate the organic matter mainly in the top few inches of soil to help prevent surface crusting, a common problem in silty soils after heavy rains. Compaction can also be a problem, so avoid unnecessary tilling and walking on garden beds, or consider constructing raised beds.

Composting

Making Compost

Organic gardeners know that if you feed the soil, the soil will feed the plant. What do you feed soil with? Actively decaying organic matter, better known as compost.

Compost is made from yard clippings, leaves, sawdust, wood chips, manure, and vegetable parings from the kitchen. Composting changes the nutrients in these materials to a form that is available for uptake by the roots of growing plants. Microorganisms such as soil bacteria and fungi accomplish this task by secreting enzymes and acids that dissolve cell walls. The contents of the plant cells —along with the decomposing bodies of generations of bacteria and fungi— feed huge populations of microorganisms in the compost pile. In fact, the activity of the billions of microorganisms in a well-constructed compost pile can generate so much heat that interior temperatures can exceed 130°F, temperatures high enough to kill most weed seeds and disease organisms.

Humus, or finished compost, is the end product of the composting process. Humus has the ability to hold nutrients in the soil like a sponge and release them to plants as they need them. It also contains great numbers of beneficial microorganisms that enhance plant growth.

Humus is the ultimate soil conditioner, improving soil structure and, thus, both tilth and aeration. Humus-rich soil is a haven for earthworms and other beneficial soil-dwellers. Fin-

ished compost also holds nutrients and water in the soil and makes them available to growing plants. For example, humus improves the drainage and aeration of clay soil by helping create large pores that can fill with air; it slows nutrient leaching and the flow of water through sandy soils, therefore providing much-needed nutrient-holding ability and buffering the soil against drought. Finished compost also is the great equalizer as far as soil pH is concerned, because it tends to bring the pH of any soil closer to neutral.

Making a Compost Pile

The simplest way to make compost is in a pile of alternating layers of leaves, green matter, manure, and soil. The best piles start with a layer of brush to hold the pile off the ground and aerate it. That's topped with alternating layers of slow-decaying materials such as leaves, woodchips, and sawdust, and fast-decaying material such as grass clippings, manure, and food wastes. Your compost pile can be as simple or as complicated as you wish, but for best results it should measure at least 3-by-3-by-3-feet. It can be larger, but piles taller than about 5 feet tend not to get enough oxygen in the center, thus slowing down the activities of microorganisms that turn clippings into gardeners' gold. Shorter piles are also easier

to turn. A covering of straw helps to hold in heat and moisture.

If you prefer something neater than a simple compost pile, consider building a compost bin. Bins, which can be square or circular, can be constructed of just about any material that's handy—lumber, chicken wire, hardware cloth, bricks, concrete blocks, hay bales, or railroad ties. It's best to build at least two bins, if you have the space, one to hold finished compost, the other for the "working" pile. If you're pressed for space, consider using a garbage can. (See "Garbage Can Compost" on page 22.) There are also several ready-made composters available commercially. For instructions on build-it-yourself models, see pages 25 and 27.

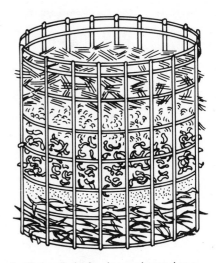

A cylinder of wire fencing can be used as a simple compost bin.

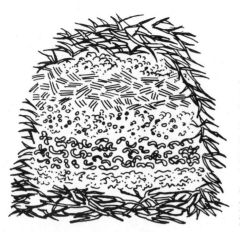

A compost pile in cross section. Brush holds the pile off the ground to aerate it, while alternating layers of slow-decaying green matter and fast-decaying manure keep the pile "cooking" evenly. A covering of straw holds in heat and moisture.

Whether you choose a pile or a bin, select a level, well-drained spot, preferably in full sun. Choose a location that will be convenient for you, such as in the middle of your vegetable garden, but one that won't annoy neighbors.

Although you can produce compost in a trench or pit, these methods rely on anaerobic organisms, and they work more slowly than aerobic organisms. It's better to build your pile above ground.

What to Compost

You can feed your compost pile with nearly anything that once was alive —grapefruit rinds, leaves, grass clippings, eggshells, plant remains from the vegetable garden, dried seaweed, manure, kitchen parings—the list is endless. It's best to avoid fats and meat scraps because they decompose very slowly, create unpleasant odors, and attract vermin to the compost pile. Most gardeners also avoid adding diseased plant materials and any weeds that might have seeds, even though temperatures inside a good compost pile will destroy most of them. Whatever you add, remember that small pieces decompose most quickly; use a shredder to break up twigs and clippings, or run your lawn mower over leaves before adding them to the pile to speed the composting process. (For a list of desirable ingredients and what to avoid for your own pile, see "Compost Ingredients" on the opposite page.)

If you have alkaline soil, remember that organic matter such as sawdust, composted oak leaves, leaf mold, cottonseed meal, and peat moss are especially effective in lowering pH. Pine needles and wood chips from coniferous trees are acidic and will lower pH; add lime to counteract this unless you want to use the compost to lower pH or to feed acid-loving plants. Wood ashes, especially those from slow-growing hardwoods such as oaks and hickories, will help raise the pH of acid soils.

It's a good idea to keep the carbon-to-nitrogen (C-to-N) ratio of the materials you're working with in mind while you're building your pile. Microorganisms can decompose organic matter with ratios of 25 to 30 parts of carbon to 1 part of nitrogen most quickly and efficiently. Sweet clover, for example, has a near ideal C-to-N ratio of 23:1, so it will break down rapidly. Sawdust, on the other hand, is rated at 500:1 and is slow to decompose because microorganisms use up all of the available nitrogen and then the decomposition process stops. (For more information, see the chart "Carbon-to-Nitrogen Ratios of Organic Materials" on page 24.) It's a good idea to combine slow-to-compost materials such as sawdust and wood chips with materials that will compost more quickly. If you have an abundance of slow-to-compost materials, add bone- or bloodmeal, cottonseed meal, or manure to provide extra nitrogen to the mixture.

Building and Turning

Whatever materials you're using, they must be layered. Start with a bottom

GARBAGE CAN COMPOST

Compost can be produced easily in a garbage can tucked out of the way in the corner of the yard or in the garage. Buy a 20- or 30-gallon can and punch several holes in the bottom with a hammer and a large nail. Put the can on a few bricks, and place a pan underneath to catch any liquid that might drain out. Next, spread a 3-inch layer of soil or peat moss on the bottom of the can. Add 2 to 3 inches of kitchen scraps, then a 2-inch layer of grass clippings, shredded newspaper, and/or shredded leaves. Keep a lid on the can, and each day or every few days as you collect them, add more layers of soil, kitchen scraps, grass clippings, newspaper, and/or leaves until the can is full. The ripe compost will be ready in about three or four months. You don't need to worry about the moisture content of this kind of pile, nor does it have to be turned.

Start with a 1-foot-thick layer of rough corn-stalks or brush, 5 to 7 feet square. Follow with a layer of high-nitrogen material such as manure or grass clippings. Then add a layer of garden soil, then more rough material such as hay or straw, more clippings, and so on.

Water between layers if the material you are adding is dry. A handful of compost in a working pile should feel about as moist as a squeezed sponge.

Turn with a pitchfork every few days and keep the pile moist.

layer of rough cornstalks or brush. Follow with a layer of high-nitrogen material such as manure or grass clippings. Then add a layer of garden soil, then more rough material such as hay or straw, more clippings, and so on. If the materials you use are dry, sprinkle them with water as you add them.

Systematically turning the pile to move composted material out of the hot center of the pile and replacing it with the partially composted material from the sides greatly speeds the composting process. A well-constructed compost pile will heat up to at least 130°F within 3 or 4 days after turning. After hitting peak temperatures during the first few days, the pile starts to cool down, heating up again with each new turning. Although you can make compost without the extra effort, turning a pile with a fork every 3 days can produce usable compost in as little as 12 days. The pile is fully composted when it fails to heat up after being turned. Then it's ready to use.

COMPOST INGREDIENTS

What to Use
Coffee grounds
Eggshells
Ground corncobs
Hedge trimmings
Kitchen wastes (vegetable and fruit peels)
Lawn clippings
Pine needles
Sawdust
Shredded leaves
Shredded twigs
Straw
Tea leaves
Weeds and disease-free plant debris
Wood shavings

What to Avoid
Material thicker than ¼ inch (shred or chop large pieces to speed up decomposition)
Diseased or pest-laden materials

Plant debris carrying pesticides or herbicides
Meat, bones, grease, other fatty substances (these are slow to decompose and attract undesirable creatures)
Seeds and fruit pits (attractive to rodents)
Cat or dog manure, bird droppings (handling fresh manure and droppings and subsequent use of compost may transmit parasites harmful to humans)

Sources of Nitrogen (to increase bacterial activity)
Bloodmeal
Bonemeal
Cottonseed meal
Manure
Tankage

Making Quick Compost

Gardeners who can't afford to wait three to six months for finished compost, or who want to get several "batches" of compost a year, can build a quick-composting pile.

To make quick compost, you need to stick to materials whose C-to-N ratios average out to about 30:1. For example, a mixture of equal parts grass clippings (19:1) and leaves (from about 80:1 to 40:1), roughly average out to about 40:1. You could speed the composting process by adding manure (20:1) or sweet clover (23:1) to the leaves and grass mixture.

Here are some steps you can take to speed up the composting process.

1. Begin by chopping all materials thoroughly. If you're working with leaves and grass, start the pile with a layer of leaves because they are more absorbent.

2. Alternate layers of leaves and grass, or whatever materials you're using, keeping in mind that low C-to-N materials will speed the process of decomposition. When the pile is 3 to 4 feet high, it's finished. Bear in mind that your carefully made layers will completely disappear when the pile is turned the first time.

3. Cover the top with a tarp, black plastic mulch, or empty plastic bags held in place with boards or branches. The plastic holds in water vapor to keep the pile moist. It also prevents rain from waterlogging the pile and leaching out nutrients.

4. Stick a dial-type thermometer with an 8-inch stem into the side of the finished pile. A good mix will reach 110° to 120°F three days after it's completed.

5. The thermometer will tell you when to turn the pile. As soon as the temperature begins to drop a little, the pile has run out of oxygen and needs to be turned, or aerated. If it doesn't get hot enough, the pile needs more nitrogen, so add more grass clippings or other low C-to-N materials the first time you turn. After the first turning, the pile should reach 130° to 140°F, and should be turned about every second or third day. The compost pile will stay hot for the next 2 to 4 weeks, depending on how promptly and thoroughly you aerate it.

6. The compost is nearly ready when it won't heat up no matter how much you turn it. When it drops to 110°F, it's ready to go onto the garden, or to be bagged in plastic for future use as naturally pasteurized potting soil.

CARBON-TO-NITROGEN RATIOS OF ORGANIC MATERIALS

Alfalfa	12:1
Alfalfa hay	13:1
Cornstalks	60:1
Food wastes (table scraps)	15:1
Fruit wastes	35:1
Grass clippings	19:1
Humus	10:1
Leaves	80:1 to 40:1
Legume–grass hay	25:1
Manure, rotted	20:1
Oat straw	80:1
Paper	170:1
Sawdust	500:1
Sewage sludge, activated	6:1
Sewage sludge, digested	16:1
Straw	80:1
Sugarcane residues	50:1
Sweet clover, green	16:1
Sweet clover, mature	23:1
Wood	700:1

Green Thumb Tip

BLENDER COMPOST

For extra-quick results, start with pureed kitchen scraps for your compost pile. As kitchen scraps accumulate, put them in the blender, add enough water to cover them, and blend until finely chopped. Then, pour the "liquid compost" into a bucket with a lid to keep it until you can take it out to the garden. Pour it into a shallow hole dug in your pile and cover it with a shovelful of compost. Or, if your gardening space is limited and you don't have room to make conventional compost, dump your liquid gold directly into trenches dug in the garden and cover with a shovelful of dirt.

Making a Barrel Composter

For small composting operations, the barrel composter is ideal. The composter is easy to build and use. The compost is easy to turn by rotating the drum.

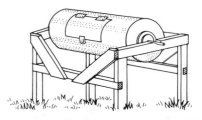

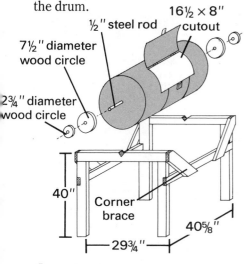

16½ × 8" cutout

½" steel rod

7½" diameter wood circle

2¾" diameter wood circle

40"

Corner brace

40⅝"

29¾"

1. Obtain a 55-gallon drum that has not been used for toxic chemicals. (Paint barrels are ideal.)

2. Drill a ½-inch hole in the exact center of both ends of the drum to accommodate the ½-inch steel rod. Make a simple gauge to find the center by cutting a 6-inch diameter circle out of heavy cardboard or wood. Mark the exact center of the circle and cut out a 90-degree wedge. Attach a piece of wood so that one edge bisects the cut-out wedge. Hold the gauge with the cut-out edge against the edge of the drum. Draw a line where the piece of wood bisects the end of the drum. Move the gauge 90 degrees and draw another line. The intersection of these lines will be the exact center.

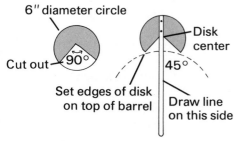

6" diameter circle

Cut out 90°

Disk center

45°

Set edges of disk on top of barrel

Draw line on this side

3. Draw the lines for the barrel opening, rounding the corners slightly. Drill a ¼-inch hole on one line to make a starting place for the

saber saw. Cut through the barrel, following the line. If the barrel has ribs, cut a 1-inch vee notch on each rib to facilitate opening the door. Attach the hinges and the hasp to the barrel and lid with ¼-by-1-inch stove bolts.

4. From ¾-inch pine, cut two 7½-inch-diameter circles (bearings) and two 2¾-inch-diameter circles. Drill a ½-inch hole in the center of each and apply glue to the 2¾-inch circles. Glue each 2¾-inch circle to a 7½-inch one. (It's a good idea to temporarily slip them over the ½-inch steel rod and clamp them.) After the glue has dried, remove the bearings, insert the rod through the barrel, and assemble as shown in the illustration (at top left). Use four ¼-by-1¼-inch stove bolts in each bearing to bolt them to the drum.

5. To build the support frame, use a corner lap joint to fasten the legs to the horizontal pieces. (To make a corner lap joint, remove one-half the thickness of the stock to a length comparable to the width of the stock on the ends of both pieces to be joined.) Use two 1½-inch #10 wood screws in each joint. Cut grooves (dadoes) on the legs 23 inches from the bottom to fit the 1-by-3-inch cross braces. Cut 45-degree angles at both ends of the 23¾-inch long corner braces and attach across corners as shown with 1½-inch #10 wood screws. Cut a ½-inch notch in the center of each top horizontal piece to accommodate the rod.

6. Drill several rows of ¼-inch holes along the bottom of the barrel underneath the door opening to eliminate excess moisture. Paint the barrel unit inside and out with black, rust-retardant paint.

TOOLS REQUIRED

Electric drill

Saws (saber saw with metal-cutting blade and handsaw or circular saw)

Screwdriver

Pliers

Paintbrush

MATERIALS

LUMBER–CUT LIST

You'll need to cut lumber into the following lengths. Use pressure-treated lumber or, if you prefer, untreated pine painted with a preservative or flat black paint. It's best to measure and then cut the pieces as you assemble them to be sure they fit together correctly.

4 pcs. 2 × 4 × 40" (legs)

4 pcs. 2 × 4 × 29¾" (frame horizontals)

2 pcs. 1 × 3 × 40⅝" (cross braces)

4 pcs. 1 × 3 × 23¾" (corner braces)

2 pcs. ¾ × 7½"-diameter wood circles (bearings)

2 pcs. ¾ × 2¾"-diameter wood circles (bearings)

HARDWARE

1 55-gallon drum (composter)

2 pcs. 1½ × 2" hinges

1 small hasp

1 pc. ½ × 40½" steel rod

8 pcs. ¼ × 1¼" stove bolts

12 pcs. ¼ × 1" stove bolts

28 pcs. 1½" #10 wood screws

1 pint black rust-retardant paint

Using a Three-Bin Composter

You can "cook" the food for your soil—compost—in an "oven" you build in your own backyard. A covered, three-bin composter can speed the process of decomposition, and it's also neater than a conventional compost pile.

A covered bin helps keep out excess moisture, which could slow the composting process and leach out nutrients in wet regions. At the same time, it retains much-needed moisture in hot, arid regions. Side-by-side bins allow you to turn the pile and supply it with oxygen without too much trouble by scooping and transferring layers from one bin to the next. The three compartments in our design provide space for continuous composting: Two bins are used for processing, and the spare bin for collecting.

Each bin in this composter holds 27 cubic feet of organic materials—the ideal size for making quick compost.

Open the hatch and toss table scraps and weeds into the holding bin. Remove the front slats a few at a time for working in an existing pile or all at once for forking layers from one bin to the next. Because the bin rests on a sturdy base and includes a floor, the unit can be moved to another site when necessary.

This handy composter makes it easy to turn kitchen wastes and garden trimmings into finished compost in as little as five weeks. In cold months, it may take longer to generate finished compost.

USING YOUR THREE-BIN COMPOSTER

The following week-by-week schedule will help you get the most from your three-bin composter. The schedule is self-perpetuating. Check moisture content when you transfer compost from bin to bin. Add dry material if it seems soggy; water if it's too dry. To boost microbial activity, mix some soil or active compost into the material from the holding bin when you transfer it to the center bin.

Week 1: In the center bin, build a traditional layered compost heap, including high nitrogen materials such as manure or bonemeal. Spread a base layer of dry leaves or straw in the holding bin; toss in kitchen wastes or garden trimmings every day or so.

Weeks 2 and 3: Remove a few front boards from the center bin and stir the compost. Keep adding to the holding bin.

Weeks 4: Remove all front boards from the center and end bins, and transfer the compost to the end bin to speed the composting process. Then remove the front boards from the holding bin and shovel that material into the center bin. Finally, spread a new layer of dry matter in the holding bin.

Week 5: Check the compost in the end bin. It should be ready to use on your garden.

Making a Three-Bin Composter

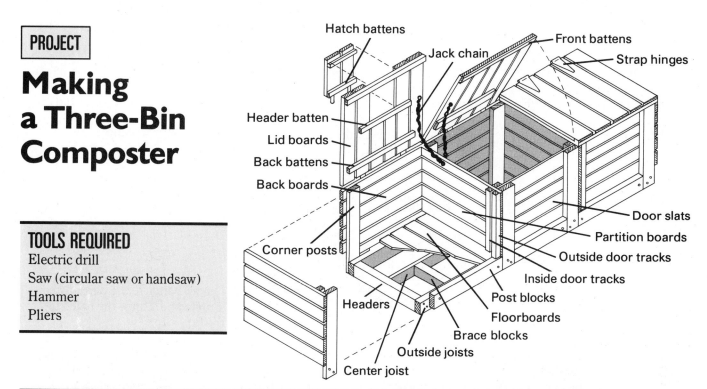

Hatch battens
Jack chain
Front battens
Strap hinges
Header batten
Lid boards
Back battens
Back boards
Corner posts
Headers
Door slats
Partition boards
Outside door tracks
Inside door tracks
Post blocks
Floorboards
Brace blocks
Outside joists
Center joist

TOOLS REQUIRED
Electric drill
Saw (circular saw or handsaw)
Hammer
Pliers

MATERIALS

LUMBER—CUT LIST
Cut lumber into the following lengths. Use pressure-treated lumber or untreated pine painted with a preservative or flat black paint. Measure and cut the pieces as you assemble them to be sure they fit together correctly.

FOR BINS
1 pc. $2 \times 6 \times 108''$ (center joist)
2 pcs. $2 \times 6 \times 30''$ (headers)
2 pcs. $2 \times 6 \times 111''$ (outside joists)
2 pcs. $2 \times 6 \times 14\frac{1}{4}''$ (brace blocks)
4 pcs. $1 \times 6 \times 33''$ (short floor boards)
8 pcs. $2 \times 6 \times 41\frac{1}{2}''$ (corner posts)
24 pcs. $1 \times 6 \times 36''$ (partition boards)
6 pcs. $2 \times 2 \times 34''$ (inside door tracks)
2 pcs. $2 \times 2 \times 35\frac{1}{2}''$ (outside door tracks)
1 pc. $2 \times 6 \times 96''$ (cut to fit for post blocks)
14 pcs. $2 \times 6 \times 34\frac{1}{2}''$ (floorboards)
6 pcs. $1 \times 6 \times 111''$ (backboards)

18 pcs. $1 \times 6 \times 35\frac{1}{2}''$ (door slats)
3 pcs. $1 \times 3 \times 35\frac{1}{2}''$ (door slats)

FOR LIDS
18 pcs. $1 \times 6 \times 37''$ (lid boards)
3 pcs. $1 \times 2 \times 36''$ (front battens)
3 pcs. $1 \times 2 \times 34''$ (back battens)
2 pcs. $1 \times 2 \times 11\frac{1}{4}''$ (hatch battens)
2 pcs. $1 \times 2 \times 22''$ (header batten)

HARDWARE
FOR BINS
22 pcs. $\frac{1}{4} \times 3\frac{1}{2}''$ carriage bolts with nuts and washers
galvanized nails 16d
galvanized nails 8d

FOR LIDS
6 strap hinges 8'' (lids)
2 strap hinges 4'' (hatch)
4 lengths jack chain, approximately 36'' each
8 heavy eye screws
4 snap hooks
1 box $1\frac{1}{4}''$ #6 galvanized screws

BUILDING THE BINS

1. **Base.** Nail a header to each end of the center joist, using 16d nails. Nail the outside joists, front and back, across the ends of the headers. Nail the brace blocks in place between the joists. Locate and nail the four short floorboards across the joists where the partitions will be located, using 8d nails.

2. **Partitions.** For each of the four partitions (two outside and two inside), nail six partition boards to connect two corner posts, spacing them evenly. Nail the inside door tracks to the partition boards, 1 inch back from the corner posts.

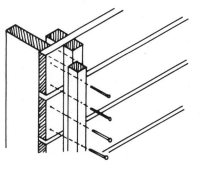

Nail the outside door tracks flush with the front of the two interior partitions. Position the assembled partitions—one on each end of the base and one on each side of the interior compartment; drill and bolt the corner posts to the outside joists.

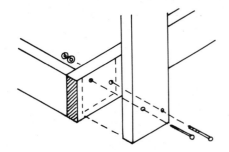

3. **Post Blocks.** Cut the 2 × 6 × 96″ post block board in three pieces, to fit snugly between the bottoms of the front corner posts. Bolt the post blocks in place, flush with the floor surface.

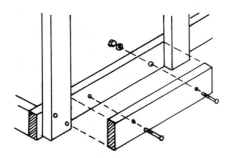

4. **Floor.** Space the floorboards evenly across the joists and nail them in place. There will be five for each of the two end compartments and four for the middle compartment.

5. **Back.** Nail the backboards in place, covering the back corner posts.

6. **Front.** Feed door slats horizontally into the door track.

BUILDING THE LIDS

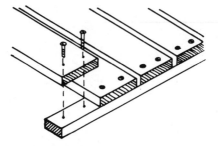

1. **Lids.** Construct two of the three lids. Using a drill and galvanized screws, fasten six lid boards to the front and back battens; allow about ½ inch between boards. Each lid will measure 36 inches across. Construct the third lid in the same manner, but leave out the two middle boards.

2. **Hatch.** Fasten the hatch battens to the two remaining lid boards, one batten about 2 inches from the end of the boards and one batten 18 inches from the same end. Fasten the header batten to the boards, 20 inches from the end, just behind the back hatch batten. Cut between the

header batten and the back hatch batten to separate the hatch. Fasten the two remaining boards and the

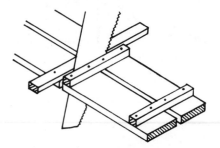

header batten to the partially constructed lid. Hinge the hatch to the lid.

3. **Finish.** Attach the three lids to the bins with the 8-inch hinges, so that they are centered over the compartments. Use eye screws to attach a chain to the bottom of the lids of the two end bins. Attach the chains on the inside edge at about the middle of the boards, on the side near the center partition. Attach chains underneath both sides of the lid of the middle bin. Mount snap hooks on the ends of the chains. Use pliers to attach eye screws to the bin partitions.

Starting Seeds

Soil Mixes for Starting Seeds

The best crops of seedlings and garden transplants start with good soil mixes. When you think "good," do not think "rich." In fact, it's probably better if the mixtures in which you sow your seeds aren't rich in nutrients. It is much more important that they be light and well aerated, provide enough support so seedlings can grow upright, and retain adequate moisture. Seed-starting mixes should also be free of weed seeds and soil-borne diseases and fungi.

There are two schools of thought concerning soil mixes for starting seeds. Some gardeners prefer to sow seeds in special seed-starting mediums—such as straight vermiculite or a mixture of equal parts vermiculite, milled sphagnum moss, and perlite—and then to transplant the seedlings into a potting or growing mix that contains more nutrients. Others prefer to plant seeds directly in a mix that contains nutrient-rich components such as compost or commercial potting soil. If you're undecided, experiment with both methods to determine which gives you the most satisfactory results. You can make your own seed-starting or potting mixes from the recipes listed in this chapter, but there are many commercial mixtures to choose from as well.

Ingredients

The following are the most common ingredients in both seed-starting and potting mixtures. Experiment with ingredients and mixtures for germinating your seeds. Only you can decide which materials and mixtures are most easily available to you, which ones you like working with, and which ones give you the best results.

Vermiculite

This is an excellent medium for germinating seeds that can even be used by itself. If you look at it closely, you'll see that it's composed of shiny, flakelike particles, which indicate its origin; vermiculite is a form of mica that has been heated and "popped" like popcorn. Seed-starters appreciate vermiculite's light texture and ability to absorb large quantities of water, as well as its ability to soak up plant nutrients from fertilizers and slowly release them to plants. For seed-starting mixes—or any horticultural uses, for that matter—be sure to avoid the vermiculite sold in the building trade. It is coarser in texture than horticultural vermiculite, can be extremely alkaline, and may contain substances that are toxic to plants.

Sphagnum Moss

This popular material is actually a type of moss that is collected live from acid bogs and dried. It is sold in two forms: whole, dried plants, most often packaged in blocks or bales; and milled sphagnum, the most popular form for seed-starters. Milled sphagnum, as its name suggests, consists of very finely chopped sphagnum moss plants. Both are light brown or tan in color, are relatively sterile, and have excellent moisture-holding capacity. There is some evidence that sphagnum moss, as well as milled sphagnum, helps control bacterial diseases of seedlings.

Peat Moss

Don't confuse milled sphagnum or sphagnum moss with peat moss or sphagnum peat, which are the *decomposed* remains of bog-dwelling mosses and other plants. Peat moss, which is dark brown in color, is often used in mixtures because it holds moisture well, is relatively sterile, and is readily available. It can be very difficult to wet, however. If allowed to dry out, it tends to form a crust and is very difficult to rewet.

Perlite

Despite its artificial appearance, perlite is a form of volcanic ash that, like vermiculite, has been "popped." Perlite's main asset is its ability to promote good drainage in seed-starting mixes. It is also relatively sterile and doesn't carry diseases or fungi.

Sharp Sand

Another ingredient added to mixtures to promote drainage, sharp sand is coarse sand sold in the building trade. Don't substitute the sand used in children's sandboxes, collected along roadsides, or gathered at the seashore. All are too fine and will form a cementlike crust. Seashore sand is also too salty.

Compost

The finished compost listed in the recipes in this chapter is the black, granular, end product of the composting process also called humus. Whether called compost, leaf mold, or humus, if you decide to use this material in your mixtures it's important to make sure your compost pile attains temperatures high enough to kill disease-causing organisms and fungi (120° to 140°F). Avoid using walnut leaves in your compost pile; they contain a chemical called juglone that is toxic to many plants, including tomatoes, peppers, rhododendrons, and azaleas.

Potting Soil

The potting soil mentioned in the recipes in this chapter could be any one of the many commercial mixes offered for sale—either specifically for seed-starting or for general house-plant use. You could also use home-mixed potting soil with good results. Whatever you use, once again, it's important that it be free of fungi, soil-borne diseases, insects, and weed seeds. Also, it should be well drained.

Don't use plain garden soil for germinating seeds or growing seedlings. It is usually much too heavy when used in containers and tends to pack and crust. Unsterilized garden soil harbors fungi that cause damping-off, a disease that kills seedlings by rotting them at soil level. Sometimes it even attacks before seedlings emerge from the soil. It's a good idea to use fresh potting soil for each new seedling crop, and add the old soil to the compost heap.

Seed-Starting Mixes

For a good all-around seed-starting mix, combine equal parts vermiculite, milled sphagnum, and perlite. When combined, these three materials provide a moist but well-drained seedbed that is relatively sterile and will provide good support to germinating seeds. It's important to remember that mixtures such as this, which don't contain compost, potting soil, or other nutrient-rich ingredients, can't provide seedlings with the nutrients necessary to support growth. You will need to feed seedlings germinated in

these substances regularly until they're transplanted to a richer mix.

You can make equally good seed-starting mixtures by combining equal parts of milled sphagnum moss and vermiculite; or 1 part milled sphagnum, 2 parts vermiculite and 2 parts perlite.

Potting Mixtures for Transplants

Good potting mixes don't have to be fancy, but don't be afraid to experiment. Seedlings generally don't live in them longer than eight weeks before they're moved to the garden, so as with seed-starting mixtures, structure and texture matter more than the exact proportion of ingredients. Most have ingredients such as screened compost that contribute to the nourishment of growing plants, however. If you suspect your compost or leaf mold is extremely acid, be sure to test the pH of the mix.

Use one of the basic potting mix formulas listed here, or develop your own.

● One part screened, finished compost or leaf mold and 1 part vermiculite or perlite.

● One part finished compost or leaf mold; 1 part good potting soil; and 1 part of either sharp sand, perlite, or vermiculite, or a mixture of all three.

● One part commercial potting soil, compost, or leaf mold; 1 part sphagnum moss or peat moss; and 1 part perlite or sharp sand. You can make a richer version of this mix by combining 1 part good potting soil; 1 part compost or leaf mold; 1 part sphagnum moss; and 1 part sharp sand or perlite.

● One part compost or leaf mold; 2 parts of good potting soil; and 1 part compost or well-rotted, sifted manure makes an especially rich potting mix.

MICROWAVING SOIL

You can use your microwave to sterilize up to 10 pounds of potting soil at a time, using a technique developed by scientists at the University of Kentucky.

The soil should be moist and crumbly, not squishy; if it's dry enough to work, it's dry enough to microwave.

Place the soil in a plastic bag (polypropylene bags, the kind used for baking, are less likely to break than polyethylene bags) or in a large, loosely covered, microwave-safe mixing bowl. Give the top of the bag a twist, but don't seal it or it might explode as steam builds up.

With the oven turned to full power, heating a 2-pound batch

of soil for two and a half minutes or a 10-pound batch for seven minutes will kill most pathogens.

If you've had problems with damping-off or other soilborne diseases, you can extend, even double, the heating time. The high water content and abundant pore spaces of organic materials make them slow to heat, so doubling the treatment time may be necessary to sterilize compost or leaf mold.

After sterilization, let the soil stand uncovered until cool; then store in sealed containers. After microwaving soil, thoroughly clean the oven, especially the door seal.

Mixing Mixes

Combining the ingredients in a seed-starting or potting mix is a relatively simple operation, but a few tips will make things easier and also improve your results.

Since the amounts in recipes listed in this chapter are given in parts, decide how much of the finished mix you'll be using, and select a container—anything from a cup to a coffee can to a bucket—with which to measure. It doesn't matter what you use, just so long as you're consistent. Since homemade media will decrease by 15 to 20 percent in total volume when mixed and moistened, make up more soil mix than you think you'll need.

Mix the ingredients together thoroughly in a large bucket or tub placed on newspapers. As you mix, you'll find that milled sphagnum and some of the other ingredients are quite dusty. Spraying the mixture down regularly with water or covering the bucket or tub loosely with plastic or a tarp and reaching underneath it may help contain the dust that rises as you mix.

It is important to thoroughly wet these mixtures before using them, so you'll need to prepare your soil mixture several hours before you intend to plant seeds. One of the main reasons for premoistening mixtures is that dry mixes are so difficult to wet; they'll either float out of containers when you water from below, or the water will run through them so quickly seedlings don't have a chance to use any of it. Dry mixes can quickly suck the moisture out of tender seedlings, severely damaging the roots and/or killing the plants.

The easiest way to premoisten a mix is to add hot water to the finished mix and soak it for several hours before filling containers and transplanting seedlings. Warm water is absorbed more quickly than cold water. This is especially important for mixtures containing either sphagnum moss or peat moss, both of which are difficult to wet. In fact, many gardeners soak peat moss for 12 to 24 hours *before* mixing it with other materials.

Judge the wetness of potting mixtures just as you would garden soil, by squeezing a handful of the mix. It should form a ball that shatters easily under fingertip pressure. If it doesn't form a ball, it's too dry; if it doesn't shatter, it's too wet. If you've added too much water, simply pour off any that puddles on the surface, and allow the excess to drain away through holes in the bottoms of the containers before planting.

Feeding Seedlings

Seedlings grown in mixtures that include compost, rotted manure, or soil (either commercial or garden soil) may not need supplemental feeding. Those in mixtures without these ingredients definitely do, starting with the appearance of the first true leaves. Feed with a weak solution of liquid fertilizer every two weeks. Half-strength solutions of liquid kelp, fish emulsion, and manure or compost tea are good sources of nutrients, although the latter two are low in phosphorus and potassium.

Starting Seeds Indoors

Each winter brings a blizzard of seed catalogs, each enticing you to try a few more plants. Displays of colorful packets bewitch you at the checkout counter. Once you give in to these temptations, you'll have a hefty stack of seed packets. Here are some helpful hints to turn them into a healthy crop of transplants.

Sowing Schedules

It's almost as important to know *when* to sow as *how* to sow. Seeds started too early too often result in unhealthy, overgrown transplants; starting too late delays fruiting and flowering. The best time to sow seeds will depend on the climate in your area, specifically the average date of the last spring frost. If you don't know what your average last frost date is, find out by calling your local county extension agent.

You'll also need to take into account what you're growing and how you plan to germinate and grow your seed. Since different types of seeds germinate at different rates and have different requirements, it's a good idea to read the seed packets for tips that will improve your success several weeks *before* you're ready to start sowing. That way, you won't be surprised by germination times or pretreatments required. (For more information on these treatments, see "Pretreating Seeds" on page 34.) Many mail-order companies also send booklets that provide germination information with their orders or offer books devoted to the subject.

Most packets will provide guidelines that recommend starting dates in terms of the number of weeks before the last average frost date. They also offer suggestions on when to transplant based on that date. For example, peppers can be started indoors 8 to 12 weeks before the last frost, and are best transplanted outdoors a week or so *after* the last frost date, once the soil has warmed. To determine the best sowing date in your area, count back the recommended number of weeks for each plant from your last average frost date. Once you've figured out schedules for all your seeds, jot notes on your calendar to remind you when and what you need to sow.

How you grow your seedlings—whether indoors on a windowsill or under lights or outdoors in a cold frame or hotbed—will also determine your timing. (For more information, see "Designing and Using Cold Frames and Hotbeds" on page 50.) Plants grown under fluorescent lights will receive more light than ones grown on a windowsill and are less apt to get spindly and overgrown if started a bit early. It's also easier to control the light, heat, and humidity levels of seedlings grown under lights on a plant rack than on windowsills. Keep notes from year to year to determine the best timing under your particular conditions.

Sowing Seeds

You can either sow your seeds in flats and transplant them to pots when they are large enough, or you can use individual containers such as plastic bedding plant "six-packs," empty cottage cheese containers, or half-pint milk cartons, sowing one or two seeds per container. Seeds sown in individual containers won't need transplanting if you use a mixture containing nutrient-rich ingredients such as compost. Many gardeners use individual pots as flats; they sow many seeds per pot and then transplant the sturdiest ones to individual containers.

Start by collecting all the supplies you'll need to sow your seeds—seed-sowing mix, seeds, a spray bottle or watering can, newspaper, labels, and markers. The flats or containers you select should have drainage holes in the bottom. You'll also need trays to catch dripping water if you will be germinating your seeds anywhere but in a greenhouse.

Seed-sowing can be a messy operation, so choose a spot where you'll have plenty of space to spread out and cover the area with newspaper. Premoisten the seed-sowing or potting mix you'll be using.

Take a minute to look over your seed packets again, make labels for each type, and remind yourself of important germination instructions. You can make your own labels from things like wooden Popsicle sticks or strips cut from plastic jugs, or buy ready-made labels from your garden supply store. Use a nursery marking pen or a pencil to write the names on the labels; labels written with felt-tip pens can fade and run.

To keep soil from sifting out through the drainage holes in the flats or containers, start by spreading a layer of newspaper, paper towels, or torn, premoistened sphagnum moss on the bottom. Cut the newspaper to fit the bottom of the flat; if it protrudes above soil it will draw off soil moisture. Add a layer of perlite to improve drainage and fill the flats or containers up to about ½ inch from the top with the premoistened seed-starting or potting mix you've selected. Then gently firm the surface with a flat object such as a board.

Either sow seeds in rows, or space them over the entire surface, but don't sow too thickly. Space tiny seeds about ⅛ inch apart; medium seeds, ½ inch apart; large seeds, 1 inch. Although

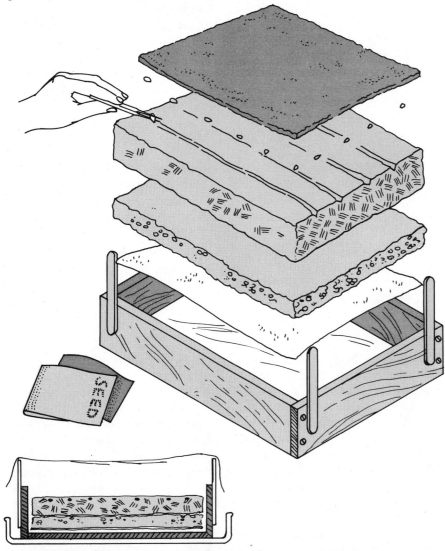

To sow seeds in a flat, begin with a layer of newspaper or paper towels on the bottom of each flat or container. Be sure containers have drainage holes or slits in the bottom. Add a layer of perlite to provide drainage and fill to within ½ inch of the top of the flat with the growing medium of your choice. Plant the seeds in rows or scatter them evenly over the surface, but be sure to space tiny seeds about ⅛-inch apart; medium seeds need ½ inch, and large seeds, 1 inch. Unless the seeds you're sowing need light to germinate, cover them with sand or soil to a depth of three times their size. Slip the flat in a plastic bag or loosely cover it with plastic to maintain humidity, but support the plastic with a wood or wire frame so that it does not touch the soil surface. You can make a simple frame by stapling or taping wooden Popsicle sticks to the four corners of the flat.

SEED GERMINATION AND LIGHT

One of the important factors to keep in mind when sowing seed is whether the seed germinates best when exposed to light and should not be covered with soil when sowing, or whether the seed requires darkness to germinate and must be thoroughly covered. The following lists of common vegetables, herbs, annuals, perennials, and biennials include plants that germinate best in light and those that require darkness for germination.

Plants That Germinate Best in Light

Don't cover these seeds with soil when sowing.

Annuals

Ageratum spp.
Antirrhinum majus (snapdragon)
Begonia spp.
Browallia spp.
Celosia cristata (cockscomb)
Cleome hasslerana (spider flower)
Coleus × hybridus (coleus)
Gerbera jamesonii (African daisy)
Helichrysum bracteatum (strawflower)
Impatiens spp. (impatiens)
Kochia scoparia (kochia)
Lobularia maritima (sweet alyssum)
Matthiola spp. (stock)
Mimulus spp. (monkey flower)
Nicotiana spp. (flowering tobacco)
Petunia spp. (petunia)
Reseda spp. (mignonette)
Salvia splendens (scarlet sage)
Tithonia spp. (Mexican sunflower)

Perennials and Biennials

Achillea spp. (yarrow)
Aquilegia spp. (columbine)
Arabis spp. (rock cress)
Aubrieta spp. (false rock cress)
Aurinia saxatilis (basket-of-gold)
Campanula spp. (bellflower)
Chrysanthemum parthenium and *C. × superbum* (feverfew, shasta daisy)
Gaillardia spp. (blanket flower)
Hesperis matronalis (sweet rocket)
Leontopodium alpinum (edelweiss)
Lychnis chalcedonica (Maltese cross)
Papaver orientale (Oriental poppy)
Physalis alkekengi (Chinese lantern)
Platycodon grandiflorus (balloon flower)
Primula spp., except *P. sinensis* (primrose)

Herbs and Vegetables

Anethum graveolens (dill)
Capsicum spp. (peppers)
Lactuca sativa (lettuce)
Satureja spp. (savory)

Plants That Germinate Best in Darkness

When sowing, cover seed with at least ¼-inch fine soil and firm it gently.

Annuals

Calendula officinalis (pot marigold)
Centaurea cyanus (bachelor's-button)
Lathyrus odoratus (sweet pea)
Nemesia spp.
Phlox spp.
Salpiglossis sinuata (painted-tongue)
Schizanthus spp. (butterfly flower)
Tropaeolum spp. (nasturtium)
Verbena × hybrida (vervain)
Viola spp. (pansy, violet)

Perennials

Delphinium spp.
Papaver spp., except *P. orientale* (poppy)
Phlox spp.
Saponaria ocymoides (soapwort)

Herbs and Vegetables

Borago officinalis (borage)
Coriandrum sativum (coriander)
Foeniculum vulgare (fennel)

---

you can always thin out excess seedlings, crowding encourages disease and reduces vigor, so taking the time to space them out at the beginning will result in huskier seedlings.

As a general rule, seeds should be covered to a depth of three times their size. Very fine seeds should only be pressed into the soil surface. Some seeds require light to germinate and should not be covered.

SANDY SUGGESTION

When planting tiny seeds in a flat, add 1 or 2 teaspoons of white sandbox sand to the seed packet. When you pour the mix on the flats, you can tell when the seeds are evenly distributed.

If you presoaked the growing medium, then it's not necessary to water just after sowing seeds. Most seeds germinate better at warm temperatures (70° to 80°F). Set your flats or containers under grow lights or on windowsills over heating cables.

Germinating seeds require high humidity and moist soil, so cover the containers with a plastic sheet or bag slipped around the flat. Only cover

33

them loosely, since closely covered seedlings tend to be succulent and weak. Use a wire or simple wood frame to prop up the plastic and prevent it from touching the leaves or soil surface. Watch carefully for mold, and, if it develops, provide better ventilation.

Watering the containers from below also helps discourage disease. Place the containers in a shallow dishpan of water, wait for the water to rise to the surface level of the con-

tainers or just below, and then lift the containers out, letting the water drain away. That way, the soil surface remains somewhat drier than the rest of the medium, which helps prevent damping-off. If you prefer watering from above, use a gentle spray from a rubber bulb sprinkler or a spray bottle to avoid dislodging the seeds.

Once the seeds germinate, you'll need to begin fertilizing regularly. (For more information, see "Feeding Seedlings" on page 31.)

Pretreating Seeds

Some types of seed will germinate more quickly if given a little head start before sowing. For example, seeds that need warm temperatures in order to emerge will get off to a quick start if germinated in moist paper towels *before* they are planted in soil. Soaking slow-to-sprout seeds can also speed germination time. Many perennials, shrubs, and trees require periods of cool, moist storage, called stratification, so they can break dormancy and begin to grow. It's a good idea to read seed packets, as well as other books or pamphlets you may have that list germination requirements, to determine which seeds will benefit from presowing treatments.

such seeds in small muslin bags to soak overnight before planting.

The purpose of scarifying seed is to nick the seed coat to speed water uptake without damaging the embryo. You can either use a file or a knife, or you can accomplish the same purpose by rubbing seeds between two pieces of sandpaper.

Vegetables and herbs that benefit from presoaking or scarification before sowing include beans, carrots, celery, okra, parsley, parsnips, and peas. Annuals and perennials that should be presoaked include thrift (*Armeria* spp.), Job's-tears (*Coix lacryma-jobi*), mallow (*Hibiscus* spp.), morning glory (*Ipomoea* spp.), sweet

pea (*Lathyrus* spp.), lilyturf (*Liriope muscari*), and lupine (*Lupinus* spp.). As a general rule, small seeds should be presoaked; large seeds are either presoaked or scarified.

Stratification

Many perennial, shrub, and tree seeds require a period of cold, moist storage, called cold stratification, to overcome dormancy before they will germinate. Some more difficult to germinate species require one or two periods of cold stratification interspersed with a period of warm, moist storage, called warm stratification.

Presoaking and Scarifying

Many seeds are slow to sprout because their hard seed coats prevent them from taking up the moisture necessary for germination. Pretreating such seeds—either by soaking them in water or scarifying the seed coats—is often the difference between success and failure.

To presoak, pour just-boiled water over the seeds, let them stand in water overnight or until the water is cool, and mix the seeds with dry sand to avoid clumping. Some gardeners put

Presoaking cuts several days of germination time for slow-sprouting seeds such as carrots, celery, and parsley. To speed things along, pour just-boiled water over them.

Drain the seeds when cool and mix with dry sand to avoid clumping.

To cold stratify seeds indoors, mix them with a small quantity of moist peat moss, place the mixture in a plastic bag in the refrigerator, and store for the recommended amount of time. Or sow the seeds in moistened medium in the pots or flats in which they will germinate, cover them with plastic, and store them in a cold frame, unheated basement, or the refrigerator—in short, anywhere that the temperature remains at or slightly below 40°F. Seeds that require a period of warm stratification should be mixed with moist peat or sown in pots or flats where they are to grow and placed in a warm (70° to 75°F), dark place. In either case, check the seeds periodically to be sure they remain moist and free of mold.

Presprouting Seeds

Plants that need especially warm conditions to germinate—cucumbers, squash, pumpkins, and melons, for example—respond well when their seeds are presprouted before planting. Presprouting gives plants a head start and also generally results in a high germination rate because the seeds receive constant warmth and moisture. Presprouting is also an excellent way to check the germination percentage of seeds you have stored or collected.

To presprout seeds, space them out on a layer of damp paper towels—

two or more are best—or several thicknesses of paper napkin. (Since no two seeds should touch, it's best not to try to germinate too many on one towel.) Then roll the towel up carefully, making sure the seeds stay as well separated as possible. Tuck the roll into a small plastic bag. You can put more than one species or cultivar in each bag if you label each roll as you go.

Put the plastic bags full of rolled-up paper towels in a warm place such as on top of the refrigerator, a fluorescent plant light fixture, or an insulated water heater.

Check the seeds daily. Although they will not begin to germinate for several days, the small amount of air that wafts in while you check on the germinating seeds is beneficial. The first sign of germination is development of the root. It is important to remove the sprouted seeds from the towels and pot them up as soon as they begin to germinate, because the root hairs have a tendency to grow together and tangle. If the roots get tangled in the paper towels, don't try to separate them, just tear up the towel and plant it right with the seed.

Planting

Presprouted seeds should be potted up in individual containers filled with a rich mix that has been premoistened. Individual milk cartons are ideal, because at transplanting time it's a

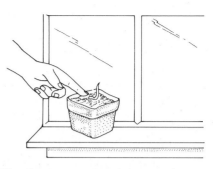

Plant the presprouted seeds in pots or in the garden.

simple matter to remove the bottom and set the whole plant in the garden with little disturbance. You can also plant them in small plastic pots, peat pots, or other containers as long as they drain well. When planting presprouted seeds, be sure to cover the roots lightly but firmly with soil. Move the pots to your sunniest windowsill or place them under lights immediately.

Cucumbers, squash, and pumpkins, which can be difficult to transplant because of their fleshy, easily bruised roots, can be planted directly in the ground after presprouting. Melons bear earlier if pregerminated and then grown in individual pots for a couple of weeks before transplanting outdoors.

To presprout seeds, first spread them on a double layer of damp paper towels.

Roll the towels carefully so the seeds don't touch each other.

Place the rolled, seed-filled paper towels in a plastic bag. Keep them in a warm place, checking daily until germination occurs.

Using a Soil-Block Maker

Homemade soil blocks are the most economical way to produce large crops of transplants, although they take time and special equipment to make. You'll need a soil-block mold, which is a metal device with a plunger used to form the blocks, as well as a tub or wheelbarrow for mixing the soil-block medium and the ingredients to make it. You'll also need trays to hold the finished blocks.

Blocks work well for starting most seeds, and they produce transplants with healthy, well-branched root systems. Because blocks interfere with root elongation, however, it's inadvisable to use them to start carrots or beets. Most plants probably shouldn't be in the blocks for more than six weeks or they will become too crowded. Transplant to the garden or into larger pots when the plants get too big.

There are four keys to success with a block maker: Mixing the right soil, forming the blocks, planting the seeds, and watering carefully.

Mixtures. The proper mixture for making soil blocks is able to hold its shape after leaving the mold, provides nutrients for plant growth, and

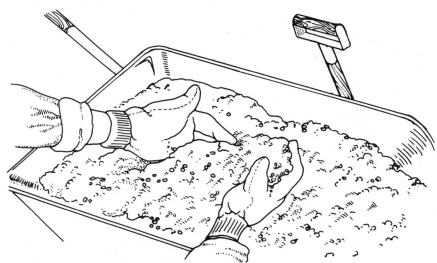

A wheelbarrow is perfect for mixing screened peat, compost, and a bit of lime. Before adding water, mix the dry ingredients thoroughly. Add water gradually. Finished mix should be the consistency of peanut butter.

has a pH between 6.0 and 6.5. Peat moss is the primary ingredient that holds the blocks together. It also lightens the mix, retains water, and is relatively sterile. An ideal mix is composed of 2 parts peat moss that has been screened through ¼-inch hardware cloth, 1 part vermiculite, and 1 part compost. Equal parts of screened peat moss and compost will also work well. You will also need ground limestone to adjust the pH of

the mix. Figure about 1 cup of limestone per 15 gallons of mix, but to be certain of the amount to add, test the pH level of the finished mix first with a pH meter or litmus paper. Then add some limestone, test again, and repeat the process until the pH is correct.

Making Blocks. You can make your mix in a tub, but a wheelbarrow is ideal. To form the blocks, mix the

Load the blocker by jamming it into the mix. Press it against the bottom of the wheelbarrow to pack it and force away excess mix.

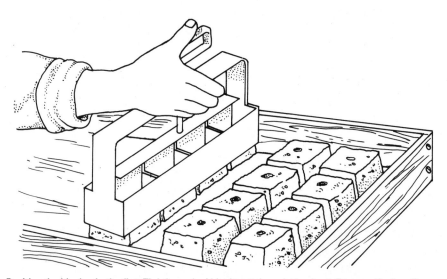

Position the blocker in the flat. Tightly packed blocks retain moisture best. Depress the handle and lift the block maker away.

dry ingredients and then add water. The mix is right when it is thoroughly wet but still stiff enough to stand on its own with little slumping. Next, push the block maker in to fill it, then push it against the floor of the tub or wheelbarrow to compress the mix. Wipe the excess against the side of the container or with your hand, check to be sure the forms are completely filled, and press the blocks out onto a tray or flat.

Seeding. Plant a single seed in each block, or plant two and cut off the extra seedling if both germinate. To handle the seeds, try picking them out of a dish using the tip of a moistened stick or pushing the seeds out of the packet with a dry pencil.

Cover the seeds by sprinkling each flat with peat moss. Water the flat thoroughly and transfer it to a hotbed or to whatever light and heat setup you have for getting your seedlings started.

Watering. Water the blocks very carefully using a can equipped with a misting nozzle. Watch them closely and water frequently from above to be sure the blocks don't dry out. Flood the flat to rewet them if they do. Once the roots fill them, blocks are nearly indestructible.

Proceed until flat or tray is full. The blocker will automatically punch dimples in which to sow the seed.

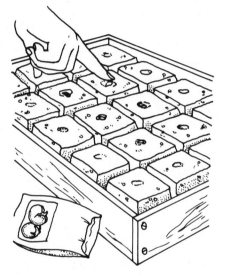

Put one or two seeds in each block. Cover the seeds with a sprinkling of peat moss, water the flat thoroughly, and move it to where you plan to germinate the seeds.

Transplanting Seedlings into New Containers

Unless you sow your seeds directly in individual pots, they'll need transplanting soon after they germinate. As a general rule, seedlings should be transplanted shortly after they produce their first pair of true leaves. Seedlings started in a mix that lacks compost or soil need to be moved to a richer medium so they can obtain the nutrients needed for growth. (For the healthiest plants, continue to provide regular applications of fertilizer even after transplanting to a richer mix.)

Transplanting to individual pots (or if you find you need to move plants along from too-small containers to larger ones) also provides seedlings with the room they need to develop into strong, healthy plants with well-developed root systems.

Transplanting also provides an opportunity to select the most vigorous seedlings, for undoubtedly you'll have more seedlings than you have space for in the garden. In most cases, plants that sprout quickly, healthy-looking green leaves, and a compact habit are the signs to look for. Select seedlings with compact, well-developed root systems, because plants with well-branched feeder roots will be more vigorous than ones with thready, trailing roots. Also, it's harder to transplant a seedling that has only one long root, which can easily become tangled or damaged. Deformed cotyledons, or seed leaves, can be a sign that the seed was damaged either before or during germination. However, if you're growing plants with variegated leaves—hostas, for example—or looking for unusual flower colors in a mix of seeds, it's best to grow on as many of the transplants as possible. Plants with variegated leaves, and sometimes those with unusual flower colors, may grow more slowly.

Transplanting Tips

A few days before you transplant, it's a good idea to harden your seedlings a bit to get them ready for transplanting. To do this, remove the plastic that covers the flats for a few hours each day.

Transplant only when you won't be in a hurry. It's easy to damage a root or shoot of a young seedling, and such injuries can set plants back for weeks or leave them open to attacks by diseases. Start by gathering up all the materials you'll need. The containers should have drainage holes in the bottom and be deeper than the germinating flats. Select a rich potting medium from one of the recipes on page 30 and premoisten it. You will also need your flats of seedlings and a small transplanting tool such as a wooden Popsicle stick, pencil, the handle of a spoon or fork, or an old screwdriver to gently separate the roots of the seedlings.

Spread a double layer of newspaper or paper towels on the bottom of each container if soil sifting through the drainage holes will be a problem. There are two good ways to deal with filling containers. For small seedlings, you can fill the containers to within ½ inch of the top before you start transplanting. For larger plants, you can start with empty containers, suspend the plants over the pots, and spoon the mixture in around the roots. Either way, it's best to start with premoistened potting medium, because dry mixes can suck the moisture out of delicate roots very quickly, thus damaging or killing them.

Gently dig up the seedlings one at a time, using the transplanting tool

When transplanting, hold the seedlings by their first leaves, called cotyledons or seed leaves. That way, you won't bruise or break the fragile stem. Use a small utensil such as a wooden Popsicle stick, pencil, or the handle of a spoon or fork to gently loosen the roots.

to loosen the roots, and lift the plants to the new containers. (Seed-starting mixes, which are very light in texture, make this operation easier, because they crumble away quite readily.) When handling seedlings, hold them by their first leaves, called cotyledons or seed leaves, and support the root ball with your hand. That way, you won't bruise or break the fragile stem. Don't expose the roots to air for more than a few minutes, because it can dry and damage them. If you disturb a large clump of seedlings while extracting one, make sure the roots stay moist by misting them with a spray bottle.

Set most seedlings just slightly deeper than they were in their original container. Grasses, sweet peas, lilies, and other plants that bear seed leaves that stay below the soil surface are the exception. They should be planted at the depth they were in the flats. Gently firm the soil around the seedlings after transplanting.

Aftercare

Keep a close eye on newly transplanted seedlings for a few days. To give them time to get over the shock of transplanting and get adjusted to their new homes, keep them out of direct sun for a day. If they begin to wilt even though the soil is damp, don't pour on more water. Instead, mist the flat lightly and cover it with a plastic bag supported on a frame so that it

DEALING WITH THE DIFFICULT TO TRANSPLANT

Some plants are harder to transplant successfully than others. Sowing recommendations on seed packets will often serve as warning—either they state, "Difficult to transplant, do so with care," or they advise outdoor sowing where the plants are to grow. These plants can be started indoors if you take extra care to handle them gently during the transplanting process. Peat pots are a good choice for plants that don't transplant well, because seedlings can be set in the garden, pot and all, with little disturbance. Be sure the rim of the pot doesn't extend above the soil level, however, because it can act as a wick, sucking all of the water out of the peat and creating a nearly impenetrable prison for the roots.

Difficult-to-transplant vegetables include beans, Chinese cabbage, corn, cucumbers, melons, pumpkins, squash, and root crops except beets, turnips, and celeriac. Perennials with taproots, including balloon flower (*Platycodon grandiflorus*), butterfly weed (*Asclepias tuberosa*), and flax (*Linum* spp.), are hard to move, too. Hard-to-transplant annuals include California poppy (*Eschscholtzia californica*), cockscomb (*Celosia cristata*), and moss rose (*Portulaca grandiflora*). Annual and perennial poppies resent transplanting, also. Difficult-to-transplant herbs include borage, burnet, caraway, chervil, coriander, and dill.

will not rest on the plants. Wilted plants should be kept shaded and cool until they perk up, which shouldn't take more than a day or two.

Once the plants are again growing actively, continue watering from below and providing regular applications of a weak fertilizer.

Setting Up a Grow-Light System

Starting seedlings under fluorescent light is one of the best ways for gardeners to get a jump on spring. A good grow-light system will produce transplants as healthy as greenhouse-raised specimens—with excellent color and stocky growth. Since seedlings grown this way receive the same amount of light day after day, regardless of the weather outside, you won't have to worry about leggy, unhealthy plants during a dark and gloomy spring. Grow-light systems also mean you'll be starting seedlings under the same conditions each year, so you can fine-tune your methods and improve your results each year.

Fluorescent fixtures duplicate the color spectrum of sunlight more closely than any other type of artificial light. Cool-white bulbs are quite satisfactory when used alone and are the most efficient lights available, short of the costly high-intensity discharge (HID) lamps sometimes used in commercial greenhouses. Incandescent bulbs produce too much heat to be practical and also provide only red light, which causes leggy growth. Specially designed plant lights (sometimes called grow lights) don't necessarily produce more vigorous plants than cool-white fluorescent bulbs, and they're also less efficient and more expensive.

The grow-light system you choose will depend on the space you have available, your budget, and how many seedlings you want to grow. You may choose to grow a flat of seedlings under lights on the kitchen counter or decide on a rack in the basement (such as the one illustrated on page

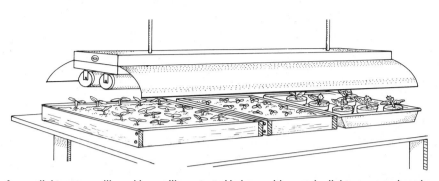

A grow-light system will provide seedlings started indoors with a regular light source and can be used to produce healthy, compact transplants for the garden. Keep seedlings as close to the light as possible, without touching the tubes, and use a timer to ensure they receive 16 hours of light a day.

40). Whatever you decide, here are a few tips for getting the most out of your lights.

● Growing seedlings need lots of light. Keep the lights on 16 hours a day and suspend the lights as close to the leaves of the seedlings as possible without allowing the tubes to touch the leaves—never more than 3 or 4 inches. Buy an inexpensive timer so you won't have to remember to turn them on and off.

● Since tubes produce less light at the ends than in the middle, choose the longest ones you have room for, and rotate seedlings near the ends into the middle every few days. Shop light fixtures, which generally have two 48-inch bulbs, reflect more light toward the seedlings where you want it to go than bulbs without reflectors.

● Keep the tubes clean, because dust can decrease the amount of light available. Reflecting surfaces,

in addition to the reflectors on the fixtures, also increase efficiency. Paint surfaces near the fixtures such as shelves and walls with white paint to reflect more light.

● Tubes last longest if they aren't turned on and off unnecessarily. As they age, however, they produce less light, so it's a good idea to replace them before they burn out completely.

Green Thumb Tip

TRICKS WITH MIRRORS

You can use a mirror to make double use of the light from a window or fluorescent fixture. Just position it so that it will reflect light back onto your seedlings. If you are growing seedlings on a windowsill, this technique helps them grow more evenly, so you won't have to turn them as often. You can also use aluminum foil to reflect light onto plants.

Making a Plant Rack

If you're sold on the benefits of starting seedlings under lights but need to conserve space in your basement or plant room, building a plant rack may be the solution. Ours is inexpensive and relatively easy to build.

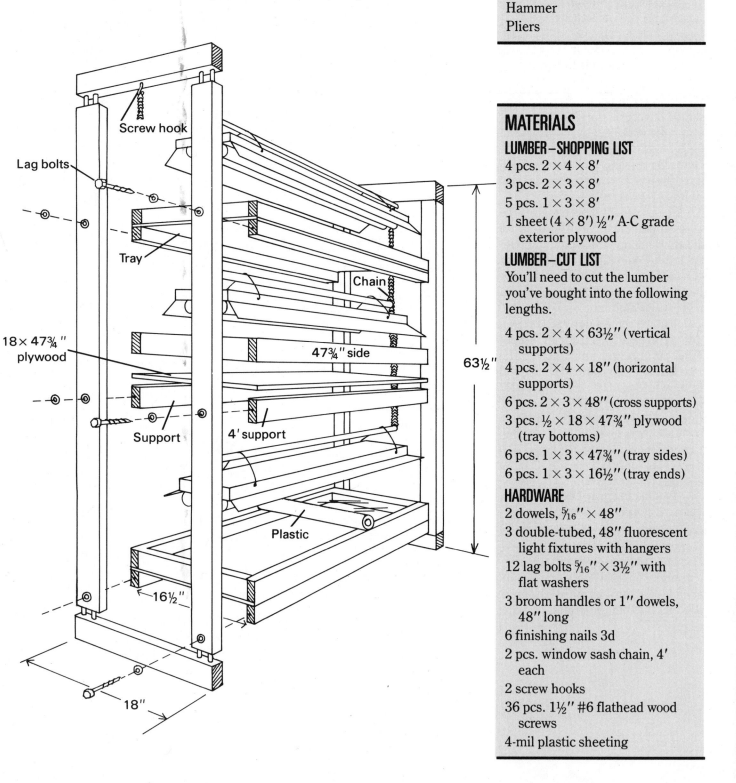

Screw hook

Lag bolts

Tray

18 × 47¾ "
plywood

Support

4' support

Chain

47¾" side

Plastic

63½ "

16½ "

18"

TOOLS REQUIRED
Electric drill
Saw (circular saw or handsaw)
Hammer
Pliers

MATERIALS
LUMBER–SHOPPING LIST
4 pcs. 2 × 4 × 8'
3 pcs. 2 × 3 × 8'
5 pcs. 1 × 3 × 8'
1 sheet (4 × 8') ½" A-C grade exterior plywood

LUMBER–CUT LIST
You'll need to cut the lumber you've bought into the following lengths.

4 pcs. 2 × 4 × 63½" (vertical supports)
4 pcs. 2 × 4 × 18" (horizontal supports)
6 pcs. 2 × 3 × 48" (cross supports)
3 pcs. ½ × 18 × 47¾" plywood (tray bottoms)
6 pcs. 1 × 3 × 47¾" (tray sides)
6 pcs. 1 × 3 × 16½" (tray ends)

HARDWARE
2 dowels, $\frac{5}{16}$" × 48"
3 double-tubed, 48" fluorescent light fixtures with hangers
12 lag bolts $\frac{5}{16}$" × 3½" with flat washers
3 broom handles or 1" dowels, 48" long
6 finishing nails 3d
2 pcs. window sash chain, 4' each
2 screw hooks
36 pcs. 1½" #6 flathead wood screws
4-mil plastic sheeting

1. Drill 5/16-inch holes for the lag bolts in the vertical supports, making sure they are spaced evenly so the trays they support will be level.

2. Drill holes for dowels in the ends of the vertical supports and corresponding holes in the horizontal supports as shown in the illustration below. Cut dowels to 4-inch lengths and glue the assembly together.

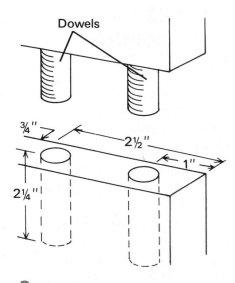

Dowels

¾"

2½"

1"

2¼"

3. Drill ¼-inch pilot holes that are 2 inches deep in the ends of each cross support. Bolt the rack together with the lag bolts and washers.

4. To make the tray bottoms, drill and countersink pilot holes through the tray bottoms into the tray sides and ends. Fasten tray bottoms to sides with flathead wood screws. For a waterproof liner, spread 4-mil plastic on the tray bottoms and up the sides, and staple or tack

it in place. Slide the finished trays onto the rack.

5. To mount the fluorescent lights, first twist screw hooks into the underside of the horizontal supports at the top of the rack. Hang a 4-foot piece of window sash chain from each hook. Drive finishing nails partway into the ends of three broom handles, slip the broom handles through the hangers on the light fixtures, and insert the nail ends into loops of the sash chain. Adjust the lights up or down by moving the nails to higher or lower loops.

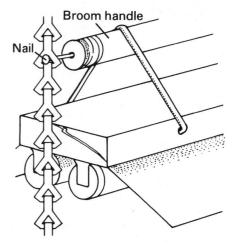

Broom handle

Nail

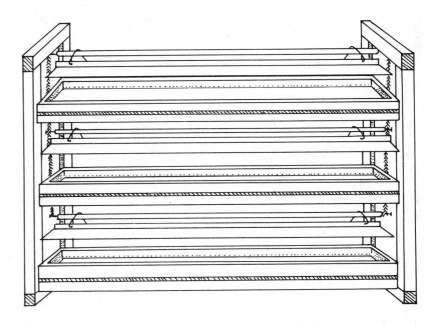

The three lights combined use about 260 watts per hour (40 watts per tube plus ballast).

For quick germination, start your seeds on the rack's top level, where the soil can be warmed by heat rising from the lower lights. Once the seedlings have sprouted, move them to a lower level and start a fresh seed tray on top.

Hardening-Off Seedlings

Indoors, you can control the light, water, temperature, and humidity to which your seedlings are exposed. However, seedlings need to be ready to withstand the more rigorous conditions that prevail in your garden—brighter light, wider extremes of temperature, as well as wind and rain—before they can be transplanted successfully. Sun, wind, and cold temperatures can kill succulent seedlings very quickly, or damage them enough to set them back for weeks. So, seedlings grown indoors need to be hardened off before they are moved to the garden permanently. Hardening off is a technique used to gradually introduce seedlings to their new environment. It also helps toughen them up by thickening succulent leaves and causing them to build food reserves.

Begin the process of hardening off your seedlings about a week before they're to be transplanted to the garden. If you have a cold frame, you can use it to graduate your seedlings from their cloistered conditions indoors. (For more information on cold frames, see "Designing and Using Cold Frames and Hotbeds" on page 50.)

1. Slow Down Plant Growth. Start hardening off your plants by watering them less often during the last week before transplanting and allowing them to dry out slightly between waterings. Also, don't feed them during their final week indoors. Another way to slow down growth is to keep temperatures on the cool side—if possible, a few degrees lower than what the plants have become accustomed to thus far. These steps will help thicken leaf surfaces and build food reserves.

2. Blocking Out. If you are growing any plants in flats, a few days before transplanting, use a knife to cut between the seedlings—a crisscross pattern from left to right and from back to front will suffice. Each plant should end up centered in a cube of soil, but leave them in the flat and otherwise undisturbed.

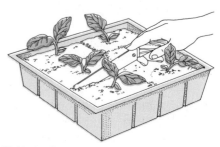

To block a flat of seedlings, cut through the soil between plants. Then allow the plants to sit undisturbed in the flats for two or three days to recover before setting them out in the garden.

Blocking out helps promote a well-branched root system and also cuts roots that would be broken during transplanting. Give blocked seedlings two or three days to begin their recovery before moving them to the garden.

3. Acclimate Plants to the Garden. After a week of cooler temperatures, as well as reduced watering and feeding, your seedlings are ready to be gradually exposed to the conditions outdoors. Start by exposing them to filtered sun outdoors on the north side of your house, in the shade of a bush, or under some other improvised shelter. Choose a spot that is protected from wind, which can dry seedlings out very quickly and cause them to wilt. Gusty spring winds can also break stems and whip seedlings around enough to damage roots. The first day, move them outdoors for about an hour in the morning or afternoon and gradually increase the exposure until at the end of a week or ten days they can withstand a full day of direct sun.

You'll need to keep a sharp watch on your seedlings during this process. They will need watering nearly every day because sun and wind cause the shallow flats to dry out quickly. Keep the soil moist enough to avoid wilting.

DON'T RUSH TO TRANSPLANT

Although every spring gardeners rush to plant their gardens, late spring frosts and cool soil conditions can take their toll with many new plants. Many plants grow well in cool temperatures—cole crops such as cabbage, broccoli, and cauliflower, as well as peas, lettuce, spinach, and many annuals and perennials; however, others are very sensitive to cold, which can check growth or kill plants. When you begin the hardening-off process, be sure to bring your plants in each night. Seedlings that thrive in cool weather can be left out all night once they are fully hardened, but have boxes ready to cover them if frost threatens. Warm-weather plants such as tomatoes, peppers, eggplant, melons, and tender annuals and perennials also should be left out all night the last day or so of the hardening process. However, it's often best with these plants to wait an extra few days after the average last frost date before transplanting so that all danger of frost has passed and the soil has warmed.

Planting Seedlings into the Garden

There comes a day in early spring when your seedlings have been hardened off and you're ready to plant them in the garden. Although clear, breezy spring days are beautiful, they're not the best kind for transplanting seedlings. Sun and wind cause seedlings to loose large quantities of water, which newly disturbed root systems have difficulty replacing. It's a far better idea to wait and transplant seedlings at the beginning of a spell of warm, damp, cloudy weather. That way, they'll have a chance to recover and put on root growth before having to withstand sun and wind.

Try not to rush seedlings into the gardens if cold weather still threatens unless you're prepared to cover them nightly with boxes or other protective devices when the weather turns cool. Jumping the average date of last spring frost pays off some years; in others, late spring frosts take their toll of newly transplanted seedlings. Although many plants grow well in cool temperatures, others are sensitive to cold and won't begin growing until the weather (and the soil) warms up. If you can't bear to wait, be sure to hold back a few of each kind of plant as insurance against a late cold snap.

Transplanting is a stressful operation for plants, and the more you can do to ease the stress a plant suffers in being put out in the garden, the sooner it will be off and growing. Here are some tips to make your transplanting day a success.

- Dig a generous hole for each seedling so that there is ample space for the plant's roots.

- If you're planting an entire bed of plants, work plenty of compost into the soil before planting, or add a handful to each hole as you plant, mix it in, and cover with ordinary garden soil before planting.

- Water seedlings before you transplant and try to keep as much soil around the plants' roots as possible so they will not dry out. If the potting mix falls away from the roots, it's a good idea to dip them in a slurry of thick, muddy water to be sure the roots stay moist.

- As you place each plant in its hole, take time to make sure the roots fan out evenly in all directions.

Dig a generous hole—one that will provide ample space for the plant's root ball.

If the seedling is hard to get out of the pot, cup the pot in your hand and turn it upside down. Sharply rap the bottom with your hand or knock the edge of the pot with your trowel.

Set the plant into the hole, making sure the roots are spread evenly in all directions.

Fill the hole with soil and gently firm it around the roots. Leave a saucerlike depression to funnel rain toward the roots.

After the seedling has been positioned in the hole, pour at least a quart of water on it to settle it in the hole.

They shouldn't double back on each other or stick up toward the top of the hole.

● Water the seedlings as you go, rather than waiting and watering after you've finished transplanting. If the soil is unusually dry, moisten it slightly before planting, because dry soil can quickly pull the water out of tender roots and damage them.

● To settle seedlings in their holes, fill the soil with loose, well-tilled soil, sprinkle at least a quart of water on each transplant, and gently firm the soil to eliminate large air pockets, so the roots will be in contact with the soil and there are no root-drying air spaces. A shallow, saucerlike depression will help catch rain and direct it toward the roots.

● As a general rule, set seedlings in the soil at the same depth they were growing in their pots. Tomatoes are an exception to this rule; if planted in a shallow trench on their sides with the top one or two sets of leaves above ground, the stems will grow roots and the plants will be less leggy.

Planting in Peat Pots

Seedlings grown in peat pots can be planted pot and all: That's why they are such a good choice for difficult-to-transplant species. However, keep in mind that the rim of a peat pot that sticks out of the soil will draw moisture away from the plant's roots. If this happens, the pot can become so dry it becomes a barrier that roots can't penetrate. When transplanting seedlings in peat pots, tear off the top inch or so of the pot so the remaining portion will be entirely underground. Cut slits down the sides to help roots penetrate them. Some gardeners prefer to gently tear away the entire pot if roots haven't already grown through. If you've started your seedlings in peat pellets encased in plastic netting, cut the netting off before planting. Then plant as you would any other seedling.

Plant Protection

The transplanting operation doesn't end when the last seedling is in place in the garden, however. Sun and wind can still wreak havoc with your seedlings for the first week or so after transplanting, and freak, late spring frosts can reduce your carefully tended plants to mush. Be sure to keep them well watered and, if possible, screen them from heavy wind. Pale yellow leaves indicate sunscald. Cover afflicted plants promptly with screens, plastic sheeting, or anything else that will provide shade. Then gradually increase exposure to sun over several days.

Outdoor Sowing

Many kinds of seeds will germinate and grow perfectly well if sown outdoors in the garden. Vegetables such as beans, beets, corn, carrots, melons, peas, radishes, and zucchini are all direct-seeded. Annuals such as sweet alyssum, California poppies, cosmos, marigolds, nasturtiums, sweet peas, and zinnias, as well as many perennials, can also be sown outdoors where they are to grow. Plants that are difficult to transplant, including poppies, corn, cucumbers, parsley, melons, and dill, often are best sown outdoors.

Scheduling

Deciding when to sow seeds is as important for outdoor sowing as it is when you're starting seeds indoors. Check seed packets for recommended sowing dates and any other planting tips that will help improve your results. Plants that grow best when temperatures are cool, such as sweet peas, beets, carrots, and radishes, for example, can be sown as early as you can work the soil in spring. Other species, including marigolds, zinnias, squash, melons, and beans, are less tolerant of cool temperatures and should be sown after danger of frost has passed. Seed of many perennials and hardy annuals such as larkspur, poppies, and cleome, can be sown outdoors in late fall for germination the following spring.

Soil Preparation

The key to outdoor sowing success is providing seeds with a well-prepared seedbed. Seeds sown outdoors need rich, well-tilled soil in which to germinate. Before tilling in spring, make sure the soil is ready to work by squeezing a handful of it. If it forms a dense ball that doesn't crumble readily, the soil is too wet to work. Tilling wet soil can damage its structure, so if the soil is wet, wait a few days and test it again. If the soil is ready to work, use a shovel or rototiller to dig or turn it to a depth of 6 to 8 inches. Then spread a layer of compost or leaf mold over the bed and work it into the top 2 or 3 inches of soil. Compost will increase the amount of water held in the soil and will help prevent crusting after heavy rain. If you prepared your soil in the fall, you may need only to fluff up the top inch or so of soil before seeding.

When planning your garden and preparing your soil, you might consider the benefits of raised beds. Raised beds improve drainage and aeration, provide a warmer germinating area for plants, and prevent soil compaction because you can reach the center of the bed from either side and consequently don't need to walk where you planted. Raised beds can be edged by wooden boards, bricks, cement blocks, stones, or railroad ties. Structured sides make gardening easier on you because you can sit on the sides when you work on the bed rather than stooping and bending. When you are planning the dimensions of your bed, make it 3 to 5 feet wide so that you can easily reach across from different sides to work on it. (For more on raised beds, see "Making a Raised Bed" on page 5.)

Sowing

In a vegetable garden or cut-flower garden, you can sow seeds in rows marked off with string or a board. (Rows running north-south take best advantage of the sun.) In ornamental plantings, you'll want to arrange seeds in a more free-form pattern. Whatever you do, check the seed packets for recommended spacing and sow seeds thinly so the seedlings won't become crowded. Spacing the seeds properly from the start will reduce thinning chores later. After sowing, firm the soil in place around the seeds and water with a fine spray. Keep the bed weeded at least until seedlings can fend for themselves. Spring-sown seeds should be kept evenly moist until seedlings are well on their way. Autumn-sown annuals such as larkspur and cornflowers should be watered once when they are sown and can be left to germinate the following spring.

There are several methods for sowing seeds. Large seeds are often sown individually by hand. Smaller seeds can be planted in rows, scattered in broad strips, or broadcast over a large area.

Conventional Rows

Vegetable gardens have been traditionally planted in straight rows marked off with string or a board.

NURSERY BEDS

One of the best ways to start seeds outdoors is in a specially prepared nursery bed. That way, all of your seedlings are growing in one place and can be weeded, watered, and fertilized at one time. No more rushing around the garden with a hose or watering can while trying to remember where each batch of seed was sown. Once the plants are large enough, they can be transplanted to where they'll grow and bloom in the garden.

To make a nursery bed, start by preparing well-tilled, loamy soil that is rich in compost or leaf mold. If you have clayey soil, plan on constructing a raised bed and filling it with a mixture of soil, peat, compost, sand, and leaf mold. Then level the bed, plant the seeds, and keep the seedbed evenly moist until germination occurs. Shade with wood lath if the bed is located in hot sun.

After marking the row, make narrow V-shaped grooves or trenches, called furrows, for planting. Use the corner of a hoe to make furrows for large seeds or a garden tool handle to make them for smaller seeds. The rule of thumb is to sow seeds to a depth equal to 2 or 3 times the diameter of the seed. Sometimes, however, it's hard to apply this guideline with oddly shaped seeds, so check seed packets for planting depths. Packet information will also indicate if a plant requires light or darkness for germination. It's important to plant the seeds at the correct depth; they may dry out if sown too close to the surface or not be strong enough to break through the soil if sown too deeply. You can plant seeds a bit deeper in the summer if the soil is hot and dry to protect the seeds from the sun.

For small seeds, sow directly from the packet by tapping it and dropping the seeds out one at a time or drop them in pinches from your fingers. You might want to use old spice shakers to spread seeds evenly. Large seeds can be placed individually.

When you complete a row, you can pinch together soil from the sides of the furrow to cover the seed or work along the row with a hoe and tap soil from the sides of the furrow to cover the seed. Don't forget to mark each row so you will know what crop is there. Water lightly, and keep the

seedbed evenly moist until germination occurs.

Seed Tapes. If you really want to ensure correct seed spacing, you can use easy-to-handle seed tapes. Many companies offer both flower and vegetable seeds that are prespaced on tape, so you just trim the tape to fit the length of the furrow. Plant the tape at the correct depth and the tape will eventually dissolve. You can find seed tapes in well-stocked garden sup-

Vegetable gardens have traditionally been sowed in straight rows, but this system is equally effective for a cut-flower garden.

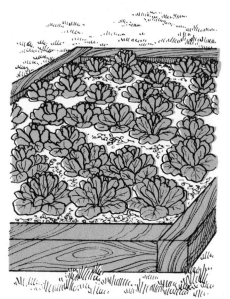

Broadcasting is an effective way to sow seeds in broad strips or when covering a large area.

ply centers or through mail-order catalogs.

Broadcasting

Broadcasting is an easy method that's best for single-crop beds or broad strips of plants instead of conventional rows. It works best with fast-growing, small-seeded plants such as carrots, turnip greens, radishes, beets, and leaf lettuce. It is especially effective for sowing cover crops and lawn grasses. This method of scattering seeds lets you sow large areas quickly, but frequent weeding the first three weeks and some thinning or transplanting might be necessary.

Fling seeds outward in even motions the full width of the bed, letting seeds scatter in midair so they fall evenly on the soil. It's a bit difficult to sprinkle the small seeds evenly at first, so you might want to practice. To prevent seeds from sticking together, you can mix them with fine sand, dry coffee grounds, or dry soil and spread the mixture. White play sand, the type used in children's sand boxes, is especially useful for this purpose, because it lets you see where you've already sown. Using a mixture also makes it easier to handle very fine seeds. Next, gently press the seeds into the ground with the back of a hoe. Seeds need close con-

tact with the soil so they can take up water necessary for germination. Gently tamp the seedbed again with a hoe and water with a gentle spray from a watering can or sprinkler. Very fine seeds do not need to be covered at all. Just rub soil between your hands, letting it lightly cover seeds, or mist with water. It's important to keep the seedbed moist until the seedlings poke up. This is fairly easy in early spring, but will be harder as the days get longer and hotter in summer.

Hill Planting

Hill planting is a good way to provide space for vines like watermelon, squash, melons, pumpkins, and cucumbers because it gives room for them to spread. It also provides them with the rich, loamy soil they require for best performance.

To build a hill, form a 6- to 12-inch-high mound of loamy, fertile soil 1 to 1½ feet square. Amend the soil with plenty of organic matter such as compost to make sure it is porous and loose. Flatten the mound on the top so water won't erode it during heavy rains. A light covering of mulch, such as salt hay, will also help prevent rains from washing the mound away before plant roots bind it together.

Plant six to eight seeds in the mound at the correct depth, spacing them along the tops and sides. Later you can thin out your plants, leaving the two or three strongest. If the soil is poor or if you'd like to provide an especially rich environment for your plants, dig a hole 12 inches deep and 12 inches square before forming each hill. Fill it with well-rotted compost, manure, or other organic material. Then build a mound on top.

Spacing and Thinning

There are many factors to consider when determining seed spacing. In the end, you have to use your judgment and experience. You can start out spacing according to packet directions, observe how much certain plants expand as they grow, and decide if you can afford to tighten up your spacing next year. If you space too closely, they'll have to compete with neighboring plants for water and nutrients. If you space too far apart, you waste valuable garden space and leave room open for weeds.

Climate is a factor to consider. Wider spacing is recommended for planting in unusually dry climates, for example, because plant roots need

The main benefit of hill planting is that it provides heavy feeders such as melons with rich, highly organic soil that encourages deep rooting.

to search farther for water. If your soil is not very fertile, heavy feeders also will benefit from wider spacing.

If your growing seedlings need more elbow room than you have allowed, you'll need to thin them. Overcrowded conditions result in competition for moisture and nutrients, which leads to weak, unhealthy plants. Try to thin as early as you can, because the longer you wait, the harder it is to disentangle roots of neighboring plants. You may have to go back and thin again as the plants grow. With many vegetable crops such as carrots, lettuce, and spinach, the thinnings are a blessing in disguise, for they make tasty additions to summer salads.

To thin, you can clip the seedling with scissors at the soil level, thus avoiding the problem of damaging entangled roots of the plants you are leaving in the row. Or you can simply use one hand to hold down the good seedlings and the other to gently pull out the extra seedling. This is easier to do when the soil is moist. You can also use a putty knife to carefully dig up the unwanted seedlings. Plants removed in this manner often can be moved elsewhere in the garden or given away.

Intensive Spacing

One way to maximize yields is to use intensive spacing. This technique involves spacing plants closer together than normally recommended on seed packets. Plants are spaced equal distances from each other so that when they mature, the leaves just touch and the entire bed is covered with foliage. Although vegetables planted in this manner will yield less per plant, because of the efficient use of space, overall yield is much higher. Intensive spacing also serves to shade the soil and help hold moisture in the soil.

Raised beds are an essential component of intensive spacing. They provide the deep, rich, well-prepared soil required to encourage plant roots to grow down, rather than sideways to compete with neighboring plants.

As with conventionally spaced plantings, your experience and judgment are the best guidelines. Pay attention to factors like shading, companion planting, and planting combinations. For example, lettuce is a perfect choice for intensive spacing, because it benefits from some additional shade. To use underground space efficiently, it's a good idea to alternate rows of leaf and root crops such as spinach and onions.

INTENSIVE SPACING FOR VEGETABLES

Here are some broad guidelines for intensive spacing. The best spacing guide is, of course, experience and knowledge of your particular climate and soil conditions. Carefully observe how well plants grow at different spacings and use that as your guideline.

Crop	Spacing (in.)
Beans	4-9
Beets	2-6
Broccoli	15-18
Brussels sprouts	15-18
Cabbage	15-18
Carrots	2-3
Cauliflower	15-18
Chinese cabbage	10-12
Collards	12-15
Corn	18
Cucumbers	18-36
Eggplant	18-24
Kale	15-18
Leeks	2-6
Lettuce, leaf	6-9
Melons	24-36
Okra	12-18
Onions, bulb type	4-6
Onions, bunching	2-3
Parsley	4-6
Peas	2-6
Peppers	12-15
Potatoes	10-12
Pumpkins	24-36
Radishes	2-3
Spinach	4-6
Squash	24-36
Sweet potatoes	10-12
Swiss chard	18-24
Tomatoes	18-24
Turnips	4-6

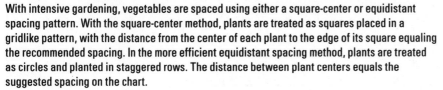

With intensive gardening, vegetables are spaced using either a square-center or equidistant spacing pattern. With the square-center method, plants are treated as squares placed in a gridlike pattern, with the distance from the center of each plant to the edge of its square equaling the recommended spacing. In the more efficient equidistant spacing method, plants are treated as circles and planted in staggered rows. The distance between plant centers equals the suggested spacing on the chart.

Growing Ferns from Spores

Unlike most garden plants, ferns do not reproduce by bearing flowers, fruit, and seed. Instead, they bear spores that germinate and develop into an intermediate stage that, in turn, produces ferns as we know them. Because of their unique, two-step life cycle, gardeners who wouldn't think twice about growing other plants from seed often find ferns intimidating. However, they are not as difficult to grow as they may appear. They require adequate humidity and light, and perhaps most importantly, as near sterile conditions as possible. The procedures are simple, and the key to success is patience.

The Life Cycle of a Fern

Spores are tiny and dustlike—hardly visible to the unaided eye—and a single plant can produce them by the millions. These tiny particles are produced inside spore cases, called sporangia, that are $\frac{1}{16}$ to $\frac{1}{8}$ inch across and generally located on the underside of the fronds. (Some species bear them on spikes or stems held above the foliage.) Sporangia are usually grouped together, either randomly or in defined patterns, in clusters called sori.

When a sporangium matures, it ruptures and releases its spores into the environment. If there is sufficient sunlight and moisture, the spores will germinate within a day or two. The first sign of germination is the development of one or many greenish threads. Within several weeks, a heart-shaped, leaflike structure about $\frac{1}{4}$ inch across, called a prothallium, appears.

The prothallium has two missions in life: to produce eggs and sperm and to house and nourish emerging fern plants following fertilization. Once both eggs and sperm have formed, fertilization can only take place if the sperm can transport itself to the egg. This can only occur if a thin film of water covers the surface of the soil and the prothallium; adequate moisture is essential to success. This process generally takes place within two or three weeks of the initial appearance of the prothallium.

If fertilization occurs, a fern will germinate on the prothallium. The prothallium will then provide nourishment to the developing fern until it reaches a size that will allow it to survive on its own—generally two or three months after fertilization has taken place.

Sowing Spores

Since algae and fungi also thrive in the warm, moist conditions that spores require to germinate and grow, it is very important to provide the spores with growing conditions as near to sterile possible. Otherwise, algae and fungi will grow rampantly, completely overwhelming the young ferns. Containers and any tools that will come in contact with the plants should be baked in an oven set at 250°F for 30 minutes or thoroughly soaked in a 10 percent Clorox solution (1 part bleach

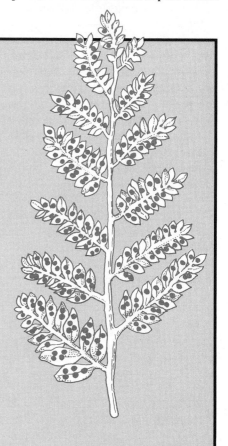

COLLECTING SPORES

1. Select a frond that contains mature sporangia that have not yet ruptured and spread their spores. Immature sporangia are usually greenish in color and rather flat; those that have already ruptured are dark brown or black and have ragged edges. Look for fronds with sporangia that appear plump, shiny, and brown or purplish in color.

2. Select a clean frond and place it in a small paper bag. Seal the bag and set it aside for several days in a warm, dry place. This will cause the sporangia to open and release their spores into the bag.

3. Once the spores have been shed, gently empty the bag by tapping the dustlike spores onto a sheet of white paper that is creased in the center.

4. Remove contaminants by adding the spores to a 5 percent Clorox solution (1 part bleach and 19 parts water). After about five minutes, pour the spores into a strainer lined with a paper towel or coffee filter, rinse with cooled, boiled water, and allow to air dry.

5. Once the spores are dry, tap them onto the desired sowing medium or into a clean paper envelope for storage in the refrigerator. (Viability will range from several days to several years. It's best not to delay sowing too long.)

to 9 parts water). Spores and soil medium should also be sterile.

For sowing, virtually any shallow container will do, as long as it allows drainage and is sterile. The sowing medium must hold moisture, provide anchorage, and allow for root penetration and air circulation. A mixture of ⅓ sphagnum peat moss, ⅓ vermiculite or perlite or coarse sand, and ⅓ commercial potting mix will provide all of these qualities.

Place the medium within the container, moisten with cooled, boiled water, and gently disperse the spores over its surface. Next, place a piece of sterilized glass or polyethylene film

As the fern sporelings grow, the prothalli will eventually cover the surface of the container. Transplant to give them room to grow.

over the top of the container to prevent contamination.

Place the container in a warm environment (65° to 85°F) where there is indirect light (2 feet below a fluorescent tube is ideal), and keep the medium evenly moist. Water the sowing container from the bottom by placing it in a larger container of water; the depth of the water in the larger container should not exceed ⅓ the height of the sowing container.

When the prothalli have formed a dense mat over the sowing medium, it's time to separate them and transplant ¼-inch sections into new containers. Using a sterilized tweezers or knife, lift the individual sections and place them ½ inch apart in a container of the same type of medium as previously used (sterilized and premoistened). Cover with glass or polyethylene.

You'll probably need to transplant again as the ferns grow, but individual plants will not be ready for their own pots until they reach a height of about 1 inch, at which time a 2½-inch pot is recommended. Hardy ferns can be transplanted outdoors about two to four weeks after they've been moved to individual pots. As with any seedling, it's important to harden off the plants before transplanting. (For more information, see "Hardening-Off Seedlings" on page 42.)

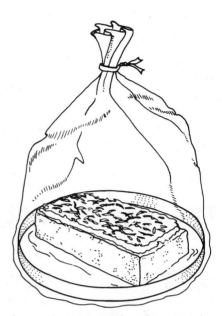

One popular way to start ferns from spores is to sterilize a brick in the oven (bake 30 minutes at 250°F), cool the brick, and cover the top with about 1 inch of milled sphagnum moss or other sterile germination medium. Set the brick, soil medium side up, in a shallow container of water and cover loosely with plastic to increase humidity. Be sure to keep the container full of water (one-third the height of the brick is fine) and keep the plastic propped up so it doesn't touch the emerging plants. Water will be drawn up to the surface of the brick, keeping the medium moist at all times but never soggy.

Cold Frames and Hotbeds

Designing and Using Cold Frames and Hotbeds

Cold frames and hotbeds are among the most useful of gardening structures, regardless of the type of gardening you do. Although most commonly used in early spring for starting or hardening-off seedlings, both can be used year-round for a multitude of purposes. Throughout much of the country, these structures can help extend the growing season by three months or more. Cold frames, and to a lesser extent hotbeds, can also be used for winter storage of container-grown plants that might not survive the rigors of winter above ground, holding over not-quite-hardy herbs or perennials, or for cold-treating spring bulbs potted up for forcing. Some models are also very useful for rooting cuttings of woody plants or perennials. Furthermore, cold frames and hotbeds—both of which are often referred to as frames for convenience—are inexpensive to build and easy to maintain.

Picking a Design

The type of frame you decide to build will depend on how you want to use it, as well as the space and site you have available. Your design can be as simple or elaborate as you wish; many cold frames and hotbeds are designed around materials on hand or ones that can be easily salvaged. Depend-

ing on the type of gardening you do, you may decide on a combination of cold frames and hotbeds, as well as permanent and portable models. There are also a variety of ready-made models for sale. Consider the following selection and design factors when making your choice.

Cold frames and hotbeds are basically rectangular, boxlike structures with glass sash on top. Most frames are designed with slanting sash roofs, with the high end toward the north, so that the sun's rays strike the glass at nearly a 90-degree angle in late winter and water and snow slide off the lids easily. Most frames are designed with lids sloping at an angle between 35 degrees and 45 degrees, which, for a 3-foot-deep model, translates to a frame that is 9 to 12 inches lower in front than in back. A slope of 35 degrees is most efficient for catching the late winter to early spring sun; a 55-degree slope catches more autumn sun, which is at a lower angle. It's possible to fine-tune your frame to catch more autumn sun by designing wedge-shaped inserts that change the angle of the glass.

The inside of the frame is usually painted white to increase the amount of light reflected onto the plants. You'll also need blocks or other props for holding the lids open to ventilate the frames.

Hot or Cold?

From a structural point of view, hotbeds and cold frames are identical, with the exception that hotbeds are supplied with some form of artificial heat. Traditionally, rotting manure served as the heat source, but today, electric heating cables are commonly used. Because hotbeds have a regular source of heat, they can be put into use earlier in the season than most cold frames and provide ideal conditions for starting most types of seeds. Also, they can be easily converted to cold frames during times of the year when heating isn't necessary. (The design suggestions provided here for frames in general apply to both cold frames and hotbeds, but for more on design and use of hotbeds, see "Making and Using a Hotbed" on page 55.)

Permanent or Portable?

There are two basic types of frames: permanent structures or portable ones. Permanent models are built over a foundation, either dug in the ground or constructed on the surface. Aboveground models provide less frost protection than ones built over a dug foundation, but both provide more reliable protection from the cold than

portable frames. Permanent frames are generally sturdier and last longer as well.

Portable frames, which are basically bottomless boxes with clear lids, can be used in much the same way as permanent frames, but are not as well insulated and are therefore subject to wider temperature fluctuations. They're most often used for hardening-off seedlings grown indoors in spring, either alone or in combination with permanent frames, to help handle the spring rush of plants being gotten ready for the garden. For gardeners with limited space, one advantage is that they can be collapsed and stored during times when they're not in use. In the vegetable garden, portable frames can be used to extend the season for spring or fall crops such as lettuce or spinach, or to keep frost away from late-ripening crops such as melons that need a few more weeks to mature in autumn. In areas with mild winters, portable frames can be used to grow winter crops of cold-tolerant vegetables. They can be erected over garden beds to protect plants that might not be quite winter-hardy and will provide adequate protection for many perennials and herbs. Use them to keep rain away from plants that dislike "wet feet" in winter. In summer, use portable frames to grow seedlings in a cool, shady part of the garden.

Site Selection

Although site selection is more crucial with permanent frames than portable ones, basic considerations apply

to both types of frames. Cold frames are essentially passive solar collectors, and in order to get maximum benefit from the heat and light of the sun, they should face south (southeast or southwest exposures are next best). Ideally, the site should receive full sun from midmorning to midafternoon during the winter and early spring months. Hotbeds, despite their artificial source of heat, need a full-sun exposure as well.

The site should also be fairly level and well drained. Water accumulating around a cold frame will quickly rot and kill plants, as well as damage the foundation or base of the frame. For protection from winter winds, locate your frame with a building, fence, or hedge on the north side. Although frames built right against the foundation of a house will receive some escaping heat, leaving a foot or two between frame and foundation is a good idea. That way, you can easily get behind the frame to remove the sashes. Mount a hook on the wall behind the frame for holding the lids completely open.

For the sake of convenience, select a site near a water supply and somewhere that's easy to keep an eye on all year long. Deciduous trees overhead aren't necessarily a liability; they'll provide summer shade without blocking winter sun.

Materials

Use the best materials available, especially when constructing a permanent frame. For permanent frames, a concrete block foundation topped with

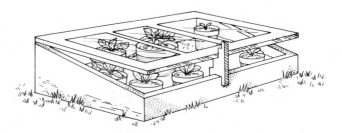

Portable frames are often used for hardening-off seedlings in spring. They are hinged on the high side, which should face north, and can be propped open for ventilation.

a frame made of decay-resistant wood painted with a nontoxic wood preservative such as Cuprinol is ideal. For portable frames, you'll need to weigh both the life expectancy of the materials and their weight. Try to use rustproof hardware in construction whenever possible.

Glass window sash are most often used to cover frames, but fiberglass, Plexiglas, or heavyweight polyethylene can be substituted. A layer of polyethylene on the underside of the glass sash can be added for extra insulation.

Proper drainage is essential, especially for permanent frames, so plan on placing at least a 6-inch layer of coarse gravel in the bottom of the frame for drainage. Incorporating drain tile into the design of the foundation is a good idea on sites where drainage may be a problem. On top of the gravel, you can add 8 inches of builder's sand in which to sink pots and other containers.

Dimensions

The size of most frames is determined by the sizes of standard window sash, and often by the sizes of salvaged or surplus windows on hand. Although 3-by-6-foot sash is traditional, smaller windows such as 2-by-4-foot or 3-by-3-foot are much lighter and easier to handle. With large sash, or in areas of heavy snowfall, plan on rafters or other supports between each sash. A bed width of about 3 feet is convenient, so you can reach the back of the frame without having to step into it. Frames can be of any length, for more than one sash can be mounted side by side. (Separate hotbeds and cold frames can also be constructed side-by-side, by dividing the foundation between heated and unheated sections and mounting a sash over each section.) Hinges at the back of the frame and handles in the front make for easy opening. Be sure the lids extend slightly beyond the frame in front so that water drains off instead of into it.

OTHER TYPES OF FRAMES

There are many variations of the simple rectangular frame, including double-glass frames, temporary flat-topped frames, and specially designed propagating frames such as the Nearing frame described here.

Double-Glass Frame

This style of frame looks much like a conventional greenhouse. It can be twice as wide as a conventional frame, since plants can be reached from either side. It is especially useful for gardeners who don't have a directly south-facing exposure. (If the length runs north and south, for example, the sun will shine on plants from the east in the morning and the west in the afternoon. If the length runs east and west, plants will still get day-long sun from the south.) Double-glass frames can be designed as portable units or built as permanent frames over a dug foundation. Pairs of sash are hinged in the middle along a ridgepole that forms the peak of the "roof." (The inside edge of the sash generally must be beveled to a 16-degree angle if the pairs are going to fit tightly.) End and side walls can be built of wood. (To increase the available light, use glass, fiberglass, or other material in the south wall.) These frames can be of any length, for any number of pairs of sash can be mounted on a ridgepole, provided there are enough rafters or central supporting poles. When used as portable units, double-glass frames can be set up directly over beds. In this case, side and end walls are held in place by stakes driven in the ground, and the "roof" is set in place across the staked-together frame.

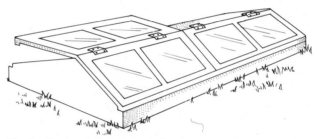

The double-glass frame can be designed as a portable or permanent model, and the hinged "roof" provides access from both sides.

Tent-Style Frame

A tent-style frame, which is similar to double-glass frames, can be constructed by attaching a glazing surface to a wooden ridgepole that runs the length of the frame. The ridgepole is supported by a post at each end that is driven into the ground or attached to the outside edge of a raised bed. Sheets of acrylic, fiberglass, or corrugated fiberglass are nailed or screwed to the frame as glazing. The ends can be covered as well, but it's best to have one end that can be opened for ventilation and closed at night or during cold weather.

The depth of the foundation and/or the height of the frame you decide on will depend on the plants your frame is designed to accommodate. When determining how much space you'll need, take into account the maximum height (including pots) of the plants you'll be growing, as well as the distance from the top of the layer of gravel added for drainage to the lowest part of the sash. A foundation dug to a depth of 2½ feet coupled with a cement block foundation that extends 8 inches above the ground will accommodate a wide variety of plant sizes. (Keeping the wooden portion of the frame off the ground also will reduce rot.) A deeper frame will

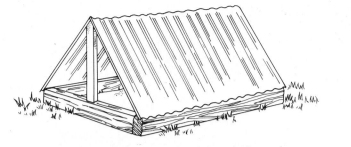

Tent-style frames can be erected over beds and covered by corrugated fiberglass. They will accommodate tall vegetables and provide early spring or fall protection.

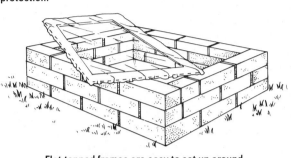

Flat-topped frames are easy to set up around garden beds and can be used to provide protection from frost for early spring or late fall crops.

Flat-Topped Frame

This type of frame is a temporary structure, easy to set up around existing garden beds and used to provide extra frost-free weeks in spring or fall. Most often, they're improvised from found materials such as cinder blocks, bricks, boards, or even hay bales. Storm windows, sheets of flexible but rigid plastic, a double layer of clear polyethylene stretched over a frame, or corrugated fiberglass are then laid over the top. Such frames will be adequate for providing extra protection for early spring or fall crops.

Nearing Frame

This type of frame, named for rhododendron hybridizer Guy C. Nearing, was designed for rooting cuttings of evergreen and deciduous trees and shrubs. Nearing frames are built exactly like conventional cold frames but are located so direct sun never strikes the glass or causes heat to build up inside. Nearing frames are not ventilated like conventional cold frames and hotbeds, because a function of the frame is to retain humidity necessary for rooting cuttings. A shady site or one along the north side of a wall or building is ideal. Nearing frames are usually sunk into the ground to help retain moisture and control temperature extremes.

cut out some light, but will accommodate small trees or shrubs.

Managing Your Frame

The first step toward learning to use your cold frame or hotbed effectively is to familiarize yourself with its own particular personality. A thermometer mounted inside the frame where the sun will not shine directly on it will provide useful information about temperature. Check it frequently under various weather conditions and at different times of day. A record of temperature extremes, prevailing weather, and other environmental conditions both inside and outside the frame will help you identify trends and establish schedules for your frame. For most effective light transmission, wipe away condensation each time you check the frame. Also, clean the glazing, inside and out, with clear water when it becomes dusty or splashed with mud.

Temperature Control

Controlling the temperature inside a cold frame or hotbed is of vital importance because on a bright, sunny day, whatever the outdoor temperature, inside temperature in an unvented, insulated frame can rise to 100°F or more, quickly killing plants inside. Until recently, the only way to regulate the temperature was manually —by watching it closely, propping the lid open when the temperature began to rise, and lowering the lid when it began to fall. Fortunately for today's two-career families, automatic vent openers are now available.

To control the temperature manually, you'll need to follow daily weather forecasts and use your own knowledge of local weather patterns to judge how much air to give your plants. The object is to keep the plants from cooking without chilling them. For example, if the morning sun is bright and the sky cloudless, promising continued sun, raise the lid and prop it open 4 to 6 inches. If it's windy or a bit cloudy, open the frame only slightly, so cold winds don't chill the plants. By midafternoon in late fall or early spring, or as early as noon in the dead of winter, check the thermometer inside the frame, and close the lid to conserve daytime heat. Temperature should be checked at least twice daily until you are well acquainted with your frame's personality.

If you're away from home during the day and unable to check the frame, a solar-powered automatic opener will do the opening and closing job for you. There are models with preset temperatures and ones that will allow you to select the temperature yourself. These are available through most general mail-order nursery catalogs and from local garden centers. They'll generally lift sashes up to a specified weight limit, but must be disconnected before the sashes can be opened completely. It is still a good idea to check the frame regularly, however, for vent openers will not perform the other essential chores of checking for signs of disease or insect problems.

In unusually cold weather, or if you have an uninsulated, aboveground frame, you can bank leaves, bales of hay, or soil around the frame. Be aware that this may attract unwanted rodents. Bricks or plastic gallon jugs filled with water can be stacked against the north wall to serve as passive solar collectors. You can enhance the heat absorption of either with a coat of black paint. Both will absorb heat during the day and release it slowly at night.

Containers

Although plants can be grown in a soil mixture placed directly on the layer of gravel in the bottom of the frame, using containers has several advantages. Plants grown in pots, seed flats, or other containers can be easily added, moved about, or removed without disturbing the frame's other inhabitants. Soil mixes can be tailor-made to suit individual plants, as can watering and fertilizing schedules, so the frame can be used for plants with a variety of requirements. Using individual pots also helps control diseases, which can spread quickly in both cold frames and hotbeds. Pots can be set on the layer of gravel at the bottom of the frame, or sunk to the rim in a 4- to 6-inch layer of sand on top of the gravel.

Watering

Until you become familiar with the conditions that prevail in your cold frame or hotbed, you'll need to check plants frequently to be sure they have enough water. This is especially important in warm weather when plants are actively growing. Check the moisture of the soil between 1 inch and ½

inch deep; for most plants, it should remain moist, but not soggy, at all times. Water whenever plants look droopy, but avoid watering on cold, cloudy days. To discourage fungal diseases, water early in the day so plants and surface soil can dry out before nightfall. Use water of approximately the same temperature as the medium in which the plants are growing, because cold water can shock plants and slow their growth. If you're using your frame to store dormant plants over winter, water well before the onset of cold temperatures, and then check every few weeks through the winter. You can tailor a miniature drip system to the size of your cold frame if it's used principally for starting seedlings in spring and summer.

Pests and Diseases

During your regular visits to your frame, carefully check for evidence of disease or insect infestation. In mild climates or during mild seasons, insects, slugs, or other pests will thrive in a cold frame or hotbed if left uncontrolled. Check each pot carefully before placing it in the frame to look for hitchhiking slugs or sowbugs. The moist conditions inside a frame also are ideal for plant diseases, and the warmer the temperatures (up to a point), the greater the danger of diseases. Generous spacing and proper ventilation can help avoid disease problems. Remove and discard infested, diseased, or sick-looking leaves and plants as soon as you spot them, because problems will spread very rapidly. If serious problems develop, remove all the plants and take steps to sterilize the inside of the frame. Pour boiling water into the gravel and/or sand at the bottom of the frame, or leave the glass lids in place and tightly closed during the summer to allow heat to build up inside the frame. If you've chosen to grow plants directly in soil in the bottom of your frame, it can be treated by either method, but it is also a good idea to dig it out

completely every two or three years and replace it with fresh soil.

Caring for Your Frame

Although maintenance tasks are minimal, they are essential because the moist, warm environment inside a cold frame or hotbed makes it subject to rot and rapid deterioration. Whenever paint starts flaking, repaint as soon as the frame is free of plants. Allow a newly painted frame to air for several weeks before putting it back into use, because fumes from the paint may harm plants. Recaulk as necessary to maintain airtight conditions. Watch for signs of rusted hardware and nails.

Replace caulking and check regularly for places where air could leak into the frames. Keep the glass and inside of the frame clean to increase the amount of light available to plants.

Year-Round Uses

How you use your frame will depend upon not only what types of gardening you enjoy, but also where you live, what exposure you have available, and what type of frame(s) you select. Experiment to discover the best way to use your cold frame and/or hotbed as well as the optimum annual schedule for your area. Keep in mind that cold frames and hotbeds can be used in much the same way, but as a general rule, you can start the season earlier or extend it longer with a hotbed. You can convert your hotbed to a cold frame during the summer or for applications where heat isn't necessary.

Spring

Spring (or late winter for southern gardeners) is the busiest season in both cold frames and hotbeds, for that is the time of year most gardeners are getting ready for the rush of spring planting.

To harden-off seedlings started indoors before transplanting them to the garden, move them to a cold frame a week or two before they're scheduled for transplanting. Gradually open the vent for longer periods each day. Shade the seedlings at first—using wood lath, burlap, or a mixture of clay soil and water painted on the glass—to keep them from burning. Expose them gradually to full sun.

Cold frames are also good places to germinate seeds in early spring—especially those of cold-tolerant vegetables, perennials, and annuals. Sow seed in flats or pots placed directly in the frame about two months before the last spring frost date. For an even earlier start, sow seeds in a hotbed or indoors and move seedlings to a cold frame after their first transplanting. This not only frees up space for more tender plants indoors, it also eliminates the succulent, rank growth that seedlings grown at warm temperatures can produce. Later in the season, more tender annuals can be sown in the frames.

In the North, where the growing season is short, cold frames can be used to start plants that require long growing seasons (such as melons) that otherwise might fail to mature. They can also be used to grow very early spring crops of lettuce or spinach.

Summer

During the summer, the glass sash that cover a cold frame are generally stored away and replaced with screens or other coverings to keep out leaves and other debris. Frames shaded with a grid of wood lath over the screens can be used in late summer to start fall crops of heat-sensitive vegetables such as lettuce. Raise seedlings in pots or flats, then transplant to the garden when temperatures begin to cool. Summer-sown perennials or biennials such as foxglove (*Digitalis* spp.) or Canterbury-bells (*Campanula medium*) can be germinated in pots or flats, held over their first winter under the protected conditions offered by a cold frame, and moved to the garden the following year. Cold frames can also be used for rooting cuttings taken any time of year.

Fall and Winter

As the days shorten and temperatures drop, glass sash are replaced and cold frames become an ideal place to sow seed of hardy annuals, perennials, wildflowers, shrubs, or trees. With seed sown in fall or early winter, the object is not to germinate the seed immediately, but to provide a cold treatment so that it will germinate promptly the following spring. Sow seed just before the ground freezes so it won't germinate before winter arrives.

Cold frames are also ideal for growing a fall crop of lettuce or spinach. Fall is also the time to move perennials, herbs, and container-grown plants that might not be quite hardy outdoors undercover for winter protection. Semihardy herbs such as parsley can be dug from your garden and guarded in a cold frame over winter. Use your cold frame for forcing pots of hardy spring bulbs. (For more information, see "Forcing Hardy Bulbs" on page 127.)

Making and Using a Hotbed

Hotbeds are designed and used much like cold frames, but as their name suggests, they are supplied with a regular source of heat.

Traditionally, hotbeds were heated by a layer of fresh, fermenting manure spread in the bottom of a frame. Temperatures remained high for several weeks and then slowly dropped off. To reheat the bed, the old manure had to be dug out and replaced with a fresh mixture.

Today, most gardeners use hotbeds heated with specially designed electric cables—the high-tech alternative to the manure hotbed—because of the labor involved in a manure hotbed and because fresh manure is not always easy to find and haul. Any cold frame built over a dug foundation can be made into a hotbed by adding an electric heating cable, assuming a source of electricity is available. Portable models can be used as hotbeds, although they don't conserve heat as well as permanent frames do, but a pit at least 1 foot deep needs to be dug underneath the frame to contain the heating cable.

To convert a cold frame to a hotbed, spread a 2-inch layer of vermiculite for insulation on top of the layer of gravel at the bottom of the pit. Spread the cable on the vermiculite, using long loops to provide an even source of heat. Don't allow the heating cable wires to cross, and keep loops at least 8 inches apart and 3 inches away from the edges of the frame. Cover the heating cable with

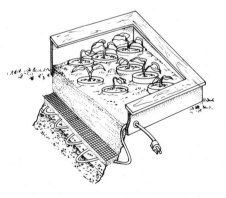

When installing a heating cable, spread a 2-inch layer of vermiculite on top of the gravel that drains the bottom of the bed. Spread the cable on top of the vermiculite, and add another inch of sand. Next, add a sheet of screen or hardware cloth to protect the cable, topped by another 4 to 6 inches of coarse builder's sand in which to sink containers.

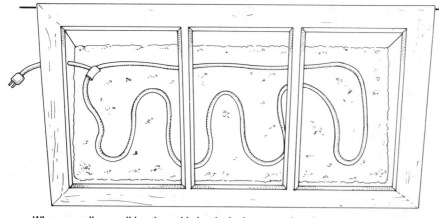

When spreading a soil-heating cable in a hotbed, arrange the wires evenly, so they'll provide a uniform source of heat. Keep wires at least 8 inches apart and 3 inches from the edges of the frame.

an inch of sand, followed by a layer of screen or hardware cloth to keep it from being dug up accidently. Cover the heating cable with 4 to 6 inches of coarse builder's sand in which to sink pots. A 30-foot heating cable is sufficient to heat a 3-by-6-foot frame. Cables with built-in thermostats provide an extra measure of control. Tender plants prefer a medium temperature of between 60° and 75°F; temperatures between 50° and 60°F are sufficient for more cold-tolerant annuals and perennials. Disconnect the cable during seasons when heat isn't necessary, and convert back to a conventional cold frame.

To make a manure-fueled hotbed, start with a pit 2 to 2½ feet or more deep and slightly larger than the bed that sits on top of it. Mix the manure with straw, and spread it in a 6- to 8-inch layer at the bottom of the frame. Water it lightly and cover it with soil or sand. Within a few days, the fermenting mixture will raise the temperature in the frame to 70° or 80°F. The temperature will remain high for several weeks, then drop off. To reheat, remove the old manure and straw and replace with a fresh mixture.

Gardeners who heat their homes (or a greenhouse) with steam or hot water have another option for heating a hotbed, provided it is located next to the house. A pipe system connected to the heating system in the house can be used to heat a hotbed. A single loop of pipe can be run around the inside perimeter of the bed on the surface of the soil, about 2 inches from the outside wall, or several lengths of pipe can be buried under the soil, about 16 to 18 inches apart and 8 to 10 inches from the outside wall.

Using Cloches and Row Covers

Stretching the growing season is an age-old goal of gardeners. The quest for the earliest lettuce or the first ripe tomato is universal. Like portable cold frames, cloches and row covers are designed to help extend the season by protecting plants right in the garden. You can use them to get a head start on spring by protecting germinating seedlings or young transplants from spring frost. They're also perfect for protecting maturing crops from autumn cold snaps.

Forms of these portable coverings, sometimes called season extenders, have been used for centuries to protect individual plants or shelter entire rows. In fact, nearly every gardener has devised some sort of temporary season extender when faced with an unusually late spring frost that threatens newly transplanted tomatoes or tender annuals. Everything from cardboard boxes to blankets to paper bags has been pressed into service. Today, season extenders are made from new types of plastic and other materials, which makes them versatile, easy-to-use, and inexpensive. The terms portable cold frames and cloches are often used interchangeably when referring to such structures as the double-glass frames used to cover entire rows, for example. Here, however, we've distinguished between the two by calling the heavier, mostly glass-glazed structures portable cold frames. The light, plastic- or other fabric-covered season extenders are called cloches or row covers.

The basic principle of cloches and row covers relies on the greenhouse effect. Short ultraviolet rays from the sun pass through the glass and warm the soil and the air inside. The soil collects and stores the heat, then releases it slowly. This creates a greenhouselike atmosphere and provides frost protection to plants. The warmer conditions under a cloche or row cover increase the growth rate.

By using these coverings, you can plant seed or transplants—especially of cool-weather-loving crops such as broccoli, peas, cabbage, cauliflower, lettuce, spinach, and radishes—outdoors earlier than normal. You'll need to consider how much frost protection the type you're using provides, however, especially for cold-sensitive plants like tomatoes. Generally, row covers only provide protection from 1° or 2°F of frost.

Cloches and row covers can also be used to extend your fall growing season. They can provide warmth and frost protection to melons and other crops that need a long growing season to ripen. Or, use them to protect a late sowing of such cool weather crops as lettuce or spinach.

In spring or fall, cloches and row covers can easily be moved from crop to crop. In spring, for example, when cool-loving vegetables are well established, use them to protect tomatoes, melons, or other warm-weather vegetables.

Making a Portable Cold Frame

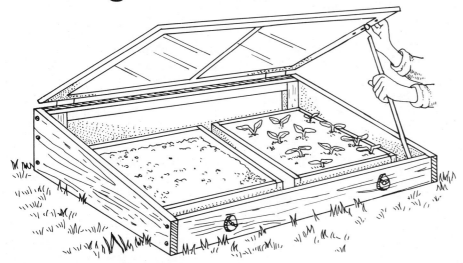

TOOLS REQUIRED
Electric drill
Saw (table or circular saw)
Hammer
Pliers
Screwdriver

MATERIALS
LUMBER—SHOPPING LIST
1 pc. $1 \times 4 \times 10'$
1 pc. $1 \times 2 \times 5'$
1 sheet $(4 \times 8')$ $\frac{1}{2}''$ A-C grade exterior plywood

LUMBER—CUT LIST
You'll need to cut the lumber you've bought into the following lengths. Use pressure-treated lumber or untreated pine painted with a preservative. See the diagram on page 58 for instructions on cutting the plywood. It's best to measure and then cut the pieces as you assemble them to be sure they fit together correctly.

2 pcs. $1 \times 2 \times 18\frac{1}{2}''$ (rear vertical cleats)
2 pcs. $1 \times 4 \times 58\frac{1}{4}''$ (front and rear horizontal cleats)
2 pcs. $1 \times 2 \times 6''$ (front vertical cleats)

HARDWARE
2 hardwood dowels $\frac{5}{8}'' \times 36''$
1 wood-frame storm window $32\frac{1}{4}'' \times 62\frac{3}{8}''$
10 pcs. $1\frac{1}{2}''$ #8 flathead wood screws
2 carriage bolts $\frac{5}{16}'' \times 2''$ with flat washers and wing nuts
3 pcs. $3''$ tee hinges with fasteners
4 pcs. $1\frac{1}{2}''$ eye screws
12 finishing nails 4d
$1\frac{1}{4}''$ aluminum nails
$\frac{1}{2}$ pint waterproof glue
1 quart exterior-grade primer/sealer
1 quart exterior-grade enamel
1 quart copper naphthenate wood preservative

This simply designed cold frame is tried and true—as well as easy and inexpensive to build. Its dual window-positioning system is a convenient feature; rods attached to both sides of the frame can be raised to any of three positions to hold the glazing open wide when full ventilation is desired or while tending the plants inside. When only a small amount of ventilation is needed, wooden cams attached to the front adjust to hold the lid open from 1 to 3 inches.

This frame is designed to use an old storm window measuring $32\frac{1}{4}$ by $62\frac{3}{8}$ inches as the glazing. If you have a window with different measurements on hand, adjust the width and length of the frame accordingly. The width of the frame should be 1 inch less than the width of your window; the length of the frame should be $1\frac{1}{8}$ inches less than the length of your window. When adjusting the design, retain the height of the front and rear walls used here, but allow the slope of the window and the width of the box to change as necessary.

This frame can be easily dismantled for storage. The only maintenance it should need is periodic repainting and caulking.

1. Lay out the front-, rear-, and side-wall panels on the sheet of plywood as shown on page 58. Cut out all four pieces. The rear-wall panel will be $\frac{1}{2}$ inch wider than its final size, so its upper edge can be beveled (see step 4).

2. Fasten the vertical cleats across the ends of the rear-wall panel (see the exploded view on page 58), using waterproof glue and $1\frac{1}{4}$-inch aluminum nails. Avoid nailing at the three points on each end where screws will be inserted to hold the side panels in place in step 7, as shown in illustration A on page 59.

3. Fasten the horizontal cleat to the upper edge of the rear-wall panel, between the two vertical cleats and flush with the top of the rear wall, using waterproof glue and $1\frac{1}{4}$-inch aluminum nails. Avoid putting nails in areas where hinges will be attached in step 9, or near the upper edge of the panel, which will be trimmed away in step 4.

4. To bevel the top edge of the frame, start by laying the rear-wall panel down with the cleats facing up. Position one of the side panels against it, overlapping the edge and making sure the bottom and back

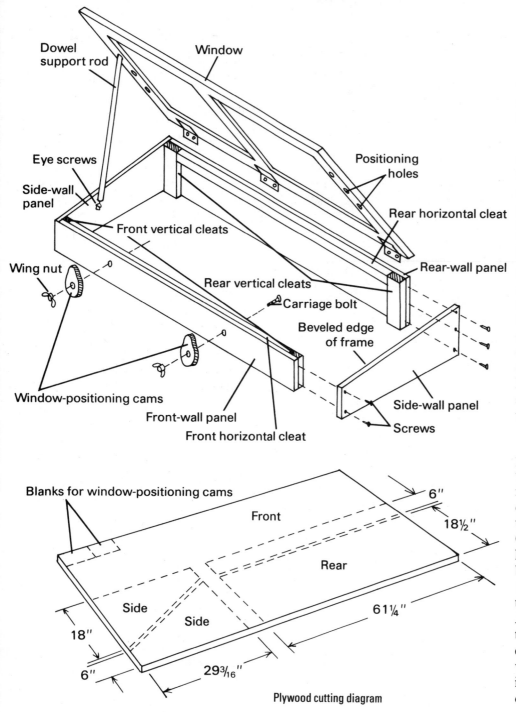

Dowel support rod

Window

Eye screws

Side-wall panel

Front vertical cleats

Positioning holes

Rear horizontal cleat

Wing nut

Rear vertical cleats

Carriage bolt

Rear-wall panel

Beveled edge of frame

Window-positioning cams

Side-wall panel

Front-wall panel

Screws

Front horizontal cleat

Blanks for window-positioning cams

6"

18½"

Front

Rear

Side

Side

61¼"

18"

6"

29³⁄₁₆"

Plywood cutting diagram

edges of each panel are aligned flush. Scribe or draw a line across the end of the rear-wall panel and vertical cleats where they are crossed by the upper edge of the side-wall panel. Do the same using the other side-wall panel on the opposite end. This establishes the angle of the bevel. Now connect the two slanted lines by scribing or drawing across the length of the rear-wall panel on the front and back. Using a table

saw or portable circular saw, rip and bevel the top edge of the rear panel.

5. Attach the front vertical cleats to the front-wall panel using waterproof glue and 1¼-inch aluminum nails. Avoid nailing where screws will be inserted from the side in step 7, as shown in illustration A.

6. Attach the front horizontal cleat to the front-wall panel, flush

with the upper edge of the panel, using waterproof glue and 1¼-inch aluminum nails.

7. Temporarily fasten the side-wall panels to the rear- and front-wall panels using 4d finishing nails or small brads. Drive the nails only part way into the wood for easy removal later. Drill a pair of ³⁄₃₂-inch-diameter pilot holes centered ¹³⁄₁₆ inch from the front edge of each side panel, as shown in illustration A. Drill the first hole 1½ inches above the base of the panel and the second 5 inches above. Center and drill three pilot holes of the same diameter through the back edge of each side panel, also as shown. Install 1½-inch #8 flathead wood screws in the holes; then remove all temporary fasteners.

8. Cut the two window-positioning cams out of ½-inch plywood by following the pattern shown in illustration B. Drill a ⁵⁄₁₆-inch-diameter hole through each cam at the point shown in the illustration. Center and drill two ⁵⁄₁₆-inch-diameter holes each 4¼ inches above the bottom edge of the front panel and 15 inches from the ends to accept the bolts for fastening the cams. Attach the cams to the outside of the front panel, using ⁵⁄₁₆- by 2-inch carriage bolts with flat washers and wing nuts. Install the bolts from inside the panel, as shown in the exploded view at left.

9. Position the window on top of the cold frame so the rear edges of each are flush. Center the window over the frame so both edges hang slightly over the outer edges of the frame sides. Fasten the window to the frame using three 3-inch tee hinges. Attach a hinge 4 inches from each end and one in the center. Check to make sure the window opens and shuts properly.

10. To attach the dowel support rods, fasten the 1½-inch eye screws

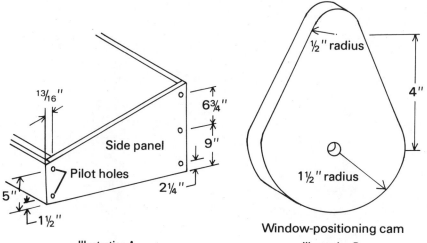

Illustration A

Side panel

Pilot holes

$^{13}/_{16}$"

6¾"

9"

2¼"

5"

1½"

Window-positioning cam

½" radius

4"

1½" radius

Illustration B

Support rod positioning holes

Storm window

4"

4"

65-degree angle

16"

Illustration C

into two linked pairs. Install one end of each pair into a front panel vertical cleat, 4¼ inches above the base of the cold frame. Then drill a ⅛-inch-diameter pilot hole into one end of each 36-inch wooden dowel. Screw the remaining eye screws into the dowels to fasten them to the frame.

11. Drill six 1¹/₁₆-inch-diameter holes into the window frame, on the underside about halfway through the wood. You'll need three holes on

either side. Locate one pair of holes 16 inches from the rear edge of the window; space the other two pairs on 4-inch centers toward the front, as shown in illustration C. Drill the holes at an angle (approximately 65 degrees) to accommodate the dowel support rods when the window is in the open position.

12. Dismantle the cold frame to prepare it for painting. Sand all sharp edges and coat all bare wood surfaces with copper naphthenate

wood preservative. After allowing the preservative to dry completely, paint the entire frame and, if necessary, the window frame with an exterior-grade primer/sealer.

13. Reglaze the window if the glazing is loose. Fill in any cracks or holes in the window or frame with caulk. Paint the wooden parts of the cold frame with two coats of good quality exterior-grade enamel. Reassemble the cold frame when you are ready to use it.

Cloches

The first cloches (*cloche* means bells in French) were glass bell jars. They were heavy, unventilated, and breakable, but nevertheless useful in extending the growing season. Today, there are many different types of cloches, ranging from those for individual plants to those for rows. Glass models are still occasionally available, but most used today are made of plastic or fiberglass. You can make your own or buy them ready-made. You'll have to determine for yourself if the time and expense you put into buying or building cloches is worthwhile.

No matter what kind of cloche you buy or make, there are a few basic guidelines to keep in mind. Like cold frames, cloches must be ventilated to prevent overheating, so you need to pay careful attention to the temperature inside the cloche. A thermometer is helpful for keeping track of how much the area under the covers warms up. In sunny weather, you'll need to partially vent or completely remove the covers during the day. Be aware that small cloches placed over individual plants will heat up fastest.

Since cloches remain in place for several weeks, be sure plants have enough elbowroom to grow. Finally, make sure the cloches are securely anchored so they don't blow away.

Homemade Cloches

The possibilities for homemade cloches for individual plants are endless. You can use plastic milk jugs with the bottoms cut out. Remove the cap to prevent overheating. To make sure they do not blow away, dig the edges of the bottoms into the soil or weight them down by tying stones or fishing weights to the jug handles. You can use wood, fiberglass, wire, or any other material to construct round, conical, or square frames to protect individual plants or entire beds. Cover them with plastic or fiberglass. Tomato cages can also be covered with plastic—even just on the sides, with the top open—to provide wind protection and a warm atmosphere. Whatever you do, be sure to anchor

Homemade cloches can be constructed many different ways. Here, left, fiberglass has been bent into a tunnel and held in place with wire. Right, wood frames with plastic stretched over them also make fine cloches.

everything so it won't blow away, and make sure you have ventilation so the plants don't overheat.

You can use wire fencing to form a Quonset-hut-type tunnel to shelter an entire row and cover it with 4-mil polyethylene. Fiberglass also can be made into a similar structure. Take a panel of translucent corrugated fiberglass and bend it into a semicircle. Wrap stiff wire (#8 or #9 gauge) around it, making a wicket that will secure the fiberglass, and stake the wire into the ground. If you make these in 4-foot segments, you can handle them easily.

If you have glass sash left over from a house renovation project, consider making a portable cold frame/glass cloche. (For more information, see "Other Types of Frames" on page 52.) Glass frames provide more frost protection than plastic ones, but they're heavier and harder to move around.

With any cloche that covers an entire row, be sure to close up each end or the row will become a mini wind tunnel. On warm days, you can open the ends to provide ventilation. Make sure plant leaves don't touch the sides of glass cloches in cold weather.

Commercial Cloches

There is a wide variety of commercial cloches available, both for covering individual plants or for sheltering

entire rows. Commercial coverings for individual plants include cone-shaped "hats," mini hothouses, and a plastic cylinder that uses water for insulation called Wall O' Water. Kits for plastic tunnel cloches are sold at most garden centers and garden supply mail-order companies. They are easy to erect. Generally you need only set wire hoops 6 or 8 inches into the ground at about 4-foot intervals along the row. Then dig trenches 6 inches deep along the edges of the row. Lay the plastic over the wires with its edges in the trenches and weigh them down with dirt or stones. Close the ends of the tunnel by tying them to stakes. Make uniform slits in the plastic for ventilation. (You can water plants without removing plastic if you have slits.)

Row Covers

Row covers are made of light permeable material, usually polypropylene or polyester, loosely laid right on top of plants or supported above them with wire hoops. They are anchored in place with stones or soil to keep them from blowing away. Sometimes called "floating" row covers because they are so light, polypropylene or polyester covers block out about 20 percent of the sun's rays, but are permeable and let in rain and air. They can be used to extend your season and protect your crops from frost

Plastic can be stretched over entire rows of plants and staked in place to provide a greenhouselike atmosphere for emerging seedlings and transplants.

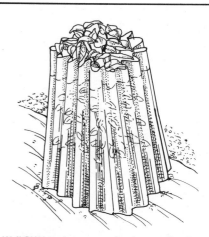

Wall O' Water is an example of a covering for individual plants. It is an upright ring of narrow plastic tubes that are filled with 3 gallons of water. The water in the tubes stores heat and releases it at night.

damage, but they provide only a few degrees of protection from frost. On the plus side, they "breathe," thus making overheating during the day somewhat less of a problem. (In hot, sunny weather, temperatures can rise 10° to 30°F underneath row covers, so you still need to watch for overheating.)

Row covers also can be used to protect plants from insects and birds, because they don't need to be slitted or vented unless the weather is warm. If you know from experience that an insect will start munching on your crops at a certain time, you can anticipate this and protect your plants with a row cover. Unfortunately, insects in the soil may also benefit from the nice growing environment under the cover. Crop rotation will help prevent them from attacking the same crop each year.

There are several brands of row covers made from different materials.

Polyester row covers, popularly known by the brand name Reemay, were the first to be released. They are very light and permeable, but break down rather rapidly when exposed to ultraviolet light, so much so that they can only be used for one season. They are also abrasive and can damage tender plant parts. Polypropylene

covers, such as Agronet, Agryl P17, and Kimberly Farms, are less abrasive to plants and last longer—from two to three seasons. All are delicate and can be ripped by the wind or torn by growing plants. Generally, they're used for about a month in spring and again in fall, then cleaned and stored until the following season.

Lightweight floating row covers are breathable, allowing air and water to penetrate, and provide protection from frost.

Care during the Season

Drip Irrigation—Use and Design

To many gardeners, drip irrigation is a puzzling system of tubes and other gadgetry somehow used to mysteriously water plants. However, drip systems are relatively easy to understand and well worth learning about, for they are the most efficient way to deliver water to plants. Drip systems can be used for much more than sending water along the straight rows of a vegetable garden. You can custom-design a system that will water all or any part of your landscape, including trees and shrubs, patio container gardens, and flower gardens. Also sometimes called trickle or weep irrigation, drip systems are as beneficial for dryland gardeners in the arid Southwest as for those in the northern, eastern, and southern parts of the country. They more than make up for the cost and effort involved in design and installation, for using them not only saves time and water, it also results in increased plant growth.

A drip irrigation system delivers water directly to the root zone of a plant and allows it to seep slowly into the soil one drop at a time. That way, little water is lost through surface runoff, and soil particles have plenty of opportunity to absorb and hold water for plants. It also means fewer nutrients are washed away through leaching. Drip irrigation reduces the water lost through evaporation as well, when compared to other methods. Conventional sprinklers distribute water by shooting it into the air, which means it can evaporate before it even hits the ground or can dry from foliage and the soil surface before it has a chance to trickle down to the roots. Furthermore, since drip irrigation delivers water directly to the plants you want to grow, less is wasted on weeds. The soil surface between plants remains drier, which discourages weed seedlings from sprouting. All these benefits add up to the fact that drip irrigation systems can save a great deal of water—and money, in terms of reduced water bills. Studies show that well-designed drip systems use at least 30 percent, and in some cases 50 percent, less water than other methods of watering such as sprinkling.

For busy gardeners, the main benefit of installing a drip irrigation system is the savings of both time and effort. Drip systems eliminate the need to drag hoses and sprin-

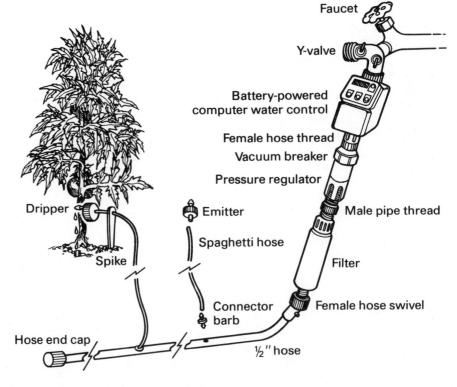

Faucet
Y-valve
Battery-powered computer water control
Female hose thread
Vacuum breaker
Pressure regulator
Male pipe thread
Dripper
Emitter
Spaghetti hose
Spike
Filter
Connector barb
Female hose swivel
Hose end cap
½" hose

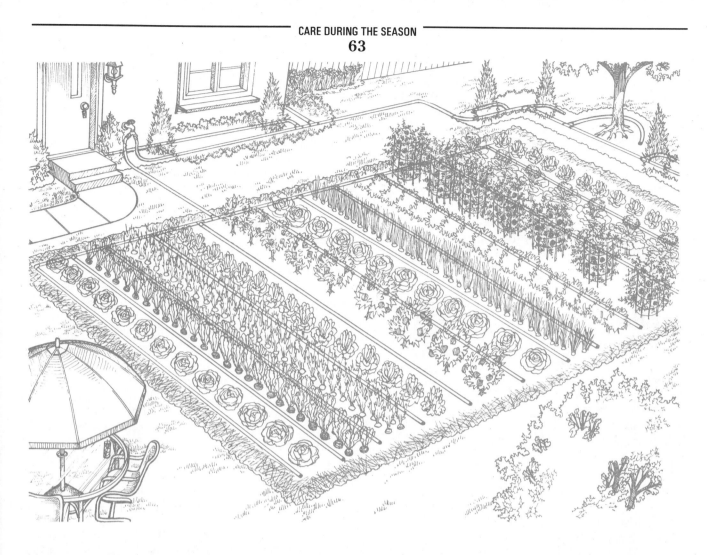

klers around. With systems that use a timer, gardeners need only spend a few seconds to turn the system on; the timer automatically turns it off.

Plants watered with drip systems grow more quickly and are more productive because they have all the water they need and their growth rates never slow down because of water stress. (This is especially true when drip irrigation is used in conjunction with mulch.) These systems also keep water off the foliage, which helps prevent some foliage diseases such as powdery mildew.

Drip Irrigation—How It Works

Unlike conventional sprinkler systems that shoot water at high pressure to distribute it over a large area, drip systems move water at low pressure through a series of tubes and other hardware and deliver it to precise locations and specific plants of the gardener's choosing. Water generally flows out of your faucet through a timer (which is optional), a filter, a pressure regulator, and into a series of hoses or pipes that carry water to emitters that deliver water to the plants. Some systems use soaker hoses, which leak water all along their length, instead of emitters. A complex system may contain two or more individual lines as well as valves that allow for watering specific parts of the garden.

Careful planning is the first step in developing a successful system,

TRADITIONAL DRIP SYSTEMS

Pitcher irrigation is a method of providing a regular supply of water to individual plants or small groups of plants, traditionally used by Indians in the Southwest. A large, unglazed earthenware jug or pitcher is sunk near the plant to be irrigated with its mouth at soil level. The pitcher is filled with water and covered to prevent evaporation, and water seeps slowly out through the porous pottery into the root zone. It is refilled every few days. For a modern-day substitute, try a large, unglazed clay pot (with the bottom hole securely plugged) covered with a saucer. Or set a plastic, gallon-size milk jug with one or two tiny holes poked in the bottom near plants (don't sink it) and keep it filled with water.

but before proceeding with your design you'll need to know more about the parts that make up a drip system. Let's take a piece-by-piece look at its components.

There are three basic sections of each drip system: the head, which attaches the system to your main water supply; the supply and feeder lines, which carry the water to individual beds; and the emitters, which deliver water to your plants.

The Head

Adapter. Since you'll want to be able to use your outside faucet for more than just your drip system, the first stop after the faucet is an adapter that allows you to divide your single water supply into two or more lines. There are Y-shaped adapters that provide a second line, as well as ones that provide four or more separate channels.

Backflow Preventer. This device prevents water from entering the drip system and then backing up into your home's water supply. This is essential if you use your system for applying liquid fertilizer, but a good idea in any system.

Pressure Regulator. Most systems require a pressure regulator to equalize water pressure throughout the system. Otherwise, some plants end up with too much water; others, not enough. City water supplies generally flow at 50 to 80 pounds per square inch (psi), and most drip systems require only 10 to 20 psi. The simplest type of pressure regulator is a disk pierced with a small hole. Preset regulators are more accurate and are the best choice for simple systems, however. You can buy this type of regulator at a variety of preset settings, including 10, 15, or 20 psi. Adjustable pressure regulators, which are more expensive, can be set at any psi level with a twist of a knob and generally have test valves

so you can check the adjustment with a pressure gauge.

Timer. A timer is optional but very convenient and well worth the cost. The simplest models work either by water pressure—metering out the gallons you dial—or simply by time—you dial in the length of time you want to water. Both shut off automatically. You can also buy more expensive battery-powered timers that let you set the frequency and duration of watering, or an even more expensive one that senses soil moisture and waters automatically. One such device allows you to dial the number of gallons you want in each bed right at the faucet.

Fertilizing Siphon. Simple, relatively inexpensive siphoning devices can be attached at the head of the system and be used to feed plants with liquid fertilizer as you water. Some models come with built-in backflow preventers.

Filter. Minerals and other particles that come through your water pipes can clog the tiny holes in the emitters and stop the flow of water. Hose washers with screens aren't fine enough—you'll need a 150- to 200-mesh filter. There are simple, in-line models and larger Y-shaped ones with removable filtering canisters, both of which are relatively inexpensive. A filter at the head of the system (installed after the fertilizing siphon) as well as additional filters throughout the system—such as at the beginning of each feeder line—are a good idea. You'll need to clean them every few weeks.

Supply and Feeder Lines

Supply Lines. You can use an ordinary garden hose to carry water to your drip system or a length of flexible ½-inch polyvinyl chloride (PVC) tubing. The main supply line can be run underground, so that it's out of

sight. It will also last longer if kept out of the sun.

If you have a large drip system, you'll have to consider whether or not you need more than one main supply line in order to maintain uniform water pressure throughout the system. For example, most city water systems provide about 6½ gallons of water per minute, or about 390 gallons per hour. If your emitters give off 2 gallons of water an hour, that means you can use about 195 emitters (390 divided by 2) at one time and still maintain uniform pressure. If you have use for twice that many emitters, plan for a second main supply line. Also, keep in mind that if you use a pressure regulator to decrease the force of the water in your system, you will also reduce the total amount per hour that passes through your lines. You may need to test the number of gallons per minute that flow through the pressure regulator before you calculate how many emitters the main can supply.

Feeder Lines. Smaller diameter lines can be used to carry water from the main supply line to garden beds or around plantings of shrubs and trees. Flexible PVC tubing about ⅜ inch in diameter is a good size because it can be snaked through the beds.

Valves. Although you can always stop the water flow by merely turning it off at the faucet, it's a good idea to have a valve at the garden end of the main water supply so you can turn the system off and on from there as well. In addition, gate valves can be located throughout the system—such as at the beginning of each feeder tube. That way, you'll be able to water crops such as cucumbers or celery that need a great deal of water while other vegetables in the same bed or row don't receive any water at all.

Fittings. There are a variety of fittings—elbows, T's, and Y's—that make laying out and expanding a system fairly easy. Leaky joints waste water, though, so make sure you use compression fittings that provide watertight seals where lines are joined.

Emitters

As their name suggests, emitters are the part of the system that emit or discharge water to plants. They can be plugged directly into the main supply line, into the feeder tubes, or installed at the end of lengths of ⅛-inch poly tubing. There are several types of emitters, all of which release water slowly.

Orifice Emitters. The least expensive and most common type, orifice emitters are just holes sized for a certain water flow at a specific pressure. There are models that mist plants, spray them, or simply drip. Orifice emitters are prone to two problems—clogging and water pressure changes. Clogging occurs when the tiny openings that allow the water to seep out fill with mineral deposits, soil, algae, or other particles loosened from the soil or the pipes. (Filters help control clogging but don't eliminate it.) Secondly, to function properly, orifice emitters need constant water pressure. Except for short runs over flat ground, the water pressure in a system varies, building up when hoses run downhill and dropping off when they run uphill. On rolling land, emitters located in dips can overwater while emitters on high ground run dry.

Labyrinth Emitters. Also called tortuous-path or laminar flow emitters, these limit flow by sending water through a maze and have larger holes to reduce clogging. The water flow of this type changes as the pressure does.

Vortex Emitters. These spin water in a circular chamber, creating low pressure at the outlet in the whirlpool's center. The result is reduced flow, in spite of a larger hole, and an emitter that compensates fairly well for pressure changes.

Diaphragm Emitters. This type of emitter has a diaphragm with a slot inside that is open wide at low pressure. As the pressure rises, the slot narrows, keeping water flow constant. Diaphragm emitters, the most expensive type, compensate fully for pressure changes from 5 to 50 psi, even on slopes and over long runs. They are also self-cleaning to a degree because at pressures near zero, particles flush through the open slot. Drip systems using diaphragm emitters don't require a pressure regulator.

Designing Your Drip System

First you'll need to decide what you want to water. Do you want a system just for your vegetable garden, or would you like to have one that takes care of your entire landscape? Topography is also a consideration: If your garden is hilly, you'll probably need to use emitters that compensate for pressure changes in the line.

You can design your own system, but most companies that sell drip irrigation equipment will design systems for you if provided with a scale drawing of your garden, information on what you're growing, your soil type, and garden topography. Their design comes complete with a list of parts and spacing for emitters. Whatever method you choose, you'll need to start by making a fairly accurate drawing of your garden to determine how many feet of tubing and how many and what type of emitters are best for you.

It's important to keep in mind what effect drip watering has on your plants. They can become "addicted" to the method, because roots will concentrate where the water is available. When designing a drip system to carry water along the rows of a vegetable garden or to the roots of a prized rhododendron, it's important that the water, and thus the roots, be spread uniformly throughout the area you are irrigating. For example, if you

are irrigating larger plants such as trees and shrubs, you'll need to place emitters on two or more sides of each plant to encourage roots to grow out in all directions rather than cluster on one side. Using your system for frequent short waterings rather than long slow ones isn't a good idea for the same reason: The water doesn't have a chance to spread far in the soil, and consequently the roots will form a tight, ball-like mass around the emitters.

Beginners Kits

A starter kit is an easy way to set up a drip irrigation system. Most companies have kits for both small and large gardens, which come with all of the essential components. However, they often don't include parts such as pressure regulators, timers, backflow preventers, and line filters. Be sure to buy a kit that you can add on to, so you can expand your system.

Soil Types and Water Profiles

The type of soil you have comes into play when designing a drip irrigation system because of the different ways water travels through a sandy, loamy, or clayey soil. Water seeping out of an emitter into sandy soil will travel straight down, creating a watering profile that is tall and thin. Root growth will mirror the water profile and form a columnlike mass instead of spreading out through the soil. In a clay soil, water spreads sideways, but doesn't travel down too far, creating a short, fat profile. Loamy soil creates an ideal, nearly round profile, for it has plenty of organic matter to hold water in the soil and enough pore space to allow it to seep out and down. Adding organic matter to sandy or clayey soil will improve the watering profile. (For more information, see "Improving the Soil—Texture and Structure" on page 17.)

To spread water uniformly throughout the area you are irrigating, make sure the watering profiles of the emitters overlap. To compensate for the tall, thin water profile of sandy soil, you'll need to space emitters closer together than you would with a loamy soil to get even coverage.

Emitter Spacing. If you're planning a system for your vegetable garden, you can space emitters anywhere from 16 to 24 inches apart depending on your soil type. To test to see if your emitters are spaced properly for your soil, turn your system on for an hour or so, and then stick your finger in the soil or dig down between two emitters. You should feel the moisture in the soil about 2 inches down, where the watering profiles of both emitters meet. Placing emitters too close together, on the other hand, can waste water and lead to waterlogged soil.

Above or Below Ground?

Although most gardeners who water with drip systems are content to leave the tubes on the soil surface, emitter systems and even some types of soaker hoses can be buried underground or hidden under a layer of mulch. This not only hides the hoses, it reduces evaporation even further and can extend the life of the system because hoses aren't exposed to sun. Lines can be buried from 2 inches to a foot beneath the surface. Cultivating in tube-laced soil can be difficult, and you'll need to keep track of where the lines are located. Drip systems on the surface tend to clog less than ones buried underground.

Soaker Hoses

Soaker hoses provide many of the advantages of emitter drip systems at a fraction of the cost. Some ooze water over their entire length, others spurt water through tiny holes. Systems using these hoses need no assembly, and the hoses can be laid down between small plants and narrow rows without much difficulty.

Soakers save water, reduce loss through evaporation, and slowly seep water into the root zone while keeping leaves dry. However, since water emerges evenly along the length of the hose, water delivery can't be directed as precisely as it can be with an emitter system. Soaker hoses can be used for short runs (100 to 200 feet) over flat surfaces. They're useful for closely spaced crops such as carrots.

Also known as dew hoses, soaker hoses can be made of canvas, various types of plastic, or rubber. Some soaker hoses are more flexible than others and consequently easier to weave in and out between plants. Those made of rigid plastics or rubber can be hard to lay flat or to bend around corners. Plastic and rubber soakers are resistant to fungal attack and seldom develop leaks at couplings or seams, so they can be left in the beds for long periods of time without deterioration. In contrast, canvas hoses are susceptible to mold and mildew and should be drained and dried after each use.

Installing a Drip System

Drip systems are relatively easy to assemble. If yours is designed for watering your vegetable garden, it can be installed before you plant in spring, covered with mulch, and left in place for the season. You can install it well before the last spring frost; just don't run water into the lines until danger of freezing weather has passed.

You'll need to have your plan, a sharp hand pruner and/or a hacksaw to cut the PVC pipe or hose, a measuring tape, and a punch to install the emitters. About an hour before you start, unroll the tubing and lay it in the sun to make it more pliable and easier to handle. Then, using the following steps, start your installation from the water source.

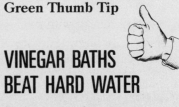

Green Thumb Tip

VINEGAR BATHS BEAT HARD WATER

If the water in your system is hard, it could precipitate calcium carbonate, which eventually plugs the emitters. Instead of discarding the plugged emitters, soak them in muriatic acid or vinegar. Either one will dissolve the deposits, so you can use the emitters over and over for years to come.

1. Connect the timer, if you have one, the backflow preventer, pressure regulator, fertilizer siphon (again, if you have one), and the filter to the main water outlet. Hand tighten all parts as you go.

2. Next, attach and lay out the main supply line. Depending on the system you buy, you'll have either plastic screw fittings to put together or compression fittings that snap together. Teflon tape wrapped around screw fittings helps reduce leaks. For compression fittings, dip the end of the hose in hot water, and gently push it into the fitting by rocking it back and forth. Compression fittings should snap together, forming a watertight seal that doesn't need glue.

3. Continue to lay the hose according to your garden plan, keeping in mind where plantings will be. Measure, cut, and install the feeder tubes as well as additional valves and filters you've planned for.

4. If you're going to run your lines underground, dig the trenches and lay the lines, but don't cover them until you've finished installing and checking out the system. Use stakes or U-shaped ground hooks to keep aboveground lines in place.

5. Try to keep dirt out of the lines while you're working. Once a line has been run, flush it with running water.

6. Use a hand punch to make small holes in the line for installing emitters. There are specially designed "goof plugs" if you make a mistake. Once emitters are in place, flush the line with water again and put a cap on the end of the line.

7. Turn on the water and check for leaks. If you dug trenches, fill them in. You're ready to go.

Caring for Your Drip System

No drip system is perfect. Hoses and pipes rot or deteriorate and need to be replaced, and a clogged emitter can cause problems from spotty watering to major erosion. You'll need to check regularly to be sure all the emitters are in working order, and unclog them if necessary.

Drip systems will be damaged if they freeze. Even small quantities of water freezing in the connections can cause leaks, so in cold climates drip systems must be drained at the end of the season. Store the pressure regulator, timer, and fertilizer siphon (if you use one) indoors over the winter months.

How Much to Water

The amount you water will depend on what you're growing, what kind of soil you have, how much rain has fallen during the week, and the part of the country in which you live. It takes time to get the feel of drip watering, so plan to watch your system closely the first few times you use it, and jot down notes so you'll be able to determine the best watering schedule. Remember, the object of drip watering is to spread the water uniformly through the area being irrigated—both sideways and down through the soil—so plant roots will

follow suit. Each time you water, you need to run the system long enough for the water to seep through the soil to wet the area between emitters. Short, frequent waterings will lead to plants with tightly bunched root systems; long, less frequent waterings will encourage plant roots to spread evenly through the soil.

Start by turning your system on and checking emitters in various parts of the system to see how far the water has spread through the soil. Check at half-hour or 15-minute intervals to get a good idea of how quickly the water spreads. As you gain experience, you will be able to water more by feel. Use a rain gauge to keep track of how much rain falls, and take a look at the plants and the soil to judge how much to water. Don't neglect these steps if you use a timer, because that can lead to over- or underwatering.

Making and Using Organic Fertilizers

What happens when you push a spading fork into your soil? Does the fork sink easily into rich-smelling earth populated by a host of well-fed earthworms? Or is your ground hard to penetrate, dry and unyielding? If the latter is true, making and using organic fertilizers is one way to turn your soil into a plant lover's dream.

The most important goal of any soil improvement program is the promotion of microbial activity, because it's the activity of microorganisms in the soil that makes nutrients available to plants. That's why adding organic matter to the soil in the form of compost or green manure is so important to fertility. Fertilizers not only feed plants, they also feed generations of bacteria and fungi that help break down organic matter and make it available to plants. Organic fertilizers differ from chemical ones

in that they tend to release nutrients more slowly and in lower concentrations than chemical fertilizers. They also tend to leach out of the soil more slowly than chemical ones. Unlike their chemical counterparts, many organic fertilizers add organic matter to the soil as well.

Whether you make them yourself or buy them prebagged at your local nursery or garden center, organic fertilizers benefit your soil and plants by slowly and gradually releasing nutrients. The organic matter present in many types of organic fertilizers also improves soil structure and tilth, as well as nutrient- and water-holding ability.

No matter what kind you choose, though, remember that fertilizers can't make up for basically poor soil. Like vitamin supplements for the body, they can help supply missing nutri-

ents, but they can't compensate for gross deficiencies such as lack of organic matter and poor drainage. To improve poor soil, you'll need to add compost and other organic matter to the soil. Then you can count on organic fertilizers to fill in the gaps.

Selecting Organic Fertilizers

Your first goal is to supply the soil with the three major plant nutrients: nitrogen (N), phosphorus (P), and potassium (K). A soil test will tell you the amounts of each element your soil needs. Different fertilizers contain different ratios of these three basic nutrients. Choose one basic type to correct a particular deficiency or mix your own blends to suit your particular needs. (See the chart "Organic Fertilizers Catalog" on page 72 for

details on many of the most important organic fertilizers.)

Sources of Nitrogen

Animal Manure. Manure is a good source of nitrogen and other soil nutrients. Because of the organic matter it contains, it's also a real boon to soil structure. There are three basic ways manure is sold: fresh, composted, and air-dried. Fresh is cheapest; dried most expensive because the percentage of nutrients and humus per pound is correspondingly higher. Bagged, dried cow manure is available at any garden supply store. Some suppliers may also carry such exotic preparations as bird and bat guano.

In addition, gardeners distinguish between hot and cold manures. Although to some, hot manure means relatively fresh manure, normally the term refers to manure that contains a relatively high percentage of nitrogen. Poultry and sheep manures are examples of hot manure. Cold manures contain relatively low percentages of nitrogen. Cow and horse manure are examples of cold manures.

If you have access to a source of fresh manure, it's best to compost it for three to six months before using it near plants. Composting also kills weed seeds in manure and allows salt, which is often fed to livestock, to leach away. Applied directly to growing plants, fresh manure can burn plant tissue and even kill seedlings. The best time to apply fresh manure to your garden is in the fall, after the growing season is over. Or you can work it into the soil in spring, no less than a month before planting. You can also use it to side-dress planting rows. Never apply it directly to plants. Dried or well-rotted manure can be worked into the soil at planting time or when you're preparing your beds.

Fish Emulsion. Fish emulsion fertilizer is a by-product of the processing of menhaden, a small, oily, bony fish related to herring. The nitrogen it contains is in the form of amino acids, which plants can take up directly. Fish emulsion isn't a complete fertilizer, though. It is low in calcium, and gardeners with soil naturally low in calcium who depend on fish emul-

sion exclusively may end up with deficiency disorders such as blossom end rot on tomatoes or tip burn on lettuce. Fish emulsion can be applied diluted to the soil at planting time, as a side dressing, or sprayed on as a foliar feed.

Other Sources of Nitrogen. Dried blood or bloodmeal and cottonseed meal are two other good sources of nitrogen. Cottonseed meal lowers soil pH as well, making it especially suitable for acid-lovers like blueberries and azaleas. Both can be added to the soil at planting time or worked into the soil during the growing season.

Leaves and grass clippings are two other free sources of nitrogen, and both also provide valuable organic matter to the soil. Chopped or whole leaves can be composted or worked directly into the soil in the fall or several weeks before planting in spring. Adding leaves directly to the soil will slightly reduce yields the first year, but as you add leaves each season, the amount of organic matter in your soil rises along with yields.

Grass clippings can be composted, used as a mulch, or worked into the soil in the fall or several weeks before planting.

Sources of Phosphorus

Bonemeal. Bonemeal is a good slow-release source of phosphorus, which is vital for flowering, fruiting, and root development. It should be worked into the soil at planting time to get it close to the root zone. (Although it also supplies a small amount of nitrogen, bonemeal is best applied as a supplement to manure or compost, which are less expensive sources of nitrogen.) Bonemeal will raise soil pH and shouldn't be used on acid-lovers like blueberries.

Several factors influence the availability of phosphorus from bonemeal to plants. Commercial bonemeal has been steamed and crushed. The more finely ground the product, the easier it is for plants to use. The microorganisms in soil break the particles down and make the phosphorus available to plants. For this reason, bonemeal breaks down faster in a healthy

soil with lots of microbial activity faster than in poor soil. Work bonemeal into the soil in spring when the soil is warming and microorganisms are active and can begin to break it down. Finally, soil pH affects availability, for if soil is too acid or too alkaline, phosphorus combines with other elements and becomes unavailable to plants. Phosphorus is most available in slightly acid soil, with a pH between 6.2 and 6.5.

Bonemeal can be used as a top-dressing or worked into the soil at planting time. It tends to be expensive and is probably best used in small applications. Add a handful to the hole when planting roses, shrubs, or trees, and a sprinkling to the holes for perennials or large bulbs such as tulips, daffodils, and lilies. Scientists have recently found that bulbs need more nitrogen than phosphorus, so be sure to provide a source of nitrogen as well.

Phosphate. Phosphate is available in two forms: colloidal phosphate and rock phosphate. Both are considerably cheaper sources of phosphorus than bonemeal. Colloidal phosphate, also called soft phosphate, is the residue left after phosphate-containing limestone has been washed. The washed, crushed limestone is then sold as rock phosphate or converted into one of the enhanced chemical phosphate fertilizers. The phosphorus in colloidal phosphate is more readily available to plants than rock phosphate, but the latter works well over the long haul.

Sources of Potassium

Langbeinite. A mineral mined in New Mexico, langbeinite is an excellent source of potassium. It contains much more potassium than greensand and granite dust, which are the two most common organic sources of this essential nutrient. It's also a more readily available source of potassium than greensand, a mineral-rich sediment, and granite dust, both of which break down very slowly. Langbeinite

can be worked into the soil at planting time or used as a side dressing.

Other Sources of Potassium. In addition to langbeinite, greensand, and granite dust, seaweed is also a good source of potassium. It is most commonly available in liquid form, and in addition to potassium also contains a large percentage of essential trace minerals. It can be applied as a liquid directly to the soil or as a foliar spray. Wood ashes also contain potassium and can be mixed with other fertilizers, worked into the soil at planting time, added to the compost heap, or used as a side-dressing. Ashes tend to raise soil pH and shouldn't be used on acid-loving plants.

Applying Fertilizers

There are several different ways to apply fertilizers, and the best method will depend on what type you're using and what plants you are growing. Obviously, liquid and dry fertilizers are applied differently, and the methods and applications suitable for an intensively managed vegetable garden wouldn't be appropriate for a lawn.

How often to fertilize depends on the plants you are growing. A vegetable garden where crops are harvested and plants are removed one or more times a year will have a much greater need for fertilizer than a perennial border, for example. As a general rule plants are fertilized when they are first planted. Heavy feeders can be given supplemental feedings approximately once a month throughout the growing season. With hardy plants such as perennials, trees, and shrubs, it's important to taper off toward fall so the plant can become dormant. Fertilizing late in the growing season can trigger lush growth, which is susceptible to frost damage.

Dry Fertilizers
Many organic fertilizers are best applied by digging them into the soil when beds are being prepared for planting in fall or early spring. Dry fertilizers such as manure, colloidal

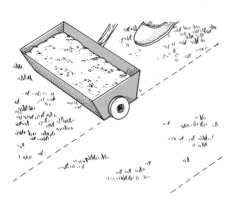

Lawn spreaders are a handy tool for applying rock powders.

phosphate, langbeinite, bonemeal, dried blood, and wood ashes, as well as compost, can all be incorporated into the soil in this manner. If you're preparing an entire vegetable garden, spread the fertilizer evenly over the whole bed—either by broadcasting or shoveling and raking—into an even layer. Then rake or dig it into the soil. Another alternative, especially useful with expensive materials like bonemeal, is to amend the soil along rows where the plants will be growing.

When planting perennials, shrubs, or trees, fertilizers can be added to the individual holes at planting time or worked into the soil surface around plants.

You might want to use a lawn spreader to apply rock powders over a large area. Simply put the powder into the hopper and the machine does the spreading for you. Hand-held spreaders are available for small jobs. Spreaders have the advantage of producing a consistent, even layer.

Side-dressing is an effective way to apply fertilizer, especially for supplemental feedings during the season or alongside new rows of plants. Work the fertilizer into the soil in a shallow furrow beside a row or work it into the surface around plants just outside the root zone. Plant roots grow toward the fertilizer and take it up gradually. Side-dressing is also a safe way to apply "hot" fertilizers such as fresh manure, which can burn plant roots if applied directly.

Liquid Fertilizers

One of the easiest ways to apply liquid fertilizers such as manure tea or fish emulsion is to use a watering can with a perforated sprinkler head, called a rose, attached. You can also deliver liquids by means of drip irrigation systems (make sure to filter the liquid to prevent it from plugging up the system).

Foliar feeding is a quick and safe way to apply liquid fertilizer. It's nothing more than spraying dilute liquid fertilizer onto the leaves of plants, which take it up readily. Use a dilute solution of fish emulsion, liquid seaweed, or compost or manure tea, and spray it directly on the leaves of a plant. You can use a commercial sprayer of the type used to apply insecticides, but be sure to filter the liquid before spraying. You can also use a watering can with a perforated sprinkler head to do foliar feeding.

Wood ashes, which will help raise pH and are also a good source of potassium, can be spread around plants and lightly worked into the soil.

Liquid fertilizers can be applied with a watering can to the soil around plants. Use a perforated sprinkler head to ensure a gentle stream.

MAKING MANURE TEA

One of the best liquid fertilizers you can use is manure or compost tea. It's also easy to make. Just put a shovelful of fresh or dried manure or well-seasoned compost in a burlap sack—the teabag—and tie it closed. Then put the sack in a rain barrel or some other large container filled with water. Keep the container covered, and steep the sack for one to seven days.

Use the tea full strength for periodic feeding or dilute it and use to water plants. Manure tea can also be used for drip irrigation systems; be sure to filter it, though, so it doesn't clog the system.

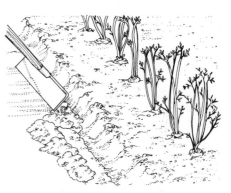

Side-dressing encourages root development and prevents fertilizer burn because the fertilizer is applied to the side of plantings rather than directly on top of the roots.

Plants can absorb dilute liquid fertilizer sprayed directly on their leaves. For foliar feeding, use a sprayer or a watering can with a perforated sprinkler head.

ORGANIC FERTILIZERS CATALOG

Organic Fertilizer	Nutrients Supplied	Rate of Application	Uses and Comments
Bloodmeal, dried blood	Bloodmeal: 15% nitrogen, 1.3% phosphorus, 0.7% potassium. Dried blood: 12% nitrogen, 3% phosphorus, 0% potassium.	Up to 3 lbs. per 100 sq. ft. (more will burn plants).	Source of readily available nitrogen. Add to compost pile to speed decomposition. Repels deer and rabbits. Lasts 3-4 months.
Bonemeal	3% nitrogen, 20% phosphorus, 0% potassium, 24-30% calcium.	Up to 5 lbs. per 100 sq. ft.	Excellent source of phosphorus. Raises pH. Best on fruit trees, bulbs, and flower beds. Lasts 6 to 12 months.
Cottonseed meal	6% nitrogen, 2-3% phosphorus, 2% potassium.	2-5 lbs. per 100 sq. ft. (For trees, apply 2-4 cups around drip line for each in. of trunk size.)	Acidifies soil, so it's best for crops that prefer low pH, such as azaleas, blueberries, citrus, dogwoods, hollies, and strawberries. Lasts 4-6 months.
Dolomite	90-100% MgCa $(CO_3)_2$ (51% calcium carbonate, 40% magnesium carbonate).	To raise pH one point, use 7 lbs. per 100 sq. ft. on clay or sandy loam, 5½ lbs. on sand, and 10 lbs. on loam soil.	Raises pH and adds magnesium, which is needed for chlorophyll production and photosynthesis. Repeated use may cause magnesium excess. Also sold as Hi-Mag or dolomitic limestone.
Fish meal, fish emulsion	Fish meal: 10% nitrogen, 4-6% phosphorus, 0% potassium. Fish emulsion: 4% nitrogen, 4% phosphorus, 1% potassium.	Fish meal: up to 5 lbs. per 100 sq. ft. Fish emulsion: dilute 20:1 water to emulsion.	Fish meal: Use in early spring, at transplanting, and any time plants need a boost. Lasts 6-8 months. Fish emulsion: Apply as a foliar spray in early morning or evening. Also sold as fish solubles.
Granite dust	0% nitrogen, 0% phosphorus, 3-5% potassium, 67% silica; 19 trace minerals.	Up to 10 lbs. per 100 sq. ft.	Very slowly available. Releases potash more slowly than greensand, but lasts up to 10 years. Improves soil structure. Use mica-rich type only. Also sold as granite meal or crushed granite.
Greensand	0% nitrogen, 1% phosphorus, 5-7% potassium, 50% silica, 18-23% iron oxide; 22 trace minerals.	Up to 10 lbs. per 100 sq. ft.	Slowly available. Lasts up to 10 years. Loosens clay soils. Apply in fall for benefits next season. Also sold as glauconite or Jersey greensand.
Guano, bat	8% nitrogen, 4% phosphorus, 2% potassium average, but varies widely; 24 trace minerals.	Up to 5 lbs. per 100 sq. ft; 2 T. per pint of potting soil; 1 lb. per 5 gal. water for manure tea.	Caves protect guano from leaching, so nutrients are conserved.
Guano, bird	13% nitrogen, 8% phosphorus, 2% potassium; 11 trace minerals.	3 lbs. per 100 sq. ft. Fruit trees: 3-6 oz. per inch of trunk diameter. Houseplants: 1-2 oz. per gallon of water.	Especially good for roses, bulbs, azaleas, and houseplants. Also sold as Plantjoy.
Gypsum (calcium sulfate)	23-57% calcium, 17.7% sulfur.	Up to 4 lbs. per 100 sq. ft.	Use when both calcium and sulfur are needed and soil pH is already high. Sulfur will tie up excess magnesium. Helps loosen clay soils.

Organic Fertilizer	Nutrients Supplied	Rate of Application	Uses and Comments
Hoof and horn meal	14% nitrogen, 2% phosphorus, 0% potassium.	Up to 4 lbs. per 100 sq. ft.	High nitrogen source, but more slowly available than blood-meal. Odorous. Takes 4-6 weeks to start releasing nitrogen; lasts 12 months.
Kelp meal, liquid seaweed	1% nitrogen, 0% phosphorus, 12% potassium; 33% trace minerals, including more than 1% of calcium, sodium, chlorine, and sulfur, and about 50 other minerals in trace amounts.	Meal: up to 1 lb. per 100 sq. ft. Liquid: dilute 25:1 water to seaweed for transplanting and rooting cuttings; 40:1 as booster and for fruit crops.	Contains natural growth hormones, so use sparingly. Best source of trace minerals. Lasts 6-12 months. Also sold as Thorvin Kelp, FoliaGro, Sea Life, Maxicrop, Norwegian SeaWeed, liquid kelp.
Langbeinite	0% nitrogen, 0% phosphorus, 22% potassium, 22% sulfur, 11% magnesium.	Up to 1 lb. per 100 sq. ft.	Will not alter pH. Use when there is abundant calcium and sulfur. Magnesium and potassium are needed. Also sold as Sul-Po-Mag or K-Mag.
Leatherdust	5.5-12% nitrogen, 0% phosphorus, 0% potassium.	½ lb. per 100 sq. ft.	2% nitrogen is immediately available; rest releases slowly over growing season. Does not burn or leach.
Manure, composted cow	2% nitrogen, 1% phosphorus, 1% potassium.	40 lbs. per 50-100 sq. ft. as soil conditioner; 2 parts to 6-8 parts loam as potting mix.	Low level of nutrients and slow release makes it most valuable as a soil conditioner. Use as winter fertilizer for houseplants.
Phosphate, colloidal	0% nitrogen, 18-22% phosphorus, 0% potassium, 27% calcium, 1.7% iron; silicas and 14 other trace minerals.	Up to 10 lbs. per 100 sq. ft.	More effective than rock phosphate on neutral soils. Phosphorus availability higher (2% available immediately) than rock phosphate because of small particle size of colloidal clay base. Half the pH-raising value of ground limestone. Lasts 2-3 years.
Phosphate, rock	0% nitrogen, 33% phosphorus, 0% potassium, 30% calcium, 2.8% iron, 10% silica; 10 other trace minerals.	Up to 10 lbs. per 100 sq. ft.	Releases phosphorus best in acid soils below pH 6.2. Slower release than colloidal phosphate. Will slowly raise pH one point or more. Also sold as phosphate rock.
Sulfur	100% sulfur.	1 lb. per 100 sq. ft. will lower pH one point. As fungicide: dilute at 3 T. per gallon of water.	Lowers pH in alkaline soil. Increases crop protein. Ties up excess magnesium. Also sold as Dispersul.
Wood ashes	0% nitrogen, 0-7% phosphorus, 6-20% potassium, 20-53% calcium carbonate; trace minerals such as copper, zinc, manganese, iron, sodium, sulfur and boron.	1-2 lbs. per 100 sq. ft.	Nutrient amounts highly variable. Minerals highest in young hardwoods. Will raise soil pH. Put on soil in spring, and dig under. Do not use near young stems or roots. Protect ashes from leaching in winter. Lasts 12 or more months.

Using Cover Crops

"Use it or lose it" is a phrase that could be applied to garden soil. Soil left without a protective covering of plants slips away like sand through an hourglass. Wind blows it away; rain washes it down hills and leaches nutrients out of the root zone. Fortunately, there is an easy way to not only stop this process but also to actually improve your soil to benefit future crops: Grow cover crops.

What exactly are cover crops? They're crops grown exclusively to feed, improve, and protect the soil. Also called green manure, cover crops —generally legumes such as clover and grains such as rye—are sown, allowed to grow, and then tilled into the soil either with a rotary tiller or by hand before they flower and set seed. In addition to stopping erosion, cover crops also prevent nutrients from leaching out of the soil. Planted into a mature crop or immediately after the ground is cleared, they act as holding tanks, taking up nutrients

and keeping them near the soil surface. In spring, after the cover crop has been tilled under, new plantings will draw on this reservoir as the cover crop breaks down. Cover crops do more for the garden, though. Those that make a fast, dense stand keep weeds from getting a foothold after the fall harvest. As they decompose,

they enrich the soil with vital organic matter, which improves structure as well as nutrient- and water-holding ability. Legumes such as sweet clover also convert atmospheric nitrogen into a form that is taken up by the crop, and then released into the soil when the legumes are tilled under. Cover crops also help to retain mois-

A SUPPRESSING STORY

How can time spent planting a cover crop next fall save you hours of weeding the following summer? According to researchers at Michigan State University, annual rye turned into the top few inches of soil in spring can drastically suppress emergence of ragweed, green bristle grass, rough pigweed, and purslane for more than a month.

But beware. Don't sow small-seeded crops like lettuce and carrots in the same plot where you grew rye. The toxins released from decaying rye are too much for any small seed. Researchers suggest reserving a rye-planted area for transplants and for sowing corn, beans, peas, and other larger-seeded crops, all of which will grow unharmed.

COVER CROP CLOSEUP

Legumes

Bean, broad, fava, or field (*Vicia faba*). A winter annual legume suitable for maritime Canada and along the U.S. Pacific Coast. Must have cool weather and ample water. Can withstand temperatures to 15°F. Prefers well-drained, heavy loams high in humus and lime. Turn under when growth is succulent for fastest breakdown. Fixes 71 pounds nitrogen per acre per year; inoculate with *Rhizobium* spp. bacteria to encourage nitrogen fixation, either by dusting the inoculant along the furrow or on the seeds. Sow on 8-inch centers, covering seed ⅛ to ¼ inch deep.

Clover, crimson (*Trifolium incarnatum*). An annual legume that will grow through the winter from New Jersey south. Must have adequate soil moisture for good germination and growth. Prefers loam soils that are high in humus, but will grow on any well-drained soil except muck or extremely acid soils. Will withstand shade and low fertility. Fixes 94 pounds of nitrogen per acre per year; inoculate with *Rhizobium* spp. bacteria to encourage nitrogen fixation. Sow ½ to ⅔ ounce per 100 square feet, covering seed ½ inch deep.

Clover, white (*Trifolium repens*). A hardy perennial legume that grows throughout Canada and the United States south to the Gulf of Mexico. Thrives in cool, moist climates. Prefers humus-rich, well-drained clay, clay loam, and loam soils. Grows well in shade. Needs high lime, phosphorus, and potash. Fixes 103 to 133 pounds of nitrogen per acre per year; inoculate with *Rhizobium* spp. bacteria to encourage nitrogen fixation. Sow ¼ ounce per 100 square feet, covering seed ½ inch deep.

Lupine, large white (*Lupinus albus*). An annual legume best grown in the Deep South, Northeast, and North Central states. The most winter-hardy lupine species. Prefers sandy loam soils and acid soils. Excellent soil-builder for barren, sandy, and worn-out soil. Good for opening up heavy clay. Inoculate with *Rhizobium* spp. bacteria to encourage nitrogen fixation. Sow 6½ ounces per 100 square feet, covering seed 1 inch deep.

Pea, Austrian winter (*Pisum arvense*). Also called Canadian field pea, this legume is a winter annual. It grows all over the United States and Canada; winterkills in the North but grows through the winter in the South. Requires cool, moist conditions and grows best in loamy soils high in lime. Fixes 48 pounds of nitrogen per acre per year; inoculate with *Rhizobium* spp. bacteria to encourage nitrogen fixation. Sow 4 ounces per 100 square feet, covering seed 1½ inches deep.

ture in the soil and help to moderate temperature fluctuations. Both of the effects protect earthworms and other soil microorganisms.

Planting Cover Crops

There are several different ways to use cover crops in the garden. You can sow a winter legume like sweet clover or winter rye in fall after you've harvested your vegetables and turn it under in early spring. Another option is to rotate garden beds by planting vegetables in a bed one year and a cover crop the next. You can also sow a cover crop directly under a vegetable crop, but the trick is to sow the cover crop after the vegetable crop has become well established so that they don't compete. For example, clover can be broadcast under sweet corn or other big vegetables after the last cultivation (about five weeks after corn has been sown). The clover can then be left to protect the soil in winter and tilled under in spring.

To sow a cover crop, lightly work the soil with a tiller or a spade, or just rough up open spaces between plants with a hoe, to prepare a seedbed. Then scatter the seed evenly, and rake or hoe lightly to cover it. For clovers, tamp the soil after sowing to provide a firm seed bed. If you're sowing in late summer or fall, the seeds will sprout and grow until temperatures get too cold. Some cover crops are winter-killed, others resume growing in spring. Either way, they're tilled under a few weeks before planting.

Tilling It Under

The first step in turning under a cover crop is to cut back the topgrowth with a sickle, scythe, or mower. This is generally done in very early spring. Make several passes with a rotary mower to chop up the plants. A layer of compost or manure spread over the top will also help speed decomposition. Then, use a rotary tiller to work the plants into the soil. You can also hand-dig the crop under, although if your garden is large this can be a daunting task. If the tops of the plants were very lush, stop after two passes with the tiller and let the soil dry out for a few days. Then till the soil again until you have a manageable seedbed.

You'll need to wait 7 to 10 days after tilling under a legume cover crop before you plant vegetables or other crops; 14 days or more after a grain crop. That's because the decomposing cover crop releases ethylene gas for the first few days, which inhibits seed germination. Also, the microorganisms breaking down the crop tie up nitrogen, and the temporary deficiency will hinder the growth of seeds or transplants.

What to Grow

Basically, there are two types of crops that can be grown for green manure:

Vetch, hairy or winter (*Vicia villosa*). An annual legume that can be grown in all parts of the United States. The most winter-hardy of the cultivated vetches. Will grow on any well-drained soil, including acid soils, alkaline soils, and soils of low fertility. Will tolerate drought. Fixes 80 pounds of nitrogen per acre per year; inoculate with *Rhizobium* spp. bacteria to encourage nitrogen fixation. Sow 2½ ounces per 100 square feet, covering seed ¾ inch deep.

Grasses

Barley, winter (*Hordeum vulgare*). An annual grass that grows all over the United States and overwinters in mild climates. Well adapted to high altitudes and semiarid regions. Prefers well-drained loam soils. Tolerant of salinity and alkaline soils; does not grow well on sandy or acid soils. Sow 4 ounces per 100 square feet, covering seed ¾ inch deep.

Oats (*Avena sativa*). An annual grass that grows all over the United States and is especially good in the South where it overwinters. Prefers cool, moist climates. Will tolerate acid soil. Will grow on many soils, but does not do well on heavy clay. Provide a firm seedbed to prevent frost-heaving in winter. Sow 4 ounces per 100 square feet, covering seed 1 inch deep.

Rye, winter or cereal (*Secale cereale*). An annual grass that will grow all over the United States, but is especially well suited for the North because of its ability to tolerate extreme cold. Grows best on well-drained loams, but will grow on any soil. Will tolerate acid soil. Prefers ample moisture. Sow 4 ounces per 100 square feet, covering seed ¾ inch deep.

Ryegrass, annual or Italian (*Lolium multiflorum*). A weak grass grown as an annual. Will grow all over the United States, but is best adapted to the areas from New Jersey south. Prefers loam or sandy loam soils, but will grow on any soil. Will tolerate acid soil. Makes rapid growth and holds soil well with heavy, fibrous roots. Sow 1½ ounces per 100 square feet, covering seed ¾ inch deep.

Wheat, winter (*Triticum aestivum*). An annual grass that will grow all over the United States. Does well at high elevations. Prefers loam soils. Grows best in fertile soil, but will tolerate moderately fertile soil. Sow 4 ounces per 100 square feet, covering seed ¾ inch deep.

legumes and grains. Legumes such as white clover or hairy vetch have the special ability to fix atmospheric nitrogen and add it to the soil by virtue of the *Rhizobium* bacteria that live in their root systems. The nitrogen becomes available to plants after the legume is tilled under. Grains such as winter rye, winter wheat, barley, or oats are grown for green manure because they produce lots of succulent growth that provides organic material when the plants are turned under to help build soil and boost microbial activity. They also have extensive fibrous root systems that take up and hold potassium in the soil. Buckwheat is a good source of phosphorus. Another advantage of grain crops—especially winter rye—is that they can grow quickly in the fall when temperatures are cool and rapidly absorb easily leached nutrients and hold them until spring. Rye seeds can germinate at temperatures above 33°F, and will grow in the fall until temperatures drop below 40°F. They then resume growing in the spring, providing lots of green manure for tilth- and nutrient-building. If you allow rye (especially winter rye) to grow too tall in spring, you'll need machinery to turn it under.

Combinations of grains and legumes, such as rye and hairy vetch, hairy vetch with winter barley or wheat, or clover and barley, offer the best of both worlds. They provide nitrogen fixation from the legume and organic matter from the grain. When seeded together, the fast-growing grain protects the legume until it becomes established.

Mulching the Garden

Want a surefire way to improve your garden and landscape plantings and save yourself hours of work? Try mulching. This one technique provides an abundance of benefits for both plants and gardener. It's a no-lose proposition.

According to the dictionary, the word "mulch" is probably derived from a seventeenth-century English dialect word meaning soft or mild. Good mulches do have a softening effect, cushioning plants against the vagaries of the environment. And although they won't eliminate all your gardening chores, they do make life easier for you, too.

Why Use Mulch?

● **Mulch helps hold moisture in the soil.** During dry spells, mulched plantings often pull through while their unprotected counterparts bite the dust. Mulches help protect the soil from the evaporative effects of sun and wind, thereby keeping the soil from crusting over. Well-mulched soils tend to be loose and crumbly rather than hard-packed. Mulch also helps prevent heavy rains from pelting the soil and leaching out nutrients and helps curb soil erosion.

● **Mulch keeps weeds in check.** Weeds have no place in the well-tended landscape. Besides being aesthetically unpleasing, they compete with other plants for moisture and nutrients. Mulch prevents many weeds from growing at all, and whatever weeds make it through a layer of mulch tend to be weak and spindly and easy to pull.

● **Mulch modulates soil temperatures.** Mulch is also valuable to help keep soil cool in the heat of summer and warm (relatively speaking) when it begins to get cold outside. A good layer of mulch can help extend your growing season by a few weeks, and though it won't keep your ground from freezing, it will help protect the roots of your perennial plantings.

● **Some mulches improve soil structure.** Organic mulches begin to decompose after they've been set out, and this breakdown helps improve soil tilth. You can further this process by working organic mulch into the soil at the end of the growing season. Don't worry that decaying mulch will tie up available nitrogen—the percentage of nitrogen that might be lost is minuscule and the loss won't affect healthy soil.

What Kind to Use?

The best kind of mulch to use depends on the primary effect you want to achieve. The material should be cheap, readily available, and, for the purposes of creating a beautiful landscape, attractive (or at least not offensive to the eye).

If you're looking to improve soil structure, contribute nutrients, and activate soil microorganisms, use an organic mulch such as compost, shredded bark, straw, chopped leaves, pine needles, or grass clippings. On the other hand, for total weed kill, black plastic is hard to beat. You can even lay it down in the fall and, come spring, you'll have a fairly workable, weed-free bed to plant. Organic mulches and newspapers can be left on the soil and worked into it as they decompose. Plastic and foil mulches should be removed at the end of the growing season; they're generally too full of holes to be reusable.

Mulch Tips

● One of the best all-around mulches is compost. If you have a

Organic mulch such as compost or grass clippings contributes to soil tilth and encourages the growth and activity of soil microorganisms.

Black plastic mulch is great for warming the soil in spring and does an excellent job of keeping the weeds down.

has a high carbon-to-nitrogen ratio, so it locks up nitrogen in the soil. Oat straw contains more nitrogen and therefore breaks down more quickly. Hay has twice as much nitrogen as straw, but is also likely to contain weed seeds, so it's best used on the compost pile, not as mulch. Rain-spoiled hay is sometimes offered for sale at bargain prices.

● Tree-trimming crews who work for the phone company or electric utility company often can be persuaded to dump wood chips on your property as they clear around phone and electric wires. (If black walnuts are common in your area, be aware that wood chips from these trees can be toxic to some plants, including rhododendrons, azaleas, and tomatoes.)

● If you have a short supply of an aesthetically pleasing mulch, such as wood chips, and an abundance of less attractive material, such as newspapers, lay down the newspapers first and cover them with the chips. The newspapers do all the work but the eye sees only the neat layer of chips. For more information on mulches, see the chart "Choose Your Mulch" on page 78.

large enough compost pile, using this soil-building material to topdress your beds will allow you to feed and mulch at the same time.

● If you have an abundance of trees, you have an abundance of leaves, which you can save for the next growing season. Don't use whole leaves, though, because they'll mat. Chop them up with a shredder or run the lawnmower over them several times. It's a good idea to leave them outside (not in plastic bags) to weather for several months. Leaves contain growth-inhibiting phenols that should be allowed to leach away before they're used.

● Material such as hay and straw is often for sale by the bale at farms and garden centers. Wheat straw

Staking Plants

Staking is a simple technique but an important one for vegetable and flower grower alike. For large-flowered plants such as dahlias, asters, and peonies, staking allows the blooms to show to best advantage and keeps them from getting top-heavy after a rain. Tall, fragile-stemmed plants like delphiniums often need help weathering storms. In the vegetable garden, supporting plants with stakes or other supports will mean the difference between a good harvest and a poor

one. If you've ever tried to grow tomatoes without staking the plants or growing them in cages, you know how hard it is to salvage a decent crop. Whatever tomatoes you are able to find under the heavy weight of the plants often succumb to attacks from insects and larger animals or rot.

Staking doesn't have to be unattractive, an important consideration in the flower garden. In fact, if done correctly, it's not in the least bit an intrusion. Properly staked plants

have no visible means of support—the foliage grows up to hide the stakes, strings, and wires.

What to Use

There are several different ways to stake plants. As a general rule, it's best to start early in the season, so the leaves have a chance to cover the supports and you can train the plant as it grows. It's not easy to stake a plant that has sprawled on the ground
(continued on page 80)

CHOOSE YOUR MULCH

The following are some of the best mulches to consider for your garden. Some are suitable for vegetables; others are best used in ornamental plantings. We've distinguished between biodegradable ones, which will add organic matter to the soil, and synthetic mulches like black plastic, which won't.

Material	Primary Benefits	When to Apply	How to Apply
Biodegradable Mulches			
Chopped leaves	Suppresses weeds well. Modulates soil temperature.	At planting time and as needed throughout the season.	Apply in 3-inch layers; best if chopped and composted, then allowed to sit outside for several months.
Compost	Builds tilth. Suppresses weeds. Fertilizes. Warms soil.	At planting time and as needed throughout the season.	Spread 1 or more inches as a topdressing around plants or along rows.
Grass clippings	Builds tilth. Modulates soil temperature.	At planting time and as needed throughout the season.	Apply a 1-4-inch layer around plantings. Make sure clippings are herbicide-free. May burn tender seedlings if placed too close.
Horticultural paper	Permeable to water and air. May warm soil.	At planting time.	Comes in various types, such as black or with peat. Some types may crust in wet climates. Lay down in sections and anchor with soil or stones.
Newspaper	Suppresses weeds well. Retains moisture.	At planting time.	Lay down whole sections of the paper and anchor with soil or stones, or shred paper and apply 4-6-inch layers. Good to use under more attractive mulches. Do not use colored newspaper; some inks can be toxic.
Pine needles	Builds tilth. Suppresses weeds well. Some control of fungal diseases.	At planting time and as needed throughout the season.	Apply in 2-4-inch layers. Needles tend to acidify soil; don't use around non-acid-loving plants.
Shredded bark, wood chips	Retains moisture. Suppresses weeds well.	As needed around established plantings or at planting time.	Apply a 2-4-inch layer around established plantings of trees or perennials. Can tie up nitrogen in soil, so not for vegetable garden. Composted bark or wood chips are best.

78

Material	Primary Benefits	When to Apply	How to Apply
Straw	Builds tilth. Suppresses weeds well. Cools soil.	At planting time and as needed throughout the season.	Lay down 8-inch layers of material around but not touching plants. Mulch heavily between rows to keep weeds at bay. May tie up nitrogen in soil; oat straw best.

Inorganic Mulches

Material	Primary Benefits	When to Apply	How to Apply
Aluminized paper	Suppresses weeds well. Modulates soil temperature; cools soil but warms air. May repel aphids and squash borer moths.	At planting time.	Lay down single sheets and cut slits to plant through. Make sure mulch extends at least 6 inches out from plants.
Black plastic	Warms soil. Suppresses weeds well.	At or before planting time.	Lay down single sheets of 4-6-mil plastic over whole planting area or between rows of plants. Anchor with soil or stones. Cut slits to plant through.
Clear plastic	Warms soil.	At or before planting time.	Lay down single sheets of plastic. Anchor with soil or stones. Cut slits to plant through. Weeds will grow beneath plastic.
Geotextile mulch	Suppresses weeds well. Permeable to water and air.	At or before planting time.	Difficult to cut. Lay down in single sheets and anchor with soil or stones. Cut slits to plant through.
Pebbles and stones	Suppresses weeds well. Modulates soil temperature. Retains moisture.	At planting time and as needed.	Put down pebbles (such as marble chips) in 1-inch layers. Good for mulching trees, shrubs, and rock gardens.

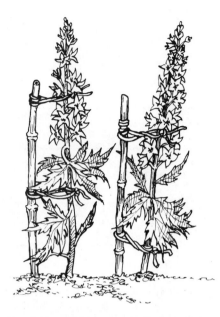

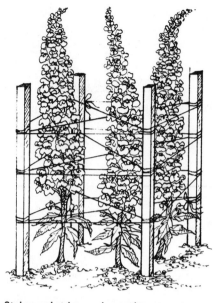

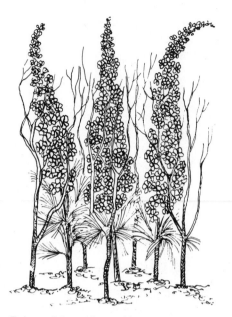

Use single stakes to support tall, single-stalk plants such as delphiniums. The stake should be about 6 inches shorter than the flower will be at full height. You can always cut off a too-tall stake when the plant begins to flower. Tie the flower stalk loosely but firmly to the stake with soft fabric or twine.

Stakes and string can be used to support clumps of flowers. Place stakes around each clump and use twine to support the plants. Criss-crossing twine through the center of the clump can provide additional support.

Twiggy sticks can be used to create an unobtrusive support system for not-too-tall but bushy plants. For this technique, called pea staking, place twiggy branches in the ground when the plants are small. The plants cover the twigs as they grow.

or has flopped over after a heavy rain. You can easily break or crush stems. Furthermore, leaves and flowers won't look quite as graceful as they would if properly trained from the start.

Bamboo Canes

Bamboo canes are lightweight, sturdy, and available in several thicknesses —from pencil-thin to ½-inch canes suitable for staking tomatoes or large-flowered dahlias. Use the thinner ones for supporting stems of delphiniums or other top-heavy beauties. Select a bamboo cane about two-thirds as tall as the plant will be at maturity and insert it into the ground close to the base of the plant. Then use yarn, strips of soft fabric, or strips of old pantyhose to tie the flower stem to the stake. Add more ties as the plant grows taller.

For multistemmed flowers such as chrysanthemums, use a single stake to support more than one stem. Tie

twine or yarn to the stake, gather the stems, and loop the twine loosely around them.

You can also use bamboo canes to make a sort of cat's-cradle around clumps of flowers such as peonies. Insert four or five canes around the plant. Again, they should be two-thirds as tall as the plant at maturity. Then tie twine to one and wrap it around the others in turn. Tie it off on the first cane. Add rings of twine every 6 to 12 inches as the plant grows. You can also weave the twine through the plant foliage from one stake to its opposing one to create an extra network of support.

Pea Staking

When you prune your trees in early spring, don't burn those trimmings. Instead, save them and use them to stake such weak-stemmed perennials as coreopsis or gypsophila and such annual climbers as sweet peas. When the plants are still small, sim-

ply stick twiggy brush into the ground near them. As they grow, the plants will climb over the network of twigs and their foliage will soon hide the twigs from view. Pea staking is most successful for plants that don't grow taller than about 2 feet. The twigs should be about 6 inches shorter than the plant at maturity. (A caution: Never use diseased prunings as stakes. Burn or destroy them to prevent the spread of disease.)

Wire Cages

Round or square wire cages similar to but smaller than the ones used to grow tomatoes are available for perennials such as peonies. Ready-made cages have wire legs that you simply push into the ground. You don't need to tie plants to wire frames; they simply grow up and through the wire and get all the support they need from the enclosure. Cages need to be put in place in early spring, while the plants are still small. You can buy cages ready-made or make your own using galvanized large-mesh (4- by 6-inch) wire fencing.

Wire Rings

It's also possible to support plants by attaching a ring of heavy gauge wire to two or three stakes. Stick the stakes in the soil and then, as the plants grow, slide the ring up the stakes. You can make your own or buy them ready-made in several models and sizes.

Training Climbing Plants

Vines and other kinds of climbing plants are a wonderful addition to any landscape. They make striking accents on walls and fences, can provide flowering canopies on porches and patios, and can be used to conceal unattractive views.

Providing appropriate support for a climber isn't hard if you understand the nature of the plant. Vines that climb by means of tendrils, tendril-like structures, or twining stems—

Wire frames or cages, which are usually painted green, are available for clump-forming plants such as peonies, whose flower heads often bend to the ground after heavy rains.

such as clematis, wisteria, or grapes —need to have a trellis or other means of support to grow best. Be sure the size of the trellis matches the plant, though. While clematis have relatively light stems, wisteria is a heavy, woody vine that requires considerable sup-

port. Annuals don't require as much heavy-duty support as perennial vines. You can train annuals such as scarlet runner beans or morning-glories on a lightweight string trellis.

To get such vines started, tie the leader to its support using soft twine. Tie a loop around the support, using a figure-eight knot; then tie the ends of the twine around the plant stem, attaching it loosely but securely to its support. Later you may want to tie individual branches to shape the vine's growth. After that, you don't need to tie such vines to their supports—just keep training the tendrils in the direction you want them to go, and the plants will take it from there. Climbing roses, although not true vines, can be trained to grow up over an arbor, but since they don't have twining stems, they'll require tying. Other vines—such as English ivy (*Hedera helix*) and climbing hydrangea (*Hydrangea anomala*)—climb by clinging holdfasts and need neither pole nor trellis to grow. They'll happily scale brick, stone, tree trunks, fences, or trellises without any support.

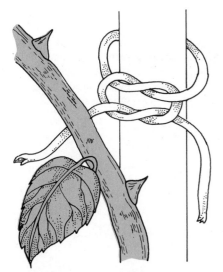

Attach vines to a trellis or other support by tying a piece of soft twine firmly to the support. Tie a single knot, as if you were tying a shoelace, then make two loops and pass the end of each piece through the opposing loop.

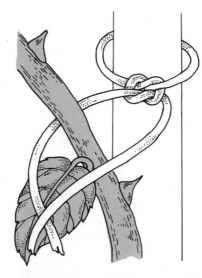

Bring the loose ends of the twine around the vine. Pull the vine close to the support but not right up against it.

Tie a secure knot, but leave enough slack to prevent the twine from binding the vine as it grows and to keep the vine from chafing against the support.

CONTROLLING INSECT PESTS

There is nothing as disheartening as lavishing hours of care and attention on your favorite plants only to discover they are infested with insect pests. The following chart lists common pest insects, what they look like, what damage they cause, and what steps you can take to control them.

Insect	Description	Host	Damage	Control
Aphids	Small, pear-shaped, soft-bodied insects of various colors, with long antennae.	Many vegetables, annuals, perennials, trees, and shrubs.	Insects suck plant juices, causing puckered or curled leaves, stunted growth, or deformed buds and flowers. Transmit plant diseases. Secrete honeydew, which encourages mold.	Spray plants with water in early morning, once every other day for 3 days. For heavier infestations, use insecticidal soap for 2-3 days. Lure aphids away from plants by planting nasturtiums a distance away. Ladybugs eat aphids.
Apple maggots	White or yellowish ¼-in.-long larvae. Adults are ¼ in. black flies with white or yellow markings on abdomen, zigzag black stripes on wings, and yellow legs.	Apples, apricots, blueberries, crabapples, cherries, pears, and plums.	Larvae make brown tunnels in fruit; damage hard to see on surface of fruit.	Collect dropped fruit. Trap flies with a red sticky trap made of a red ball coated with Tanglefoot or other sticky substance; hang 2-4 in tree. Can also trap flies in jars filled with 1 part blackstrap molasses and 9 parts water.
Armyworms	Brown or green caterpillars with dark stripes, mottled brown head; 1½ in. long. Adults are night-flying 1-1½-in. moths with gray-white mottled wings.	Various vegetables and grasses.	Caterpillars chew leaves, stems, and buds, usually at night. May appear in large numbers.	Handpick and drop in soapy water. Trichogramma and braconid wasps will parasitize the larvae. Use Bt (*Bacillus thuringiensis*) for larvae.
Asparagus beetles	Adult beetles are blue-black with 4 yellow squares and reddish margins on wings; ¼ in. long. Plump larvae are gray or greenish with black head and legs; less than ⅓ in. long.	Asparagus.	Adults chew spears and leaves of asparagus.	Clear away plant debris; turn over soil in fall. Handpick adults. Use pyrethrum for severe infestations.
Bagworms	Larvae of moths that surround themselves with bags of silk covered with pieces of leaves. Adult male moths are black, with transparent wings; females are yellow and wingless.	Various trees including evergreens, some maples, locust, linden, and citrus trees.	Larvae defoliate trees.	Handpick and destroy bags. Use Bt (*Bacillus thuringiensis*) in spring; pheromone traps in late summer.

Insect	Description	Host	Damage	Control
Cabbage loopers	Light green caterpillars with yellow stripes. "Loop" as they walk. Adults are brown moths with a silver spot on each wing.	Members of the cabbage family; vegetables such as beans, lettuce, parsley, peas, spinach, and tomatoes; and flowers.	Caterpillars chew ragged holes in leaves; bore into developing heads of cabbage family members.	Handpick caterpillars and eggs and drop in soapy water. Use Bt (*Bacillus thuringiensis*) for serious infestations.
Codling moths	Pink, 1-in.-long larvae with brown heads. Adults are gray-brown moths with delicate brown lines on their forewings and fringed, pale hind wings.	Apples and pears (serious pest); also other fruits and walnuts.	Larvae cause early drop of fruit; form tunnels to core of fruit.	Use sticky traps made of red balls coated with Tanglefoot or other sticky substance. Wrap trunks with corrugated cardboard in spring; remove weekly to kill cocoons formed underneath. Pheromone traps for moths are effective. Bt and horticultural oil are preventives.
Colorado potato beetles	Yellow ⅜-in.-long beetles with black stripes, orange heads, and rounded backs. Plump red larvae have two rows of black spots on sides, black heads. Yellow eggs in rows under leaves.	Various vegetables such as potatoes, tomatoes, peppers, or eggplant.	Adults and larvae chew foliage, defoliating plants.	Mulch heavily with clean hay or straw. Handpick and remove eggs in spring. Use pyrethrum for serious infestations. Ladybugs prey on them.
Cucumber beetles	Actually two species of insects. One type is ¼ in. long, yellow with black spots; larvae are slender and white; ¼ in. long. The other beetles are ¼ in. long, yellow-orange with black stripes; larvae are beige with brown head and a brown spot on the last body segment; ½ in. long.	Vegetables, trees, flowers, and fruits.	Larvae feed on roots. Adults chew holes in leaves, flowers, fruits. Beetles may spread bacterial wilt of cucurbits and cucumber mosaic.	Clear away plant debris, especially spent cucurbit plants. Cover plants with floating row covers or other covers from germination to bloom. Use rotenone for serious infestations.
Cutworms	Larvae of nocturnal moths. Fat, grayish to brown caterpillars, usually curled; 1-2 in. long. Overwinter in grass or debris.	Seedlings, transplants of most vegetables, annuals, perennials, and some grasses.	During night, larvae chew stems at or below ground level.	Protect seedlings and transplants with 3-in. paper collars. Beneficial nematodes and trichogramma wasps prey on cutworms.
Flea beetles	Small, black, shiny beetles, some with curved yellow or white stripes. Hop quickly away when disturbed.	Broccoli, cabbage, cauliflower, eggplant, potatoes, spinach, tomatoes, and watermelons; some ornamentals.	Adults chew tiny holes in leaves and may transmit viral and bacterial disease. Larvae chew roots.	Cover crops in spring with floating row covers. Use pyrethrum for severe infestations. Beneficial nematodes prey on larvae.

(continued)

Insect	Description	Host	Damage	Control
Gypsy moths	Larvae are hairy, gray or brown, with five pairs of blue spots and six pairs of red spots. Male moths are gray, females are white and cannot fly well.	Serious pest of many deciduous and evergreen trees.	Defoliation by larvae weakens trees; severe infestations for a few years in a row may cause death.	Use Bt (*Bacillus thuringiensis*) in late spring. Wrap a foot-wide strip of burlap around trunk, tie with string, fold upper half down; destroy caterpillars caught in burlap. Pheromone traps are also effective.
Japanese beetles	Adults are shiny, ½-in.-long, metallic green beetles with copper-colored wings. Larvae are plump, 1-in.-long, grayish-white grubs with dark brown head, usually curled in C-shape.	Adults feed on many fruit and shade trees, shrubs, flowers, and a few vegetables. Larvae may be a pest of lawns.	Adults eat foliage or fruits. Grubs chew roots of lawn grasses and other plants. Very destructive in masses.	Handpick and drop in soapy water. For long-term grub control, use milky spore disease (*Bacillus popilliae*) or beneficial nematodes. Use pyrethrum for severe infestations.
Leafhoppers	Various tiny, wedge-shaped insects in a variety of colors, which hold their wings in a rooflike position and fly or hop away quickly when disturbed.	Many vegetables, annuals, perennials, trees, and shrubs.	Insects suck sap from leaves, buds, or stems, causing white or yellow spots. Plants are weakened, may drop leaves. May transmit several diseases.	Weed area and clean up debris. Spray leaves with insecticidal soap with isopropyl alcohol (1 T. alcohol to 1 pint of soapy mixture). Various parasitic wasps prey on leafhoppers.
Leaf miners	Small larvae of various insects. Usually green or black; ⅛ in. long. Adults are tiny, grayish or shiny black flies.	Various trees, shrubs, annuals, and perennials.	Larvae eat inside of leaves, leaving winding white or brown trails or blisters. Leaves may turn yellow or brown and fall off. May also attack fruit.	Remove and destroy infested leaves. Insecticidal soap is also effective if applied just as eggs hatch, before larvae enter leaves. Ladybugs prey on eggs.
Mexican bean beetles	Adults have copper-colored, ladybug-like bodies, ⅓ in. long, with 16 black wing spots. Larvae are yellow and spiny.	Beans and cowpeas.	Both larvae and adults skeletonize leaves of beans from underneath. May also attack stems and pods.	Handpick early in season. Destroy the bright yellow eggs found under leaves. Clear away debris in fall; pull up infested plants immediately after main harvest. Use pyrethrum for severe infestations.
Nematodes, plant-parasitic	Various wormlike parasites, usually microscopic. Many present in soil. (There are also beneficial nematodes.)	Vegetables such as beans, carrots, potatoes, and tomatoes. Many other plants.	Deformed flowers, leaves, roots, or stems; abnormal tissue growth; knots on roots. Nematodes may transmit diseases.	Add plenty of organic matter to soil. Turn severely infested beds over to planting of French marigolds for a season, then till under. Rotate crops to avoid planting susceptible plants in infested soil.

Insect	Description	Host	Damage	Control
Plum curculios	Adults are ¼-in.-long beetles with curved brown snout, mottled gray back with 4 humps. White larvae are legless grubs with brown heads.	Serious pest of stone fruits, such as plums and cherries, and apples. Also may be found on other fruits.	Adults make crescent-shaped cuts in fruit to lay eggs in spring. Hatching larvae eat within fruit, usually causing fruit to drop.	Collect dropped fruits and destroy. Shake adults from trees onto tarp on ground, then drop in soapy water or crush. Use rotenone for severe infestations.
Sawflies	Several species of wasplike flies with 2 pairs of wings. Can be ⅝-1½ in. long. Larvae look similar to caterpillars; may be black or green; ½ in. long. Feed in groups.	Various trees, shrubs, grasses, fruits, and flowers.	Larvae feed on fruit and leaves. Some may roll or mine leaves or spin webs.	Collect fallen fruit. Hand-pick larvae on smaller plants. Insecticidal soap is effective. Cultivate soil to expose larvae to predators. Use pyrethrum or rotenone in extreme cases.
Scale	Round, legless insects with waxy shells in various colors; ⅛ in. across. Resemble small bumps on plants.	Many types of plants, depending on species of scale.	Suck plant sap from stems, leaves. In masses, may cause plants to be stunted and leaves to yellow. Their honeydew encourages dark sooty molds that may interfere with photosynthesis.	If infestation not severe, scrape off with fingernail or cotton swab with rubbing alcohol. Insecticidal soap and alcohol will help with severe cases. Horticultural oil in late winter will kill eggs or larvae. Chalcid wasps prey on scale.
Slugs and snails	Soft-bodied, usually black, brown, or gray adults with tentacles, often with hump on back; ½-3 in. long. Snails have a single shell. Both leave a slimy trail.	Many vegetables, fruits, and flowers.	Most feed at night, creating holes in leaves and stems, pits on fruit.	Handpick at night early in season; drop in soapy water or sprinkle with salt. Bury saucers or shallow bowls with rims at surface in garden; bait with stale beer. Place boards or cabbage leaves in garden, destroy slugs underneath in day. Diatomaceous earth will repel them.
Spider mites	Tiny, 8-legged relatives of spiders; 1/150-1/50 in. long. White, green or rust-colored, several different species.	Many vegetables, annuals, perennials, trees, and shrubs.	Suck sap from leaves, fruits, roots. Leaves may become discolored, curled, and may be covered with webs. Fruit may be russeted, dry, or deformed.	A forceful spray of water on leaves in early morning, repeated for 3 days, will deter pests. Insecticidal soap is an effective control. Frequent light watering of soil will help limit attacks during hot, dry weather. Green lacewings or ladybugs will prey on these pests.

(continued)

CONTROLLING INSECT PESTS – *Continued*

Insect	Description	Host	Damage	Control
Spittlebugs	Adults are dull brown, green, or black, sometimes striped; ¼-⅓ in. long. Resemble leafhoppers. Green nymphs are surrounded by froth.	Many vegetables, fruits, flowers, trees, and grasses. Some favor strawberries.	Nymphs and adults suck juices of plants. Some are harmless, others are destructive, causing deformed leaves, needles, stems, fruits.	Spray with insecticidal soap. Use rotenone for severe infestations.
Spruce budworms	Brown, ½-¾-in.-long caterpillars with yellow warts on their backs. Adult moths are mottled buff or gray; ⅞ in. long.	Various evergreens.	Caterpillars tunnel into opening buds, feeding on pollen, causing deformed growth. Overall weakening of trees. Serious pest in northern U.S.	Handpick caterpillars. Prune out infested areas. Use Bt (*Bacillus thuringiensis*) in spring for caterpillars.
Squash bugs	Flat, dark brown to black bugs with orange-brown on the abdomen; nearly ¾ in. long. Malodorous when crushed. Nymphs have red heads, antennae and legs, and a green abdomen or are dark greenish gray.	Various vine crops, especially squash and pumpkins.	Both adult and nymphs suck plant juices, causing leaves to wilt, blacken, and dry.	Clear away spent crops after harvest. Use barriers such as floating row covers on young plants. Place boards in garden, destroy bugs that hide underneath in day. Insecticidal soap is effective. Use rotenone in severe cases.
Squash vine borers	White, 1-in.-long larvae with brown heads and tiny brown legs. Adults are orange and black clear-winged moths; 1-1½ in. long.	Pumpkins, gourds, squash, cucumbers, muskmelons, and watermelons.	Boring larvae cause wilted runners and vines. Deposits of yellow-green, sawdust-like material near the bases of stems and around wounds.	Protect young plants with floating row covers. Inject Bt (*Bacillus thuringiensis*) into infected stems. Poke a flexible wire into entrance hole to kill larvae. Slit stems and kill worm inside; pile soil over wound to encourage rooting. Destroy vines after harvest.
Stinkbugs	Small or medium-size, odoriferous shield-shaped bugs that are green, brown, or gray.	Various vegetables and flowering plants.	Adults and nymphs suck out juices causing wilting; distorted seeds, fruits, or vegetables; and premature fruit dropping.	Clear away debris and weeds. Use sabadilla dust when necessary. Some species are beneficial, preying on Colorado potato beetles.

Insect	Description	Host	Damage	Control
Tent caterpillars, eastern	Black, 2-in.-long caterpillars with white, brown, and yellow stripes and a row of blue spots. Adults are reddish brown moths with white stripes.	Various trees and shrubs.	Webbed tents in crotches of trees. Larvae feed on foliage. Weakens trees and may cause irreparable damage if attacks occur for several years.	Scrape off egg masses (gray foamlike material encircling young twigs). Destroy tents. Use Bt (*Bacillus thuringiensis*) for the larvae.
Thrips	Thin, $\frac{1}{25}$-in.-long insects with fringed wings. Usually present in great numbers.	Many flowers and vegetables.	Nymphs and adults of some species scrape plant tissue and feed on sap. Discolored, twisted leaves; withering flower buds; pitted fruit.	Insecticidal soap is an effective control. Use pyrethrum in severe cases. Green lacewings prey on thrips.
Tomato hornworms	Green, 3-4-in.-long caterpillars with 8 diagonal stripes on either side and a black horn protruding from behind. Adults are gray-brown moths with white zigzags on rear wings and orange or brown spots on body; 4-5-in. wingspan.	Tomatoes, dill, eggplant, peppers, and potatoes.	Caterpillars chew holes in leaves and fruit.	Handpick early in season. Clear away plant debris and turn over soil in fall. Use Bt (*Bacillus thuringiensis*) when caterpillars are small. Braconid wasps prey on these pests. Use pyrethrum if infestation is severe.
Whiteflies	Tiny, white mothlike insects. Noticeable if plant is disturbed, as they fly away in large groups. Nymphs are green, transparent, and flat.	Many flowers and vegetables.	Adults and nymphs suck plant juices, causing discolored foliage; weakened growth. Secreted honeydew encourages growth of black sooty mold.	Spray with insecticidal soap. Use yellow sticky traps to spot infestations early in season. Use pyrethrum in severe cases.
Wireworms	Thin, brown, hard-shelled, wormlike larvae; $\frac{1}{2}$-$1\frac{1}{2}$ in. long. Adults are brown or gray click beetles, with dark spotted heads; $\frac{1}{2}$ in. long.	Vegetables, fruits, grass, and flowers.	Worms feed on underground stems, roots, or seeds of many plants, causing wilting and death.	Remove plant debris in fall. Handpick adults in spring. Trap larvae by putting half a potato on a stick in a 3- by 3-in. hole. In 3-4 days, drop potato and worms into bucket of soapy water. Repeat until no longer a problem.

CONTROLLING PLANT DISEASES

A variety of common plant diseases can become a problem in the garden, causing symptoms such as spotted or disfigured foliage, blighted petals, or rotted stems. The following chart provides a guide to symptoms, the conditions that promote the disease, and what steps you can take to control it.

Disease	Symptoms	Conditions	Control
Anthracnose	Dark circular spots or lesions on stems, leaves, fruit. White to pink spores ooze out of wounds. Leaves may shrivel and die. Stems, petioles, or fruit may have mushy sunken depressions.	Many plants are susceptible. Wet weather promotes spreading as spores are carried by windblown rain or on seeds.	Destroy infected plants. Rotate crops. Work in garden only when plants are dry to avoid spreading disease.
Azalea petal blight	Small white or brown spots on petals enlarge, causing entire petal to become slimy. Usually lower petals are affected first. By the second day, flowers have collapsed but remain on plant. Fungus overwinters in dead flowers and soil under shrubs.	Quick-spreading disease confined to flowers, usually on azaleas, sometimes rhododendron or mountain laurel. Prevalent in southeastern states. Transmitted by wind, rain, and insects. Encouraged by warm, wet, humid conditions.	Pick infected flowers as soon as you notice condition. Clear away debris. Avoid overhead watering while in flower. Cover soil with mulch.
Bacterial leaf spot	Small brown or purple spots on leaves, often numerous. Leaves eventually yellow and fall.	Affects cauliflower, cabbage, turnip, and others, especially in seedling stage.	Destroy infected plants. Rotate crops in a 3-year cycle to avoid planting susceptible plants in infected beds.
Bacterial wilt	Large irregular patches appear on leaves, which eventually wilt. May spread to stems and branches, and could cause death of whole plant. Infected stems contain thick ooze.	Attacks all cucurbits such as cucumbers, pumpkins, and squash (except watermelon). Transmitted by cucumber beetles.	Cover young plants with floating row covers. Rotate crops; beetles overwinter in soil.
Black rot	Leaves have yellowed, V-shaped wedges; dark veins. Growth may be one-sided. Eventually all but top leaves may drop. If severely infected, yellow ooze may be squeezed from stem.	Attacks all crucifers. Bacteria transmitted by seeds, soil, and rain, eventually finding its way to the vascular system.	Buy certified disease-free seeds. Treat homegrown seed for 30 minutes in a 122°F bath. Plant in well-drained, nutrient-rich soil. Clear away debris. Use three-year crop rotation.
Black spot	Round black spots, usually on upper surfaces of leaves, that are up to ½ in. wide. In more susceptible cultivars, leaves eventually yellow and fall off. Generally weakens plants as they try to regrow lost leaves. Fungus may also cause lesions in canes.	Common disease of roses. Encouraged by moist or wet conditions.	Prune and destroy infected areas in dry weather with sterilized tools. Remove fallen leaves. Apply flowable sulfur spray weekly throughout season. Plant resistant cultivars. Space plants far enough apart to maintain good air circulation; mulch in spring. Water early in day; avoid wetting leaves.

Disease	Symptoms	Conditions	Control
Canker	Red or yellow spots on canes or stalks of plant which eventually dry out and turn brown and wrinkled. These areas may burst, revealing greenish-brown spore masses. Stem may die back to injury.	Common disease of rose canes.	Prune out diseased areas. Always prune roses just above bud or leaf axil so that plant can heal quickly before possible diseases set in.
Crown gall	Round, rough galls up to several inches form, usually near soil or graft union.	Bacterial disease of many plants. Enters through wounds, encouraged by warm weather and alkaline soil conditions.	Prune out diseased areas. Sterilize tools with bleach after each cut. Destroy seriously infected plants. Check plants for galls on crowns before buying. Plant new ones away from previously infected area.
Curly top virus	Virus disease of many vegetables and ornamentals that has various symptoms. Beets have curled leaves, clear veins, and sharp formations under leaves. Tomato leaves twist and curl upward, petioles downward, stems become yellow with purple veins.	Transmitted by beet leafhopper. Encouraged by sun and heat, low humidity. Most common in areas where sugar beets are grown.	Destroy infected plants. Cover seedlings with floating row covers or equivalent.
Damping-off	Water-soaked or necrotic lesions on seedling stems close to soil. Roots look small and rotted. Stems may fall over.	Disease of many seedlings caused by various fungi. Common in wet conditions.	Plant in well-drained, sterile soil. Maintain good air circulation. Don't overcrowd seedlings.
Downy mildew	Upper sides of leaves have brown or yellow spots; undersides have downy white or purple mold in wet conditions. Stems may become discolored.	Many plants susceptible. Caused by various fungi.	Destroy infected plants or plant parts. Dust or spray with sulfur. Water plants at soil level. Avoid wetting leaves when watering.
Fireblight	New shoots curve downward, turn black or brown, eventually die. Blossoms and fruit also affected; blackened fruit remains on tree. Cankers emit ooze. Overall scorched effect.	Bacterial disease spread by rain and insects into flowers, where it spreads throughout tree. Fruit trees such as apple and pear commonly attacked.	Cut diseased branches 3-12 in. below infected area during dormant season (depending on plant size). Destroy any severely infected plants. Plant resistant varieties.
Fusarium wilts	Darkening veins. Wilting, yellowing, and eventual death of leaves and stems. Rotting roots.	Fungal disease; various plants affected. Fungi live in soil; many types have specific hosts. Encouraged by hot, dry weather.	Destroy infected plants. Rotate crops for several year intervals. Clear away debris. Plant resistant cultivars.

(continued)

CONTROLLING PLANT DISEASES –*Continued*

Disease	Symptoms	Conditions	Control
Gray mold blight	Pale, water-soaked spots on flowers, leaves, or stems. Spots turn into soft tan or gray mold. Brown lesions may appear on stems.	Encouraged by warm, damp, cloudy conditions. Transmitted by wind and water. Attacks fruits, vegetables, flowers, and shrubs.	Remove and destroy any spent or infected plant parts. Prune off any leaves touching soil or other plants. Maintain good spacing, air circulation, and soil drainage. Avoid wetting foliage when watering.
Mosaic	Mottled green and yellow foliage or veins. Leaves may be wrinkled or curled; stems may be banded. Stunted growth.	Virus disease. Attacks various plants from vegetables to flowers. Often transmitted by aphids or leafhoppers.	Destroy infected plants. Buy certified disease-free plants. Plant resistant cultivars. Clear away plant debris. Wash hands and clothes after handling. Control leafhoppers or aphids that spread the virus.
Powdery mildew	White powdery spots or blotches on leaves that eventually cover leaf surfaces. Leaves pale, brown and shriveled. Fruits also may be covered. Reduced yield, stunted growth.	Fungal disease affecting many plants. Transmitted by wind, splashing rain, or on seeds.	Destroy infected plants or prune infected area in trees. Spray weekly with flowable sulfur once "bloom" appears. Rotate crops. Clear away debris. Plant resistant cultivars.
Root rot	Leaves may yellow, growth slows, plants wilt and die. Roots become soft and black.	Caused by various fungi. Attacks many plants. Usually transmitted through soil. Encouraged by hot, dry conditions.	Encourage healthy growth by maintaining good soil drainage and aeration and providing necessary nutrients.
Rust	Reddish-brown powdery spots; yellowed leaves. Stunted growth.	Fungal diseases that often have very specific hosts or alternate hosts. Plants such as apples, asparagus, beans, carrots, corn, lettuce, onions, and spinach are affected. Transmitted by wind; high nitrogen and humidity encourage infection.	Destroy infected plants. Dust or spray with sulfur. Plant resistant cultivars. Space plants appropriately for good air circulation. Keep soil moist. Clear away debris.
***Verticillium* wilt**	Wilting leaves and stems on one or more branches. Margins of leaves may curl upward before they yellow between veins and drop off. Small fruit. Darkened veins.	Fungal disease affecting many plants. Enters through soil into roots and wounds.	Destroy infected plants. Rotate crops to uninfested soil. Clear away debris.

Plant Propagation

Propagating Plants

One of the easiest and most economical ways to increase your plant collection is to learn how to propagate them yourself. You can start new plants in a variety of different ways—sow seed, root cuttings, layer, or divide them. Propagating plants is a fascinating hobby that requires little in the way of supplies or equipment, and the techniques involved are straightforward and relatively easy to master. Best of all, creating new plants is fun and rewarding and provides an opportunity not just to create but to share plants with other gardeners.

There are two types of propagation techniques: sexual and asexual propagation. Plants grown from seed or spores have been sexually propagated, because most seed is the result of cross-pollination and contains genetic information from two different parents. Vegetative propagation is the term used for the many different asexual ways plants can be propagated, such as division, cuttings, or layering. All vegetative techniques involve removing sections of stems, roots, or leaves from a parent and inducing them to develop into new plants by providing conditions that encourage the production of roots and shoots. Plants propagated vegetatively are genetically identical to the parent plant. For this reason, vegetative propagation is used to make exact copies of plants that have special features such as taste, color, disease resistance, size, or form. Since many

cultivars do not come true from seed (because seeds resulting from cross-pollination are not genetically uniform), and others do not produce seed at all, vegetative propagation is an important way to perpetuate valuable cultivars. For example, 'Bartlett' pear was created in 1770 and is enjoyed today only because of vegetative propagation. Another benefit of vegetative propagation techniques is that they generally yield much quicker results than growing plants from seed.

Vegetative Propagation

What makes it possible for individual plant parts to transform themselves into complete plants with roots, stems, foliage, and flowers of their own? All plants have specialized clusters of cells that can divide very quickly and differentiate into all the structures a plant needs to grow. These clusters of cells, called meristem or meristematic tissue, are found in the growing tips of roots, stems, and branches. As the plant grows, it is the meristematic cells that differentiate into new stems, roots, foliage, and flowers. Meristematic tissue also lies dormant in the plant, most notably in dormant buds, which will begin to grow if given the proper stimulus. For example, the moist, humid conditions needed to root a cutting will awaken the meristem in dormant buds

and cause it to begin producing roots and shoots. Plants such as orchids propagated by a specialized technique called meristem or tissue culture are grown from single cells of meristem tissue. Certain types of plant cells can also turn into meristemlike tissue, causing roots to arise on the cut surface of a stem even if dormant buds are not present.

Supplies

The first task is to assemble the tools and supplies you'll need. You'll probably need the following items:

● **Propagation knife.** For taking cuttings or making cuts to encourage roots to form on a layer, you'll need knives of various sizes and shapes. Specially designed propagation knives usually have a thin, straight blade. They must be kept very sharp.

● **Pruning shears.** You'll also need one or several different sizes of pruning shears and/or scissors for cutting stems, leaves, or other plant parts.

● **Containers.** In some cases, new plants can be propagated and planted directly into the garden, but you'll need containers for rooting cuttings or potting up new plants. Many different sizes and shapes of containers will work, as long as they are deep enough to hold the base of the cuttings, provide drainage, and can be covered in some manner to maintain humidity. At least 2 inches deep is best. Try using plastic garden flats and pots or plastic food containers. Plastic shoe or sweater boxes also are very useful because cuttings can be stuck in rooting medium spread in the bottom, and with the top in place they provide the humid conditions cuttings need.

● **Rooting medium.** A good rooting medium provides enough support to hold the cutting firmly and also retains moisture, but is porous enough to drain well and allow roots to penetrate. Many mixtures will work, but a mixture of equal parts sterile, coarse sand (not builder's or beach sand) and vermiculite or perlite are recommended as the initial medium. After rooting, cuttings can be transplanted to a medium that is richer in nutrients—a mixture of one or several of the above ingredients with an equal amount of sterile potting soil is fine.

A container of water will serve as an effective rooting medium for many plants—coleus or philodendrons, for example—but this approach has drawbacks. Roots that are produced in water tend to lack the structure and strength of roots produced in other media, and they do not transplant to soil well since they tangle together and are easily damaged.

● **Dibble.** This is a pencil-like instrument that is used to make a cylindrical hole into the rooting medium for the cutting. Making a hole with a dibble (or the end of a pencil) prevents the cut end of the cutting from being damaged when it is stuck into the soil. It also prevents rooting hormone from rubbing off.

● **Atomizer.** A simple atomizer or spray bottle will make the task of increasing humidity around the cuttings quick and easy.

● **Disinfectant.** Bleach or alcohol are excellent disinfectants for cleaning pruning shears and knives. Make a solution of 3 parts water to 1 part bleach or alcohol. Dip implements into a container of this disinfectant after taking each cutting to avoid transporting fungi, bacteria, or other diseases from plant to plant.

● **Heating cable.** Although this piece of equipment is optional, many kinds of cuttings will root more quickly if provided with bottom heat. You can provide bottom heat by setting propagation containers on heated surfaces, such as the top of a radiator, refrigerator, or hot water heater. Or invest in a commercial heating cable like the ones sold for speeding the germination of seeds. These are available from most mail-order nurseries or well-stocked local garden centers. They will generally keep the temperature of the medium about 5° to 10°F above the temperature of the surrounding air, and can be easily positioned along the bottom of a propagation box beneath the soil.

● **Rooting hormones.** Rooting hormones are very useful in encouraging hardwood and other difficult-to-root cuttings to form roots, but they must be used sparingly and carefully. Generally, only the tip of the cutting is dipped into the powder; in this case, more is not necessarily better. It's also important to realize that these hormones can be contaminated with fungi and other organisms. When using them, pour a small amount into a separate container, use it to treat the cuttings you're planting on a given day, then throw away the excess. It's best to store rooting hormones in the refrigerator to extend the shelf life, which ranges from six months to a year. Some formulations include chemical fungicide, but you can purchase ones that don't and use sulfur to control fungal diseases.

● **Antitranspirants.** Often used to protect evergreen foliage from water loss and windburn in winter, antitranspirants will reduce the amount of moisture lost through foliage. For this reason, they help prevent a cutting from drying out before roots have a chance to form. Antitranspirants are also quite useful when transplanting cuttings to larger pots or to the outdoors, because they reduce water loss and help plants overcome stress.

● **Propagators and mist beds.** If you're serious about getting professional results, you may want to invest in a propagation box, which is much like a miniature greenhouse. It provides uniformly high humidity, and most models come equipped with heating cables. You can also make one yourself with plastic stretched over a wood or wire frame and a heating cable spread under a layer of vermiculite or sand. You can suspend fluorescent lights over the box if necessary. Be sure to provide for ventilation to prevent excessive humidity from building up.

A mist bed is a more sophisticated piece of equipment, which is relatively expensive and is generally used in a greenhouse. A heating cable regulates bottom heat while a timer and a series of small mist nozzles spray the cuttings with a fine mist of water at intervals throughout the day. A mist bed isn't enclosed, because the frequent misting provides all the humidity the cuttings require.

Rooting Cuttings

Rooting cuttings is one of the easiest, most popular ways to propagate plants. Although there are several different types of cuttings, two basic concerns apply to all types. First, since cuttings are removed from the parent plant before roots develop, they dry out easily. To root them successfully, you'll need to provide a rooting medium that is well drained but remains moist at all times. They also require high humidity to reduce water loss. Second, it's important to provide as antiseptic conditions as possible to discourage disease organisms and fungal spores from invading the wound(s) made when taking the cutting.

Taking Stem Cuttings

Regardless of the type of stem cutting you're taking, it's best to start with short ones, between 3 and 6 inches in length. Remove all flowers and flower buds so that the plant's energy will go toward root rather than flower production. Also remove the bottom leaf or set of leaves so that the foliage won't touch the rooting medium.

It's important to make a clean cut without crushing the stem. Use a knife on soft and semihardwood cuttings; shears on thick stems or for hardwood cuttings. Make the cut at a 45-degree angle, so that the cut has more surface area from which the roots will grow. The top of the angled cut should be between ¼ and ½ inch below a leaf node (where leaves emerge from the stem). Be sure to sterilize your knife or shears with disinfectant between cuttings to avoid transporting fungi or disease organisms from plant to plant.

Fill the containers you'll be using with rooting medium, water thoroughly, and allow excess water to drain away before sticking in the cuttings. Use a dibble or the end of a pencil to make holes to insert the cuttings, spacing the holes 2 to 4 inches apart depending on the size of the cuttings. Insert the cuttings at least 1 inch into the medium, and make sure the bottom set of leaves is not in contact with the medium.

After planting the cuttings, don't let the rooting medium dry out. There are several different ways to water the cuttings. You can gently water the surface of the medium using a watering can with a fine-spray nozzle. Another method is to water from below by setting containers in a pan or tray of water and allowing water to seep upward through the drainage holes. Either way, be sure to allow the containers to drain after watering because they should not be left sitting in water. A third method is to set the propagation container atop a water-filled pebble tray, with one or several wicks running from the medium, through drainage holes in the bottom of the container, into the water. (Strips of nylon stockings work fine as wicks.) Be sure the bottom of the container

To take a herbaceous cutting, remove a 3- to 6-inch-long stem with from two to six leaf nodes. Cut the stem just below a node.

Remove any flowers or flower buds from the cutting to direct plant energy into root growth. Also remove all but the top few leaves to reduce water loss.

Treat the cutting with rooting hormone, if needed, and stick it into the rooting medium in a hole made with a dibble or the blunt end of a pencil.

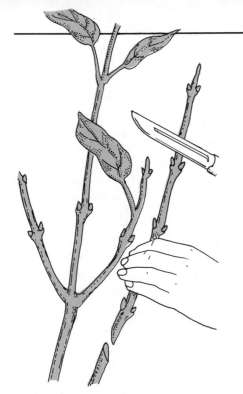

For any kind of cutting, it's important to keep track of which is the top and which is the bottom of the cutting. Hardwood cuttings can be taken in early winter with a sharp knife.

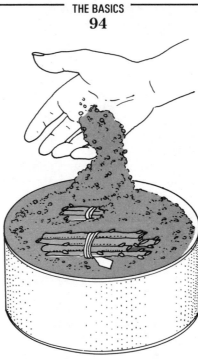

After taking hardwood cuttings, bundle, label, and then bury them in moist peat moss or vermiculite. Be sure to keep all of the cuttings pointing in the same direction.

Store the cuttings in a cool but frost-free place until spring, when they will have developed callus on the ends. Dip the bottom of each cutting in rooting hormone.

doesn't make direct contact with the water.

Cuttings require high humidity (near 100 percent) in order to root without drying out. You can place a plastic bag over a single pot or group of pots and support it with thin strips of wood or heavy gauge wire to keep it from touching the foliage. Or use garden flats with clear plastic covers, sweater boxes, a cold frame or hotbed, a propagation box, or a mist bed to maintain humidity.

Ideally, the air temperature within the propagation container should be 70°F or less. Within the rooting medium, between 60° and 70°F is best. Adequate light is important, but bright light will literally cook the cuttings. Either natural, indirect sunlight or light from fluorescent fixtures is fine. Make sure fluorescent lights are suspended approximately 6 to 10 inches above the propagation container.

Types of Cuttings

Herbaceous Cuttings. These are stem cuttings taken from herba-

ceous plants, meaning plants that do not develop woody tissue. Many houseplants, annuals, perennials, herbs, and vegetables can be propagated by this type of cutting. Herbaceous cuttings can be taken at any time of the year, but late spring and early summer are probably best. Most plants are in active growth at this time of year and actively growing shoots that will yield the best results.

Softwood Cuttings. Similar to herbaceous cuttings, softwood cuttings are taken from woody plants such as ornamental shrubs, small-fruit bushes, and many trees. Softwood cuttings should be taken from actively growing shoots in late spring or early summer. These cuttings should be 2 to 4 inches in length.

Semihardwood Cuttings. This type of cutting is similar to softwood cuttings but is taken later in the year, when active growth has slowed down and no new leaves are being produced. The stems are becoming woody (hard) at the base, but the stem tips are still soft. Also called semiripe cuttings,

these should be between 4 and 6 inches long and should be taken in late summer. They will usually require the addition of a rooting hormone for best results.

Hardwood Cuttings. These are stem cuttings taken from outdoor deciduous trees and shrubs after the leaves have dropped. They are taken from new wood that is thoroughly ripe or woody and dormant. These are taken in late fall to early spring and should be between 5 and 12 inches long.

Because they are dormant, hardwood cuttings are treated quite differently than softwood or semihardwood cuttings. Place them singly (or in bundles of the same species or cultivar) in a large container filled with moist sand or vermiculite. Place the container in a cool (35° to 45°F), dark location for the winter months. When lifted in spring, the cuttings will have developed a protective callus over the cutting wound, from which roots will emerge upon planting. Dust the callus with rooting hormone and root the cuttings in a manner similar

Stick the cuttings in moist, sterile rooting medium. Cover them with plastic held a few inches above the cuttings to provide adequate humidity.

Once the plants have rooted, they will begin to produce topgrowth. They're then ready to move to individual pots or into the garden.

to that recommended for the other types of cuttings listed above. Bottom heat is often effective at this stage. Once rooted, cuttings will be ready for transplanting to individual pots or outdoors. (For more information, see "Propagating Trees and Shrubs" on page 342.)

Leaf Cuttings

Not many plants will propagate from leaves, but those that do (primarily a limited number of houseplants) provide a quick and easy way to increase numbers. Like stem cuttings, described earlier in the chapter, leaf cuttings require as sterile conditions as possible to discourage fungi and other disease organisms. They also need high humidity and a rooting medium that remains evenly moist.

The simplest type of leaf cutting consists of the leaf alone, without the petiole, or leaf stalk, attached. The base of the leaf is placed in the medium, which is kept evenly moist until one or more plantlets appear. Once the new plants have produced

an adequate root system, the leaf can be removed and they can be potted and grown on. Jade plants (*Crassula* spp.) and piggyback plants (*Tolmiea menziesii*) are easy to propagate by simple leaf cuttings. There are several other types of leaf cuttings, which are described below. (See the list of plants that can be propagated from different types of leaf cuttings in "Plants and Propagation Methods" on page 98.)

Leaf and petiole cuttings.
These consist of an entire leaf with at least ½ to 1½ inch of the petiole (leaf stalk) attached. Place the petiole into the rooting medium of a propagation container, and follow the standard procedures listed above for stem cuttings. One or more new plantlets will develop from the petiole, at which time the original leaf can be removed and the plantlets grown on in the propagation container until ready for transplanting. African violets are often propagated this way.

Leaf–bud cuttings.
As the name suggests, this type of cutting con-

sists of a mature leaf, a dormant bud in the leaf axil, and a small amount of stem tissue (¼ to ½ inch in length) to which the leaf is attached. Place the base of the leaf into the rooting medium, covering the bud and the stem. The stem may be softwood, semihardwood, or hardwood. Then follow the same procedures described earlier in the chapter for leaf and petiole cuttings. The new plant will develop from the dormant bud. English ivy (*Hedera helix*) is especially easy to propagate in this manner.

Split vein cuttings.
The leaves of some plants will produce new plantlets anywhere along their undersurface where a cut vein is in contact with rooting medium. For these, remove a leaf from the plant and make slits across individual veins—one slit per vein, effectively severing a vein with each cut. Lay the leaf flat on the surface of the medium, right side up, with the underside in direct contact with the medium. You may need to tack down the leaf with hairpins or bent pieces of wire to be sure the leaf is touching the medium. Rex begonias are often propagated in this manner.

Rex begonias are often propagated by leaf cuttings. For this technique, the leaf is pinned faceup in a container filled with sterile rooting medium. Make a slash across the major veins in the leaf, then cover with plastic to provide high humidity.

Leaf sections. Some plants can even be propagated from small pieces of a leaf, as long as each piece includes a section of a large vein. For these, simply cut the desired number of leaf sections and place them vertically into the rooting medium. Be sure to place them right side up—with the end that was closest to the base of the plant in the medium. New plantlets will develop from the base of the primary vein. *Sansevieria trifasciata,* commonly called snake plant, is the plant most often propagated in this manner.

Cane Cuttings

Plants that produce canelike stems can be propagated by softwood cuttings, but one of the most productive approaches is to cut the cane into 2-inch-long sections, each of which must have a node (an old leaf scar and a dormant bud). Place each cutting horizontally into the rooting medium, with about ⅓ of the cutting (including the dormant bud) located above the surface of the medium. Use bottom heat to promote rooting, and follow the same procedures recommended for other stem cuttings. Dieffenbachias (*Dieffenbachia* spp.) and dracaenas (*Dracaena* spp.) can be propagated in this manner.

Root Cuttings

Many fleshy-rooted plants can be propagated from the simple technique known as root cuttings. Root cuttings are taken once the plants have become dormant at the end of the growing season. Lift the parent plant and root prune it by severing several of the large, fleshy roots. Then replant the parent plant. This root pruning will not harm the plant, provided you don't remove too many roots.

Cut each root into 2- to 3-inch sections (4 to 6 inches long for trees). It's important to keep track of polarity, which end of the root was closest to the parent plant (up) and which was farthest from the plant (down). That's because the oldest part of a root cutting (generally the widest end) must

be placed at the surface of the propagation medium with the youngest part of the cutting placed into the medium. They won't root upside down. One easy way to keep track is to make the cut at the "top" or oldest end of the root horizontal and the "bottom" cut at a 45-degree angle. That way, each cutting will have a recognizable top and bottom for planting.

To plant root cuttings, fill a container with equal amounts of peat and ordinary sterilized potting soil. Thoroughly moisten the soil and let the water drain away. Then dust the bottom of each cutting with powdered sulfur to control fungi. Use a dibble to make insertion holes, allowing no less than 1½ inches between holes, and place the cuttings into the holes. Again, make sure that the cuttings are oriented with the oldest or top part nearest the surface. Cover the container with ¼ to ½ inch of pea gravel or coarse sand.

If you are propagating hardy plants, you can place the container in a cold frame. Keep cuttings of tender plants in a frost-free place. Water only when the medium begins to become dry; too much moisture can promote the growth of fungi, which is the prime cause for loss of root cuttings. When new shoots appear, provide a mild dose of fertilizer such as manure tea. Once the plants have become established, they can be transplanted to individual pots or moved to the garden.

Division

One of the easiest ways to propagate clump-forming plants is to divide them, that not only serves to propagate, but also helps rejuvenate clumps that have spread and left an old, overcrowded center that has ceased blooming. Plants propagated in this manner are dug, separated into individual plantlets, each with its own shoot(s) and roots, and then replanted. Many perennials are divided in early spring, when plants are just beginning to awaken from winter dormancy

and begin actively growing. However, spring-blooming plants are best divided in early summer, just after bloom in the case of irises, or in late summer or early fall as they approach dormancy, as in the case of such plants as peonies or hostas.

To divide a plant, dig the parent plant and either gently pull or cut apart sections of the crown. You can cut with pruners or use the sharp edge of a spade or trowel. Replant the divisions as soon as possible, and keep them well watered both until you get them back into the ground and until they become established.

A number of plants such as raspberries and lilacs produce suckers or offsets that root either before or after they are cut away from the parent plant. Use a knife to cut them away from the parent plant or use a shovel and dig the sucker or offset if it has already rooted. Make sure the cut is as close to the parent stem as possible. Replant at the same depth as when attached to the parent plant.

Bulbs can also be propagated by yet another form of division; bulbs such as daffodils that produce offsets at the base of the main bulb can be dug and separated. Once the bulb has finished blooming and the foliage is turning brown, it's a simple matter to lift the parent bulb, remove the offsets, and replant. Offsets will generally take one to several years to reach blooming size. (For more information on propagating bulbs, corms, and tubers, see pages 124-27.)

Layering

Most plants that have long, flexible stems are candidates for another propagation technique called layering. Layering is a method to encourage roots to develop on a section of a plant where they would not normally grow (such as on aboveground stems) while the stem is still attached to the parent plant. This process can occur naturally, such as when a forsythia branch arches downward, touches the soil, and roots. It's also easy to induce the process.

To layer a plant, start with a young, vigorously growing outer stem. In mid- to late spring, dig a small, shallow hole or trench (1 to 3 inches deep) several feet from the center of the parent plant. Arch the young stem downward so that its tip or a portion near the tip can be placed into the hole. Then fasten it down with a wire wicket or a rock if necessary and cover it with soil. Keep the soil evenly moist, and by the end of fall a complete root system should have formed at the base of the buried portion of the stem. The offspring plant can then be severed from the parent plant, either that fall or the next spring, and planted elsewhere. Some stems will root more readily if a slanting cut is made partway through the stem at the point where it touches the soil.

Serpentine layering is a very similar technique used to produce many plants from a single, flexible stem. In this case, make a slanting cut every 8 to 10 inches along the length of the stem. Then bury the stem along the ground, fastening the cut portions into the soil in holes dug at intervals away from the plant. Leaf nodes buried underground will generate roots; those left above will grow shoots. When lifted in spring or fall, a root system should exist at each point along the stem where it was cut, and each new plant can be severed from the original parent stem and replanted. (For illustrations and step-by-step instructions for layering shrubs, see page 342.)

Air Layering. Some plants that do not have flexible stems can be

To air layer a favorite houseplant, make a shallow cut in the main stem just below a leaf node, dust with rooting hormone, wrap damp sphagnum moss around the stem, and cover it with plastic taped in place. Once roots are visible beneath the plastic, you can remove the plastic, sever the stem below the roots, and pot up the new plant. Don't throw away the parent plant: Most will resprout from dormant buds.

layered in yet another way, through a technique called air layering. To air layer a plant, cut a small horizontal wedge on one side of a healthy stem, partway through the stem just below an old leaf scar (node). Dust the wound with rooting hormone, and pack a ball of moist sphagnum around the stem, thickly covering the wound. Hold the sphagnum in place by wrapping black plastic around the stem and securing it with twist ties or tape. Keep the sphagnum evenly moist until roots develop. Once the roots begin to emerge from the sphagnum, you can sever the offspring from the parent and replant. Air layering is often used to root the tops of houseplants

such as dieffenbachia (*Dieffenbachia* spp.) that have lost their lower leaves. The parent plant will usually resprout below the cut.

Stooling. Another form of layering, called stooling or mound layering, involves wounding each stem of a multistemmed plant about 6 inches above ground level, and then mounding soil over the base of the plant and the wounds. This is usually performed in spring. By fall, each stem will have developed its own root system from the point of the wound and can be severed from the parent plant and replanted.

PLANTS AND PROPAGATION METHODS

The following are some of the easiest houseplants, annuals, herbs, and perennials to propagate vegetatively. For more information on propagating trees and shrubs, see page 342.

Herbaceous or Softwood Cuttings

Achillea spp. (yarrow)
Alchemilla spp. (lady's-mantle)
Aster spp. (aster, perennial species)
Begonia spp. (begonia)
Bougainvillea spp. (bougainvillea)
Campanula spp. (bellflower)
Centaurea spp. (centaurea)
Chrysanthemum spp. (chrysanthemum)
Coleus × *hybridus* (coleus)
Erigeron spp. (fleabane)
Euphorbia spp. (spurge)
Ficus spp. (fig)
Geum spp. (avens)
Helenium spp. (sneezeweed)
Heuchera sanguinea (coralbells)
Hoya spp. (hoya)
Iberis spp. (candytuft)
Lantana spp. (shrub verbena)
Lavandula spp. (lavender)
Lupinus spp. (lupine)
Monarda didyma (bee balm)
Oenothera spp. (evening primrose)
Philodendron cordatum (heart-leaf philodendron)
Plumbago spp. (leadwort)
Rosmarinus officinalis (rosemary)
Salvia spp. (salvia, perennial species)
Sedum spectabile (stonecrop)
Silene spp. (campion, perennial species)
Solidago spp. (goldenrod)
Thymus spp. (thyme)
Tradescantia spp. (wandering jew)
Verbena spp. (vervain)
Veronica spp. (speedwell)

Leaf or Leaf and Petiole Cuttings

Asplenium bulbiferum (hen-and-chickens fern)
Begonia spp. (begonia)
Crassula arborescens (silver jade plant)
Echeveria spp. (hen-and-chickens)
Gesneria spp. (gesneriad)
Gloxinia spp. (gloxinia)
Peperomia caperata (emerald-ripple plant) and *P. metallica*
Saintpaulia ionantha (African violet)
Sedum spp. (stonecrop)
Streptocarpus × *hybridus* (cape primrose)
Tiarella cordifolia (foamflower)
Tolmiea menziesii (piggyback plant)

Leaf-Bud Cuttings

Aphelandra squarrosa (zebra plant)
Codiaeum variegatum (croton)
Haberlea spp. (haberlea)
Hedera helix (English ivy)
Hypoestes phyllostachya (polka-dot plant)
Kalanchoe spp. (kalanchoe)
Pelargonium spp. (geranium)

Leaf Section

Sansevieria trifasciata (snake plant)

Cane Cuttings

Codiaeum variegatum (croton)
Cordyline terminalis (good-luck plant)
Dieffenbachia maculata (spotted dumb cane)
Dracaena marginata (dracaena)

Root Cuttings

Acanthus spp. (bear's-breech)
Achillea spp. (yarrow)
Alcea rosea (hollyhock)
Anchusa spp. (bugloss)
Anemone japonica (Japanese anemone)
Anemone pulsatilla (pasque-flower)
Aralia spp. (aralia)
Armoracia rusticana (horseradish)
Asclepias tuberosa (butterfly weed)
Baptisia australis (blue false indigo)
Dicentra spectabilis (bleeding-heart)
Echinops ritro (small globe thistle)
Erodium spp. (heron's-bill)
Eryngium amethystinum (eryngium)
Gaillardia spp. (blanket flower)
Geranium spp. (cranesbill)
Gypsophila paniculata (baby's-breath)
Hypericum spp. (St.-John's-wort)
Limonium spp. (sea lavender)
Limonium spp. (statice)
Nicotiana alata (flowering tobacco)
Pachysandra terminalis (Japanese spurge)
Paeonia spp. (peony)
Papaver orientale (Oriental poppy)

Phlox spp. (phlox, perennial
  species)
Primula spp. (primrose)
Rheum rhabarbarum (rhubarb)
Rubus spp.(blackberry)
Rubus spp. (raspberry)
Salvia spp. (salvia, perennial
  species)
Saponaria spp. (soapwort)
Stokesia laevis (Stokes' aster)
Thermopsis caroliniana (Carolina
  lupine)
Verbascum spp. (mullein)
Yucca filamentosa (Adam's-
  needle)

Layering
Aristolochia durior
  (Dutchman's-pipe)
Begonia spp. (begonia)
Chlorophytum comosum (spider
  plant)
Cissus spp. (grape ivy)
Duchesnea indica (Indian
  strawberry)
Fittonia verschaffeltii (nerve
  plant)
Hedera helix (English ivy)
Jasminum spp. (jasmine)
Lonicera spp. (honeysuckle)
Maranta spp. (prayer plant)
Philodendron spp.
  (philodendron)
Pothos spp. (pothos)
Rosmarinus officinalis
  (rosemary)
Rubus spp. (blackberry)
Rubus ursinus var. *loganobaccus*
  'Boysen' (boysenberry)
Rubus ursinus var. *loganobaccus*
  'Logan' (loganberry)
Saxifraga stolonifera (strawberry
  begonia)
Tolmiea menziesii (piggyback
  plant)

Vinca minor (myrtle)

Air Layering
Codiaeum variegatum (croton)
Cordyline spp. (dracaena)
Dieffenbachia spp. (dumb cane)
Ficus elastica (rubber plant)
Monstera deliciosa (Swiss-cheese
  plant)
Schefflera spp. (umbrella tree)

Stooling
Cotoneaster spp. (cotoneaster)
Hydrangea macrophylla
  (French hydrangea)
Potentilla spp. (cinquefoil)
Ribes spp. (currant)
Ribes spp. (gooseberry)

Division
Achillea spp. (yarrow)
Aster spp. (aster, perennial
  species)
Boltonia asteroides (boltonia)
Campanula spp. (bellflower)
Chrysanthemum spp.
  (chrysanthemum)
Doronicum spp. (leopard's-bane)
Geum spp. (avens)
Helianthus spp. (sunflower,
  perennial species)
Heliconia spp. (false bird-of-
  paradise)
Hemerocallis spp. (daylily)
Hepatica spp. (liverleaf)
Hosta spp. (hosta)
Hypericum calycinum (rose of
  Sharon)
Hypoxis spp. (star grass)
Iberis spp. (candytuft)
Iris spp. (iris)
Kerria japonica (Japanese rose)
Kniphofia spp. (torch lily)
Lavandula angustifolia
  (English lavender)

Liatris spp. (blazing-star)
Linaria spp. (toadflax, peren-
  nial species)
Liriope spp. (lilyturf)
Lychnis spp. (campion)
Lythrum spp. (loosestrife)
Mentha spp. (mint)
Mertensia virginica (Virginia
  bluebells)
Mimulus spp. (monkey flower)
Monarda didyma (bee balm)
Nephrolepis spp. (sword fern)
Nymphaea spp. (waterlily)
Pachysandra terminalis (Japan-
  ese spurge)
Paeonia spp. (peony)
Parnassia spp. (grass-of-
  Parnassus)
Phlox spp. (phlox, perennial
  species)
Physalis spp. (ground cherry)
Physostegia spp. (false
  dragonhead)
Platycodon spp. (balloon flower)
Polemonium spp. (Jacob's-ladder)
Polygonatum spp. (Solomon's-
  seal)
Polygonum spp. (knotweed)
Primula spp. (primrose)
Pulmonaria spp. (lungwort)
Rodgersia spp. (rodgersia)
Saponaria spp. (soapwort, peren-
  nial species)
Sedum spp. (stonecrop)
Smilacina spp. (false
  Solomon's-seal)
Stachys officinalis (betony)
Tanacetum spp. (tansy)
Teucrium spp. (germander)
Thalictrum spp. (meadow rue)
Thermopsis spp. (false lupine)
Trollius spp. (globeflower)
Xanthorhiza simplicissima
  (shrub yellow-root)

Saving Seed

Although many gardeners depend on the annual winter deluge of seed and nursery catalogs for the seed they sow each year, there are at least two good reasons to save your own seed from year to year. First, by saving seed you can harvest, store, and replant seed of a cherished plant year after year. This is especially important when saving seed of antique or discontinued cultivars that may no longer be offered by seed companies. Second, saving seeds is the easiest way to experiment with plant breeding. You can cross-pollinate two different plants to create your own hybrid, then harvest, save, grow, and evaluate the offspring of your cross.

Harvesting Seed

Before harvesttime rolls around, you'll need to take time to learn about and observe the plants whose seed you'd like to collect and save. The more you know about the plants from which you will be harvesting seed, the better your chances of success.

Flowering

If you know approximately when flowering occurs, you'll find it much easier to prepare for the harvest. You should know if the plant is an annual (produces seed in the single year of its life), a biennial (produces seed only in its second and final year of life), or a perennial (produces seed each year).

Fertilization

If you wish to collect pure seed to preserve a species or special cultivar, try to find out if it is easily cross-fertilized by other species or cultivars. If so, cover the immature flower before it opens with a lightweight paper bag or other covering to prevent pollen from other plants from pollinating the flower. Then make sure the flower is pollinated with its own pollen or that from another bloom of the same type to ensure pure seed.

Seed

You'll also need to know how long it takes for the seed to ripen and the manner in which it is normally disseminated. Tiny seed can be easily lost during collection, so simply arch a seed head or pod into an envelope or other container, tap a few times to dislodge loose seed, and remove the seed head from the stem—taking seed head and seed together for cleaning afterward. Some plants dispel their seed from pods that abruptly pop or shatter and scatter the seed in all directions. For these, place an envelope around the pod or seed head before it is ripe and ready to discharge its seed. Remove the seed pod and seed from the stem once it has ripened. Seed that is difficult to harvest can often be collected easily if entire branches are removed from the plant, placed into a large paper bag, and thrashed back and forth by shaking the bag. If the seed is mature the thrashing action will dislodge it readily. Also, most plants will signal the approach of seed maturation by losing flower petals, splitting pods or capsules, and changing the color of fruit, pods, or seeds. Be aware of these signals and use them in timing the harvest.

Keep in mind that many improved cultivars sold through catalogs don't come true from seed. They may be hybrids created by crossing specific parents or color forms that must be propagated vegetatively by means such as division or cuttings. Feel free to experiment with these plants, but don't be disappointed at the results.

Regardless of when the harvest takes place, there are several important points to keep in mind:

- Collect seed only from healthy plants.
- Harvest on a dry, calm, sunny day.
- Use a separate container for each different type of seed.
- Clearly label each collection container with the name of the plant and the collection date.

● If you are collecting seed of wildflowers or other native plants, don't be guilty of eliminating a unique species from its native habitat. Be sure you leave ample seed behind for the continuation of the species or variety.

Cleaning Seed

Before storing seed, remove all debris that might introduce contamination during storage.

Separate seed from fleshy fruit by gently working the fruit over a fine mesh screen with your fingers, and then rinsing the resulting mixture with water. The spray will force the fruit through the mesh, leaving the seed behind.

Remove fine chaff from seed by gently dropping it onto a large sheet of paper, from a height of 4 or 5 feet. When this task is performed on a slightly breezy day or in the presence of a fan, the light chaff will be removed in the air and the heavier seed will fall onto the collection paper.

Separate fine seed from large chaff and debris by gently working the combination through a fine screen; the fine seed will fall onto the collection paper and the chaff and debris will be held behind.

Drying Seed

Seed must be absolutely dry during storage or it might germinate prematurely. Moist conditions will also encourage mold. Air drying on newspaper in a dry, airy location works well, but often requires one to two full weeks to accomplish. This time frame can be reduced to three or four days if the seed is dried on newspaper located 6 to 12 inches below a light bulb; the air temperature around the seed should be no more than 90°F, otherwise the seed may be burned or injured. Oven drying is not recommended, since rapid drying usually results in cracking of the seed coat.

After drying, add a small amount of silica gel (equal in weight to the seed) to the storage container. The

silica gel is a desiccant, and will remove additional moisture that might be introduced during storage. You can substitute powdered milk wrapped in a paper towel, but it must be replaced about every six to eight weeks.

Seed Storage

Seed that has been cleaned and dried should be placed in a clean, dry container. Glass jars with screw tops work well; use small jars (baby food, medicine, or spice jars are ideal) for a single type of seed, or larger jars for holding envelopes of several different types. Remember to properly label each envelope or container.

Place the containers in the refrigerator (32° to 41°F). As long as the seed remains dry, it will maintain its viability. Most seed will survive for at least a full year, and some will last for several to many years.

Upon removal from storage, allow seed to adjust to room temperatures for a few days before sowing.

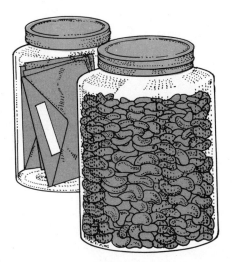

PART 2

Flowers

Annuals

Caring for Annuals

Annuals are bountiful beauties loved by gardeners for their long blooming season, easy culture, and many uses. Annuals are distinguished from other flowers such as perennials and biennials because they will germinate, flower, set seed, and die, all within one growing season. Unlike most perennials, which generally bloom for only two or three weeks, many annuals flower week after week from spring until they are cut down by frost. Ageratums, fibrous-rooted begonias, marigolds, impatiens, and petunias all provide long blooming seasons.

There are many ways to use annuals in the garden. Many expert perennial gardeners fill summertime color gaps in perennial plantings with generous splashes of annuals. Annuals also can make a fine cover over a springtime bulb garden, for they are generally shallow-rooted and will hide the bulb foliage as it fades. Other gardeners prefer to use annuals alone in colorful masses. For small terraces, porches, or patios, containers and hanging baskets filled with annuals provide garden greenery and color.

Each year the newest geranium, petunia, and impatiens cultivars vie for the number one position in the bedding plant industry. Seed packets of these popular plants are available in stores and from mail-order catalogs across the country. Many of the most common and reliable annuals are also offered as bedding plants.

Bedding plants are an easy and inexpensive way to add instant color to the garden. All you need to do to create an "instant" garden is take your garden plan to the garden center and select your plants.

Many gardeners like to raise their annuals from seed. Growing plants

---

Green Thumb Tip

BUYING HEALTHY ANNUALS

If you're buying annual bedding plants, get your garden off to a good start by selecting the healthiest plants you can find. The extra time you spend looking for bedding plants that have been well cared for and are disease- and insect-free will be well worth it. Here are some pointers that will help you make your choice.

- Look for plants with deep green leaves and bushy, compact growth.
- Choose plants whose buds aren't yet open. Although plants that are in full flower are attractive, they take longer to establish than plants that haven't yet begun blooming.
- Wilted plants displayed on a hot supermarket sidewalk aren't a bargain. Heat and drought can damage roots and will severely stress plants. Stressed plants won't get off to a running start in your garden.

- Don't buy by the yard. With annual bedding plants, bigger isn't necessarily better. Overgrown plants that have long outgrown their pots probably have roots circling the stem and have already had their growth severely checked.
- Buy plants that are clearly labeled, unless you're game for a gamble. Labels help you choose the cultivars you'd like to grow, and therefore flower color, bloom size, height, and other characteristics.
- Finally, always look carefully for signs of insect infestations or disease. Don't buy plants that show evidence of whiteflies, aphids, spider mites, or other pests. Disease symptoms to look for include rotted lesions on the stem or leaves and yellowed or spotted foliage.

from seed is the most thrifty way to produce annuals. It's also great fun, and it provides an opportunity to try many new or unusual cultivars not otherwise available, since seed catalogs offer many more selections than the average bedding plant display.

Some annuals, like marigolds and zinnias, are so easy to start from seed they can be planted directly in the garden. Others, including geraniums and impatiens, need to be sown indoors well before the last frost. (See the chart "Selecting Annuals" on page 106 for germination times, and see "Starting Seeds" on page 29 for directions on how to grow your own annuals from seed.)

Planting Annuals

If you've grown annuals from seed, be sure to harden the plants off before moving them to the garden. This is also a good idea for greenhouse-grown bedding plants, which haven't been exposed to the rigors of life in the outdoors. You can move them to a cold frame a week or so before they're scheduled to go into the garden; build a simple hoop shelter out of wire and polyethylene; or move them to a sheltered spot outdoors for longer and longer periods each day.

Most gardeners transplant seedlings or bedding plants just after the last average date of frost in their area. If you put them out earlier, be prepared to cover your tender plants with burlap, newspaper, or some other protective layer if frost threatens. Listen to the weather reports during those changeable spring days. Very tender annuals such as impatiens won't really begin to grow until soil temperatures warm.

Routine Care

Once in the garden, annuals need minimal maintenance. One of the best ways to reduce the amount of work they require is to find annuals that are adapted to the conditions that generally prevail in your garden. Plants that are naturally inclined to grow in dry, sandy soil, for example, will be healthier and require less care than those that aren't. There are annuals suited to every climate and every type of garden. There are several ways to identify the best ones for your garden: Talk to other gardeners, visit gardens and note which plants are thriving, call your local cooperative extension service, and look for lists in pamphlets, magazines, or other publications that recommend plants for similar conditions. Try growing some new annuals each year and keep notes about their performance.

In a well-prepared bed with enriched soil, most annuals seldom need any additional fertilizer. However, some, like petunias, respond well when cut back in midsummer and given a boost of a balanced fertilizer.

Mulch helps keep moisture in the soil, and it also cuts down on weeding.

Most annuals will need to be pinched at least once early in the season to encourage branching and compact growth. To pinch a plant, use your fingernails or a small pair of shears to pinch the bud, or the bud and youngest set of leaves, off the tip of each stem. Annuals that become tall and leggy can be cut back to just above a leaf node. It's best to use shears for this purpose to make sure you make a clean cut.

Deadheading, which means removing spent flowers as they fade, prevents the plants from going to seed. This keeps the garden more attractive and encourages the annuals to produce more flowers. It also is a way to keep annuals that will reseed prolifically in check. Only let a plant set seed if you want to save the seed.

(continued on page 110)

Pinch young plants early in the season to encourage branching, bushy growth, and more flowers.

Use pruning shears to cut back annuals that have become overgrown; otherwise you're liable to tear or damage the stem.

SELECTING ANNUALS

Annuals can be employed in every part of the garden. Grown in containers, mixed with perennials, or in a bed or border by themselves, they are a very versatile component of garden design. Annuals can provide color when perennials are not in bloom. They can quickly and inexpensively turn an eyesore into a visual treat or help deter garden pests from demolishing your harvest. What's more, these plants can be combined in totally new ways the next year for endless variety. The following is just a sampling of the annuals you can choose from to make your garden the most colorful.

Annual	Height	Flower Color	Description	Culture
Ageratum houstonianum (Ageratum)	6-18 in.	Blue, pink, white	Heart-shaped leaves with many small fluffy flowers.	Full sun to partial shade. Average soil. Sow seed indoors 6-8 weeks before last frost. Borders. Containers. Exposed sites. Good for cutting. Will root from cuttings.
Amaranthus caudatus (Love-lies-bleeding)	4-5 ft.	Red	Red, bottlebrush-like flowers with red or green leaves.	Full sun. Any well-drained soil. Sow seed indoors 6 weeks before last frost or sow outdoors when night temperatures remain above 50°F. Beds. Good for cutting. Brilliant colors may overwhelm garden.
Anchusa capensis (Bugloss)	16-18 in.	Bright blue	Biennal with hairy lancelike leaves. Clusters of small 5-petaled flowers.	Full sun to partial shade. Any well-drained soil. Sow seed indoors 6-8 weeks before the last frost or sow outdoors when danger of frost has passed. Containers. Good in masses. Cut plants back after first flush of bloom to encourage new flowers.
Antirrhinum majus (Common snapdragon)	6-48 in.	Reddish purple, white, pink, yellow, orange	Perennial grown as an annual. Tall spikes of unusual two-lipped flowers. Flowers at bottom of spike open first.	Full sun to partial shade. Rich well-drained soil. Sow seed indoors 6-8 weeks before last frost. Buy rust-resistant cultivars. Borders. Good for cutting. Good in masses. May need staking.
Begonia × semperflorens-cultorum hybrids (Wax begonia)	6-12 in.	Red, white, pink	Glossy, round leaves that are maroon or green, with waxy, heart-shaped flowers.	Full sun to partial shade. Rich, moist soil. Best propagated by cutting. Or sow seed indoors 12-14 weeks before last frost. Beds. Borders. Containers. Houseplant. Almost continuous bloom. Will root from cuttings.
Browallia speciosa (Browallia)	12-15 in.	Blue, white	Large bell-shaped flowers in clusters.	Full sun to partial shade. Rich, well-drained soil. Sow seed indoors 6-8 weeks before last frost. Beds. Borders. Containers. Can be brought indoors in fall as a houseplant.
Calendula officinalis (Pot marigold)	6-24 in.	White, yellow, orange	Large single or double daisylike flowers with thick, light green leaves.	Full sun to partial shade. Any moist soil. Sow seeds in early spring where plants are to grow. Beds. Good for cutting. Best where summers are cool.

Annual	Height	Flower Color	Description	Culture
Callistephus chinensis (China aster)	6-36 in.	Blue, white, pink, red, yellow	Single or double flowers on tall stems.	Full sun. Rich, sandy, moist, alkaline soil. Borders. Containers. Good for cutting.
Celosia cristata (Cockscomb)	6-36 in.	Red, yellow, purple, orange	Unusual crested or plumed flower heads ranging from 2-10 in. wide.	Full sun. Rich, sandy, well-drained soil. Sow seed indoors 4-6 weeks before last frost or sow outdoors. Beds. Borders. Good for cutting, drying.
Centaurea cyanus (Bachelor's-button)	1-3 ft.	Blue, pink, white, red, purple	Flowers have many small petals that give them a pincushion look. Gray-green, slightly fuzzy, straplike leaves.	Full sun to partial shade. Rich, light, well-drained soil. Cool conditions. Sow seed outdoors in fall or early spring. Drought and salt tolerant. Deadhead for further bloom.
Chrysanthemum coronarium (Crown daisy)	1½-2 ft.	White, pale yellow	Many large daisylike flowers with fernlike foliage. Some flowers semi-double.	Full sun. Rich, moist, well-drained soil. Sow seed outdoors in early spring. Borders. Good for cutting. Will tolerate alkaline soil.
Cleome hasslerana (Spider flower)	3-5 ft.	Pink, white	Tall spikes of spidery flowers. Clusters 6-8 in. across. Leaves palmate.	Full sun to partial shade. Cleome will grow in nearly any soil. Will withstand heat and drought. Sow seed outdoors when danger of frost has passed. Background plants. Borders. Will reseed.
Coleus × hybridus (Coleus)	6-36 in.	Grown for white, green, purple, red, yellow, pink, gold foliage	Square stems with variegated leaves of unusual color combinations. Insignificant flowers in spikes.	Full sun to partial shade. Rich, moist, well-drained soil. Sow seed indoors 10 weeks before last frost. Borders. Containers. Houseplants. Remove flowers and pinch to maintain compact shape. Will root from cuttings.
Consolida spp. (Larkspur)	1-3 ft.	Blue, pink, purple	Tall spikes of large frilly flowers. Finely cut leaves.	Full sun to partial shade. Rich, moist soil. Grows best in cool weather. Sow seed outdoors in fall or very early spring. Borders. Good for cutting. May need staking. Will reseed. Will tolerate alkaline soil.
Coreopsis tinctoria (Calliopsis)	2-3 ft.	Yellow, maroon, red, pink, purple, with brown center	Daisylike flowers, sometimes with different bands of color. Threadlike foliage.	Full sun to partial shade. Light, sandy, well-drained soil. Sow seed outdoors in very early spring. Drought tolerant. Borders. Good for cutting. Will reseed.
Cosmos bipinnatus (Common cosmos)	2-5 ft.	White, yellow, pink, red, orange, with yellow center	Large daisylike flowers with lacy leaves.	Full sun. Poor, dry, well-drained soil. Sow seed outdoors after danger of frost has passed. Back of borders. Good for cutting. May need staking.
Eschscholzia californica (California poppy)	1-2 ft.	Yellow, gold, orange, pink, white	Large saucer-shaped flowers above finely dissected gray-green leaves.	Full sun. Well-drained, somewhat sandy, soil. Sow seed outdoors in fall or early spring. Drought and heat tolerant. Beds. Borders. Containers. Good for cutting. Many cultivars available. Will reseed.

(continued)

Annual	Height	Flower Color	Description	Culture
Gypsophila elegans (Annual baby's-breath)	8-18 in.	White, pink, red	Upright annual with masses of tiny flowers on wiry stems with linear leaves.	Full sun. Moist, well-drained, alkaline soil. Sow seed outdoors after danger of frost has passed. Borders. Rock gardens. Good for cutting. Sow seeds at 2-4-week intervals for continuous bloom.
Helianthus annuus (Common sunflower)	6-10 ft.	Yellow with prominent brown centers	Bushy and upright with coarse, large leaves. Daisylike, 3-6-in. flowerheads are borne singly or several per stem.	Full sun. Any soil. Sow seed outdoors in spring after danger of frost has passed. Drought tolerant. May need staking. Attracts birds as seeds ripen. Dwarf cultivars (1½-2 ft.) available.
Helichrysum bracteatum (Strawflower)	2-4 ft.	White, red, yellow, orange	Large flowerheads with stiff petallike bracts.	Full sun. Any well-drained soil. Sow seed indoors 4-6 weeks before last frost or sow outdoors after danger of frost has passed. Heat tolerant. Borders. Good for cutting and drying.
Impatiens wallerana (Impatiens)	1-3 ft.	White, red, pink, pale purple	Large lance-shaped leaves; fleshy stems. Single or double, waxy spurred flowers.	Full sun to partial shade. Rich, sandy, organic, moist soil. Sow seed indoors 4-8 weeks before last frost. Heat tolerant. Beds. Borders. Containers. Houseplant.
Lobelia erinus (Edging lobelia)	4-8 in.	Deep blue, pale blue, red, white	Trailing or compact with many small flowers.	Full sun to partial shade. Rich, sandy, moist soil. Sow seed indoors 10-12 weeks before last frost. Do not cover seed. Beds. Containers. Edging.
Lobularia maritima (Sweet alyssum)	6-12 in.	White, purple, pink	Perennial often grown as an annual. Mounds of linear leaves with many small fragrant flowers.	Full sun. Average, well-drained soil. Sow seed outdoors in very early spring or sow indoors 4-6 weeks before last frost. Drought and heat tolerant. Borders. Containers. Rock gardens. Shear plants back when flowers fade to encourage new bloom. Will reseed.
Lychnis coeli-rosa (Rose-of-heaven)	1-3 ft.	Red, white	Linear leaves. Single 1-in.-wide flowers.	Full sun. Average, well-drained soil. Sow seed outdoors in spring. Exposed sites. Good for cutting.
Mirabilis jalapa (Four-o'clock)	2-3 ft.	White, yellow, red, pink, some speckled	Perennial grown as annual. Tubular flowers that open in late afternoon. Tuberous roots with succulent stems.	Full sun. Light, well-drained soil. Sow seed in spring. Beds. Borders. Roots can be dug in fall just before frost and overwintered in frost-free place.
Moluccella laevis (Bells-of-Ireland)	2-3 ft.	White and green	Unusual plant with small fragrant flowers that, when gone, leave green bell-shaped calyxes arranged along hairy stems.	Full sun to partial shade. Average, well-drained soil. Sow seed outdoors after danger of frost has passed. Borders. Good for cutting and drying. Best in cool-climate areas.
Myosotis sylvatica (Garden forget-me-not)	6-18 in.	Blue, white, pink	Biennial or annual with many tiny flowers that bloom on a compact mound of leaves.	Partial shade. Rich, moist, well-drained soil. Sow seed outdoors fall or early spring. Tolerates wet conditions. Borders. Edging. Will reseed.

Annual	Height	Flower Color	Description	Culture
Petunia × hybrida (Common garden petunia)	6-24 in.	White, red, pink, orange, purple, some striped	Trailing or compact plants with large, single or double, trumpet-shaped flowers.	Full sun. Sandy well-drained soil. Sow seed indoors 8-10 weeks before last frost. Beds. Borders. Containers.
Phlox drummondii (Annual phlox)	8-18 in.	White, pink, red, purple	Mound-shaped plant topped with clusters of tubular, 1½-in.-long, 5-petaled flowers.	Full sun. Rich, sandy, well-drained soil. Sow seed outdoors after the last frost date. Beds. Borders. Rock gardens. Good for cutting. Deadhead to encourage repeat bloom.
Portulaca grandiflora (Rose moss)	4-8 in.	Red, pink, white, purple, yellow	Mound-shaped plant with succulent linear leaves and ruffled single or double flowers. Blooms open only during sunny weather.	Full sun. Sandy, dry, well-drained soil. Sow seed outdoors after last frost or indoors 4-6 weeks before last frost. Drought and heat tolerant. Beds. Rock gardens.
Salvia splendens (Scarlet sage)	1-3 ft.	Red, white, pink, purple	Glossy leaves with spires of tubular flowers.	Full sun to partial shade. Rich, moist, well-drained soil. Sow seed indoors 4-6 weeks before last frost. Beds. Containers.
Tagetes spp. (Marigold)	6-36 in.	Yellow, orange, red	Large group usually with finely dissected foliage and single or double, strongly scented flowers.	Full sun. Average, well-drained soil. Sow seed indoors 4-6 weeks before last frost or outdoors after danger of frost has passed. Borders. Containers. Edging. Good for cutting.
Tropaeolum majus (Garden nasturtium)	1-4 ft.	Orange, red, yellow	Compact or vinelike plant with round leaves and large trumpetlike flowers.	Full sun to partial shade. Poor, sandy, dry, well-drained soil. Grows best in cool, dry conditions. Sow seed outdoors where plants are to grow after danger of frost has passed. Beds. Containers. Walls. Foliage and flowers are edible.
Verbena × hybrida (Garden verbena)	8-18 in.	Red, white, pink, yellow, purple, blue	Toothed leaves with flat clusters of tiny tubular flowers.	Full sun. Rich, well-drained soil. Sow seed indoors 12-14 weeks before last frost. Containers. Edging. Rock gardens. Good for cutting. Will root from cuttings. Can dig and overwinter indoors.
Viola × wittrockiana (Garden pansy)	6-12 in.	Red, purple, yellow, pink, white, orange	Annual or biennial usually with large flowers with characteristic facelike dark patches on petals.	Full sun. Rich, moist soil. Grows best in cool conditions. Sow seed indoors 10-12 weeks before last frost. Beds. Borders. Containers. Edging. Deadhead or pick flowers to further encourage bloom.
Zinnia elegans (Common zinnia)	6-36 in.	Red, yellow, pink, orange, white	Large, single to very double flowerheads in various forms borne above hairy leaves.	Full sun. Rich, loamy, moist, well-drained soil. Sow seed outdoors after danger of frost has passed and night temperatures remain above 50°F., or sow indoors 4-6 weeks before last frost. Beds. Borders. Containers. Good for cutting. Will tolerate hot, dry conditions.

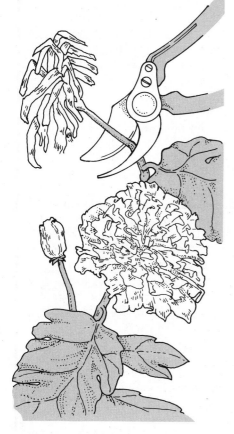

Deadheading is removing spent flowers as they fade. It helps direct the plant's energy into new flowers rather than seed production.

In weeks when there is less than an inch of rain, you'll probably need to water the garden. In parts of the Southeast, Southwest, and California, where there is no rain for months at a time, traditional gardens need to be on a regular watering schedule. Using drip irrigation may be a feasible way to reduce water use.

Today, many gardeners are selecting plants able to survive with a limited supply of water. Drought-resistant annuals, such as African daisy (*Gerbera jamesonii*), sunflowers (*Helianthus* spp.), and moss rose (*Portulaca* spp.), are very useful for adding color to a garden that uses modest amounts of water.

Ending the Season

After enjoying the season of color and beauty annuals provide, there is one final job for the gardener—putting the garden to bed for winter.

Before frost threatens, consider rooting cuttings or digging and potting annuals that are actually perennials and can be brought indoors for the winter. These include wax begonias, impatiens, and verbena. You can enjoy the color they'll provide indoors and also use them to propagate new plants for next spring. You can select annuals to overwinter that have unusual flower color or other attractive features and perpetuate these characteristics for next season. Roots of four-o'clocks can be dug, dried for a few hours, and stored indoors in a cool, frost-free place through the winter.

When frost kills the impatiens, petunias, and marigolds to the ground, it's time to remove the debris from the garden. Pick up or rake off all of the spent plants and toss the remains on the compost heap where they will decompose and be returned to the garden another year in the form of rich brown compost. Leaving the garden clean during the winter is more attractive, and it minimizes insect and disease problems during the next gardening season. If you've grown French marigolds for nematode control, now is the time to till the plants into the soil.

Overwintering Geraniums

In all but the warmest, frost-free corners of our country (USDA Zone 10), geraniums (*Pelargonium × hortorum*) are grown as ordinary annuals. In truth, they are tender perennials that can be overwintered in several different ways.

For gardeners who have a cool greenhouse, keeping geraniums from year to year is a simple matter. They put the pots on the greenhouse bench or hang baskets of geraniums from the rafters and water occasionally. Geraniums thrive in sunlight and cool but not freezing temperatures.

If you don't have a greenhouse, you may have a cool bay window or a

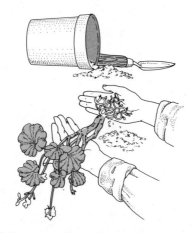

To force a geranium to become dormant, withhold water until the soil is dry, and then gently shake the soil from the roots.

For best results, place each plant in a paper bag and tie the bag shut before storing in a cool, humid place.

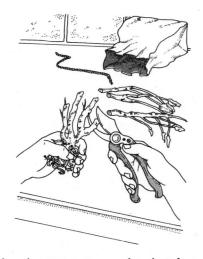

In spring, remove your geranium plants from the paper bags and prune the stems back to living green tissue.

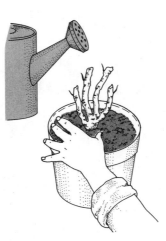

Repot the plants in standard houseplant potting mix, water, and set them in a cool, bright window or other well-lit spot until they begin to grow.

sunny, unheated basement room that provides the perfect conditions for maintaining geraniums in full growth. Early in the new year, take cuttings from these "mother" plants and raise a new crop of geraniums for the coming garden season.

If you have neither the space nor the ideal conditions for overwintering potted geraniums, you can turn to a method grandmother used to use. Because modern geraniums come from species native to areas of the world that are extremely dry, these

plants can drop their leaves, conserve water in their succulent stems, and survive without care during the winter months. You can force your plants into dormancy by withholding water in order to store them over winter.

During the cool, crisp fall days before the first frost, dig the plants and set them in a bushel basket or bring potted specimens indoors. Be sure to select only healthy specimens. Discard any plants that show mottled or puckered leaves that are evidence of virus diseases.

When the soil is thoroughly dry, gently knock the soil off the roots. At this point, you can simply hang the dry plants from the rafters in a cool, frostfree place. You will have a better survival rate, however, if you place each geranium in a paper bag and tie the end of the bag shut. Store the bags in a cool, humid place, like a basement or crawl space, where the plants will not freeze.

Check on the plants regularly. The leaves will turn yellow and dry up, but if the stems become very shriveled, mist them lightly with water to keep them from drying up completely. If you see mold or rot, they are too wet. Cut out any molded or rotted spots, move the plants to a drier (but still cool) place, and leave the bags open for a day or two until the plants dry out. Early in the spring, take the plants from the bags, prune the stems back to healthy green tissue, and repot in fresh potting soil. Then water the plants well until they begin to grow.

You can put the pots under fluorescent lights, in a bright window, or in a cold frame until they begin to grow. Water regularly and gradually move them into full sunlight. When all danger of frost is past, move them outdoors.

Bulbs, Corms, and Tubers

Planting Bulbs, Corms, and Tubers

Bulbs are about as foolproof as a gardener can get. You plant the bulb; it blooms. Growing bulbs is easy enough for beginners and gratifying enough for lifelong gardeners. And the wide range of color and variety means that there are bulbs to fit everyone's garden.

A handful of sunny daffodils are a great way to welcome spring, but don't stop with the old reliables. Tuck in a few of the lesser-known spring bulbs: a dozen blue grape hyacinths (*Muscari* spp.) to accent a sunny forsythia; graceful windflowers (*Anemone blanda*) to soften a brick wall; a sprinkling of snowdrops (*Galanthus* spp.) where you'll be able to spot them from the kitchen window. These early bloomers are great for the spirit after a season of winter drab.

Consider the summer bulbs, too. Dahlias and gladioli brighten up the late-season garden just when it needs it most. Lilies add exotic beauty and long-lasting flowers to the summer border. Pink magic lilies (*Lycoris squamigera*) spring up suddenly from beneath annuals or perennials after a late summer rain. And there are dozens of others.

Although we commonly call all these plants bulbs, they actually arise from several types of structures. Depending on their structure they're classified as true bulbs, corms, tubers, or rhizomes. All are underground storage systems, full of food to nourish the growing plant.

Which Side Is Up?

Bulbs get off to the fastest start if you plant them right side up. The general rule: Plant with pointed tip up. But not all bulbs have points, and that's where confusion sets in. If you're ever in doubt, you can always plant the bulb on its side. Although you might not be able to tell which side is up, the bulb will know which way to send roots and and which way to send shoots. Bulbs planted sideways will have a better chance of growing than a bulb planted upside down.

True Bulbs

Onions are one of the most familiar true bulbs. These structures consist of layers of scales, which are modified leaves designed to store food for the plant over winter. They surround a heart from which the aboveground leaves and the flower stem will rise. True bulbs also have a narrow pointed tip, which makes it easy to determine which side is up. Roots grow from the edges of the basal plate, the flat, hard part on the bottom of the bulb.

Tulips, hyacinths, daffodils, and lilies—and onions and garlic—all have true bulbs. If you compare a daffodil bulb with a lily bulb, however, you'll notice that there are two types of true bulbs. Like onions, daffodils have scales so tightly packed they seem solid. Lilies, on the other hand, have loose scales that are joined at the base and easily removed. They also usually have fleshy roots attached to the base of the bulb, which should be left intact when planting.

Many bulbs hide their scales under a papery covering called the tunic. (The tunic is especially evident on tulip bulbs.) To protect the scales,

True bulbs

Tulip   Daffodil   Lily

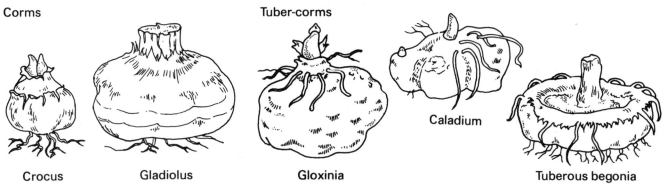

Corms

Crocus Gladiolus

Tuber-corms

Gloxinia

Caladium

Tuberous begonia

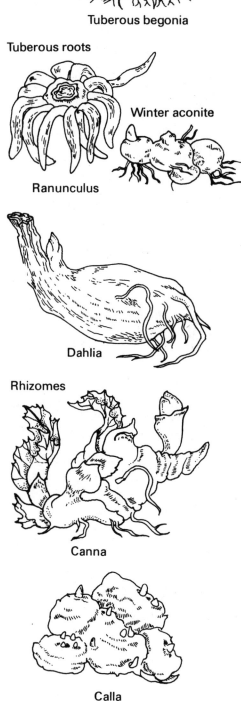

Tuberous roots

Winter aconite

Ranunculus

Dahlia

Rhizomes

Canna

Calla

be sure to slip the tunic back on if it falls off during planting or handling.

Corms

At first glance corms may look like true bulbs: They are squat, flattened, and covered with a papery brown skin or tunic. The big difference is that a corm is a solid chunk of stored food, not a bundle of wrapped scales. It is actually a swollen, underground stem. At the top of the corm is a tip or bud, from which will sprout the leaves and flowers. Crocuses, gladioli, and dog-toothed violets arise from corms.

Each season, as the plant grows, it eventually uses up the corm entirely. But at the same time, new corms are forming around it—you'll have crocuses and gladioli next year. Gener-

ally one large corm forms to replace the corm from the current year (to bloom the following year). Other, smaller corms form around it, which will produce foliage and grow for several seasons before they reach blooming size.

Tubers

Tubers are fleshy underground stems that have "eyes" or buds and take many forms. Tuberous begonias and anemones arise from tuber-corms, which are rounded, often flattened tubers with a lumpy appearance. Roots grow freely out of the sides, the bottom, and sometimes the top. Some tuber-corms such as caladium have a pointed bud on top; others such as those of anemone are woody-looking, almost barklike, and have eyes from which the leaves and flowers grow. Tuberous begonias have a shallow, dish-shaped top with a bud or buds in the center.

Tuberous Roots

Tuberous roots are swollen, fleshy roots that store food and have a pointed bud on top and roots that sprout from the bottom. Dahlias are probably the best-known garden plant that sprouts from tuberous roots. The center stalk of a dahlia plant is surrounded by the long, fat tuberous roots. When the plants are dug and divided at season's end, the clumps of roots can be used to propagate the plants provided a piece of the stem is left attached to each tuberous root. Plant dahlias horizontally, with the bud tip pointing up and the roots down.

Green Thumb Tip

BUYING HEALTHY BULBS

Damaged or deteriorating bulbs are no bargain. Bulbs that are left in bins in stores, or trapped in plastic bags, soon go from prime to worthless. The bulbs to buy are firm and solid, not marred with mold, soft spots, or cuts— and not dried out to a withered shell. Heft a bulb in your palm. A healthy bulb should feel solid and heavy for its size.

SELECTING BULBS, CORMS, AND TUBERS

A glance at the bulb display at a well-stocked nursery will confirm that there are hundreds of bulbs, corms, and tubers from which to choose. Spring bulbs such as daffodils and tulips are familiar to almost everyone, as are summer-blooming bulbs such as cannas and gladioli. The following list provides a guide to some of the best of these popular plants a home gardener can grow.

Bulb	Height	Flower Color	Description	Culture
Spring-Blooming				
Anemone spp. (Windflower)	6-8 in.	White, pink, blue	A low-growing plant with divided leaves and large daisylike flowers. Tuber-corm.	Partial shade. Rich, humusy, well-drained soil. Propagate by division, seeds. Planting depth: 3 in. Zones 6-8. Borders. Containers. Meadows. Will naturalize. *A. coronaria* is a popular but less hardy (Zone 8).
Chionodoxa luciliae (Glory-of-the-snow)	3-6 in.	Blue, white	Delicate-looking plant bearing 4-6 flowers atop a short stalk. Narrow leaves. Bulb.	Full sun to partial shade. Sandy or loamy, well-drained soil. Propagate by offsets, seeds. Planting depth: 3 in. Zones 4-8. Meadows. Rock gardens. Will naturalize. Blooms very early in spring.
Crocus spp. (Crocus)	3-6 in.	White, yellow, pink, purple, lilac	Genus of low-growing plants with cup-shaped flowers borne close to the ground. Dark green, grasslike leaves. Corm.	Full sun to partial shade. Sandy or gritty, well-drained soil. Propagate by cormels, seeds. Planting depth: 3-4 in. Zones 3-8. Beds. Borders. Rock gardens. Woodland areas. Will naturalize.
Erythronium spp. (Dog-toothed violet)	6-12 in.	Yellow, white	Genus of native wildflowers with nodding lilylike flowers 1 in. across with 2 linear leaves that are usually mottled. Corm.	Partial shade. Deep, well-drained soil rich in organic matter. Propagate by cormels, seeds. Planting depth: 5 in. Zones 4-9. Rock gardens. Woodland areas. Will naturalize.
Fritillaria imperialis (Crown-imperial)	2½-3 ft.	Red, yellow, orange	Striking plant bearing a cluster of nodding bell-shaped flowers at the top. Leaves narrow. Bulb.	Full sun to partial shade. Deep, well-drained soil rich in organic matter. Propagate by offsets. Planting depth: 6 in. Zones 5-9. Borders. Rock gardens. Woodland areas. Leaves and flowers have an unpleasant smell.
Galanthus elwesii (Giant snowdrop)	5-10 in.	White and green	Nodding 1-1½-in. flowers borne atop leafless stalks. Foliage is grasslike. Bulb.	Full sun to partial shade. Deep, well-drained soil rich in organic matter. Propagate by offsets, seeds. Planting depth: 3 in. Zones 4-8. Borders. Rock gardens. Woodland areas. Will naturalize. One of the first to bloom in spring.
Hyacinthus orientalis (Common hyacinth)	1-1½ ft.	White, pink, blue, yellow	Columnar clusters of small, densely packed fragrant flowers. Foliage is fleshy and straplike. Bulb.	Full sun to partial shade. Deep, well-drained soil rich in organic matter. Propagation difficult; best to buy new bulbs. Planting depth: 4-5 in. Zones 5-9. Beds. Borders. Containers.

Bulb	Height	Flower Color	Description	Culture
Leucojum aestivum (Summer snowflake)	9-12 in.	White with green tips	Attractive delicate looking plant with clusters of 2-5 bell-shaped flowers. Grasslike leaves. Bulb.	Full sun to partial shade. Sandy or loamy, well-drained soil. Propagate by offsets. Planting depth: 5 in. Zones 4-8. Rock gardens. Woodland areas. Will naturalize.
Muscari spp. (Grape hyacinth)	8-12 in.	Purplish blue, white	Tiny, bell-shaped flowers borne in dense spikes that resemble clusters of grapes. Foliage is grasslike. Bulb.	Full sun to partial shade. Sandy, well-drained soil rich in organic matter. Propagate by offsets, seeds. Planting depth: 2-4 in. Zones 3-8. Borders. Edgings. Rock gardens. Woodland areas. Will naturalize. Some are good for cutting.
Narcissus spp. (Daffodil, narcissus, jonquil)	6-15 in.	White, yellow, orange, pink, bicolor	Large genus with many species and forms. Showy, cup-shaped flowers with 6 surrounding petallike segments. Stiff, narrow strap-shaped leaves. Bulb.	Full sun to partial shade. Deep, well-drained soil rich in organic matter. Propagate by offsets. Planting depth: 4-8 in. or 1½ times as deep as the height of the bulb. Zones 5-8. Beds. Borders. Meadows. Woodlands. Rock gardens. Will naturalize. Good for cutting. Many cultivars available. Bulbs poisonous; avoided by rodents.
Ornithogalum spp. (Star-of-Bethlehem)	9-12 in.	White and green	Clusters of 2-in.-wide, nodding, starlike flowers on leafless stalks. Leaves narrow and straplike. Bulb.	Full sun to partial shade. Well-drained soil. Propagate by offsets, seeds. Planting depth: 4 in. Zones 5-9. Borders. Containers. Rock gardens. Will naturalize; can become invasive.
Scilla siberica (Siberian squill)	4-6 in.	Blue, pink, white	Bell-shaped, ½-in. flowers in clusters on top of thin leafless stalks. Leaves are grasslike. Bulb.	Full sun to partial shade. Deep, well-drained soil rich in organic matter. Propagate by offsets, seeds. Planting depth: 3-4 in. Zones 4-8. Woodland areas. Borders. Edgings. Will naturalize. Early spring bloom.
Tulipa spp. (Tulip)	3-15 in.	Many colors available, including red, yellow, pink, white, maroon, orange	Large genus with many species and forms. Flowers usually solitary, cup-shaped, from 1-4 in. across. Leaves broadly straplike, blue-green, sometimes mottled. Bulb.	Full sun. Sandy, well-drained soil rich in organic matter. Propagate by offsets. Planting depth: 6-10 in. Zones 2-9. Beds. Borders. Rock gardens. Many good for cutting. Many cultivars available.

Summer-Blooming

Bulb	Height	Flower Color	Description	Culture
Achimenes spp. (Achimenes)	1-2 ft.	White, purple, red, pink, violet	Genus of African violet relatives that bear masses of flat-faced, tubular flowers that have 5 petals and are 2 in. across. Leaves dark green. Scaly rhizome.	Partial to deep shade. Light, well-drained soil rich in organic matter. Propagate by division, cuttings, seeds. Planting depth: ½ in. Not hardy, grown as an annual; rhizomes dried and overwintered indoors. Containers.
Allium spp. (Ornamental onion)	6-48 in.	Lilac, yellow, white	Large genus with many species bearing round clusters of tiny flowers on tall stalks. Flat or hollow linear leaves. Bulb.	Full sun to partial shade. Sandy, well-drained soil. Propagate by division, seeds. Planting depth: 3-8 in. Zones 4-9. Borders. Containers. Rock gardens.

(continued)

Bulb	Height	Flower Color	Description	Culture
Summer-Blooming—continued				
Begonia × *tuberhybrida* (Tuberous begonia)	1-1½ ft.	Red, pink, yellow, orange, white	Showy single or double 2-4-in. flowers with succulent green leaves. Some cultivars have cascading habit. Tuber-corm.	Partial shade. Rich, well-drained soil with plenty of organic matter. Propagate by division. Planting depth: 1-2 in. Not hardy, grown as an annual; tuber-corms dried and overwintered indoors. Beds. Containers. Many cultivars available. May need staking.
Caladium spp. (Caladium)	8-20 in.	Grown for white, red, pink, green foliage	Genus with many hybrids grown for large, heart-shaped leaves with boldly colored veins or other decorative patterns. Tuber-corm.	Partial to deep shade. Well-drained soil rich in organic matter. Propagate by division. Planting depth: 1 in. in south, 2-3 in. in north. Not hardy, grown as an annual; tuber-corms are dried and overwintered indoors. Borders. Containers. Grown for foliage only; remove flowers. Many cultivars available.
Canna spp. (Canna)	2-8 ft.	Red, yellow, pink, white, some speckled	Genus with many hybrids grown for showy clusters of 4-in.-wide flowers on tall stems. Large, broad leaves. Fleshy rhizome.	Full sun. Rich, moist, well-drained soil. Propagate by division. Planting depth: 3-5 in. Not hardy, grown as an annual; rhizomes dried and overwintered indoors. Borders. Containers. Heat tolerant.
Colchicum spp. (Autumn crocus)	4-12 in.	White, rose, purple, yellow	Genus of crocuslike plants with 3-4-in.-long flowers and narrow, dark green leaves. Corm.	Full sun to partial shade. Rich well-drained soil. Propagate by cormels. Planting depth: 3 in. Zones 5-9. Blooms late summer to fall. Many cultivars available. Belongs to the lily family, Liliaceae; *Crocus* spp. are in the iris family, Iridaceae.
Dahlia hybrids (Dahlia)	2-8 ft.	Yellow, red, pink, purple, white, bicolor	Large group of hybrids grown for showy flowers ranging from 1-12 in. across. Many flower shapes and sizes. Fleshy, compound leaves. Tuberous roots.	Full sun. Rich, light, well-drained soil. Propagate by division. Planting depth: 4-6 in. Cover roots with 2 or 3 in. of soil when planting; add soil as shoots grow to fill hole. Not hardy; roots dried and overwintered indoors. Borders. Containers. Good for cutting.
Gladiolus spp. (Gladiolus)	2-4 ft.	Yellow, orange, red, pink, white	Tall spikes of trumpet-shaped, 2-3-in.-wide blooms. Leaves straplike. Corm.	Full sun. Rich, sandy, well-drained soil. Propagate by cormels. Planting depth: corms ½ in. or less in diameter, 3 in.; corms ½-1 in., 4-5 in.; corms 1¼ in. or more, 6-8 in. Most not hardy; corms dried and overwintered indoors. Beds. Borders. Good for cutting.

Bulb	Height	Flower Color	Description	Culture
Hyacinthoides spp. (Wood hyacinth)	15-20 in.	Blue, pink, white	Several species with loose spikes of bell-shaped flowers ¼-½ in. wide. Leaves straplike. Bulb.	Full sun to partial shade. Deep, well-drained soil rich in organic matter. Propagate by division, offsets. Planting depth: 4 in. Zones 4-9. Accent. Borders. Rock gardens. Woodland areas. Also listed as *Endymion* spp.
Hymenocallis narcissiflora (Peruvian daffodil)	1½-2 ft.	White	Delicate, fragrant daffodil-like flowers with thin, curly, petal-like segments surrounding cup. Flowers 4-8 in. wide; leaves straplike. Bulb.	Full sun. Deep, well-drained soil rich in organic matter. Propagate by offsets. Planting depth: 6-8 in. Hardy to Zone 7; in North, can be grown as an annual with bulbs dried and overwintered indoors. Borders. Containers. Also called spider-lily, basket flower.
Iris spp. (Iris)	4-48 in.	Blue, red, purple, yellow, orange, greenish, white	Large genus of plants, with several species arising from bulbs; all have 6-petaled flowers with 3 upright and 3 descending petals. Sword-shaped leaves. Bulb.	Full sun. Deep, well-drained soil rich in organic matter. Propagate by offsets. Planting depth: 2-6 in. Zones 3-9. Borders. Rock gardens. Woodlands. Some species are good for cutting. Many cultivars available.
Lilium spp. (Lily)	2-5 ft.	White, yellow, orange, red, purple, some spotted	Large genus with many species and forms. Flowers are trumpet or bell shaped, about 2-6 in. wide. Usually borne in clusters on tall stems. Leaves fleshy, straplike. Bulb.	Full sun to partial shade. Light or loamy, moist, well-drained soil rich in organic matter. Propagate by division, offsets. Planting depth: as a general rule, plant bulbs 3 times as deep as the height of the bulb—there are exceptions. Zones 4-10. Borders. Good in masses. Many are good for cutting. Many cultivars available.
Lycoris squamigera (Magic lily)	1½-2 ft.	Pink	Showy, trumpet-shaped, 3-in.-long flowers borne in clusters atop leafless stems. Straplike leaves appear in early spring, then die back; flowers appear in mid- to late summer. Bulb.	Full sun to partial shade. Sandy, well-drained soil rich in organic matter. Propagate by offsets. Planting depth: 5 in. Zones 5-10. Borders. Containers. *L. radiata,* red spider-lily, is hardy to Zone 7.
Zantedeschia spp. (Calla)	1-3 ft.	White, pink, yellow	Tropical plant with unusual blooms that have a showy petal-like spathe ranging from 5-10 in. long. Leaves are large, glossy, and arrow-shaped. Sometimes spotted white. Fleshy rhizome.	Full sun to partial shade. Moist, well-drained soil rich in organic matter. Propagate by division. Planting depth: 2-4 in; rhizomes dried and overwintered indoors. Borders. Containers. Good for cutting.

Rhizomes

Often mistaken for ordinary roots, rhizomes are actually horizontal stems, fat with stored food. Roots grow downward from the bottom; stems, leaves, and flowers sprout from the top. But which is which? Remains of last year's roots or bits of stem will give you a hint. If you're planting Japanese, Siberian, or bearded irises, cannas, or callas, you're planting rhizomes.

Plant rhizomes horizontally in the ground, root side down.

Time of Bloom

Anticipation is half the fun of gardening, and bulbs—planted weeks or even months before they grow and bloom—give you plenty of it. Bulbs fall into two general periods of bloom. By selecting a variety of species and cultivars from each, you can plan for a lengthy display of color.

Spring-Flowering Bulbs

This large group of bulbs, familiar to northern gardeners, includes the ever-popular tulips, daffodils, and hyacinths. There also are many lesser-known small or "minor" bulbs, such as crocuses, squills (*Scilla* spp.), snowdrops (*Galanthus* spp.), and glory-of-the-snow (*Chionodoxa* spp.), from which to choose. All make charming additions to the garden.

All these bulbs, adapted to survive hard winters, must have several weeks of cold temperatures for successful flowering. They are planted in the fall. If you're a southern gardener willing to put in some extra effort, you can enjoy these traditional harbingers of spring by forcing them or providing an artificial period of winter chill in your refrigerator.

Summer-Flowering Bulbs

The backbone of the late-season garden, summer bulbs provide easy and reliable color from summer through frost. This group includes both cold-hardy and tender bulbs. Lilies, for example, can be left in place all year long, but tender bulbs, such as dahlias, gladioli, and tuberous begonias, must be dug before the first frost of autumn, dried, and stored indoors in a cool, frost-free place through the winter. Peruvian daffodils (*Hymenocallis narcissiflora*) are hardy to Zone 7 and must be dug and overwintered indoors in the North.

Using Bulbs in the Landscape

There are almost as many ways to use bulbs in the landscape as there are bulbs to choose from. The following are a few considerations to keep in mind when deciding how, when, where, and what to plant.

A Bulb for Every Garden

Bulbs can fit happily into nearly any garden situation, whether it's a sunny spot with loamy soil or a shady, woodland garden. The trick is selecting the right bulbs for your needs. Most bulbs don't like wet feet, so good drainage is a must. Wet sites or waterlogged, clayey soil will lead to rot unless you are growing bog-loving species. (For information on improving wet, poorly drained soil, see "Improving the Soil—Texture and Structure" on page 17.)

Sun and regular garden soil will satisfy most of the spring-blooming bulbs, although they'll appreciate a generous supply of organic matter added to the soil at planting time and periodically thereafter. Daffodils and crocus do fine under deciduous trees (such as in woodland gardens), where the foliage can ripen in dappled shade as the trees come into leaf. Some of the spring-flowering bulbs, especially the smaller bulbs like dog-tooth violets (*Erythronium* spp.), are happiest in shade. Vibrant blue Siberian squill (*Scilla siberica*) will spread over a shady area, too, as long as some slanting sunlight finds its way under the trees.

Summer-blooming bulbs have a wide range of cultural needs. Some, like dahlias and gladioli, bloom best in full sun and require rich, well-drained soil. Tuberous begonias, caladiums, and achemenes, on the other hand, do best with shade and evenly moist soil that is very rich in organic matter.

In addition to the chart "Selecting Bulbs, Corms, and Tubers" on page 114, be sure to consult mail-order catalogs, local nursery owners, and your local cooperative extension service for suggestions on the right bulbs for your garden.

Avoiding Toy Soldier Syndrome

All spring-blooming bulbs—tulips, daffodils, crocuses, even hyacinths—look best planted in groups. Try for a single good splash of color rather than stretching out your bulbs as far as they will go, with one here and two there. Six red tulips planted in a loose clump beside your front door will make a cheerful bouquet that will greet you every time you go in or out. But six red tulips spaced along the front walk one by one will look like a row of toy soldiers.

Combining different spring bulbs in a setting, or adding early-blooming perennials, is where the creativity of the gardener comes into play. Six red tulips with pale blue creeping phlox (*Phlox stolonifera*) foaming beneath them and quiet bells of grape hyacinths nodding nearby will mark you as a gardener and an artist.

Think background when you're deciding on a planting plan. Fragrant, creamy-white "Mount Hood" daffodils will get lost against a classic picket fence or a white-painted house. Put them in front of a slate wall, or let them poke up through a tangle of common periwinkle (*Vinca minor*) with its glossy deep-green leaves and lilac-blue blossoms, and you multiply the impact.

Making Room for Summer Bulbs

Summer-blooming bulbs can be a little trickier to work into the landscape.

Hardy ones, such as lilies, are easy: The plants can stay in place for years, so all you need to do is pick a sunny spot and decide a color scheme. (Gardeners in Zone 4 and colder will have to lift these for winter storage.)

For northern gardeners, the tender bulbs, such as tuberous begonias, dahlias, cannas, and gladioli, present more of a challenge, since they must be planted each year and overwintered indoors. But, the flowers are well worth it, since they come in the late summer and early autumn when the garden can be very bare of bloom. Plant them where you won't disturb their neighbors at digging time.

The tall and showy summer bulbs are a bit more difficult to weave into the garden than a handful of daffodils. The 4-foot swords of gladioli, ready to flop over at the first excuse, take some thinking: Will you want a row of glads in the garden just for cutting? Or will you be happy to fool with stakes and string for the pleasure of those lovely colors in the late summer border? Dahlias also can be quite overwhelming and all but the dwarf cultivars require staking to look their best.

Naturalizing Spring Bulbs

Naturalizing is a technique that strives to imitate the best plantings of nature, the grand sweeps of color, the uncounted abundance. A wash of golden daffodils across a meadow, a casual scattering of snowdrops among the trees: Naturalized plantings are planned and planted so that the hand of the gardener is unapparent.

Pick an out-of-the-way spot that can remain undisturbed until the bulbs finish their cycle of ripening. You can plant in loose clumps, or gently toss handfuls of bulbs where you want them to go and then plant them where they fall. For instant effect, ignore the usual recommendations about spacing and plant the bulbs thickly.

Daffodils are ideal for naturalizing. They endure for decades and multiply slowly but reliably. 'Carlton'

is a classic yellow and a strong grower; 'Ice Follies' is always dependable.

The minor spring bulbs are even easier to naturalize because many of them seed themselves readily, filling in bare places with a wealth of flowers. Try some of the early-blooming species crocuses for a colorful effect. White and blue drifts of color are nice around the feet of trees and shrubs. Choose from white snowdrops (*Galanthus* spp.), snowflakes (*Leucojum* spp.), and dog-tooth violets (*Erythronium* spp.); or blue grape hyacinth (*Muscari* spp.), Siberian squill (*Scilla siberica*), and glory-of-the-snow (*Chionodoxa* spp.). All are determined multipliers.

The Right Tool

You can plant your bulbs by digging individual holes for them, or you can dig a big hole and plant a whole group at once. You can even remove enough soil to plant a bedful. (The chart "Selecting Bulbs, Corms, and Tubers" on page 114 will help you to decide planting depths.) Mix in a handful of bonemeal and aged manure or compost in your holes to give your bulbs a good start.

If your ground is full of rocks, stones, or tree roots, or if you are only placing a few bulbs, planting one-by-one makes sense. Picking the right tool makes the job easier. Bulb planters look like a metal can with a handle on top and come in both hand-operated and foot-operated models. If you need the extra force to break through sod, the step-on type is best. These planters cut out a cylinder of earth and leave a nice hole for a big bulb or a few little ones. A dibble is a thick wooden stick with a point at one end and a handle at the other. Poking holes is quick and easy in a well-prepared bed. But using a dibble in rocky soil or among tree roots is asking for frustration. An all-purpose tool, good for loose soil and tough spots alike, is the hand trowel. The pointed metal blade slices

SPRING BULBS WITH A SOUTHERN ACCENT

If you are a southern gardener who yearns for the scent of hyacinths in your garden, you can fool your bulbs by giving them a false winter that will trick them into blooming. Place the bulbs in paper bags and put them in your vegetable bin. Don't store fruit in the same drawer (apples and other fruits can give off ethylene, a gas that may damage the bulbs). Keep the bulbs in the bin for at least ten weeks. Then they'll be ready to plant outdoors for a classic touch of spring.

You can try just about any spring bulb that strikes your fancy, though the blooms won't last as long as in the cool northern spring. Hyacinths and daffodils do well in the South. For flowers next year, lift all spring-blooming bulbs in fall after the foliage has ripened and the bulb has had time to cure, and repeat the big chill.

Southern Tulips

Many tulips are well-suited for southern gardens. The strong-growing Triumph tulips, the reliable Darwins, and even, with a bit of luck, the romantic, late-flowered Peony tulips, have all proved themselves in the South.

Even better are the species tulips, sometimes called botanical tulips. These are the wild tulips and their cultivars, with all their heat-tolerant qualities intact. The flowers and plants are smaller than the familiar hybrids, but they are nice in rock gardens or along the front of a border where passers-by can admire them close up.

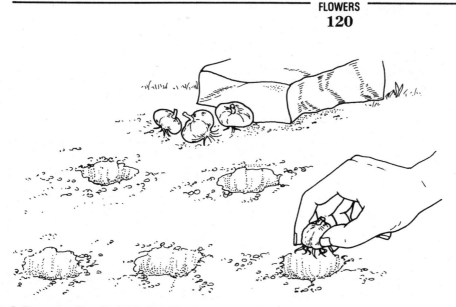

Bulbs can be planted individually by digging separate holes for each plant.

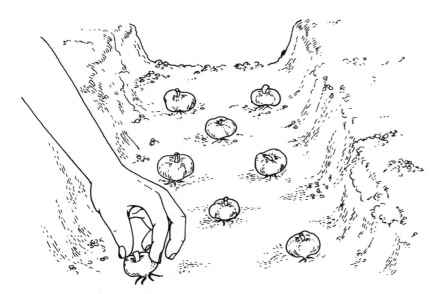

For mass plantings, you can dig a trench and plant an entire bed at once.

Trenches work well if you are planting a row of bulbs, especially the more formal hyacinths, tulips, or gladioli. Dig a wide trench so there is room for more than one bulb across. Always use care in covering a group of bulbs. Add soil a little at a time at first so that you don't dislodge the bulbs.

Do Not Feed the Animals

Chipmunks, mice, and the rest of the furry gang love tulips—and hyacinths, crocuses, and anemones. Luckily, daffodils are somewhat poisonous, so they'll leave them alone except when they're really hungry. Unless you have a strong enough constitution to shrug off the sight of a bed of ready-to-bloom tulips dug and gnawed to pieces, you'll have to take precautions.

You can try planting the bulbs deeper than usual or interplant the tastier bulbs with daffodils. You can try drenching the ground with hot-pepper tea or tobacco juice. But the only guaranteed-to-almost-always-work method is caging. Bend galvanized wire netting, with holes just big enough for the new shoots to grow through, to make a loose cage around the delectable bulbs.

If you are planting in groups, make a cage in two sections. Lay the wire mesh in the bottom of the hole. Place the bulbs, then fashion the rest of the cage, bending the edges down to make sides.

To protect established plantings

through turf and, with a little wiggling, works its way past roots and stones.

To plant bulbs in groups, you can make individual, closely spaced holes or use a spade to make one big hole. Plant groups in odd numbers for an informal look. Groups of five or seven large bulbs or more than a dozen small bulbs make a good-sized clump.

You can even combine large and small bulbs in the same hole. Place pink cottage tulips, cover them with an inch or two of soil, and then add bulbs of grape hyacinths or other small favorites right on top of the tulips.

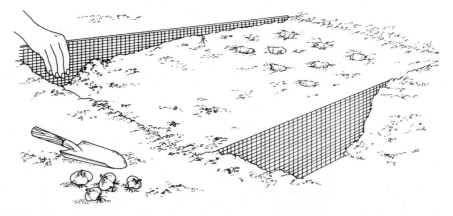

To discourage rodents from eating bulbs, you can line an entire bed with wire hardware cloth.

from rodents, place a piece of wire hardware cloth on top of the soil. Anchor with more soil or compost, and bend the edges into the ground at least 2 inches to deter tunneling critters.

Timing Is Everything

Northern gardeners should plant spring-flowering bulbs as soon as they can get them in autumn. The little bulbs, such as snowdrops, species tulips, Dutch iris, and species crocus, dry out fast. They should be tucked into the ground in a hurry. Lilies shouldn't be allowed to dry out before planting time, either. Most lilies are best planted in fall.

You can be a little lazier with the bigger bulbs of narcissus, daffodils, hyacinths, and tulips, although sooner is better is the rule for these, too. If you know you are not going to plant right away, bulbs may be stored loosely in paper bags in a cool spot. If you need to store your spring bulbs longer than a week or two, keep them safe in your refrigerator's vegetable bin until you're ready to plant.

Caring for Bulbs, Corms, and Tubers

Unlike some of the prima donnas of the garden, most bulbs are not very fussy. Plant them at the right depth in the right place and you can leave them alone for the rest of the growing season, and in the case of hardy bulbs, for years. That's why you can find Madonna lilies (*Lilium candidum*) planted 50 years ago still blooming among the crumbled foundations of an old homestead.

But like all garden plants, bulbs will do even better with a little attention to their needs.

Care Basics

The bulb is a storage system, a fat underground root or stem full of stored food. These underground pantries were a defense against the harsh climates where bulbs originated. An internal "clock" within the bulb evolved, to teach it to sleep during the baking heat of an African summer or the icy cold of winter in the Chinese mountains. When rain and warmth come again, the clock signals the bulb to start growing, using the stored food. After flowering is done, the leaves make food to replenish the bulb for next year. Then the bulb goes into its dormant period, waiting out the extremes. Successfully growing bulbs is a matter of understanding this cycle of growth and dormancy.

Watering

If you have planted your bulbs at the recommended depth and given them a good drink to get them started, you will have to water only when the plants look thirsty or during a long dry spell. (Foliage that wilts and stays wilted the next day is a clue that the bulb needs water.) It's also a good idea to give your bulbs a long, thorough soaking when the flower buds show.

Don't bother with sprinklers or hand-held spray nozzles. You need to get that water to the roots of the bulb. Either lay the hose among the bulbs to soak into the ground, or use a soaker

Hardy spring bulbs are planted in fall and begin to grow roots from the time they are planted until the ground freezes. By spring, the roots are well developed and ready to support foliage and flowers.

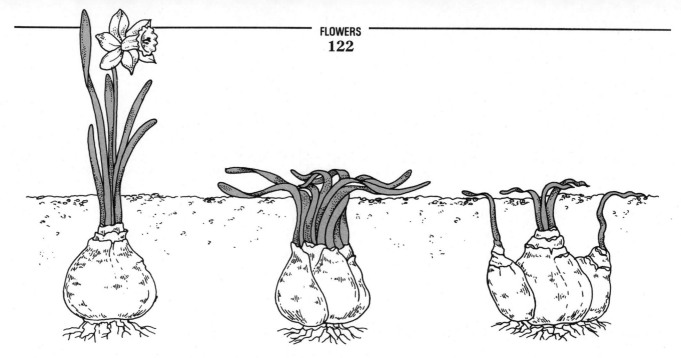

The plants flower in early spring and the flowers fade, but the foliage continues to grow and produce food for the following year. Many bulbs also produce natural divisions called offsets.

hose so the water isn't wasted in evaporation. Water long enough to be sure it soaks deep into the ground where the roots of the bulb can drink.

Fertilizing

Fertilizing is especially useful soon after planting, when the roots are beginning to form. That's why it's a good idea to add some aged, well-rotted manure and bonemeal while planting new bulbs or to give old bulbs a boost. Slow-release fertilizers such as bonemeal or special bulb food can be scratched in in the fall.

For summer bloomers, an all-around fertilizer can be used in the spring when the first shoots appear above ground. Gladioli and dahlias are heavy feeders and need regular fortification with compost and aged manure to do their best. Flowers will be bigger if fed regularly after the buds form. (For more information on suitable fertilizers, see "Making and Using Organic Fertilizers" on page 67.)

Mulching

A deep mulch over winter is a good idea for hardy bulbs if your soil is susceptible to frost heaving. Unmulched bulbs may be forced out of the ground by repeated cycles of freezing and thawing. If your soil is dry, a mulch during the growing season will help retain water.

Chopped leaves make a perfect mulch and can be left in place to decompose into humus. Straw, grass clippings, or evergreen branches are other possibilities.

Don't worry about new shoots that poke up before freezing weather is over. They are unlikely to be damaged by cold or snow. Sometimes newly planted small bulbs such as grape hyacinths throw out a lot of leaves soon after planting. These leaves will not be harmed by winter weather and do not need to be protected by mulch.

Deadheading

Snip the faded flowers from your large spring bulbs as they finish blooming. If you allow the seedpods to remain, tulips, daffodils, and hyacinth bulbs may exhaust themselves with the effort of making seeds. Deadheading directs the plant's energy into producing food for next year's flowers.

Most summer-flowering bulbs also benefit from deadheading, since more of the plant's energy can go into producing food.

Removing dead flowers from the small spring bulbs like scilla and snowdrops isn't necessary, unless you don't want them to self-sow. But who doesn't want more of these first flowers of spring?

Ripening Foliage

Bulb foliage must be allowed to ripen without being cut, tied, or braided. The leaves make food to replenish the bulb for next year. Remove the leaves before they shrivel and die back, and you sap the vigor of the bulb. After the foliage has turned yellow or brown, you can cut it down and add it to the compost heap.

There are plenty of ways to draw attention from the ripening foliage, which can look unkempt and unattractive as it lengthens and then turns yellow. You can plant bulbs among ground covers such as bugleweed (*Ajuga* spp.) or wild ginger (*Asarum canadense*). Late peony-flowered tulips ('Angelique' is an ethereal pink) are lovely overplanted with ferns. Or you can interplant perennials or annuals to mask the maturing foliage. Hostas and daylilies work well to camouflage daffodil leaves.

Lifting Tender Bulbs

Bulbs that are not hardy in cold winters, such as cannas, gladioli, dahlias, and tuberous begonias, must be dug up in fall for storage. After the first light frost, when the foliage has begun to blacken, track down all of your tender summer bloomers and carefully lift them from the beds. A garden fork will do the job nicely. Be sure to dig deep enough to get beneath the bulbs, to avoid that sickening *crunch* of a fat tuber being sliced in half. (See "Storing Bulbs, Corms, and Tubers" below for information on storage.)

Replanting Stored Bulbs

The new shoots of summer-blooming bulbs such as dahlias and glads are vulnerable to frost, so wait until the weather has warmed and night temperatures stay around 50°F before you put your winter-stored bulbs back into the ground in midspring. You can plant your summer bulbs in pots or shallow boxes of damp peat to give them a head start. They can be set in a sheltered spot outdoors during the day, but be sure to protect them from frost on chilly nights.

Storing Bulbs, Corms, and Tubers

If you live in an area where frost hardens the earth in winter, you will need to store your tender bulbs in a place protected from the cold. Storage temperatures should range between 45° and 60°F to keep plants from beginning to grow while in storage. (Dahlias are fussier; they need temperatures between 40° and 45°F to prevent sprouting.)

Most bulbs are well on their way to dormancy when cold weather sets in. They can be dug and saved in a sheltered place in nothing fancier than cardboard boxes, paper bags, bushel baskets, or old pantyhose. Even plastic trash bags will work, if you keep the top open and folded back so the bulbs remain dry. Dormant bulbs in pots can even be stored right in their pots.

A dusting with a copper-based fungicide or simply sulfur dust is a good precaution against disease and decay. For quick application, use the "Shake-and-Bake" method: Put bulbs and fungicide in a Ziploc storage bag and shake gently to lightly coat the bulbs. Or fill an old sock with sulfur dust and dust away.

Storing bulbs for winter is a rewarding job. Baskets and boxes of bulbs are just as satisfying to contemplate as a pantry full of homemade preserves. It makes a gardener feel like Midas to see how the crop of bulbs has increased over the year.

Storing Thick-Skinned Bulbs and Corms

Gladioli and Peruvian daffodils (*Hymenocallis narcissiflora*) and other thick-skinned corms and bulbs ask only for a cool, dry area with good air circulation to keep them happy all winter. Their protective coverings help retain moisture and keep the bulb in good shape through the winter.

You may keep your tender bulbs in containers of loose, dry sand, peat, vermiculite, or perlite. A cardboard box of peat or sand works just fine. Don't place the bulbs too close together—the spread of disease is lessened if bulbs don't touch.

Mesh onion bags make good storage containers for gladioli and the larger corms. Cut-off pantyhose legs or stockings allow plenty of air circulation and are just the right size for little cormels.

Storing Tubers and Rhizomes

Thin-skinned beauties like dahlias, callas, cannas, and tuberous begonias need slightly different treatment to keep them from drying out. Store them buried in containers of loose sand, peat, vermiculite, or perlite, and add a few drops of water now and then. Don't keep them bone-dry, but don't add enough water to encourage them—or fungi—to start growing. Remember to keep dahlias below 45°F to prevent sprouting.

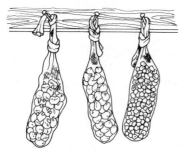

Corms and bulbs of nonhardy plants can be stored in nylon net bags or old pantyhose over the winter.

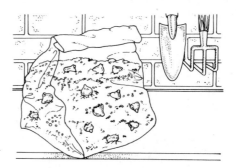

You can also store bulbs, corms, and tubers over winter in a paper bag filled with sand or vermiculite.

Propagating Bulbs

Most bulbs will multiply themselves in the easiest way possible: Just leave them alone and in a few years they'll form thick clumps. If there's lots of foliage but flowers get scarce, it's a sign that things are getting too crowded and the bulbs can't all get enough nutrients or space to reach blooming size. The solution is simple: Wait until the foliage has ripened, lift the clump, gently separate the crowded bulbs, and replant with more breathing room.

But if you want to speed up the multiplication, or if you want lots of your favorite lilies but not at $5-and-up per bulb, propagating the bulbs yourself is the answer.

You can increase your bulb supply in two ways. Dividing is a simple and rewarding way of making more flowers for your garden. The dividing technique will vary depending on whether you are propagating true bulbs, corms, tubers, or rhizomes. Growing from seed, in many cases a tricky task, is not for those in a hurry —some bulbs may take seven years to flower from seed.

Dividing means you will get no surprises. The lily you propagate from the mother bulb will look just like its parent. Whether you're propagating true bulbs, corms, or tubers, a vegetative division is a clone, an exact genetic copy of the mother plant.

Growing from seed is a riskier business. You never know what that lily had in its family tree—and after waiting for years to see a flower, you may wind up with an unwanted throwback.

An out-of-the-way corner of rich, loose soil makes a good nursery bed where you can nurture your bulblets till they reach blooming size. A cold frame can be handy, too. You may want to anchor metal hardware cloth over your baby bulbs to protect them from becoming a rodent feast.

Just one warning before you start: Once you see how easy it is to multiply your bulbs, how easy to grow 20

new lilies or 10 new crocuses from a single bulb, you'll be addicted.

Propagating True Bulbs

Daffodils and most other spring-blooming bulbs have the generous habit of producing little bulblets, or offsets, around the original bulb. As soon as the leaves have died back in early summer, lift the clump of bulbs and separate the bulblets from the mother bulb. (Use a knife if you need to; often, they pull apart easily.) Be sure each bulblet has a section of basal plate on its bottom to grow roots next year. Dust any cuts with a copper-based fungicide or sulfur dust to prevent decay and replant. Big offsets may bloom the next year; small ones may take two or three years to produce a flower.

Offsets produced by true bulbs such as daffodils can be gently pulled apart and planted.

It's not worthwhile to try to grow tulips and daffodils from seed. Allowing the seedpod to develop weakens the bulb. And the seeds will take several years to grow into blooming-size bulbs, which won't be true to their parents anyway. But many of the smaller spring bulbs grow fast and easily from seed, and differences in color or size are usually not noticeable. They'll seed themselves well if left to their own devices. But if you want to help things along or raise plants for another site, try grape hyacinths (*Muscari* spp.), squill (*Scilla* spp.), and star-of-Bethelehem (*Ornithogallum* spp.). Collect the ripe seedpods and plant the seed shallowly in

a cold frame, or hold for spring sowing. Most species will bloom in their second spring.

Many ornamental onions (*Allium* spp.) have a unique way of multiplying. That old flowerhead you see atop the allium stalk is not full of seeds: It's actually tiny bulbs. These offspring drop to the ground and root to make new plants. You can collect them yourself and pamper them in the cold frame or nursery bed.

Propagating Lilies

Because of their scaled structure, lilies are propagated differently from the rest of the true bulbs. They often yield the most new plants—as many as 20 or more from one mother bulb. In fact, there are several ways to propagate lilies. As with the true bulbs, wait till the foliage has ripened before you lift or disturb any bulbs for propagating.

Bulblets and Bulbils. One way to add to your lily collection is by collecting and planting the bulblets that form at the top of the mother bulb on some lilies. Gently brush the soil away from the stem of a lily in late summer and check for pea- to marble-sized bulblets where stem joins bulb. Pluck them carefully and plant in the nursery bed. The mature plants will be identical to the mother plant.

Many lilies, such as the familiar tiger lily, produce what look like shiny dark beads in the leaf axils where their leaves join the stem. These are aerial bulbils, the start of a fine garden of lilies, all clones identical to the mother plant. If left to themselves, they'll fall off when ripe, sprout roots, and begin to grow. If you want to give them less of a haphazard start in life, pick the bulbils in late summer or fall (wait till they detach easily) and plant 1 inch deep in a mix of equal parts soil, peat moss, and sand, in pots or dishpans or cold frame. Bury them outside under a deep mulch for the winter, then move into nursery beds

Many lilies produce small bulbils along the stem above the leaves. These can be harvested and grown into full-sized plants.

Lilies also produce bulblets at the base of the stalk, which can be planted and grown on.

Scaling is another way to propagate lilies. Remove up to half of the scales from the mother bulb.

Place the scales in a shallow container with the end that was nearest the base of the mother bulb in the soil.

Tiny bulblets will form at the base of each scale and can be potted up when they are large enough to handle.

or the garden in spring. Flowers will appear the second or third year.

Scaling. You can grow more new lilies by carefully removing as many as half of the scales from the mother bulb (discard the dried-up outer scales). Place them basal-plate-down, about halfway covered, in loose, moist vermiculite or peat moss. Add a lid of clear plastic to keep in moisture.

(A Ziploc bag full of moist peat makes an instant propagating bed.) In a few weeks at room temperature, you'll see tiny bulblets forming at the bases of the scales. When the bulblets are big enough to handle, usually in about 10 to 12 weeks, plant them scale and all about 2 inches deep and 6 inches apart in the nursery bed or cold frame for the winter. (You can also give them a "false winter" in the refrigerator if

you are propagating in spring.) Add a couple of inches of loose soil on top of the bed at the end of its first year, after a killing frost. Some of the new lilies will bloom their second spring, others will wait another year. These, too, will be identical to the mother plant.

Seed. Some mail-order companies offer seed for the easily grown Asiatic and Trumpet lilies, or you can harvest your own. Just shake out the seeds from a ripe seedpod and sow them ½ inch deep in moist, sterile soil. You can also save the collected seed for spring planting. The first leaf may sprout in as little as three weeks. Add them to the nursery bed after the second leaf forms, or when big enough to handle.

Propagating Corms

Corms shrivel and die to a withered shell each year, but don't worry: Each corm makes a large replacement corm to bloom next year and also produces offsets called cormels around the old corm. Special roots work to position new corms by pulling them deeper into the ground so that the new corm stays at the right depth.

Lift corms with a garden fork as soon as the leaves have died back or been killed by frost. Hardy corms like the spring and autumn crocuses should be replanted immediately. Tender corms like gladioli may be replanted right away in mild areas, but in the North they must be cured for winter storage.

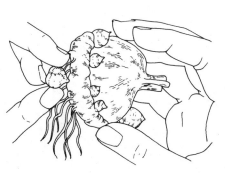

Each corm will produce a cluster of small new corms, called cormels, each year.

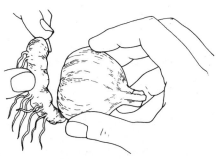

When harvesting and storing corms, break the old, spent corm from the previous year away from the base of the new corm formed for next year's growth.

Hardy Corms

Hardy corms like crocuses (*Crocus* spp.) and autumn crocuses (*Colchicum* spp.) multiply so fast on their own that interfering hardly seems worthwhile. A single crocus corm may multiply into a bouquet of 30 flowers from 30 corms in as little as three or four years, provided their foliage is allowed to ripen and other conditions (such as soil and light) are to their liking. Crocuses often seem perfectly content squeezed in cheek-by-jowl. But if you hunger for hundreds of crocuses, removing their cormels after the leaves have died is a surefire method. Plant the cormels right away in a nursery bed where they'll have plenty of elbowroom, and they'll usu-

ally reach blooming size in a year or two. Dig them up that fall and you'll see how much they've grown. Replant wherever you want crocuses next spring.

Dog-toothed violets (*Erythonium* spp.) are slower-growing hardy plants that can be propagated by their corms in the same way as hardy crocuses. The depth-adjusting roots sometimes pull the corms far into the ground, so be sure to dig good and deep when you're lifting them.

Tender Corms

After digging tender corms, such as those of gladioli, cut off the tops and spread the corms in an airy, shaded place to dry. (A window screen raised up on blocks works well.) Allow them to dry for two to three weeks, then peel the new corm off the old useless one at its base. Gently rub off any dried soil and collect the cormels clustered around the larger corm.

In mild climates (Zones 9 and 10), tender corms may be replanted immediately. Cormels may be put in the nursery bed or into a row in the vegetable garden to mature into corms. In areas with cold winters, tender corms and cormels must be stored in a cool, dry place and replanted in spring. (See "Storing Bulbs, Corms, and Tubers" on page 123 for details on how to store them.)

Propagating Tuber-Corms, Tuberous Roots, and Rhizomes

The quickest way to get a garden full of caladiums, dahlias, or begonias is by division. In this case, division is just what the word means: Chopping the tuber or rhizome into pieces. Raising new plants from seed is also a possibility for some species, and even stem cuttings will work to start some of the tuberous plants.

But a strong, sharp knife is the tool of choice. The big payoff for all your propagating work with tubers and rhizomes is that because there's no waiting for a bulb to mature, most divisions will flower the next year.

Propagating Tubers and Tuberous Roots

Each division of a tuber or tuberous root must have a living bud or eye from which the new plant will grow. Imagine a potato, a familiar tuber: To grow a new plant, you must use a chunk with an eye.

Propagate tubers and tuberous roots in spring, before planting, when you can see the buds best. (You can

Propagate tuberous-rooted plants such as dahlias by cutting apart the roots, but make sure each piece has a bud or eye.

Tuber-corms such as caladiums can be cut apart with a sharp knife. Dust cut edges with sulfur to prevent rot.

divide them in fall, if you prefer.) Tuberous roots like dahlias will have all their eyes at one end—where the old stem was connected. Cut them apart at the juncture of tuber and stem, making sure each has a bud or eye. Dust with a copper-based fungicide or sulfur dust and let the cuts toughen for a few hours. Then plant into the garden.

Chop tuber-corms, such as caladium and tuberous begonia, into pieces, making sure each piece has a bud. Dust with fungicide, as above, and let the cuts harden off for two days in a shady, airy place. Then plant as usual.

Stem cuttings, another type of vegetative propagation, may also be used to start more of your favorite tuberous begonias and dahlias. Slice off a healthy shoot a few inches long and strip the lower leaves. Dip the end in rooting hormone powder for quick results. Insert the cuttings in pots of sandy compost and keep them well watered. Plant in the garden after several new leaves have formed.

Propagating Rhizomes

Plants that grow from rhizomes, such as cannas and iris, can get crowded in a hurry. Dividing them will mean bigger and better flowers—and more plants. In late summer, dig up the clump with a spade or garden fork. A strong, sharp knife is essential for slicing through the thick, tangled rhizomes.

Cutting iris rhizomes into pieces of a single fan of leaves stretches the plants the farthest, but some of them may not bloom the next year and that may create dead spots in the garden. A three-fan division, with two new rhizomes connected to an old rhizome, guarantees a spot of bloom next season.

Dust with a copper-based fungicide or sulfur dust to prevent decay and lay the pieces in a shady spot for a day or two to dry the cuts. You may trim the leaves to about 6 inches before replanting.

To make more cannas or callas, cut them in spring into sections with four or five eyes. Again, dust with fungicide or sulfur for good health and harden the cuts for a few days. For earlier bloom, northern gardeners may bury their divisions in damp sand or peat moss indoors in pots to get them off to a good start.

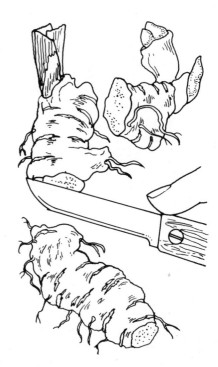

Rhizomes can also be cut apart with a sharp knife. Leave four or five eyes per section for best results.

Forcing Hardy Bulbs

A garden full of daffodils is a beautiful sight, but a single pot holding half-a-dozen yellow trumpets in February is worth its weight in gold.

There's nothing mysterious about forcing hardy bulbs. It's all a matter of giving them a compressed life cycle: Cool fall for root growth, cold winter dormancy, followed by the warmth and water of spring. The trick is in manipulating the "seasons" to shave off a few weeks and get early bloom. (Some mail-order catalogs offer precooled bulbs, which have already had their cold treatment and are ready for forcing.)

Growing an Early Spring

Start in the fall with the biggest, fattest, healthiest bulbs you can find. (See "Bulbs for Forcing" on page 128 for help in making your selections.) Once you've decided on your flowers, pick appropriate containers. Shallow, wide pots, often called bulb pans, work best and won't tip over when the bulbs grow tall and top-heavy. Plastic pots work well because they won't be damaged by freezing treatment and can be slipped inside other more decorative containers later. (If you are using precooled bulbs, you can plant them in as fragile a container as you like.) Drainage holes are a must.

The food stored in the bulb is enough to nourish and produce a flower, so you can even force some bulbs in nothing but water. Cultivars

BULBS FOR FORCING

Force only the best bulbs, the plumpest, firmest, biggest ones you can find. Look in the catalogs for cultivars recommended for forcing and for those types that bloom the earliest of their kind.

All hardy spring bulbs will force well. Try the traditional tulips and the botanical or species types, hyacinths, daffodils, and crocuses (these are especially easy). Don't forget the other spring bloomers like grape hyacinth (*Muscari* spp.), snowdrops (*Galanthus* spp.), glory-of-the-snow (*Chionodoxa* spp.), squill (*Scilla* spp.), *Iris reticulata* (a miniature dark blue and yellow charmer), and Dutch iris (*I. xiphium* hybrids). The tender bulbs of *Anemone coronaria* and freesia (*Freesia* × *hybrida*), unbeatable for fragrance, also force well.

of *Narcissus tazetta,* including paperwhite narcissus, can be grown in a dish of pebbles and water. A special little vase called a hyacinth vase, which has a flared top in which the bulb sits, can be used to bring a sweet-smelling hyacinth (*Hyacinthus orientalis*) or two into bloom on a child's windowsill.

Potting Up

Most bulbs will require a pot filled with soil. You can make a good basic potting medium from the following recipe: Mix equal parts of potting soil, peat moss, and perlite, and then add 1 part of coarse sand or fine gravel to each 2 parts of soil mix. The top of the soil must be firmed down well, to keep the bulbs from heaving out. But the soil must be loose below, to let the roots grow easily. If you want to save the bulbs for next year, add some fertilizer, such as bonemeal, when planting.

You'll be planting to make a show, so crowd the bulbs into the container, leaving only a little space between. Odd numbers of bulbs are more pleasing to the eye than a pot of two or four. Plant the bulbs shallowly, with their "noses" poking out of the ground, to encourage fast growth.

Tulip bulbs, which usually have one side less well-rounded than the other, should be planted in a circle with the flat sides towards the outside of the pot. That way, the first leaf of each bulb, which grows from the flat side, will be to the outside, and the flower stems will be bunched in the middle.

To squeeze more daffodils into a container, plant in two layers. Place the bottom bulbs on a 2-inch layer of potting mix, cover them to their necks, then set more bulbs between them and cover to the top. This is a good trick for Dutch iris and the small spring bulbs, too.

Remember to press firmly around the bulbs to settle them in place. Then get ready to move them for the cold treatment.

Cold Treatment

Most spring bulbs need at least a 12- to 15-week period of cold temperatures (between 33° and 50°F) and darkness to give them time to grow a healthy set of roots. The bulbs must have time to grow roots *before* being exposed to freezing temperatures, which will stop root growth. Don't cheat on this end of the forcing cycle; good roots are essential for good bloom. Keep the bulbs moist during the cold treatment.

Pots can be left outside under their blanket of mulch or in a cold frame until it's time to bring them indoors. Or you can dig a trench and store the pots placed up to the rim in coarse sand. (You'll be bringing the pots indoors in the middle of winter, so sinking them to the rim in soil may result in pots frozen in place until spring.) Be sure to take steps to protect the pots from bulb-hungry rodents. Tulips need a total of 14 to 20 weeks of cold, including the cool fall period. Daffodils take longest, from 16 to 22 weeks. Hyacinths will root at warmer temperatures than others, and take 10 to 14 weeks to root well. Crocuses, snowdrops, and other small bulbs need about 12 weeks of cold. Bring them indoors when the tips have grown an inch or so high.

When you bring the pots inside, wake the bulbs from their sleep slowly by putting them in a cool but bright place, at no more than 50° to 55°F. Higher temperatures will rush new growth, making it pale and spindly.

Once the flowers bud and bloom, move your containers anywhere you want a touch of early spring. They'll last longer in a cool spot, however, and moving them back into their cool room at night will also prolong bloom.

When the flowers are finished, give the bulbs a dose of fertilizer to strengthen the leaves and thus the bulb. Plant them outside when the ground thaws.

For forcing, plant bulbs shallowly, with the nose of the bulb poking out of the soil.

After planting, water well and move the pots to a cold location for 12 to 15 weeks so they can grow roots.

Growing Amaryllis

First, let's get the name straight. Amaryllis, the giant bulb with the tall, showy flower, though a member of the Amaryllis family, really belongs to the genus *Hippeastrum*. But since *Hippeastrum* hasn't quite made it to common usage, we'll use the common name amaryllis to refer to the showy hybrids in *Hippeastrum*.

No matter what you call it, amaryllis is a spectacular flower. The trumpet-shaped blooms come in red, white, pink, and salmon, and often exceed 5 inches across. Bulbs are shipped ready to bloom and often prepotted.

If you're planting your own, a soak in tepid water before planting will give the bulb a head start. Use a pot slightly bigger than the diameter of the bulb and heavy enough not to tip once the fleshy flower stalk elongates. Clay pots work well. Put a handful of potting soil or compost in the bottom, then carefully settle the bulb so that about a third of the bulb is sticking up above the rim. Try not to damage the fleshy roots that may still be attached to the base of the bulb. Fill the pot with soil, covering most of the bulb but leaving the top of its shoulders and the stem exposed. Firm the soil and soak with water. Then set the pot in a cool (55° to 60°F), dark place so it can begin to grow roots. You won't need to water again until the bulb sprouts in about a week or two.

Amaryllis plants grow so fast you can almost watch them getting taller. It takes only six to eight weeks from potting to full flower, and sometimes growth is even faster. Start bulbs at the middle or end of November to have bloom for the holidays. Planting bulbs at one- or two-week intervals will ensure an eyecatching, winter-long display.

The broad, strap-shaped leaves will begin to emerge either before or at flowering time. After flowering, cut the flowering stalk back to 2 inches, but be sure to leave the leaves intact. The plants aren't very attractive after flowering, so a sunny window in a cool, unused room is ideal. Once spring arrives and temperatures remain above freezing, you can move the plant —pot and all—to a shady spot in the garden. Just be sure to bring it in before frost in fall. Water and fertilize lightly until the leaves die back and the bulb becomes dormant. Store the bulb in a cool, dry place, protected from freezing. (If you garden in a mild climate, you can plant the bulb outside after flowering.)

Around Thanksgiving, you can repot in fresh soil, give it a good drink, and wait for the next show.

Some growers have good luck and even increase their bulb supply by eliminating the dormant period. When the flower is done and roots fill the pot, they repot the amaryllis into a container 2 inches larger. When that is full of roots, they move the bulb to a still larger pot, and still again, until the amaryllis is growing in a 12-inch pot. The plant should be lightly fertilized every two weeks. The lush, strapping leaves may be staked or tied up (a wire hoop is ideal). Flowers—about one to every four leaves—appear in late January or February.

Plant amaryllis so that about one-third of the bulb is above the soil.

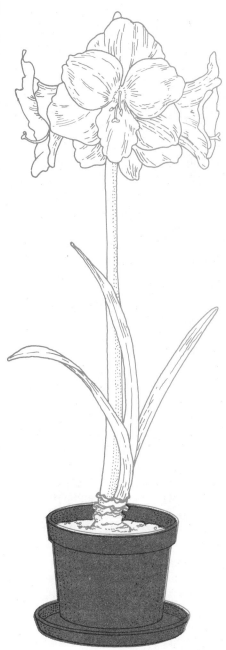

Perennials and Biennials

Selecting and Planting Perennials

Planting perennials is common sense. Most of them are long-lived and become familiar friends in the garden, showing up spring after spring. All they ask in return is some basic annual care and maintenance and that their basic cultural requirements are met. With some planning, you can tailor a garden of perennials to provide plenty of bloom all season long.

The widest range of perennials will do best in a garden that has deep, well-drained, fertile soil, with a good amount of sun. So cast a critical eye upon your garden before sending off that wish list or making a trip to your local nursery. You'll get the best results for the least work if you match cultural needs to the conditions that exist naturally in your garden. Also, take time to make your garden plan on paper first. It's much easier to move plants with an eraser and pencil than a spade and wheelbarrow! (See "Garden Design" on page 172 for tips.)

If your garden site isn't ideal—perhaps you have sandy or heavy clay soil, deep shade, or only damp, boggy areas—take heart, and take your time. No matter how bad you think your site is, some kind of perennial will be happy to call it home. The easiest way to work with a problem garden is to narrow your selections to those plants that have been proven in a similar site. (See the chart "Selecting Perennials and Biennials" on page 134 to help make the right choices. There are also several good reference books listed in "Recommended Reading" on page 406 that will provide an even more extensive list.)

But if you don't want to limit yourself to plants that do well in the conditions your garden has to offer—if you yearn for a towering stand of royal-blue delphiniums but your garden has hard, sun-baked clay—then you will need to spend time solving your garden problems before adding plants. Raised beds filled with loose, rich loam could be the answer; double-digging and adding organic matter such as compost is another way. (See "Double Digging" on page 7 or "Improving the Soil—Texture and Structure" on page 17 for more information on either of these topics.)

It's a good idea to prepare the perennial bed a couple of weeks before you plant. Spade deeply and dig in compost, leaf mold, and some aged manure to give your plants a good start. When you get your plants, set them in the locations you have planned, step back, and visualize the garden at blooming time. Need to add another plant or two of *Coreopsis* 'Moonbeam' to make more of a splash of yellow in front? Revise the plan as needed, then plant. After planting, water is the magic ingredient until your perennials settle in. Don't worry *too* much about achieving a perfect plan before beginning; you can always move plants next spring.

Planting Perennials

Most mail-order perennials are shipped dormant in early to midspring. Plants that become dormant during the hot summer months, such as Oriental poppies, are shipped in time for fall planting. You can also plant dormant crowns of peonies or hostas in late fall. Dormant plants may arrive bare-root, plastic-bagged in peat, or in pots.

Bare-Root and Bagged Plants

Don't be fooled by the meager bunch of dead roots you find inside those exciting packages of bare-root perennials. Those "dead" roots will come alive fast, though it may take them a year to catch up to the plants depicted in catalog centerfolds.

Get dormant plants into the garden as fast as you can. Many nurseries will allow you to specify a shipping date, so you'll be prepared. If you must hold dormant plants for a few days, take them out of their plastic bags, find a well-shaded spot, and bury the roots in moist peat.

When you're ready to plant, it's best to work with no more than a half-dozen plants at a time. Gently shake off any clinging packing material. Then snip off any rotten or moldy roots and set a few plants to soak in a wheelbarrow or bucket of water while you dig the holes according to your plan.

Make a mound in the bottom of the hole to support the crown of the plant, from which the stems and leaves will grow. Add a sprinkle of bone meal, then place the plant in the hole, gently spreading the roots over the mound. Fill the hole with soil (don't bury the crown) and firm it with your hand.

Water thoroughly, soaking the ground. Mulch to hold moisture in the soil. Then place a box or bushel basket over the plant (hold it down with a rock or brick). This will give the new plant a dark, sheltered place to rest for a few days while root growth begins.

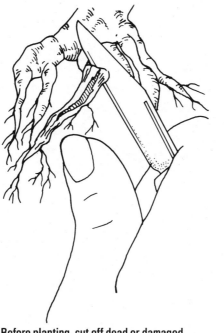

Before planting, cut off dead or damaged roots. Also inspect the roots carefully and cut off moldy or diseased ones.

When planting bare-root perennials, work with only a few plants at a time and soak the roots in water before planting.

GARDENERS BEWARE

You can buy perennials through the mail sight unseen, collect a wagonload as you wander through the local garden center, or inherit a bucket of plants from a neighbor over the backyard fence. Each method has its advantages—and its drawbacks.

Hand-Me-Downs

The generous neighbor is usually handing out perennials classed as "invasives"—which means, if left alone, they will sooner or later take over your garden. (See "Controlling Invasive Perennials" on page 143 for more about these eager beavers.) The good news is, hand-me-downs will probably do as well in your garden as in your neighbor's. And they're free.

The Blind Date

If you don't know the reputation of a mail-order nursery, start with a small order to judge the quality and size of the plants they supply. Always look for a money-back guarantee. In this field, there's sometimes not much correlation between the price you pay and the stock you get. Don't be swayed by pretty catalogs—sometimes the smaller nurseries, with their hand-typed plant lists, will supply better plants than big businesses with slick advertising. Some unscrupulous nurseries will even picture one cultivar and send you another. Make sure you get what you've paid for—and that the guarantee allows you enough time to find out.

Practicing Self-Control

The trip to a nearby garden center or nursery can be hazardous, especially for impulse buyers. You've considered your site, planned your garden, made your list —but when you see perennials in bloom, it's hard for a gardener to think rationally.

The big advantage to picking plants in person is that you can see the stock and buy the healthiest and biggest plants. Look for good, thick growth, not tall, spindly plants (unless you're looking for garden phlox [*Phlox paniculata*] or similar plants, which are by nature tall and spindly). Leaves should be green and unblemished, not yellowing or curling.

The other plus of nursery shopping is that you are buying potted plants. They won't mind sitting in a shady corner till you're ready to plant them—next week or next month—provided you keep them well watered in the interim. If you're a lazy gardener, potted perennials are the way to go.

Set the plant on a mound of earth in the center of the hole and gently spread the roots out evenly.

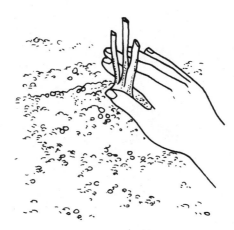

Fill the hole, making sure the plant's crown is at the surface of the soil. Firm the soil to ensure that there is good contact between roots and soil.

Water thoroughly to settle the soil around the roots and encourage root growth.

Mulch to conserve soil moisture.

PROBLEM PLANTING

If your garden spot is near a tree, you may be in for trouble. Tree roots often grow near the surface of the ground, competing for nutrients and water with your garden plants. Extra fertilizer and regular, deep watering may help keep both tree and perennials happy, or you can try sinking potted perennials —still in pots—between the tree roots. Place a scrap of window screening in the bottom of the hole to keep out exploring tree roots.

Maples are very shallow-rooted and, consequently, difficult to plant under. Oaks, on the other hand, are deep-rooted and pose less of a problem. If that tree near your garden is a black walnut, you have more to worry about. Black walnuts give off toxic juglone from their roots, a natural way of keeping competition for growing room and nutrients in check. Some perennials are known to be tolerant of juglone, and many others are worth experimenting with. Try bellflowers (*Campanula* spp.), bugleweed (*Ajuga reptans*), coralbells (*Heuchera* spp.) blanket flower (*Gaillardia* spp.), daylilies, hostas, lily-of-the-valley (*Convallaria majalis*), and *Sedum* spp.

Plants in Pots

Potted perennials, dormant or growing, can be kept in the shade for a few days until you're ready to plant, as long as you keep the plants watered. If you can, wait for a drizzly, overcast day to plant, or plant in the early evening. Hot sun is hard on new transplants.

Dig a hole the size and depth of the pot before you remove the plant. Fill the hole with water and let it soak in. Fill the hole with water again to "muddy in" the plant.

Trim off any broken stems or leaves. Hold the pot upside down with one hand spread across the surface, supporting the stem of the plant between your fingers. *Never* pull on the stem. Wiggle the pot or give it a whack on the bottom. Most often, the plant will slip right out, with its ball of roots intact. If it doesn't, hit the pot harder with your trowel a few times. The most stubborn plants can be removed by gently pushing with a stick through the drainage hole. Remember, those are live roots you're poking through, so only use as much force as necessary.

If the roots have grown into the shape of the pot, comb them gently with your fingers to untangle them. Severely root-bound plants will have lots of white roots circling around the root ball. To encourage the roots to branch out into the soil, score the root ball on three or four sides with a sharp knife to cut circling roots and encourage branching. You can trim extra-long roots off with scissors. Then place the root ball in the planting hole to the same depth it was growing in the pot. Add soil to cover, and firm it with your hands. Water the plant once more, then mulch. A bushel basket makes a good cover to shelter the plant for a day or two.

Once the potted plants are in the ground, they are quick to recover from any hard knocks they might have received during shipping. By the third day, your new perennials should be perked up and ready to grow.

Caring for Perennials

Most perennials are not low-maintenance plants. Though they'll struggle along if left to their own devices, the reward for regular care and feeding is bigger and better bloom.

Spring—Preparing for a New Year

The perennial year begins in early spring, when new arrivals are added to the beds and old residents are spruced up. If you've left the grooming chores of cutting back and removing debris from last year, now is the time to clean up the garden for the new season.

Cleanup

Make sure the cycles of freezing and thawing have come to an end, and steady, warmer temperatures have arrived before you remove the layer of winter mulch that has protected your plants through the cold months. Then clip the dead leaves and stems from all plants that died back to the ground during the winter. Divide and replant overgrown clumps or pushy plants on the verge of invading their neighbors (see "Dividing Perennials" on page 141). This also is the time to renew clumps of plants such as chrysanthemums, which may have died out in the center. Dig the clumps, discard the old, woody center portion, and replant the newer plants at the edges of the clump.

Cultivating

Use a cultivator tool, long- or short-handled, to loosen the earth around your perennials. When you see the first new shoots peeping up, fertilize the perennials liberally with compost or other slow-release fertilizer.

Watering

Deep, thorough watering—at least an inch at a time—is important to most perennials, especially during the growing season. The best time to water is early morning, when the sun isn't high enough for instant evaporation. Watering at night may encourage fungus disease and mold because the leaves don't dry off quickly.

An inconspicuous soaker hose snaking its way through the perennial bed makes the job easier and can even be left in place all season. Water long enough to penetrate down to the roots. If you only soak the top inch of soil, drinking roots will learn to seek water there, and the plant will be in trouble when a hot, dry spell comes.

A thick mulch will cut down on watering chores and conserve water.

Weeding

As Shakespeare said in *King Henry VI:* "Now tis the spring, and weeds are shallow-rooted. Suffer them now and they'll o'ergrow the garden." The year-round job of weeding starts in spring, and the more thorough you are now, the less you'll have to do later (when you should be lying on your chaise lounge, sipping iced tea, and admiring the garden). There are three rules to remember to make weeding easier.

● Little weeds are easier to pull than big weeds.
● Never let a weed set seed.
● Mulch, mulch, mulch.

Mulching

Put down a good, thick layer of mulch in late spring, after the garden has had a long soaking with rain or hose. Compost, grass clippings, and layers of newspaper covered by soil or compost are three of the best. The mulch will retain water in the soil and smother most weeds that try to sprout.

Staking

Floppy flowers, such as peonies, yarrow (*Achillea* spp.), and baby's-breath (*Gypsophila paniculata*), need a support system to look their best. Tall, regal perennials, like delphinium and foxglove (*Digitalis purpurea*), need sturdy stakes to hold them up as they grow.

Strong bamboo stakes, wire mesh cylinders, twiggy branches, and cages of string all have their place. Consider the growth habit of the plant you are staking and choose a method that will allow it to keep a natural look. Wire mesh cylinders or cages are ideal for peonies, for example. Airy *Achillea* won't look its best if tied to a single bamboo stake; try a web of string and stakes. When staking perennials, try to avoid damaging the crown of the plant when you drive the stakes into the ground. (See "Staking Plants" on page 77 for more support tips.)

SELECTING PERENNIALS AND BIENNIALS

Perennials make popular additions to home gardens. The plants below are divided by blooming season: spring, spring to summer, summer, and summer to fall. By selecting plants listed in each category, you can plan for bloom throughout the growing season. Be sure to check other charts in this book, such as herbs, bulbs, wildflowers, ornamental grasses, and groundcovers, for other useful perennials to add to your display.

Perennial	Height	Flower Color	Description	Culture
Spring-Flowering				
Anemone spp. (Windflower)	6-48 in.	White, pink, red, purple, yellow	Wide variety of perennial species with pastel to brightly colored, cup-shaped flowers and attractive leaves that may be covered with silvery hairs.	Full sun to partial shade. Rich, moist, humusy, well-drained soil. Propagate by division, root cuttings, seeds. Zones 3-8 (depending on species). Borders. Rock gardens. Woodland areas. Some are good for cutting. Some species bloom in late summer to fall. May need winter protection.
Arabis procurrens (Rock cress)	6-8 in.	White	Creeping, mat-forming perennial with glossy green leaves and many-flowered spikes of tiny flowers with 4 petals.	Full sun. Gravelly, well-drained soil. Propagate by division, seeds. Zones 3-7. Rock gardens. Spreads quickly. *A. caucasica* is a similar species with fragrant flowers and double-flowered forms.
Armeria maritima (Common thrift)	6-12 in.	White, dark pink	Clump-forming perennial with blue-green grasslike leaves. Ball-shaped flower heads, ½ in. across, arise above foliage on leafless stalks.	Full sun. Sandy, well-drained soil. Propagate by division. Zones 4-7. Coastal areas. Rock gardens. Clumps will rot in damp soil.
Aubrieta deltoidea (False rock cress)	3-6 in.	Purple, red	Thick, mat-forming perennial with loose clusters of tiny, ¾-in. flowers with 4 petals held above leaves.	Full sun to partial shade. Sandy, well-drained soil. Propagate by division, seeds. Cool, moist conditions. Zones 5-8. Edging. Rock gardens.
Aurinia saxatilis (Basket-of-gold)	6-10 in.	Yellow	Dense, mat-forming perennial with small, fuzzy, gray-green leaves. Bears large clusters of bright yellow, ⅛-in., 4-petaled flowers.	Full sun. Light, well-drained soil. Propagate by cuttings, seeds. Zones 4-10. Cuttings. Edging. Rock gardens. Formerly listed as *Alyssum saxatile*.
Baptisia australis (Blue false indigo)	3-4 ft.	Blue	Large, clump-forming perennial with blue-green, cloverlike leaves and blue pealike flowers followed by attractive seedpods.	Full sun to partial shade. Humusy, moist, well-drained soil. Propagate by cuttings, seeds. Zones 4-8. Borders. Cuttings. May need staking. Plants resent disturbance; try not to divide. Seedpods used in arrangements.
Dicentra spp. (Bleeding-heart)	1-2 ft.	White, cream, pink, purplish pink	Delicate-looking perennials with feathery foliage and loose spikes of unusual heart-shaped flowers.	Full sun to partial shade. Rich, moist, well-drained soil. Propagate by division, root cuttings, seeds. Zones 3-7. Shady borders. Rock gardens. Woodland gardens. Popular species include *D. spectabilis* (bleeding-heart) and *D. eximia* (wild bleeding-heart), which will bloom spring through fall.

Perennial	Height	Flower Color	Description	Culture
Digitalis purpurea (Common foxglove)	2-5 ft.	Purple, white, pink, yellow, red	Biennial with tall spikes of large, nodding, bell-shaped flowers borne atop a clump of hairy basal leaves.	Partial shade. Rich, well-drained soil. Propagate by seeds. Zones 4-10. Backs of borders. Good for cutting. Will reseed.
Helleborus orientalis (Lenten rose)	15-18 in.	White, green, pink, purple	Clump-forming perennial with glossy, evergreen leaves and nodding 2-in.-wide flowers that appear in late winter to early spring.	Partial shade. Rich, moist, well-drained soil. Propagate by division, seeds. Zones 4-8. Shady borders. Woodland gardens.
Iris spp. (Iris)	4-60 in.	Blue, red, purple, yellow, orange, greenish, white	Large genus of perennials with many hybrids and species organized into groups, including the Tall Bearded Iris, Crested Iris, Japanese Iris, and Siberian Iris. Flowers have 3 upright and 3 descending petals. Bearded irises have a colorful fuzzy beard down the middle of the descending petals; crested irises have a fleshy crest. Swordlike leaves.	Full sun. In general, irises like deep, moist, well-drained soil rich in organic matter; specific requirements vary with species. Propagate rhizome-forming plants by division; bulbous species by offsets. Zones 3-9 (depending on species). Borders. Woodland areas. Most irises bloom in spring; some may last into summer or fall. Many cultivars available.
Paeonia officinalis (Common peony)	2-3 ft.	Red, yellow, white	Sturdy, clump-forming perennial with attractive, leathery foliage and large 3-5-in.-wide flowers that come in many forms from single to double.	Full sun for best bloom; will tolerate partial shade. Rich, humusy, well-drained soil. Propagate by division. Zones 3-8. Accents. Borders. Specimen plants. Many cultivars available.
Papaver orientale (Oriental poppy)	2-4 ft.	Red, orange, pale pink, white	Perennial with fuzzy, low clumps of foliage and very large, brilliantly colored flowers with black centers.	Full sun. Average, well-drained soil. Propagate by root cuttings, seeds. Zones 3-8. Borders. Foliage dies after flowering and reappears in late summer or fall.
Primula spp. (Primrose)	4-18 in.	Pink, purple, yellow, white, orange	Large genus of perennials usually with oval leathery leaves, and clusters of trumpet-shaped, 1-2-in.-wide flowers.	Partial shade. Rich, humusy, moist, well-drained soil. Propagate by division, seeds. Zones 4-8. Beds. Borders. Wide range of colors available. Requires moist conditions.
Trollius spp. (Globeflower)	2-3 ft.	Orange, gold, yellow, white	Perennial with finely cut dark green leaves and 1-2-in.-wide globe-shaped flowers that have a waxy texture.	Partial shade. Rich, moist to boggy soil high in organic matter. Propagate by division, seeds. Zones 5-8. Near water. Shady borders. Deadhead to prolong bloom. Best in areas with cool summers.

Spring- to Summer-Flowering

Perennial	Height	Flower Color	Description	Culture
Aquilegia spp. (Columbine)	1-3 ft.	Red, yellow, white, purple, blue, many bicolored	Genus of heavily hybridized perennials with delicate-looking, bluish-green leaves. Showy flowers have long spurs and are borne on delicate stems atop the foliage.	Partial shade. Moist but well-drained, somewhat sandy to average soil. Propagate hybrids by division. Zones 3-8. Borders. May require winter protection. A favorite of hummingbirds. Will reseed, but hybrids don't come true from seed.

(continued)

Perennial	Height	Flower Color	Description	Culture
Spring- to Summer-Flowering—continued				
Dianthus spp. (Pinks)	6-36 in.	Pink, red, white	Perennials and biennials with tufts of grasslike or broad lance-shaped leaves. Fragrant flowers held singly or in clusters on upright stalks. Blooms range from ½-2 in. across, depending on species.	Full sun. Average, well-drained, slightly alkaline soil. Propagate by cuttings, layerings, seeds. Zones 4-10 (depending on species). Borders. Rock gardens. May need winter protection. Some good for cutting.
Geranium spp. (Cranesbill, hardy geranium)	6-36 in.	White, blue, rose pink, purple	Large genus of low-growing perennials with lobed leaves and showy, 5-petaled flowers.	Full sun to partial shade. Average, moist, well-drained soil. Propagate by division, seeds. Zones 4-9. Borders. Ground covers. Rock gardens. Often confused with common garden geraniums, *Pelargonium* spp., which are grown as annuals and are not hardy.
Hemerocallis hybrids (Daylily)	12-48 in.	Yellow, orange, red, pink, maroon	Heavily hybridized genus of stout perennials with clumps of sword-shaped leaves. Clusters of large buds borne atop tall stalks open consecutively into 2-6-in., trumpet-shaped flowers, each fading after a day.	Full sun to partial shade. Moist, well-drained soil rich in organic matter. Propagate by division. Zones 3-8. Banks. Borders. Good in masses. Many cultivars available.
Heuchera sanguinea (Coralbells)	1-2 ft.	Pink, red, white	Perennial bearing many-flowered spires of dainty ¼-½-in., bell-shaped blooms on tall stems above roundish, evergreen leaves.	Full sun to partial shade. Rich, moist, well-drained soil. Propagate by division, seeds. Zones 4-8. Edging. Woodland areas. Deadhead to prolong bloom.
Iberis sempervirens (Edging candytuft)	6-12 in.	White	Mound-shaped perennial with evergreen, needlelike, dark green leaves. Plants bear many 1½-in. clusters of tiny flowers.	Full sun. Any well-drained soil. Propagate by division, cuttings, seeds. Zones 4-10. Banks. Borders. Walls. Trim back hard after flowering to promote branching. Will stop flowering if too dry.
Myosotis scorpioides (Forget-me-not)	12-20 in.	Blue	Perennial with tiny, ⅓-in. flowers borne in loose clusters above elliptical leaves.	Partial shade. Rich, moist soil with plenty of organic matter. Propagate by division, cuttings, seeds. Zones 3-8. Along shady streams. Woodland areas. Can be planted with spring-blooming bulbs.
Summer-Flowering				
Achillea spp. (Yarrow)	6-48 in.	Yellow, white, pink	A large genus of perennials with feathery, gray-green foliage. Tiny flowers are in flat many-flowered clusters from 1-4 in. wide.	Full sun. Poor to average, dry soil. Propagate by division. Zones 3-10. Borders. Drought tolerant. May be invasive. Good for cutting and drying. Deadhead to prolong bloom. Some may bloom into fall. Many cultivars available.
Astilbe × arendsii (Astilbe, false spirea)	1-4 ft.	Pink, white, red, mauve, reddish purple	Clump-forming hybrid perennials with fernlike green or bronze leaves and fluffy, spike-shaped flower heads.	Full sun to partial shade. Moist, well-drained soil rich in organic matter. Propagate by division. Zones 3-8. Borders. Good for cutting. Many cultivars available.

Perennial	Height	Flower Color	Description	Culture
Boltonia asteroides (White boltonia)	3-5 ft.	White or purple with yellow center	Tall vigorous perennial with small, narrow, blue-green leaves and abundant clusters of small, ½-in., daisylike flowers.	Full sun. Tolerates average soil, grows best in moist, fertile soil. Propagate by division. Zones 4-8. Borders. Meadow gardens.
Campanula spp. (Bellflower)	6 in.-4 ft.	Blue, white, pink, purplish blue	Large genus of sprawling to erect perennials and biennials with spikes of bell-shaped flowers and lancelike leaves. Some flower in late spring to early summer.	Full sun to partial shade. Average to rich, moist, well-drained soil. Propagate by division, seeds. Zones 3-8. Borders. Containers. Good for cutting. Small species good for edging or rock garden.
Delphinium elatum (Larkspur)	4-6 ft.	Blue, purple, white	Tall stately perennials with dense spikes of 2-in.-wide flowers.	Full sun to partial shade. Rich, moist, well-drained, slightly alkaline soil. Good conditions. Propagate by division, seeds. Zones 3-7. Borders. May need staking and winter protection. Cut back after bloom to encourage flowering.
Echinacea purpurea (Purple coneflower)	2-3 ft.	Pink or white with orange or copper centers	Stout perennial with hairy stems and leaves and large 3-4-in. daisylike flower heads with drooping outer petals and cone-shaped centers.	Full sun to partial shade. Sandy, well-drained soil. Propagate by division, root cuttings, seeds. Zones 3-10. Borders. Meadow gardens. Will tolerate sunny, dry, windy sites. Good for cutting.
Echinops ritro (Small globe thistle)	1-2 ft.	Blue	Perennial with woolly, thistle-like leaves and spiny, globe-shaped, 1½-2-in.-wide flower heads.	Full sun. Average to poor, well-drained soil. Propagate by division, root cuttings, seeds. Zones 4-9. Borders. Drought tolerant.
Gypsophila paniculata (Baby's-breath)	3-4 ft.	White	Delicate-looking perennial bearing myriads of tiny ¼-in. flowers that appear cloudlike. Stems are wiry and leaves are tiny and gray-green.	Full sun. Moist, well-drained, slightly alkaline soil. Propagate by cuttings, seeds. Zones 4-8. Rock gardens. Good for cutting. Cut back a bit after bloom to encourage more flowering.
Hosta spp. (Hosta, plantain lily)	6-36 in.	White, lilac, blue	Large genus of clump-forming perennials grown for ornamental leaves, which can be blue-green, bright green, or variegated. Leaves vary in size from 2-15 in. Plants bear clusters of bell-shaped flowers.	Partial to deep shade. Rich, moist, well-drained soil. Propagate by division. Zones 4-9. Borders. Edgings. Specimen. Grown for ornamental foliage. Many cultivars with different leaf patterns available. Some have fragrant flowers.
Lychnis chalcedonica (Maltese-cross)	2-3 ft.	Red	Perennial with dense clusters of small, 1-in.-wide cross-shaped flowers borne atop rigid stems.	Full sun to partial shade. Average, moist, well-drained soil. Propagate by division, seeds. Zones 4-8. Borders. Accent.
Platycodon grandiflorus (Balloon flower)	2-3 ft.	Blue, pink, white	Perennial with unusual 2-3-in.-wide buds resembling balloons before opening. Flowers bell-shaped on opening. Leaves are bluish green.	Full sun to partial shade. Moist, well-drained soil rich in organic matter. Propagate by division, root cuttings, seeds. Zones 4-9. Borders. Rock gardens. Long blooming period. Double-flowered forms available.

(continued)

SELECTING PERENNIALS AND BIENNIALS—*Continued*

Perennial	Height	Flower Color	Description	Culture
Summer-Flowering—continued				
Rudbeckia spp. (Coneflower, black-eyed Susan)	2-9 ft.	Golden yellow with brown, black, or green centers	Perennials and biennials with large, coarse, dark green leaves. Daisylike flowers have cone-shaped centers and drooping petals.	Full sun. Average, well-drained soil. Propagate by division, seeds. Zones 4-9. Borders. Meadow gardens. Good in masses. Some species may be invasive.
Sempervivum spp. (Houseleek, hen-and-chickens)	4-12 in.	Yellow, green, red	Succulent mat-forming perennials grown for their fleshy ½-5-in.-wide rosettes of leaves which spread by off-sets on runners surrounding a central plant. Foliage green, maroon or bicolored.	Full sun. Poor to average, well-drained soil. Hot, dry conditions. Propagate by division. Zones 5-10 (depending on species). Ground covers. Edgings. Rock gardens. Walls. Containers. Drought tolerant.
Stachys byzantina (Lamb's-ears)	10-12 in.	Pinkish purple	Vigorous perennial grown for its soft, fuzzy, silver-gray leaves that resemble lamb's ears. Small ½-in.-long flowers borne in spikes.	Full sun. Poor to average, well-drained soil. Propagate by division, seeds. Zones 4-9. Edging. Ground cover. Rock gardens. Grown primarily for foliage; many gardeners remove bloom stalks when they appear.
Veronica spp. (Speedwell)	1-3 ft.	Pink, lavender, blue	Low-growing or erect perennials with lance-shaped leaves and dense, showy 6-8-in.-long spikes of ⅛-½-in.-long flowers.	Full sun to partial shade. Average, moist, well-drained soil. Propagate by division. Zones 4-8. Borders. Low-growing species suitable for edging or ground covers. Deadhead to prolong bloom. Several species and many cultivars available.
Yucca filamentosa (Adam's-needle)	4-6 ft.	White	Clump-forming perennial with stiff, sword-like, evergreen leaves. Waxy, fragrant, bell-shaped flowers, 2 in. across, borne in large clusters atop tall, branched stems.	Full sun. Sandy, dry soil. Propagate by offsets, seeds. Zones 5-10. Accent. Beds. Large containers. Cultivars with variegated foliage available.
Summer- to Fall-Flowering				
Aster spp. (Aster)	1½-5 ft.	Purple, white, pink, blue	Stiff-stemmed perennials with lance-shaped leaves and masses of daisylike, ½-2-in. flowers.	Full sun. Average, well-drained soil. Propagate by division. Zones 4-9. Borders. Woodland areas. Wild gardens. Cut back after flowering. May need staking. Popular species include *A.* × *frikartii, A. novae-angliae,* and *A. novi-belgii.*
Chrysanthemum × morifolium (Hardy chrysanthemum)	1-4 ft.	Red, pink, white, yellow, orange, lavender, maroon	Heavily hybridized, clump-forming perennials with daisylike flowers in many forms from single to double.	Full sun to partial shade. Rich to average, moist, well-drained soil. Propagate by division. May need winter protection. Zones 3-10. Borders. Edgings. Containers. Good for cutting. Pinch to encourage branching and more flowers.
Coreopsis spp. (Tickseed)	1-3 ft.	Yellow, orange, red, red-brown	Genus of somewhat weedy perennials with daisylike single or double flowers and lance-shaped or finely divided leaves.	Full sun to partial shade. Average, well-drained soil. Propagate by division, cuttings, seeds. Zones 5-9. Beds. Borders. Meadow gardens. Deadhead to prolong bloom. Good for cutting. Some are drought tolerant. Will reseed.

Perennial	Height	Flower Color	Description	Culture
Gaillardia × grandiflora (Blanket flower)	1-3 ft.	Red, orange, or yellow; petals may be bicolored	Perennial with showy, 3-4-in.-wide daisylike flowers. Centers may be red, yellow, brown, or purple.	Full sun. Poor to average, dry, well-drained soil. Propagate by division, root cuttings, seeds. Zones 3-8. Borders. Coastal areas. Drought tolerant. Good for cutting. Tall forms may need staking; dwarf cultivars mound-forming. Cut back after flowering.
Helenium spp. (Sneezeweed)	5-6 ft.	Yellow with golden centers	Tall, somewhat rangy perennial with many-branched stems and numerous, 2-in.-wide daisylike flowers with prominent, buttonlike centers.	Full sun. Rich, moist, well-drained soil. Propagate by division, seeds. Zones 3-9. Borders. Meadow gardens. Good for cutting. May need staking.
Liatris spp. (Blazing-star, gay-feather)	3-4 ft.	Lavender	Perennial with tufts of dark green, grasslike leaves and tall, feathery spikes of flowers that open from the top downward.	Full sun. Rich, moist, well-drained, somewhat sandy soil. Propagate by division, seeds. Zones 4-8. Borders. Meadow gardens. Good for cutting. Good in masses.
Monarda didyma (Bee balm)	2½-3 ft.	Red	Perennial with tall square stems, aromatic leaves, and 2-3-in. clusters of small tubular flowers.	Full sun to partial shade. Rich, moist, humusy soil. Propagate by division. Zones 4-9. Borders. Woodland areas. May become invasive. Attracts bees and hummingbirds.
Phlox paniculata (Garden phlox)	2-4 ft.	White, pink, lavender, purple	Perennials with showy, trumpet-shaped flowers, 1 in. across, borne in large clusters.	Full sun to partial shade. Rich, humusy, moist, well-drained soil. Propagate by division, root cuttings. Zones 4-9. Borders. Good for cutting. Deadhead to prolong bloom. Many cultivars available. Other species of phlox bloom in early spring to summer.
Salvia spp. (Sage)	2-8 ft.	Blue, purple, red, white	Perennial or biennial plants with small 2-lipped flowers arranged in dense spikes.	Full sun. Poor to average, well-drained soil. Propagate by division, cuttings, seeds. Zones 4-9 (depending on species). Borders. Some good for cutting. May need staking.
Sedum spp. (Stonecrop)	2-36 in.	White, pink, red, yellow	Large genus of succulent-leaved perennials, some of which trail along ground, others of which are upright. Tiny, star-shaped flowers borne in dense or flat clusters.	Full sun to partial shade. Grows in any well-drained soil. Hot, dry conditions. Propagate by division, cuttings. Zones 4-10. Rock walls and gardens. Some are good in flower beds. *S. spectabile* and its cultivars most often grown for fall bloom.
Tradescantia × andersoniana (Spiderwort hybrids)	1-2 ft.	Red, white, blue, purple	Clump-forming perennial with grasslike leaves and clusters of 1-in., 3-petaled flowers.	Full sun to partial shade. Average to rich, moist, well-drained soil. Propagate by division. Zones 5-9. Borders. Woodland areas. Often sold as *T. virginiana*. May be invasive.

There are many ways to support perennials that sag or flop over. Tie spike-forming plants such as delphiniums or lupine to stakes driven in the ground.

Summer—Maintaining the Garden

Summer brings the rewards of spring preparation. Many perennials are at their peak bloom, the spring rush to get the garden going is over, and there's more time to enjoy the flowers and fragrances that make a perennial garden so alluring. Make notes about what plants you'd like to add to your garden for next season, and take time to enjoy the butterflies that flit from flower to flower, too.

Weeding

Not only perennial flowers are in peak growth now; weeds are also racing to set seed and renew themselves for next year. Make once-a-week weeding a routine. If you have only a minute or two to spare, at least make a once-through pass and pull all weeds that are about to set seed. You'll thank yourself next year!

Mulching

Keep renewing the mulch to maintain a thick layer that will hold moisture in the soil, keep the soil cool, and discourage weeds. As the mulch decomposes, it's enriching the soil.

Watering

Even with mulch, you should keep an eye on soil moisture. Wiggle your finger an inch or two into the earth. If it's dry, then it's time for a long, deep soaking.

Staking

Keep those tall plants secure by adding another layer of twine or wire as the plants grow. Be sure the stakes are pushed deep into the ground so the plant doesn't keel over when it gets top-heavy with bloom.

Pinching

Beginning in late spring or early summer, encourage perennials like chrysanthemums to branch by pinching out the tips of the stems. The plants will be bushier and produce more flowers. Removing side buds on plants like delphinium (*Delphinium* spp.) and foxglove (*Digitalis* spp.) will lead to a bigger single flower. On the other hand, disbudding—by removing the main flower bud on these same plants—will produce a wealth of smaller side flowers.

Deadheading

A plant's goal in life is to reproduce itself, and making seeds takes a lot of energy. Removing faded blossoms will help your perennials remain vigorous. It also means a bonus of extending the blooming season for most perennials—or even causing another flush of bloom in late summer. Deadheading prevents invasive plants from self-sowing themselves throughout the garden, and it keeps the garden looking neat.

Snip off the faded blossoms individually, if there are more buds or blooms on the stem. Trim a stem with leaves, such as Japanese anemone (*Anemone × hybrida*), to the first leaves below the dead flower. Stalks that lack buds or leaves can be sliced off at ground level.

Deadheading, or removing spent blooms as they fade, helps extend the blooming season and directs a plant's energy into flowers and foliage rather than seed.

Pruning

Cutting back perennials stimulates new growth and prevents straggly, weak plants. Mat-forming plants, such as edging candytuft (*Iberis sempervirens*), rock cress (*Arabis* spp. and *Aubrieta* spp.), garden pinks (*Dianthus* spp.), moss pink (*Phlox subulata*), and creeping phlox (*P. stolonifera*), benefit from a crewcut when they're done flowering. Prune them back hard with a pair of shears to about one-half their original height to keep them neat and attractive and also to encourage bushy growth. This technique is often referred to as shearing.

Taller plants that bloom in one flush of flowers, like golden marguerites (*Anthemis tinctoria*), painted daisies (formerly *Pyrethrum* or *Chrysanthemum coccineum* but now *Tanacetum coccineum*), cranesbills (*Geranium* spp.), and sundrops (*Oenothera* spp.), respond well to a trimming. Cut these back to about one-half their height after flowering. Removing the spent flower spikes from delphiniums stimulates blooming of side flowers, just like the broccoli in the vegetable garden.

Fall—Get Ready for a Long Winter's Nap

Too often, fall is a forgotten season in perennial gardens. If your garden has faded by the end of summer, think about adding some fall color for next season. Native New England asters (*Aster novae-angliae*), chrysanthemums, and *Sedum* 'Autumn Joy' all bloom in fall. Also consider adding ornamental grasses, which come into their glory late in the season. (See "Ornamental Grasses" on page 168.)

Maintenance

Continue deadheading and trimming back. If autumn is dry, water your perennials thoroughly as usual.

After frost, you can cut to the ground your perennials that normally die back—or you can let the stems and flower heads stand, to add interest to the winter landscape. Old flower heads of *Sedum* 'Autumn Joy', purple coneflowers (*Echinacea* spp.), and black-eyed Susans (*Rudbeckia* spp.) are lovely when they catch the snow.

Mulching

Perennials are mulched deeply for winter after the ground has frozen, not to protect them from the cold but to insulate them from alternating cycles of freezing and thawing. Repeated freezing/thawing cycles can damage roots and crowns and even heave your plants right out of the ground. Use a mulch that won't mat down and smother the crowns. A blanket of chopped oak leaves, salt hay, or pine branches, alone or in layers, will all add insulation.

Winter— The Gardener's Time to Dream

Plan on Paper

This is the season to plan that perfect garden you'll have next year, the one with no drought, no bugs, no disease, and perfectly color-coordinated flowers that bloom from spring to frost. Send for catalogs and make lists and diagrams.

The Perfect Winter Mulch

It's also the time to make your neighbors wonder about your mental stability. If you can bear funny looks, take advantage of the wonderful natural insulation when snow falls and shovel as much of it as you can *onto* your perennial beds. A thick snow quilt is great for a gardener's peace of mind—no worrying about whether your leaf mulch has blown away or if the layer of pine branches is thick enough. Snow is perfect protection.

Dividing Perennials

It is rewarding to see the lush clump of fragrant 'Hyperion' daylilies grown from the puny bare roots you planted only a few years ago. But you have noticed that you are not seeing as many flowers as you did last year. And the daylily has elbowed out its neighbors on both sides, threatening the whole corner of the garden. It's time to divide.

Many perennials become overgrown in only a few years, taking up too much space or becoming so crowded that flowering is affected. Others spread on the edges but stop blooming at the centers of the clumps —either because they're too crowded or because the center is old and woody. Root division is the way to revitalize your favorite perennials for better bloom—and make more of them at the same time.

Spring is the best time to divide most perennials, when growth has just begun and the plants are only a few inches high. The general rule here is the sooner, the better. Early fall, with its cooler temperatures and more frequent rain, is also a good time for dividing, and the best time to divide early spring bloomers like the low-growing *Phlox* species (*P. sub-ulata, P. stolonifera,* and *P. divaricata*). With careful treatment, though, most perennials can be divided any time it fits into your schedule, though they'll need coddling to get through hot, dry spells.

FAST-GROWING PERENNIALS

Revitalize the following perennials and keep them in bounds by dividing every year or at least every two years.

Achillea spp. (yarrow)
Anthemis tinctoria (golden marguerite)
Artemisia spp. (wormwood)
Aster spp. (aster)
Boltonia asteroides (white boltonia)
Cerastium tomentosum (snow-in-summer)
Chrysanthemum spp. (hardy chrysanthemum, daisy)
Eupatorium spp. (boneset)
Helenium spp. (sneezeweed)
Helianthus spp. (sunflower)
Lysimachia spp. (loosestrife)
Monarda didyma (bee balm)
Physostegia virginiana (obedient plant)
Rudbeckia spp. (coneflower, black-eyed Susan)
Solidago spp. (goldenrod)

When possible, use your fingers to gently tease apart entwined roots to divide a clump of perennials.

Use forks to force apart clumps of perennials with thickly matted roots.

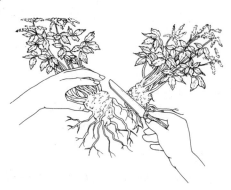

Thick, fleshy rhizomes can be sliced apart with a sharp knife.

Before you begin dividing, prepare the new homes for your divisions. The sooner you replant the divisions, the quicker they'll recover. If you're going to be giving the baby plants away, dampen some newspaper for wrapping the divisions.

How to Divide

Whatever the season, there are two ways to approach the task of dividing perennials. You can either dig the entire clump with a garden fork or sharp spade, or remove sections of the plant while the mother plant remains in the ground relatively undisturbed. If you're dividing in late summer or early fall—after the plant has bloomed—clip the foliage back to make it easier to handle.

When you're breaking a clump apart into manageable divisions, as with many garden chores, the best tools for the job are right at the ends of your wrists. Your own two hands are gentler and more sensitive than a spade or fork, especially when it comes to teasing apart tangled roots.

Low-growing plants with small or shallow root systems—like many of the violets and sedums—can be divided by hand. You can simply break pieces from the clump or dig sections while the main plant remains in the ground. Always make sure two or three healthy growing shoots are attached to the division. Plants with

creeping roots, such as bee balm (*Monarda didyma*) and sundrops (*Oenothera* spp.), are even easier. Just use a spade to remove a piece of the mother plant—stems, roots, and soil—and plop it into the soil in a new spot. You can do this with or without digging the entire plant.

Deeper-rooted clumps can be brought back to size by using a spade to slice off divisions from the outside of the plant. If the plant needs a complete overhaul, though, it's best to lift the entire clump from the ground with a spade or garden fork. Loosen the clump from all sides before lifting,

INDIVISIBLE PERENNIALS

Some perennials, especially those with fleshy taproots that are easily broken, resent being disturbed. Avoid dividing these plants; if you must, dig deeply and take precautions to minimize stress.

Aconitum spp. (monkshood)

Alcea rosea (hollyhock)

Anemone × hybrida (Japanese anemone)

Aquilegia spp. (columbine)

Asclepias tuberosa (butterfly weed)

Campanula spp. (bellflower)

Delphinium spp. (delphinium)

Dianthus spp. (garden pinks)

Dicentra spectabilis (bleeding-heart)

Dictamnus albus (gas plant)

Gypsophila paniculata (baby's-breath)

Iberis sempervirens (edging candytuft)

Kniphofia uvaria (red-hot-poker)

Lavandula spp. (lavender)

Limonium spp. (sea lavender)

Linum perenne (perennial flax)

Lupinus spp. (lupine)

Papaver orientale (Oriental poppy)

Penstemon spp. (beard-tongue)

Perovskia spp. (Russian sage)

Platycodon grandiflorus (balloon flower)

Ruta graveolens (rue)

Sedum spectabile (showy stonecrop)

Stem cuttings, root cuttings, basal cuttings, seed: There's more ways than root division to fill your garden with new perennials. See "Plant Propagation" on page 91 for more information.

and be sure to dig deep enough to get beneath the roots.

After lifting the clump, consider the best way to divide it. If the roots are not too intertwined, you may be able to pull sections apart by hand. But if the roots are a matted, solid mass, you will have to resort to stronger methods. Plants with tough crowns or rhizomatous growth can be divided by using a strong, sharp knife to sever the crown into sections, each with roots and growth buds. Perennials with matted roots, such as daylilies, hostas, and garden phlox, are best divided by using the power of leverage. After lifting, force two garden forks —closely back-to-back—down into the clump. Then push the handles apart (this may take a few tries) to split the clump of roots. Repeat as often as needed to separate the plant into divisions of manageable size.

With a knife or pruner, trim any damaged, dead, or rotten roots from your division. Replant and water liberally until new growth begins. If you are dividing a perennial that has died out in the center of the clump, cut away and discard the portion at the center of the plant that has ceased blooming. Then replant the new growth found at the edges of the clump.

Growing Biennials

What would a June border be without the drooping bells of foxglove (*Digitalis purpurea*), cheerful, old-fashioned hollyhocks (*Alcea rosea*), or an abundance of pink and lavender Canterbury-bells (*Campanula medium*)? Biennials like these offer some of the best flowering plants, many of them familiar from old cottage gardens, if you can spare a little space in the garden and a little patience. Biennials help the gardener learn the virtues of delayed gratification. They produce only leaves the first year, follow with flowers and seeds the second year, and then the plants die.

Most biennials are as easy to grow as marigolds. They can be sown outdoors in spring or late summer. Just sprinkle a packet of seeds into a nursery bed or right where you want the plants to bloom, and water with a fine spray. If you sow seeds into a nursery bed in spring, transplant the seedlings to where they are to bloom at least six weeks before the first hard frost to give the plants time to settle in. Mulch well over winter. If you sow into a nursery bed in summer, move the plants to where they are to bloom as early in spring as you can lift them from the ground.

Some biennials will survive another year if you cut back the flowering stems to the basal rosette of leaves as soon as the flowers fade. But you'll get better bloom by sowing new seed. In fact, if you add the sowing of biennials to your yearly garden calendar, you'll have an ongoing supply of these undemanding flowers. Many biennials such as sweet William (*Dianthus barbatus*), Johnny-jump-up (*Viola tri-*

color), honesty (*Lunaria annua*), English daisy (*Bellis perennis*), foxglove (*Digitalis purpurea*), Canterbury-bells (*Campanula medium*), and hollyhocks (*Alcea rosea*) are happy to seed themselves in the garden, if you let a few seedheads mature on the old plants.

Controlling Invasive Perennials

If yours is the ideal garden soil—rich, loose loam, high in organic matter— the perennials called invasive mean trouble. But if you struggle along with heavy clay soil, you may welcome the vigor that invasive perennials might bring to your garden. And if you're a new gardener on a tight budget, invasives are a sure way to fill out a border in a hurry.

Invasive perennials are just that: If you turn your back, they'll take over your garden. Some move more quickly than others; some are easier to control than others. Since many spread by creeping underground runners, loose soil means they'll move fast to colonize a big area.

With these plants, control is the key. Some of the most dependable garden flowers belong to the group

INVASIVE PERENNIALS

The following perennials are infamous for their ability to run rampant through the garden. Keep your eye on them.

Acanthus spp. (bear's-breech)

Achillea spp., especially *A. ptarmica* 'The Pearl' (yarrow)

Anchusa spp. (bugloss)

Artemisia spp., especially *A. ludoviciana* var. *albula* 'Silver King' (wormwood)

Aster spp. (Michaelmas daisy)

Campanula spp. (bellflower)

Cantanache caerulea (Cupid's-dart)

Centaurea cyanus (bachelor's-button)

Chelone glabra (turtlehead)

Chrysanthemum spp. (hardy chrysanthemum, daisy)

Echinacea spp. (purple coneflower)

Echinops ritro (small globe thistle)

Eupatorium coelestinum (mist flower)

Euphorbia spp. (spurge)

Lysimachia spp. (loosestrife)

Macleaya cordata (plume poppy)

Mentha spp. (mint)

Monarda didyma (bee balm)

Nepeta spp. (catmint)

Oenothera spp. (evening primrose, sundrops)

Physalis alkekengi (Chinese-lantern)

Physostegia virginiana (obedient plant)

Rudbeckia spp. (black-eyed Susan)

Stachys byzantina (lamb's-ears)

Solidago spp. (goldenrod)

Tradescantia virginiana (spiderwort)

Verbascum spp. (mullein)

of scorned invasives, but they can be invited to your garden if you use a few precautions and remain alert.

Barriers are the only sure way of keeping invasives with creeping runners in check. A fence or wall can form one side of the barricade, although the most determined invasives will creep through that fence eventually. Strips of galvanized sheet metal, sunk to a depth of at least 12 inches, can form the perimeter of a planting. Lawn edging sunk deep in the ground will be somewhat discouraging, too. A bucket or plastic pot, with holes poked in the bottom for drainage, buried in the garden with the top at surface level or even a bit above, can keep most enthusiastic perennials where you want them as long as the container is at least 12 inches deep. Otherwise, the roots and

Pots, buckets, or dishpans with holes punched in the bottom can also be put into service for containing invasive perennials.

runners will just go under to get around. Another alternative is lengths of ceramic pipe buried in the garden.

Other invasives spread throughout a garden by self-sown seeds. Vigilant deadheading will keep these in check, and seedlings are easy to scratch out in spring.

Wildflowers

Growing Wildflowers

Anyone who has enjoyed the beauty of a spring woodland carpeted with Virginia bluebells (*Mertensia virginica*) and bloodroot (*Sanguinaria canadensis*), or a colorful autumn meadow bursting with butterfly weed (*Asclepias tuberosa*) and goldenrod (*Solidago* spp.), has felt the magic of wildflowers. These plants also hold a special fascination because they thrive in all sorts of conditions—from dry, desert soils to boggy sites, and from full sun to deep shade—all without a gardener's helping hand. Not only are there wildflowers for nearly every part of the garden, they also require little maintenance, provided they're happy with the conditions in which they've been planted.

The key to growing wildflowers successfully is understanding the conditions they require in their native habitats. Wildflowers will grow best in locations that duplicate their native environments. Soil type, monthly rainfall, annual temperature range, and sunlight or exposure are all important. To pick the best wildflowers for your garden, try to find plants that naturally thrive in the conditions your garden has to offer. If you have a tree-shaded lot with loamy soil, for example, perhaps some of the Eastern woodland wildflowers such as wild columbine (*Aquilegia canadensis*) or Jacob's ladder (*Polemonium* spp.) would be suitable. Or, if you have a dry, sun-baked spot, consider planting California poppies (*Eschscholzia californica*), a reseeding annual, or one of the hardy prickly-pear cacti

(continued on page 148)

WILD PLANTS FOR CULTIVATED GARDENS

It's not likely you'll forget wildflowers when planning your flower garden. Many native plants are so much a part of our gardens that we often forget that they're wildflowers. You may decide to grow one of the improved cultivars of the species listed below, such as a fancy form of garden phlox (*Phlox paniculata*) or *Rudbeckia* 'Goldsturm', for example. But for an authentic wildflower garden, choose the species rather than an improved form. Don't forget they are all originally native Americans.

Aquilegia spp. (columbine)
Aster novae-angliae (New England aster)
Baptisia australis (blue false indigo)
Coreopsis spp. (coreopsis, calliopsis)
Echinacea purpurea (purple coneflower)
Eschscholzia californica (California poppy)
Gaillardia aristata (Indian blanket)
Geranium maculatum (wild geranium)
Helenium spp. (sneezeweed)
Helianthus annuus (common sunflower)
Liatris spp. (blazing-star, gay-feather)
Mertensia virginica (Virginia bluebell)
Monarda didyma (beebalm)
Oenothera spp. (evening primrose, sundrops)
Penstemon spp. (beard-tongue)
Phlox spp. (garden phlox, wild sweet William)
Rudbeckia spp. (coneflower, black-eyed Susan)

Native or Naturalized?

Surprisingly, many of the plants we call wildflowers are not native to this country at all. Many species have escaped from cultivation and have made themselves at home—spreading throughout the countryside in habitats that suit their liking. These plants, called alien or naturalized species, may be pictured in field guides with notes about their origin. They include oxeye daisy (*Leucanthemum vulgare*), yarrow (*Achillea* spp.), Japanese honeysuckle (*Lonicera japonica*), turtlehead (*Chelone* spp.), teasel (*Dipsacus* spp.), and Queen-Anne's-lace or wild carrot (*Daucus carota* var. *carota*).

145

SELECTING AND GROWING WILDFLOWERS

There are literally hundreds of native wildflowers from which to choose. As you'll read in the pages that follow, the best wildflowers for your garden are ones naturally adapted to your site. The following plants (listed for sun and shade) are a good place to start because they'll grow throughout much of the country. Also see "Wild Plants for Cultivated Gardens" for a list of wildflowers so often grown in gardens we sometimes forget they're wildflowers. You'll find cultural information for many of these plants in the charts at the beginning of the annuals and perennials sections.

Wildflower	Height	Flower Color	Description	Culture
For Sun				
Asclepias tuberosa (Butterfly weed)	1-3 ft.	Orange	Perennial species related to milkweed with clusters of tiny, bright orange flowers in summer. Shrubby habit.	Full sun. Poor, well-drained soil. Propagate by root cuttings, seeds. Deep rooted, resents division. Zones 4-8. Meadow gardens. Borders. Attracts butterflies. Drought tolerant.
Aster novae-angliae (New England aster)	1½-6½ ft.	Violet-purple	Perennial species with lance-shaped leaves and stiff stems that support late-fall clusters of 2-in., daisylike flowers.	Full sun. Average, well-drained soil. Propagate by division. Zones 4-9. Meadow gardens. Borders. Many cultivars available. Cut back after flowering. *A. novi-belgii* is another popular native aster.
Coreopsis spp. (Tickseed, calliopsis)	2-3 ft.	Yellow with maroon, purple, or brown centers	Perennials and annuals with single or double, daisylike flowers with toothed petals borne in summer to fall.	Full sun to partial shade. Any well-drained soil. Propagate by division, cuttings, seeds. Zones 4-9. Meadow gardens. Borders. Drought tolerant. Good for cutting.
Oenothera spp. (Evening primrose, sundrop)	1-5 ft.	Yellow, white	Perennials or annuals with 2-3-in.-wide, glossy, often fragrant, flowers borne in clusters in summer.	Full sun to partial shade. Poor, well-drained soil. Propagate by division, seeds. Zones 4-10 (depending on species). Meadow gardens. Borders. May be invasive. Drought tolerant. Flowers of some species open in the evening; others during the day.
Lupinus spp. (Lupine)	1-3 ft.	Blue, violet, white, pink, yellow	Perennials and annuals with silky, palmate leaves and small pealike flowers borne in spikes in spring and summer.	Full sun to partial shade. Well-drained, rich soil. Requires cool, humid conditions. Propagate by division, seeds. Zones 3-10. Meadow gardens. Borders. Good for cutting. Will tolerate dry or alkaline soil.
Opuntia spp. (Prickly-pear cactus)	4-8 in.	Yellow	Hardy perennial with flat, fleshy leaves, and showy, yellow, 2-4-in. flowers in summer followed by red or purplish fruits.	Full sun. Sandy, very well-drained soil. Propagate by division, cuttings. Zones 5-10. Rock gardens. Very drought tolerant. Usually prostrate in habit. Some species lack spines.
Penstemon spp. (Beard-tongue)	2-4 ft.	Blue, white, red, purple, yellow	Large genus of perennials with spikes of snapdragon-like flowers borne in summer.	Full sun to partial shade. Moist, well-drained soil. Propagate by division, seeds. Zones 4-10. Meadow gardens. Woodland gardens. Borders.
Ratibida columnifera (Prairie coneflower)	1-3½ ft.	Red or yellow with brown centers	Summer-blooming perennial with daisylike flowers that have cone-shaped centers.	Full sun. Any well-drained soil. Propagate by seeds. Zones 3-10. Meadow gardens. Borders. Drought tolerant.

Wildflower	Height	Flower Color	Description	Culture
Sisyrinchium spp. (Blue-eyed grass)	4-20 in.	Violet-blue with yellow centers	Grassy-looking, clump-forming perennial related to irises with tiny 6-petaled flowers borne in loose clusters from spring to summer.	Full sun to partial shade. Loamy well-drained soil. Propagate by division, seeds. Zones 3-10. Meadow gardens. Borders. Drought tolerant. Will reseed.
Solidago spp. (Goldenrod)	1-7 ft.	Golden yellow	Perennial species related to daisies with showy, plumelike clusters of tiny flowers borne in late summer to fall.	Full sun. Average to poor, well-drained soil. Propagate by division, seeds. Zones 4-10. Meadow gardens. Borders. May be invasive.

For Shade

Wildflower	Height	Flower Color	Description	Culture
Arisaema triphyllum (Jack-in-the-pulpit)	1-2 ft.	Purple and green	Unique perennial that grows from a corm. Spring-borne flowers consist of spathe (the pulpit) surrounding a spadix (the "Jack").	Partial to deep shade. Rich, moist soil. Propagate by seeds. Zones 5-9. Woodland gardens.
Cimicifuga racemosa (Black snakeroot)	6-8 ft.	White	Summer-blooming perennial with dark green leaves and tall stalks topped by bottle-brush-shaped flowers.	Partial to deep shade. Rich, moist, well-drained soil. Propagate by division. Zones 3-9. Woodland gardens. Shady borders.
Dicentra eximia (Wild bleeding-heart)	1-2 ft.	Pinkish purple	Delicate-leaved clump-forming perennial with spikes of nodding, 1-in.-long flowers in spring and summer.	Partial shade. Rich, moist, well-drained soil. Propagate by division. Zones 3-10. Woodland gardens. Borders. Rock gardens.
Iris cristata (Dwarf crested iris)	1-3 in.	Lilac-purple with yellow and white crests	Low-growing perennial with sword-shaped leaves and attractive 1½-in-long flowers borne in early spring.	Partial shade. Rich, well-drained soil. Propagate by division. Zones 4-10. Woodland gardens. Edgings. Borders. Rock gardens.
Mertensia virginica (Virginia bluebells)	18-24 in.	Blue	Perennial with broad, blue-green leaves and early spring clusters of pink flower buds that turn blue as they open into nodding trumpets.	Partial shade. Rich, moist, humusy soil. Propagate by seeds. Zones 3-8. Shady beds. Woodland areas. Becomes dormant in summer.
Phlox stolonifera (Creeping phlox)	8-12 in.	Violet, purple, pink	Creeping perennial with clusters of 1-in. flowers borne in spring.	Partial shade. Rich, moist, well-drained soil. Propagate by division. Zones 3-9. Woodland gardens. Shady borders. Groundcover.
Polygonatum spp. (Solomon's-seal)	2-3 ft.	White or greenish yellow	Perennial grown for its arching stems of paired leaves and spring-borne, trumpet-shaped flowers borne along the stems.	Partial to deep shade. Rich, humusy, well-drained soil. Propagate by division, seeds. Zones 3-8. Woodland gardens. Blue berries form after flowering. Variegated-leaved forms available.
Tradescantia virginiana (Common spiderwort)	1-3 ft.	Blue-purple	Perennial with grasslike leaves and small clusters of 1-3-in.-wide flowers borne spring to summer. Each opens for a day.	Partial shade. Rich, humusy, well-drained soil. Propagate by division, seeds. Zones 4-10. Woodland gardens. Borders. May be invasive. Cut back plants after flowering.
Viola spp. (Violet)	2-5 in.	Lavender, purple, yellow, white	Perennial species generally with heart-shaped leaves and ½-1-in. flowers resembling tiny pansies.	Partial to deep shade. Rich, moist soil; some species will tolerate boggy sites. Propagate by division, seeds. Zones 3-10. Woodland gardens. Rock gardens.

(*Opuntia* spp.), which bear brilliant flowers followed by interesting fruit.

Tips for Success

One good way to start developing a list of wildflowers to try in your garden is to look around you. Look at the plants that spring up in vacant lots, along roadsides, or in natural areas of nearby parks or gardens. Although often thought of as mere weeds, if they are growing in conditions similar to what your garden has to offer, they might be perfect prospects. Use a field guide to identify them, if necessary, and then look for them at your local nursery or in a mail-order catalog. You'll be surprised at how many common weeds are offered for sale.

Beware of weeds that live up to that name, however. Many native plants are quite aggressive and can spread very quickly—either by abundant reseeding or by wandering rhizomes—if not kept in check. If you have an out-of-the-way corner, this might be just what you want, but keep these plants away from areas where their thuglike tendencies might pose a problem. Members of the daisy family, Compositae, such as golden-rod (*Solidago* spp.), are notorious.

Don't try to improve upon a wildflower's natural environment. Too much moisture may be stressful for a plant adapted to withstanding summer droughts, and rich soil may lead to lush foliage but little bloom if a plant is native to areas with sandy, poor soil.

Like other plants, wildflowers are sold as seeds, bare-root, or potted. Handle new plants just as you would any annual, perennial, or bulb. (They can also be propagated by many of the same methods described in "Plant Propagation" on page 91.)

Don't forget the many wildflowers that make superb additions even to formal beds and borders. In fact, many of these plants are grown in gardens so often, we forget they are actually wildflowers. (See "Wild Plants for Cultivated Gardens" on page 145 for some suggestions.)

Acquiring Wildflowers

There are several ways to obtain wildflowers to add to your garden. They're offered for sale everywhere. One sad fact to consider when purchasing wildflowers, however, is that many plants offered for sale were collected in the wild at the expense of native populations. Virtually all of the pink lady's-slipper orchid (*Cypripedium acaule*) plants offered for sale have been wild-collected. And these beautiful native orchids have exacting requirements that nearly always doom them to death once they're dug and moved to a garden. Other plants to avoid are other native orchids; native lilies (*Lilium* species, not the popular hybrid forms); *Trillium* spp.; and carnivorous plants, such as pitcher plants (*Sarracenia* spp. and *Darlingtonia californica*).

Don't buy collected wildflowers. Ask nursery owners about the source of the native plants they sell. Do not dig plants in the wild yourself unless you are participating in an organized conservation program.

So where should you buy? Reputable nurseries are now beginning to refuse to deal in wild-collected plants and are labeling their plants as horticulturally propagated. You can also buy wildflowers from plant sales organized by botanical gardens or local native plant societies. Or propagate your own—many are easy to grow from seed, and fellow gardeners are often happy to share plants via division.

Growing a Wildflower Meadow

For most people, the word meadow brings to mind scenes of large fields filled with grasses, daisies, and other flowering plants. Or perhaps it suggests a vast expanse of prairie with head-high grass as far as the eye can see. More recently, however, the word has been linked to gardening, and gardeners across the country are experimenting with creating their own meadows, both small and large.

Meadow Options

There are many ways a meadow or meadow-style garden can be incorporated into the home ground. You can create a stylized meadow border with ornamental grasses and cultivated forms of native plants such as *Rudbeckia* 'Goldsturm', purple coneflowers (*Echinacea purpurea*), and sneezeweeds (*Helenium* spp.). If you have an uncultivated area, orchard, or old field that you simply mow to keep neat, consider letting it grow up, and sow seed or plant small potted wildflowers to add color.

If you're starting from scratch, you can use a seed mix or start with potted plants. Seed is less expensive and easier to distribute than plants, so it's is the choice of most meadow gardeners. The best mixes to select are ones designed especially for your region or garden.

Sowing a Meadow

Today many seed companies, as well as the seed rack at your local nursery, offer a wide range of wildflowers, which you can buy either as single species or in meadow mixes. Mixes are available for specific geographic (regional) hardiness ranges or for specific cultural conditions—sun or shade, dry or moist. There are also mixes selected for height and ones designed to attract birds or butterflies. Most meadow mixes will include an annual "nurse grass," which will germinate quickly and help to keep out weeds until the meadow plants have the opportunity to become established.

The key to success is in knowing what plants will do well in your specific gardening environment, and avoiding those that will not do well or that might prove invasive. Contact your local cooperative extension service or wildflower society for plant lists and other recommendations for developing a meadow in your area. Nearby botanical gardens in your area may also have demonstration meadows that you can learn from.

Compare the meadow mixes and wildflower seed offerings from several catalogs. Look at species included, the seed origin, and the price tag. Species that are native to your area will have the best chance of survival and should be tops on your list; avoid potentially invasive species. Since much of the seed offered is wild-collected, look for a statement that indicates the seed has been collected conservatively, so that collection hasn't harmed wild populations. If you collect seed yourself, be sure to do so responsibly: Always harvest much less than you leave behind.

Sowing Season. The next item on your agenda is to select the best time for seeding your meadow. Both fall and spring seeding are recommended, since cool daytime temperatures and not-too-cool nights are best for germinating seedlings. As a general rule, fall sowing is best if you live in the southern states (Zone 7 south); spring sowing in the North.

Site Preparation. You'll need to remove existing vegetation to prepare the seedbed. For a small area, try spreading black plastic over the entire site, secure it in place with dirt and rocks around the edges, and leave it for several months. This will kill existing weeds and cause weed seeds in the soil to germinate and die. You can also dig up existing weeds and cut

out turfgrass to get ready for sowing. For a large area, you'll probably need to till the area, although deep tilling will often bring dormant weed seeds to the surface. If you do decide to till, plan on tilling several times at two- to three-week intervals to kill weeds that germinate.

Prepare the Seedbed. The next step is to lightly rough the soil's surface, so that the seeds can make good contact with the soil. If you have matched your seed mixture to the site, you shouldn't need to improve the soil unless you really want to.

Spreading Seed. Next, mix the seed with light sand (the white sand used for sandboxes is ideal), using 1 part seed to 4 or 5 parts sand. This will help you keep track of where the seed has been spread and also helps ensure that it's evenly distributed. For small meadows, you can spread by hand; use a crank seed spreader (available in most seed catalogs) for larger meadows. Look at the seed packet for the recommended application. Usually, 6 pounds of seed per acre or 4 ounces per 1,000 square feet are about average. Don't sow more thickly than recommended, because seedlings will become crowded and quick-to-germinate species will crowd out ones that get off to a slower start. After sowing, lightly sweep the seedbed with a broom or nearby tree branch to settle seed just below the soil surface.

Aftercare. For best results, a newly seeded meadow will require adequate moisture—either by rain or watering—to ensure that germination takes place and young seedlings have a chance to become established. A good soaking from the lawn sprinkler every several days is often the difference between success and failure in starting the meadow. Seeds will begin to germinate within seven to ten days after sowing.

Annual Maintenance

Once established, a meadow should require little in the way of annual maintenance. Healthy, established meadow plants don't need watering and fertilizing.

Change Is Natural

Change is a fact of life in a meadow, and in a meadow garden. New plants arrive, add new color, perhaps outcompeting other inhabitants. Some plants spread quickly via their abundantly produced seeds; others disappear because of competition from neighboring plants. Shrub and tree seedlings can move in and begin the transformation from a sunny meadow to a woodland. The changing appearance—both from season to season and year to year—is one of the fascinations of a meadow. It's also one of the reasons for annual maintenance.

You'll need to weed as the need arises. If one species takes over, reestablish a balance by weeding or even removing it altogether. You may need to resow some annuals each year to keep populations healthy. Plan on a bit of hand weeding on a regular basis to remove undesirable plants.

Your meadow also will require an annual mowing to control trees and shrubs that find their way into the meadow, before they can become established. Mow in late fall or late winter when the plants are dormant. Many gardeners prefer mowing in late winter, because they enjoy the texture and color of the winter meadow and the birds and other creatures it attracts.

The best tool for the job will vary with the size of the meadow. A weed wacker or lawn mower will prove adequate for a small meadow; you'll need a tractor and mower for large meadows. Double-cutting a tractor-mowed meadow (once at a height of 18 inches and once at a height of 6 inches) will produce an excellent seedbed mulch for all of the seed that has dropped to the meadow floor.

Herbs

Planting an Herb Garden

Herbs are among the easiest plants to grow in a garden—and the most useful. Perhaps best known for their role in cooking, where they add flavor to stews, soups, vinegars, jellies, relishes, and all types of recipes, herbs also have many other uses. They have been used medicinally and in cosmetics. In arts and crafts, they lend color and fragrance to potpourris, herb baths, wreaths, and sachets. However you use herbs in your garden, you'll find that they offer fragrance, flavor, color, a sense of history—and more.

Designing an Herb Garden

You can incorporate herbs in the garden in many different ways. Combine them with annuals and perennials in beds and borders. Plant them in a kitchen garden or perhaps a cutting garden. Grow a more traditional herb garden—perhaps in a formal knot pattern (see the knot garden illustrated on the opposite page). Or simply tuck some commonly used cooking herbs in a half-barrel or a small bed outside the kitchen door so you can dash out quickly for an easy supply of fresh herbs.

The success of any good garden is based on the quality of the design and the implementation of that design. Take time before you plant to think about what herbs you want to grow, what you'll use them for, and what

sites you have that would suit their cultural needs. For example, if you want a steady supply of fresh herbs for cooking, choose a convenient place for daily harvest. If you are growing a large supply for drying, on the other hand, convenience isn't such an issue.

Style

Select a style that complements the house or building nearest to the garden. Herb gardens are often used for historic sites because they can be used to represent almost any time period. A dooryard garden would be suitable for a colonial-style house. This informal style of herb garden, actually a type of cottage garden, provides a warm welcome to all visitors coming to the house. This style came to America with the early colonists and was primarily utilitarian. Herbs were planted near the front door for easy access; herbs such as tansy (*Tanacetum vulgare*) also had value in keeping insects out of the house.

A Victorian garden displaying herbs in containers or in flower beds is another possibility. Although the Victorians did not grow herbs in great quantity, there was some carryover from colonial gardens. They especially loved herbs used for fragrance, as well as those with special meaning. (Perhaps the best known herb for this purpose is rosemary, for remembrance.) A garden using herbs in the Victorian style should include some

of the Hybrid Perpetual roses that were so popular during the Victorian era and are a symbol of love.

Modern herb gardens tend to blend herbs with complimentary plants. Herbs can create a lovely garden at the entrance to any house or building and can be blended beautifully with other plants, particularly old roses or perennials. At long last, herbs are being recognized as important ornamentals worthy of being grown in all types of gardens—formal or informal, historic or modern. Use herbs as border plants along walkways to soften harsh edges or in containers, on balconies, rooftops, or patios. There are limitless possibilities for the use of herbs in the landscape.

Herbs in Nooks and Crannies

Although the subject of herb lawns is often covered in gardening books, using herbs in this manner generally works better in theory than in reality. Even in the finest of English gardens, an herb lawn is something that requires a great deal of work and considerable maintenance.

That said, if you still want the challenge of a thyme or chamomile lawn, plan on starting with plants rather than seeds to avoid severe weed competition. The two best plants to use are Roman chamomile (*Chamaemelum nobile*) and caraway thyme (*Thymus herba-barona*) because they are both durable and fragrant. Plant Roman chamomile on 6-inch centers in a moderately rich, well-drained soil. Be aware that Roman chamomile sometimes dies out in spots, leaving bare areas. Caraway thyme, on the other hand, is about the toughest herb for a lawn. It will create a thick, dark green mat within one year if planted in full sun in moderately rich, well-drained soil. Because the plants attract bees when in bloom, be sure to block off the lawn during their flowering time or prune back the blossoms. You'll need to water regularly until the plants become established.

Roman chamomile and caraway thyme are also excellent to use on benches constructed so that the seat is actually a bed in which plants are grown, a tradition in many European gardens. These and other herbs can also be included for planting in the nooks and crannies between rocks in a wall or along a walkway. Some are fine for rock gardens. The best of the very small thymes to grow in between bricks or stone on a walkway is mother-of-thyme (*Thymus praecox* subsp. *arcticus*), which comes in a red-, white-, or pink-flowered form. Again, it's best to begin with plants rather than seeds because it gets the planting off to a good, quick start. In fact, many herbs such as thymes are variable when grown from seed, producing many inferior hybrids. So it's best to avoid seed-grown plants altogether.

Other herbs to consider for use as groundcovers include sweet woodruff (*Asperula odorata*), which will grow well in moist shade; wild strawberry (*Fragaria virginiana*), which is perfect for a sunny spot in a naturalized garden; pennyroyal (*Mentha pulegium*), another sun-lover hardy only to Zone 7; and golden lemon thyme (*Thymus × citriodorus* 'Aureus'), a creeping thyme grown for its attractive golden foliage.

Knot Gardens

A traditional knot garden is another possibility for a small, formal herb planting. Knot gardens were at their peak of popularity in Elizabethan England, when it was fashionable to include a knot as an essential component of any garden. All knot gardens featured fragrant herbs, the clippings of which were used for scenting linens and fabrics. There are a variety of knot garden styles from which to choose. (One pattern is illustrated below.)

Here are the main points to consider when thinking about and planning a knot garden.

● Place the garden where it can be viewed from above so the interlocking chains will be fully appreciated.

● Be sure the site has excellent drainage before you plant. If there is any doubt, either relocate the garden or consider adding a system of drain tiles.

● Select only plants that thrive in your area and that are completely hardy.

● Do not plan a large knot garden because when plants die, replacement plants are often hard to locate.

● Be sure to use plenty of evergreens so your knot will be interesting to look at in the winter as well as summer.

● Plan on pruning the plants in the knot from early spring through midsummer, as needed. Don't sim-

(continued on page 155)

Low-growing shrubs are traditionally used to edge a knot garden, with individual "strands" of the knot planted in different colors. Consider green santolina (*Santolina virens*) combined with silver gray-leaved lavender cotton (*S. chamaecyparissus*). Other edging plants include English lavender (*Lavandula angustifolia*), germander (*Teucrium chamaedrys*), crimson pigmy barberry (*Berberis thunbergii* 'Crimson Pigmy'), or dwarf cultivars of juniper (*Juniperus* spp.).

SELECTING AND GROWING HERBS

The plants we call herbs are among the most useful in the garden. They are essential ingredients for flavorful dishes, and also in such diverse activities as crafts and medicine. Herbs are attractive in any garden, providing interesting textures and colors. Some offer delightful scents when you brush by them; others attract pollinators. Many have interesting histories. The following are a few of the most common and useful herbs. Give them a try in your garden!

Herb	Height	Description	Culture	Comments and Uses
Basil, sweet (*Ocimum basilicum*)	1-2 ft.	Bushy annual with fragrant, oval, 2-3-in.-long leaves. Yellow-green leaves; maroon-leaved cultivars available.	Full sun. Rich, moist, well-drained soil. Propagate by seeds.	Excellent fresh or dried in tomato-based dishes; pesto. Plant in herb or flower gardens. Thought to benefit tomato plants when grown near them. Can be stored frozen.
Bay, sweet (*Laurus nobilis*)	10-40 ft. (to 5 ft. in pot culture)	Fragrant evergreen shrub with thick, dark green, leathery leaves.	Full sun to partial shade. Moderately rich, well-drained soil. Propagate by cuttings. Zones 8-10.	Fresh or dried leaves add wonderful flavoring to foods, sauces. Dried leaves used in wreaths. Plant in containers and winter indoors in north.
Borage, common (*Borago officinalis*)	2-3 ft.	Annual with hollow, hairy stems and large, hairy leaves. Attractive star-shaped, blue flowers.	Full sun. Fairly rich, moist, light soil. Sow seed outdoors after last frost. Will reseed.	Leaves and stems have cucumber-like flavor and are used raw or steamed. Plant in wildflower garden. Attracts bees.
Catnip (*Nepeta cataria*)	1-3 ft.	Perennial mint-family member with square stems and coarse, gray-green leaves that are fragrant when crushed.	Full sun to partial shade. Average, sandy, well-drained soil. Propagate by division, seeds. Zones 3-9.	Cats enjoy toys stuffed with dried leaves.
Chamomile, German (*Matricaria recutita*)	2-3 ft.	Annual with fuzzy feather-like leaves and daisylike flowers.	Full sun. Sandy, well-drained soil. Sow outdoors in spring or fall. Will reseed.	Makes a soothing tea. Adds applelike fragrance of leaves to sachets or arrangements. Fragrant when crushed. Thought to benefit cucumbers and onions when grown near them.
Chamomile, Roman (*Chamaemelum nobile*)	9-12 in.	Low-growing perennial with single or double, daisylike flowers on fuzzy stems.	Full sun. Rich, well-drained soil. Propagate by division, cuttings, seeds. Zones 3-10.	Makes a soothing tea. Can be used as a lawn substitute. Garnish salads with edible flowers. Thought to benefit cabbages and onion plants when grown near them.
Chervil (*Anthriscus cerefolium*)	1-2 ft.	Annual with delicate fern-like foliage and small white flowers.	Partial shade. Humusy, moist, soil. Propagate by seeds sown where the plants are to grow. Seed requires light to germinate.	Add to soups, stews, just before serving for best flavor. Flowers are used in bouquets. Sow seeds at 2-week intervals for consistent supply.
Chives (*Allium schoenoprasum*)	1-1½ ft.	Clump-forming, grasslike perennial with tiny bulbs and hollow leaves. Flowers borne in round, ½-in. clusters.	Full sun. Average, sandy, dry, well-drained soil. Propagate by division, seeds. Zones 4-10.	Use leaves fresh or dried for mild onion flavor. Dried flowers attractive in arrangements. Ornamental for borders, edging.

Herb	Height	Description	Culture	Comments and Uses
Clary (*Salvia sclarea*)	3-4 ft.	Biennial with hairy, square stems and heart-shaped aromatic leaves with a balsamlike fragrance. Spikes of ½-1-in.-long, 2-lipped flowers.	Full sun. Average, sandy, dry, well-drained soil. Propagate by seeds.	Use leaves and flowers in food or tea. Adds balsamlike fragrance to potpourris. Plant in herb or flower garden.
Coriander (*Coriandrum sativum*)	2-3 ft.	Annual with bright green carrot-like bottom foliage and tiny linear top leaves.	Full sun to partial shade. Moderately rich, light, well-drained soil. Propagate by seeds sown where the plants are to grow.	Leaves and roots are added to foods for a bold flavor. Seeds have citrus taste. Attractive plant for borders. Attracts bees; makes good honey.
Dill (*Anethum graveolens*)	2½-3 ft.	Annual with feathery, blue-green foliage with a tangy fragrance. Flat, pale yellow flower clusters yield seeds also used for flavoring.	Full sun. Moderately rich, moist, well-drained soil. Propagate by seeds sown where the plants are to grow. Will reseed.	Seeds and leaves are used in all types of cooking for their strong, tangy flavor. Flowers and leaves dry well. Can be stored frozen.
Fennel (*Foeniculum vulgare*)	3-4 ft.	Nonhardy perennial with feathery, blue-green foliage with a mild, aniselike flavor. Usually grown as annual.	Full sun. Average, well-drained soil. Propagate by seeds sown where the plants are to grow. Will reseed. Zones 9-10.	Use fresh leaves in salads; seeds in desserts, bread, beverages. Stems can be eaten like celery.
Horseradish (*Armoracia rusticana*)	2-3 ft.	Perennial with white, hairy, wrinkly root and large, fleshy, dark green leaves.	Full sun. Rich, moist, heavy soil. Propagate by division, root cuttings. Zones 5-8.	Grate root and add vinegar for a sharp, mustardy condiment. Can be very invasive if left unchecked.
Lavender, English (*Lavandula angustifolia*)	2½-3 ft.	Bushy shrub with silver-gray linear leaves and spikes of tiny fragrant purple flowers.	Full sun. Light, well-drained, somewhat sandy soil. Propagate by division, cuttings. Zones 5-8.	Popular for its fragrant flowers. Used in potpourris, soaps, perfume. Dries well. Repels moths. Edgings, rock gardens. Attracts bees.
Lavender cotton (*Santolina chamaecyparissus*)	1½-2 ft.	Compact evergreen perennial with attractive silver-green leaves and clusters of yellow buttonlike flowers, ½-¾ in. across.	Full sun. Light, well-drained, somewhat sandy soil. Propagate by division, cuttings, seeds. Zones 6-8.	Adds musky scent to sachets. Dries well. Good for borders, edging. Often used to edge knot gardens.
Lemon balm (*Melissa officinalis*)	1½-2 ft.	Loosely branched, somewhat floppy perennial with square stems and scented, toothed, roundish leaves that are 1-3 in. long.	Full sun to partial shade. Average, well-drained soil. Propagate by division, cuttings, layering, seeds. Zones 4-5.	Fresh leaves used in cooking for their minty lemon taste. Add dried leaves to potpourri.
Lemon verbena (*Aloysia triphylla*)	5-10 ft.	Fragrant, nonhardy shrub with light green, lance-shaped leaves and spikes of pale purple flowers.	Full sun. Rich, moist soil. Propagate by cuttings. Zones 9-10.	Dried leaves make a lemon-lime tea and are good in potpourris. Grow as a houseplant in containers in colder climates.
Marjoram, sweet (*Origanum majorana*)	1-1½ ft.	Bushy perennial often grown as an annual. Fuzzy, pale, grayish green leaves. Tiny white or pink flowers.	Full sun. Light, dry, well-drained soil. Propagate by division, cuttings, seeds. Zones 9-10.	Use fresh or dried leaves and flowers for a mild oregano flavor. Add to potpourris or wreaths.

(continued)

Herb	Height	Description	Culture	Comments and Uses
Mint (*Mentha* spp.)	1-3 ft.	Square-stemmed perennials with fragrant leaves and spikes of tiny flowers.	Full sun to partial shade. Rich, moist, well-drained soil. Propagate by division, cuttings, layering. Zones 5-10.	Many types available—spearmint, pineapple mint, peppermint, apple mint. Refreshing flavor in tea, jelly, candy. Invigorating in sachets. Attractive, but can be invasive.
Oregano (*Origanum* spp.)	1-2 ft.	Square-stemmed perennial with oval, aromatic leaves and spikes of tiny tubular flowers.	Full sun. Average, well-drained soil. Propagate by division, cuttings. Zones 5-10.	Used in cooking—tomato sauce, egg dishes. Fragrance and flavor varies; plant named cultivars or strains selected for flavor.
Parsley (*Petroselinum crispum*)	1-1½ ft.	Bright green-leaved biennial with finely-cut foliage that comes in curly or flat-leaved forms.	Full sun to partial shade. Moderately rich, moist, well-drained soil. Propagate by seeds.	Rich in iron, vitamin A and C. Blends well with other flavorings. Adds color to foods. Used as a garnish.
Rosemary (*Rosmarinus officinalis*)	5-6 ft.	Evergreen shrub with aromatic, gray-green, needle-like leaves. Purplish blue flowers are tiny, tubular, and borne in spikes.	Full sun to partial shade. Light, well-drained soil. Propagate by division, cuttings, layering. Zones 8-10.	Excellent flavoring in lamb, veal, beef, vegetables. Good in sachets. Can be grown in containers.
Sage, garden (*Salvia officinalis*)	12-30 in.	Wiry-stemmed, low-growing shrub with fuzzy, aromatic gray-green leaves.	Full sun. Moderately rich, well-drained soil. Propagate by division, cuttings, layering, seeds. Zones 4-8.	Used as flavoring alone or with other herbs. Leaves dry well. Attractive in gardens. Variegated forms available.
Savory, summer (*Satureja hortensis*) **Savory, winter** (*S. montana*)	Summer 1-1½ ft. Winter 6-12 in.	Summer savory is a bushy annual with soft, gray, linear leaves. Winter savory is a compact shrubby perennial with shiny, dark green leaves.	Full sun. Summer savory grows in average soil and is propagated by seeds. Winter savory prefers light, dry, well-drained soil; propagate by division, cuttings, layering, seeds. Zones 6-10.	Both used in cooking. Summer savory has a peppery-thyme flavor and blends well with other flavorings in vinegars, herb butters, and vegetables. Winter savory has a stronger, more piny taste.
Scented Geranium (*Pelargonium* spp.)	1-3 ft.	Nonhardy perennials with clusters of small flowers. Grown mostly for their aromatic leaves which may be nearly round or heavily divided.	Full sun. Rich, humusy, dry, well-drained soil. Propagate by cuttings.	Leaves have many different scents including rose, mint, lemon, lime, apple, and nutmeg. Can be used in teas or jellies. Useful in potpourris and sachets. Attractive potted plants.
Tarragon (*Artemisia dracunculus*)	1½-2 ft.	Perennial with linear fragrant leaves on wiry stalks.	Full to partial shade. Rich, loamy or sandy, well-drained soil. Propagate by division, cuttings. Zones 4-10.	Adds strong flavoring to fish, beef, lamb, vegetables, sauces. Plant near vegetables for healthy growth.
Thyme, common (*Thymus vulgaris*)	9-12 in.	Small prostrate shrub with tiny, roundish, aromatic leaves that are hairy underneath.	Full sun to partial shade. Light, dry, well-drained soil. Propagate by division, cuttings, layering. Zones 5-9.	Adds delicate flavoring to lamb, veal, beef, butter, vegetables. Dried flowers repel insects. Leaves and flowers good in sachets.

ply shear the surface of the plants each time. Plucking some of the branches near the center of the plant allows air and light into the center, which helps avoid serious disease problems and encourages new branches and thick growth.

● Use an attractive, appropriate material, such as cobblestone or brick, to edge the bed. The edging will help accentuate the design and perhaps help drainage.

Selecting a Site and Preparing the Garden

It's important to keep a few basic points in mind when selecting a site and planting your herb garden. With the exception of shade-loving herbs, most herbs require at least six hours of direct sunlight. The soil should be slightly acid, with a pH of approximately 6.5, and should be moderately rich and well drained. It also should be free of encroaching tree roots.

To prepare a new bed for herbs, follow the steps below. You'll have to make adjustments depending on your own garden and the conditions available. For example, if you have extremely sandy or acid soil, start with the basic soil improvement suggestions described in "Knowing Your Soil" on page 12.

Start by laying out the bed you've designed; ideally, you'll have a detailed design on paper to follow. Remove all sod or top growth from the site. Dig the soil either by double garden digging (going two spade depths into the soil) or digging as deep as possible with a garden fork. Then apply a generous amount of organic material over the top of the area; well-rotted manure and/or well-rotted leaves are best. Adjust the pH as necessary. If the soil is heavy clay, apply generous amounts of medium-size chicken grit because this will help to break up the heavy clay and improve aeration, especially important in wet winters. The addition of gypsum will help improve the drainage in heavy clay soils. If the area is extremely wet, consider making a raised bed to help improve

the drainage. The best height for a raised bed is from 12 to 18 inches. Avoid higher beds, because the soil can become too dry in winter.

Planting and Caring for Herbs

Herbs are really no different than annuals, perennials, biennials, or bulbs when it comes to planting and propagation techniques. For planting, seed sowing, or propagation information, see the appropriate sections earlier in this book for directions.

The main consideration in keeping the herbs beautiful is to keep them well pruned. For the most part, herbs love to be cut back, and they will reward you with beautiful form and habit as long as their pruning requirements are met. With cooking herbs, of course, you'll want to use the trimmings in the kitchen. For best results, prune plants on a cool, shady day so that underlying growth is not suddenly exposed to hot, baking sun.

Harvesting, Drying, and Storing Herbs

Historically, knowledge about how to harvest and dry herbs was considered essential. People with herbal knowledge were highly regarded, for their ability to keep herbs well preserved through techniques such as drying was essential if the plants were to maintain their effectiveness.

Tips for Success

The aim in drying herbs is to remove the water they contain but at the same time conserve as much of the oils and compounds within the plant parts as possible. Although not a difficult process, this must be done with care in order to prevent the herbs from "cooking," which would make them

ineffective. The following tips will get you off to a good start.

● It's best to cut the herbs in the morning of a cool, cloudy day. Wait until the dew has dried, but harvest before the sun has become very bright. Usually the best time is around 9:00 A.M. Only cut the amount of material you will be able to handle that day so you won't waste any.

● Use sharp pruning shears and cut the plant so that it will still look beautiful even after it has been pruned. On some plants such as parsley or chives the leaves are cut right back to the base; cut the

outside leaves all the way around the plant to encourage further growth. The entire clump of chives can be cut to 1 inch high; it will grow again.

● As you're cutting, keep the herbs fresh and unwilted by placing them in a bucket of cool water.

● If the plants are clean and free of pesticides, you can bundle them immediately after picking. If not, wash them in water and pat dry with a towel.

● If you plan to dry the herbs by hanging them upside-down suspended from a line or cord, you'll need to separate them into small bunches and fasten them together with string or a rubber band at the base. Don't make the bunches too large, for there is a risk that they won't dry properly and will mildew if not enough air is able to reach the leaves.

● You can also dry herbs by laying them flat on screens or baskets to dry. In fact, if you are drying flower petals, such as roses, it's best to dry them in this manner because they need good air circulation to dry evenly. With flowers, it's a good idea to occasionally move them around gently to avoid moisture buildup.

Drying and Storing Herbs

The ideal place to dry herbs is warm, dark, and well ventilated. The ideal temperature for drying is approximately 90°F. If the temperature is too low or the location too humid, there's a risk the plants will mildew; if it's too hot, there's a risk they'll cook rather than dry, which would render them useless. Exposure to sun-

light also will lessen the quality of dried herbs, so always dry them in a dark place. Air circulation helps to speed up the drying process.

An attic is often the ideal location for drying as long as it's not too dusty. The oven is a bit risky, unless it is heated only by a pilot light, since it's difficult to control the temperature at very low heat. If you only have a shed or other location that has a humid environment, supplemental heating is a possibility. Food dryers and dehydrators have been used with success for herbs, as have microwave ovens. To dry herbs in a microwave, place them between two paper towels and dry for approximately two minutes or more. Timing will depend on the thickness of the plant part and your own particular oven. Test for correct dryness by crushing the herb. It should not be so dry that it totally crumbles when touched, but it should

be evident that it is sufficiently dry and free of water, ready for packaging.

Keep dried herbs out of direct sunlight to prevent their color from fading. You can package them in glass or ceramic containers, but herbs stored in glass should be kept out of direct sun. Label each container with the

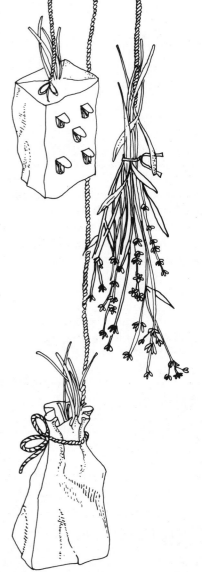

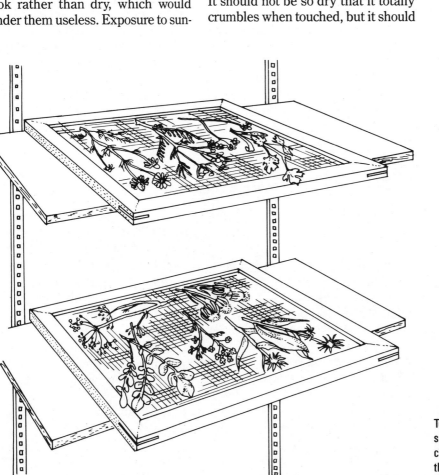

Herbs, rose petals, and other ingredients destined for potpourri can be spread on screens and left in a warm, dark, dry place to dry.

To hang herbs or flowers for drying, tie them in small bunches and hang them. To keep them clean and out of direct sunlight, you can cover the plants with brown paper bags. Cut holes in the bags to ensure proper ventilation. Herbs harvested for seeds also must be covered with a paper bag to catch the seeds as they dry.

herb name and date. This step is very important since many dried herbs look very similar. The date will help you make sure you're not using herbs that have been in storage too long. The amount of time an herb can be stored will vary depending on the kind of tissue it has. For example, rosemary, with its thick waxy coating, will hold its flavor for three years or more. Basil, on the other hand, with its thin, tender leaves, may lose its flavor in six months.

Freezing Herbs

Freezing herbs is an especially valuable alternative for herbs that do not dry well, such as basil, chives, French tarragon, parsley and chervil. Once the herbs are clean and dry, you can freeze them either whole or chopped. An efficient method is to mix the herbs with water or olive oil and place the mixture in an ice tray for freezing. Just pop out the cubes as needed for soups, stews, or sauces.

Harvesting Seeds and Roots

Harvest herbs grown for their seeds just before the seeds are about to fall off the plant. Cut off seed heads, tie the bases of several stems together, and hang them upside-down in a paper bag so that as the seeds fall they will remain in the bag. They should be ready for packaging in approximately two weeks. Test for dryness. If there are insect problems, freeze the herbs and redry.

Roots of plants such as sweet flag (*Acorus calamus*) or orris (*Iris* × *germanica* var. *florentina*) should be harvested in the autumn, after the plant compounds have made their way down to the roots. At this time they will have the maximum fragrance or flavor. Dig the roots and scrub clean before drying on screens. Because roots are thick tissue, they tend to take a longer time to dry.

Making Tussie-Mussies

Tussie-mussies or herbal bouquets are beloved combinations of fragrant, meaningful herbs that lift the spirits and improve the senses of all who give or use them. Their fascinating history takes us back to the old European courtrooms where judges carried a bouquet of fragrant herbs to protect them from jail fever. Such combinations would have included southernwood (*Artemisia abrotanum*) or rue (*Ruta graveolens*). More elegant tussie-mussies were carried for their perfuming effect by many of the ladies of the manor. The selection of plants used in a tussie-mussie has always been tied into the language of flowers, which was no doubt greatly promoted by the writings of Shakespeare, who described the meanings of many herbs. A typical Shakespearean bouquet might have included rosemary for remembrance, violets for faithfulness, roses for love, carnations for graciousness, cowslips for counsel, or marigolds for marriage.

American colonists were known to carry to church tussie-mussies made with a combination of herbs they could nibble on to stay awake during long sermons. People of the Victorian era were most renowned for their love of tussie-mussies and their emphasis on the meanings of flowers. Collections of elaborate tussie-mussie holders made during the Victorian period can be seen at the Smithsonian Institution in Washington, D.C. These elegant hand-held holders or pin holders are made of a variety of metals, many of the finest in silver and gold. Most are able to hold water so that plants can stay fresh for an extended period.

Some have a hook on the side so that a woman could attach the tussie-mussie to the side of her ball gown while dancing.

Tussie-mussies can range from exquisitely beautiful and colorful bunches of flowers to more simple combinations of fragrant, less showy plants and flowers. However, in order to fit the true representation of tussie-mussie, they shouldn't be too elaborate, because then they become more like flower arrangements.

Today, the resurgence of interest in tussie-mussies goes hand in hand with the renewed interest in herbs and their meanings and fragrances. Tussie-mussies can have great effects on people. For example, one Connecticut gardener uses tussie-mussies made with herbs from her garden to lift the spirits of people with terminal illnesses. These simple fresh bouquets can have a profound effect, because they bring back memories and associations from less complicated times.

How to Make a Tussie-Mussie

A little practice is the only recipe you need for making tussie-mussies. Remember, these are not formal bouquets and should not look like a flower arrangement. They should vary depending on the occasion, and each individual making a tussie-mussie will have his or her own style.

To create your tussie-mussie, gather a varied sampling of foliage and flowers from the garden. Begin with a cluster or flowers or foliage at the center of the bouquet, and then continue by placing herbs one around the other (in concentric circles) to develop a balanced arrangement. Use a circle of herbs with beautiful leaves around the edges, such as scented geraniums (*Pelargonium* spp.), lady's-mantle (*Alchemilla* spp.), or parsley.

Hold the cluster of stems together

and surround the tips with a moistened piece of cotton. Cover the base of the bouquet in plastic, then wrap with floral tape. Push the base through a purchased or homemade doily, secure it with a florist's pin, then tie a ribbon around the top of the base. The plastic between the flowers and

the doily will protect the doily from dampness. Spray the tussie-mussie frequently or remove the doily and immerse in water to keep it fresh. Small tussie-mussies can be pinned on a blouse or jacket, while larger ones can be hand-held or put in a small vase.

To make a tussie-mussie, gather herbs and flowers from the garden. Arrange them in a small bouquet, surrounded by leaves from fragrant-foliaged herbs. A moistened piece of cotton wrapped in plastic provides moisture while protecting the doily and ribbon from dampness.

Herbal Baths

Herbal baths are a soothing and healthful way to relax and enjoy the varied benefits and earthy aromas of herbs. Herbs can be combined to create the bath of your own choice and needs.

There are several categories of herb baths. Healing baths were described by Hippocrates, who recommended them to aid with muscle and joint diseases. A variety of herbs are suggested for stiff muscles and aching joints, including chamomile, sage, strawberry leaves (*Fragaria* spp.), mugwort (*Artemisia vulgaris*), and agrimony (*Agrimonia eupatoria*). Tonic herbal baths help to refresh the skin, especially during winter, and should be taken several days in a row to be effective. Some of the choice tonic herbs are blackberry or raspberry leaves, patchouli leaves (dried), orange peel, and jasmine flowers. In Asia, herbal baths are quite common, and ginger is the principal ingredient in herbal baths used to help promote circulation. Chop, grate, or slice fresh ginger root, and then cook it for 20 minutes in 1 gallon of water before adding it to the bath. By far the most popular use of the herbal bath is to

relieve stress and tension. Suggested herbs for this use include valerian (*Valeriana officinalis*), sweet flag (*Acorus calamus*), hops (*Humulus lupulus*), queen-of-the-meadow (*Filipendula ulmaria*), rose petals, and sweet violet (*Viola odorata*). Certain herbs are known to help heal skin inflammations. These include mint, plantain (*Plantago major*), dandelion leaves, and lady's-mantle (*Alchemilla* spp.). Antiseptic herbs such as eucalyptus (*Eucalyptus* spp.) and sandalwood (*Santalum* spp.) are helpful in clearing up congestion when added to the bath. Inhaling the steam is especially beneficial.

To make an herbal bath, gather the herbs you've selected and combine them in a large muslin bag with a drawstring that can hang from the faucet into the bath water. Then fill the tub with extremely hot water so that the herbal combination can steep for five to ten minutes before you get into the bath. A hot bath will make you sleepy; a cold bath will be stimulating. By the time you get in, the bathroom will have filled with the fragrant steam. Carefully test the water temperature to be sure it's cool

enough. Then use the bath as a time for total relaxation. Your skin will benefit from its soaking in herb water.

Another method for preparing an herbal bath is to make a strong infusion of herbs and then blend that liquid into the bath water. Another possibility is adding essential oils to the bath. Some of the favorite oils to use in the bath are rosemary, lavender, and citrus. These and other combinations are described at great length in books on aromatherapy.

FRAGRANT, REJUVENATING HERBAL BATH

Combine the following ingredients in equal parts:

Lavender flowers

Tangerine peel (one high in oils)

Rose petals (petals of fragrant, old roses such as damask are best)

Rosemary leaves

Allow to steep in the bath. Soak in this herbal delight for as long as you like.

Making Herbal Tea

Throughout the world, herbs have provided the flavoring for mankind's beverages for centuries. Today, herbal teas provide the best alternative to caffeinated coffee. Experiment with mixing teas from a variety of herbs, or make tea with a single herb like spearmint or beebalm.

Before you make tea with any herb, be sure you know exactly what it is. Gathering plants in the wild can be dangerous. Distinguishing safe from harmful plant species requires tremendous knowledge of botany as well as extensive experience in the

field. For this reason, it's best to grow the plants for tea in your own garden so that their safety and identification is beyond question.

Most herbal teas are made by placing the herb, fresh or dry, in a tea ball, muslin bag, or loose in a teapot, and allowing it to steep for approximately four minutes until the tea has the desired flavor and color. Herbal teas can be served with honey or lemon or are usually delicious on their own. Most dry herbs used for tea will hold their flavor for six months to one year if properly stored.

THE BEST HERBS FOR TEA

• Chamomile has a pleasant pineapple flavor and is known for its calming effect.

• Lemon verbena can be blended with other herb teas.

• Spearmint is very refreshing, especially as an iced tea. Try spearmint tea with lemonade.

• Anise seeds make a delicious licorice-flavored tea.

Roses

Selecting and Planting Roses

Roses have been called the "queen of flowers." Perhaps not surprisingly, they are the oldest cultivated ornamental plant and our national flower. Although many other flowers share the word *rose* as part of their common names, true roses are members of the genus *Rosa,* which contains over 100 species and literally thousands of cultivars. Their showy flowers, thorny stems, and leathery green leaves are familiar to all gardeners. Blooms come in white, red, pink, orange, yellow, lavender, and all shades in between; some bear bicolored blooms. The flowers can be single or double, large or small, and may be borne singly or in dramatic clusters. In addition, many roses also provide attractive hips that turn red in fall. Rosehips are used in jams, jellies, and teas for their high vitamin C content and tart, cranberrylike flavor.

Making the Right Choice

Probably the most important decision you'll make regarding roses in your landscape is selecting the right plant for the right place. There are so many types of roses available that choosing them requires some knowledge of each group and its distinguishing characteristics. There are roses to blend into a flower or perennial garden, or even a sunny spot in a natural garden. They make fine companions for herbs. Climbing roses are often the most suitable plant for covering a trellis or training as pillar roses on posts or old tree trunks.

The information in this chapter about some of the major classes of roses will help you make your selection. Rose hybridizers are constantly introducing new cultivars of roses with more attractive, longer-lasting flowers, ornamental hips, and better habit. They are also selecting for plants that exhibit disease- and insect-resistance characteristics. Although you'll find examples of cultivars listed in the sections that follow, ask your cooperative extension agent or local nursery owner for a list of the best roses to consider for your area. Since hardiness varies from class to class and cultivar to cultivar, it's also a good idea to find out which ones will survive best in your area.

Hybrid Tea Roses

Hybrid tea roses are the most common roses grown today. The first hybrid tea, 'La France', was produced in 1867, the result of complex crosses between Chinese and European roses. Hybrid tea roses gradually gained in popularity because of their long season of bloom and the beauty of their unfurling buds. Hybrid tea roses are 3 to 5 feet tall and are primarily grown for their spectacular, many-petaled blossoms, which are borne singly or in small clusters on long, straight stems. Blooms range from 3½ to 5½ inches wide. Hybrid teas are not reliably hardy in the North and require winter protection if they are to survive in areas where temperatures routinely go below 10°F.

Hybrid teas probably require the most maintenance of any of the roses. Most hybrid teas are highly susceptible to insect and disease problems, and therefore require regular applications of insecticides and fungicides to look their best. Today, the trend is toward cultivars—both old and new—that require less maintenance and have more disease resistance. 'Miss All-American Beauty', 'Mister Lincoln', 'Pink Peace', 'Tiffany', and 'Tropicana' are all examples of hybrid tea roses. (All show resistance to black spot and powdery mildew, the two most prominent diseases of hybrid teas.) New and beautiful hybrid tea cultivars that show superior pest and disease resistance are introduced every year.

Floribunda and Grandiflora Roses

These two classes of roses are closely related to hybrid teas. Floribunda roses, which were created by crossing polyantha roses with hybrid teas, are about 2 to 3 feet tall. The individual flowers range from 2½ to 3½ inches wide but are borne in large, many-flowered clusters. Floribundas are generally quite hardy, and can be easily grown anywhere hybrid teas are grown.

Grandiflora roses are the result of crosses between hybrid teas and floribundas. They are shrubs that can reach 6 to 8 feet in height and are about as hardy as hybrid teas. Grandifloras bear large clusters of hybrid-tea-size blooms. Both floribunda and grandiflora roses are among the most floriferous roses in the garden. 'Europeana', 'First Edition', 'Rose Parade', and 'Razzle Dazzle' are examples of Floribunda roses. 'Queen Elizabeth' and 'Prominent' are both Grandiflora roses. (All of these cultivars exhibit resistance to black spot and powdery mildew.)

Climbing and Rambling Roses

Because of their tremendous versatility and adaptability, climbing and rambling roses are extremely popular. They can be trained to climb over fences, on trellises, against buildings, or up tree trunks. They're not true climbers, though, because they have no natural way to grip or hold onto supports. Instead, they must be tied in place. These roses come in many forms. Some bear clusters of small flowers; others have blooms like those of hybrid teas. Hardiness varies from type to type. Rambling roses tend to have a much more rampant and vigorous growing habit than climbers, and bloom once a season, generally on two-year-old canes. Some climbers, on the other hand, will bloom twice. 'Don Juan' and 'Improved Blaze' are examples of large-flowered climbing roses. 'Chevy Chase' is a rambling rose that is resistant to powdery mildew.

Shrub Roses

Shrub roses make up one of the best groups of roses to blend with other plants in a landscape. This is a catch-all class for many of the newer roses, which often are hybrids between old roses and new roses. They tend to be excellent, low-maintenance shrubs that are easy to blend into a variety of landscape settings. Many shrub roses also are highly resistant to insect and disease problems and quite cold hardy. (The shrub roses bred by Griffith Buck, such as 'Carefree Beauty',

are particularly good.) 'Bonica' is a popular shrub rose that grows very well with little care. It is approximately 3 to 4 feet tall with medium-pink flowers.

Old Roses

Old garden roses comprise a very large group of increasingly popular roses that have been grown since long before modern roses (such as hybrid teas) came into existence. They have been subdivided into many different subgroups, including Gallica, Alba, Centifolia, Moss, Bourbon, Hybrid Perpetual, China, Musk, Noisette, and Species. Although old roses vary a great deal, they possess many unique characteristics. The plants closely resemble shrub roses and range from 2 to 8 feet in height or sometimes more. Blooms may be single or double, solid or striped, and are borne in clusters. Fragrant blooms are another feature of many of the old roses. In addition, many have attractive hips that add fall interest. Hardiness is variable. *Rosa* 'Mundi', 'Reine des Violettes', and 'Mary Washington' are all examples of old roses.

Miniatures

These useful roses are excellent as edging plants, in containers, and just about anywhere you want a floriferous, low-growing plant. Often called minis, they range in height from 1 to 2 feet and are easy to grow. Although tiny, they require much the same care as their larger cousins, the hybrid teas.

Planting Pointers

Once you've made your choice, proper site selection and planting are the next steps to getting your roses off to a good start. The following pointers will help you on your way to success.

Site Selection

Roses absolutely require a location that has been carefully planned and prepared. Select a site that gets at least six hours of direct sunlight. Good air circulation is also important, so

avoid damp, stagnant spots where there is little breeze. This will help prevent excessive problems with powdery mildew and black spot—the two most serious fungal diseases of roses. Pruning is one way to improve air circulation, but good site selection and a garden design where roses have plenty of room to grow are equally important.

Avoid spots where competition from encroaching tree roots, especially the greedy, shallow roots of trees such as silver maple, will sap the strength of your roses. However, roses are able to compete with smaller, less overpowering plants, such as many types of herbs and perennials, because their roots tend to go deep into the soil.

Soil pH should be somewhere between 6.0 and 6.5 for best growth. If the soil becomes too alkaline, you'll see chlorosis on the leaves because the plants are unable to take up the nutrients they need. Other signs of nutrient deficiencies will also appear. (For information on how to measure and adjust the soil pH, see "Testing the Soil" on page 12.)

Soil Preparation

To prepare the soil, either double-dig the bed by hand, going as deep as possible, or use a rotary tiller. You'll need to add plenty of organic matter. Mix in generous quantities of well-rotted manure (cow or chicken are best) and/or well-rotted leaf mold. Spread a layer on top of the bed and then work it into the soil.

Excellent drainage also is a priority. Roses grow best in well-aerated soil that retains moisture but drains well. If you are gardening in heavy clay soil, consider raised beds to improve drainage. Organic matter improves soil structure and improves drainage. Chicken grit, composed of small, sharp pieces of granite, also will help to break up clay soil. (See "Improving the Soil—Texture and Structure" on page 17 for more on organic matter as it applies to clay soil.)

After amending the soil, carefully smooth the bed so that it's slightly higher in the center and carefully graded so that water won't form puddles in the middle of the beds after a heavy rain.

When to Plant

Roses can be planted in early spring or in autumn. Generally, dormant, bare-root roses are shipped in autumn, and it's best to plant them as soon as they arrive. (Although bare-root roses are offered for sale in spring, it's best to buy and plant them in fall.) The roots of roses planted at this time of year will begin growing in very early spring, long before you'll be able to spot signs of growth aboveground. If you can't plant in fall (or if you can't plant right away), heeling-in and plant-ing the following spring is the next best alternative. Dig a trench in a convenient area, lay the plants in the trench at about a 45-degree angle, and cover the roots with soil. Be sure that all the roots are adequately covered because new rose plants often dry out if exposed to cold, dry winter winds, but don't mound soil over the entire plant. It's also important to avoid overcrowding. Plants that have been heeled-in need to be moved to their permanent location before mid-spring to avoid root damage.

Container-grown roses can be purchased from garden centers in spring and planted at that time.

Planting

As a general rule, roses can be planted just like shrubs and trees. With bare-root plants, it's important to keep the roots from drying out. Unpack the plants as soon as possible and check to see that the packing material is damp. Make sure the roots remain damp until you are able to plant.

To plant bare-root roses, dig a hole large enough to accommodate the plant's roots and make a mound of soil in the center of the hole. Before planting, inspect the plant carefully. Remove broken or split roots or canes. Also remove weak, thin, or badly placed canes, such as those that cross the center of the plant. Most bare-root roses will be properly pruned on arrival, so if you've bought good-quality plants, you may not need to do any pruning at all. When cutting off canes, be sure to cut back to healthy wood and make cuts ¼-inch above a

After preparing the soil for planting roses, dig a hole that is large enough to accommodate the plant's roots. Create a mound of soil in the center of the hole.

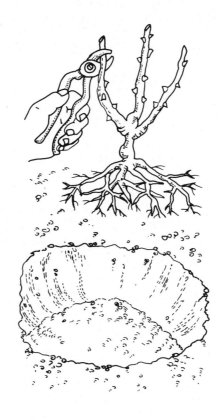

Use sharp pruning shears to remove any broken, diseased, or damaged canes and roots. When pruning canes, cut to healthy wood and be sure to cut just above a bud that points toward the outside of the plant.

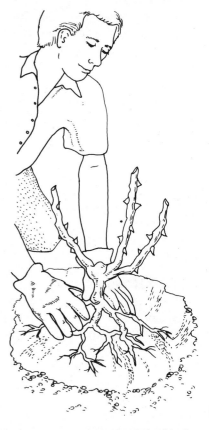

Set the plant on top of the mound of soil in the center of the hole, and spread the roots out evenly.

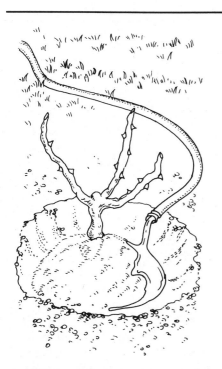

Fill the hole by gently working soil around the roots and firming it in place to eliminate air pockets. Water thoroughly when the hole is two-thirds full, then finish filling with soil.

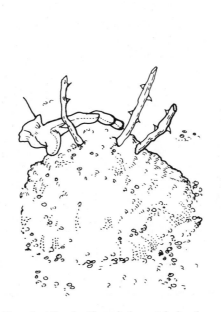

To protect the plant from drying out during the first winter, mound soil around the crown.

have been grown in containers, the roots of these plants have not yet begun to grow, and it's likely the potting mix will fall from the roots if you remove the plant from its pot. To minimize transplant disturbance, dig a hole the size of the pot, cut the bottom out of the pot, and cut partway up the sides of the pot. Hold the bottom of the pot in place while you set the plant in the hole, then remove the bottom. Cut the rest of the way up the sides and remove the pot. Firm soil around the roots and water thoroughly.

Mulching

There are several reasons for mulching roses. A layer of mulch will help conserve moisture and prevent weed growth. Mulch also looks attractive, and if applied in autumn, it can help to regulate soil temperature. Mulch can also help prevent fungal spores in the soil from splattering up onto the foliage. Use shredded hardwood bark or bark chips for mulch. Keep in mind that these materials can gradually change soil pH, so be sure to check for pH changes periodically.

Winter Protection

Protect tender roses in winter by tying up the canes and surrounding them with a burlap-covered collar of chicken wire. Stuff with leaves all around the roses. This helps prevent damage to the canes by moderating temperature changes around the plants.

bud eye. Then set the plant in the hole and spread the rose roots evenly in all directions. Be sure to check the depth of the bud union, if you're planting a grafted plant, or crown, if you are planting a plant grown on its own roots. (Usually, all roses except shrub roses and old garden roses are grafted onto an understock.) Where winter temperatures fall below 0°F, the bud union should be planted 1 or 2 inches below the surface of the soil. In the South, the bud union should be planted even with the surface of the soil. Roses grown on their own roots should be planted with the crown at the surface of the soil.

Carefully fill the hole, firming the soil around the plant to eliminate pockets of air around the roots. Water thoroughly when the hole is about two-thirds full, then finish filling. To keep the plant from drying out during the first winter, mound soil up around the base of the plant to protect it. Be sure to uncover the plants in early spring.

When planting container-grown roses, remove the pot and set the plant in place with as little disturbance to the root ball as possible. Many nurseries pot bare-root roses in late winter and then offer them in pots the following spring. Unlike roses that

Pruning Roses

If you're going to grow roses, you'll need to love—or at least like—pruning. Since the best time to prune roses is late winter, many gardeners look forward to pruning as an annual ritual of spring.

Proper pruning is vital for healthy growth—and for gorgeous flowers—so

make an annual pruning appointment with your roses in late winter, just as the buds begin to swell. Annual pruning benefits plants by removing dead and diseased canes as well as crossing and weak branches. It keeps the plants well shaped and encourages vigorous growth that will lead to large,

abundant flowers. On grafted plants, it's important to regularly remove any suckers that arise from the understock onto which the plant has been grafted. First- and second-year plants will need little pruning, but all other roses will benefit from some annual attention. In addition to late winter pruning, you may also need to prune in summer to keep plants from getting too tall. Remember, too, that deadheading and cutting roses for indoor bouquets is a form of pruning. Here are the supplies you'll need to begin.

- **Sharp pruning shears.** It's a good idea to dip shears in alcohol, bleach, or another disinfectant between pruning cuts to prevent spreading diseases.
- **Loppers.** Although most pruning is done with pruning shears, the larger, older branches may need to be cut with loppers to ensure a clean cut. Be very careful not to rip rose canes when cutting.
- **Wood glue or shellac and a paint brush.** After cutting back canes, paint them with wood glue or shellac in order to prevent cane borers from invading the stems.
- **Gloves.** Heavy leather gloves will help prevent too much damage to your hands and make it easier to remove large canes.
- **Garden rake.** Use this tool to rake out any debris under and around the plants after you've finished pruning. A rake also is useful for keeping the area clean and smoothing out mulch.
- **Vinyl-coated wire fencing.** This may come in handy for taller-growing roses that have problems with flopping over. After pruning, place a cylindrical cone of wire around the rose, up to around 3 feet, to support the rose during the growing season. Wire it together and use hooks of bendable wire to attach the cylinder in place.
- **Large basket or garden cart.** You'll need either or both of these to remove the prunings.

Generally, roses can be placed into one of two categories when it comes to pruning. There are the roses that bloom on old growth (also called old wood) and those that bloom on new growth produced the current season (new wood). Most roses fall into the latter category and are pruned hard in late winter, before the beginning of the growing season.

Roses that bloom on old wood include primarily old garden roses and species roses. These roses should only be pruned lightly in late winter, so that not too many of the flowers are removed. But a late-winter pruning does benefit these plants and results in larger, showier blossoms and fuller, better-shaped plants.

Roses should not be pruned in fall, because pruning at this season removes food reserves that will help the plant survive the winter. Fall pruning also encourages growth at a time the plants should be preparing for winter dormancy. The new stems produced late in the year will not harden properly before winter and will be killed by freezing temperatures.

The general guidelines for pruning vary depending on the type of roses you are growing and where you are growing them. Begin any pruning job by thoroughly studying the plant to decide which canes are to be removed and how the plant can be made more attractive. You should plan on removing old canes that are no longer flowering well, and any diseased or damaged wood. Also remove canes that cross the center of the plant, to improve air circulation, and eliminate any spots where canes rub and damage one another.

Pruning Techniques for Specific Roses

Hybrid Teas

Ideally, hybrid tea roses should be pruned back to a height of 18 to 24 inches in late winter. Be sure to remove all dead, diseased, and damaged growth. Also remove any crossing branches to increase air circulation at the center of the plant. Gardeners who grow roses for exhibition often cut back more severely in order to get fewer, larger flowers for show, but this is not recommended; it will shorten the life of the plant. Remember, regular deadheading and cutting blooms is also a form of pruning. During the growing season, don't let stray branches grow so long that the plant looks straggly.

Grandifloras and Floribundas

Grandiflora and floribundas need only very basic pruning to keep them healthy. In late winter prune back all dead, diseased, and damaged growth. Also remove any crossing branches to increase air circulation at the center of the plant. These roses don't need to be cut back to reduce height. Throughout the growing season, as

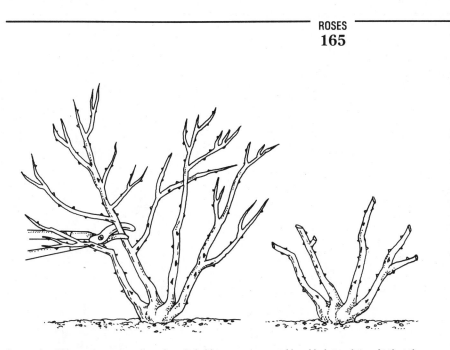

Roses that bloom on new wood, such as hybrid teas, are pruned hard in late winter. At that time, cut all dead and diseased canes back to healthy wood, remove weak, thin canes, and eliminate branches that cross the center of the plant to increase air circulation.

You can increase flowering on a hybrid tea rose by deadheading. Cut faded blooms off just below the flowers and ¼ inch above a large bud (left). Unless you're cutting fresh flowers, which will require long stems, don't cut blooms off farther down the stem, because the buds will not be as large and vigorous (right).

Green Thumb Tip

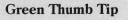

CUTTING ROSES FOR INDOOR USE

It is best to cut roses in the early morning before the sun is very bright. Cutting roses is a form of pruning, so be sure to use sharp pruning shears to avoid ripping and bruising the stems of the plant. Make a slanting cut about ¼-inch above a leaf bud. Choose a bud that is facing the outside of the plant if possible, to encourage branching in the same direction. When you cut the flower, leave two to three leaf buds on the plant stem.

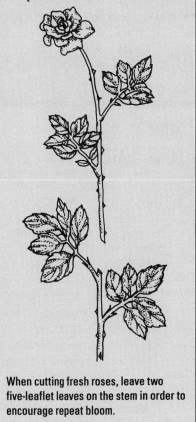

When cutting fresh roses, leave two five-leaflet leaves on the stem in order to encourage repeat bloom.

you remove spent blooms or cut flowers for indoor display, keep in mind that you are also shaping the plant.

Climbing Roses

When pruning climbing roses, it's best to remove all ties that hold the rose to its support and lay down all canes. Then shape the plant by bringing selected canes back up and tying them in a pleasing, graceful appearance.

For best flowering, always try to have one-, two-, and three-year-old canes on the plants at all times. For example, select at least one or two three-year-old canes for training, one or two two-year-old canes and one or two one-year-old canes. All canes selected to remain on the plant should be healthy and vigorous.

Some of the more rampant climbing roses can become an impossible tangled mess if left unpruned. You can cut these back hard each winter. ('Silver Moon' or 'Dr. Van Fleet' can be treated in this manner.) Since most blooms are borne on new wood, this harsh treatment will not greatly affect flowering. Climbing hybrid teas, on the other hand, are much less vigorous than other climbers and require only a light annual pruning. On these plants, just remove dead, diseased, or damaged growth.

With tall ramblers, it's impractical to pull the whole plant down for pruning. Apply the same principles as for climbing roses—removing diseased and old, woody canes—and prune in place. Nearly all rambling roses bloom only on second-year wood, so be sure you leave young wood to encourage blooming. You can cut the ends of long canes to encourage lat-

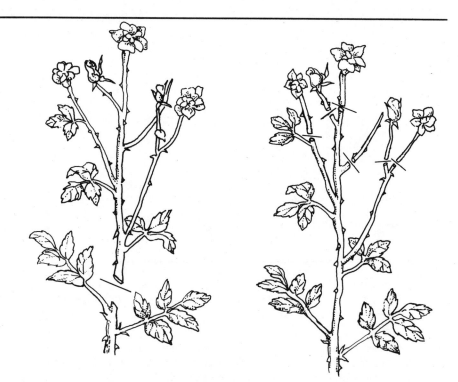

When deadheading floribundas, cut to a healthy bud just below the entire flower cluster (left) instead of simply removing the tips of the shoots just below the blooms (right).

HOW TO MAKE ROSE WATER

Making rose water is a wonderful way to enjoy the delightful fragrance of roses and capture its essence for use in cooking, perfumes, and cosmetics. As a food flavoring, it is especially famous for its use in flavoring the candy known as Turkish delight. Rose water is also delicious in sauces, on chicken, and as a flavoring for sherbet and cakes.

In ancient Egypt and Greece, perfumes were originally made by oil extraction using sesame oil. To make rose oil, they would gather fragrant rose petals (damask roses, a type of old rose, were preferred) and crush them with a mortar and pestle. Petals were added to sesame oil in a covered pot, stirred, and kept warm. The combination was stirred occasionally, and after one month, was heated up to the temperature of a warm bath. It was then strained through a fine sieve and put in an airtight container. This oil was used as a perfume or for potpourri.

Today, rose oil is extracted by complex chemical processes, and it takes an acre of roses to produce a single pound of pure oil. But you can use one of these simple recipes to make your own rose water. For best results, use only fragrant rose petals gathered in the early morning. Do not use roses that have had pesticides applied to them.

Kettle Method

1. Fill a large kettle half full with water. Add 1 pound of fragrant rose petals.

2. Attach a 4-foot-long piece of rubber tubing to the spout of the kettle and place the other end in a large jar on the floor.

3. Place the middle section of the tubing in a bowl of ice water on a chair. This will condense the steam passing through the tubing.

4. Maintain the kettle at a gentle simmer until most of the water has evaporated and the petals are almost dry. Turn off the stove, and carefully drain the condensed steam from the tube.

5. Place the rose water in a jar, label it, and use as needed.

Jug Method

1. Place rose petals into a ceramic jug and pour 1 to 2 cups of boiling water over them.

2. Cover the jug and allow the mixture to cool.

3. Once cold, strain and press out all liquid from the rose petals.

4. Place the rose water in a jar, label it, and use as needed.

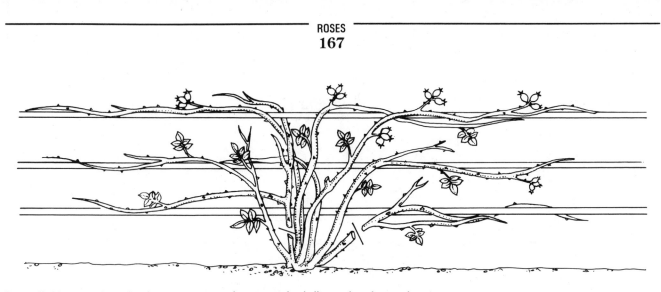

Prune climbing roses for a pleasing appearance and to remove dead, diseased, or damaged canes.

eral branches, which will bloom the following year. Many ramblers produce too many canes and become thick and tangled at the base; remove excess canes at the base of the plant. Rambling roses can be pruned in summer after they finish blooming.

Old, Shrub, and Species Roses

There is such tremendous variation within these groups of roses that you'll need to depend on your own judgment and be sensitive to the growth habits of individual plants when pruning. Don't treat these plants as you would treat other modern roses such as hybrid teas. They don't appreciate hard pruning. Instead, it's best to leave the natural shape of the plants intact, and use pruning simply to enhance their shape and beauty, as well as to keep them under control and healthy. Restrict yourself to a late-winter pruning to remove diseased, damaged, and very old wood. Thin the growth at the center of the plant to increase air circulation, and eliminate crossing branches. You can also cut back any excessively long canes to improve the shape of the plant.

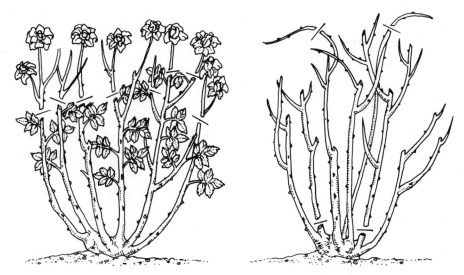

Remove spent blossoms of shrub roses when they fade (left). Don't deadhead roses if you are growing ones that will produce attractive hips in fall. Shrub roses benefit from light annual pruning in late winter. Remove one or two old, woody canes, along with any that are diseased or damaged. Cut back excessively long shoots and any canes that cross the center of the plant (right).

Ornamental Grasses

Growing and Using Ornamental Grasses

Ornamental grasses have become a popular ingredient in gardens in recent years. It's easy to understand why. They're extremely versatile plants that are quite undemanding when it comes to care and maintenance. But what exactly are they? Most are members of the immense grass family, Gramineae, which includes lawn grasses as well as a number of weedy species. Members of two other families—the sedge family, Cyperaceae, and the rush family, Juncaceae—are also commonly added to the general classification of ornamental grasses.

Design Considerations

Ornamental grasses add subtle beauty of form, texture, and color to gardens whether they are used in beds, borders, rock gardens, meadows, as edgings, or as specimens. Most are hardy perennials, although there are annual species grown for their seed heads. Their delicate foliage may be green, blue-green, or variegated with yellow, cream, or red. In fall and winter, the foliage turns buff or brown and adds interest to the dormant garden. Many species have ornamental seed heads that are attractive through winter or can be cut and dried for indoor display. Height ranges from several inches to several feet. The best ornamental grasses are clump-forming. Large, clump-forming species such as maiden grass (*Miscanthus sinensis*) combine delicate texture with a striking fountain-shaped habit. Some species spread by wandering rhizomes and can become invasive, however.

Ornamental grasses are most often combined with other plants such as shrubs, perennials, and annuals. Whether you're selecting them for a perennial garden, as specimens, or combining them with shrubs or other landscape plantings, consider all of the elements of design—color, texture, line, space, light, pattern, size, and form—just as if you were selecting any other plant. Most have an airy texture and a casual look that makes them especially suited to contemporary gardens. They work well in front of evergreens and in combination with other drought-resistant perennials. One popular combination that is especially effective in autumn is maiden grass (*Miscanthus sinensis*) planted with *Sedum* 'Autumn Joy' and *Rudbeckia* 'Goldsturm'. Blue fescue (*Festuca ovina* var. *glauca*) is a compact, 8-inch-tall, mound-shaped plant perfect for a spot at the front of a rock garden or edging a perennial bed. Taller grasses, such as 8-foot-tall maiden grass (*M. sinensis*), belong at the back of a perennial garden or among other drought-tolerant plants in a low-maintenance design. Large, beautiful clumps of grass can be singled out for specimen status. In addition to maiden grass, fountain grass (*Pennisetum* spp.) and Japanese blood grass (*Imperata cylindrica* var. *rubra*) are suited to this use. Pampas grass (*Cortaderia selloana*), which is hardy only to Zone 8, also is often displayed in this fashion.

Caring for Ornamental Grasses

Grasses are not demanding, fussy plants. They will survive in a wide range of conditions and have no disease or pest problems. They grow best in full sun, but many will also thrive in light shade, particularly in the South. They'll flourish if planted in rich soil that has been double-dug and thoroughly prepared, but they will do reasonably well planted in almost any soil. Ornamental grasses are tough, adaptable, drought-resistant plants that can stand weeks without water. A few true grasses, along with sedges and rushes, thrive in boggy conditions, but most prefer drier sites. Even variegated Japanese sedge (*Carex morrowii* 'Aureo-variegata'), a sedge frequently suggested for moist soil, will do well at the edge of a dry southern woodland, unwatered through 10 to 12 weeks of drought.

The only regular maintenance perennial ornamental grasses need is an annual trim to keep them neat and remove the previous season's foliage. Generally this is done in late winter, just before the plants begin to grow, because of the texture and color the dry clumps add to the winter landscape. Cut the plants back to the base; short plants like blue fescue should be cut to 1 or 2 inches, tall clump-forming plants to 6 or 8 inches.

Unlike irises and other perennials that require routine dividing every two or three years to keep them healthy, perennial ornamental grasses can remain untouched for ten years or more. When it is time to divide them, the process can be as simple as lifting small clumps with a garden fork and tearing each clump into smaller pieces. For the larger grasses, you'll need an ax or a saw and a strong back to chop the tough, large clumps into reasonable divisions.

Annual grasses will need to be planted each spring. Direct sowing into a prepared seedbed is best. (See the chart "Selecting Ornamental Grasses" on page 170 for germination information for some annual grasses. Follow directions in "Starting Seeds" on page 29 for sowing indoors or out.)

Harvesting and Using Grasses

Although most annual grasses aren't as spectacular landscape plants as the perennial species, they are treasured for their beautiful flower and seed heads, which are very useful in flower arrangements. Big quaking grass (*Briza maxima*), feathertop (*Pennisetum villosum*), and foxtail mil-

Dried seedheads of ornamental grasses make attractive, long-lasting arrangements. They can be combined with roadside plants such as teasel (*Dipsacus sylvestris*).

let (*Setaria italica*) are three of the more popular annual grasses grown for their seed heads. Of course, perennial grasses such as maiden grass (*Miscanthus* spp.) and pampas grass (*Cortaderia selloana*) also make fine additions to winter bouquets.

Harvesting grasses is a simple process. Just cut the stems, tie them in small bunches, and hang them in a dry place. For those species like foxtail millet or quaking grass that look best with a naturally curved stem, simply stand the grass stems in a tall, dry container.

Experiment with timing of the harvest. For example, wheat is beautiful if collected at the early, green stage, but can also be collected when it is gold in midseason or beige in autumn. Many grasses are best cut just before the seed heads open to disperse the seed, because the heads will last longer. Spritz fluffy panicles that might fall apart with hair spray to help them hold together through the winter. Use grasses alone or with other dried flowers for attractive winter bouquets.

SELECTING ORNAMENTAL GRASSES

Ornamental grasses are grown for many reasons. The seed heads of both annual and perennial species add attractive texture to garden beds and also to dried arrangements. These plants are at their glory in the fall and winter garden, when their ripening foliage and plumy heads add tawny yellows, tans, and browns to the landscape. The following are some of the best of these undemanding, easy-to-grow plants.

Grasses	Height	Season of Interest	Description	Culture
Annuals				
Briza maxima (Big quaking grass)	1-2 ft.	Summer to fall	Narrow, 4-6-in. leaves. Seeds borne in a loose cluster. Seed heads ripen to yellow or brown; quiver and quake in breeze.	Full sun. Poor soil. Propagate by seed. Does not transplant well. Sow seed outdoors in spring after last frost where plants are to grow. Good additions to dried arrangements. *B. media* is a perennial relative, hardy to Zone 5.
Coix lacryma-jobi (Job's tears)	3-4 ft.	Summer to fall	Sword-shaped, erect, 1-2-ft. long leaves. Clusters of drooping, ¾-in. beadlike seeds that are white streaked with gray or black.	Full sun to partial shade. Moist soil. Propagate by seed; soak in water 24 hours then sow indoors in early spring or outdoors after last frost. Relative of corn. Seeds can be strung like beads. Best where summers are long and hot.
Pennisetum villosum (Feathertop)	2 ft.	Summer to fall	Feathery, 4-5-in. spikes are creamy white with purple cast.	Full sun. Average, well-drained soil. Propagate by seed; sow indoors in early spring or outdoors after last frost. A perennial grown as an annual. Hardy to Zone 9. Can be dug and wintered indoors where not hardy. Seed heads shatter when dried.
Setaria italica (Foxtail millet)	2-4 ft.	Summer to fall	Dense, fuzzy, 1-ft.-long seed heads borne on arching stems.	Full sun. Moist, well-drained soil. Plants will not tolerate drought. Propagate by seed; sow outdoors where plants are to grow after last frost. Seed heads are attractive and long-lasting when dried.
Perennials				
Calamagrostis acutiflora* var. *stricta (Feather reed grass)	3-5 ft.	Summer through late winter	Narrow, green, 2-ft.-long leaves. Upright clump-forming habit. Narrow 1-ft.-long seed heads are purplish.	Full sun. Will tolerate moist or heavy clay soil. Propagate by division. Zones 5-10. Seed heads dry well; attractive in bouquets. A good background plant.
***Carex* spp.** (Sedge)	6-24 in.	Spring through fall	Low-growing, grasslike plants that form tufts or mounds. Narrow, arching leaves are often variegated with yellow or white.	Full sun to partial shade. Rich, moist soil. Propagate by division. Zones 3-8. Attractive groundcover or accent plant. Grown for ornamental foliage.

Grasses	Height	Season of Interest	Description	Culture
Chasmanthium latifolium (Northern sea oats)	3-5 ft.	Summer through fall	Narrow, light green leaves. Showy, drooping seed heads are green when new, then ripen to brown in fall.	Tolerate shade. Rich, moist soil. Propagate by division, seeds. Zones 4-10. Frequently listed as *Uniola latifolia*. Dried seed heads attractive in bouquets. Will reseed.
Festuca ovina var. *glauca* (Blue fescue)	6-12 in.	All year long	Evergreen, clump- or tuft-forming grass with threadlike, silvery blue foliage.	Full sun. Well-drained soil. Divide clumps if centers die out. Propagate by division. Zones 4-10. Grown for ornamental foliage. Also listed as *F. caesia* and *F. cinerea*.
Hakonechloa macra 'Aureola' (Golden variegated hakonechloa)	12-18 in.	Spring through fall	Attractive, arching habit. Leaves narrow, 8 in. long; brightly variegated with yellow and green. Ripen to tan in fall.	Partial shade. Rich, well-drained soil. Propagate by division. Zones 4-10. Grown for ornamental foliage. Color fades in full sun.
Imperata cylindrica var. *rubra* (Japanese blood grass)	10-12 in.	Spring through fall	Upright, clump-forming grass. Leaves narrow; green at base, deep red to tip.	Full sun to partial shade. Rich soil that is moist but well drained. Propagate by division. Zones 5-10. Grown for ornamental foliage.
Miscanthus sinensis (Eulalia or maiden grass)	4-8 ft.	Spring through mid winter	Vigorous, clump-forming plant with narrow, fine-textured foliage. Plumy, ornamental seeds heads appear in late fall.	Full sun to partial shade. Rich soil that is moist but well drained. Propagate by division, seeds. Zones 5-10. Many cultivars available; 'Variegatus' and 'Zebrinus' have variegated leaves.
Molinia caerulea var. *altissima* (Tall purple moor grass)	1-2 ft.	Summer to fall	Mound-forming grass with narrow leaves. Delicate-looking seed heads are purplish, appear in summer, and can reach 6 ft.	Full sun to partial shade. Rich, moist soil. Propagate by division. Zones 4 or 5-8. 'Variegata' has leaves striped with creamy white.
Panicum virgatum (Switch grass)	5-6 ft.	Late summer through winter	Narrow, upright grass that spreads by rhizomes. Seed heads buff-colored when ripe; foliage golden brown in fall.	Full sun. Well-drained soil. Propagate by division, seeds. Zones 4 or 5-10. Prairie native. Can become weedy. Dried seed heads attractive in bouquets.
Pennisetum spp. (Fountain grass)	2-3 ft.	Summer through winter	Many narrow, green leaves in wide, dense clumps. Graceful, arching habit. Ornamental seed heads fuzzy in texture; silver with a purplish cast.	Full sun. Rich, moist soil. Propagate by division. Zones 5-9. Excellent for mass plantings.

Garden Design

Designing a Flower Garden

Nothing can add sparkle and beauty to a landscape like a garden. A flower garden can be as as simple as petunias planted around a birdbath, as elaborate as a formal perennial border, or somewhere in between—perhaps clumps of bold perennials arranged strategically around your yard. But designing a flower garden can be a complicated undertaking. There are literally thousands of flowers to choose from, and new cultivars are constantly being offered. There are also unlimited possibilities for combining them in the garden. No wonder so many gardeners are attacted to the irresistible challenge of creating an attractive flower garden that satisfies their taste and needs. But your gardening will be more fun and your triumphs sweeter if you take time to ponder certain matters long before taking trowel and plants in hand.

The ABCs of Good Design

The best and most satisfying gardens are the result of careful planning and sound design. A flower garden should not only be a pleasing focal point, it should also fit into the total garden picture, harmonizing with background trees and shrubs, fences, paths, lawns, and with your house and other structures.

The best place to start any design project is on paper. Plot out a basic plan of your property. Nothing will inspire you to look more closely and critically at your landscape. It's best to make as accurate a plan as possible and include all your garden's features—paths, trees, buildings, fences, and the like. Draw it to scale, measuring distances with a 100-foot tape measure and transferring this information to graph paper. A scale of ¼ inch per foot is workable; tape sheets together if your property is large. This will make a valuable permanent record that you can work from and give you the best idea of where your garden is heading.

Use sheets of thin tracing paper as overlays to sketch in ideas and see how they fit while you work on the design. That way, you can use your master plan again and again until you decide on the best arrangement of pathways, flower beds and borders, and other landscape features. You can then transfer the final design to your master plan.

Design Principles

There are a few basic aesthetic principles to keep in mind that will help you make decisions as you develop your plan. They aren't unique to garden design; you'll find evidence of these principles in any good design. They also apply to decisions about adding walls or walkways to your garden. They're not hard-and-fast rules, although they will be helpful when making tough decisions. In the end, trust your own instincts and plan the garden you'll be happiest with—it's your garden, after all.

Balance. When elements on one side of a central point are of comparable size or weight as those on the other, they are said to be in balance. Balanced design gives the viewer a peaceful, restful feeling; unbalanced, lopsided design is unsettling.

In the garden, balance can be put into practice in many different ways. Two identical plants planted on either side of a path are symmetrically balanced. But two small plants on one side of a path can be balanced with one larger plant of comparable size and visual weight on the other. In this case they are asymmetrically balanced. Symmetrical balance is a hallmark of formal gardens; asymmetrical balance, of informal gardens.

Proportion. Elements of a design are said to be in proportion when their scale is in good relationship to their surroundings. A row of tall evergreens in a small lot creates a picture that is out of proportion because the size of the evergreens overwhelms the surrounding lot. Small trees or shrubs are a better choice for a small lot, because their scale is in better proportion to the space.

Repetition. Repeating one element in a design, such as color, texture, or shape, gives a feeling of unity and harmony. In a garden, repetition can be accomplished in a variety of ways. For example, if red is the dominant color in a flower bed, repeating it at intervals leads the eye onward and creates a feeling of wholeness and rhythm throughout. You can repeat the same plant or use several different species with similarly colored blooms to achieve the same effect.

Style

There are two general types of garden design styles—formal and informal. Gardens designed in an informal style are dominated by curved and free-form flower beds that sweep along the natural swell of the ground. Lawns, terraces, walkways, and other features also follow this style, with one gentle arc leading to another to create a feeling of harmony and unity. Naturalistic meadow or wildflower gardens are informal in style. If the lay of your land is irregular—with slopes, different levels, or rock outcroppings—it will lend itself to an informal design.

A formal garden contains classical symmetry, and flower beds and borders follow linear walks and terraces in strict rectangular shapes. Just as informal does not mean unplanned, formal does not necessarily mean grand. Actually, a formal design that is unfussy and simple is usually the easiest to work with for a small lot.

If your yard is fairly flat, you can choose whatever style you want. Here the architecture of your house might suggest the appropriate tone. A traditional house with a central hallway and distinct rooms calls for a more formal garden than a modern ranch house. Consider a garden with a central path that serves as an extension of the main hallway, with rectangular borders symmetrically flanking it. This simple design will repeat the harmonious plan of the house. A contemporary house with an open floor plan could have an informal garden with sweeping beds and a seeming disregard for symmetry.

Plants and Design

But building a flower garden isn't just a matter of putting design principles into practice. You need to con-sider the characteristics of the plants—most importantly color, height, form, and texture—when developing your basic design. Keep in mind that, perhaps more than in any other form of gardening, there are no guarantees in flower gardening. Plants will not bloom on schedule; some will grow taller than expected, some shorter; their colors will not be as you imagined them; some will disappear altogether. Even veteran gardeners must constantly fine-tune their gardens and cope with the unexpected; that is the challenge and lure of gardening.

Color. There are about as many theories on how to use color in the garden as there are gardeners. In the end it's pretty much a matter of personal preference. The riot of color one gardener strives for is considered garish by another; a pastel haze of soft pinks, blues, and lavenders is highly romantic to some, but others may find it insipid or boring. Regardless of personal taste, there are several ways you can use color in your garden. Learn how to manipulate the colors you like to make your garden more pleasing to you.

Color has the capacity to influence the mood of a garden. Hot, vibrant colors such as reds, oranges, and yellows will help evoke a happy, exciting mood. Cool colors—greens, blues, and purples—create a feeling of serenity and quiet.

Color can also influence perceived perspective. To the eye, hot or warm colors advance and bring an object or scene closer; cool colors tend to recede and push the object farther away. You can take advantage of this phenomenon in various ways. If you want to make your yard appear larger, plant flowers in cool colors at the back of your garden; warm colors would make it seem smaller.

Cool colors are best used for close-up viewing; hot colors for dramatic effect. Use cool colors in masses to catch the eye, and keep in mind that the cooler colors can be easily overwhelmed by the warm.

You will have to think hard about how you combine different colors in your design, particularly with flowers that bloom at the same time. Some colors enhance each other; for example, blue flowers are quite attractive next to pale yellow ones. But if your orange lilies are an eyesore next to magenta-colored phlox, try planting a gray-leaved plant such as Russian sage (*Perovskia* spp.) between them. The soft gray foliage of the sage will act as a peacemaker, and its tiny blue flowers will help balance the combination. Some gardeners use white in a similar way. White is a strong color; use it to define and organize bright colors.

Try to apply the principles of design in your color scheme. Strive for balanced distribution of color. For example, avoid having a massive planting of red flowers on one side of the garden without balancing it with a planting of equal weight on the other. A massive planting of one color can also overwhelm the other colors in a design, thus affecting proportion. Use repetition to unify the design by repeating the same color at balanced intervals. You don't need to use the same plant again and again, though. For example, you could repeat clear yellow by planting 'Lemondrop' marigolds near the front of the garden, evening primroses (*Oenothera* spp.) farther along toward the center, and tall, yellow-flowered heliopsis (*Heliopsis helianthoides*) at the back on the opposite end.

Height. The shape of your garden will dictate what rule of thumb you should use when arranging plants according to height. Again, the aim is to develop a design that is balanced and in proportion for your garden. For example, when planting a traditional border in front of a fence or other backdrop, stair-step the design with the tallest plants in the back and the shortest in front. You can soften any feeling of regimentation by planning an occasional "surprise" effect: Try placing a tall, airy plant that you can see through at the front of the border. Meadow rue (*Thalictrum* spp.) can be used for this purpose. In beds and borders that are not uniform in width, plan on having the tallest plants at the widest parts of the border. In island beds, on the other hand, the tallest plants should be in the center of the bed.

Form. The term form refers to the shapes of different plants—round, vertical, open, upright, creeping, weeping—and can be used to describe the entire plant or just the flowers.

For example, delphiniums are vertical plants with spike-shaped blooms, while marigolds are generally mound-shaped with round blooms. As with color, a particular form can affect balance and proportion. Form also can be repeated at intervals to strengthen unity and harmony. Spiky, vertical forms, for example, such as salvias (*Salvia* spp.) and speedwells (*Veronica* spp.), make pleasing complements when repeated along a border or when balanced with the more rounded forms of phlox or shasta daisies (*Leucanthemum maximum*). Daylilies have a bold form that can be repeated throughout a garden to lend stability and character to the whole design.

Texture. Plants also have different textures that can be used to strengthen a design. Their leaves can look coarse and crinkled, medium, or fine. They reflect light in different ways. Flowers can be feathery and delicate-looking or waxy and bold. Astilbes (*Astilbe* spp.) and cockscomb (*Celosia cristata*) have flowers with a plumy, featherlike texture, while tulips and lilies (*Lilium* spp.) have flowers with a waxy, less airy look.

Both form and texture are subtle characteristics to work with, not as dramatic as color. But they are well worth experimenting with. (For more information on how to select plants for color, height, form, texture, and period of bloom, see "Designing a Flower Border" on page 176.)

Questions to Ask Yourself

Once you've begun thinking about principles of design such as balance, repetition, color, and texture, the next step is to decide how a garden will fit into your landscape. Here are a few questions to help you decide what character it should take.

Where Should You Place Your Flower Garden?

Fortunately flower gardens can be planned for almost any site, as long

as the plants are matched to the sun, soil, and other cultural conditions present. Most flowers need a spot in the sun for best bloom. A site facing south or southeast that is sunny for at least six hours is ideal. If you only have a spot with partial shade available, don't despair. You can still have a flower garden, but the choice of plants is a bit more limited. Some of the flowers that can add pools of color to a shady spot are astilbes (*Astilbe* spp.), impatiens, flowering tobacco (*Nicotiana* spp.), wax begonias (*Begonia semperflorens*), and woodland wildflowers. These are effective when used with plants with bold or variegated foliage, such as hostas.

Put your flowers where you can see and enjoy them. Perhaps you want a pretty view from inside the house or from the terrace. If you want to be able to fully appreciate the colors, shapes, and textures of the flowers, site the garden within 25 feet of the house; farther away, the details will blur. Be sure to consider the direction from which you will most often be viewing the garden and orient it so it can be viewed to best advantage.

Consider what role you want the flower garden to play in your landscape. You might want it to define a work or play area, to enhance a swimming pool, or embellish a fence. If your yard is small and you prefer open space, plan a border at the perimeter of the lawn rather than a freestanding island bed in the middle.

What Size Should It Be?

There are several factors that play a role in determining the best size for your flower garden. Available space may be the determining factor, but if that isn't a problem, then ask yourself when you want your garden to bloom. Perhaps you and your family spend a month at the shore every July or August. If so, it makes sense to plan a garden that will be abloom from spring to early summer and have a final show in the fall.

If you want a garden that blooms all season, then you'll need a relatively large space so you can include many different plants that will provide an extended period of bloom. There is no set size for a garden designed for season-long bloom, but about 125 square feet will give you enough room to mass flowers for a succession of color. This could be a rectangle—perhaps 5 by 25 feet —or a circle 12 feet in diameter. Or you could plan several related beds divided by paths; each could be designed individually, or they all could be incorporated into one overall design. In general, don't plan gardens that are less than about 4 or 5 feet wide if you want a lush effect. Don't plan them any wider than that if you want to be able to tend the plants without stepping into the bed, or else plan on an access path on either side.

The last consideration is critical: How much time and money do you want to spend on your garden? Flowers require regular care—weeding, staking, watering, pruning—that takes time. Plants and other supplies cost money; decide how much you want to spend before you start to dig. If you want several flower gardens, consider designing separate beds that can be completed in stages over a long period, as time and budget permit. If you're not realistic about what size garden you can control, it will end up controlling you. Plan your flower garden so that you will have time to smell the roses.

What Kinds of Plants Do You Want?

No doubt you have many favorites— annuals, perennials, bulbs, herbs, and even vegetables—but your yard isn't large enough to accommodate sepa- rate gardens for each group. Include them all in your flower garden. Consider the different ways you can use plants from each of these categories in the flower garden.

Annuals. A planting of all annuals can provide an almost instant garden that will make a bright, showy display from June to frost. The plants then die, and the bed is torn up and replanted the following year.

Perennials. A flower garden designed with all perennials provides a more subtle color display and blooms for a shorter period. Peak bloom usually lasts a few weeks. Because the bloom period for each plant is limited, select plants with attractive foliage, since that is what you'll be looking at much of the season. The plants reappear year after year, but it usually takes them a year or two to fill their assigned spot in the flower bed. After they become established, most perennials will need to be divided every few years to keep them healthy and under control.

Annuals and Perennials. Most gardeners find that mixing annuals and perennials works best. A few favorite perennials in a bed of annuals will provide stability and textural contrast. On the other hand, annuals planted in pockets among perennials —or as edgings along a bed or border —will guarantee color when the perennials are in between bloom periods.

Bulbs, Corms, and Tubers. Interplanting flowering bulbs, corms, and tubers (all commonly referred to collectively as bulbs) with annuals and perennials is the perfect way to add color in early spring and fall. Spring-blooming bulbs, such as daf- fodils or crocuses, should be planted with fairly vigorous perennials, such as hostas or hardy geraniums (*Geranium* spp.), that have substantial leaves. The perennials can hide the yellow foliage of the ripening bulbs.

Summer-blooming bulbs, such as magic lilies (*Lycoris* spp.), ornamental onions (*Allium* spp.), or true lilies (*Lilium* spp.), add color to any planting. There are also tender bulbs that must be lifted and stored over winter, such as dahlias, which grow from tuberous roots, and Peruvian daffodils (*Hymenocallis* spp.). These are well worth the extra trouble for the color they add to the summer garden.

Herbs. Herbs not only add their distinctive fragrances to the flower garden, many have interesting foliage textures and colors as well. Herbs with silvery gray foliage, such as lavender cotton (*Santolina chamaecyparissus*), catmint (*Nepeta mussinii*), and English lavender (*Lavandula angustifolia*), are wonderful edging plants and can be used as a buffer between clashing colors.

Vegetables. Many new vegetable cultivars such as 'Vulcan' Swiss chard, ornamental cabbages and kales such as the 'Color Up' hybrids, and malabar spinach (*Basella alba*), a climbing vine with spinachlike leaves, are ornamental as well as edible. Even tomatoes—particularly the patio types with either small red or yellow fruit—can be decorative. You might have to sacrifice the design element of balance in your garden after your vegetables are harvested, but if you are willing to pay this price, consider adding an edible element to your ornamental garden.

Designing a Flower Border

If you have your heart set on a perennial border, the first decision you'll have to make is where to place it. Perennial borders can be used in many different ways, both in large or small properties. Borders can be used to edge walkways, terraces, and pool areas, or can be planted in front of walls, fences, or shrubbery. If you've decided on a formal garden, plan on a rectangular border. For an informal garden, a free-form border with curved edges might be in order. Borders are stunning when placed on one or both sides of a lawn.

Nothing can set off a perennial border better than a solid, neutral background—a wall, a board fence, the side of a building, or a mass of dark green shrubs. The backdrop will set off the details and colors of the border in a way open space beyond the flowers cannot. The architectural background also gives more stability to the border, anchoring it to the ground, so to speak. Such borders are best viewed from the front and are planted with the taller plants at the back. If the border is to be more than 4 feet wide, be sure to plan on a 2-foot-wide path at the back, between the border and the wall, to allow access for maintenance. This space will also allow air and light to reach the plants at the back of the planting, essential for the health of wide borders.

Getting Started

By this point, you'll have an idea of how large your border will be, what style you want, and whether it's to be in sun or shade. Now you're ready to sit down and develop the design.

Designing your perennial border will give you a chance to let your imagination soar and give vent to your creative talents. As you make lists and doodle with shapes and sizes, you'll be making decisions according to season of bloom, plant colors, and heights. At the same time, you'll want to keep in mind the precepts of good

design—balance, proportion, and repetition. Don't be intimidated by the many details you have to remember or the wide range of plants from which to select. There are basic steps to follow to make the design process a manageable and stimulating task. These techniques are the same whether you are designing a larger border, or one as small as 4 by 10 feet.

First, assemble the materials you'll need to make a plan. You'll need regular pencils, colored pencils or crayons, ruled paper for making lists, graph paper, a pad of tracing paper, and a soft eraser. Use graph paper with a scale of ½ inch for each foot; tape two sheets together if necessary.

Making a Plant List

The first step is making a list of all the perennial plants that are possible candidates for your border. Leave plenty of space between plants for notes. If your border is to be located in full sun on a spot with rich, loamy soil, then you can pretty much let your imagination run free. But if you are planning a border for less ideal conditions—a shady spot or dry, sandy soil—then be sure to keep these conditions in mind when selecting plants, and eliminate plants that will not tolerate the conditions you have to offer.

First, think of your own favorites, then add plants you have admired in other gardens, in nurseries, and in photographs, books, and magazines. Consult seed and nursery catalogs to find more plants to add to your list. These sources also give important descriptions of plant characteristics and tips for growing them. Jot down all that you can learn about a plant. When and how long does it bloom? How high is it? What color? How much space will it take up in the border when it matures? Is it hardy in your area? These are all facts you must know to decide which plants will best suit your purposes.

If you love blue, for example, now is the time to load your list with

bellflowers (*Campanula* spp.), balloon flower (*Platycodon grandiflorus*), purple-blue salvias like *Salvia × superba,* Stokes' aster (*Stokesia laevis*), asters, delphinium, irises, and others, depending on your climate. Don't forget blue-flowered spring bulbs *Iris reticulata* and grape hyacinths (*Muscari* spp.). To combine with blue-flowered plants, consider including white flowers and the versatile silvery-leaved artemisias 'Silver King' and 'Silver Mound'. You may want to add the blue-foliaged ornamental grass *Festuca ovina* var. *glauca.*

Whatever your color scheme, be alert for perennials with good foliage and long season of bloom. For example, *Achillea taygetea* 'Moonshine' has finely-cut leaves that are useful foils for any plant, and its yellow flowers will rebloom in September if cut back in July. *Sedum* 'Autumn Joy' has gray-green foliage and long-lasting flowers, which are borne in fall. The blooms turn from pink to russet over many weeks. (See the chart "Selecting Perennials and Biennials" on page 134 for some suggested perennials.) If you've decided on combining annuals, herbs, or wildflowers with perennials, be sure to add these plants to your list as well. Don't worry about making your list too long.

When you feel you have exhausted your resources, review your list and eliminate any plant that does not fit your conditions and needs. Do you go away every June? Cross off peonies and irises. Do you detest sulfur yellow? Get rid of *Coreopsis* and *Achillea* 'Coronation Gold'. Do you have a hot, sunny site with dry, sandy soil? Cross off delphiniums and astilbes, which need rich, moist loam and cool temperatures to do well.

Charting Selections. The next step is to organize your plants into categories that will help you select the ones that will add the most to your design. Begin by making a column for the bloom times you want.

To do this, take a fresh sheet of paper and, on the left side, make a column titled "Season of Bloom". Then subdivide the column according to when you want your garden to be in bloom. For example, for a succession of bloom all summer, write "Early Summer" just under "Season of Bloom," then farther down the column write "Midsummer," and farther down, "Late Summer." Or you can make it more specific and make a heading for each month that you want bloom. Do whatever is logical for your climate and wishes. Leave enough space under each subhead to list plant names.

Next to the "Season of Bloom" column, you'll need columns indicating plant heights. Move to the right on the page and make columns headed: "Under 1 foot," "1 to 2 feet," "2 to 3 feet," and "Over 3 feet." Last, make columns for each of the color groups you want to include in your color scheme. You may have columns such as "Pink-Salmon-Rose-Red," "Blue-Lavender-Purple-Mauve," "Yellow-Orange-Bronze," "White," and "Silver Foliage."

Now take the first plant on your list and enter it under the appropriate bloom category on your newly made chart. Also indicate its height and color by placing an *X* in the appropriate columns. Do this for each of the plants on your list. When you finish, look the chart over to make sure you have a fairly equal representation of *X*'s under each column. Will some flowers of each color be blooming in each part of the season? Are almost all of your plants 2 to 3 feet tall? Add and subtract plants until you have a good balance in all the plant categories and a manageable number of plants to grow. Last, number the plants on your list in consecutive order.

Sketching the Border
Draw an outline of your border to scale on the graph paper. As you look at your sketch, you are probably wondering how many plants it will take to fill your border. Let's assume that

it contains 125 square feet. Allowing 1½ to 2 square feet of space for each plant when it reaches maturity, this means that you can fit from 60 to 70 perennial plants into the border. The rate at which plants grow and their size at maturity varies, of course, but this will give you some idea of how many individual plants are needed.

This sketch will also help you determine if your plant list is too long to make an effective border. Plants are generally arranged in clumps of several, and the basic design principles of repetition and balance dictate that you'll probably want to repeat clumps of at least some species. As a general rule, you'll probably want one-third as many types of plants (species or cultivars) on your list as you can fit in your border. In the example above, that would mean about 20 to 25 types of plants.

The next step is to draw nameless shapes on the graph paper to indicate where each plant will grow. (Draw on a piece of tracing paper placed over your design on the graph paper if you like, so you can easily start over if you need to.) Instead of drawing neat circles or blocks, try to use oval or oblong shapes placed in horizontal drifts so that the plants will eventually merge and flow into one another. If your shapes begin to "puddle up" as you sketch, erase them and leave a little more space in between. Then, beginning with the first plant on your list, study its profile and decide where you want to plant it in the border. Transfer its number (number 1) to the corresponding shape—or shapes if you want to repeat it in more than one spot—on your diagram. Do this with all the plants on your list.

At the same time, you will have to decide how many of each plant you want. You may wish to follow the "rule of three" for perennials that are relatively small at maturity. Three plants will make an attractive clump. For large plants, such as peonies or Japanese anemones, you may want only one plant; for others two.

Design Considerations
Height. Remember to place the tall plants in the back of your diagram. Will a 7-foot-tall sneezeweed (*Helenium* spp.) overwhelm your border? Probably. For the most pleasing proportion, keep your tallest plant to a scale of two-thirds the width of the border—no taller, certainly, than 4 feet in a 5-foot-wide border—unless you want to experiment with an airy plant such as meadow rue (*Thalictrum* spp.) as a surprise focal point.

Instead of rigidly sticking to the stair-step profile, with medium heights in the center and short plants up front, let some tall plants extend forward into the middle group, and plan on clumps or drifts of some of the shorter ones up front. Used with discretion, this will give the border a less regimented look without destroying its unity.

Shapes and Textures. Now is also the time to play with shapes. Plants with spikey blooms, such as speedwells (*Veronica* spp.), salvias, and delphiniums, are wonderful accents for adding rhythm to your design. Intersperse them among the softer, rounded forms of baby's-breath (*Gypsophila* spp.), yarrow (*Achillea* spp.), or blanket flower (*Gaillardia* × *grandiflora*), to move the eye through your planting in either syncopated or slow movement, as you like. Use plants with attractive foliage in a similar manner. Contrast them with one another by planting glossy, dark green-leaved peonies next to *Achillea* 'Moonshine', which has gray-green, fernlike foliage.

Color. Try to dream up pleasing color patterns as well. For example, the lemon yellow flowers of *Achillea* 'Moonshine' are attractive paired with violet-purple salvia. This color scheme can be echoed by pairing *Geranium* 'Johnson's Blue' with *Coreopsis verticillata* 'Moonbeam', another lemon-yellow flowered plant. Pink and blue always mix well, too. Unless your border is hot and dry, try rosy pink *Astilbe chinensis* 'Pumila' with blue

Stokesia. If you like bright, primary colors, use white-flowered plants in between them to organize them and soften clashes. The possibilities are almost endless.

Color and Season of Bloom.
When you plan a border for a succession of bloom over several weeks or months, you are in effect creating a different garden for each bloom period. You can visualize how your border will look at each season with the help of tracing paper. Put a sheet of tracing paper over your completed design. Check your chart to find out which plants bloom in the first season in your column—early summer, for example. Locate the plants that bloom at that season by number on your master diagram, and trace them on your tracing paper. Then color them the appropriate color. Do the same for the other seasons of bloom on your chart, using a separate sheet of tracing paper for each. Each sheet will indicate how the border will look during the desired bloom periods.

Getting your colors right for each season of bloom will be difficult. You should strive for a balanced composition in every season, with the color weaving throughout the border during each bloom period. The color should not only be evenly distributed, it should make pleasing patterns. Are all the reds or yellows off to one side of the border so that the design looks lopsided? Are the color combinations pleasing to you? Do you have the magenta phlox planted next to orange-flowered *Rudbeckia* 'Goldsturm'? Would placing a plant of gray-leaved artemisia 'Silver King' make the color combination acceptable? Are major color combinations repeated at rhythmic intervals to tie the border together? Would it help to add more plants of a particular color?

As you grapple with these problems and refine your design, be sure to make changes on both tracing paper and master diagram. Expect to have to redo your design several times before you feel you have it right. Think

of it this way: Each sheet of crumpled paper brings you closer to your goal of creating a beautiful garden—tailor-made by and for you.

Preparing the Site

Thorough soil preparation is the foundation of a luxuriant perennial border. What good is a beautiful design if your plants can't grow well? Soil preparation is especially critical in a perennial border where the soil will remain relatively undisturbed for years. Ideally, you should prepare the soil in the fall so the border will be ready for spring planting. Whatever you do, don't order plants and then try to prepare the soil after they arrive. For best results, you want to have a home ready and waiting for plants when they arrive in the mail or you bring them home from the nursery.

If your border is to be rectangular, you can measure and mark it out using stakes and string to mark the boundaries; where there is only bare earth, draw lines on the ground with lime. If your border has irregular, flowing edges, use hose or pieces of heavy rope to outline the edges. Adjust them until you're pleased with the shapes you've outlined, then mark the edges with lime.

If the border abuts the lawn, insert a barrier (metal or rubber edging materials are readily available in garden centers) in the ground along the edges to keep grass at bay. Or you could edge the bed with brick, stone, or landscape pavers—whatever material would look well with your house, terrace, or walks. A 1- to 1½-foot-wide edging will accommodate one wheel of a lawn mower and make mowing along the border easier.

Planting Your Border

With your design in hand, the soil prepared, and well-watered plants at the ready, it is time to plant your garden. Set each plant on the soil, still in its container, according to its position in your master plan. Allow

enough room for the spread of each plant at maturity. Since you are now looking at your border in three dimensions instead of only two, you might want to do some last-minute fine-tuning. When you are satisfied that all is well, begin planting at the back of the border and work forward. (See "Selecting and Planting Perennials" on page 130 for tips.) Step out to the front every so often to see how things are shaping up, and try to visualize the scene as it will look in a couple of years.

The Question of Annuals
Whether you decide to plant your border all at one time or in stages, consider putting a few annuals into service—at least for the first few

---

ACQUIRING PLANTS

Once you've completed your design, it's time to acquire the plants. You will be able to purchase some from nurseries, others through the mail. (See "Sources" on page 401 for addresses of some mail-order nurseries.) You also might want to grow some yourself from seed. When you estimate how many plants you will need, and figure on paying about $5 each, your cost for plants for an average-size border will probably fall between $200 and $300. You might well decide to grow your own from seed.

Another budget-saving device might be to use annuals in place of many of your perennials the first year and complete your design the following year. You can also cut down on costs if you plant one perennial instead of two or three of the same kind, then wait a couple of years until the "mother" plant can be divided to fill in the design. The only drawback is that you'll have to wait a bit longer to see the final results of your plan.

seasons, while your border becomes established. Afterwards, try slipping a few of these dependable plants into your scheme each year; the continuous bloom annual flowers contribute to a border is invaluable. Even in successful borders, there will inevitably be a quiet period as the flowers rev up for the next display. Somehow, if there are colorful annuals in the front row, all seems well within the border. Try scattering seeds of white sweet alyssum (*Lobularia maritima*) or *Phlox drummondii* along the front; the tiny white flowers of alyssum are especially effective because they complement everything. Petunias add a cheerful note as well as fragrance; use single colors you can integrate into your color scheme, or use white. Annual salvias will add spirelike flowers farther back in the border, and cosmos (*Cosmos* spp.) and spider flower (*Cleome* spp.) could be seeded directly in the soil in June where bare spots are apparent. Work from your basic diagram to see where annuals might strengthen your design, and use it to decide appropriate colors.

If you want to use annuals only if trouble occurs, such as a failed or sluggardly plant, it's a good idea to keep a few growing in pots in a small nursery area or in containers on your porch or patio. If necessary, you can then pop them into your border.

Designing an Island Bed

An island bed is nothing more than a freestanding bed placed in the open space of a garden. It can be walked around and viewed from all sides and is generally surrounded by lawn. In fact, the best island beds entice the viewer to walk around them and enjoy them from all sides. Plants are exposed on all sides to light and air, so they generally grow sturdy and straight. With careful selection, plants grown in island beds require little or no staking. Another advantage of island beds is that plants are accessible for easy maintenance.

Design Considerations

Island beds are less formal than conventional perennial borders. Usually, they're free-form in shape, which makes them perfect for informal gardens. However, there isn't any reason why you can't plan a rectangular, round, or square island bed that would suit a formal garden. Often they're planned in groups, with two or more related shapes that interact visually but are separated by strips of lawn. As with any type of flower planting, good planning and design will pay off with attractive plantings that are pleasing to the eye. Here are basic questions to consider and design guidelines to assist you in planning.

Location

Island beds are especially effective in gardens surrounded by trees and shrubs planted around the boundaries for privacy. Placing an island bed—or beds—in the lawn in the center of the yard will provide an attractive, colorful focal point. Unless your yard is tiny, putting an island flower bed out in the center will make it look larger than if you design your flower plantings to hug the edges.

However, don't take center of the lawn literally, unless you're planning a formal garden, in which case you may decide on a pair of rectangular islands or a single one at the end of a walk. For an informal effect, place your island bed slightly to one side in the open space—this might be a lawn or a graveled or paved area—so that the resulting spaces around the bed vary in their dimensions. These un-

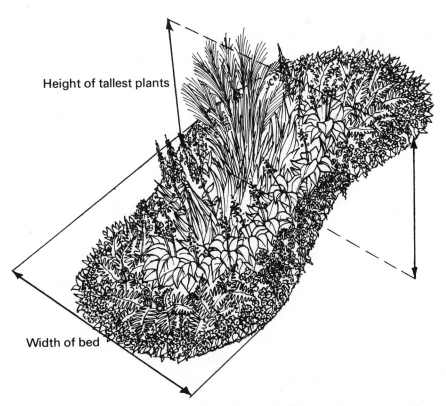

Height of tallest plants

Width of bed

Design your island bed so that the height of the tallest plants will equal approximately half the width of the bed.

even spaces can add a dynamic element to your property and lure the viewer into other parts of the garden as well. To achieve a pleasing asymmetrical balance, locate your bed in relation to other garden features and buildings. A garage or a large oak tree diagonally across from the proposed bed can serve as a balancing element.

Size

Although island beds can be small, for best effect make them as large as space, budget, and maintenance will permit. Two yardsticks of good design apply: Width should be twice the height of the tallest plant in the bed; and length should be about half the distance from the house or terrace to the bed itself. If you keep the tallest plant to about 4 feet and make the bed 8 by 16 feet, this would provide a nice manageable bed for a backyard of modest size. These dimensions offer a cohesive shape in which to arrange colorful and interesting plant pictures for viewing from all sides.

A large property could support a dramatic bed with large plants such as 8-foot-tall black snakeroot (*Cimicifuga racemosa*) or cow parsnip (*Heracleum* spp.) in the center. A bed with plants this tall would demand a width of 16 feet and a length long enough to be in pleasing proportion to both the width and the distance from the main viewing point. An alternative would be to plan two or more smaller beds that would swerve and curve toward each other, leading you on over the landscape. These could be treated the same way as a series of borders: Design them thematically according to color—one bed containing predominantly blue flowers, one white, and so on—or according to season of bloom. This method would avoid fussiness and color clashes and preserve a mood of unity in the garden.

Shape

For a formal garden, island beds should be regular in shape—rectangular or round beds are ideal. In an informal garden, irregular beds with curving shapes provide a more natural look. An island bed with flowing, curved edges is a good choice because it gives a feeling of movement to your garden and is particularly pleasing to walk around. Curving lines create the illusion of more space and make a small garden appear larger.

After you know the maximum width and length of your island bed, you can begin sketching ideas on paper. For a free-form shape, begin with a rough oval set to your dimensions, and then refine your design by adding curved edges that bulge in places. Also consider creating a "hook" or two in the bulges; these will become pockets to entice the viewer to enjoy the plants up close. Be sure to keep all the curves and hooks heading in the same direction for a nice flow. When you've developed a design that pleases you, check it again against your total garden picture to make sure it will fit in well. It's also a good idea to go out to the spot you've selected, use a hose or heavy rope to outline the pattern you want, and place a few stakes representing your tallest plants in the center of the bed. This will help you visualize how the bed will look in three dimensions. Walk around your proposed bed and study the changing views in the landscape as well as the shape of the bed itself. Then plot your final design on graph paper.

Planting Design

An island bed can be planted with with almost any mix of plants that suits your fancy—perennials, annuals, herbs, bulbs. If the bed is large enough, consider including small shrubs to add winter interest—evergreens for color mass, deciduous shrubs for skeleton shapes and mood. Vines such as clematis can romp over shrubs and clumps of lilies can add stature in the center.

To develop a plant list and plan your design on paper, follow the steps described in "Designing a Flower Border" on page 176. You must know the bloom time of each plant and its color, height, cultural and climate requirements, and other special features. Then decide how to make the most pleasing harmonious and contrasting patterns while working with these qualities in your allotted space.

Try to select plants that are self-supporting and won't need staking. A few suggestions include leopard's-bane (*Doronicum* spp.), speedwell (*Veronica* spp.), bellflowers (*Campanula* spp.), hardy geraniums (*Geranium* spp.), and daylilies. Select low-growing species or cultivars of taller plants that are normally rangy, such as asters or phlox. For example, there are low-growing cultivars of our native asters, and species of phlox such as *Phlox subulata* and *P. sto-*

Green Thumb Tip

WINTER INTEREST

Since island beds are located in open areas, they are highly visible year-round. With a bit of planning, they can become a garden attraction in both winter and summer. Select a few large rocks or stepping stones with unique shapes and texture, then position them in an attractive pattern in the bed. During the growing season the plants will camouflage the rocks, but you can use them to step on while weeding or removing spent flower heads—especially if your garden is wider than 8 feet. If you add one or two small deciduous shrubs or dwarf evergreens, you'll have a pretty winter feature to look at while most of the garden is "quiet."

lonifera are low-growing and won't need staking like tall garden phlox (*P. paniculata*).

Once you've narrowed your list and are deciding where each plant will go in the bed, it's important to remember that an island bed will be seen from all sides, not just the front. Put the tallest plants in the center of the bed and taper the smaller plants around them until the lowest-growing ones edge the bed. Avoid building a solid ridge of tall plants across the middle of the bed; instead strive for a peak or "crescendo" at the center. Once you're happy with your design on paper, you can prepare the bed, obtain the plants, and plant them just as you would a perennial border.

Creating a Water Garden

A garden without water—whether a birdbath, small pond, or stream—seems somehow incomplete. Adding a water garden to your landscape opens a whole range of soul-satisfying experiences. What can instill a feeling of repose and peace better than gazing at the reflection of clouds wafting by on the still, cool surface of a pond? The sight of goldfish glinting among water lilies? Or the sound of splashing water mixing with birdsong? A water garden also offers a chance to grow exciting aquatic plants such as hardy and tropical water lilies and lotus, and a variety of shallow-water bog plants, including blue-flowered pickerel weed (*Pontederia cordata*), sweet flag (*Acorus calamus*), and yellow water iris (*Iris pseudacorus*).

Not too long ago, unless you already had a natural pond or stream on your property, creating a water garden was an expensive, high-maintenance undertaking. Luckily, water gardens are a possibility for nearly any yard today because of the availability of easy-to-install pool liners that are relatively inexpensive.

Design Considerations

The principles of balance and proportion discussed in "Designing a Flower Garden" on page 172 apply to the planning of a water garden in much the same way as a flower garden. You'll need to consider proportion just as if you were adding a flower bed or border to your landscape. A water garden should be in proportion to the size of your yard, without overwhelm-ing it. A large garden may have room for a large pool, but in a small garden there may only be room for half a whiskey barrel in a sunny corner of the patio—even so, this will suffice for a dwarf water lily, some smaller plants, and two or three fish.

Also consider the principle of balance when deciding where the water garden will go, and position it in relation to other landscape elements. A water garden can be balanced with an island bed, trees or shrubs, or a shed or other structure, for example.

Style and Placement

There are water gardens for both formal and informal gardens. For an informal garden, consider a naturalistic pond located in an open area and designed to blend with the existing landscape. It could be kidney-shaped or a combination of geometric and free-form shapes. Natural stone or grass could be used to soften the lines of the pool edging.

If your garden is more formal, a geometric pool—perhaps with a fountain or statue—could make an ideal focal point for a squarish terrace, or in the middle of a velvet lawn. Face it with brick, flagstone, or other cut stone to match your terrace or walks.

Whether your water garden will be formal or informal, large or small, pick a location away from trees if you do not want to spend hours scooping out leaves; otherwise place black netting or mesh screening over the pool to catch falling autumn leaves. A position away from trees is essential if you want to grow water lilies, because they require at least six hours of sunlight to bloom well.

If the site you've selected is a low area, groundwater may run into the pool after rainstorms, upsetting its ecological balance and muddying the water. You can prevent this by building up the rim of the pool so that it will be a few inches higher than the ground around it.

You will want the site to be within reach of the garden hose, for refilling the pond. Place the pool within reach of an electrical source if you're going to use a pump.

Movement

If you want the added drama of a splashing fountain in your pool or would just enjoy hearing the gentle trickle of water in the background, a wide variety of pumps and fountains are available from mail-order companies specializing in water gardening. (See the source list on page 401.) All come with instructions and are usually simple to install. For safety, pumps for recirculating water should be used in conjunction with a ground fault circuit interrupter installed by an electrician.

If your property is on different levels and has rock outcroppings, it's even possible to build a cascading chain of small pools with the aid of a submersible pump for recirculating water. Naturalistic waterfalls are more ambitious, requiring expertise and perhaps a consultation with a professional.

Keep in mind that you'll need a larger pool if you want to grow water lilies *and* have a fountain or waterfall. This isn't just for aesthetic reasons: Water lilies can't tolerate moving water. Your pool must be big enough so you can keep water lilies away from moving water, or consider a fountain that only provides a gentle trickle of water.

Materials and Construction

Before beginning the excavation for your water garden, you'll need to decide what kind of pool to install. Pools can be made of concrete, rigid, prefabricated pool liners, or flexible liners made of polyvinyl chloride or butyl rubber. Plan on at least a 16- to 24-inch-deep pool if you intend to grow hardy water lilies in areas where there are winter freezes. It's also a good idea to plan on building some shallow ledges around the edges for bog plants. In fact, prefabricated liners come equipped with them.

Concrete Pools

Concrete pools are the most expensive, but they are sturdy and long lasting, and you can create whatever shape you want. Building a formal rectangular pool requires a level of technical skill beyond the abilities of most gardeners. It involves constructing a wooden form, laying drains and an inlet pipe, and perhaps shaping niches or pedestals for various kinds of aquatic plants. It's best to have this type of pool built by professionals. On the other hand, an informal concrete pool with rounded irregular sides can be made without building a form. Two layers of cement are poured, each 3 inches deep, with reinforcing mesh between the layers. Before the top layer is dry, rocks can be embedded in the concrete to provide footholds for plants that will grow along the edges. New concrete ponds must be treated to neutralize lime and calcium to make them safe for fish. It's a good idea to coat the pool with waterproofing before filling it with water.

The disadvantage of concrete pools is that they tend to crack and spring leaks as the surrounding soil settles. This is particularly true where there is winter freezing and thawing. While cracks can be repaired, draining the pool, repairing the cracks, and re-waterproofing is a time-consuming process. Companies specializing in water gardening offer materials for repairing and treating concrete.

Prefabricated Pools

Both landscaping supply stores and mail-order firms specializing in water gardening sell prefabricated pools made of fiberglass in a variety of styles, shapes, and sizes. A large prefabricated pool can be roughly 16 inches deep, 13 feet long, 6 feet wide, and hold 550 gallons of water; small pools holding as little as 60 gallons are also available.

Prefabricated pools are relatively easy to install. Dig a hole the size and shape of the pool, line it with sand, and fit the fiberglass pool into the hole. It's important to check periodically to make sure the pool will be level, both while digging and lining the hole with sand. Use a level placed on a board to measure rim to rim. Once the pool is in place, check carefully again to make sure it's level; if not, remove the liner and adjust the sand until it is. A pool that's not level won't fill evenly and the uncovered pool rim on the high side will look unnatural. Fill soil in around the edges of the pool and under any ledges to support the fiberglass. Once you've finished, edge the pool with rocks or bricks or conceal the edges with trailing plants, and fill with water.

Fiberglass pools hold up well in winter extremes and are long-lasting. Make sure soil drainage around the pool is good enough to prevent freezes that might pop the pool right out of the ground. Although the liners are expensive, they cost less than installing a concrete pool.

Flexible Liners

Pools lined with flexible liners are easy to design and install because the material will conform to whatever shape you want. They're also relatively inexpensive. The best, most long-lasting liners are made of heavyweight polyvinyl chloride (PVC) or butyl rubber between 20 and 32 mils (1 mil = $\frac{1}{1000}$ inch) thick. They are manufactured in neutral colors such as gray, black, and green. PVC liners are less expensive than butyl rubber but their life expectancy is also less: 20 mil PVC lasts seven to ten years; 32 mil, 15 years or more. Liners are available from companies specializing in water gardening. (For step-by-step instructions to create a pool with a PVC or butyl rubber liner, see "Building a Pool with a Liner" on page 185.)

Water Garden Plants

Aquatic plants fall into several categories, with water lilies being perhaps the best known. There are also other floating-leaved plants, lotus, and bog plants to consider. You'll also need oxygenating plants to keep the pool balanced and healthy.

Restrain yourself when you make your plant list. For the health and beauty of your pool, no more than half the surface of the water should be covered with lily pads and other plants. Overplanting will also hide the sight of sparkling water and fish darting along the bottom. The water gardening specialists in the source list on page 401 offer plants in each of the categories below.

Floating-Leaved Plants

Perhaps you fantasized about growing water lilies after seeing French Impressionist Monet's paintings of his beautiful water garden at Giverney. Water lilies are easy to grow if you have a site for a pool that has a minimum of six hours of sun daily. There are both hardy and tropical water lilies, all belonging to the genus *Nymphaea*. They are grown with their roots planted in submerged containers while their leaves and flowers float on or just above the water's surface. Their spectacular flowers come in shades of white, pink, red,

PLANTING WATER LILIES IN CONTAINERS

The best time to plant water lilies is during the warm weather of mid- or late spring. Most mail-order companies will ship them at the proper time for your area, complete with step-by-step directions. Tropical water lilies should not be planted until the water reaches a minimum stable temperature of 70°F.

Planting lilies in containers will allow you to move them about easily. Use a large dishpan, a plastic pot at least 12 inches across, or one of the planting containers offered by companies specializing in water gardening. Plant water lilies in heavy garden soil—do not use commercial potting mixes and do not add organic material which might decompose in the water. Sift through the soil to remove any roots and leaves, partially fill the container, then position the water lily crown so it just protrudes above the soil. Gently fill the container with soil and tamp it firmly around the plant. Top-dress the container with ½ inch of pea gravel and saturate it with water from the pool. Slowly lower the container into the pool until the rim is about 6 inches below the surface of the water. Use bricks or plastic crates to support the container initially. (Do not use concrete blocks, which may cause a pH imbalance.) Once the plant has begun growing, lower the container so the water depth over the crown is 12 to 18 inches.

Before planting a water lily, inspect the rhizome carefully and cut away any dead or damaged roots.

Fill the container with heavy garden soil. If you're using one of the mesh baskets designed for planting lilies, line it with burlap before filling. Plant the rhizome horizontally near the surface.

Before slowly lowering the newly planted lily into the water, cover the surface of the soil with a ½-inch layer of pea gravel. Initially, the container rim should be about 6 inches below the water's surface. Once the plant is growing, lower the container so that the rim is 12 to 18 inches beneath the surface.

orange, yellow, bronze, and blue and appear from June through August. Some have scented blooms. Tropical water lilies are generally replaced each year much like annuals. They are usually more flamboyant than the hardy lilies; some will bloom at night. Hardy lilies are perennial and can overwinter in the pond if their roots do not freeze.

Other smaller floating-leaved plants include four-leaf water clover (*Marsilia mutica*) and yellow-flowered floating heart (*Nymphoides peltata*).

Emergent and Marginal Plants

Commonly called bog plants, emergent and marginal plants are all tall plants that root beneath the water or in the shallow water at the edges of the pond and carry their lush foliage and colorful flowers skyward. There are hardy and tropical species from which to choose. Hardy species include pickerel weed (*Pontederia cordata*), arrowheads (*Sagittaria* spp.), cattails (*Typha* spp.), and yellow water iris (*Iris pseudacorus*), as well as shorter species like golden-club (*Orontium aquaticum*), parrot's-feather (*Myriophyllum aquaticum*), and spike rush (*Eleocharis* spp.). Dwarf papyrus (*Cyperus isocladus*), taro (*Colocasia esculenta*), and umbrella palm (*Cyperus alternifolius*) are some of the tropical bog plants from which to choose.

Although they generally are planted in deeper water than bog plants, at least 4 inches below the surface, lotus (*Nelumbo* spp.) have large, round leaves carried up to 5 feet above the water surface. Their large, bowl-shaped blossoms are followed by intriguing seedpods.

Since water lilies and garden pools are horizontal, use emergent and marginal plants in masses for vertical accents and as interesting backdrops for shorter plants. Don't crowd them, though, so the water can frame and reflect them.

Oxygenating Plants

Oxygenating plants maintain an ecological balance in your pool. They control algae by depriving them of minerals and sunlight; trap debris in their leaves; and use up carbon dioxide produced by fish while giving off the oxygen these animals require.

Oxygenating plants are sold in bunches of cuttings and can be planted in containers along with water lilies or in containers of their own. Use one bunch for every 1 or 2 square feet of pool surface. Plants to consider include anacharis (*Elodea canadensis*), cabomba (*Cabomba caroliniana*), dwarf sagittaria (*Sagittaria subulata*), and vallisneria (*Vallisneria americana*).

Fish

Fish are not only decorative—and fascinating to watch—they join with the plants to balance the ecology of your pool. They are good scavengers, eating mosquito larvae and insects, algae, and plant debris. The best candidates are common goldfish, golden orfe, and different kinds of fantail fish. A good stocking ratio for a new pool is 2 inches of fish to every square foot of pool surface. Your pool should be filled with water and allowed to settle for several weeks before you add fish. This is especially important if you are ordering fish through the mail, because the pool needs to be waiting and ready when they arrive. You'll also need to treat the water for chlorine, chlorine dioxide, or chloramine, all of which are toxic to fish, before adding the fish to their new home. Chlorine will dissipate naturally if the water is aged overnight; chlorine dioxide and chloramine, both of which are used in municipal water systems, will not. Pet stores and mail-order firms specializing in water gardening offer products to neutralize these chemicals.

Release the fish by submerging the unopened bag in which the fish were purchased for about 15 to 20 minutes, so the water in the bag can reach pool temperature. Then open the bag and release the fish. Although you can feed the fish daily, they can survive on insects and underwater plants for several days at a time. Overfeeding can foul the pond, so waiting a day or two between artificial feedings is a good practice. Feed fish from spring, when the water warms, through autumn. As the water cools in late fall, stop feeding; fish cannot digest food properly in cold water. They will overwinter on the bottom of the pool, provided it doesn't freeze completely to the bottom. If you're unsure, you can purchase a de-icer from water garden suppliers.

Plants for around the Pool

Plantings around your pool can help tie it to the landscape. It's a good idea to avoid planting anything that will shed leaves into the pool. Consider clumps of ornamental grasses placed in sunny spots around an informal pool; the movement of grasses waving in the breeze will echo water rippling in the pool. Try ferns and hostas around a shady pool. Small shrubs and trees—especially those with a weeping habit such as cherries or Japanese maples—are suitable, although they will shed leaves into the pool. Plant them on the north side of the pool to avoid shading it, and balance the planting on the opposite side with prostrate junipers, which will hold the scene all winter, or clumps of evergreen azaleas, which will make a dazzling spring show.

Maintenance and Seasonal Care

Water gardens require very little regular care once they've become established. You'll need to regularly remove yellowed leaves of water lilies and lotus; pinch the stems off at the base of the plant. Oxygenating plants such as anacharis can become overgrown; prune it back if it seems to be restricting the movement of the fish. Periodically scoop leaves and debris off the bottom of the pond; this helps keep the water clear and also prevents the buildup of organic matter. In winter, decomposing organic matter can suffocate fish when the surface of the pool is covered with ice. Water lilies and lotus should be divided and repotted when they become overgrown. This is best done in spring. Finally, you'll need to drain the pool every year or two to clean it out. To clean a pool, take out the plants and set them in a tub or buckets of water so they don't dry out. Catch the fish and place them in a container of seasoned water from the pond. Then siphon or pump the water out of the pool. Remove leaves and other debris at the bottom. Then replace the plants and refill with clean water. Reintroduce the fish after you have treated the water to eliminate chlorine and related chemicals.

Building a Pool with a Liner

Building a water garden lined with a plastic liner is a quick and easy way to install a pool. Just follow these steps.

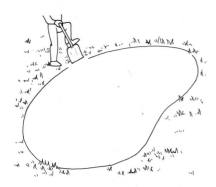

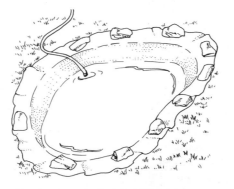

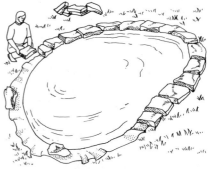

When installing a pool with a flexible liner, first outline the shape with hose or rope, mark the edges with lime, and dig out sod or weeds covering the area.

Then lay down the liner, holding it in place with rocks placed around the edges. Adjust the liner for a smooth fit as you fill the pool with water.

Once the pool has been filled, trim and conceal the edge of the liner and hold it in place with stones or bricks.

1. Once you know the rough shape of the pool, you'll need to determine what size liner you'll need. Use these formulas: Liner length equals pool length plus double the maximum depth of the pool; liner width equals pool width plus double the maximum depth of the pool. For example, for a pool 12 feet long by 6 feet wide by 3 feet deep, you would need a liner that is 18 feet (12 plus 6) by 12 feet (6 plus 6).

2. Next, mark the outline of the desired shape of the pool with garden hose or rope. As you dig, shape shelves around the pool edge so you'll have plenty of room for shallow water plants—about 9 inches wide and 9 inches below water level is fine. The sides of the pool should slope slightly inward from top to bottom at about a 75-degree angle.

3. After you've finished digging, check the depth and width of the shelves at the edges of the pool.

Also remove sharp stones or roots from the sides and bottom of the pool.

4. Check to be sure that the pool is level by laying a plank across the top of the hole and using a level on top. Do this several times, moving the plank to a new position each time. Where the edge is low, build it up with soil.

5. To protect the liner, place a ½-inch layer of sand over the bottom of the hole. Press wet sand into any holes or crevices in the sides.

6. Drape the liner loosely into the hole, leaving at least a 6-inch overlap all around.

7. Place bricks or smooth stones around the edges to anchor the liner while you slowly fill the pool with water. As the pool fills, move some

of the stones to pleat and smooth the liner.

8. When the pool is full, adjust the liner and trim the edges to 6 inches, if necessary. Cover the edge of the liner with bricks, stones, sod, or whatever is in keeping with your garden style. Treat the water for chlorine and related chemicals before planting and adding fish.

Plant the finished garden with a variety of plants such as water lilies and shallow-water bog plants. Fish add color and movement to the garden while consuming algae, mosquito larvae, and other insects.

Creating a Rock Garden

A rock garden can add natural beauty to a landscape in a way few other gardens can. The combination of rocks with diminutive, delicate-looking plants brings to mind rugged natural scenes—windswept mountaintops or craggy cliffs. In fact, the best rock gardens start with a natural-looking construction of rocks as the backbone. They're then planted with a wide variety of tiny, low-growing plants with compact growth habits, fine-textured foliage, and colorful flowers. For this reason, rock gardens are usually naturalistic in style and best suited to an informal landscape. Traditional rock garden plants are native to alpine cliffs and mountainous areas the world over. Other species thrive in rocky conditions in sun or shade at lower elevations. However, there are many easy, undemanding plants suitable for rock gardens from which to choose.

Why bother building a rock garden when there are already so many tempting flowers and shrubs to grow? Well, if you love plants and have a small yard, even a tiny rock garden can easily hold over a hundred plants—compared with a mere handful of perennials in a conventional garden of the same size. Also, in the different micro-environments of a rock garden—between rocks and among miniature ridges and valleys you create—you can grow unique plants that might not survive elsewhere in your garden or would be overwhelmed by more aggressive plants. Once the garden is planted, all that's required is faithful weeding, watering during extended droughts, and light pruning.

Design Considerations

There are many ways to incorporate a rock garden into your landscape. It's easy to build one where a natural slope exists, such as a steep bank that's awkward to mow or a gravelly slope with poor soil. If you have only a level lawn, you can add interest to your landscape by bringing in rocks and topsoil and building your own slope. You may be able to design one near a pond or rocky woodland. Or plant a few evergreens such as gnarled pines or spreading junipers, or a clump of birch or dogwood, to use as a background for a rock planting. If you're lucky enough to have a rock outcrop, use it as the nucleus of a simulated mountainscape. Weed it, then expose soil-covered rocks or add more rocks of matching color and texture. Then amend the soil and tuck in your plants.

If a conventional rock garden would look awkward, or if you haven't the space, time, or resources for a full-fledged garden, you can grow rock plants in a raised bed 2 feet or more high, using stone, brick, or railroad ties for walls. A hidden bonus is that raised beds bring gem-sized plants closer to eye level.

Picking a Site

For best results, start with a site in full sun or one with some dappled shade during hot summer afternoons. A location several yards away from overhanging trees is best, so tree roots won't compete with your plants. If your yard is mostly shaded, you can still have a lovely rock garden—choose shade-loving plants such as small wildflowers and ferns.

Good drainage is also important. Many rock plants have long roots that reach deep into the soil behind and under rocks; they like moisture about their roots, but can't tolerate constantly wet soil. If the site isn't well drained naturally, you'll need to improve drainage before planting.

Soil is another important consideration. Rock plants growing in the wild are usually found in soil that contains rock debris with a considerable amount of organic matter. Such soil provides excellent drainage but retains moisture long after the surplus water has drained off. Overly sandy or clayey soils are unsuitable. For best results, start by amending the soil you have or making a special growing mix that's satisfactory for the largest number of plants. A good basic mix is ⅓ loam or topsoil, ⅓ humus such as screened leaf mold, and ⅓ gravel. You can amend the basic mix to suit plants with special needs by adding ground limestone for plants that prefer a high pH or peat moss and sulfur for plants that prefer acid soil (it's a good idea to plan a separate area for each of these groups).

Selecting Rocks

For the most pleasing, natural effect, stick to one type of rock. Repeating the same color and texture of rock throughout the garden will unify its design. Rocks that have weathered to a neutral gray or tan color are ideal for an informal rock garden. Limestone and sandstone, both of which can be stratified, or layered, are popular. Granite, a hard volcanic rock that may be reddish, blue-gray, green, and purplish, is useful for plants that cannot stand the high pH caused by limestone.

The best choice is stone native to your area. Not only will it look most natural, it will be easier to obtain and cheaper than rocks transported over a long distance. You may find someone within hauling distance who is eager to part with some of the rocks on their property. Rockyards, quarries, and construction sites are other good sources. Rocks are sold either by weight or cubic yard. If you are buying from a landscape supply center, tell the supplier the size of the area you want to cover. Try to pick out the rocks yourself. Choose mostly large irregular shapes that are weathered, but keep in mind you'll need smaller sizes, too.

Plan First

Even though you'll undoubtedly have to modify your design somewhat as you construct your garden, any time spent planning before you're actually moving rocks about is time well spent. One good way to visualize your garden without hauling stone hither and yon is to make a three-dimensional scale model with small stones and sand on a large tray or box. Mound the sand and arrange your rocks in the model. Or use graph paper, if you prefer. You might want to start with a photograph of a favorite mountain scene. Try to answer some of the following questions: How many rocks —and what sizes—do you need? Where do you want the outcrops? Which rocks will go where? Will there be a path though the garden, or will a few unplanted ledges serve as stepping stones for working in the garden?

Try to alternate and balance elevations and depressions throughout the design. If ground space is limited and you want more room for plants, make the garden higher and dig out paths or steps. You may have to rearrange or sketch the contours and the placement of rocks several times before you find the design that looks right to you. The key to a successful rock garden—one that is harmonious and natural-looking—is studied irregularity.

Construction

Once you've selected a site and have a basic plan in mind, the next step is to begin construction. Mark out the area you've selected and remove any weeds or sod. Excavate it to a depth of a foot or so, saving the soil for fill. You'll need to have an extra load of topsoil on hand for filling in between rocks and building up level areas. (If the subsoil doesn't drain freely, lay in about 8 inches of rubble or small rocks; you may have to remove more soil to accommodate this drainage layer. Cover this with sod turned upside-down, coarse gravel, or salt hay, to prevent soil from washing down and clogging the drainage.)

Unless the rocks are very small, you'll need some tools to move them. You can move good-sized rocks with a garden cart or on a small dolly. Or use iron pipes about 4 inches in diameter as rollers. You'll need a crowbar to use as a lever and a block of wood for a fulcrum to position rocks. If you're determined to start with massive rocks, a professional with a backhoe might be the answer.

When installing rocks for a rock garden, it's important to position them so they will be as stable as possible. Angle them so water will run back into the garden, not out of it.

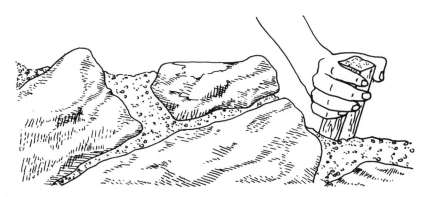

To anchor the rocks firmly, pack soil firmly in and around them. Finish with a layer of prepared soil mix that will drain quickly and also retain water.

Working from your plan or model, place some of the larger stones on the perimeter. These will serve as the foundation stones of the garden. Save many for use in the center of the garden or farther up the slope to avoid a building-block look. It's important to position rocks so they will be as stable and firmly placed as possible. Place them with the wider, heavier part of the rock against the soil. Angle the rocks so water is channeled back into the garden, not out of it. Try to lay the rocks so any strata lines run horizontally and along parallel planes throughout the garden.

Once you've placed the rocks and they are arranged to your satisfaction, check to make sure they are relatively stable. Then bury them by shoveling fill soil in and around them. The traditional practice is to bury two-thirds of the rock, simulating the way stones look in nature.

After you've laid the foundation stones, position the next tier of rocks, make sure they're stable, and shovel fill soil around them. Continue until you've reached the top of the garden. As you work, try to create miniature ridges and valleys and intersperse small level areas; this will be artistically pleasing and is a good chance to provide microclimates for a variety of plants. For example, you can provide sun-baked southern exposures on a small ridge for plants that like hot, dry conditions. Plan to plant species that require protected locations in north-facing "valleys." Keep the effect irregular, including the top. End with a series of flat ledges at different levels rather than a peak—unless you want your construction to resemble an Egyptian pyramid.

After you've placed all the rocks, shovel your prepared soil mix around them, making deep planting pockets that reach back to the fill. Then tamp it in. Wait a week for the soil to settle, then add more if necessary. Spread a 1-inch layer of pea gravel over the area, or if you have plants ready and waiting, apply the gravel after planting. Use chopped leaves as mulch for woodland rock gardens. The mulch should come up to but not cover the crown of each plant. Mulch will help conserve moisture, keep the soil cool, reduce weeds, prevent soil from muddying the leaves, discourage crowns from rotting, and add a tidy finish.

Building on a Slope

If you are building on a sloping site, start by clearing weeds from the entire area. Contour the slope as much as possible before placing your rocks. Drainage should not be a problem unless the subsoil is heavy clay. (In heavy clay, provide drainage by digging trenches 1 to 1½ feet deep and 3 to 6 feet apart. Fill them with stones or rubble and cover with upturned sod or smaller stones to prevent the upper soil from clogging the drainage. Finally, cover with soil.)

When placing rocks, dig a hole larger than the rock so that there will be some leeway for moving it to get the most effective position. Place each rock with the wider, heavier portion down to ensure stable construction. Place the largest, most attractive rock —the keystone—first. When it's in place, walk around and examine it from all angles. The keystone will set the stage for the rest of the garden. Is it facing the main viewing point? Is it tilted inward slightly so water will run into the garden? When you're satisfied the keystone is positioned correctly, shovel soil in and around it, ramming the soil with a pole to remove air pockets and to assure it is firmly anchored. A good portion should be buried in the soil and it should look as though it is not simply perching on the surface. Add rocks, working outward from the keystone, and match strata, color, and angle as much as possible. Arrange groups of rocks as outcrops rather than individually, with small "alpine meadows" in between. Finish by adding prepared soil mix, plants, and mulch.

Rock Garden Plants

Above all, rock garden plants should be low growing and compact. They may trail over rocks or have foliage held close to the soil and flowers borne on short stalks above it. Fortunately, there's no need to be particular about what's considered a proper plant for your rock garden as long as it stays in scale and looks more or less at home among rocks—that is, unless you decide to specialize in plants native to a particular region or decide to grow only true alpines. True alpines can be difficult to accommodate. They grow best when they have a blanket of snow all winter and a short, dry growing period in summer. They're also hard to grow where summers are hot, humid, and long (a growing season of more than 140 frost-free days). However, there are literally hundreds of plants to try—low-growing annuals, diminutive perennials, dwarf shrubs, and miniature bulbs. Many are easy-to-grow choices perfect for beginning rock gardeners. As you become more knowledgeable and experienced, you can gradually introduce more difficult-to-grow species. (For more information, see "Easy Plants for Rock Gardens" on the opposite page.)

Use the basic design principles for creating a flower garden to develop a plant list and plan a beautiful rock

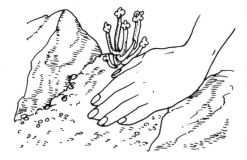

Fill the pockets between rocks with compact, slow-growing perennials and miniature spring bulbs.

garden. Start with a scale drawing and plot your color scheme on tracing paper. Or go out to the garden armed with labeled sheets of newspaper or construction paper and lay out your "plants," adjusting your design as you visualize it for each season. Be sure to record your decisions on paper.

A few dwarf conifers such as pygmy spruce (*Picea* spp.), dwarf pines (*Pinus* spp.), or other minia-

If your rock garden is large, plan on stepping-stone paths or unplanted ledges so you'll be able to care for the plants and enjoy them up close.

ture evergreen shrubs should form the backbone of your planting scheme. Perennials with evergreen foliage also add winter interest; consider the stonecrops (*Sedum* spp.; avoid *S. acre*, a pernicious spreader), hen-and-chickens (*Sempervivum* spp.), and candytuft (*Iberis sempervirens*). Where soil is acidic, heaths and heathers are good choices. Many rock plants have attractive foliage and cushionlike habits; group these to complement one another and place evergreens behind them for contrast. Against this framework, plan for spring bloom provided by miniature bulbs such as crocus, daffodils, and species tulips. Plan on planting a few annuals over the bulbs to fill the space they leave after flowering. Choose annuals that have single, simple flowers and delicate form such as cupflower (*Nierembergia* spp.), sweet alyssum (*Lobularia maritima*), browallia (*Browallia speciosa*), or Dahlberg daisy (*Dyssodia tenuiloba*). Then select a variety of spring- and summer-blooming perennials to carry the garden through the summer and into autumn.

Take time to learn about the microclimate in which the plants will be growing. For many rock garden plants, a south or southeasterly exposure is best, but a few like to cook in noonday sun. You can control the conditions somewhat by carefully placing plants among the rocks and ridges. You can also use dwarf evergreens and shrubs to provide shade and serve as windbreaks. Alpines will do better with a north to northeasterly exposure. While many creeping rock plants, such as saxifrages (*Saxifraga* spp.), thymes (*Thymus* spp.), and hen-and-chickens (*Sempervivum* spp.), can withstand rough weather, wind and rain can break the tall flower stems of others such as windflowers (*Anemone* spp.), primroses (*Primula* spp.), and columbines (*Aquilegia* spp.).

Rocks and Plants

The rocks in a rock garden provide a dramatic, year-round design feature, and rock plants have forms and habits that fall into distinct categories.

EASY PLANTS FOR ROCK GARDENS

There are many ways to determine what plants will be suitable for your rock garden. One of the best is visiting specialty nurseries and public gardens that feature rock garden displays. Early spring is the best time since that is when most rock plants flower. If you know of a private rock garden nearby, ask to see it; like most plant-lovers, rock gardeners are usually eager to share their gardens and their tales of triumphs and trials. Visiting local gardens will give you a good idea of what grows well in your area. Garden catalogs, books, and magazines are other sources.

The American Rock Garden Society is another good source of information. It offers an excellent publication, a seed exchange, regional meetings, and also has local chapters, many of which hold annual plant sales. Membership is $20 per year; write Miss Buffy Parker, 15 Fairmead Road, Darien, CT 06820 for an application.

The perennials listed here are a good place to start. All are relatively easy to grow, hardy, and easy to obtain. There are improved cultivars available for many of them as well. Don't forget dwarf shrubs and trees, too. There are many diminutive cultivars of conifers whose dwarf or ground-hugging habits will add interest to your rock garden. Consider dwarf and low-growing forms of false cypress (*Chamaecyparis* spp.), junipers (*Juniperus* spp.), spruce (*Picea* spp.), pines (*Pinus* spp.), and hemlock (*Tsuga canadensis*). Also look for dwarf or creeping barberries (*Berberis* spp.), cotoneasters (*Cotoneaster* spp.), and azaleas and rhododendrons (*Rhododendron* spp.). (See "Sources" on page 401 for a list of mail-order nurseries that specialize in rock garden plants.)

Plants for Sun

Although some of the following plants may spread a bit rapidly, all are good specimens for a sunny rock garden. Also add hardy bulbs such as snowdrops (*Galanthus* spp.), dwarf narcissus (*Narcissus* spp.), squill (*Scilla* spp.), and low-growing species tulips (*Tulipa* spp.).

Achillea tomentosa (woolly yarrow)

Ajuga reptans, A. genevensis (bugleweed)

Alchemilla alpina (alpine lady's-mantle)

Anemone apennina, A. blanda, A. pulsatilla (windflower)

Antennaria dioica, A. rosea (pussy-toes)

Arabis alpina, A. caucasica (rock cress)

Armeria maritima (common thrift)

Aster alpinus (rock aster)

Aurinia saxatilis (basket-of-gold)

Campanula, many species, including *C. carpatica,* and *C. rotundifolia* (bellflower)

Dianthus alpinus, D. deltoides (pinks)

Festuca ovina var. *glauca* (blue fescue)

Geranium, many species, including *G. dalmaticum, G. endressi,* and *G. sanguineum* (hardy geranium)

Gypsophila repens (creeping baby's-breath)

Helianthemum numullarium (rock rose)

Iberis saxatilis, I. sempervirens (candytuft)

(continued)

EASY PLANTS FOR ROCK GARDENS—*Continued*

Plants for Sun—*continued*

Iris tectorum (Japanese roof iris)

Lavendula angustifolia 'Nana' (dwarf lavender)

Leontopodium alpinum (edelweiss)

Nepeta mussinii (catmint)

Phlox subulata (creeping phlox)

Opuntia humifusa (prickly pear cactus)

Saxifraga spp. (saxifrage)

Sedum, many species, including *S. album* and *S. spurium* (sedum)

Sempervivum spp. (houseleek, hen-and-chickens)

Thymus, many species, including *T. serphyllum* and *T. pseudolanuginosus* (thyme)

Veronica incana, V. repens (speedwell)

Plants for Shade

There are plenty of plants to consider for a rock garden that receives partial shade. In addition to the plants listed here, consider adding ferns and hardy bulbs such as snowdrops (*Galanthus* spp.), dwarf narcissus (*Narcissus* spp.), squill (*Scilla* spp.), and low-growing species tulips (*Tulipa* spp.).

Anemone nemorosa, A. parviflora (wood anemone)

Aquilegia, many species, including *A. canadensis* and *A. chrysantha* (columbine)

Arisaema spp. (Jack-in-the-pulpit)

Asarum canadense, A. europaeum (wild ginger)

Astilbe spp. (astilbe)

Aubrieta deltoidea (purple rock cress)

Bergenia cordifolia, B. crassifolia (bergenia)

Corydalis lutea, C. nobilis (corydalis)

Cyclamen hederifolium, C. coum (hardy cyclamen)

Dicentra eximia (wild bleeding-heart)

Helleborus orientalis (lenten rose)

Heuchera sanguinea (coralbells)

Hosta, many dwarf species and cultivars (hosta, plantain lily)

Iris cristata (crested iris)

Liriope muscari, L. spicata (lilyturf)

Phlox divaricata, P. stolonifera (phlox)

Primula, many species (primrose)

Sanguinaria canadensis (bloodroot)

Tiarella cordifolia, T. wheeryi (foamflower)

Viola, many species, including *V. blanda, V. cornuta, V. pedata,* and *V. rotundifolia* (violet)

Take advantage of these elements and plant your garden for the most appealing effects. Place prostrate, spreading, or creeping plants—rock jasmines (*Androsace* spp.), small bellflowers (*Campanula* spp.), and thymes (*Thymus* spp.), for example—so they will cascade down a rock. Emphasize the stately, upright forms of perennials such as astilbe by placing them at the base of a rock. Wedge rosette-forming saxifrages and sempervivums into vertical crevices by firming the soil ball underneath the plant and filling in from above with soil and gravel. Fill the open spaces with mats of bugleweed (*Ajuga* spp.), sedums, *Cotula* spp., shrubbier thymes, and pussy-toes (*Antennaria* spp.) Use dwarf shrubs to soften the harshness of rocks and as green backdrops to the flowering plants.

Making a Stone Trough

You can create a miniature rock garden that will require only a few square feet of space with a trough garden. Not only can you display dwarf trees, delicate alpines, and other plants in a trough, this type of garden allows you to escape the heavier weeding and watering tasks that a larger garden requires. Also, for a plant collector, trough gardening offers an embarrassment of riches: A rectangular, 2-by-3-foot garden can accommodate a wealth of fascinating plants, including a few miniature shrubs or trees.

Originally, trough gardens were planted in stone sinks once used for watering livestock. Today, these antique troughs are hard to find and expensive. Fortunately, you can make attractive, inexpensive troughs with hypertufa, a mixture that simulates stone but can be molded into lighter, more portable troughs. Hypertufa containers are also rustic-looking, weatherproof, and relatively easy to make.

The standard mix for a hypertufa planter is 1 part portland cement, 1½ parts perlite, and 1½ parts fine peat moss. Mix the dry materials together first, then slowly add water until the mixture resembles a spreadable paste. Don't prepare the hypertufa until you are ready to begin construction! A 1-cubic-foot bag of portland cement is enough to make at least several large troughs. If you like, you can change the gray color by tinting it with limeproof cement-coloring powders, available at hardware stores.

CASTING A RECTANGULAR TROUGH

The simplest way to make a rectangular trough is to use two cardboard boxes as the form, or mold, for casting the trough. The main advantage of boxes is they're easy to tear away after the hypertufa hardens. You will need two boxes, one slightly larger than the other. (The large box determines the size of the outside of the finished trough. You can make a small, portable trough that will hold about a dozen plants with a large box that is 11 by 15 inches and 6 inches deep.) When one box is nested inside the other, there should be a gap of about 1½ to 2 inches between the sides—this determines the width of the walls. It's best to keep the depth of the trough between 4 and 6 inches; if necessary, trim the larger box to the appropriate depth. Be sure to add a 2-inch allowance for the concrete that will form the bottom. In addition to the boxes, you will also need the following materials.

MATERIALS
½" mesh or 1" chicken wire
Wire or heavy tape
½" wood dowels
Sharp knife, trowel, or scraper
Rubber gloves

1. Wrap wire or tape around each box near the top and bottom to strengthen it and to prevent it from buckling when wet cement is applied.

2. Mix the hypertufa with water. Place the larger box on a firm, flat surface, and cover the bottom with a 1-inch layer of hypertufa.

3. Embed a piece of mesh or chicken wire, precut to fit the bottom of the box, in the hypertufa at the bottom of the box. Then cover this reinforcing wire with another inch of hypertufa.

4. Insert several dowels into the wet hypertufa to create drainage holes. Make sure they are pressed firmly against the bottom of the box so the holes will go completely through the bottom.

5. Turn the smaller box upside down, centering it over the larger box, and place it inside the larger box. Press its rim into the hypertufa.

6. Cut a piece of mesh or chicken wire to the dimensions of the inner box and wrap it loosely around the small box in the space between the two cartons. Press the lower edge firmly into the hypertufa.

7. Allow the hypertufa to harden for about half an hour, then pack the space between the boxes with hypertufa until it covers the edge of the mesh or chicken wire at the top. Eliminate air bubbles by tamping the hypertufa with a stick.

8. Keep the hypertufa moist while it is curing. (Don't expose it to freezing temperatures during this period.) After two to three days, peel away the boxes and remove the dowels by twisting them out. Wait another ten days for the hypertufa to harden completely. Allow the completed trough to age outdoors for several weeks before planting, so the excess lime in the hypertufa can be leached away by rain.

CASTING A ROUND OR FREE-FORM TROUGH

You can make a round or free-form trough over a mold made of damp sand by following the steps below. In addition to hypertufa mix, you will also need the following materials.

1. Pack damp sand over one or several bowls to form a mold in the shape of the trough you'd like to make.

2. Cut enough chicken wire to generously cover the shape, and put it aside.

3. Cover the sand with a large plastic sheet, then add water to the hypertufa mix.

4. For a small trough, spread a ½-inch-thick layer of hypertufa over the form; use a 1-inch layer for a larger one.

5. Embed the reinforcing chicken wire in the hypertufa.

6. Press dowels into the bottom for drainage, making sure they extend to the plastic sheet. They should protrude above the hypertufa at all stages.

7. Trim away any excess chicken wire, and add another layer of hypertufa over it.

8. Bring the ends of the plastic sheet up around the sides of the trough—not the bottom, however—and hold it in place with more damp sand.

9. After a day, when the hypertufa is partially hardened, remove the plastic sheet and the dowels. Gently scrape the bottom of the trough with a board to level it and brush the surface for a clean finish. Turn it right side up and follow the steps for curing and weathering as described for a rectangular trough.

PLANTING

Once the trough has cured, you're ready to plant. The plants you select can be as difficult or easy to grow as you'd like. (See "Easy Plants for Rock Gardens" on page 189 for a list of easy, adaptable species.)

Cover the drainage holes with broken pottery or screening and fill the trough to within 2 inches with a soil mix that will drain readily. A good general mix for troughs is 1 part compost, 1 part fine stone chips, and 1 part loam. Adjust the mix to suit the type of plants that you intend to grow. For best results, don't mix plants with different soil needs in the same trough.

To transform your planting into an "authentic" alpine landscape, you'll need a few pieces of rock. As with a conventional rock garden, stick to one type of rock, and pick several sizes. One or two pieces of reasonable size used to simulate a miniature outcrop will be more effective than sprinkling smaller pieces. You can plant in the crevices between the rocks as you set them, so the plants will grow over the rocks. Arrange your plants, still in their pots, around the rocks. Set trailing plants in the corners and near the edges, and be sure to include one or two dwarf evergreens. When you are satisfied with your rock and plant arrangement, remove the plants from their pots, set them in place, and fill around each with the prepared soil mix. Water thoroughly and top-dress with an inch or more of gravel mulch for good drainage and a tidy appearance.

Place your finished trough in sun or a spot with dappled shade that will protect it from the hot afternoon sun. A spot on a terrace or flanking a path, where it's easy to see, is ideal. Avoid spots where overhanging structures, awnings, or trees might drip moisture. Your trough with its lilliputian mountainscapes should last for years.

Building a Stone Wall

Stone walls add to the garden a feeling of age and permanence that stirs the imagination. They offer perfect backdrops for perennial borders, rose gardens, ferns, and wildflowers. They can even be planted with rock garden plants that will add color and charm. Carefully crafted stone walls are valued for their utility, beauty, and longevity. Consider building a freestanding wall to separate one part of your garden from another or to surround your property at its boundaries. One of the most practical and attractive uses of a stone wall is as a retaining wall at the bottom of a slope. This prevents erosion and offers a superb opportunity for creating a vertical rock garden. You can even build a series of retaining walls on a steep slope and plant low-growing evergreen shrubs, flowers, or lawns on the level terraces between them.

You don't need to be a stonemason or professional to build a low stone wall. It's actually relatively easy and inexpensive. (For walls higher than about 3 feet, it's best to call in a professional.) Aside from rocks, a few tools, and step-by-step instructions, all you need is determination, time, and a fairly strong back. In addition to a trowel, a level, some stakes, and string, you may want rollers, ramps, and levers to ease the task of carrying heavy rocks. No mortar is needed; joints can be filled with earth or small rocks.

Selecting Stones

The best stones for walls are large and flat and easy to split into manageable blocks. Look for stratified rocks such as limestone and sandstone, which are available in most parts of the country. Avoid large, irregularly shaped boulders, because they're more difficult to work with. Look for rocks that one person can lift and handle.

If you already have suitable stones on your property, you're lucky. If not, check the yellow pages for quarries in your area; sometimes stones perfectly proportioned for stone walls can be picked from their scrap heap at practically no cost. In areas of the country where stone buildings are common, search the newspaper for advertisements by contractors who may offer stone free for the hauling from demolished structures. If all else fails, buy the stones you need and don't stint—they'll last longer than a lifetime, and the beauty and character they will add to your garden will repay you many times over. Stone is sold either by the cubic yard or by weight. To buy stone by the cubic yard, measure the length of your wall in feet and multiply by the height and the width. Divide the total by 27 to get the cubic yards needed, and add about 5 percent for waste. To buy stone by weight, figure about a ton of rocks for every 25 square feet of wall face.

You'll need three basic types of rocks. You'll need rocks that are flat, squarish, and relatively regular for the ends, corners, and top of the wall. Long stones whose length is equal to or greater than the width of the wall are used to "tie" the wall together across its width. Finally, you'll need small, wedge-shaped stones to use as shims under larger stones and to chink gaps. Once you've acquired your rocks, it's a good idea to sort them into piles by type.

Whenever you handle rocks, be conscious of lifting and handling them safely. When lifting a rock, bend your body and your knees into a crouch, then be sure to have your legs do the work, not your back. Always carry the stone close to your body, and watch your footing.

Tricks of the Trade

Water, freezing and thawing, and gravity are the natural forces that stone walls have to contend with. The earth in the slope behind a retaining wall exerts considerable pressure on the

wall, particularly when the soil is wet. Fortunately, there are basic structural tactics to counter these forces.

Perhaps the best-known principle of stone wall construction is "one over two," which means that the stone on one layer, or course, should always cover the space between at least two stones under it. As in bricklaying, staggering the spaces avoids creating vertical fissures in the wall, which would be weak points where the wall could separate.

For stability when building a retaining wall, arrange each stone so it is tilted downward slightly toward the slope. This allows the slope to help carry the weight. The wall itself should also be tilted or tapered with a backward slant from base to top so that it leans into the slope. This counters the weight of the earth in the slope pushing against it. Called battering, this slant becomes more critical as wall height increases; a 2-inch batter for every foot of height is the recommended norm.

Low stone walls, whether freestanding or retaining, are best built on a gravel foundation to provide better drainage and help protect against frost heaving. For retaining walls, it's also a good idea to make water outlets, or weep holes, through the wall between the rocks of the first course, at the base of the wall.

The following guidelines will help you determine the size of the base or foundation of the wall. For a wall 3 feet or slightly less, the suggested width for the base is 24 inches. For each additional 6 inches of height, add 4 inches to the bottom width. Because of battering, the width of the top of a finished wall should be about one-fourth narrower than the bottom; a 3-foot wall, then, will be about 18 inches wide at the top.

Building a Retaining Wall

To construct a stone retaining wall, start by cutting into the slope to make a vertical face for placing your stone

wall. Save the topsoil from your excavation; the rest can be hauled to your compost pile. Lay out the wall area with stakes, placing the foot of the wall far enough away from the foot of the vertical face to allow for the backward slant (the battering) of the wall from bottom to top. Also allow enough room on top for a planting area behind the wall if you want one.

Dig a trench 6 to 12 inches deep, to the dimensions of the base of your wall. Spread a layer of coarse gravel in the trench, almost filling it. Angle this fill toward the bank so that the first course of rocks, and therefore each successive course, will dip toward the bank. Lay some of the largest, flattest stones on the gravel to make an even, stable base. Make sure they tilt inward and that you have left gaps of a few inches between them for weep holes. Be sure the stones do not teeter. If necessary, knock off a ridge or bump on a stone with a chisel and a lightweight mason's hammer or with a small pick. Fill the weep holes with small rocks or gravel.

Use a level to check that the first course of stones is horizontal, and check after each course is laid to make sure it remains level throughout the construction. A cord strung between the stakes about a foot above the ground will help maintain the level; raise it as your wall progresses.

Put loose small rocks, pieces trimmed from other stones, or gravel in the space between the wall and the slope behind to improve drainage behind the wall. Shovel soil over this rubble and in the joints between the stones, tramping on it and packing it firmly to eliminate air holes. A broken broom handle is a good tool for this. Shovel a thin layer of soil on top of the stones—an inch or two is fine—making sure that the weep holes are left open. If you intend to plant the wall, now is the time to begin adding your plants. (See "Planting a Stone Wall" on the opposite page.)

Follow the one-over-two rule when you start positioning the stones in the second course. Set the stones with the flattest sides on top and bottom, and turn the next largest flat dimension toward the front of the wall. Also begin to batter the wall by placing the front edge of each stone in the course slightly behind that of the course under it. Every few feet, span the width of the wall with a tie stone—one placed with its longest dimension across the wall. Ideally, tie stones should be placed on the ends of every course. Where possible, have the tie stones extend into the slope as well to anchor the wall. From time to time you may have to correct unevenness by adding or removing soil underneath the course as needed.

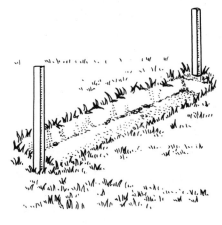

When building a freestanding stone wall, start by marking out the base of the wall with stakes. Then dig a foundation for the wall and fill it with several inches of coarse gravel.

Before laying the first course, or layer, of stone, check to be sure the foundation is level.

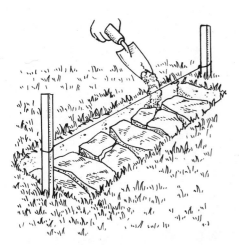

After laying each course, spread a thin layer of soil over the stones. Use thin rocks as shims to provide a stable, level surface for rocks above.

Use stones that span the width of the wall on either end and at intervals throughout the length of the wall to tie it together and form a stable structure.

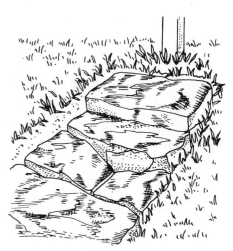

Use small rocks to fill chinks between courses. Lay the stone in a bricklike pattern so large stones cover the spaces between stones in the level below.

If you need more than 2 inches of soil between courses to maintain level, add a couple of thin rocks as shims to help carry the weight of the upper stone. As each course is completed, continue filling the space between the wall and the slope with rubble and packing it with soil. Also, continue spreading a thin layer over each course.

Save your choicest large, flat stones for the top of the wall, for both strength and beauty. Their weight will help hold the lower layers in place. If all are tie stones spanning the entire width of the wall, so much the better.

Position small stones as wedges under the top layer to make the top perfectly level. The only remaining task is to bank soil around the base of the wall and the edges. Let your own taste determine how best to mold your stone wall into the natural contours of the site.

Corners and Ends. Corners and ends demand special attention because this is where any shifts in the wall will meet. Save your flattest and biggest stones for these places; those with right-angled ends should be hoarded for use as corners. Use tie stones for corners and ends—placed with their length perpendicular to the length of the wall—for stability.

Irregular Stones. If you have round or irregular stones that you want to use, begin each course by hiding the worst ones toward the back or down the middle of the wall. Be sure to position them so that they don't teeter, and stagger the joints over those of the course underneath. The stones placed in front of these "undesirables" should have a flat, straight side turned outward to make a pleasing face.

Planting a Stone Wall

A sunny stone wall planted with sprawling rock plants has a charm that is irresistible. The best time to plant a stone wall is while it's being built, because it's easy to add soil mix and plants between courses of stone as you build. It's more difficult, but not impossible, to insert plants later, although the survival rate for plants with long roots will not be as high.

Any newly planted wall—especially a sunny one—will need to be syringed frequently with a gentle

spray of water until the plants become established. If a long dry spell follows your planting, stretch a soaker hose across the top of the wall and leave it running until the moisture reaches the bottom niches. It might be necessary to shield the wall from hot sun for a few days with a burlap screen or a drape of cheesecloth over the wall. Once the plants are established, about the only care you need to worry about is plucking the occasional weed and shearing back plants after flowering.

Planting as You Build

If you are going to plant a wall as you build, have hardened seedlings and small divisions of established plants in flats or pots, well watered and waiting in the shade. Mix up an adequate supply of rock plant soil. A good basic mix is 1 part loam or top soil; 1 part humus, such as screened leaf mold; and 1 part gravel.

Planting can begin after the first course of stones is laid and you've spread soil over the stones. As you plant, slightly loosen the roots from the soil, then spread them out horizontally in the soil pocket between two stones, directing the roots back as far as they will go. Set each plant so the crown is about an inch back from the front edge of the stone. Along with the backward tilt of the stones, this will help prevent rainwater from falling over the face of the wall, settling in the crown, and causing the plant to rot. Cover the roots with another thin layer of soil—½ inch to 1 inch is adequate. Then water thoroughly with a fine spray and place a stone for your second course firmly over it, overlapping the joints.

As you work your way down the face of the wall, and as you plant each succeeding course, try to position the plants in an artistically irregular pattern. Don't overplant; leave much of the stonework exposed to set off the contrast in textures and to savor the way in which the plants soften the wall. Save some pockets for adding new plants later on, and allow room for your seedlings to grow and billow over the wall. Many plants will self-seed in crevices and crannies of their own choosing, adding to the naturalness that is so beguiling in a stone wall.

Planting an Existing Wall

You'll need some dexterity to add plants to an existing wall. You can poke holes in the soil with a long, slim dibble and insert the roots in the crevice, tamping it in firmly. A spoon is useful for ladling moist soil into the larger niches and packing it in around the plant. It's a good idea to wrap wet sphagnum moss around the plant's roots before wedging it in the crevice. Houseleeks or hen-and-chickens (*Sempervivum* spp.) are about the easiest plants to get started in a wall. Insert a few pebbles around them to prevent the soil from washing out before they become established. You can also sow seeds by mixing them with a little soil and spooning this into the wall. Or try putting small seeds into one end of a beverage straw and blowing them (gently!) into the crevice. Finish by tamping moist soil around the seeds.

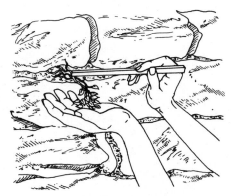

When planting an existing stone wall, gently work the roots into the crevice with a dibble. Ideally, the roots should extend far into the wall and the crown of the plant should be positioned so it is about 1 inch in from the edge of the stone.

Plants for a Stone Wall

Most rock plants will thrive on the surface of a stone wall. Choose those suited to the exposure and microenvironment your wall provides. As with rock gardening, it's best to start with easy-to-grow species; as you become more experienced, experiment with more difficult species. (See "Easy Plants for Rock Gardens" on page 189.)

It's a good idea to develop a plant list as you would for any flower garden. This will also be a chance to look up the habits of the plants you choose, so you can position them to best advantage. Allow room along the top of the wall for plants to overflow and cascade over the lower niches. Don't place trailing or creeping plants such as rock roses (*Helianthemum* spp.),

Don't overplant a stone wall. Be sure to leave plenty of space open so you can enjoy the texture and structure of the stone.

purple rock cress (*Aubrieta* spp.), or creeping phlox (*Phlox subulata*) directly over more compact plants, which will be smothered by them. You can also plant creeping species near the bottom of the wall, where they can billow out and wander on the ground, melding the wall with the rest of your garden.

For a sunny low wall about 2 feet high, confine yourself to growing smaller plants such as the creeping thymes (*Thymus* spp.), houseleeks (*Sempervivum* spp.), creeping baby's-breath (*Gypsophila repens*), creeping phlox (*Phlox subulata*), and the lower-growing sedums and bellflowers (*Campanula* spp.). For higher walls, you can use larger rock plants and still hold to a suitable scale; try some of the rock roses (*Helianthemum* spp.), pinks (*Dianthus* spp.), pasque flower (*Anemone pulsatilla*), and gray-foliaged woolly yarrow (*Achillea tomentosa*).

Stud north-facing walls with the smaller species of primroses (*Primula* spp.), woodland wildflowers, small ferns, and some of the new dwarf hosta cultivars that grow only several inches high. *Corydalis lutea* will bloom most of the summer in light shade.

Building a Walkway

Walkways give a finishing touch to a garden. Depending on their design, they can visually unify or divide a garden and invite visiters to follow wherever they lead. A well-built, well-designed walkway combines beauty and function, whether it is a mulched path, a series of stepping stones, or concrete, brick, or stone.

Design Considerations

Before you begin construction, take time to consider how a walkway will fit into your overall garden plan. If you are considering a system of walkways for a large property, or a long walk to wend through several areas of your yard, first draw a detailed plan on paper and then transfer the design to the ground as you build each section. (Keep basic design principles such as balance and proportion in mind.) A simpler walkway can be "designed" directly on the ground: For a straight path, use taut string and stakes; for a curved path, outline its contours with a garden hose or rope. Adjust curves by holding a string marked with the desired path width at right angles across the path (this will take two people holding the string on either end and moving the hose or rope to the correct position). Then mark the line with lime.

Style and Placement

Like any other garden feature, walkways have different styles. Straight walkways provide a direct route from one point to another and are geometrically suited to formal gardens. Regardless of the style of the landscape, straight lines are best for walks that are designed primarily for a practical purpose, such as for taking out the garbage or walking to the garage. Informal gardens lend themselves to curving walks. A wide walk that sweeps gracefully up to your front door makes a more agreeable approach than a rigidly straight one. Or you can plan a walkway to meander through the garden, alternately hiding focal points and views.

Make the width of main walks at least 4 or 5 feet, so that two people can walk along side by side; other pathways can be 2 or 3 feet wide. Where walks will also be used for garden carts and other equipment, make sure that you will be able to maneuver them easily, with space to pass without damaging plants.

Materials

Any walkway should be safe and stable, fairly level, and provide enough traction to walk upon comfortably. A well-tended earth path can be charming in a rustic garden, but isn't practical for a well-traveled path because it will alternate between dust and mud depending on the weather. Mulched or paved paths are neat looking and eliminate dust and mud. Wood chips or gravel (dark gray, not white) are both good-looking practical mulches; they will have to be raked and replaced periodically and are not entirely weedproof. You can reduce maintenance by edging a mulch or gravel path with landscape ties or flexible lawn edging.

Poured concrete is versatile and durable if you welcome the challenge of a complicated project that involves some heavy work. Other materials to consider include brick, concrete pavers, and cut slate or flagstone. Flat native stones that match the color and texture of local outcroppings give the most natural look. Walks laid without mortar look soft and pretty when mosses, thyme, or other creepers are established in the cracks.

Brick remains the most popular paving material and works well with any garden style, formal or informal. It is durable, versatile, and comes in a variety of sizes, textures, and colors. Furthermore, it can be laid in many different beautiful patterns. Bricks are easy to lift and handle, and you can work in stages to suit your own schedule. However, unless you can obtain bricks from a demolition site, most brick is expensive.

These are some of the many patterns that can be used when laying brick.

BUILDING
A BRICK WALKWAY

Mark out the walkway with stakes and string, then remove the sod.

To square the edges, pound a board against the edges of the walkway.

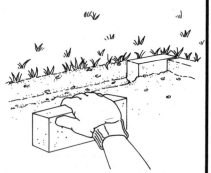

Lay edging bricks on their sides along the end and edges of the path.

Building brick comes in three grades: SW (severe weathering), MW (moderate weathering), and NW (no weathering). If your area has severe frosts, choose SW for longevity. Like stone, brick must be set in a few inches of sand or it will heave out of place in the winter. Even if the ground does not freeze in your area, a layer of sand under the brick helps water drain away quickly—and it provides a more stable base for a level walk.

You can calculate how many bricks you'll need by laying a course of bricks in your chosen pattern. Count the bricks across the path, including the edgers. Multiply this by 1.5 (the number of bricks in a running foot), and then by the length of the path in feet. (Or figure by drawing the pattern on graph paper, measuring, and calculating.)

Follow the steps below to make a straight brick walkway.

1. Use stakes and string to mark off the outline of the walkway you'd like to build.

2. Remove the sod covering the area with a flat spade. Then excavate the area to 4 inches.

3. Pound a short length of board, such as a 2-by-4, against the ground where the edging will be placed.

4. Lay the border bricks on their sides along the tamped, bared earth around the edges of the path. Place them with the tops at ground level for easy mowing if the walk abuts a lawn. Check to make sure the width of the path between the edging bricks is wide enough to accommodate the pattern you've chosen. Plan the width so you don't have to cut bricks to fit.

5. Spread 2 inches of sand between the edging bricks. Smooth and level it, using a piece of 2-by-4 to match the width between the edgers. Then wet the sand thoroughly with a fine spray from a hose and tamp it down hard.

6. Lay the brick, tamping and tapping with a rubber or wooden mallet to get the tightest fit.

7. From time to time, check your work with a spirit level. If a brick sits too high, remove a little sand from underneath; if it's too low, add sand until it's flush with others.

8. As you progress, lay the edging bricks along each side first, then add the walkway in between.

9. When the path is laid, dump dry sand over the bricks and

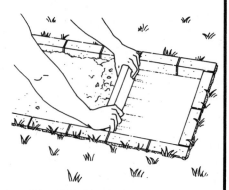

Spread 2 inches of builder's sand between the edging bricks and smooth it with a board.

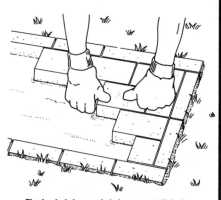

Fit the bricks as tightly as possible in your chosen pattern. You can use a rubber mallet to tap them in place.

sweep it over the walk to fill the cracks. You can hose down the path gently or wait for the first few rains. Add more sand as it settles. Install a plastic or metal barrier strip between bricks and lawn, with the top flush to the brick, to keep grass from encroaching on the walk.

Harvesting and Using Flowers

Cutting and Conditioning Flowers

When the flower garden you've planned and nurtured finally bursts into bloom, you'll want to enjoy the blossoms to their fullest. Bouquets of cut flowers are the perfect way to bring the delicious fragrances and glorious colors of the garden indoors. Although flowers last longest when left in the garden, with just a little special care you can lengthen the life of cut flowers —adding days of enjoyment from floral arrangements. Longer vase life begins with something as simple as how you cut the flowers.

There are a number of conditioning techniques that will also help lengthen vase life. Although the additional treatments listed below may seem like too much bother, many flowers will benefit from them. Try them, and you'll find they make a difference. Treat blooms immediately after cutting, before you soak them overnight.

Cutting

Scissors and fingers are not the tools of choice for harvesting flowers. Picking flowers by pinching them off with your fingers tends to tear the stems or uproot the plants. It also generally crushes the stem rather than severing it cleanly. Even scissors can bruise stems and close off the channels that carry water to the bloom. For best results, use a very sharp knife to cut flowers. As a general rule, cut across

the stem at an angle to provide as wide a cut surface for water uptake as possible. This also prevents the stem from resting squarely on the bottom of the container, which would prevent water uptake. It's a good idea to have a bucket of water handy to receive your freshly picked flowers.

Lukewarm water (100° to 110°F) is best; icy-cold water is a bit of a shock for the cut blooms.

Good timing also makes a difference in the vase life of flowers. Don't cut flowers during the heat of the day, when they may already be drooping. Instead, cut them during the

cooler hours of early morning or in late afternoon or evening when they are not under stress from the sun.

Flower maturity is also an important consideration. Mature blooms that are full of pollen will not last as long as newly opened flowers. Choose blossoms that are just about to open fully. With some happy exceptions (daffodils and forsythia, for example), tightly closed buds will not open after they've been cut; they'll simply wilt when cut and put in water. Roses generally will open if cut once one outside petal has unfurled. Daisies last longest if picked when the flowers are fully open but the centers are still firm and slightly green. Spiky flowers like gladiolus, lupine, and delphinium will have the longest vase life if you select stems with lower flowers in full bloom and upper buds just on the threshold of opening. Snip off lower flowers as they wilt.

Conditioning

You can lengthen the vase life of flowers by conditioning them properly. That means allowing them to absorb as much water as possible as soon as they've been picked. Immediately after cutting and before arranging, stand flowers in deep water for six to eight hours—or, even better, overnight—in a cool, dark place. Immerse the foliage, but be sure to keep the flowers dry. Most flowers will take up warm water (around 100°F) more quickly. Conditioning will let the flowers drink in the water and be at their sturdiest for you to work with them. If the flowers have been out of water, recut the stems at an angle before plunging them in tepid water.

Surprising as it may sound, some flowers benefit from a hot bath immediately after cutting. Flowers that benefit from this treatment include windflower (*Anemone* spp.), broom (*Cytisus* spp.), bellflower (*Campanula* spp.), rose campion (*Lychnis coron-*

aria), columbine (*Aquilegia* spp.), daphne (*Daphne* spp.), hellebore (*Helleborus* spp.), lobelia (*Lobelia* spp.), beard-tongue (*Penstemon* spp.), primrose (*Primula* spp.), and periwinkle (*Vinca* spp.).

To give your flowers a hot water bath, start by cutting the stems at an angle. Pour 1 inch of boiling water into a heat-resistant container. Protect the blossoms from steam with a collar of newspaper, then submerge the tips of the stems in the water for about one minute. Then plunge the stems up to the base of the flowers into tepid water (100° to 110°F) and give the flowers a good deep soak.

There are specific techniques suitable for different types of flower stems. Stems are generally classified as woody, milky, hollow, or soft.

Woody Stems. The blossoms of flowering trees, shrubs, and some vines have woody stems that have difficulty taking up water unless they are specially prepared. To increase water uptake, strip off the bark 1 inch above the cut, then lightly crush the tip of the stem to break down the fibers so they can more readily take up water. A wooden rolling pin or mallet will do the job with a few gentle taps; use a sturdy block of wood or a chopping board to save your countertop. An alternative method is to cut a series of slits up through the center of the base of the stem—again, to about 1 inch. After splitting the stems, soak them in tepid water for several hours. Dogwood (*Cornus* spp.), mountain laurel (*Kalmia* spp.), forsythia (*Forsythia* spp.), honeysuckle (*Lonicera* spp.), and fruiting trees such as apples and crab apples all benefit from this treatment.

Some other types of flowers have fibrous stems that also benefit from splitting before soaking. These include thistle (*Cirsium* and other genera), mallow (*Malva* spp.), and chrysanthemum.

Milky Stems. Stems that exude milky sap when cut must be sealed at the tip before they are arranged. To condition poppies (*Papaver* spp.), hydrangea (*Hydrangea* spp.), poinsettia (*Euphorbia pulcherrima*), or any other milky-stemmed flower, singe the stem tips immediately after picking for a second or so over a match or candle flame. With a sizzle, the cut will be sealed. You can also seal the ends with a hot water bath. Return flowers to water until time for arranging. If you need to cut the stems to length for the arrangement, you'll need to seal them again.

Hollow Stems. One of the secrets of flower show winners is filling the hollow stalks of plants such as dahlias, delphinium, and lupine with water, then plugging the opening. Hold each stalk upside down to receive water from a medicine dropper or narrow-spouted watering can. Release any air bubbles by tapping the stem firmly with your finger. Use a tightly twisted wad of absorbent cotton as a stopper. Then stand flowers upright in deep water before arranging.

Soft Stems. Hyacinths, daffodils, and other soft-stemmed flowers last longer if you recut their stems under water to avoid the formation of an air lock. A basin or wide, shallow bowl full of water is perfect for dunking the stem while you cut it with your sharp knife. Be sure to cut stems at an angle. Then condition these flowers in cold water before arranging. When picked, the stems of daffodils exude a runny, clear sap that can clog the stems of other flowers arranged with them. To avoid this, soak daffodils in a separate container of cold water for two to three hours after cutting and before arranging. Try to cut the stems to the length you'll need in the arrangement before soaking them, to avoid recutting them.

Flower Arranging

Flower arranging doesn't have to be difficult. In fact, probably the hardest part is overcoming the fear of designing your first bouquet. Arrangements can be as simple as daisies in a milk jug or as elaborate as a mixed bouquet for a buffet table, but if you're a beginner, it's best to start simple and work up. Just remember, flowers are always beautiful—it's hard to make them look ugly!

All good arrangements start with a few basic materials—fresh, properly conditioned flowers and foliage, tools, and containers. Knowing a few simple styling principles will help steer you in the right direction and encourage you to experiment.

Materials

Take a tip from nature to inspire your designs and help you select the plant materials you use in arrangements: Your garden and the fields and forests nearby contain a wealth of colors, textures, and fragrances. Don't be afraid to try to recreate this natural beauty in your arrangements. Mix several types of flowers or foliage, select a variety of colors, or try new color combinations. Experiment with many types of materials to blend texture, color, and fragrance. For example, when selecting flowers, consider combinations of wildflowers, perennials, annuals, flowering shrubs and trees, roses, and herbs. Look to trees and shrubs, ferns, perennials, grasses, and herbs for foliage to add to your arrangements. Don't overlook the showy heads of ornamental grasses, seedpods, or shrubs with berries for unusual color and texture. Bring fragrance indoors with sweet-smelling blooms, but don't overlook pungent herbs—many of them make wonderful additions to bouquets. Crush a leaf between your fingers now and then to release their fragrance. Using flowers in varying stages of development will enrich the texture of an arrangement—combine unopened buds with fully blown flowers, for example.

Containers

The choices for a container are almost limitless. Just remember that the container and flowers must complement each other to form an artistic unit. Often a container in a neutral color with simple lines is most effective, since it doesn't compete with your plant material for attention. That doesn't mean you should avoid a container with some individuality. Consider baskets, handmade pottery, and vessels of wood, pewter, or brass. Even seashells and rocks can hold flowers, especially in oriental or contemporary arrangements. All of these containers have the advantage of being opaque and will hide the mass of stems and any mechanical support system you've used.

A clear glass container lets the flowers take center stage. Stems showing through a transparent bowl make the flowers appear larger. Glass—cut crystal particularly—reflects light and makes flowers glow.

Some containers are so ornate that putting many colors in them creates confusion. But a monochromatic arrangement in one of these could be stunning—an all-white bouquet in an oriental vase, for example.

Tools

The tools you need for flower arranging aren't numerous, nor difficult to find. In addition to plant materials and containers, you'll need tools for cutting flowers, as well as mechanics, the tools used to hold flowers in place in their containers. Mechanics such as floral foam, pinholders, or chicken wire provide much-needed stability. They allow you to place stems exactly where you want them and hold flowers in position for best effect. (See

EQUIPMENT BASICS

A small investment in a few basic tools will help you improve your results dramatically. All are generally available from local florist-supply or craft-supply stores. (See "Sources" on page 401 for mail-order suppliers.)

Cutting Tools
- A well-sharpened knife for cutting soft stems
- Pruning shears to cut woody stems
- Wire cutters for cutting floral wire
- A rolling pin or rubber mallet for pounding woody stems

Mechanics
- Floral foam
- Pinholders
- Chicken wire
- Marbles or pebbles

Other Supplies
- Waterproof floral tape
- Floral clay
- Floral wire
- Corsage tape
- Lazy Susan

"Equipment Basics" above for a list of basic tools you'll need to make flower arrangements.)

Mechanics

Experiment with some or all of the following mechanics in future arrangements.

Floral Foams. Perhaps the most widely used mechanic, floral foam bricks come in two forms, for either fresh or dried flower arranging. The bricks used for arranging fresh flowers absorb water and stems can be stuck in place anywhere in the brick for support. You can cut the bricks to fit any container. Use waterproof flo-

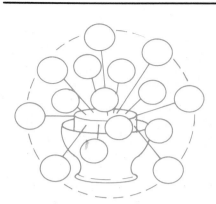

Round arrangements are the simplest to make. The stems of the flowers all point to a central spot, from which they appear to grow.

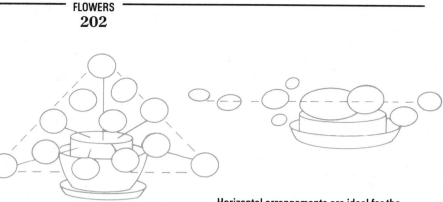

Triangular arrangements are nearly as easy as round ones. Use spiky flowers to establish the points of the triangle, then fill with rounder flowers.

Horizontal arrangements are ideal for the center of a dining table. Start with round flowers in the center, then add spiky material on either side. The completed arrangement should appear oval when viewed from the top.

ral tape fastened to the edges of the container and across the top of the foam to hold it in place. (The container must be dry when you fasten the tape to it.) For best results, soak the foam for several hours in water before arranging flowers; it takes time for water to soak in, and sticking stems in dry foam can cause them to wilt.

Floral foam can be reused, so don't throw it away after a single use. After your arrangement has passed its prime, remove the spent flowers, taking care not to break the foam apart. Then store foam wet in a plastic bag if you'll be using it within a few days; otherwise, store it dry. When reusing, don't place new flowers in old stem holes in the foam. Air pockets there could stop the flow of water up the stem.

Pinholders. These are small, heavy implements that have round, oval, square, or rectangular metallic bases with many closely set pins molded into them. They're used primarily in low or flat containers such as those used in Japanese and contemporary arrangements, because they can be concealed in small containers. Secure the pinholder to its container with waterproof floral clay. Remember that container, pinholder, and clay must be dry when you fasten them together, to remain tightly in place.

Grid Mechanics. Chicken wire, the best known grid mechanic, is often used to hold flowers in position in large vases. To use chicken wire, cut a square of wire and fold the edges to fit tightly inside the mouth of the vase. Hold wire in place with waterproof floral tape. (The container must be dry when you fasten the tape to it.) You can also use waterproof floral tape to create grids over wide-mouthed vases, helping flowers to stay more upright.

Other Mechanics. Use marbles, pebbles, gravel, shells, or sand as mechanics by filling the container and using them to support flowers. These materials can provide interesting highlights to arrangements when used in clear or colored glass containers. Use clear marbles if you don't want mechanics to be so easily seen.

You can also design arrangements without mechanics. Flower and foliage stems, along with twiggy branches stuck in the mouth of the container, will hold flowers in their artistic poses.

Wiring

For most arrangements, wiring isn't necessary, but for some styles—especially formal ones—you may want to strengthen or bend a stem so it stays in position. To wire a bloom, insert the end of a piece of floral wire into the flower head. Then loosely wrap the remaining wire down around the stem. An alternative method used with some types of flowers is to guide the wire from the head down through the stem; this technique hides the wire and does not deter water flow.

Styling Principles

Whether you're planning a flower garden or making a flower arrangement, there are some basic design principles that will help you create a pleasing design.

Balance

Flowers have visual weight of size and color that must be balanced in a pleasing manner if an arrangement is to be attractive. For example, the visual weight may be distributed evenly throughout the bouquet or may be used at the base of an arrangement to provide a stable foundation. Balance is important in designing an arrangement regardless of the shape or style you've selected. Even though some styles are not symmetrical, all should be balanced. Otherwise, the arrangement will look top-heavy or lopsided. In applying these principles, the general rule is to place flowers with more visual weight closer to the focal point of the arrangement. Other, less weighty flowers can be used to lead out and away from the center.

Flower Color. Generally, dark and bright colors carry more weight than light colors. Dark colored flowers, such as maroon tulips or deep purple bearded iris, or bright colors, such as brilliant orange marigolds or flaming pink peonies, have more weight than blooms of equivalent size in light colors such as white, lilac, or pale yellow. Try to balance the distribution of each throughout the arrangement. An arrangement with large, brilliantly col-

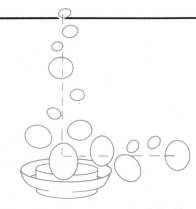

L-shaped arrangements are especially effective for spiky foliage, branches, and flowers. Establish the L shape with several pieces of spiky material, then fill in with rounder and smaller flowers.

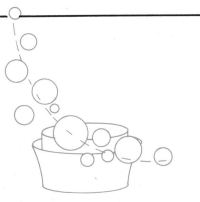

A crescent-shaped arrangement is just like an L-shaped one, but it lacks the 90-degree angle. A pair of crescent-shaped arrangements is effective on a mantle.

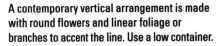

A contemporary vertical arrangement is made with round flowers and linear foliage or branches to accent the line. Use a low container.

ored blooms at the top and white or other light flowers at the bottom will look top-heavy; one with dark flowers all to one side will look lopsided.

Dark colors can also be used to add visual weight to the base of an arrangement to add stability. Intersperse light colors throughout a bouquet to reflect more light and add an airy effect. This will also break up heavy masses of color.

Flower Size. Of course, large flowers have a heavier appearance, or visual weight, than small flowers. Try to avoid the top-heavy look of an arrangement with large flowers at the top and smaller, more delicate-looking flowers beneath. (If you want to repeat the color of a large flower at the very top of an arrangement, use a bud or partially opened flower that won't "weigh" as much.) You can use several small flowers to balance a larger one. Large flowers are effective when used to create visual weight near the center of an arrangement. Increase the visual weight of small flowers by allowing them to protrude farther from the center of the arrangement than large flowers. Small flowers often are used as fillers in arrangements—they're interspersed throughout the arrangement to add a feathery touch and delicate color.

Flower Shape. You'll also want to balance the many different shapes of the flowers in the arrangement. Use tall, spiky flowers to direct the eye outward, by placing them around the outside of a bouquet. Or use them

to make a flourish at the tips of a design, making the arrangement "reach." Round, denser flowers draw the eye toward the center of the arrangement.

Flower Texture. Finely textured flowers add an airy quality to bouquets; coarser flowers give the arrangement a more solid appearance. In most cases, it's best to intersperse the various textures you're using so that they are distributed evenly throughout the bouquet. However, you can also use texture to create an accent. For example, seed heads of ornamental grasses can be used to create an attractive plume in an arrangement.

Proportion

An arrangement is said to be in proportion when its scale is in good relationship with its surroundings. This means that the different elements of an arrangement—flowers, foliage, and container—should all go well together and create a harmonious composition. A huge bouquet in a tiny container would be out of proportion just as would an arrangement mixing only 3-inch-wide zinnias with tiny tufts of baby's-breath. Mix a variety of sizes of flowers and foliage, and choose a container that is appropriate in size and style to the flowers you're using.

Repetition

Repeating one element in a design helps unify an arrangement and create a cohesive whole. You can repeat particular flowers—red zinnias, for example—or repeat a color using

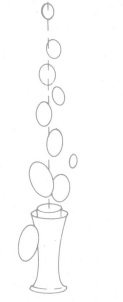

A traditional vertical arrangement is made in a tall vase. Use larger, fuller flowers near the base of the arrangement, and allow one or two blooms to droop beneath the rim of the vase.

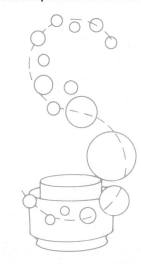

Make an S-shaped arrangement by building gentle curves above and below a central mound of flowers. Use spiky flowers and vines for the curve.

many different flowers all of the same or closely related colors, such as yellow marigolds, yarrow, and chrysanthemums. You can also repeat specific combinations of flowers throughout a bouquet, or repeat lines in a geometrical arrangement.

Styles and Shapes

Floral designers use many different styles and shapes of arrangements to suit various tastes. An arrangement can have an airy, informal style, with flowers gathered in a loose bouquet—a handful of mixed wildflowers placed in a vase, for example. Formal arrangements tend to have a more compact and regular style—such as a low composition for the center of a dining room table.

There are eight traditional shapes for arrangements: round, triangular, L-shaped, crescent, horizontal, contemporary vertical, traditional vertical, and Hogarth or S-curved. (These are illustrated on pages 202-3.) Some shapes are particularly suitable for certain kinds of occasions. The horizontal arrangement, for example, is the best choice for a centerpiece on a formal dining table. This low arrangement won't interfere with conversation across the table.

Whatever shape arrangement you're making, start by deciding where to put the center of your design. This will be the imaginary source from which the flowers appear to grow. When you place flowers in the container, aim stem tips at this focal point to give the bouquet a more natural appearance. As you work with the flowers, be sure to remove foliage that would be below the water line.

How to Make a Flower Arrangement

A simple round arrangement makes an excellent centerpiece for informal dining. You can create a compact, formal Colonial-style mound of flowers, or a colorful, loose, informal array of your garden favorites. Whatever the style, the round arrangement is a good choice for learning floral design. Just follow the steps listed here.

1. Begin by preparing the container for designing. Cut a piece of wet floral foam to fit snugly in the container you've selected. Then fix it in place with two strips of floral adhesive tape. (Or use a pinholder secured with clay instead.) Fill the container with water. Place the container on a lazy Susan so that you can rotate it with ease while designing to view the arrangement from all sides.

2. In a round arrangement, the focal point is the center of the foam block or pinholder. Aim your stem tips toward this point. Start by placing some of the foliage you've gathered to cover the foam base.

3. Place the largest flowers next. Position some very close to the focal point and some farther away at various distances out and up from the center, roughly outlining the round shape of the arrangement. Check to make sure the arrangement is balanced, with visual weight evenly distributed throughout the bouquet.

4. Create contrast by adding linear material such as tall, spiky flowers, seed heads of ornamental grasses, and twigs or berry branches alongside the first few flowers placed in the center.

5. Define the roundness further by filling in large gaps with medium-size flowers and foliage.

6. Check to make sure the floral foam is covered with foliage.

7. Round out the bouquet by filling any spaces with small, dainty flowers. Baby's-breath (*Gypsophila* spp.) makes a good filler for this purpose.

Making a Dried Arrangement

The steps are almost reversed in making a dried arrangement. You may need to use floral wire to strengthen the stems of dried flowers, or wire small clusters of flowers together and insert them all together. First, cover the mechanics with sheet moss, which is available from floral suppliers. Then define the round outline with small filler material such as dried baby's-breath or statice. Build the arrangement by adding medium-size flowers and then large flowers. Last, carefully place the linear material such as ornamental grass seed heads or dried spikes of lavender for accents to soften the edges.

How to Press Flowers

Pressing is one of the best ways to preserve flowers and retain them as treasured keepsakes, whether they're from your wedding bouquet or a child's walk in the woods. You can use pressed flowers to make a variety of decorative items such as pictures, candles, frames, stationery, cards, and bookmarks. These items can hold their color and artistic value longer than dried flower arrangements, wreaths, or potpourri.

Selecting Plant Material

You can gather an abundance of materials for pressing in meadows and forests, or you may already have plenty of flowers and foliage in your garden. Choose flowers with heads that will flatten well. Flowers with simple shapes such as violets are easier to press than large, trumpet-shaped lilies, for example. Various leaves, skeletonized or fresh, take nicely to pressing and add a fine contrast to colorful flowers. You can also press grasses, herbs, tree leaves, and ferns. Try pressing plants and flowers in different stages of growth: fronds and fully developed ferns; flowers and their buds. For large, double flowers such as peonies or roses, try pressing individual petals and recreating the "flower" by arranging the separate petals in your compositions. Don't be afraid to experiment. In addition to the materials listed above, try mosses and lichens or even slices of fruits and vegetables. With any new material, it's a good idea to jot down notes about what steps you take as you discover what works for you.

Harvest plant material when it is dry and stems are full of water. The best picking time is on a dry day in the late morning. Press your gatherings shortly after cutting, or keep them in a container of water until you're ready to press them. Remember not to press flowers when wet or wilted.

The Flower Press

You don't need any elaborate supplies to experiment with pressing flowers. Start with a heavy, hardcover book or a telephone directory for a press. Place the materials you're pressing between sheets of blotting paper (available in art stores) to prevent ink from staining the flowers—and moisture from the flowers from staining the book—then insert them between the pages of the book. Stack heavy books or bricks on top of the book press for extra weight.

You can construct a sturdier press from plywood. A plywood press enables you to apply more pressure to the flowers, quickening the entire process and giving better results. Cut two pieces of heavy gauge plywood to equal dimensions; rectangles that will accommodate a folded sheet of newspaper—about 14 by 16 inches—are ideal. Drill a hole in each corner, then use long bolts with wing nuts to connect the two boards at each of the four corners. Use the wing nuts to tighten and loosen the press to adjust pressure.

Plant material is pressed between the plywood boards in sandwiches of absorbent paper such as recycled paper or newsprint and blotting paper.

First, place a layer of absorbent paper on the board—several folded sheets of newspaper are ideal. Next, put down a layer of blotting paper. Arrange your flowers on the blotting paper. Try to use as much space on the blotting paper as possible when spreading out the flowers, but don't overlap the specimens—they'll stick together. Arrange flowers so that you'll end up with a variety of stem curves, as well as open flower faces and profiles, so you'll have plenty of choice for your compositions. It's best to keep all of the same type of flower, or at least all of the same color, in one layer, so you'll be able to find them easily. You may even want to label the layer. After you've arranged the flowers, add another piece of blotting paper, several more sheets of newsprint or absorbent paper, and then more blotting paper and another layer of flowers. Make as many layers as you want, as long as the corner bolts that hold the plywood pieces together will span the depth.

For best results, keep your press in a warm, dry place, because too much moisture in the environment may promote mold to form. After the first few days of pressing, change the absorbent paper between layers, but leave the blotting paper intact so you don't disturb your flowers. Check for wetness periodically for the remainder of the pressing process. Keeping the paper dry and pressure strong will quicken the drying process for most plant materials and yield more vivid colors. (Very succulent materials, however, require less pressure but more frequent paper changes.)

Materials are dry when they're crisp to the touch—this should take at least two weeks. Store your dried flowers in the press until you're ready to use them.

Making a Pressed Flower Picture

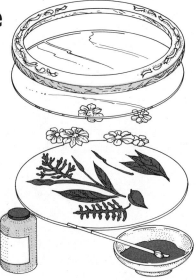

Creating a pressed flower picture is like painting one. Use the flowers as brushstrokes of color and texture; leaves as background. You can create bouquets or depict scenes with dried flowers, and it's easy to rearrange the dried materials until you have a composition that pleases you.

1. Begin your picture by choosing a paper or fabric background. The background should be simple and not overpower your picture—a sheet of mat board is fine. The background should contrast with the flowers to play up their colors. For example, use a dark background if you'll be working with mostly light flowers.

2. Cut the background to the size and shape of your frame. If you're using paper or fabric, mount it with spray adhesive on a piece of mat board or foam core. Spray adhesive, unlike regular white glue, won't leave bumps on the background surface.

3. Start building your picture by putting down the larger backdrop flowers and leaves. These can be skeletonized leaves, fern fronds, long flowers, and leaves. Move the delicate plant material carefully with forceps or tweezers.

4. Next, arrange the bolder, more colorful flowers that will form the

center of your arrangement. Layer some of these over the stems of backdrop elements. (Don't forget, unless you plan to frame with a mat, the finished picture must be flat.)

You may need to cut away the plant parts that won't be seen.)

5. Position small, dainty flowers for accent, and cover any unsightly stems with pressed leaves, lichens, or moss.

6. To assemble the picture permanently once you've created an arrangement that pleases you, turn the arrangement upside down or sketch it so you'll remember how all the elements were arranged. To turn upside down, cover it with a piece of heavy cardboard, hold tightly, and turn. Then fasten down the elements of your design one at a time, starting with the background material. Use rubber cement or water-soluble white craft glue that dries clear. Use a toothpick to dab tiny amounts on the backs of flowers and foliage. Let the glue dry overnight. Then cover your picture with glass and frame it.

Drying Flowers

Arrangements, wreaths, and other projects made from dried flowers have nearly universal appeal. Fortunately, drying flowers is easy and requires little more than adequate storage space and an abundance of plant materials. Many gardeners only think of drying annual flowers such as cockscomb (*Celosia* spp.), strawflower (*Helichrysum bracteatum*), and gomphrena (*Gomphrena globosa*) in the late summer or fall. But there are flowers suitable for drying all seasons of the year, in your garden and in the meadows and forests around your home. For example, daffodils and tulips dry well in desiccants such as silica gel. Pussy willow is another early spring feature that is easy to dry. In spring and summer, try drying blooms of ornamental onions (*Allium* spp.), astilbe (*Astilbe* spp.), and yarrow (*Achillea* spp.), all of which are easy to air-dry. In fall, ornamental grasses make wonderful additions to dried bouquets. Also try ripened seed heads from weeds, perennials such as blue false indigo (*Baptisia australis*), twigs, and vines. Don't be afraid to experiment with many different types of plant materials.

The traditional way to dry flowers is to air-dry them in bunches. The fragrance and nostalgic charm of flower bunches suspended from a drying rack are just as enjoyable as the dried blossoms and grasses will be in an arrangement later. Although air-drying is still popular, desiccants have widened the range of flowers that can be dried successfully and microwave drying has shortened the process to a matter of minutes or hours, not days or weeks. Regardless of the technique you choose, there are a few pointers that apply to all of them.

Tips for Success

● Don't harvest flowers or other plant material when the weather is cloudy and damp or the plants are wet. If you should find a few hidden drops of dew on material you've harvested, use the edge of a paper towel to gently absorb the water before drying.

● Don't harvest plant material that is wilted. If you can't dry cut material immediately, stand it in water in a cool, dark place until you can get to it.

● Select the most perfectly formed flowers you can find; drying will accentuate any flaws.

● Experiment with flowers at various stages of development—blooms often open further as they dry. But don't pick flowers which have been fully open for several days, as they're more likely to turn brown and shatter.

● Keep a notebook to jot down what works and what doesn't—what you harvested, what stage of development it had reached, how you dried it, and other methods you'd like to try to improve your results.

● If you've a specific arrangement in mind, dry perhaps twice as much material as you think you'll need. Then you'll not be caught short if some flowers do not dry perfectly or are damaged in storage.

● To protect plant material from shattering or reabsorbing moisture from the air, spray after drying with matte-finish plastic craft sealer or hair spray.

● Flowers dried with silica gel can reabsorb moisture. You'll need to display them in an airtight container, such as a Victorian bell jar, or store them until the air is less humid, such as during the winter heating season.

● If you're not using them right away, store flowers in flat boxes in one or two layers separated by tissue paper so they can be easily located later without damaging your handiwork. Add a few mothballs to repel rodents and moths. Silica-gel-dried flowers should be stored in an airtight container with silica gel or dry sand in the bottom.

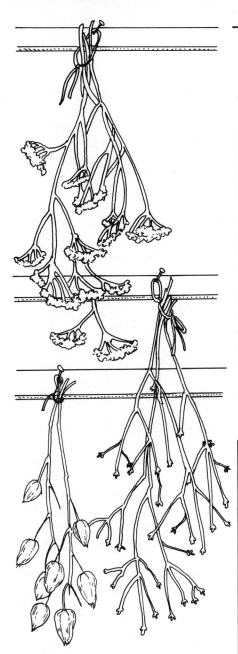

Many plants dry beautifully when simply hung upside down in a warm, dark spot.

Some plants—and petals being dried for potpourri—dry best when spread on screens.

Air-Drying

Air-drying is a simple method for preserving large quantities of plant material. Results differ from plant to plant. Some such as cockscomb (*Celosia* spp.) will dry nearly perfectly, with attractive form and brilliant color. The colors of some blossoms will fade, but these can be used to impart an antique aura to nosegays or arrangements.

Flowers with fat, moist blossoms or many petals such as peonies (*Paeonia* spp.) generally do not air-dry well. They drop their petals, fade, or shrivel past recognition. (See "Plants for Air-Drying" below for a list of the flowers to start with for each of the methods described below.

You can experiment with other flowers as you become more experienced.)

The ideal spot for air-drying is a dark room with warm, dry, gently moving air. The dryness of the air will affect whether the process takes a week or three weeks. Consider an attic, dry basement, garage, shed, or closet.

Many flowers can be hung upside down to dry. Strip foliage from their stems and make small bunches of them. Put no more than five in a bunch, and stagger flower heads so they don't touch. Make a slip knot with a string or rubber band down toward the stem ends to hold them tightly together. Then hang them from hooks, pegs, coat hangers, or racks that are either suspended from

PLANTS FOR AIR-DRYING

There are several ways to air-dry plant material, and some plants are better suited to one method than another. Here are lists of plants suited to each method.

Plants to Hang Upside Down

Achillea spp. (yarrow)
Allium spp. (ornamental onions and chives)
Ammobium alatum (winged everlasting)
Armeria maritima (thrift)
Artemisia spp. (artemisia or wormwood)
Carthamus tinctorius (safflower)
Celosia spp. (cockscomb)
Delphinium spp. (delphinium or larkspur)
Limonium spp. (statice)
Lunaria annua (money plant or honesty)
Salvia spp. (sage)
Sedum spectabile (sedum)
Solidago spp. (goldenrod)
Tagetes spp. (marigold)

Other materials that can be dried hanging upside down include seed heads of *Clematis* spp., Oriental poppies (*Papaver* spp.), and coneflowers (*Echinacea* spp. and *Rudbeckia* spp.); seedpods of many plants including blue false indigo (*Baptisia australis*); rosebuds; cattails (*Typha* spp.); and branches of pussy willow and knotweed (*Polygonum* spp.). Blooms of globe amaranth (*Gomphrena globosa*), strawflower (*Helichrysum bracteatum*), and everlasting (*Helipterum* spp.) are best wired before they're hung to dry for the stems aren't strong when dry and tend to droop.

the ceiling, along walls, or free-standing.

Some flowers and plants dry better when placed right side up in a widemouthed container. Spread the stems out so they aren't crowded or crushed, and so you'll be able to separate them easily. Try drying some of the plants you normally hang to dry, to create a pleasing curve in the stem. Other plants should be dried in a similar container, standing in ½ inch of water.

Round, flat flower heads need support to dry flat. Slip stems through a screen, such as ¼-inch hardware cloth, letting heads rest faceup on the screen. Some materials are best laid flat to dry on a wood-framed screen that lets air circulate beneath.

Or use an absorbent surface such as newspaper; turn occasionally during the drying process.

Desiccants

Drying agents, or desiccants, not only speed drying as they absorb water from petals and leaves but also expand the range of flowers that you can preserve. The flowers dried by this method much more closely resemble fresh flowers in color and form.

Of the commercially available desiccants, silica gel works fastest. It now comes very finely ground for use with flowers and can be sifted into blooms to encourage them to dry quickly without leaving bumps from coarse grains on the petals. Silica gel

is available from hobby or craft stores, florists, and garden centers, as well as mail-order suppliers. Although it's expensive, it can be reused indefinitely. It usually comes with blue "color indicator" crystals that change color when the silica gel is saturated with moisture. To reactivate it by drying it out, spread it on a flat baking pan and heat it in a 250°F oven until the original color returns.

Drying flowers with desiccants such as silica gel is easy. Just follow these steps.

1. Select an airtight container, such as a cookie tin. Since different flowers dry at different rates, plan on using a separate container for each type of flower.

2. Gather flowers as described in "Tips for Success" on page 207, and cut stems to 1 inch or so in length. If you expect to need wire stems for arranging, it's a good idea to wire them now. To wire a bloom, insert the end of the wire into the flower head. Loosely wrap the remaining wire down around the stem. An alternative method used with some types of flowers is to guide the wire from the head down through the stem.

3. Spread a ½-inch layer of silica gel on the bottom of your container. Then set the blossoms on the silica gel, bending wired stems out of the way as needed. Set daisylike flowers facedown; complex, many-petaled flowers like roses or carnations faceup. Space the blossoms so they don't touch one another.

4. With a spoon or measuring cup, gently pour silica gel around the blossoms, first filling in support underneath each bloom and then making sure all crevices in the bloom are filled. Cover with another ½-inch layer of silica gel. You can make additional layers of flowers if the container is deep enough.

5. Tightly close the container and label it with date and contents.

Plants to Dry Right Side Up

In addition to the plants listed here, grains and ornamental grasses also can be dried right side up.

Echinops spp. (globe thistle)

Gypsophila paniculata (baby's-breath)

Physalis alkekengi (Chinese-lantern plant)

Cotinus coggygria (smoke tree)

Dry the following plants right side up, but set the stems in ½ inch of water: *Calluna* spp. (heather), *Hydrangea* spp. (hydrangea), and *Moluccella laevis* (bells-of-Ireland). Florist's proteas (*Protea* spp.) and other related florist's flowers, including *Banksia* spp., *Hakea* spp., and *Grevillea* spp., can also be dried in this way.

Dry with Support

Slip the stems of the following plants through screens or hardware cloth to provide support for the flower heads.

Anethum graveolens (dill)

Daucus carota var. *carota* (Queen-Anne's-lace, wild carrot)

Foeniculum (fennel)

Heracleum spp. (hogweed)

Leontopodium alpinum (edelweiss)

Dry Flat on a Screen

Many plant materials can be spread on screens or layers of absorbent paper for drying. These include dock (*Rumex acetosa*), bamboos and grasses (which can also be dried by hanging or upright), fungi, twigs, and sprigs of lavender (*Lavandula* spp.).

When drying with silica gel, gently sift the granules over the blossoms, filling up all the crevices between petals.

6. If you're drying simple flowers such as small daisies, open the container in about two days and gently shake it until a few petals appear. If they feel like crisp paper, carefully pour off silica gel into another container and remove flowers. For fleshy or more complex, many-petaled flowers, wait several days before checking.

7. After the flowers have dried, partially refill the container with a layer of silica gel and insert flower stems up to, but not covering, the petals. Close the container and leave for another two to four days to finish drying. This is especially necessary with more complex, many-petaled flowers, like roses.

8. Check the blooms regularly, and remove them when they are fully dry. With a small camel's hair paintbrush, dust off any clinging silica gel. Protect blooms from shattering with a drop of clear-drying glue at the flower's center and base.

9. Keep a record of drying times you use for each flower type so you develop a sense of what works best. Flowers immersed in silica gel for too long will become overly dry and be very brittle, so you'll want to get it just right.

Microwave Drying

Microwave drying is not only speedy for flowers, it also solves the problem of how to preserve foliage, which shrivels or changes color when dried by any other method.

You can dry autumn leaves, fern fronds, or other foliage in your microwave. First, to protect the microwave, put a cup of water at the back of the oven. Replace the water each time you run the microwave. Fold a paper towel in half and put the leaves to be dried inside it. They should not overlap. Place the paper towel in the microwave and place a microwaveable dish on top to prevent the leaves from curling. Cook two minutes on high power, then remove the leaves. If they are dry and crisp, they are done. If they seem almost dry, overnight air-drying will most likely finish them. If they've lost color or appear too dry, try a new batch and less cooking time. Use a dry paper towel for each new batch of leaves.

You can also dry flowers in the microwave using silica gel. Dry one flower at a time, using a small microwaveable container that is about 3 inches taller than the flower. Put in a layer of silica gel, insert the blossom, then carefully cover the flower, filling in all nooks and crannies with the silica. (Don't wire blooms before putting them in the microwave. If you need to wire them, do it immediately after they're done, before they cool.) Add a layer on top, leaving about 2 inches of space between the top of the gel and the top of the container.

Place a cup of water at the back of the microwave, and replace the water each time you do a new flower.

To eliminate guesswork, place a microwave thermometer in the silica so it does not touch sides or bottom of the container. Put the container in the microwave and heat on high for 30 to 60 seconds at a time, until the thermometer reads 200° to 220°F. Use a rotating rack or turn the container every 30 seconds. Remove the container from the microwave with thermometer still in place. Allow silica to cool until the temperature reads 70° to 80°F before removing the flower. Keep a record of cooking times and results for various flower types so you can make adjustments if needed. If flowers turn beige, reduce cooking time the next try.

After the flowers have dried, carefully sift away the silica gel. Insert flower stems up to, but not covering, the petals, in another larger container with a fresh layer of silica gel. Close the container and leave the flowers for another two to four days to finish drying. Then clean the flowers with a small paintbrush and spray with sealer.

Making a Dried Flower Wreath

Wreaths are a delightful way to decorate doors or bring nature into your home. They also make treasured gifts or keepsakes, especially when the flowers are from your own garden.

There are a variety of ways to make a wreath, partly because of the many choices for wreath bases. You can start with a wire frame and cover it with small bunches of dried baby's-breath (*Gypsophila* spp.), statice (*Limonium* spp.), or dried 'Silver King' artemisia (*Artemisia ludoviciana* var. *albula*) for filler. Wrap floral wire around the stems of the bunches and wire them to the frame. Continue adding and wrapping bunches until the entire frame is covered. For a quick wreath, intersperse small bouquets of mixed dried flowers for the bunches of base material as you go. (For tips on attaching flowers to wreath bases, see "Attaching Flowers" on the opposite page.)

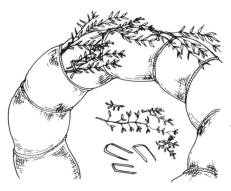

Attach small bunches to the base with hairpin-shaped floral pins or bent wires. Poke pins in to secure the stems of the bunches.

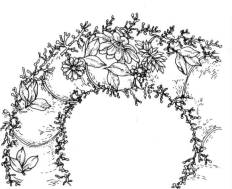

Overlap the bunches, covering the stems. Fill the inside edge of the base first, then the outside edge. Add accent materials as you fill the middle.

Spray the finished wreath with an acrylic sealer or hair spray to protect it from breaking or absorbing moisture from the air. The sealer also slows fading of colors.

You can also start with a base made of straw or Spanish moss, both of which can be purchased at craft stores or garden centers. Start with a background filler—as with a wire frame, baby's-breath, statice, or artemisia are fine—and insert it stem by stem until the entire base has been covered. Then add accent flowers to dress it up. Small bouquets of colorful dried flowers wired together—plus dried herbs for fragrance—are easy to add by poking them in place. Or you can fasten them with hairpin-shaped floral pins or bent pieces of wire. You can add just a few bright accents and intersperse them with stems of more neutral colors. Keep in mind that you want a harmonious composition of color and texture.

You can also make a wreath base from trailing vines, such as grapevine and trumpet vine. Harvest the vines in summer or fall when they

ATTACHING FLOWERS

There are several ways to attach flowers to a wreath. It's generally easiest to wire small bunches of filler or background material together and then insert them. If you're using a straw or Spanish-moss-based frame, you can wire flowers to wooden floral picks, which come with a short piece of wire attached just for this purpose. Just gather a few stems together, wrap the wire around them, and poke them in place.

To wire with floral wire and corsage tape, first fold a piece of floral wire in half. Then lay the folded wire alongside the stem with the fold at the base of the flower head. Wind half of the wire around the stem to secure it. The second half of the wire remains long, to serve as the stem. Finish by wrapping corsage tape down the length of the wire, beginning at the flower head. Corsage tape will seal in place as you stretch and twirl it as you wrap. Be sure to cut wire stems to appropriate lengths so they will be held tightly in the base without protruding.

You can also glue flowers in place with either white craft glue that dries clear or hot glue. Nuts, berries, herbs, seedpods, and other materials may also be glued in place to accent your wreath.

are pliable, and use them immediately so they don't become brittle. Trim off leaves and green growth. Begin the wreath by looping a circle with the vine in the desired size for your wreath. Continue making circles, weaving the ends in and out around the initial loop. Once you've woven one vine in place, you can add another until the wreath is as thick as you desire. Tuck the ends in when you're finished. If you like the look of dried grape tendrils poking out in all directions, save some lengths of vine with attractive tendrils until the end, then weave or wire them in place. Once you've created the vine base, add accent materials by wiring or using hot glue to fasten them in place. Don't plan on covering the entire base with dried flowers, since the vine wreath adds an attractive, woodsy touch.

Making Potpourri

You've probably discovered that on a bleak winter day an open bowl of potpourri is a marvelous bit of "aroma therapy," evoking pleasant memories of your summer garden. But have you tried creating your own mixtures?

If you feel at all romantic about the fragrance of your flowers and heady scent of your herbs, you'll enjoy making, using, and giving potpourri. Making potpourri is simpler than it seems; it's nothing more than a concoction of flowers, leaves, and seeds of plants enhanced with a few drops of one or more essential oils to intensify aroma and a fixative to retard evaporation of the oil and make the fragrance last. The principles in making potpourri are few and simple, and possibilities are endless—you're limited only by the plant material available to you.

Follow these instructions to make dry potpourri, the familiar loose mixture so pretty in an apothecary jar and fragrant in a sachet.

For a start, look over the recipes and plant materials lists and pick a main scent you think appropriate. Decide whether you want the overall effect to be floral, woodsy, or spicy. Especially at first, keep it simple. Limit a mixture to four to six different flowers and leaves and just three or four spices and other ingredients. You'll find that rose petals and lavender are especially appealing in potpourri.

COMMON POTPOURRI INGREDIENTS

Flowers and Floral Scents

Flowers add color and fragrance to potpourris. Try drying some to add attractive floral scents and brilliant color to your mixtures. Petals of these flowers form the basis of any potpourri. To make a woodsy, spicy, or citrusy scent, add the materials listed under those headings to your basic supply of crisply dried flower petals.

The most common essential oils with floral scents are jasmine, lily-of-the-valley, rose, rose geranium, honeysuckle, and heliotrope. You can add their characteristic scents with purchased essential oils.

Centaurea spp. (bachelor's-buttons)
Delphinium spp. (delphinium or larkspur)
Dianthus spp. (carnation or pinks)
Gomphrena globosa (globe amaranth)
Heliotropium spp. (heliotrope)
Lavandula angustifolia (English lavender)
Matricaria recutita (sweet false chamomile)
Paeonia spp. (peony petals)
Rosa spp. (rose petals and small buds)
Syringa vulgaris (lilac)
Tagetes spp. (marigold)

Woodsy/Earthy Scents

There are many materials you can add to give your mixtures a woodsy or earthy scent. The most common essential oils for woodsy or earthy mixes are bayberry, patchouli, sandalwood, and frankincense or myrrh, both of which have a balsamlike fragrance. If you like woodsy scents, mix petals of flowers listed above with some of the following materials.

Bayberry (berries from *Myrica pensylvanica*)
Cedar shavings
Clary (*Salvia sclarea*)

pourri because, when dried, they retain their fragrance particularly well.

Gathering and Drying

You can gather and prepare plant materials throughout the blooming season with one or more potpourri mixtures in mind. For best results, collect flowers on a sunny, dry morning just after the dew has dried. Select flowers just after they've opened. Also include buds that dry well—small rosebuds are lovely in potpourri. Cut herbs shortly before flowering. (See "Common Potpourri Ingredients" below for a list of flowers, herbs, spices, and other materials that are commonly used in potpourri. Some flowers, such as bachelor's-button (*Centaurea cyanus*), are used more for the color they add than the fragrance.)

Pull off petals or individual florets and spread them on nonmetallic screens or a stretched piece of cheesecloth to let air circulate around them. (Avoid metal screens because they can change the scent of plant materials.) Small flowers or buds are also attractive when dried whole and added to potpourri. A warm, dark spot with good air circulation is best for drying. Hang herbs in small bunches to dry.

To prepare citrus peel, scrape out the pulp and white inner peel. Dry the outer rind in narrow strips. If you've purchased a balsam wreath for the holidays, save the dried needles for use in potpourri.

When your gatherings are crisp and dry, strip leaves from stems. Store each plant type separately in airtight glass containers in a dark place.

Other Ingredients

Spices.   For long-lasting aroma, use whole spices rather than ground. Cloves, strips of sassafras roots, or curled pieces of cinnamon bark are attractive in mixtures. Store them in airtight containers in a dark place until you are ready to mix the potpourri.

Essential Oils.   There are many essential oils from which to choose, including rose, rose geranium, lily-of-the-valley, lavender, lemon verbena, sandalwood, heliotrope, and patchouli, to name a few. These oils are available from craft stores and specialty shops. The most natural choice is usually an oil made from the same plant material you've chosen as the main fragrant ingredient in your potpourri. You might enhance the bouquet with a second or possibly even a third oil. Use just a few drops per batch.

Fixatives.   There are a number of plant-derived fixatives, which you can purchase from craft or herbal-supply stores; some can even be grown in your garden. Orris root (*Iris* × *germanica* var. *florentina*) is most popular, as its violetlike fragrance blends beautifully with woodsy and exotic mixes. To make your own, dig the plants, scrub the roots, and chop them into ¼-inch pieces. Then let them dry in a warm, dark, airy place. (Some people are allergic to orris and should avoid it.)

Calamus root (sweet flag or *Acorus calamus*) will grow if you have a boggy spot. It enhances earthy, spicy, and vanilla-scented potpourris. Pre-

Juniper needles or berries (*Juniperus* spp.)
Marjoram (*Origanum vulgare*)
Pine or balsam fir needles
Rosemary (*Rosmarinus officinalis*)
Sage (*Artemisia* spp.)
Sweet woodruff (*Galium odoratum*)
Thyme (*Thymus vulgaris*)

Spicy Scents

Lavender or vanilla oils are attractive with spicy fragrance potpourri. Ground vanilla beans are also an excellent ingredient. For a spicy potpourri, mix these oils with crisply dried flowers and petals and some of the spices and other plant materials listed below. To add a spicy, citrusy scent, consider dried leaves of lemon geranium (*Pelargonium crispum*), lemongrass (*Cymbopogon citratus*), lemon balm (*Melissa officinalis*), lemon verbena (*Aloysia triphylla*), or strips of dried lemon or orange peel.

Allspice (*Pimenta dioica*)
Anise (*Pimpinella anisum*)
Basil (*Ocimum basilicum*)
Sweet bay (*Laurus nobilis*)
Caraway (*Carum carvi*)
Cinnamon (*Cinnamomum zeylanicum*)
Cloves (*Syzygium aromaticum*)
Coriander (*Coriandrum sativum*)
Mints (*Mentha* spp.)
Nutmeg (*Myristica fragrans*)
Pennyroyal (*Mentha pulegium*)
Sassafras (*Sassafras albidum*)

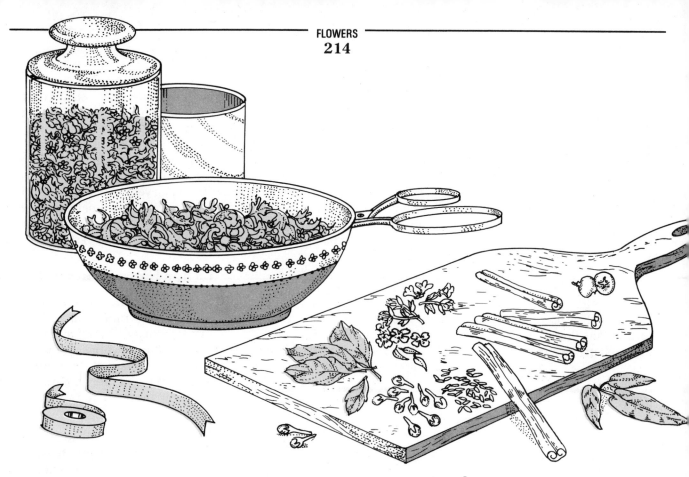

pare as you would orris root.

Oak moss (*Evernia pranastri*), a lichen, is pleasing with lavender, citrus, and floral mixes as well as those containing patchouli, vetivert, vanilla, and tonka bean.

Use 2 to 4 tablespoons of orris or calamus root or 1 cup of oak moss per quart of dried flowers and herbs.

Mixing Dry Potpourri

1. Two days before you're ready to mix, sprinkle several drops of the essential oil or oils you've selected over your fixative in a small glass jar and cap it tightly.

2. Lightly crush any whole spices you're using in a mortar and pestle. Combine them with other plant materials such as dried flowers and herbs, citrus peel, and wood chips in a large, nonmetallic bowl. Toss all the dried ingredients with your hands.

3. Sprinkle on the oil and fixative mixture and mix well.

4. Pour all this into a widemouthed "aging jar" that has enough room for potpourri to be shaken well. A widemouthed 1-gallon jar with a screw-on top is ideal.

5. Set the jar in a warm, dark place. Turn the jar over and shake it twice a week to blend the mixture well.

6. In about a month, your potpourri should be mature, with a well-blended fragrance.

RECIPES FOR POTPOURRI

Try some of these mixtures, then experiment with your own. Don't forget to add an essential oil or oils of your choice when you prepare the fixative before you mix.

Rose-Lilac
3 cups rose petals
2 cups lilac flowers
2 cups marjoram
1 ounce orris root (fixative)

Lavender-Geranium
4 cups lavender
2 cups rose geranium
2 cups rosemary
1 ounce orris root (fixative)

Lemon-Thyme
2 cups lemon balm
1 cup thyme
1 cup nutmeg
½ ounce orris root (fixative)

Herb Garden
2 cups thyme
1 cup rosemary
½ cup lavender
1 cup mint
¼ cup tansy
¼ cup cloves
½ ounce orris root (fixative)

PART 3

The Food Garden

The Vegetable Garden

Designing a Companion-Planted Garden

Most of us have heard that marigolds help keep insects out of the vegetable garden or that nothing will grow near a black walnut tree. But while some of these claims seem to hold true, others do not. Just where do these horticultural maxims come from? Is there any truth to the notion that growing certain plants together can help or hinder their growth?

Companion Planting as a Tradition

For centuries, gardeners and farmers have cultivated different crops together in the same space to maximize available resources. American Indians, for example, used a corn-bean-squash interplanting scheme that balanced the requirements of each crop for light, water, and nutrients. The practice of companion planting, growing two or more crops simultaneously in a given area to achieve a specific benefit, is still common among subsistence farmers and organic gardeners in many parts of the world today. On large-scale, mechanized farms, however, single-crop cultivation has been the norm for several decades.

In recent years, as the limitations and ill effects of pesticides, chemical fertilizers, and other modern practices have become more apparent, scientists have begun looking more seriously at companion planting and other "old-fashioned" methods once considered inefficient. Small-scale farmers and backyard gardeners who have kept the interplanting tradition alive now serve as a valuable source of information on the complex interactions of crops with each other and with the surrounding environment.

Yet even those who practice companion planting do not know why some interplanting methods seem to work while others don't. Only careful research, combined with the experience and intuition of practitioners, will reveal which plant combinations are most beneficial and why. In the meantime, gardeners are in a unique position to take advantage of what is already known and to try out new combinations in their own plots at home.

Benefits of Companion Planting

Not all crops respond to companion planting in the same way. In fact, some do worse when combined with other crops than if they are grown by themselves. In many cases, however, the positive effects of interplanting are striking.

Some crops, for example, show increased yields when combined with other plants. Studies suggest that different crops planted together may take better advantage of sunlight than those grown separately. Think of cool season crops such as lettuce or spinach. The intense light (and heat) of midsummer sun may damage their leaves. Planting in the filtered shade of a row of tomatoes can allow these plants to receive enough light for good growth, while preventing heat injury.

Scientists have also theorized that interplanted crops make better use of soil nutrients and water than do crops cultivated apart from others. Corn interplanted with soybeans may stimulate the beans, a legume, to fix more nitrogen in the soil. Whatever the reason, you can reap a greater harvest from many of your vegetables if you are willing to spend the extra time to learn about and practice companion planting.

By interplanting certain crops, you can also improve the quality of your soil. Many plants supply nutrients to the soil that are beneficial to crops nearby. In addition, some plants with thick roots work the soil, improving tilth and drainage.

Companion planting is particularly useful in keeping pest and disease problems under control. If you grow only one crop at a time, you are likely to attract only a small variety of insects or diseases, but these may be great in number and can wreak considerable havoc in your garden. On the other hand, if you plant two or more crops together, you may have a large variety of pests, but there will be few of each in number. In the first instance, you are creating a less stable environment where one disease or insect population can easily take over all the rest; in the latter case, the diversity of plants allows for a more stable environment in which the various pests keep each other in check.

You can also include certain plants in your interplanting scheme that will repel insects and thus prevent pest damage to other crops in the vicinity. Companion plants can even be used to attract beneficial insects to the garden.

Designing a Companion Garden

Selecting the right arrangements or combinations of plants for the companion garden can be tricky. You must aim for a balance between the benefits of mixing crops and the possible competition between those crops for space, sunlight, nutrients, and water. Lettuce interplanted with kidney beans may benefit from shading by the bean plants; this advantage will have little value if the beans compete too strongly with the lettuce for available water and nutrients, however.

Companion planting of reputedly repellent or attractant plants also requires careful investigation. Research has shown that some plants traditionally relied upon to repel pests may have other, harmful effects on companion crops or may actually attract some harmful insects. Some species of marigolds have been shown to repel harmful nematodes but may cause stunting of some vegetable crops. Tansy is an herb which may repel some insects but has been shown in some studies to attract other pests.

Every garden is different, too; what works in one may not work in another. Soil, available light, and many other factors will affect the outcome of any given planting. Even your own goals as a gardener probably differ from those of your neighbor. For example, what you consider a "high yield" may be a "moderate harvest" to others.

Nevertheless, certain companion planting arrangements that have worked for many gardeners are worth trying. Even if you do not see spectacularly increased yields or reduced pest damage, you will have gained a better awareness of how plants interact with one another and their environment. Gradually, as you gain more experience with your own particular growing conditions, you may want to experiment with new companion planting schemes. (See the chart "Companion Planting Options" on page 220 for some arrangements you may want to try.)

Fencing the Garden

How many times have you carefully planted a vegetable garden, only to have the fruits of your efforts devoured by the wildlife sharing your property? While plant lovers are typically wildlife aficionados as well, the different objects of our admiration are often incompatible, especially when it comes to hungry animals and edible plants. The only solution—barring exterminating the animals, an unacceptable and generally impossible option for most of us—is to provide barriers to keep flora and fauna apart.

There are many types of fencing from which to choose. What you end up erecting will depend on the culprits doing the damage and the amount of time and money you want to spend on the project. Whatever design you select, remember that you should put up fencing *before* the animals have begun rummaging in your garden; if they have already munched on your lettuce, they are likely to try to return for another meal.

Chicken Wire Fences

One of the best ways to ward off midsized animals, including groundhogs and rabbits, is to erect a 3-foot-high chicken wire fence around your garden. By digging a trench and lining it with wire mesh before you set the posts, you will keep most, if not all, of the burrowing types from entering your plot. Try spacing the posts far enough apart so that the fence is a bit floppy; animals are less likely to scale a floppy fence this size than a tight one.

Chicken wire fences are also suitable for keeping deer out of your garden. However, since this type of fencing must be 8 to 12 feet tall to be effective, it can be both expensive and difficult to erect as well as to maintain. A high chicken wire fence is often topped with strands of barbed wire to extend its height, but this tends to be aesthetically unappealing.

Double Fences for Deer

One relatively simple and inexpensive solution to the deer problem is to erect two 3-foot-high fences made of three strings each and spaced 3 feet apart. Apparently, deer are reluctant to jump over a low fence if another fence is visible just on the other side.

COMPANION PLANTING OPTIONS

Here are some companion plantings you may want to try, with information on the type of interaction between the crops and whether the pairing has been confirmed by research studies or is simply part of companion planting tradition or folklore.

Sample Combinations	Relationship	Folklore or Fact?	Tips/Comments
For Interplanting in Neighboring Rows			
Tomatoes with cabbage	Tomatoes repel diamondback moths and flea beetles. Improved flavor and growth.	Shown in research studies. Folklore.	Tomatoes will shade transplants for fall crop from summer heat and sun.
Corn with snap beans or soybeans	Beans enhance growth of corn, possibly due to capability to fix nitrogen.	Research backs this claim in certain specific planting arrangements.	Alternate double rows of corn with double bean rows to ensure good corn pollination.
Peanuts with corn or squash	Intercropping increases yields of both crops.	Shown in research studies.	Leave plenty of space at planting for heavy vegetative growth of peanuts.
Peas with spinach, lettuce, or Chinese cabbage	Peas provide shading and wind protection for young transplants.	Traditional practice.	Vining peas must be started early and trained on fence or trellis to provide good protection.
Asparagus with tomatoes, parsley, or basil	Companions help control asparagus beetles.	Folklore.	Allow 5 ft. between rows when interplanting tomatoes to avoid crowding.
For Interplanting within a Row			
Radish, onions, or beets with lettuce, beans, cabbage, or tomatoes	Various beneficial interactions including: Lettuce makes radishes tender, onions help deter weeds and repel some insects.	Mostly folklore.	Fast-growing crops can be grown around slower-growing crops. Harvest before competition between crops has detrimental effect.
Lettuce or spinach with winter squash or cucumbers	Makes better use of space and soil materials.	Traditional practice.	Lettuce and spinach are harvested before vine crops spread over bed.
Cabbage with garlic	Garlic reputedly repels many harmful insects and helps prevent disease.	Folklore; some research shows garlic contains bactericidal and fungicidal substances.	Garlic has a cold requirement for bulbing. Try as a fall planting; allow garlic to overwinter.
Corn with beans, cucumbers, melons, or squash	Makes best use of light and bed space.	Traditional practice; some research shows beans promote corn growth.	Border rows of corn with vine crops; plant beans and corn in alternating hills; 3-4 plants per hill.
Other Arrangements			
Lettuce, cabbage, bush beans, basil, seed onions, tomatoes, beets in 1-ft.-square blocks	Various beneficial interactions, good for seed-starting beds.	Mostly folklore; research shows pest repellent properties for some crops.	Block planting is best for compact, low-growing plants.
Radishes planted in a circle around a hill of bush squash or cucumbers	Radishes repel vine borers and cucumber beetles.	Folklore.	Circle planting is a way to surround crops with repellent plants.
Strips of clover or alfalfa between corn rows	Helps control weeds and conserve moisture.	Traditional practice.	Sod strips may require periodic mowing. Strip plantings of tall crops with tender low-growing plants can reduce wind damage.

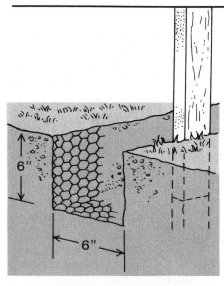

To construct a groundhog fence, first dig a trench at least 6 inches wide by 6 inches deep. Line the trench with wire wrapped along the side and bottom of the trench and extending above the soil line. Next, take 2 × 4 posts measuring about 5 feet long and set them about 2 feet into the ground. Metal or fiberglass posts can also be used to support a groundhog fence. (For a floppy fence, space posts about 8 feet apart.)

If you decide to use this design, be sure to select string that is easily seen by the animals. You may want to add height to the fences in wintertime.

Another low-profile barrier that is surprisingly effective in keeping deer away is the double mesh fence. For this design, try stringing 4-foot-high, 12½-gauge mesh fencing between metal stakes spaced 5 feet apart. Allow 5 feet between the outer and inner fences. Keep the area between the two fences bare if you want to watch for other, smaller intruders such as rabbits.

Electric Fencing

Electric fences are often the last resort for gardeners, yet many people swear by their effectiveness, especially in areas where wildlife has done extensive damage. The main thing to re-member is that this kind of fencing must be treated with respect. If there are children in the area, be sure to spend time explaining to them exactly why the fence is dangerous and where they are permitted to play. (Of course, if the children are very young, you may want to consider another kind of fencing.) A properly designed electric fence will surprise anyone or anything that touches it, not hurt them. In fact, the barrier is more psychological than real. It gives a strong buzzing feeling that makes animals back off when they've touched it once or twice, and they'll avoid it afterwards, often even if the current is turned off. Since you have to be in contact with the ground to receive a shock, birds can safely sit on the wire.

A single strand of electric wire strung at a distance of 1 foot outside your garden's chicken wire fence will give additional protection against small animals climbing over or burrowing under the wire fence. (See "Installing an Electric Fence" on page 222 for step-by-step instructions.) If deer are the main nuisance in your area, try stringing the electric wire 3 feet off the ground at a distance of 3 feet from your chicken wire fence. This fence works on the same principle as the double mesh fence and will be most effective if the chicken wire fence is at least 4 feet high.

Plants and debris that collect against the wire can drain the fence's power, so you will need to keep the area around it clean. You should also check the fence's charge periodically with a voltage tester.

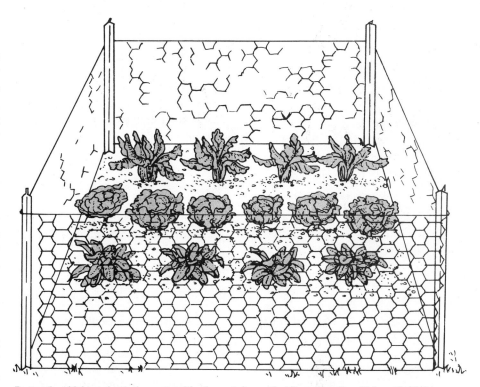

Fasten the chicken wire to the posts with wire or twine so that it overlaps the chicken wire lining the trench and extends about 3 feet above the ground. Then fill in the trench.

Installing an Electric Fence

The first step in installing an electric fence is to measure the area to be fenced and estimate the amount of wire, number of fence posts and other materials you'll need. Fence posts can be nothing more than wooden 1-by-2-inch stakes, pointed at one end. (The patented electric fence posts have an insulator loop already attached.) The length will vary according to what type of animal you are trying to keep out. As a general rule, the height of the top wire should be about two-thirds the height of the animal you are trying to exclude. You'll need posts about 1½ feet in length for a low fence designed to deter rabbits and groundhogs, for example, and about 4 feet long for deer.

There are chargers, or fence controllers, that operate from 6- or 12-volt batteries, or use 120-volt household current. **A word of caution:** Use only chargers that have the approval of either the Underwriters Laboratories, Inc., or the Industrial Commission of Wisconsin. *Never* try to make your own: Using homemade chargers has been known to result in death.

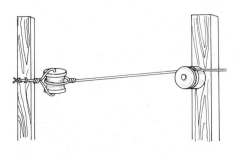

4. Attach the charger to a fence post. Then set an 8-foot-long ground rod into the ground near the charger so that about 6 inches are still above the soil line.

5. Run 6-gauge copper wire between the ground rod and the charger's ground terminal. Using the same type of wire, connect the other charger terminal to the fence wire.

6. Using wood screws, attach the lightning arrester to a post. The two lead wires go to the fence wire; connect one wire to each fence wire, if your fence has two strands.

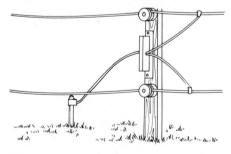

7. Next, drive an 8-foot-long ground rod into the soil near the lightning arrester, leaving about 6 inches exposed. Then attach the middle wire on the arrester (it is usually white) to the rod. Use 6-gauge wire to reach the rod and a pipe clamp to connect the wire to the pipe.

TOOLS REQUIRED
Hammer
Wire cutters
Screwdriver
Measuring tape
Shovel or posthole digger

MATERIALS
Smooth wire (12½ to 18 gauge)
Line post insulators (to attach wire to line posts)
Strain-type insulators (for end and corner posts)
Wire clips or 12-gauge galvanized wire (to fasten fence wire to the insulators)
Fence posts
Charger, or fence controller
Lightning arrester
Wood screws
2 pcs. 8 ft. pipe (ground rods)
1 pipe clamp
6-gauge copper wire

1. Set the posts 10 to 14 inches deep in the soil and at least 15 feet apart. (For a sturdier fence, brace the end posts.) Once the posts are in securely, you are ready to fasten the insulators, wire, and charger.

2. Fasten the line post insulators to the line posts at the height you have chosen. Then fasten the strain-type insulators at the same height to the end and corner posts with a loop of wire.

3. Fasten the wire to a strain-type insulator; the best way is to wrap the wire securely around itself. Then, string the wire along the line posts, pulling it tight as you go.

Making a Scarecrow

Scarecrows have been scaring birds away—or in some cases, amusing them—for as long as man has cultivated crops. Some say these whimsical stuffed figures were first used by tribes in central or northern Europe; others claim that pre-Columbian Indians were ahead of the Europeans. Whatever its origin, the scarecrow is a common fixture in gardens and farms across the world today.

Why Build a Scarecrow?

Scarecrows are fun; no one will argue with that. With just a little straw, wood, and some old clothes, it's amazing what creative designs some gardeners come up with. Not only are they an outlet for our creativity, they're also an excellent way to involve children in the garden. Young would-be gardeners who balk at the idea of "helping" in the family vegetable plot are easily enticed by a scarecrow-making project.

Yet scarecrows serve a serious purpose, too. Each year, birds destroy millions of dollars' worth of crops including wheat, corn, sunflowers, and various kinds of fruit. Individual farmers have experienced losses of up to 75 percent or more due to the voracious appetite of birds. For the backyard gardener, too, birds pose a threat to tender young plants. Crows, blackbirds, blue jays, and many other winged creatures have been known to swoop down and snatch seedlings from the ground or to peck holes in newly ripened fruit. Thanks to scarecrows, farmers and gardeners have at least a fighting chance to save their crops from being destroyed by birds.

How Scarecrows Work

It is a common joke that scarecrows attract more birds than they frighten. Indeed, it is not unusual to see a scarecrow with at least one or two birds perched on its shoulders at any given time. If properly designed and utilized, however, these human effigies can be fairly effective in protecting your vegetable garden.

The idea behind scarecrows is simple: Put up a figure that resembles a human being (one of the birds' predators), and the birds will stay away. But there's a catch: Sooner or later, birds wise up and realize that your creative masterpiece will not harm them; in fact, it takes some birds less than a week to figure things out. So you must try to be as ingenious as possible in the short time you have to scare them away. For example, by hanging aluminum pie plates or other shiny objects from your scarecrow's arms, you may be able to buy yourself and your plants a few days' time. Noisemakers, including pie plates banging together in the breeze, can also help to ward birds off a little longer.

The timing of your scarecrow's debut is important, too. You may want to bring your straw man out as soon as your seeds begin to germinate. Or if the birds in your area seem to go more for the ripe tomatoes or cantaloupes than for the seedlings, try putting it up in your garden just as the fruit begins to mature. The key is to use the novelty of your scarecrow's presence for all it's worth.

Other Bird-Scaring Devices

If you find that your scarecrow seems to have little or no effect on the birds and their destructive habits, you may want to consider other options designed to frighten birds away from the garden. Some gardeners simply nail a plastic garbage bag to a fence

The ancient tradition of building scarecrows stems from the need to protect crops from the ravages of birds. Yet scarecrows also serve a decorative purpose in our gardens, adding a whimsical touch and calling attention to our creativity.

post; the movement of the bag in the breeze seems to keep many otherwise determined birds away. Other gardeners set up automatic noisemakers or recordings that play bird-in-distress calls. There are also large nylon nets that you can place across the top of your garden to protect your crops.

Among the more innovative methods for keeping birds away is the small paper "hawk kite," which swoops like a hawk over the crops. Though very effective when suspended from a helium-filled balloon, the kites are both expensive and difficult to maintain. A more practical but no less original device is the Crow Killer, a plastic owl mounted on a rotating weathervane. Its effectiveness against crows stems from the added feature of the lifelike crow in its talons, whose wings are designed to flap slowly in the wind.

In recent years, scientists have designed a number of fairly elaborate mechanical devices to control bird damage to crops, particularly on large farms. One such device is the Pop-Up Scarecrow, which sits atop a propane cannon and literally pops into the air each time the cannon detonates. In a variation of this method, the propane cannon periodically produces loud, gunlike blasts that unnerve birds in the vicinity. Unfortunately, it also unnerves neighbors, who can hear the blasts within a half-mile radius.

How to Make a Scarecrow

To build a scarecrow from scratch, you need only a few materials and a willingness to use your imagination.

1. Select two 2 × 4 stakes measuring about 4 to 5 feet long to serve as the legs. Sharpen the ends so that they can be driven into the ground easily.

2. Find an old pair of pants and put them on over the stakes.

3. Put the stakes into the ground at an angle so that they join at the top.

4. For the backbone, take a 2 × 4 measuring about 3 feet long and nail it to the top of the legs.

5. To make the arms, take a 2 × 4 measuring about 4 feet long and nail it perpendicular to the backbone, above the legs.

6. Stuff the pants with straw, then slip a shirt on over the shoulders and fill it with straw.

7. Fill an old pillowcase with straw to make the head, and tie the pillowcase opening closed around the top of the backbone.

8. For the hands, stuff some gloves with straw, then fasten them on the ends of the arms.

9. Draw a face and add any embellishments you like, such as hair, a hat, or a pipe.

Planting Asparagus

Asparagus is one of the few common home garden vegetable crops that are perennial (rhubarb is another). A little extra care in soil preparation and planting is required to establish asparagus, but your initial hard work will be rewarded by year after year of fresh asparagus spears. Annual mulching may be the only follow-up care required to maintain your stand. Allow 10 to 20 crowns per asparagus eater. (Healthy plants normally yield at least a dozen spears.) If you have enough space, 40 crowns per person will ensure a steady supply of asparagus over a longer period.

Starting Asparagus from Crowns

The best way to start asparagus is from crowns; that is, one- or two-year-old asparagus plants, available from your local nursery. With crowns, you can pick a few spears the first year after transplanting; with seeds, you can expect to wait at least two years before the first harvest.

Begin laying out your asparagus bed after the last frost in spring. Ideally, soil should be relatively fertile, with a pH between 6.0 and 7.0. Choose a well-drained site that gets full sun. Dig a trench about 15 inches deep and slightly more than 1 foot wide. Mix sand and rotted manure, leaf mold, or compost with the soil from the trench, refilling it to a depth of about 8 inches. Make a 2-inch-high ridge in the bottom with the prepared mixture, then set in the young plants at 18-inch intervals, in double rows spaced 4 feet apart. Finally, cover the plants with about 2 inches of the soil mixture and water thoroughly.

Once the crowns start to grow, add another 1 to 2 inches of soil every few days until the trench is filled and the soil is slightly mounded. To prepare the bed for winter, mulch with shredded leaves, compost, grass clippings, or rotted manure.

Starting from Seed

Although most gardeners start with crowns, there are several advantages to growing asparagus from seed. For one, new cultivars of asparagus are often available only as seed. Also, asparagus grown from seed produces a greater harvest after a few years than that grown from crowns. And with seeds, you're less likely to encounter problems with fusarium root rot or with transplanting shock.

Plant one seed per 2- to 4-inch peat pot in late February or early March, and place the pots in a warm, sunny spot. In approximately 10 to 12 weeks, when the seedlings are about 1 foot tall, they will be ready for transplanting to a permanent bed. Be sure to wait until after the last average frost date, however, before setting them outside.

Maintaining and Harvesting Asparagus

Asparagus requires little care once it is established, besides periodic mulching with shredded leaves, straw, or well-rotted sawdust. An annual feeding in fall—a 6- to 8-inch layer of compost or well-rotted manure—is all these plants require. You may also need to weed out asparagus seedlings and other weeds, but the mulch should keep these to a minimum.

In the spring, the first spears usually appear long before the last frost. When harvesting the spears, do not use a knife, which can injure the crowns. Instead, with your fingers, snap the spears off at ground level. You can harvest for six or eight weeks; the spears will become thinner as the harvest progresses. Stop cutting when they are about the thickness of a pencil, and allow new spears that arise to grow into tall ferns. Allow the ferns to grow through summer and fall to make food for the plants, which will be stored in the roots and used to produce the following year's crop. Leave the ferns to overwinter in the bed, then cut them down in early spring, before growth begins, to clear the way for young stalks.

With proper care and the right conditions, your asparagus will continue to thrive for a good 20 years or so. Some beds have been known to last for several decades.

EDIBLE EROSION CONTROL

If you're looking for a way to halt erosion on a steep slope, asparagus may be the answer. Malaysian farmers have discovered that the large root systems of the plants keep their sloping mountain gardens from eroding, even after harvesting time. With its green stalks and wispy ferns, asparagus also makes an attractive ornamental.

COOKING ASPARAGUS

To make your asparagus uniformly tender, try the following method. Bring about ½ inch of stock to a simmer in a 10-inch sauté pan. Lay a broken chopstick across the bottom of the pan near one edge, and place the asparagus spears so that the tips are resting on the chopstick, just above the liquid. Cover loosely and simmer for approximately five minutes or until done.

If you have a percolator-type coffeepot that can sit on the stove, you may want to try this method: Pour about 1½ inches of water into the pot and bring to a boil; add the asparagus, with the tips pointing upward; cover and simmer for approximately five minutes. Serve spears with lemon and orange wedges.

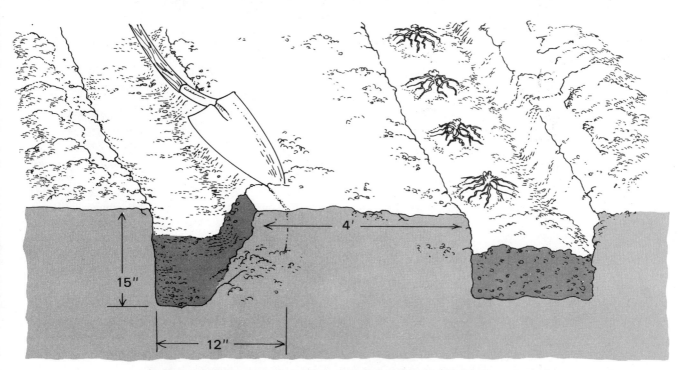

Asparagus plants are planted in trenches atop a layer of soil enriched with plenty of organic matter. The trenches are gradually filled in as the plants grow.

GROWING AND HARVESTING VEGETABLES

The best reward of a good vegetable garden comes when you can enjoy the flavor of homegrown vegetables—or share your produce with friends and neighbors. Here is a summary of tips and techniques that will improve your results. Days to harvest are from time of seed sowing.

Vegetable	Planting	Growth Facts	Culture	Comments
Asparagus (*Asparagus officinalis*)	65 crowns per 100 ft. row. 18 in. between plants; 3-4 ft. between rows. Plant crowns 6-8 in. deep.	Sow seeds indoors 12 to 14 weeks before last spring frost; transplant 4 weeks after last frost date. Or sow outdoors in nursery bed. Plant seeds 1½ in. deep, 2 in. apart, then thin. Germination takes 7-21 days at medium temperatures of 70°-80°F.	Full sun. Sandy, well-drained soil rich in organic matter. pH 6.5-7.5.	Hardy perennial usually grown from 2-year-old crowns. Don't harvest first year; harvest sparingly the second. Wait 3 years to harvest if growing plants from seed. Soak seed in warm water for 48 hours before sowing.
Beans, lima— bush and pole (*Phaseolus lunatus*)	¼ lb. lima bean seed per 100 ft. row. Bush lima beans: 3-6 in. between plants; 2-2½ ft. between rows. Pole lima beans: 12-18 in. between plants; 3-4 ft. between rows. Plant seeds 1-2 in. deep.	Sow lima beans outdoors 2 or more weeks after last spring frost once soil temperatures have reached 55°F. Germination takes 7-12 days; 65-80 days to harvest for bush lima beans; 85-90 days for pole lima beans.	Full sun. Loamy, well-drained soil rich in organic matter. Grow best in warm conditions. Mulch plants to ensure moist, but not wet, soil. pH 5.5-6.5.	In the North, select short-season lima bean cultivars for early harvest. Pole beans will require staking. Dust seed with legume inoculant to ensure nitrogen fixation. Productive until frost. Keep picking for continuous yield. Don't work around plants when they're wet to avoid spreading disease.
Beans, snap— bush and pole (*Phaseolus vulgaris*)	½ lb. seed per 100 ft. row. Bush snap beans: 2-4 in. between plants; 18-35 in. between rows. Pole snap beans: 4-6 in. between plants; 3-4 ft. between rows. Plant seeds 1-2 in. deep.	Sow snap bean seeds outdoors after last spring frost once soil temperatures have reached 55°F. Germination takes 6-14 days; 45-65 days to harvest for bush snap beans; 60-70 days for pole snap beans.	Full sun. Loamy, well-drained soil rich in organic matter. Grow best in warm conditions. Mulch plants to ensure moist, but not wet, soil. pH 5.5-6.5.	Snap beans can be sown indoors in peat pots, but direct seeding is best. Pole beans will require staking. Dust seeds with legume inoculant to ensure nitrogen fixation. Don't work around plants when they're wet to avoid spreading disease.
Beets (*Beta vulgaris*)	1 oz. seed per 100 ft. row. 1-2 in. between plants, thin to 2-4 in.; 12-18 in. between rows. Plant seeds ½-1 in. deep.	Sow seeds outdoors 2 to 3 weeks before last spring frost. Germination takes 7-10 days at soil temperatures of 50° to 85°F; 50-60 days to harvest. Can be sown indoors, but handle transplants with care; 28 days to transplant size.	Full sun; partial shade in hot climates. Light, moist but well-drained soil rich in organic matter. Do not grow well in hot, dry weather. pH 6.5-8.0.	Use thinned seedlings in salads. Will not germinate in excessive heat. Require well-tilled soil free of rocks, dirt clods, and roots. Soak seed in warm water for 24 hours before sowing.

Vege-table	Planting	Growth Facts	Culture	Comments
Broccoli (*Brassica oleracea,* Botrytis group)	45 plants per 100 ft. row. 14-24 in. between plants; 2-3 ft. between rows. Plant seeds ¼-½ in. deep.	Sow seeds indoors 5 to 7 weeks before last spring frost. Germination takes 10-12 days at medium temperatures of 70°-75°F. Set plants out 2 weeks before last spring frost; 97-154 days to harvest.	Full sun to partial shade. Rich, moist, well-drained soil. To reduce disease problems, plan a rotation so that several years elapse between plantings of any cabbage family crop in a given bed. Grows best in cool conditions. pH 6.7-7.2.	Harden off seedlings before transplanting. Mulch to keep soil moist and cool. Can also be grown as a fall crop; plan planting so that harvest will begin at least 1 month before killing frost.
Cabbage (*Brassica oleracea,* Capitata group)	55 plants per 100 ft. row. 14-24 in. between plants; 2-3 ft. between rows. Plant seeds ¼-½ in. deep.	Sow seeds indoors 5-7 weeks before transplant date. Germination takes 10-12 days at medium temperatures of 70°-75°F. Transplants can be set out as soon as soil can be worked in spring; 102-166 days to harvest.	Full sun to partial shade. Rich, moist, well-drained soil. To reduce disease problems, plan a rotation so that several years elapse between plantings of any cabbage family crop in a given bed. Grows best in cool conditions. pH 6.0-6.8.	Harden off seedlings before transplanting. Transplants exposed to prolonged cold periods may head prematurely. Mulch to keep soil moist and cool. Can be grown as a fall crop. Will withstand considerable frost.
Carrots (*Daucus carota* var. *sativus*)	½ oz. seed per 100 ft. row. 1-2 in. between plants; 14-24 in. between rows. Plant seeds ¼ in. deep.	Sow seeds outdoors in early spring as soon as the soil can be worked. Germination takes 15-20 days. Young seedlings are feathery and delicate; mixing seed with radish seed helps to mark rows. 70-80 days to harvest.	Full sun to partial shade. Deep, somewhat sandy soil that is moist but well drained and rich in organic matter. Grow best in cool conditions. Mulch to keep soil moist. pH 6.0-6.8.	Thin seedlings to 2 in. Require well-tilled soil free of rocks, dirt clods, and roots. Sow every 3 weeks until early summer for continuous harvest.
Cauliflower (*Brassica oleracea,* Botrytis group)	55 plants per 100 ft. row. 16-24 in. between plants; 2½-3 ft. between rows. Plant seeds ¼-½ in. deep.	Sow seeds indoors 5-7 weeks before transplant date. Germination takes 10-12 days at medium temperatures of 70°-75°F. Transplant seedlings as soon as soil can be worked in spring; 90-134 days to harvest.	Full sun. Rich, moist, well-drained soil. To reduce disease problems, plan a rotation so that several years elapse between plantings of any cabbage-family crop in a given bed. Grows best in cool, moist conditions. pH 6.0-7.0.	Harden off seedlings before transplanting. Mulch to keep soil moist and cool. Can be grown as a fall crop. Blanch when flower heads are 1½-2 in. across.
Corn (*Zea mays* var. *rugosa*)	3-4 oz. seed per 100 ft. row. 12-18 in. between plants; 2-3 ft. between rows. Plant seeds 1-2 in. deep.	Sow seeds outdoors in spring 2-3 weeks after the last spring frost. Germination takes 6-10 days; 70-100 days to harvest.	Full sun. Rich, moist, well-drained soil rich in organic matter. pH 6.0-7.0.	Plant crops every 2-3 weeks until midsummer for continuous harvest. Wind-pollinated; plant in blocks of short rows to ensure pollination. Separate plantings of different cultivars; cross-pollination yields ears not true to type.

(continued)

GROWING AND HARVESTING VEGETABLES—*Continued*

Vege-table	Planting	Growth Facts	Culture	Comments
Cucumbers (*Cucumis sativus*)	½ oz. seed per 100 ft. row. 12-18 in. between plants; 2-3 ft. between rows. Plant seeds 1 in. deep.	Sow seeds outdoors 1-2 weeks after last frost; or sow indoors 4-6 weeks before transplanting outdoors. Germination takes 6-10 days at medium temperatures of 70°-75°F; 48-80 days to harvest.	Full sun. Rich, moist, loamy soil that is well drained and rich in organic matter. Mulch plants to keep soil moist and control weeds; avoid disturbing roots. To reduce disease problems, plan a rotation so that several years elapse between plantings of any cucurbit family crop in a given bed. pH 5.5-7.0.	Can be planted in hills with 3-4 plants per hill, or grown on trellis. Vigilance in watering is important, especially after fruit appears on the vines, or fruits may be bitter or tasteless.
Eggplant (*Solanum melongena* var. *esculentum*)	⅛ oz. seed per 100 ft. row. 18-24 in. between plants; 2-3 ft. between rows. Plant seeds ¼-½ in. deep.	Sow seeds indoors 8-10 weeks before last frost. Germination takes 10-14 days at medium temperatures of 70°-75°F. Transplant after night temperatures remain above 55°F; 112-150 days to harvest.	Full sun. Fertile soil that is well drained and rich in organic matter. To reduce disease problems, plan a rotation so that several years elapse between plantings of any nightshade family members (potatoes, tomatoes) in a given bed. Grows best in warm conditions. pH 5.5-7.0.	Mulch plants to keep soil evenly moist and discourage weeds. Plants are susceptible to chilling and frost damage. Fruit is harvestable from ⅓-full size to fully mature size.
Lettuce, leaf (*Lactuca sativa*)	¼ oz. seed per 100 ft. row. 2-3 in. between plants; 15-18 in. between rows. Plant seeds no more than ¼ in. deep; lettuce seeds require light to spur germination.	Sow seeds outdoors in early spring as soon as the soil can be worked. Germination takes 4-10 days; 45-60 days to harvest.	Full sun to partial shade. Rich, sandy, soil that is moist but well drained and rich in organic matter. Grows best in cool conditions. pH 6.0-7.0.	Quick-growing crop that thrives in cooler conditions; make several small sowings 2 weeks apart throughout growing season. Crop turns bitter easily in hot weather. Leaf lettuce is more versatile and easier to grow than head lettuce.
Melon (*Cucumis melo*)	⅒ to ⅕ oz. seed per 100 ft. row. Plant in hills spaced 3-6 ft. apart. Plant 2-3 seedlings per hill; 6-8 seeds. Thin to 2 plants per hill.	Sow seed outdoors when day temperatures reach 80°F and nights are above 55°F. In short-season areas, start seeds indoors in peat pots 3-4 weeks before average last frost date; germinate at 70°F. Plant transplants out 1-2 weeks after last frost date. Melons do not transplant well; do so with care.	Full sun. Light, sandy, moist but well-drained soil rich in organic matter. pH 6.0-7.5.	Nonhardy annual; must be replanted each year. Muskmelons ripen 35-45 days after pollination. Winter melons take longer (and prefer cooler temperatures). Melon vines extend 6-10 ft.

Vegetable	Planting	Growth Facts	Culture	Comments
Onions (*Allium cepa*)	1 oz. seed or 400-600 plants per 100 ft. row. 2-4 in. between plants; 1-2 ft. between rows. Sow seeds ¼ in. deep, space sets or plants 1-3 in. deep.	Sow outdoors in spring as soon as soil can be worked or sow indoors in winter. Germination takes 10-12 days at medium temperatures of 70°-75°F; 42-56 days to transplant size; 92-120 days to harvest.	Full sun. Rich, moist, well-drained soil. Grow best in cool conditions. Weed often. pH 6.0-6.5.	Start from sets in areas with short growing seasons. Plant sets as early as soil can be prepared. In warmer regions, sow seeds in fall or winter for spring crop. Thin to 1 in. apart for green onions; thin to 3 in. for dry storage onions.
Peas (*Pisum sativum*)	1 lb. seed per 100 ft. row. 1-3 in. between plants; 1½-3 ft. between rows. Plant seeds 1-2 in. deep.	Sow seeds outdoors in spring as soon as the soil can be worked. Germination takes 6-15 days; 55-90 days to harvest.	Partial shade. Sandy, loamy, moist but well-drained soil rich in organic matter. Grow best in cool, humid conditions. Mulch after seedlings appear. pH 6.0-6.5.	Grow vining types on trellises. Successive plantings at 2-week intervals will help spread harvest. Dust seeds with legume inoculant to ensure nitrogen fixation. Sow until 2 months before hot (70°F) weather arrives. Make fall plantings 12 weeks before first expected fall frost.
Peppers (*Capsicum annuum*)	⅛ oz. seed per 100 ft. row. 18-24 in. between plants; 2-3 ft. between rows. Plant seeds ¼ in. deep.	Sow seeds indoors 4-5 weeks before last spring frost. Germination takes 10-20 days at medium temperatures of 75°-80°F. Transplant after night temperatures remain above 55°F; 102-146 days to harvest.	Full sun. Sandy, loamy, moist but well-drained soil rich in organic matter. To reduce disease problems, rotate crops so several years elapse between plantings of other nightshades (potatoes, tomatoes) in a given bed. Grow best in warm conditions. pH 6.0-7.0.	Mulch to keep plants moist. Select short-season cultivars in areas with cool summers. Pick early fruits when small to encourage greater yield through the rest of the season.
Potatoes (*Solanum tuberosum*)	6-10 lbs. seed potatoes per 100 ft. row. 10-15 in. between plants; 2-3 ft. between rows. Plant tubers 4 in. deep.	Cut seed potatoes into sections with 2-3 eyes a piece. After hardening overnight, plant outdoors 2 weeks before last spring frost in half-filled trench. Fill in trench as sprouts appear, which takes 1-2 weeks. 90-120 days to harvest.	Full sun. Sandy, well-drained, well-aerated soil rich in organic matter. Mound soil around stem as plant grows, protecting tubers from sunlight. To reduce disease problems, rotate crops so several years elapse between plantings of other nightshades (peppers, tomatoes) in a given bed. Grow best in cool conditions. pH 5.2-5.7.	Use certified disease-free seed potatoes. For an easier and larger harvest, try an alternate planting method; barely cover seed potatoes with soil and then spread a 1½ ft. layer of mulch over them. New potatoes will grow in mulch. Plant early-, mid-, and late-season types for a continuous harvest.

(continued)

Vege-table	Planting	Growth Facts	Culture	Comments
Radishes (*Raphanus sativus*)	1 oz. seed per 100 ft. row. 1-2 in. between plants; 1-2 ft. between rows. Plant seeds ½-¾ in. deep.	Sow seeds outdoors in early spring as soon as soil can be worked. Germination takes 3-10 days; 25-50 days to harvest.	Full sun to partial shade. Sandy, loamy, moist but well-drained soil rich in organic matter. To reduce disease problems, rotate crops so several years elapse between plantings of a cabbage family crop in a given bed. Grow best in cool conditions. pH 5.5-6.8.	Sow crops every 2 weeks until midspring; begin sowing again in late summer for fall crops.
Rhubarb (*Rheum rhabarbarum*)	20 plants per 100 ft. row. 48 in. between plants; 3-4 ft. between rows. Plant crown divisions 2-4 in. deep.	Plant divisions in early spring or fall. 2-3 years to harvest.	Full sun. Loamy, moist but well-drained, deep soil rich in organic matter. Grows best in cool conditions. pH 5.0-7.0.	Hardy perennial usually grown from divisions. Do not harvest first year; harvest sparingly the second. Remove seed-heads as soon as they form. Divide and replant every 5 years during dormancy. Only the stalks are edible; leaves and roots are poisonous.
Spinach (*Spinacia oleracea*)	1 oz. seed per 100 ft. row. 2-4 in. between plants; 1-2 ft. between rows. Plant seeds ½-¾ in. deep.	Sow seeds outdoors in early spring as soon as the soil can be worked. Germination takes 6-14 days; 40-65 days to harvest.	Full sun to partial shade. Sandy, loamy, moist but well-drained soil rich in organic matter. Grows best in cool conditions. pH 6.0-7.0.	Plant every 2-3 weeks until 6 weeks before summer temperatures regularly reach 75°F. Plant in late summer, up to 9 weeks before first frost, for fall crops. In frost-free areas grow as a winter crop.
Squash, summer (*Cucurbita pepo*)	1 oz. seed per 100 ft. row. 24-36 in. between plants; 3-5 ft. between rows. Plant seeds 1 in. deep.	Sow seeds outdoors 2-4 weeks after last spring frost or start indoors 3-4 weeks before transplant time. Germination takes 3-12 days at medium temperatures of 70°-75°F; 50-75 days to harvest.	Full sun. Rich, sandy, loamy, moist but well-drained soil. To reduce disease problems, plan a rotation so that several years elapse between plantings of any cucurbit family crop in a given bed. Grows best in warm conditions. pH 6.0-7.5.	Can be planted in hills, with 3-4 plants per hill. Weed when young.
Squash, winter (*Cucurbita* spp.)	½ oz. seed per 100 ft. row. 24-48 in. between plants; 5-8 ft. between rows. Plant seeds 1 in. deep.	Sow seeds outdoors 3-4 weeks after last spring frost, or sow indoors 3-6 weeks before transplant time. Germination takes 6-10 days at medium temperatures of 70°-75°F; 85-120 days to harvest.	Full sun. Rich, loamy, moist but well-drained soil. To reduce disease problems, rotate crops so several years elapse between plantings of any cucurbits in a given bed. Grows best in warm conditions. pH 6.0-7.0.	Winter squash obtains fuller flavor if allowed to remain in the garden to withstand a few light frosts; if picked too early, it will be watery.

Vege-table	Planting	Growth Facts	Culture	Comments
Swiss chard (*Beta vulgaris,* Cicla group)	1 oz. seed per 100 ft. row. 4-8 in. between plants; 15-24 in. between rows. Plant seeds ½-1 in. deep.	Sow seeds outdoors in early spring as soon as soil can be worked. Germination takes 7-10 days; 55-65 days to harvest.	Full sun to partial shade. Rich, loamy, moist but well-drained soil. Tolerates warm conditions. pH 6.0-6.8.	Sow in late summer for a fall crop. Mulch to keep roots moist. Cut off flower stalks when they appear.
Tomatoes (*Lycopersicon esculentum*)	50 plants or ⅛ oz. seed per 100 ft. row. 18-36 in. between plants; 2-4 ft. between rows. Plant seeds ½ in. deep. Set plants 2 in. deeper than in pot.	Start seeds indoors 5-7 weeks before last spring frost. Germination takes 6-14 days at medium temperatures of 70°-80°F. Transplant after danger of frost has passed; 96-160 days to harvest.	Full sun to partial shade. Rich, moist but well-drained soil with plenty of organic matter. To reduce disease problems, plan a rotation so that several years elapse between plantings of any nightshade family members (potatoes, eggplant) in a given bed. Grow best in warm conditions. pH 6.0-7.0.	Grow indeterminate cultivars (unlimited growth) with tall stakes; determinate types (limited growth) can be grown in cages. Mulch to keep soil moist.
Turnips (*Brassica rapa,* Rapifera group)	½ oz. seed per 100 ft. row. 1-3 in. between plants; 14-24 in. between rows. Plant seeds ½ in. deep.	Plant seeds outdoors as soon as soil can be worked in early spring. Germination takes 3-10 days; 30-60 days to harvest.	Full sun. Rich, moist but well-drained soil. To reduce disease problems, plan a rotation so that several years elapse between plantings of any cabbage family crop in a given bed. Grow best in cool conditions. Weed carefully. pH 6.5-7.0.	For fall crop, sow in late summer, up to 9 weeks before first frost. Water often.
Water-melons (*Citrullus lanatus*)	⅒-⅕ oz. seed per 100 ft. row. Plant 2-3 plants or 8-10 seeds in hills 6-10 ft. apart. Plant seeds 1 in. deep.	Sow seed outdoors when day temperatures reach 70°-80°F and night temperatures do not go below 60°-70°F. In short-season areas start seeds indoors 3-6 weeks before the last average frost date; germinate at 70°F. Watermelons do not transplant well; do so with care.	Full sun. Light, loamy or sandy soil that is moist but well drained and rich in organic matter; pH 5.5-6.5.	Nonhardy annual; must be replanted each year. Self-fertile except for seedless watermelons, which require cross-pollination by a seeded type. In short-season areas, pick off blossoms after 2-4 fruits appear.

Growing and Harvesting Broccoli

Growing a good crop of broccoli can be tricky. The key to success is to keep the plants growing rapidly and evenly by providing just the right cultural conditions—proper timing, rich soil, plenty of water and nutrients, and cool temperatures. The heads we eat are actually tight clusters of immature flower buds. Good growing conditions favor abundant bloom and, thus, large heads. The following guidelines will help you produce a bumper crop—three to six plants per broccoli eater should be adequate.

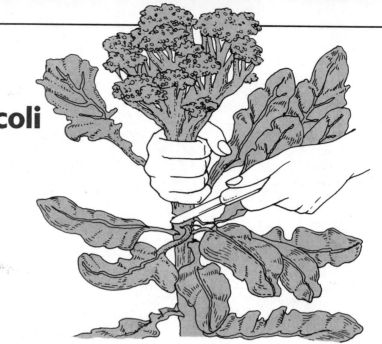

When harvesting the central head of broccoli, be sure to cut 10 to 12 inches of the stalk along with the head.

Transplant Tips

For best results, grow broccoli from seed sown indoors and then transplanted to the vegetable plot. Start seeds approximately three months before the harvest date, or 6 to 8 weeks before the transplant date. Optimal temperatures for seedlings are between 60° and 65°F. You are probably safe if you set out the more vigorous seedlings about 2 weeks before the last average frost date in spring. Seedlings can also be set out 2 to 3 weeks after the last frost. For fall broccoli, you will need to begin harvesting at least a month before the first hard frost, so start your seedlings about 18 weeks before hard frost.

It's important to minimize transplant shock, which can check growth and lead to heads that develop prematurely and are of inferior quality. If your seedlings get too large or too old before you set them out, this is likely to happen, and you'll end up with only small, buttonlike heads. Transplanting too early can also lead to problems; young plants exposed to temperatures between 35° and 50°F for prolonged periods can also form small, immature heads.

Spacing is important, too. The closer broccoli plants are to each other, the smaller the head size. For a good-sized head (8 to 10 inches wide), allow 18 inches between plants.

Cultural Requirements

The soil in which you plant your broccoli should be well drained and rich in nutrients such as calcium and magnesium. Every autumn, add a 3- to 5-inch layer of manure to your garden. Approximately three weeks before planting time in the spring, turn the rotted manure over. When you are ready to set out your transplants, prepare the soil by adding 6 pounds of cottonseed meal, 2 pounds of bonemeal, and 1 pound of wood ashes or kelp meal per 100 square feet of garden bed. Add fish emulsion or manure tea two or three weeks after planting to keep your broccoli growing rapidly and evenly. Another feeding about a week before you harvest the heads will give the plants a final boost and help stimulate the growth of side shoots.

Broccoli grows best in cool weather. Temperatures between 60° and 70°F at night, and no more than 80°F during the day, are fine. Although broccoli thrives in full sun, plants will not develop heads in hot weather. Young plants can tolerate some frost, although the stalk may rupture in cold weather.

Harvesting Broccoli

Harvest the central head when it is still compact, before the blue-green buds begin to open. Once the individual florets start to open, the broccoli will not be as tender. It takes just a few days for the flowering stage to begin, especially in the spring, so keep a close watch on your plants around harvesting time.

When harvesting the head, be sure to cut low on the plant, generally at least 10 inches below the head. By doing so, you will eliminate many potential branches and encourage the remaining nodes on the stalk to send out new shoots with large heads.

TIMING SIDE SHOOTS

Recent studies indicate that if you want to increase your broccoli yield, *when* you cut the central heads may be just as important as *how* you cut them. Instead of waiting until the center head matures, try pinching the plant when it has three leaves, or about 42 days after planting. By removing the growing point before a head forms, you will have fewer but larger side shoots, and a higher yield overall.

Growing, Harvesting, and Storing Carrots

There's nothing quite like pulling plump carrots out of the ground after weeks of wondering what's underneath those leafy green tops. Somehow, seeing those brightly colored vegetables makes the wait worthwhile. But it's important to sow carrot seeds properly if you want an impressive-looking, sweet-tasting crop.

Sowing and Growing

Carrots grow best in a fertile, sandy soil with good drainage and a pH of 6.0 to 6.5. To lighten the soil and improve moisture retention, add compost, peat moss, or well-rotted manure. Remove any rocks—even small ones —or large clods that could prevent the taproots from penetrating the soil and thus cause misshapen carrots. Be careful not to walk over the area once you have tilled it.

Begin sowing seeds directly in the ground about two or three weeks before the last average frost date in spring. For a continuous supply of carrots through the summer, plant seeds every three weeks until 2½ months before the first expected fall frost. Thirty plants per person should be sufficient.

BURLAPPED CARROTS

To keep your carrot seeds from washing away or drying out in the garden before they germinate, try covering them with burlap sheets or bags, held down at each corner with heavy rocks or bricks. Water thoroughly when you first put the burlap down, then check periodically to see if the soil needs more watering, particularly during hot, dry spells. After the seeds have sprouted, remove the burlap, preferably late in the day when the sun won't dry out the exposed seedlings.

You can grow carrots either in straight rows planted 10 to 24 inches apart, or in wider beds. If you prefer rows, mark them using string and stakes, then dig a shallow furrow for each row and distribute the seeds evenly. (To prevent the tiny seeds from coming out of the package too quickly, try tearing just a small hole in the corner.) If you plant your carrots in a

bed, mark off the area with stakes and string, then broadcast the seeds as evenly as possible. Keep in mind that you'll need to reach weeds in the middle later on, so don't make the bed any wider than 3 feet. Before scattering the seeds, try mixing them with sand for thinner and more even distribution. Mixing the carrot seeds with radish seeds has a double benefit —the quick-germinating radishes serve as row or bed markers and also provide a quick crop.

Carrots don't need much covering; a ¼-inch layer of soil or compost is sufficient. Once the seeds have germinated, thin to about 1 inch apart;

Green Thumb Tip

CARROT GERMINATOR

If you want carrots in autumn, you must plant in midsummer, when the soil temperature may be too high and the soil surface too crusty for successful germination. One solution is a "carrot germinator," an 8-foot-long box made with 1-by-6-inch pieces of lumber for the sides, two 1-by-1-inch strips across each end, and a cheesecloth cover held down with thumbtacks. When the box is placed over a bed the same size, the soil temperature is lowered, and the carrot seeds germinate in about ten days. The germinator also helps retain moisture and keeps the tiny seeds from being washed away.

in two weeks or so, thin seedlings again to 3 or 4 inches apart.

Mulch the rows or bed regularly to control weeds. If weeds do appear, remove them carefully so as not to disturb the carrots' fragile root systems. You can use scissors to snip off weeds without damaging nearby carrots.

Harvest and Storage

Carrots become sweeter as they grow larger. Depending on the cultivar, you can harvest mature carrots anywhere from 55 to 85 days after germination. However, you can begin harvesting them anytime they're large enough to eat. If the soil is moist, try pulling the carrots up with your fingers by tugging their leafy tops at ground level. If that doesn't work, simply dig them out with a trowel.

You can store carrots in a root cellar for at least six months. Ideally, the temperature should be about 34°F and the humidity about 90 to 95 percent. The following tips for storage will help keep your carrots crisp and tasty.

● Store only healthy, well-formed carrots without bruises. Eat the imperfect carrots or can them right away.

● Before storing, cut off the tops of the greens so that about 1 inch of the stem is left, then leave the carrots outside in the sun for a few hours. Do not wash them until you are ready to eat them.

● Keep carrots in a cardboard box or plastic bag lined with peat moss or sawdust.

● Arrange carrots so that they aren't touching each other.

● Keep apples and carrots in separate areas; apples release a gas that can cause carrots to become bitter.

Growing and Harvesting Cauliflower

Growing cauliflower can be an exercise in patience. One year, your plants may never form heads; the next year, you may have a high yield but the heads may be so tiny that they are hardly worth cutting. And even if your heads are an impressive size, they can turn brown from exposure to the sun. What's the secret to producing large white heads?

sure to check the covered heads frequently. They will be ready to harvest anywhere from three days to two weeks later. Whichever method or cultivar you choose, you will be rewarded for your efforts with a snow-white head to contrast with your brightly colored vegetables.

To blanch a cauliflower, choose a time when the plant is dry and the large outer leaves are pliable. Gather the leaves over the top of the young head and tie or hold them together with string, a rubber band, tape, or clothespins. Keep in mind that the head will need room to grow, so don't tie or fasten the leaves too tightly.

Keeping Cauliflower White

As the heads of cauliflower develop and grow larger, the small inner leaves that grow around them are often forced apart. Once exposed to the sun, the heads of certain cultivars, including the "snowball" types, turn an unappetizing brown. Sunlight can actually cause the curds to lose their tenderness and become bitter.

If you want snow-white cauliflower, you might choose a cultivar such as 'Self-Blanche', with long leaves that wrap around the head and shield it from the sun's rays. Or you can blanch the cauliflower yourself by tying up the large outer leaves or clipping them closed with clothespins to cover the head. (Don't tie or fasten the leaves too tightly.) For quick, temporary protection from the sun, you can break off one or two of the outer leaves and cover up the head. Be

Beating Buttoning

Buttoning, or the development of tiny cauliflower heads, is another common problem. In order for large-sized heads to develop, cauliflower must have a rapid growing period, mild temperatures (60° to 65°F), and a regular supply of water. Although many factors that check vegetative growth (such as hot, dry weather) are beyond your control, there are a few preventive measures you can take that will decrease the chances of buttoning.

● To avoid fluctuating temperatures, try growing cauliflower in autumn instead of spring. Be sure to select a cultivar suited for fall growing. Move seedlings outside about eight weeks before the first average frost date.

● Set out transplants when they are no more than four or five weeks old, or before they have begun to

develop heads. If possible, choose a cloudy day to ease the seedlings' adjustment to their new environment.

● Provide a nutrient-rich loam with good drainage and a pH of about 6.5.

● Allow 20 inches between plants and 30 inches between rows. The wider the spacing, the faster the plants mature.

● Provide an ample supply of water, particularly during hot, dry spells.

● Avoid disturbing the leaves; leaf damage can lead to buttoning.

Growing Corn

A successful corn crop depends on thorough pollination: A grain of pollen must reach each strand of silk for the ears to be completely full at maturity. Since corn is wind-pollinated, it is commonly grown only in large gardens and on farms, where the wind can distribute the pollen effectively. Yet if planted in blocks and hand-pollinated, this popular summer crop can thrive in relatively small plots, too.

Cultural Requirements

Corn will grow in most soils but yields best in loose, well-drained, loamy soil rich in organic matter. It is a heavy feeder—especially of nitrogen—so work plenty of compost or well-rotted manure, along with bonemeal and wood ashes, into the soil at planting time, and prepare the beds to a depth of about 6 inches. It's a good idea to plant corn in a bed where beans or peas were grown the previous season, or use a cover crop such as clover or alfalfa the season before planting. All will help fix extra nitrogen in the soil.

Sow seed directly into the garden where the plants are to grow. For best germination, check before planting to see if the soil has warmed to between 50° and 60°F. Try pregerminating seed of the new supersweet corn cultivars, which can be less vigorous than traditional hybrids. (See "Presprouting Seeds" on page 35 for directions.) Plant the seeds just as the root appears, when it's too short to break.

To ensure a bumper crop, space plants 15 to 18 inches apart in full sun, so they'll have plenty of room to grow. Corn roots can spread up to 2½ feet out from the base of the stalk and up to 2 feet deep.

You can extend your harvest by making several plantings. Corn grows fastest in hot weather and stops growing completely when temperatures drop below 50°F, so plants grown during midsummer will mature faster than ones sown in early spring or for late season harvest. You can plant blocks of early, midseason, and late season cultivars to extend your harvest.

Keep the soil hoed and weeded for a month after planting, then consider sowing clover beneath the plants as a cover crop. The clover will discourage weeds and fix nitrogen in the soil for next season, but won't harm your harvest.

Hand-Pollinating for a Larger Yield

If you want a high yield from your small garden, arrange your corn plantings in a square. Try planting in five short rows instead of two long ones. This way, the middle plants are likely to catch plenty of pollen when the wind blows in their direction.

Once the ears have begun to develop, you can hand-pollinate them to ensure they will be full once they mature. When collecting pollen to sprinkle on the young ears, it's best to work in the morning when the pollen comes off most easily and the wind is more likely to be calm. Look for tassels with pollen that is just beginning to shed, then cover them with a paper bag. You can either hold the tassels inside the bag at an angle and shake gently to retrieve the pollen, or tie the bags closely around the plant stems and return in a couple of hours to collect the grains. Once you have gathered enough pollen, mix it together and sprinkle a little on the silks of each young ear. Be certain you apply pollen only to silks of the same cultivar, as cross-pollination may yield ears that are not true to type.

Making a Cucumber Trellis

Consider training your cucumbers on a trellis instead of allowing them to run along the ground. Trellised cucumbers are healthier and produce a higher yield than their counterparts on the ground. They also generally bear fruits with more uniform color and better shape. In addition, trellising makes it easier for bees to find the flowers and for gardeners to find the ripe fruit.

There are a few things to remember if you decide to use a trellis. First, to avoid harming the cucumbers' sensitive roots, put the trellis up *before* you plant. Try to find a site where the trellis will not block the sun from other plants; the northern end of your garden may be suitable, as long as the cucumbers still get at least eight hours of full sun a day. Keep in mind that vines growing on a trellis take up much less garden space than they do when they are growing on the ground. A 20-foot row of cuke vines can take up to 120 square feet of space in the garden, whereas the same row growing 6 feet up a trellis may take up just 40 square feet or less. Plan on sowing seeds two weeks after the last average frost date, when the soil temperature has warmed to at least 55°F. Don't forget that cucumbers won't tolerate frost. Cucumbers have delicate roots and often don't transplant well, so outdoor sowing is best.

Sow seeds about 6 inches from the foot of the trellis. Be sure to plant on the windward side so that the trellis provides support for the fruit when the prevailing winds blow. You may need to train the plants onto the trellis at first.

Trellises come in all shapes and sizes, but one that seems to work exceptionally well for cucumbers is the all-star trellis, a star-shaped support that provides a 12-square-foot area for the spreading vines.

To build an all-star trellis, you will need the following materials.

TOOLS REQUIRED
Wire cutters
Tape measure
Shovel or posthole digger

MATERIALS
Plenty of soil and compost
8 pcs. 3½"-diameter, 7'-long posts
Heavy gauge wire (12½ to 18 gauge), enough to run from the center post out to each perimeter post
⅛" hardware cloth with 6½-by-4" rectangular mesh, enough to run from the center post out to each perimeter post
Black plastic

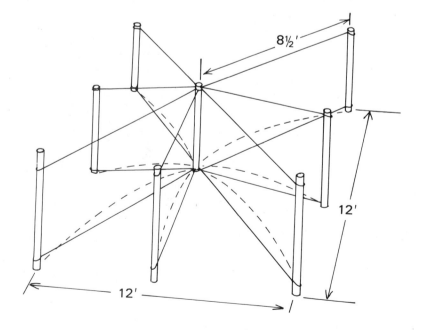

1. Select a 12-by-12-foot plot for your trellis. Form a mound of soil that measures about 1½ to 2 feet high at the center and gradually slopes down to ground level at the edges of the plot. Be sure the mixture contains plenty of organic matter such as compost or well-rotted manure.

2. Form the framework for a star by putting the posts in the ground, with one post in the center on top of the mound and the rest around the perimeter. Set the bases of all the posts 1½ feet deep; the pole in the center will be taller than the ones around the perimeter. Try to leave the sunny side open to make room for a watering hole.

236

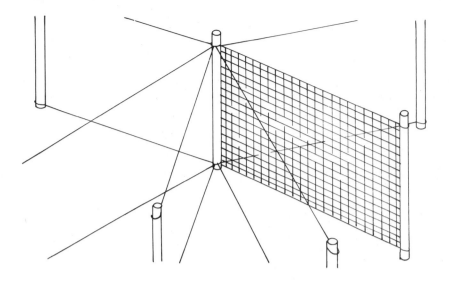

3. To help control weeds, heat the soil, and retain moisture, cover the entire plot with black plastic.

4. Run two strands of heavy gauge wire from the center out to each of the posts.

5. Then attach the ⅛-inch hardware cloth to the wires to form the arms of the star.

6. Punch holes in the plastic on the windward side of the trellis arms to sow the cucumber seeds. To water the plants, punch a hole near the center post on the side you left open, dig a small watering hole, and insert the nozzle of your hose so that water can trickle down into the mound.

Growing Garlic

If you grow garlic, you are continuing a tradition that dates back more than 5,000 years. This well-known relative of the onion has long been valued not only for its pungent taste, but also for its reputed ability to cure or prevent all sorts of ailments. Garlic has also been widely used to repel insects in the garden and elsewhere.

Cultural Requirements

Most people recognize garlic by its compound bulb, which consists of several cloves, or sections. The garlic plant also has a leaf stalk. The leaf stalk reaches about 8 inches to 2 feet tall and produces seeds and bulblets.

Although you can plant the seeds or bulblets, garlic is usually grown from the individual cloves. Save your biggest and best bulbs for planting each year, or you can order a suitable cultivar from a reputable seed company.

Garlic needs cool temperatures when the leaves first develop, followed by warm temperatures and long days as the bulbs form. Some gardeners plant cloves four to six weeks before the last average frost date in the spring.

For best results, however, set your garlic cloves in the ground several weeks before the first frost in the fall for harvesting the following autumn. A fall planting allows the plants plenty of time to produce healthy roots and leaves before the weather begins to warm up in the spring. Be sure to add a heavy layer of mulch for the winter; garlic can withstand light frost, but it needs protection from the severe cold.

Garlic is generally more sensitive to the soil conditions than onions are, so it is important to prepare the bed carefully. The soil you use should be fertile, well-drained, and finely tilled. However, a sandy loam with plenty of organic matter and a pH of 5.5 to 6.8 is ideal. Once you have planted the garlic cloves, water thoroughly.

Keep the bed free of weeds and the soil moist, but do not allow it to become soggy.

To avoid exposing the plants to excessive heat and dryness, try planting your garlic in raised beds instead of wide rows. If you do not want to devote an entire bed to garlic, you can easily interplant the cloves with other crops. Set cloves 1 to 2 inches deep (the pointed end should be up) and 4 to 6 inches apart. You will not have to plant many cloves to feed your family; five to nine plants per garlic eater should be adequate.

Growing Garlic as a Perennial

Although garlic is usually grown as an annual, it can also be treated as a perennial. Once the plants are established, you can reap a harvest each year without having to replant. Here's how.

1. When the plants are about 2 feet high, pinch off the flower buds.

2. In August, pull the largest plants out of the ground by hand, or dig them out with a trowel. Then scratch the soil surface lightly and pull up any weeds that have appeared.

3. In October, add a 3- to 4-inch layer of mulch. You may need to turn it occasionally during the winter to allow the garlic to sprout through.

4. In spring, if your soil needs fertilization, spread 1 inch of well-rotted manure over the top of the bed; do not cultivate the soil.

5. Repeat steps 1 through 4 above.

Harvesting Garlic

For large bulbs, remove the flower heads when they first appear. When the tops begin to droop and turn yellow, knock them down and refrain from watering. After a few days, when the stems feel soft, dig the bulbs out and leave them outside in a cool, dry spot for several days more. When the tops are completely dry and the skin is papery, cut the leaf stalks and roots off. (Do not trim the leaf stalks if you intend to braid the garlic.) Finally, hang the bulbs in a cool, airy location inside. Garlic may be stored for as long as a year.

For a decorative touch, you can braid your garlic into attractive strands before storing.

Braiding Garlic

To braid garlic, follow the simple steps below (see the illustration on the opposite page).

1. Take a 3-foot piece of heavy string or twine, tie it to form a loop, and hang it from a hook. Then tie the stem of a garlic bulb securely to the end of the loop.

2. Weave the stem of another bulb through the two sides of the loop: first over the right string, then over the left string.

3. Weave the stem back over the right string. Pull it tight, and move it down near the other bulb.

4. Work in a third garlic bulb, this time starting from the left side of the string. You can add 10 to 12 more bulbs, making sure you alternate sides as you go. Then hang the braid in a cool, dry, well-ventilated room.

Green Thumb Tip

OLD-TIME GARLIC REMEDIES

You may want to try some of these traditional remedies using garlic.

Garlic Tea

Add several chopped cloves of garlic to ½ cup of boiling water and let steep for six to eight hours. Gargle for a sore throat, or swallow to ease flu symptoms.

Garlic Oil

Mix a small amount of olive oil with a slice of garlic, heat briefly, and strain. Use a few drops of the warm oil to soothe an earache.

Garlic Smelling Salts

Crush a clove of garlic and sniff to relieve "hysteria."

Garlic Cough Syrup

Add 1 pound of sliced garlic to 1 quart of boiling water, and let steep for 12 hours. Add sugar—or honey and vinegar boiled with caraway and fennel seeds—until the mixture reaches the consistency of syrup.

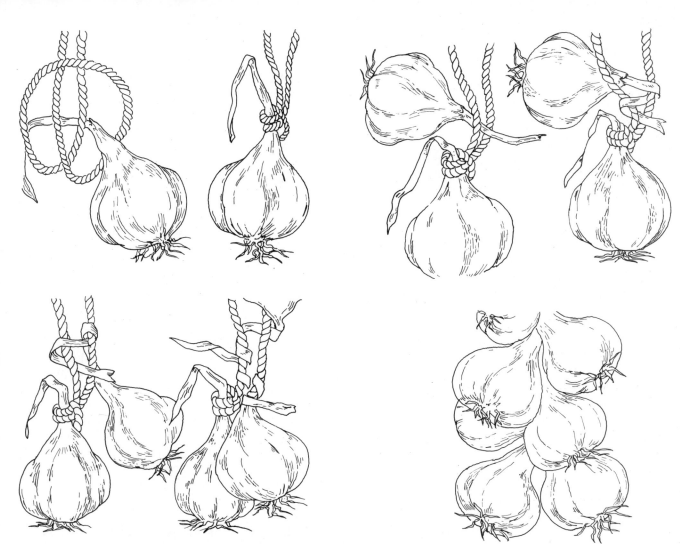

Braid garlic bulbs together for a storage method that is both decorative and practical.

Growing Onions from Seed

"In the onion is the hope of universal brotherhood; if everyone will eat onions at all times, they will come into a universal sympathy," Charles Dudley Warner, the American author, wrote. Though a universal diet of onions may not solve the world's problems, it *is* possible to eat these strong-tasting bulbs year-round if you are so inclined, thanks to their long shelf life. Some keep longer than others, depending on how you grow them, and which cultivars you choose.

Sets versus Seeds

Onions are commonly grown from sets, and for good reason. If you plant onion seed, you must start early in the season, when seeds are often lost to unpredictable weather conditions. Even if you start your seeds indoors, you still risk losing your seedlings when you transplant them outside. With sets, on the other hand, you don't have to worry about either germination loss or transplant shock. Sets are also popular because you don't have to thin the plants, and you can harvest the bulbs long before many seed-grown onions mature.

Nevertheless, there are certain advantages to growing onions from seed. For one thing, seed-started onions are less inclined to bolt than are set-grown plants. In addition, there is a greater variety of onions from which to choose if you plant seeds instead of sets. Finally, and perhaps most importantly, onions grown from seed generally fare better in storage than do those started from sets.

Starting Onions from Seed

For large, healthy bulbs, soil should be light, fertile, and well-drained, with a pH of 6.0 to 6.5. A sandy soil supplemented with well-rotted manure is ideal.

Use fresh seed every year, and choose a cultivar that is well suited to the amount of daylight in your area. Plants will not begin to form bulbs until the critical number of daylight

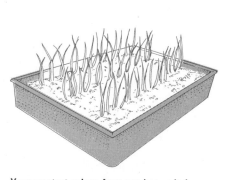

You can start onions from seed sown indoors. The tiny seedlings have grasslike leaves.

Harden off seedlings for a week before setting out. Clip long leaves back to about 6 inches before transplanting.

smallest plants and trim the tops of the remaining seedlings back to 6 inches. Plant the seedlings 1 to 1½ inches deep in the garden. Allow 4 to 5 inches between plants and 1 to 2 feet between rows.

Growing and Harvesting Onions

The key to healthy onions is to keep them growing quickly once they're planted. Water the plants thoroughly each week and keep the bed free of weeds. (Be careful not to disturb the shallow roots when cultivating near the plants.) To encourage bulb formation, snip any flowering heads or bulblets that are produced by the mature leaves.

You can tell the plants have finished bulbing when the leaf sheaths above the bulbs become weak and turn yellow. At this point, stop watering. When the tops of about half the plants begin to topple, break down the foliage with the back of a rake to accelerate ripening. If rain is predicted, cover the bulbs to keep them dry. After a few days, dig the bulbs up and use them as soon as possible or cure them for storage.

To cure the bulbs, leave them outdoors in a shady spot (or in a well-ventilated garage or shed during rainy weather) for about a week, or until the tops are completely dry and withered. For best results, spread

hours has been reached. Short-day onions require 11 to 12 hours of daylight, while intermediate-day onions need 12- to 14-hour days for the bulbs to form. Long-day onions need a minimum of 14 hours before they begin to bulb. Keep in mind that the larger and sweeter cultivars, such as Spanish and Bermuda onions, don't tend to store as well as sharp-tasting ones with smaller necks.

To direct-seed, sow seeds as soon as the ground can be worked in spring. Plant one to five seeds per inch, at a depth of ¾ to 1 inch. For large bulbs, thin plants to 3 inches apart. For scallions or small bulbs, thin to ½ inch or 1 inch apart.

You have a better chance of harvesting large bulbs if you start your seed indoors, since the plants will be larger when they reach the critical day length for bulb formation. In fact, transplants can be harvested in midsummer—even earlier than sets.

Plant seeds 12 weeks before you intend to move seedlings outdoors. For example, you can start them in January for transplanting in April. For best results, sow 10 to 12 seeds per inch in flats filled with sandy soil. Cover with about ½ inch of soil, and water thoroughly. Place the flats in a warm place (65° to 70°F) until seedlings appear, then move them to a cooler spot (50° to 65°F) that receives full sun. Do not allow the soil to dry out.

About seven to ten days before you intend to transplant, stop watering the seedlings and gradually expose them to nighttime temperatures just above 32°F. Thin out the

NO MORE TEARS

Hard, pungent onions usually store better than sweet cultivars, but their powerful chemicals can also cause the tears to flow faster. To avoid crying each time you chop a strong onion, try one of these techniques.

• Wear swimmers' goggles or a scuba mask. (If you wear contact lenses, you may already have enough eye protection.)
• Chill the onion in the freezer for 15 minutes or in the refrigerator for an hour before cutting.
• Chop the bulbs in a food processor.

Keep developing onions well watered and mulched throughout the season.

When onion tops begin to turn yellow and fall over, the bulbs are ready for harvesting.

the onions on wire mesh held above the ground by bricks underneath on either side. Be careful not to bruise the bulbs, and be sure to leave the papery outer skin intact. You can braid the tops, or cut them off about 1 to 1½ inches above the bulbs. Hang the onions on string or in mesh bags in a cool, dry spot.

One easy way to store onions for several months is to hang them from double strands of strong twine strung across your storage area. When the onion tops are still flexible, weave them through the twine: Fold each top backward over the two strings, bring the top forward underneath, then cross it over in front of the stem and insert it between the strands. Pull the knot tight from behind to keep the onion in place. Allow about 1 inch between onions.

ONIONS IN THE NEWS

Newspaper can help keep weeds out of your onion bed and save you the aggravation of spacing sets at the same time. Just take three sheets of newspaper, staple them into one thick sheet, then tape several identical pieces together to make one long sheet. Next, fold the paper into accordion-like pleats and punch holes into the folded sheet at 4-inch intervals. To punch the holes, try using a hammer and a piece of duct pipe measuring 1 inch in diameter and sharpened at one end. Spread the large sheet over the bed at planting time, place rocks and soil at the edges to hold it down, and plant one onion set in each hole. The newspaper covering not only provides a guide for spacing, it also keeps weeds to a minimum while still allowing water to reach the bed. In the fall, just till the paper under.

Growing Tomatoes

Sorting through all the literature on growing tomatoes can be a monumental and confusing task. Should you buy seedlings or start the plants from seed yourself? Is it better to use stakes or cages? Does pinching suckers really lead to a better yield? The following guidelines and tips will help get you started and will also help you cope with the some of the problems commonly encountered by tomato growers, including hot temperatures and short growing seasons.

Starting Tomatoes

You can either purchase tomato seedlings or start them yourself. Sow seeds indoors about six weeks before you intend to transplant. Tomato seed germinates within a week if the soil temperature is between 75° and 85°F; allow two weeks for germination in 60°F soil. Be sure to keep flats away from gas ovens or heaters, as tomato seedlings cannot tolerate exposure to natural gas.

Container size is an important factor in seedling health. By the time the first true leaf appears, seedlings should be in 4-inch pots. If you start seed earlier than six weeks before transplanting, use larger containers. As for store-bought plants, it's best to purchase them as soon as they are available (usually several weeks before planting time) and repot them immediately; otherwise, the plants are apt to get leggy and rootbound and may even produce flowers before it's time to transplant. Plants will establish themselves much more quickly if they are transplanted before they set flowers or fruit.

When repotting a tomato seedling, hold it by the leaves to avoid damaging the delicate stem. Set the seedling a little lower in the soil than it was before; the covered portion of the stem will eventually develop roots.

Transplanting Tomatoes

A few days before transplanting your seedlings, start the process of hardening them off. (See "Hardening-Off Seedlings" on page 42 for directions.) Choose a site with well-drained soil and a pH between 6.0 and 7.0, and work in about an inch of compost.

When transplanting tomatoes, start by hardening them off to minimize transplant shock. For plants grown together in flats, one of the first steps is to block, or cut apart, the seedlings.

When you get ready to transplant, prune a few of the lower leaves.

Plant the seedlings so that the pruned portions of the stems are underground.

Set the plants in gently, allowing 1½ to 2 feet between staked plants, 2 to 3 feet for unstaked. For best results, remove the lower sets of leaves, then set the plants horizontally in a shallow trench so that only the top one or two sets of leaves show above the ground; the buried portion of the stem will produce roots, and the top portion will develop a straight new stem. This method of planting tomatoes not only helps protect the young plants from drying winds, it also makes it easier to cover them if frost is predicted.

To keep the plants from drying out, choose a cloudy day for transplanting. When filling in the holes, be sure the soil is broken up well; clods allow the air to dry out the roots more quickly. Water each plant thoroughly as you set it in the soil and then regularly thereafter until the transplants begin growing rapidly again.

Regional Tips

Growing in Hot Conditions

If you live in the Sun Belt or any area that is subject to excessive heat in the summertime, your tomatoes may grow too rapidly and produce little fruit. To improve your chances of a successful harvest, choose a cultivar that is recommended for your area— specifically, one that can produce normal flowers under hot conditions. If the heat still seems to impede the pollination process of your selected cultivar, you can help distribute the pollen grains by gently shaking the flower clusters as they open.

Try planting your tomatoes in succession to avoid losing your entire crop during the height of the heat. If possible, plant between taller crops such as corn, which can help protect the plants from drying winds. Once your transplants are in the ground, add a deep layer of mulch, and water regularly. Even plants that drop their blossoms during a heat wave in late summer can bounce back when temperatures cool down, as long as they have had a steady supply of water.

Extending the Season

Cool temperatures and a short growing season present tomato growers with a different problem: how to speed up the growing process while still allowing the plants enough time to produce fruit. Gardeners in more temperate regions who want to give their tomatoes an early start in spring or extend the harvest in fall also can use some of these techniques.

If you live in a region with a short growing season, choose a cultivar that matures quickly. Start your seeds indoors up to 9½ weeks before the last frost date in spring (any earlier may cause the transplants to become too leggy) and begin hardening the seedlings off when outdoor temperatures reach at least 50°F during the day. Or start your tomatoes in a frost-free cold frame or hotbed and expose them to direct sunlight when temperatures exceed 50°F.

To give your transplants a boost outdoors, plant them in raised beds with southern exposure. You can also cover your plot with black plastic a few weeks ahead of time to ensure that the soil is plenty warm. If frost threatens the plants, cover them with plastic tunnels, milk jugs, cloches, or wire cylinders wrapped with plastic. (Keep in mind that protecting the foliage won't help much if the soil isn't warm.) Once your tomatoes are established, you can hasten the growth process by fertilizing with fish emulsion or manure tea every two weeks or so. Keep the plot free of weeds, and provide stakes or other support to help the plants grow efficiently.

To extend the season even further, grow tomatoes during the wintertime in a greenhouse or in a window with southern exposure and plenty of space for the spreading branches. Choose a cultivar recommended for container growing. Shaking the flower clusters gently will improve pollination indoors. If possible, choose a location where the average daytime temperature is 65° to 68°F and the nighttime temperature is 55° to 60°F.

Pruning and Training Tomatoes

There are many different ways to grow tomatoes, and each method has its devotees. There are gardeners who prune and train faithfully; others who cage plants and allow them to sprawl at will. If you're unsure of what works best for you, try experimenting with several options next season.

Pruning

To prune or not to prune? Gardeners have been debating the virtues of tomato pruning, or pinching, for as long as they have been growing tomatoes in their backyards. Some say pruned plants actually produce larger fruit, while others disagree. Regardless of fruit size, however, growers have discovered that pinching out the suckers—the side branches that sprout from the leaf axils—does have distinct advantages.

Pruned tomatoes take up less space than do tomatoes with sprawling branches; 1 foot between plants is usually sufficient. So if you prune your tomatoes, you can grow several cultivars in a limited space. In addition,

---

TRELLIS TRICKS

Here are a few ideas for easy-to-make tomato trellises.

Bamboo Tomato Trellis

If you're looking for a strong yet lightweight support for your tomatoes that you can use year after year, try constructing a bamboo trellis. For a 4-by-12-foot plot, you'll need the following:

18 pcs. 4' bamboo (crosspieces)
6 pcs. 12' bamboo (support pieces)
10 pcs. 4' bamboo (upright posts)
Nylon string

Fit the pieces together and tie them securely with string to make a two-tiered trellis. Place the trellis over your plot and set the posts into the ground about 6 inches deep. The bamboo will support the plants, and the fruit will be easy to pick as it hangs from the trellis.

Clothes-Dryer Tomatoes

For a simple tomato trellis, place an old wooden clothes dryer on its side in the garden and set your tomatoes between the racks. As the plants grow larger, they will be supported by the racks and the fruit will ripen well above the ground.

Custom Tomato Stakes

Tying up tomatoes is easy with custom-made stakes. First, take a ¾-by-1½-inch stake and make saw cuts about ½ inch deep and about 1 foot apart, staggering them on either side. Next, make strips of nylon measuring ⅜-by-10-inches, and tie knots at each end. Put the stake in the ground, then put one end of a strip in one of the slots, using the knot as an anchor. Loop the strip around the tomato stem in a figure-eight pattern and secure it in another slot on the other side of the stake.

Boarded Up

Put your scrap lumber to use in the garden by setting a row of 15-inch-tall logs (cinder blocks will also do) on end, on either side of your row of young tomato plants. Then set long boards from log to log and short boards across the row to form a kind of frame around each plant. As the plants grow larger, you can move the boards as necessary to support the branches. The fruit will hang over the boards for easy harvesting.

---

you can often harvest the fruit of pruned plants up to two weeks sooner than that of unpruned plants. And since pruned plants must be trained on stakes or other supports, they are less likely to rot than tomatoes that are allowed to trail along the ground.

If you decide to prune your tomatoes, keep in mind that you'll need to check them weekly to pinch out the suckers and tie the plants to the stakes. It's best to begin when the plants are still relatively small—specifically, when the suckers are about 2 inches long. That way, you can use your hands to snap off the suckers at the base and you'll avoid leaving large wounds. Be sure to wash your hands before you begin, especially if you've just touched cigarettes or weeds, both of which can carry tobacco mosaic virus.

The growth habit of the particular tomato cultivar you are growing will usually determine the amount of pruning necessary. Indeterminate cul-

Always wash your hands before removing the suckers from a tomato plant. Snap the suckers off at the base. Be careful not to remove the terminal bud or damage the main stem.

tivars normally require severe pruning, while moderate to light pruning is best suited for semi-determinate and determinate cultivars. Whether you prune severely or only lightly, be sure you can differentiate between the terminal bud, which should never be pruned, and the suckers, secondary shoots that grow from the juncture of the leaf stalk and the stem.

Staking and Caging Tomatoes

The easiest method for training tomatoes is to prune all the suckers down to a single stem and then tie the stem

---

Green Thumb Tip

TOMATO PLANTS FOR WINTER

For vine-ripened tomatoes in winter, prune pencil-thick branches from your best tomato plants just before the first frost in autumn. Strip the leaves from the bottom third of the branch and remove fruits and any buds that show any yellow. Then place each stalk in a deep pot of potting soil. To keep the soil moist, insert tomato cages into the potting soil and cover them with plastic. When new top growth appears, remove the plastic and add fertilizer. If you have a sunny enough window, you'll have tomatoes for your salads all winter long.

VEGETABLE HARVEST AND STORAGE

This chart gives you the facts on when and how to harvest your vegetables for maximum flavor. It also tells you how to store them properly to maintain freshness and taste.

Your refrigerator is one of your best storage options. If you have two available, set one at a cold temperature (32°-40°F) and the other at a cool temperature (45°-50°F). In a refrigerator set for normal operation, the temperature in the center storage section is usually between 38° and 42°F. The temperature just below the freezing unit is lower—often 30° to 35°F. The bottom of the cabinet is somewhat warmer than the center. Check temperatures in different parts of your refrigerator.

Your basement is another possible storage place. Temperatures in most heated or air-conditioned basements will usually be 65°F or higher in summer and 60°F or less in winter. Create partitions to vary the temperature and humidity. You can use outdoor air, dirt floors, or wet sacks to vary the temperature and humidity needs. Unheated basements, if well ventilated, can provide good storage conditions for some vegetables.

Vegetable	Harvest and Storage
Cold, Moist (32°–40°F, 90–95% relative humidity)	
Asparagus	Harvest by snapping 10-12-in. spears off at ground level. Store in plastic bag in refrigerator for up to 1 week. Freeze or can any surplus.
Beans, lima	Harvest when pods have filled. For tender limas, harvest when a bit immature; for "meaty" limas, harvest when mature. Store shelled limas in perforated plastic bags in the refrigerator for about 1 week. Surplus limas can be canned or frozen.
Beets	Begin harvest when beet is 1 in. in diameter. Tender tops make excellent greens. Main harvest is when beets are 2-3 in. Harvest spring-planted beets before hot weather; fall beets before the first light freeze. For storage, wash roots, trim tops to ½ in., place in perforated plastic bags, and store in refrigerator or cold moist cellar for 2-4 months.
Broccoli	Harvest terminal head while florets are still tight and of good green color. Smaller side heads will develop. Store in perforated plastic bags for up to 1 week in the refrigerator. Freeze any surplus.
Cabbage	Harvest when heads are solid. Store cabbage in refrigerator, cold cellar, or outdoor pit for up to 2 months.
Carrots	Harvest spring crops before hot weather; fall ones before the first light freeze. For storage, wash roots, trim tops to ½ in., place in perforated plastic bags. Store in refrigerator or cold moist cellar for 2-4 months.
Cauliflower	Tie outer leaves above the head when curd diameter reaches 1-2 in. (except purple types). Heads will be ready for harvest in about 2 weeks. Cauliflower may be stored in perforated plastic bags in the refrigerator for up to 2 weeks. Freeze any surplus.

Vegetable	Harvest and Storage
Corn	Harvest when kernels are plump and tender. Silks will be dry and kernels filled. To check for maturity, open top of ear and press a few kernels with thumbnail. If milky juice exudes, it is ready for harvest. Husk ears to conserve space; store in plastic bags for no more than 2 days in the refrigerator. The new super-sweet cultivars will store for 1 week or more. Freeze or can surplus.
Lettuce	Harvest the leaves or heads when they reach suitable size. Head, semihead, and leaf lettuce can be stored for up to 2 weeks in perforated plastic bags in the refrigerator.
Onions, green	Harvest green onions when they attain sufficient size. Cut off roots; remove tops, leaving 2 inches of green. Place in plastic bag and store in refrigerator for up to 2 weeks.
Peas	Harvest when pods have filled. For tender peas, harvest when a bit immature; for "meaty" peas, harvest when mature. Unshelled peas can be kept in a perforated plastic bag in the refrigerator for about 1 week. Freeze or can surplus.
Potatoes	Harvest when the tops have yellowed or died. Do not leave in ground exposed to high soil temperatures and sun. Wash potatoes; discard diseased or damaged ones. Cure for 1 week in a shaded, well-ventilated place (open barn, shed, garage). Avoid exposing tubers to light. Store in a cool, humid place; cool basements are ideal. Provide good ventilation; will keep 2-4 months.
Radishes	Harvest when ½-1 in. in diameter. Wash roots, trim taproots and tops, and store in plastic bags in refrigerator for up to 1 month. Store the same as carrots.
Rhubarb	Harvest leaf stalks when ½-1 in. in diameter. *Do not use leaves.* Store in perforated plastic bags for up to 3 weeks in the refrigerator. Freeze surplus.
Spinach	Harvest the leaves and leaf stems of greens when they reach suitable size. Either harvest the whole plant or the outer, larger leaves. Spinach does not store well, but may be kept in plastic bags in the refrigerator for up to 2 weeks. Freeze any surplus.
Swiss chard	This is a summer green that is harvested continuously. Merely break off outer leaves. Store up to 2 weeks in refrigerator.
Turnips	Turnips can be harvested from the time their diameter reaches 1 in. They are best as a fall crop and can withstand several light freezes. Store the same as carrots.

(continued)

loosely to a stake or pole. (Some gardeners prefer to prune the plant to two stems instead of one, since two stems provide a higher yield and produce more foliage that can protect the fruit from sunscald.) Begin staking the plant when it is about 1 foot tall, then every week or so thereafter. Small strips torn from an old bedsheet make excellent ties, since they don't damage the plant tissue and are easily removed at the end of the season. Space plants 1 to 2 feet apart; allow 3 feet between rows.

An alternative training method that requires fewer stakes is weaving.

Staked tomatoes take up less space and produce healthier fruit than tomatoes that are allowed to trail over the ground.

VEGETABLE HARVEST AND STORAGE– *Continued*

Vegetable	Harvest and Storage
Cool, Moist (45°–50°F, 80–90% relative humidity)	
Beans, snap	Pods will be most tender when seeds inside are one-fourth normal size. They become fibrous as the beans mature. Store up to 1 week in perforated plastic bags in the warm part of the refrigerator. Can or freeze surplus.
Cucumbers	Harvest cucumbers before seeds become half-size. Most cultivars will be 1½-2½ in. in diameter and 5-8 in. long. Pickling cucumbers will be more blocky and not as long as slicers. Store slicing cucumbers up to 1 week in plastic bags in the warm part of the refrigerator. Cool pickling cucumbers quickly in ice water; keep up to 2 days in a plastic bag in the refrigerator.
Eggplant	Harvest when fruits are nearly full grown, but color is still bright. Keep in warm part of refrigerator for about 1 week.
Peppers, sweet	Harvest when fruits are firm and full size. For red fruits, leave fruits on plant until ripe. Store in the warm part of the refrigerator in plastic bags for 2-3 weeks.
Squash, summer	Harvest when fruits are young and tender. Skin should be easily penetrated with the thumbnail. Store for up to 1 week in a perforated plastic bag in the refrigerator. Surplus can be frozen.
Cool, Dry (45°–55°F, 50–60% relative humidity)	
Onions, dry	Harvest when the tops have fallen over and the necks have shriveled. Remove tops, place in shallow boxes or mesh bags, and cure in open garage or barn for 3-4 weeks. Store in mesh bags in a cool place. Keep ventilated during humid, muggy weather.
Peppers, hot	Pull plants late in the season and hang to dry in sun or a warm place. Store in a dry, cool place, such as a basement.
Warm, Dry (55°–60°F, 60–70% relative humidity)	
Pumpkins; Squash, winter	Harvest when skin is hard and the colors darken. Harvest before frost. Cut the fruits from the vine with a portion of stem attached. Store spread on shelves so air can circulate.
Warm, Moist (55°–60°F, 80–85% relative humidity)	
Tomatoes	Ripe tomatoes will keep for a week at 55-60°F. Harvest green, mature tomatoes before frost, and keep at 55-70°F; for faster ripening, 65-70°F. Mature green fruits should approach normal size and have a whitish green skin color. Keep them 3-5 weeks by wrapping each tomato in newspaper. Inspect for ripeness each week.

Source: Gaus and Henry, "Grounds for Gardening: A Horticultural Guide," University of Missouri-Columbia.

Set stakes in the ground near every other plant, then run a nylon string between the stakes about 6 or 8 inches above the ground and flop the plants over it. As the plants grow larger, you can weave them through additional strings stretched about a foot apart. Weaving is suitable for both pruned and unpruned plants.

Caging, or placing wire cylinders over the plants, is a popular method for growing unpruned tomatoes. Caged tomatoes are generally healthier and have a better form than tomatoes that are left to grow on the ground. It's easier to contain the sprawling plants in cages than it is to tie them to stakes. The cages are inexpensive and sturdy enough to be used for several years. They are lightweight, however, and should be well anchored in the ground so that they won't blow over during a storm. To avoid missing any ripe fruit hidden by the dense foliage, it's a good idea to pinch off the tops of the plants before they grow over the tops of the cages.

Fruits and Berries— Small Fruits

Planting Strawberries

Gardeners with thriving strawberry beds are the envy of their neighbors; all they have to do is walk a few steps out their door to pick one of summer's most delectable fruits—or so it seems. There's a bit more to growing strawberries than just harvesting the juicy red fruit; strawberry plants require careful planning and care if they are to consistently produce a bountiful crop.

One of the first decisions you'll have to make is which types you want to grow. Garden strawberries are short-lived perennials, and there are two types from which to choose: June- or spring-bearing and everbearing. June-bearing cultivars produce one crop per season, and plant breeders have developed cultivars for early, midseason, and late harvest. Ever-bearing strawberries generally produce two smaller crops of fruit in spring and fall. They usually produce fewer runners than June-bearing cultivars. To extend your harvest, consider planting cultivars from each group.

For best results, you'll want to choose cultivars suited to your region of the country. Check with your local nursery owner or the cooperative extension service for the best ones for your area.

Planning a Strawberry Bed

Garden strawberries spread by forming runners that root and produce new plants. Although there are nearly as many ways to grow strawberries as there are gardeners, there are three main methods for growing strawberries: the hill system, the matted row system, and the spaced runner system. Which method you choose will depend on several factors, including the cultivars you've selected, the plants' susceptibility to disease, the amount of garden space available, and the amount of time you are willing to devote to maintaining the bed.

It's best not to grow strawberries in one place for more than three or four years, because the bed will eventually become overcrowded and fruit production will suffer. Soilborne diseases are also more of a problem when strawberries are grown year after year in the same spot.

Hill System

For gardeners with limited space but plenty of time and plants to spare, the hill system is ideal. Begin by setting your plants 12 inches apart, staggered in rows spaced 1 foot apart. Every three rows, be sure to leave room for a path. Then, as the plants grow, clip off all runners as they appear so the plants will put their energy into producing a big crop of berries. The hill system is especially effective with everbearing cultivars, as well as June-bearing ones that don't produce many runners, and will provide a plentiful supply of large, easily accessible berries. Your hills of strawberry plants should serve you well for three to six years. When you notice production dropping off, order new plants and start another bed in a different part of the garden.

You can vary the hill system a bit by planting your berries about 18 inches apart, in rows spaced 4 feet apart. Instead of cutting all the runners, allow each plant to set four new plants. Your bed should be productive for a good four or five years.

Matted Row System

The matted row system provides a high yield and requires less work than the hill system. In areas plagued by chronic disease problems, the matted row system is the best choice because it involves renewing your strawberry bed every one to three years with fresh plants. Start by setting plants 12 to 18 inches apart throughout the bed, staggering the rows so that the spacing is balanced. June-bearing cultivars, which are especially vigorous, should be spaced 18 inches apart; plant everbearing cultivars 12 inches apart, since they have fewer runners. Keep the bed narrow enough to allow for easy harvesting later on, and be sure to leave space near the edges of the bed for the runners to roam. Once you've planted the bed, you can sit back and allow the runners to spread freely. The following year, if you look carefully, you should see abundant fruit among the dense, or matted, rows of strawberry plants and runners.

Matted rows must be replanted periodically if the bed is to remain productive. For a continuous supply of strawberries, start a new bed in another part of the garden every year or two. (If your bed is not too crowded and your plants are still productive, you can wait until the third year.) Then till under the old bed after the spring harvest. Plant your new bed with either new disease-free plants or runners from the original plants.

Spaced Runner System

The spaced runner method requires a good deal of garden space but is an easy way to keep your strawberries healthy and productive. Set your plants 8 to 12 inches apart, in rows spaced 4 feet apart. Leave a 2-foot strip on either side of the bed so there will be room for the plants to spread. When the runners appear the first year, spread them 8 inches apart and pin the stems into the ground with hairpins, clothespins, or staples. If necessary, clip off excess runners to control crowding and maintain spacing. The first year the runners will spread out 1 foot on each side of the parent plant, leaving a 2-foot-wide path between rows.

The second year, after harvesting the berries, let the runners grow freely across the paths and space them out as before. By the third year, you'll need to walk carefully through the bed to harvest the fruit, since the

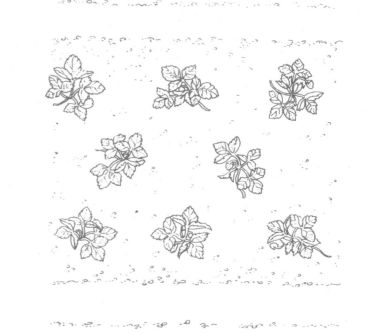

The hill system works well if you're short on space but have plenty of time to maintain the bed. Plants are spaced close together, and all runners are removed.

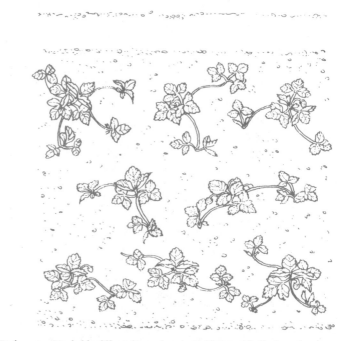

The matted row system is ideal if you have chronic problems with diseases in your area. Just let the runners roam freely, then every one to three years start over with fresh plants, preferably in another part of the garden.

plants will have spread out onto the paths. Once you've picked the berries, let the plants in the paths continue to grow and till under the rows you started originally. Add compost or manure to the cultivated soil. Repeat the same steps from the beginning, treating the old paths as your new rows, and the former rows as your new paths. Alternate rows and paths every three years, or as necessary to control crowding.

Planting a Strawberry Bed

You can purchase strawberry plants from a local or mail-order nursery. Be sure to look for certified disease-free stock, your best defense against the two most common diseases of strawberries: verticillium wilt and red stele (root rot). There are disease-resistant cultivars of both June-bearing and everbearing strawberries. You can also use last season's runners from your own garden. The roots of healthy plants should be whitish; old plants, which usually have black roots, should not be used. Be sure to dig and destroy any plants that show signs of disease, such as mottled foliage or rotted crowns.

Plant your strawberries as soon as the ground can be worked in spring. Choose a sunny location, away from low-lying areas where drainage may be poor or a late frost could settle and freeze the flowers. Mail-order plants will arrive bare-root, and it's a good idea to have the bed ready and waiting—you can even prepare it in fall for planting the following spring. Prepare the bed by working in well-rotted manure or compost. Strawberries thrive in soil with a pH of 5.5 to 6.0.

The plants will adapt to their new environment more easily if you transplant them on a cloudy day. To keep the roots from drying out, soak them in water a few hours before setting the plants in the ground.

Proper Planting Depth

How you plant your strawberries is very important to their survival. If you plant them too deep, they will rot; if they aren't set deep enough, they can dry out. For best results, use a trowel to dig a hole about 5 to 7 inches wide and deep enough for the plant's roots. Untangle the roots carefully, if necessary, and spread them out evenly around the plant. Position plants with the top of the crown just above ground level and the roots completely buried in the soil. When you're finished planting the bed, water it thoroughly and check to see if all the crowns are still in the right place. If they're too far out of the ground or if the tops are covered with soil, gently add soil or uncover the tops. Check plants again if it rains soon after planting.

Seasonal Care

Keep your strawberries well watered and pull weeds as they appear. Before the ground freezes in autumn, spread 2 to 3 inches of oat straw over the bed to protect the plants during winter and to prevent them from flowering during late spring frosts. When the foliage starts to turn yellow in spring, pull away or remove some of the straw to allow the plants to poke through. The remaining mulch will help retain moisture, control weeds, and keep the fruit clean throughout the rest of the growing season.

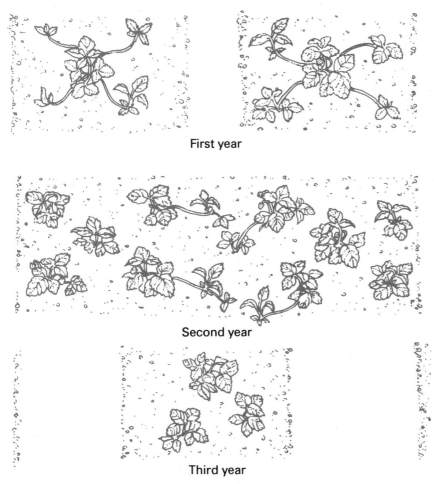

First year

Second year

Third year

The spaced runner system is an easy way to grow healthy strawberries, provided you have enough space in your garden. By leaving wide paths, spacing the runners carefully, and tilling under the original beds over a three-year period, you should have a continuous supply of good-sized berries.

(continued on page 252)

SELECTING SMALL FRUITS

Small fruits have their own unique appeal. Growing them can be a challenge, but homegrown fresh fruit has a delectable quality missing from supermarket produce. For the best cultivars for your area, check with your local cooperative extension agent. And remember, when choosing 2 cultivars for cross-pollination, make sure that they have overlapping blooming periods. Yields will vary according to weather and soil conditions; yields listed are average for 1 year.

Fruit	Yield per Plant	Culture	Harvest Information	Comments
Blackberry (*Rubus* spp.)	1-4 qts.	Full sun to partial shade. Moist but well-drained soil; pH 5.5-7.0. Buy 1-year-old, certified disease-free plants. Plant in early spring; fall or winter planting is best in areas with mild winters. Space plants 3-6 ft. apart. Avoid planting where nightshade family members have been grown within 3 years, as *Verticillium* wilt may still be in area. Zones 4-9.	Harvest in midsummer when berries are very easily pulled off canes; keep berries out of the sun and refrigerate promptly. Fruit is ½-2 in. long.	Group includes dewberries (trailing forms of blackberries); boysenberries (derived from a type of dewberry); and loganberries. May fruit up to 20 years. Some are 4-5-ft. bushes; others, vinelike with 15-ft. canes. Most have thorns. Protect fruit from birds with plastic netting. Disease-resistant types include 'Black Satin', 'Lucretia', and 'Thornfree'.
Blueberry (*Vaccinium* spp.)	2-4 qts.	Full sun to partial shade. Moist but well-drained, light, acid soil rich in organic matter; pH 4.5-5.5. Buy 1-2-ft., 2- or 3-year-old plants with root ball. Plant in early spring; fall or early winter in areas with mild winters. Space 3-8 ft. apart (rabbit-eye blueberries require more space). Mulch thickly. Zones 3-9.	Will fruit in 3 years. Fruits ripen in mid- to late summer on previous year's wood. Harvest when berries have been blue for 1-2 weeks; they should easily twist off twigs.	May fruit up to 40 years. Most require a second cultivar for pollination. Lowbush blueberries grow from 8-24 in.; highbush from 8-15 ft.; rabbit-eyes, 4-20 ft. Protect fruit from birds with plastic netting. Recommended cultivars include 'Bluecrop', 'Bluejay', 'Blueray', 'Earliblue', 'Jersey', and 'Northland'.
Grape (*Vitis* spp.)	American, French hybrids, European: 10-20 lbs. Muscadine: 20-30 lbs.	Full sun. Well-drained, sandy or loamy soil; pH 5.5-6.5. Buy 14-in.-high, 1-year-old plants. Plant in early spring; in southern areas, dormant vines can be planted in fall. Select a sunny, warm spot with good air circulation. Space 6-8 ft. apart for American, French hybrid, and European; 12-20 ft. apart for muscadine. Zones 4-9.	Vines will fruit in 3-5 years. Harvest by cutting bunches from vines; harvest muscadine grapes by shaking fruit onto a cloth. Pick fully ripe for dessert, grape juice, wine; for jelly, harvest when slightly underripe. Green grapes are ripe when they become a bit white or yellow. Red and black grapes become deep in color. Pick on a cool, dry day.	American and French hybrids grow in Zones 5-9; some American cultivars grow in Zone 4. European grapes are grown mainly in California. Muscadine grapes grow in Zones 7-9. Some muscadine cultivars require a pollinizer. Grapevines live 50-100 years. Disease-resistant cultivars include American grapes 'Canadice', 'Concord', 'Edelweiss', and 'Steuben'; muscadine grapes 'Carlos', 'Doreen', and 'Nesbitt'; and French hybrids 'Baco Noir', 'De Chaunac', and 'Foch'.

Fruit	Yield per Plant	Culture	Harvest Information	Comments
Kiwifruit (*Actinidia chinensis, A. arguta*)	*A. chinensis,* 70-120 lbs. at maturity; *A. arguta,* 100 lbs.	Full sun to partial shade. *A. chinensis* prefers loamy, well-drained soil; *A. arguta* (hardy kiwi) tolerates any well-drained soil; pH 6.0-7.0. Plant in late spring in areas that are well protected from cold winds and frost. Space plants 15-20 ft. apart. *A. chinensis* Zones 7-9 (depending on cultivar). *A. arguta* Zones 3 or 4-7.	Will fruit in 3-6 years. Harvest in early to midfall; check for ripeness by letting a sample soften for a few days, and tasting. If sweet, harvest all fruit and refrigerate. Remove from refrigerator a few days before needed to let fruit soften and develop full flavor.	*A. chinensis* has egg-sized fruits with fuzzy skin. Grown in California, it is the type normally in grocery stores. *A. arguta* fruits have smooth skin and are about 1-1½ in. long. Kiwis may fruit up to 60 years. Buy at least 1 male plant for every 8 or 9 female plants for pollination. Recommended hardy cultivars include 'Ananasnaja', 'Issai', and 'Meader'.
Raspberry (*Rubus* spp.)	1-1½ qts. per foot of plant	Full sun to partial shade. Moist but well-drained soil rich in organic matter; pH 5.5-7.0. Buy 1-year-old, certified disease-free plants. Plant in spring or late fall. Space plants 2-3 ft. apart. Avoid planting black and purple raspberries where nightshade family members have been grown within 3 years, as *Verticillium* wilt may still be in area. Will fruit following year. Zones 4-8.	Harvest fruit by gently pulling berry off the white core, which remains attached to plant. Black raspberries are red when immature. Fruit tastes best when unwashed, although will need washing if any chemicals were used.	Includes red, yellow, purple, and black raspberries. Grown as hedges or trained on trellises. Some cultivars have 1 crop per year; everbearing types produce 2 crops, bearing fruit in summer on 2-year-old canes, and on the current year's canes in fall. Raspberries grow 5-8 ft. Red raspberries are the most disease resistant. Disease-resistant cultivars include black raspberries 'Black Hawk', 'Jewel', and 'Logan'; purple raspberry 'Royalty'; red raspberries 'Amity', 'Fairview', 'Festival', 'Scepter', and 'Southland'.
Strawberry (*Fragaria* spp.)	1 pt.-1 qt.	Full sun. Moist but well-drained soil, rich in organic matter; pH 5.5-6.5. Buy certified disease-free 1-year-old plants. Plant in early spring; fall plantings are possible in areas where ground is not frozen in winter. Avoid planting where nightshade family members have been grown for 3 years, as *Verticillium* wilt may still be in area. Zones 4-9.	Pinch off flowers of June-bearing types the first year. For everbearing types, pinch off the first year's spring flowers, but leave blooms for fall crop. Harvest fully red berries by pinching off stem above them.	June-bearing cultivars usually ripen in early to midsummer and produce a large crop. Everbearing cultivars produce smaller early summer and fall crops, and are best grown in Zones 5-8. Plants bear for 2-3 years; in hot climates they may produce only 1 crop. Protect fruit from birds with plastic netting. Disease-resistant cultivars include 'Allstar', 'Darrow', 'Delite', 'Earliglow', 'Guardian', 'Hood', 'Lateglow', 'Redchief', 'Sunrise', 'Surecrop', 'Tribute' (everbearing), and 'Tristar' (everbearing).

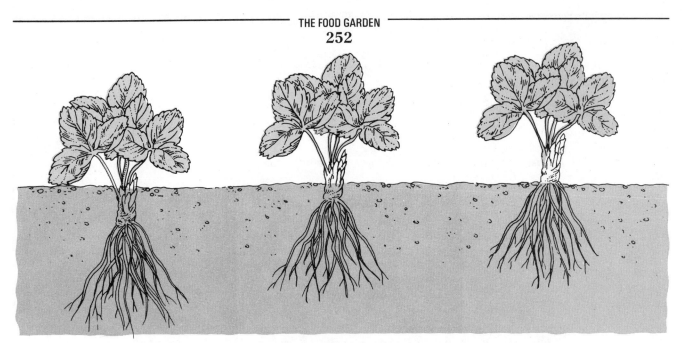

When you plant a strawberry plant, the top of the crown should be just above ground level, like the plant in the center. The one on the left is too deep, on the right, too high.

It's a good idea to remove any flower buds that appear on June-bearing cultivars during the first year of planting; remove the buds on everbearing cultivars until July 1. This will help the plants develop a stronger root system, thus encouraging higher yields the following season.

STRAWBERRY FUTURES

Autumn weather determines just how big your strawberries will be the following year. If the growing conditions are favorable in August and September, you should have large berries the next season. But if conditions are less than favorable, your fruit will probably turn out to be small.

Researchers have also discovered that a few days of rain in the fall can mean the difference between a bountiful crop and a mediocre harvest several months later. So if it looks like a dry fall, make time to water your strawberry bed thoroughly at least twice before the end of September.

Renewing a Strawberry Bed

You can prolong the life of your June-bearing strawberries by renewing the bed promptly after harvesting every year. If you get in the habit of automatically starting the renewal process within two weeks of picking the berries, you may be able to put off replanting the bed with fresh stock for up to eight years. Renewing a strawberry bed helps keep the plants from strangling one another with overgrowth, which will lead to crops of small, poorly ripened berries.

1. Start the renewal process as soon after harvest as possible—no more than 10 or 14 days. Begin by mowing your strawberry bed to remove the foliage. Set your mower blade so that it cuts the leaves but misses the crowns. Rake up the leaves, then fertilize the bed with cottonseed meal.

To renew a strawberry bed, start by mowing the bed.

2. Thin the planting by digging out most of the plants. If the weather is not excessively hot or dry and you have just harvested the fruit within the last two or three days, leave a

6-inch band of mother plants down the middle of the bed; otherwise, leave an 8- to 10-inch band.

3. Using a hoe, gently push up about ½ inch of fine soil around the crowns for added protection and to encourage vigorous new growth.

4. Mulch the bed with clean straw. As daughter plants appear, space them 6 to 12 inches apart. If necessary, gently pull them through the mulch to help them root. Once the bed is filled completely, pinch the extra runners. Weed and water regularly. By next season, your plants should be healthy and vigorous.

Turn under most of the plants and leave a narrow band of mother plants down the middle.

Push ½ inch of soil up around the crowns of the plants with a hoe.

Mulch the bed with straw and space the daughter plants 6 to 12 inches apart.

Growing and Planting Brambles

One of the joys of summertime is eating fresh raspberries or blackberries. Although these tasty berries are often unavailable in grocery stores, they're relatively easy to grow in your own backyard. With proper attention at planting time and a bit of annual pruning and training, you can harvest abundant crops of these bramble fruits—and a single planting can be productive for ten or more years.

What Are Brambles?

Bramble fruits are members of the genus *Rubus,* which belongs to the Rose family. They include red raspberries, the most popular; yellow raspberries, which are variations of the reds; black raspberries, a native American plant that has been brought into cultivation; purple raspberries, a hybrid between red and black raspberries; and blackberries, a common name used for several native and naturalized species. Dewberries, boysenberries, and loganberries are less well-known, closely related brambles.

The raspberry or blackberry fruit is composed of a cluster of tiny fruits, called drupelets, each of which contains one seed. One of the main differences between raspberries and blackberries lies in the receptacle, the core that anchors the berries to the cane. When raspberries ripen, you can slide them right off the receptacle, leaving a hollow center; when you pick blackberries, the core comes off with them.

All brambles produce biennial canes, or long, woody stems, that have a two-year lifespan. The first year, the canes grow vigorously but do not flower. During the second season, they flower and produce fruit. The canes die once the fruit matures, but each spring a new crop of canes appears, to produce fruit the next season. Although "bramble" technically means a prickly shrub or bush, not all of the cultivated varieties have thorns. In addition, despite the berries' reputation for growing into a tangly mess, many of the bramble cultivars now on the market can be grown in neat rows in the garden.

In addition to the basic types of bramble fruits, there are a variety of cultivars available of most brambles. With a little planning, you can combine several types and cultivars to spread out the harvest. For example, there are summer-bearing raspberries that ripen in June or early July, and everbearing ones that ripen from July to frost.

Planting Brambles

If you plan to grow brambles, it's important to select the best site you have available and take some extra time to prepare the soil properly. After all, a planting will last for many years, and time spent up front will increase yields for years to come. Select a site in full sun, well away from wild raspberries and blackberries, which can transmit diseases and pests to your plants. A site with rich, well-drained soil is best. If soil drainage is a problem, try growing your plants in a raised bed. When preparing the bed,

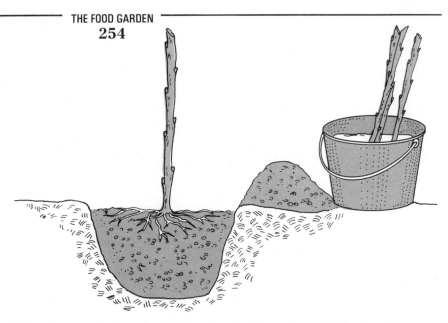

To plant brambles, dig a hole about 1½ times the size of the root mass. Set the plant at the same level it was planted in the nursery, fan out the roots, and fill the hole with organic matter and loose soil.

be sure to add plenty of organic matter to the soil—well-rotted manure or compost are ideal.

South of Zone 6, fall is the best time for planting; in the North, plan on planting in spring. Purchase plants from a nursery that offers certified disease-free stock; brambles are subject to virus diseases, and the extra expense is well worth it. Be sure to prepare the soil well ahead of time, so the bed will be ready and waiting when it's time to plant. Soak bare-root plants in a bucket of water for about two hours before planting, and leave them there up until the moment you put them in the ground.

The hole for your bramble plant should be about 1½ times larger than the root mass. Fan out the roots, then set the plant in the hole and add more soil to keep the plant in place. Add loose soil mixed with organic matter up to the level the bramble was planted at the nursery.

You can plant your brambles in either hills or rows. The best method, and the spacing, depends on the type of brambles you've selected. Red and yellow raspberries, as well as erect and semi-erect blackberries, are best planted 2 to 3 feet apart in hedgelike, 1- to 3-foot-wide rows. Leave 6 or more feet between rows at planting time. These plants spread vigorously

by root suckers, which can eventually fill in the spaces between the rows—preventing you from reaching the tasty berries! You'll need to keep the spreading under control by removing suckers that block access to the plants. Prune or pull them up throughout the season or simply mow regularly between the rows. Black and purple raspberries don't produce root suckers, but they do have branching canes that need plenty of space. It's best to plant these brambles in hills spaced 3 to 4 feet apart. Trailing blackberries should be planted 8 to 12 feet apart to allow plenty of room for the vigorous canes.

Keep plants well watered, especially during flowering, fruit ripening, and bud development stages, but do not allow the soil to become soggy; brambles will not tolerate "wet feet." Pull up weeds as they appear, and mulch periodically with rotted sawdust or shredded leaves to help retain moisture in the soil and keep the shallow roots from drying out.

After a few years, you may need to thin out the canes to ease overcrowding. For best results, thin in the spring. As a general rule, remove the thinnest canes and leave the thickest. Thin so the plants are spaced according to their type. For red and yellow raspberries, allow 6 to 8 inches between plants, or no more than eight to ten canes for every 3 feet of a narrow row. For black raspberries, leave five to ten canes per hill. For erect blackberries, five to six canes for every foot of wide row is ideal.

Training and Pruning Brambles

Once you've established your brambles, it's important to train and prune the plants to keep them healthy and productive. Training and pruning also enable you to grow brambles in a limited space and to harvest the berries more easily.

Training Brambles

There are several ways to keep raspberries and erect blackberries from falling over onto the ground as they become laden with berries.

Double-Armed T. The simplest method is the double-armed T trellis. Begin by setting two 4- to 6-foot-tall posts every 20 feet down the center of the row. (The height of your posts will depend on the vigor of the bramble cultivar you've selected.)

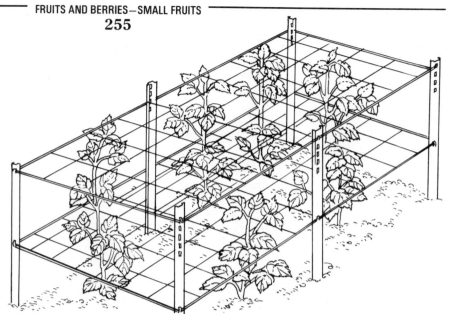

A trellis using wire mesh provides support for the canes on the inside as well as the outside of the row.

Brace the end posts for extra support by attaching a board on the inside of each post—about halfway or three-quarters of the way up—to form the second side of a triangle in the bed. Make crossbars as wide as the row, and mount one at the top of each post and another about halfway up. Run heavy wire between the arms along the edge of the rows, and add turnbuckles to keep the wire taut. Use notches or hooks to attach the wire to

the crossbars so that you can unfasten the wire and get to the canes easily. Train the canes inside the wires.

Wire Mesh. You can also use a wire mesh trellis to train your brambles. Set metal fence posts every 3 feet on either side of the row, then stretch concrete-reinforcing wire or other heavy wire mesh horizontally between the posts at the top and about halfway up. Select mesh with at least 6-by-6-inch square openings so there will be plenty of room for the canes to grow and so you'll be able to remove spent canes easily. The wire mesh provides support for the canes growing in the center as well as those along the outside edges of the row.

Wires. If you're growing brambles against a wall or have only a limited amount of space, the best way to train them is with two wires spaced 2 to 3 feet apart and fastened directly to the wall or stretched between two posts. To keep the canes productive, tie each one to the two wires with twist ties. As new canes appear, thin them to 6 or 8 inches apart and tie them to the wires. This approach requires more work than other methods, but if you're hungry for raspberries and have little space to spare, it's well worth the effort.

The basic double-armed T is the simplest trellis for brambles.

Wires fastened to the wall or stretched between two posts work well for trellising brambles against a wall or in a small space.

V-Trellis System. Yet another method, called the V-trellis system, is also effective for increasing yields and making fruit easy to pick. Drive pairs of 8-foot-long metal posts 1½ to 2 feet into the ground along the sides of the beds at 3½-foot intervals. The base of the posts in each pair should be about 1½ feet apart, but they should slant outward so they are about 3½ feet apart at the top. Add a post at each end of the bed and string two wires—one 2½ feet above the ground and the other at the top—around all the posts. The end result is a V-shaped support in which the canes can grow. It's best to erect the trellis at the end of the first season for a new planting or at pruning time for an established planting. Tie the canes that will bloom next season to the trellis so they are angled out in two directions and easy to reach. New canes will arise in the center of the bed, and can be tied to the trellis when you remove canes that have already fruited.

Wire Fan. Trailing blackberries have long, vigorous canes and require a slightly different method of training. Install one 5-foot post every 15 to 20 feet in the row, then stretch wire between the posts at 3 feet high and again at 5 feet. Fan out the canes and tie each one to the trellis. If they're extra-long, you may need to loop them over the top wire and spread them out along the lower one for better exposure to the sun. In areas where blackberries need winter protection, you can allow the canes to grow along the ground underneath a cover of mulch in winter, then train them on the trellis when the temperatures warm up in spring.

A V-trellis system allows you to tie the fruiting canes to the outside wires for support, leaving the center of the row open so sun can reach the new canes that arise at the base of the plants.

Pruning Brambles

Since bramble canes are biennial, meaning they have a two-year lifespan, it stands to reason that they need regular pruning in order to produce a reliable crop from year to year. First-year canes, or primocanes, grow foliage but don't flower. Second-year canes, called florocanes, produce fruit and then die. After the florocanes have finished producing fruit, you must cut them down to the ground to give the new primocanes a chance to develop fully in the sunlight. Be sure to remove the old wood you've pruned from the garden, since it can harbor diseases and pests.

Primocanes must also be pruned periodically. The particular technique used to prune primocanes depends largely on the type of bramble being pruned and the trellising method you're using. As you cut, keep in mind that the top half of the cane is generally the most productive. Also remember that the bigger the cane, the better the berries.

Red or Yellow Raspberries.

For summer-bearing cultivars, remove the canes that have fruited immediately after harvest. Since these plants produce an abundance of suckers, also thin out smaller and weaker canes to make plenty of room for the new primocanes—10 to 15 canes per 3 feet of row is about right. If you have summer-bearing red or yellow raspberries and don't want to bother with a trellising system, you can prune the canes back to 3 or 4 feet late in the winter season, before the cane buds appear. This will encourage shorter canes that stand up well when loaded with fruit. However, since cutting the top sections of canes reduces the plants' yield, you may want to consider simply weaving the canes through a wire trellis instead. This practice will enable you to reach the berries fairly easily while still giving you a high yield.

For everbearing red and yellow raspberries, you can cut out the canes that have fruited after the summer harvest; new canes coming on at that time will fruit in fall and again the following spring. Thin out weak canes at this time as well. When the fall harvest is over, prune the tops of the canes that have fruited to about 3 feet. These will produce a second crop the following summer. Or, if you don't mind missing a summer crop, try cutting down all the canes in the fall for an abundant harvest the following autumn.

Black and Purple Raspberries.

Remove canes of black and purple raspberries that have already fruited after harvest. Unlike red and yellow raspberries, the new primocanes of black and purple raspberries will branch their first year, and summer pruning will increase harvest. To encourage maximum branching and a higher yield of berries, pinch the top 2 to 3 inches of the primocanes in June when they are about 1½ to 2 feet tall. (You may have to do this again a few weeks later if some primocanes aren't tall enough to be pinched in June.) Then late the following winter, cut the lateral branches to 8 to 12 inches.

Blackberries.
Prune erect blackberries the same as you would black raspberries; remove canes that have fruited and pinch back primocanes 2 to 3 inches in June. (Blackberries will be about 3 to 3½ feet at this time.) Trim the lateral branches to about 12 inches late the following winter. Be careful not to cut the lateral branches too far, however, if your particular cultivar bears flowers on the ends of the branches. For trailing blackberries, forgo pruning the first year, then cut the canes back to 10 feet in late winter.

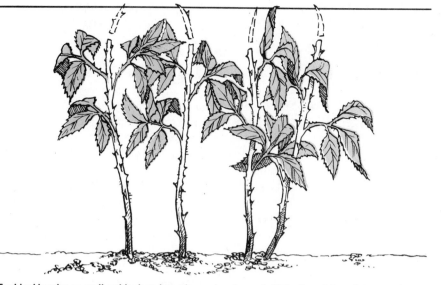

For blackberries as well as black and purple raspberries, cut off the tips of the primocanes in summer to increase the number of berries produced.

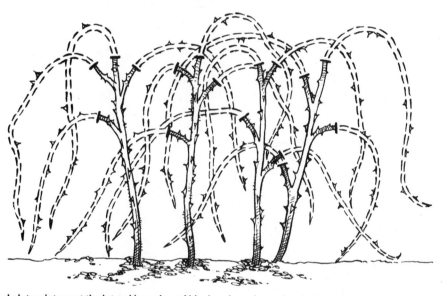

In late winter, cut the lateral branches of black and purple raspberries back to increase branching, which will increase yield.

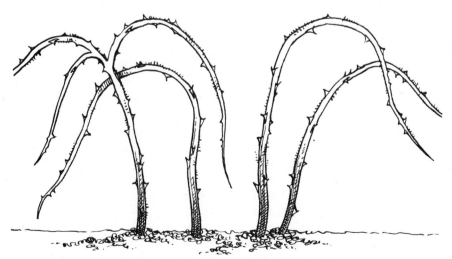

A black or purple raspberry that is left unpruned will not produce nearly as many berries as one that has been encouraged to branch by pruning.

257

Selecting, Planting, and Pruning Blueberries

If you don't mind waiting three or four years after planting for the first harvest, blueberries will reward you many times over for your patience. Just a little care in planting and occasional attention thereafter is all that's required to reap an abundant harvest of deliciously sweet berries year after year. Luckily, blueberries also make striking ornamentals, often grown for their brilliant autumn color.

Types of Blueberries

Blueberries belong to the genus *Vaccinium,* which also contains cranberries and a variety of other native shrubs such as bilberries and huckleberries. There are three commonly grown types of blueberries: highbush, lowbush, and rabbit-eye.

Highbush Blueberries

Highbush blueberries (*V. corymbosum*) are the most common in home gardens. They average 6 to 12 feet tall and are hardy to Zone 3. Each plant typically yields at least 4 to 8 pints of berries each year by its sixth to tenth season. Some especially vigorous highbush plants have been known to produce 25 pints or more in a season.

Cultural Requirements. Highbush blueberries thrive in a moist, well-drained, acid soil with a pH of between 4.2 and 5.0 and plenty of organic matter. If your soil is slightly alkaline, add sulfur or aluminum sulfate a year before planting to lower the pH. Sphagnum peat moss will acidify the soil as well as increase its organic content; simply mix it with the soil in the planting hole. Other good organic supplements are acid compost, leaves, and old sawdust.

When choosing a site for your plants, keep in mind that blueberry roots are shallow and will need an adequate water supply to withstand heat and drought. Try to plant in a protected spot where the brittle canes are not apt to be broken by accident. Select an area that receives full sun, and avoid low-lying pockets that are subject to late spring frosts.

Choosing Highbush Blueberries. It's important to choose a highbush cultivar that's suited to your geographic area. Some cultivars are bred to withstand consistently cold temperatures in winter, while others are resistant to certain diseases common in the warmer regions. There are cultivars that ripen at different seasons—very early, early, midseason, late, and very late. By selecting a variety of cultivars that ripen at different times, you can extend the harvest season.

Highbush blueberries are self-fertile, meaning a single plant will produce berries without needing pollen from another cultivar (although yields are higher if the flowers are cross-pollinated with another cultivar). Home gardeners can choose from more than 45 highbush cultivars. The best source of information about cultivars suited for your garden is your local cooperative extension service.

Lowbush Blueberries

Lowbush blueberries (*V. angustifolium*), the most popular choice among commercial growers, are very hardy plants (to Zone 2) that grow just 8 to 12 inches high. Plants prefer moist, well-drained soil that is rich in organic matter with a pH between 4.2 and 5.2. They grow from creeping rhizomes that form a dense mat under the soil surface, and for this reason make an excellent ground cover in areas with acid soil.

There are only a few cultivars of lowbush blueberries from which to choose, but you will need to select at least two, for they are not self-fertile and require cross-pollination from a different cultivar in order to set fruit. (Two plants of the same cultivar will not do, because they are propa-gated asexually and are genetically identical.)

Rabbit-Eye Blueberries

Rabbit-eye blueberries (*V. ashei*) thrive in warmer climates in the South. They're hardy to Zone 7 and can grow as high as 18 feet. Rabbit-eye blueberries perform best in soil rich in organic matter that is moist but well drained, although they'll tolerate poorer soils than other blueberries. They'll grow in soil with higher pH than other blueberries—ranging from 4.2 to 6.0—and are somewhat more drought resistant than the other types. One feature important to gardeners in the Deep South is that they require very little winter chilling to break dormancy and set fruit—as little as 18 to 20 days at temperatures of 60°F during the day and 45°F at night.

There are a number of cultivars of rabbit-eye blueberries from which to choose, including ones for early, midseason, and late harvest. Consult your local cooperative extension service for the best ones for your area. You'll need to plant more than one cultivar in order for the plants to cross-pollinate and set fruit, for, like lowbush blueberries, they are not self-fertile.

Planting Blueberries

Dormant blueberries may be planted in either spring or fall. If your plants arrive several days before you intend to plant them, heel them in temporarily by digging a trench outside and loosely covering the roots with soil. If you're keeping them for just a few hours, you can put them in a bucket of water; don't leave the plants in water for longer than that, however, or you could kill them.

Highbush and rabbit-eye blueberry plants should be spaced 6 to 8 feet apart, in rows spaced 10 feet apart. (If you're planting a hedge, plants can be somewhat closer.) Space lowbush blueberries 1 foot apart, with 3 feet between rows.

As you dig each hole, allow enough room for the root mass of the plant to spread out horizontally about ½ inch to 1 inch below ground level. Fan out the roots as you set each plant in the hole, then fill with loose soil or a mixture of soil and sphagnum peat moss. If your soil isn't acidic enough for blueberries, use a 50-50 mixture of sphagnum peat moss and soil. Be sure to use sphagnum peat, because other types may not be as acidic.

Since the blueberry's shallow roots are easily injured by cultivation, it's best to apply a heavy mulch at planting time to keep the weeds in check. Mulch will also help retain soil moisture and prevent the roots from drying out during hot, dry spells. Apply 3 to 6 inches of well-rotted pine sawdust, shredded oak leaves, or cottonseed meal, all of which are acidic and will help lower pH, as soon as your blueberries are in the ground. Add more mulch as needed during the growing season to control weeds and keep the ground moist. You can also mulch with compost or bark chips if your soil naturally tends to be acidic enough.

Pruning Blueberries

Once you've planted your blueberries, keep them healthy and productive with regular pruning. There are a few basic principles you need to keep in mind. Blueberries flower and fruit on wood produced the previous season and bear best on young, vigorous branches. There are two types of buds on the twigs: fruit buds, which are round and plump, and develop at the branch tips; and vegetative buds, which are smaller and more pointed, and found farther down on the branches. The biggest berries are borne on the thickest twigs. New unbranched shoots, called canes, appear at the base of the plant each year. In the second and subsequent years, these canes branch, each time producing thinner twigs. By the sixth year, the branches have become

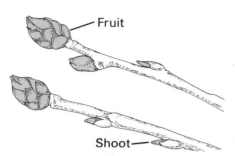

Blueberry fruit buds are round and fat, while shoot buds are small and pointed.

twiggy and small, and have few fruit buds. Pruning blueberries—a process of removing old canes to make room for new ones—will yield bigger and better harvests.

At planting time, remove only canes that have been damaged in shipping or are weak and twiggy. For best results, allow your blueberry plants to become established for at least a year after planting before you begin pruning—most don't need pruning for the first three years after planting. From then on, plan on pruning annually in late winter, before new growth begins, to keep plants thriving.

Pruning Highbush Blueberries

Begin pruning highbush blueberries the fourth year after planting. First, cut out any weak, twiggy growth, as well as canes that are five years old or older. Remove any growth that appears winter-damaged. Look for canes that are wrinkled or shriveled, or soft and dark in color. Next, remove any branches that are growing near the ground or crowding the center of the plant. Finally, to encourage larger berries, clip some of the weaker branch tips that have flower buds. Removing excess flower buds will stimulate the production of bigger and sweeter berries.

As a general rule, try to leave one cane for every year of the plant's age, plus one or two healthy new canes. (If the new canes are thinner than about ¼ inch, leave only one cane.) Eventually, to avoid overcrowd-

ing, you may want to leave only six or eight old canes and a couple of vigorous new canes. Keep in mind that the older the cane, the smaller the berries, so don't be afraid to prune the elders. Some gardeners automatically remove any canes more than three years old to allow for newer, more vigorous growth.

Pruning Lowbush and Rabbit-Eye Blueberries

Prune some of the older canes of lowbush cultivars (some growers recommend 50 percent) to the ground every year, then harvest berries from the uncut stems. Alternate the next season by clipping those canes you left uncut and picking fruit from the new shoots. This method allows you to harvest berries each year while still encouraging vigorous growth. If you don't mind forgoing a crop one season, you can cut back all the canes every three years with a lawn mower.

Rabbit-eye blueberries require a different pruning method. Begin-

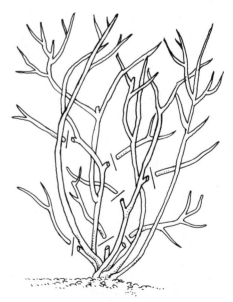

When pruning highbush blueberries, first cut out twiggy growth and canes that are at least five years old. Then remove branches growing near the ground or crowding the center of the plant. Finally, clip off a few of the weaker branch tips that have flower buds.

ning the first season, cut out any weak shoots or fruit buds that appear after planting, and prune the bush to 4 to 6 inches high. For the next four years, shorten a few branches to about half their length from the previous year,

and remove any dead or diseased wood. By the sixth year, begin removing old canes on the inside to ease overcrowding, then prune only as necessary to keep the fruit within reach.

Rejuvenating Blueberries

Older blueberry bushes that have been neglected usually produce only a small crop of tiny berries—if you're lucky. If you want your bushes to be productive again, you must be prepared to prune them severely. Simply remove any canes that are five years old or older, as well as any weak or twiggy growth. Within two years, your plants should produce a crop of fair-sized berries.

Even blueberry plants that are over 20 years old can sometimes be rejuvenated. Cut the bush all the way back to the ground; you may be surprised to find a few berries emerging from the new growth by the second year. If the plant continues to thrive, prune it as you would any blueberry bush that has just been planted.

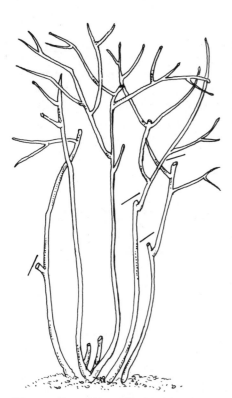

When pruning rabbit-eye blueberries, prune bush to 4 to 6 inches high the first year. Also remove weak shoots or fruit buds. The next four years, cut a few branches back to about half the length of the previous year, and remove any dead wood. By the sixth year, begin thinning out a few interior branches, and prune lightly to keep berries within reach.

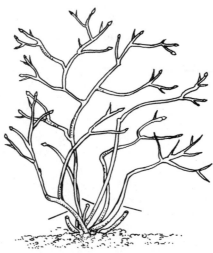

When pruning lowbush blueberries, cut some of the older canes to the ground and harvest berries from the uncut stems. The following year, clip those canes you left uncut, and pick from the new shoots that resulted from last year's pruning.

Selecting, Pruning, and Training Grapes

There are three basic types of grapes grown in gardens, all of which belong to the genus *Vitis*. Cultivars derived from *V. vinifera* include European wine grapes as well as the popular 'Thompson's Seedless'. These can only be grown in limited parts of this country, such as California, the Northwest Pacific Coast, and selected areas along the East Coast. French wine grapes, the result of crosses between *V. vinifera* and hardier, more disease-resistant American grapes, can be grown over a wider area. They make excellent wine. American hybrid grapes are derived from *V. labrusca,* commonly called fox grape. These are hardier than *V. vinifera* cultivars and can be grown throughout most

of the northern part of the country, especially in northern and northeastern portions. There are many cultivars available; 'Concord' is probably the best known. Muscadine grapes, derived from *V. rotundifolia,* are the best choice for southern gardens. They will perform well in warm parts of the country where other types will not, but won't survive temperatures below 10°F. The best way to select an appropriate type and cultivar is to ask your local cooperative extension service for a recommendation of plants that will grow well in your area. With the exception of a few cultivars, mostly muscadines, grapes are self-fertile, and you won't need a second cultivar for pollination and fruit set.

Site Selection and Planting

All grapes prefer a sunny site with well-drained soil that is not too rich. Rich, loamy soil will produce vines with large crops of fruit that mature late and are low in sugar. A gentle, south-facing slope is best, but if you don't have one, provide protection from northwesterly winds. Good air drainage is important; avoid low-lying areas that might be frost pockets. The best time to plant is late winter or early spring, so it's a good idea to prepare the soil the season before by tilling in compost or well-rotted manure. Also check the pH and adjust it to between 6.0 and 7.0. In the South, where winter injury isn't a problem, grapes can be planted in fall.

For best results, plant the best quality one-year-old plants you can find (number one grade is best). Trim away any damaged roots, then spread the roots in the hole. Be sure the plant is growing at the same depth it was in the nursery. Many *V. vinifera* grapes are grafted on disease-resistant rootstocks. If you have a grafted plant, be sure the graft is above the soil surface. (You'll need to rigorously remove any suckers that appear from the roots throughout a grafted plant's lifetime.) Fill in the hole, tamp it down firmly, and water thoroughly.

Space most grapes 8 feet apart in rows, and allow 6 feet between rows. Rampant growers like muscadines should be spaced 12 to 20 feet

TRAINING A YOUNG VINE

Pruning begins as soon as the grapes are planted. Ideally, the trellis should be in place *before* you plant. If you don't have a trellis already set up when you plant, drive a stake in the ground near the base of the vine, and tie the plant loosely to the stake. Be sure to replace this temporary support with a trellis when the plants are still dormant during the first year.

Cut the vine back almost completely at planting time, leaving a short stem with only 2 to 4 buds. Remove all other canes completely, cutting flush with the surface of the main cane or trunk to prevent the bud from developing again. Throughout the season, rub or cut off any additional buds that begin growing. Remove any flower buds that appear, to direct the plant's energy into root production. The main shoots that arise in spring will be brittle, so gently tie them to the trellis with yarn or very loosely with soft string or twist ties.

At the end of the next winter, while the plants are still dormant, cut the canes back again to just 3 or 4 upward-facing buds. Let the new shoots grow to about 8 inches long, then choose the healthiest to serve as the trunk, and cut off all the other shoots except one. Prune the extra "insurance" shoot, called a renewal spur, back to just 2 buds to keep the plant's energy directed toward the trunk. Cut off all side shoots that appear along the trunk, along with any flower buds, but allow any leaves you see to remain, since these serve as food for the plant.

When the trunk cane has grown about 1 to 1½ feet beyond the top trellis wire, prune it back to the height of the wire and tie it to the trellis. When you do this, try to cut through a bud; this will not only prevent the cane from growing taller but will also provide a handy spot for attaching the vine to the trellis. Then you're ready to establish the branching framework for the trellising system you've selected.

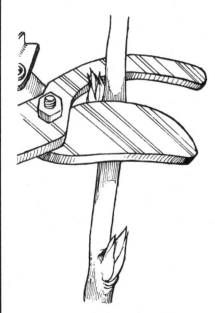

When pruning a grapevine to stop its upward growth, try to cut through a bud. You'll be left with a swollen knob around which you can wrap the wire when tying the vine to the trellis.

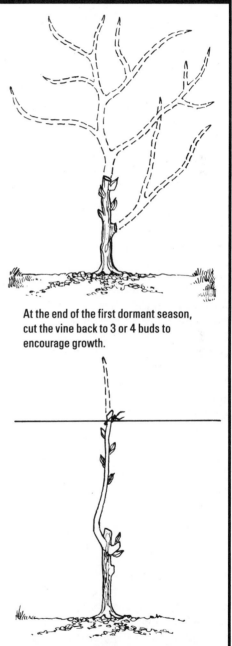

At the end of the first dormant season, cut the vine back to 3 or 4 buds to encourage growth.

When the new shoots are about 8 inches long, choose a vigorous one as the trunk. Select a trunk renewal spur; prune back to 2 buds. Once the trunk is a foot above the top wire, prune and tie it.

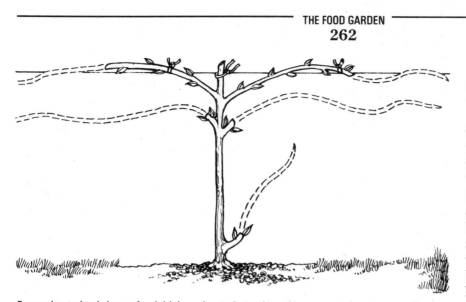

For cordon-trained vines, after initial pruning, train two lateral arms, or cordons, to grow along the wire in opposite directions.

Training and Trellising

Whether you grow grapes to make jelly, raisins, juice, or wine, or simply for table use, you'll need to train and prune the vines to keep them productive and manageable. Grapes produce fruit from shoots that arise from buds borne on one-year-old canes. The best fruit is borne on canes about the size of a pencil that arise as close to the main trunk as possible. Surprisingly, very thick canes don't fruit well; instead, they just produce lots of vegetative growth.

Vines that aren't trained or pruned will grow rampantly, producing far more foliage and fruit than the plant can support. As a result, the grapes will be small and nearly useless. Grapes need plenty of sun to ripen, and trellising opens the vines up to the sunlight. (For directions on how to establish the basic framework of a young plant so that it can be trained in one of the methods below, see "Training a Young Vine" on page 261).

There are several methods of trellising grapes. Which system you choose will depend on a number of factors including the cultivar you are growing, how many vines you intend

apart in the row, with 9 to 10 feet between rows.

to plant, the amount of space available in your garden, and your particular climate. For example, if your winters are severe, you should choose a low trellis, which can provide your grapevines with some protection from harsh conditions. Vigorous cultivars growing in warm areas, on the other hand, do best on high trellises that offer plenty of room for expansion. Ask your local cooperative extension service to recommend a method that is best for your area and the vines you'd like to grow.

Training Methods

Although there are several ways to train grapes, they can be divided into two general types—cordon-trained vines and head-pruned vines.

Cordon-Trained Vines. To establish a cordon-trained vine, tie the trunk to the trellis as described in "Training a Young Vine" on page 261. Select two lateral shoots growing in opposite directions to serve as fruit-bearing arms, called cordons, to train along the wires. Also select two additional shoots below them to serve as backups, or renewal spurs. Choose healthy shoots arising about 6 to 10 inches below the wires, growing parallel to the wire and in opposite directions off the trunk. Then cut off all other shoots except the cordons and renewal spurs. Remove any fruit clusters that appear the first year.

Allow the cordons to grow freely, then tie them *loosely* to the wire when they are about 1½ to 2 feet long. Attach them near the point at which they touch the wire; if they are tied close to their growing point, they may have difficulty growing. As the cordons lengthen, you can wrap them gently around the wire. (It's a good idea to check them from time to time to make sure they aren't pinched by the wire as they thicken.)

The following winter, cut back any new growth measuring under ⅜ inch thick. (If you have to trim back

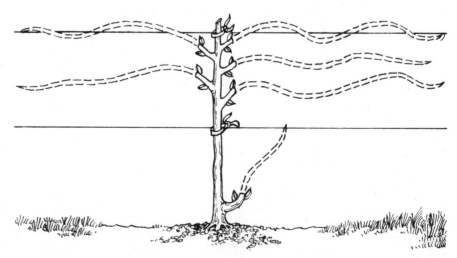

For head-trained vines, prune the trunk to the top trellis wire. Choose five lateral shoots to grow from the head of the trunk, then train the arms along the wire.

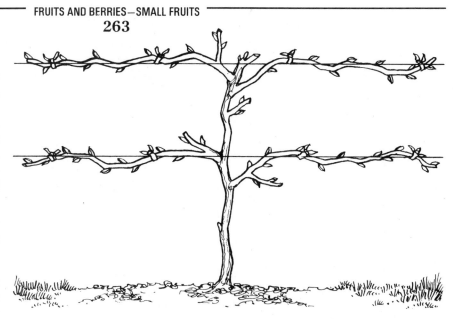

The Four-Arm Kniffin is easy and makes an attractive "living" fence.

to a point below the wire, cut to a side bud growing only a few inches from the trunk cane.) Then, in spring, remove any buds that are growing in the wrong direction. For instance, cut off the lower buds if you're using a trellising method with upright fruiting canes; remove the upper buds if you want canes growing downward.

As the cordons grow, snip off a little of one or the other to keep them the same length. When fruit appears on the vine (usually by the third season), thin out all but one fruit cluster for each cordon. If you want to encourage the cordons to grow longer, simply thin the fruit clusters even more—for example, to one cluster for every other shoot.

Head-Pruned Vines. Training a head-pruned vine requires a different procedure. Tie the trunk to the top wire as described in "Training a Young Vine" on page 261. Remove all but five lateral shoots from the trunk, and prune away the extra shoot at the bottom. Select equally spaced shoots near the top of the stem to keep as fruit-bearing arms, or cordons. When the more vigorous vines have grown to the top wire during the second growing season, thin the fruit clusters to one per shoot. Remove all fruit clusters from those shoots that have not yet reached the wire.

Trellising Systems

Regardless of the method you select, remember that the trellis should be sturdy enough to support the heavy vines for several years.

Use pressure-treated wood, steel pipe, or other strong materials, and bury the posts at least 2 or 3 feet into the ground. String your trellis with heavy galvanized wire, and attach the wire to the crossarms with heavy staples. For most systems, the top trellis wires are 5½ to 6 feet from the ground.

Geneva Double Curtain. This method is excellent for vigorous cultivars such as 'Concord' that require good air circulation as well as maximum sun exposure. To construct the trellis, you'll need three wires and two T-shaped posts that measure 4 feet wide at the top. String the first wire 4 feet high between the posts to support the vine trunks. Attach the other two wires to the arms of the posts to support the cordons.

For this system, you'll need to establish two trunks for each vine. (Be sure to leave a renewal spur for each trunk.) Allow the trunks to grow 4 feet high, then tie them loosely to the first wire. Train the trunks of the first vine to grow to the front wire, train the second vine's trunks to the back wire, and continue alternating down the row of vines. Let each trunk grow one cordon measuring about 8 feet long, then train the two cordons from the two trunks of each vine to grow in opposite directions on the wire. Soon you'll have a double curtain of fruiting shoots growing downward from the top wires.

Four-Arm Kniffin. If you want to create an attractive privacy screen with your grapevines, this is the method to use. Your harvest will probably be smaller than with other methods, since the lower parts of the vines tend to be more shaded with this system.

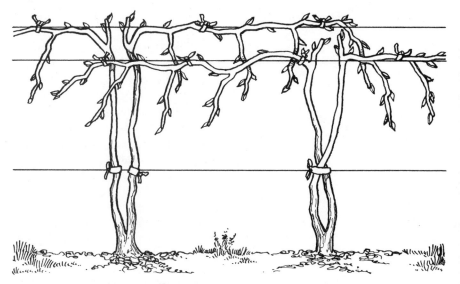

The Geneva Double Curtain is well suited for vigorous vines.

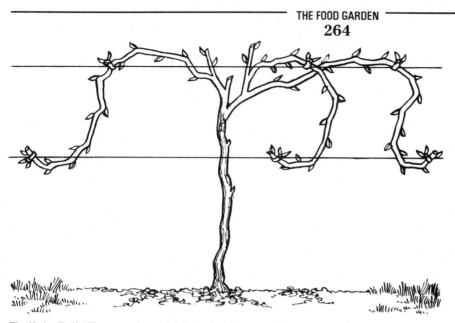

The Umbrella Kniffin system is a good choice for vigorous cultivars.

String one wire between two posts at 3 feet high; string another at 6 feet high. You'll need one healthy, upright trunk from each plant. Tie it loosely to the lower wire when it is tall enough, probably the first year after planting. When the trunk reaches the top wire, tie it again, and cut off the growing point to encourage side branches. Allow four cordons to grow away from the trunk, two along the top wire, two along the bottom. Let them grow to about 4 feet long, and keep them pruned to that length.

Umbrella Kniffin.   This method is suitable for vigorous vines. Use the same trellis as you would with the four-arm Kniffin, only this time head-prune the vine instead of training cordons. As the trunk develops, remove any shoots that appear. Tie the trunk to the lower wire when it reaches that height. When the trunk grows as tall as the top wire, cut it back 6 to 12 inches below the wire and allow shoots to grow from the head.

Bend the new canes over the top wire so that they hang downward, then tie them to the lower wire when they are long enough. As the vine grows, it will assume the shape of an umbrella.

Keuka High Renewal.   If you're growing an upright cultivar with basal buds that tend to bear lots of fruit, or if you're unfamiliar with the growth habit of the particular cultivar you've selected, this method is a good choice. The trellis consists of three wires strung between the posts at 3 feet, 4½ feet, and 6 feet high. This system uses head-pruned vines, each of which can have one or two trunks. Once the head reaches the middle wire, prune it at that level, then allow shoots to develop from the trunk. Depending upon how vigorous the vine is, you can train cordons along the lower two wires or you can encourage cordons to grow on all three wires.

Fan.   This method is appropriate for use in areas with harsh winters, where trunks are often damaged by cold temperatures, or for growing tender grapes in colder regions than they normally tolerate. (In fact, in areas with very cold winters, you can prune vines trained in this manner in late fall and then gently lay them along the ground and bury them under up to 8 inches of loose soil for protection.) Use a trellis with two wires, one at 2½ feet and the other at 4½ to 5 feet. Prune the trunk to 1 foot high. Allow four cordons to develop into arms, cut them back to about 10 buds each, and tie them loosely to the two wires. In addition, leave four renewal spurs in case the plant is injured during winter.

The second year, prune each of the canes back to 5 or 6 live buds, and remove all of the side shoots except one, which will become the renewal spur. Trim it back to 2 buds. Let each cane produce only 2 or 3 lateral shoots per foot of growth, and train them upward onto the wires.

The third year, cut each cane back to the first branch, which will produce grapes this season. Tie each cane to the wire and cut it back to 8 or 10 buds. (You'll need to cut them back farther if there has been winter damage.) Only allow one flower cluster per cane to remain.

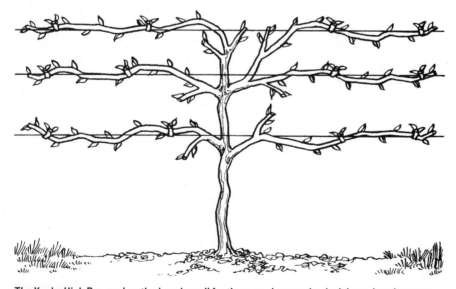

The Keuka High Renewal method works well for those gardeners who don't know how large or fast their vines will grow.

The fourth year and every year thereafter, replace one of the old canes with one grown from a renewal spur.

Annual Pruning

Once you've trained your grapevines, you'll need to prune them every year to keep them compact and open them up to the sunlight. Since grapes are borne on year-old canes, pruning is also necessary to keep the vines productive.

Pruning Basics

When you prune your vines depends on how cold your winters are. (Muscadine grapes, which should always be pruned in summer, are the exception.) If you live in an area where winter temperatures are moderate, you can prune at the beginning of the dormant season, as soon as the vine has lost its leaves. In harsher climates, however, it's best to prune in late winter, after the worst of the cold weather has passed. Not only will the wounds have a better chance to heal, you can also remove any winter-killed growth as you prune.

When pruning your grapevines, you want to remove enough to encourage productivity but not so much that the vine is weakened and cannot bear fruit. As a general rule, trim the vines when they begin to overwhelm your trellis and thin out fruit clusters when the berries become too small and are slow to ripen. That way, you will keep both vine and fruit growth in check.

Prune any shoots growing on wood that is more than two years old, as well as any wood that has been damaged during the winter. As you thin out the canes, leave the thickest behind, along with nearby renewal spurs for backup. Try to save canes that are easy to tie to the trellis, as well as those that have been exposed to the sun.

Knowing just how many fruiting buds to remove can be tricky. If you're not familiar with the bearing capacity of your vines, it's best to

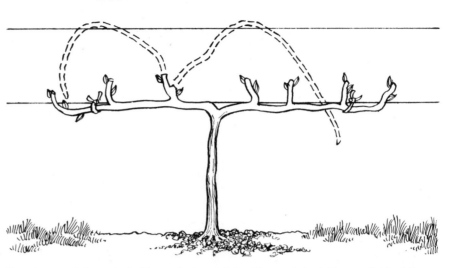

For spur-pruned vines, start with a cordon-pruned vine. Choose six to eight spurs. Cut back the fruiting arms each year to 2 buds each.

prune moderately and leave one flower cluster per shoot. (If you've left too much wood, you can still remove the flower clusters as they appear.) After a few years, you'll have a better feel for the vines and can adjust your pruning accordingly. Most cultivars of mature grapes should have about 40 to 50 buds remaining after they are cane-pruned, and 12 to 24 buds following spur pruning.

Pruning Methods

There are two basic methods of pruning grapes, spur pruning and cane pruning. The method you choose depends on the grapes you're growing.

Spur Pruning. Spur pruning is the easiest of the two basic types of grapevine pruning, though it can only be used with cultivars that have fruitful basal buds—mostly European vines. Begin with a cordon-trained vine. Choose six to eight spurs along the cordons the first bearing year. Allow the shoots to reach the top trellis wire, then tie them loosely or loop them over the wire. When it's time to prune the vine, cut back each of the canes to 2 buds. By the time you're ready to prune again, each spur should have two shoots. You can either cut the canes back to 2 buds as before or, if the vine produces large grape

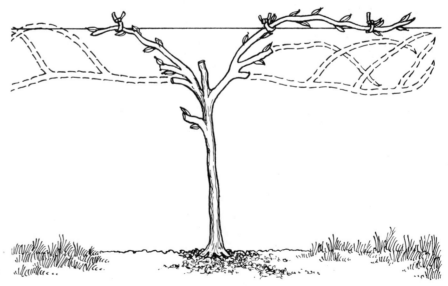

For cane pruned vines, prune canes back to 8 to 15 buds for fruiting every year and leave 2-bud spurs for next year's harvest.

clusters, remove one of the canes and leave 2 buds on the other. Continue cutting back the canes in the same way each year.

Cane Pruning.   Cane pruning may be used with many cultivars of grapes, though it is not as simple as spur pruning and usually requires more space. Every year during pruning season, choose a few canes for fruiting from among the year-old canes. Cut these back to 8 to 15 buds per cane. (Keep in mind that the best bearing canes are the darker ones, or those that have been exposed to the sun.) You will also need to leave 2-bud spurs near the bearing canes for next year's harvest.

PLANTING AND TRAINING HARDY KIWIS

For an exotic taste treat, try growing the hardy kiwi (*Actinidia arguta*). Less common than the New Zealand kiwi but bearing sweeter-tasting fruit without the fuzzy brown covering, this vigorous twining vine produces attractive, fragrant white flowers and may be grown in much the same way as you would grow grapes.

Select a site with full sun and well-drained, fertile soil. Set plants 10 feet apart in rows spaced 10 to 15 feet apart. Since kiwis are usually dioecious, you'll need to plant one male plant for every five to ten females. Keep the plants protected from the wind, and water thoroughly, especially during hot, dry spells. Prune the vines in late winter by removing damaged wood and low-lying branches. Thin out spurless branches that are at least three years old. Cut back older, spurred branches to within a few buds of the fruit from the previous year; these will produce fruit the following season.

Hardy kiwis may be trained on trellises, arbors, and many other kinds of supports, and are excellent for covering walls with their thick, glossy green foliage. Be sure the support is strong; kiwis are heavier and more vigorous than grapes. For female plants, use a trellis with 8- to 9-foot-tall posts and a network of wires strung between them. Train a single trunk to grow to the top wire, then prune it back a few inches to just above a bud so that the trunk will split to form a Y. Train subsequent growth in opposite directions on the wire and prune as needed to keep growth in check. You can also prune further to create an arbor.

Fruits and Berries— Tree Fruits

Planting Fruit Trees

Fruit trees are an investment that can yield bountiful, delicious interest for many years after planting. To get the best return on your investment, it's important to take extra care in selecting the right plants and picking the best site for them. There are many types of tree fruits from which to choose, and the best choices for you will depend on where you live and how much space you have available. Your local cooperative extension agent also may be able to recommend cultivars suitable for your area. (The chart "Selecting Tree Fruits" on page 270 will help you get started. Be sure to read "Pollination and Fruit Set" on page 274 before selecting plants to make sure plenty of the right kind of pollen is available to pollinate your trees.)

Just because you have limited space in your garden doesn't mean you can't enjoy the taste of fresh, tree-ripened fruit. Many tree fruits are grafted onto rootstocks that affect their size at maturity, and the availability of dwarf or semidwarf trees makes it possible to grow a bearing-size tree in even the smallest garden. Even if you have plenty of room available, dwarf and semidwarf plants have other advantages. Their fruit is easy to reach for picking, and it's generally easier to prune and care for smaller trees. Finally, dwarf and semidwarf fruit trees begin blooming and bear fruit sooner than standards.

Site Selection

It's important to select the best possible site for your trees. For best yields, fruit trees need full sun. Avoid areas in the shadow of large ornamental trees or tall buildings. Most fruit trees prefer deep, loamy soil that is moist but well-drained and rich in organic matter, although they'll tolerate many types of soils. Heavy clay soils, however, will impede root system formation and result in poor tree growth. If you have clayey soil, plan on adding plenty of organic matter to a large area around the planting site and working it in as deeply as possible. Or consider making a large raised bed to accommodate one or several dwarf fruit trees. (See "Making a Raised Bed" on page 5 for directions.)

Look for a site that offers good air drainage. Cold air drains downhill and settles in valleys or against barriers such as thick hedges, creating frost pockets. Frost can damage fruit blossoms, which appear in early spring, so try to plant trees near the top of a slope rather than at the bottom where chilly air often collects. A south- or southeast-facing slope is fine, although very early blooming trees sometimes are best planted on the side of a north-facing slope. This helps delay bloom and increases the likelihood that tender flowers will survive spring frosts. Although trees should be protected from strong prevailing winds, they should be planted in a site with good air circulation.

Heeling-In

You can buy container-grown fruit trees or field-grown trees dug and sold with their roots wrapped in burlap (called balled-and-burlapped or "b & b"). Fruit trees also are commonly sold bare-root, that is, with all the soil removed from the root system and with the roots packed in wood shavings or similar material.

It's best if you have the site all prepared so you can plant your fruit trees as soon as you bring them home or they arrive in the mail. However, if that's not possible, both container-grown and balled-and-burlapped trees can be set in a sheltered site out of sun and wind and watered regularly until you find time to plant. Bare-root trees, on the other hand, need immediate attention to keep the roots from drying out. If you can't plant them right away, you'll need to protect them with a technique known as heeling-in.

Soak the roots of bare-root trees in water for an hour or so before heeling them in. Then find a spot sheltered from direct wind and sun (the

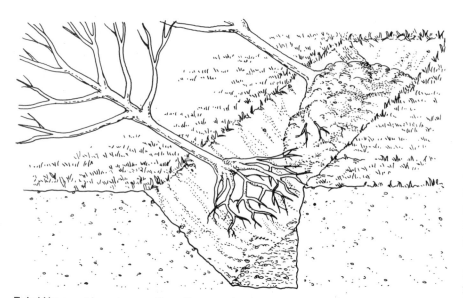

To hold bare-root trees temporarily until you can plant them, heel them in by digging a shallow trench with one sloping side. Lean the trees against the sloping side, spread the roots, and cover with soil or soil mixed with peat.

in a shaded outdoor area if the temperature is above freezing. If you use garbage bags, be sure to leave the top open so the roots have an air supply. Lightly water the peat moss or soil when it dries out.

It may seem reasonable to just put your new tree in a tub or pail of water. But roots can't breathe underwater and can be damaged if left this way for more than 24 hours. However, this method is fine for temporary storage overnight or for keeping the tree roots moist while you are preparing the planting hole.

Whatever method you use, remember that heeling-in is a temporary measure only. Try to move your trees to their permanent site as soon as possible.

north-facing wall of a house can provide good shelter) and dig a trench with one sloping side, large enough to accommodate the roots. Lean the trees against the angled side with their roots in the trench and cover the roots with soil (or a combination of peat moss and soil), pressing lightly to pack the soil around the roots. Water thoroughly and keep the roots evenly moist but not wet until you can move the trees to their permanent location.

If your soil is frozen or too wet for heeling plants into a trench, you can use a large pot, plastic bucket, or heavy plastic garbage bag to hold moist potting soil or peat moss around the roots. Keep trees in such makeshift containers in a cool (40° to 45°F), humid garage, shed, or basement, or

Planting Pointers

One of the best things you can do for your new fruit trees is to have the planting site ready and waiting for them. This minimizes transplant stress and helps get them off to a good start.

Site Preparation

Dig a hole that is at least 3 feet in diameter and 1½ to 2 feet deep. When in doubt, dig as wide a hole as you can, to encourage roots to spread out laterally in every direction. Remove any large rocks. Rough up the sides of the hole after you've finished digging, to eliminate hard-packed sides that may be impenetrable to roots.

In the past, amending the soil removed from the hole with compost, purchased topsoil, or peat was considered standard operating procedure. However, recent observations indicate that filling the planting hole with rich, amended soil encourages the roots to remain within the planting hole rather than work their way out and down into the surrounding soil. Although you may want to test the pH of your soil and adjust accordingly, or add a cup of bonemeal in the bottom of the hole, plan on filling with unamended, native soil.

SPRING OR FALL?

True or false: The best time to plant fruit trees is in the spring. The answer: It depends where you live. In areas where cold weather arrives in early autumn and temperatures often fall below -10°F, planting in the early spring will give the young tree time to grow and harden before the onset of harsh winter temperatures. Spring rains will help keep newly planted trees well watered for proper growth.

However, if your local conditions include hot, dry summers and mild winters, fall planting can give a new tree extra time to establish a healthy root system that can survive harsh summer weather. Because the tree is planted while dormant, the roots have time to become established before buds break in the spring. Fall-planted trees have a further advantage of being able to begin growth in early spring, when soil is still too wet for tree planting. Also, the soil in the fall is often drier and easier to work. For the best root growth and winter survival, fall planting should only be done in those areas where the soil temperature remains above 50°F several weeks after the trees become dormant. Plant as early in the fall as you can to take advantage of good root-growing weather.

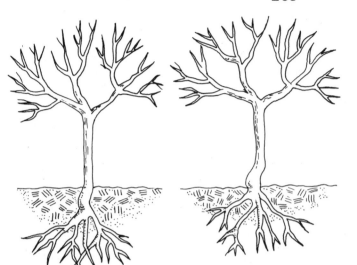

Plant standard-size trees (left) with the graft union 1 to 2 inches below the level of the soil. Plant fruit trees grafted on dwarf and semidwarf rootstocks (right) with the knobby graft union aboveground.

Determining the Proper Depth

Before you plant, examine the trunk close to the roots. If your plant has been grafted, you'll find a slight knob or crook near the base of the stem. This is the graft union. Dwarf and semidwarf trees should be planted with the graft union aboveground. Covering the graft union would allow the upper part of the tree, called the scion, to root, and you would lose the effect of the dwarfing rootstock. If you live in an area with high winds, plant the tree with the top part of the graft union knob toward the prevailing wind.

Plant standard trees so the graft union is 1 to 2 inches below the ground. (Since in this case you're not worried about keeping the plant small, it doesn't matter if the scion produces its own roots.) This provides protection from severe winter weather and gives the tree better anchorage.

To see if your tree will be at the proper depth, place it in the hole you have prepared and set a broomstick or pole across the hole to help judge the depth. Make a pyramid- or cone-shaped mound of soil in the center to spread out the roots of bare-root trees. Set container-grown or balled-and-burlapped trees in the hole, container and all. If the tree is too low, add more soil to the central mound, and remove some soil if the tree is too high.

Planting

At planting time, remove containers completely—even peat or papier-mâché ones—and check to make sure that the roots aren't circling around the root ball. For balled-and-burlapped trees, cut the burlap in several places to make it easy for the roots to grow out into the surrounding soil; remove any string or wire holding the burlap in place, along with synthetic fabrics sometimes used as burlap substitutes. Cut back any broken or damaged roots without disturbing the root ball.

Soak the roots of bare-root trees for an hour or so before planting. Then cut ½ inch off broken root tips so that healthy tissue will contact the soil and more fine roots will be stimulated to grow. Prune crushed or broken roots.

If you are planting more than one fruit tree, space dwarf fruit trees 8 to 15 feet apart; semidwarf trees, 10 to 12 feet; standard trees, 25 feet. Use the larger spacing for the dwarf or semidwarf trees if your soil is deep and fertile, as each tree's root system will expand more through the years in these soils.

It's easiest to have another person hold the tree in the right position as you start to fill in the soil. Have him or her gently shake the tree as you shovel, to help settle soil around the roots. When the roots are covered by several inches of soil, you can start to press the soil down with your hands. Do this gently, taking care not to break any roots. When the hole is two-thirds filled, soak the site with a pail of water to help settle the soil around the roots. Then finish adding soil to ground level. Press the soil so that there is a bowl-shaped indentation in the ground—this will help hold water during the first growing season—and water thoroughly.

Pruning at Planting Time

It may seem criminal to cut branches off your newly purchased fruit trees, but selected pruning will ultimately lead to better tree form and growth. You'll need to remove any dead branches, which will look shriveled and blackened at planting time. If you're not sure whether a branch has life in it, carefully scrape away a small piece of bark with your fingernail. Dead wood is brown, gray, or black; healthy wood is green.

In the past, the general recommendation was to cut back unbranched bare-root trees by approximately one-third or one-half at planting time. This was thought to balance the loss of roots that occurred when the tree was dug at the nursery. Research indicates this is not necessary: Do not prune unbranched bare-root trees at planting time.

The only pruning that branched specimens need at planting time is to establish the basic framework of the tree. Remove any damaged or dead branches, along with branches growing vertically (or nearly so) against the main trunk. The narrow crotches these branches create are weak and tend to break under heavy fruit loads. The strongest branch angles are 45 degrees or greater. Choose three to five branches that are evenly spaced around the circumference of the cen-

(continued on page 274)

SELECTING TREE FRUITS

Fruit trees are ornamental as well as useful, and homegrown fruit, whether eaten fresh, baked in pies, or preserved in jelly is a special treat. Before buying a tree, check with your local cooperative extension agent to find out what cultivars are best for your area. Consider planting some of the many disease-resistant cultivars available. Yields listed are for 1 year.

Fruit	Yield per Plant	Culture	Harvest Information	Comments
Apple (*Malus pumila*)	Standard: 10-20 bu. Semidwarf: 5-10 bu. Dwarf: 1-5 bu.	Full sun. Average, well-drained soil rich in organic matter; pH 5.5-7.0. Buy 1- or 2-year-old trees. Site should be protected from frost; the middle of a gentle, south-facing slope is ideal. Allow as much space between trees as their height at maturity. Water and mulch around young trees, but do not mulch near trunk. Zones 3-8.	Dwarf trees will fruit in 2-4 years after planting; semidwarfs, in 3-5 years; standards, in 5-7 years. Different cultivars ripen from early to late summer or early fall. Pick fruit when ripe but firm. Hold apple and stem and twist gently, while tilting upwards. Keep stems on apples. Do not damage spurs when harvesting.	Most apples sold today are grafted on rootstocks that affect growth rate; dwarf, semidwarf, and standard-size trees are available in most cultivars. Dwarf trees grow to be 8-12 ft.; semidwarf, 12-20 ft.; and standards, 20-40 ft. May live up to 35 years; some may fruit heavily every other year. Some cultivars are self-sterile (2 cultivars needed for pollination); others, partially self-fertile. Disease-resistant cultivars include 'Freedom', 'Liberty', 'Macfree', 'Nova Easygro', 'Prima', 'Priscilla', and 'Redfree'.
Apricot (*Prunus armeniaca*)	Standard: 3-4 bu. Dwarf: 3 bu.	Full sun. Deep, average, loamy soil that is moist but well drained; pH 6.0-7.0. Buy 3-5 ft., 1-year-old plants. Plant on a north-facing slope protected from cold winds if possible. Allow at least as much space between trees as their height at maturity. Avoid planting near or after member of the nightshade family, brambles, or strawberries. Prune out nonfruiting spurs. Zones 4-9.	Will fruit in 3-5 years. Fruits ripen in late summer. Harvest when fruit is almost firm and orange-yellow all over. Hold fruit and gently twist while tilting upwards.	Apricots are fast growing and may live up to 35 years. Standard trees grow 15-25 ft. high; dwarf (grafted) trees, 8-12 ft. Most are self-fertile, although a few cultivars, such as 'Moongold' and 'Sungold', should be planted together for pollination. Thin to even out annual yield. Pink flowers open in early spring but are often ruined by frost. Disease-resistant cultivars include 'Harcot', 'Harlayne', and 'Harogem'.

Fruit	Yield per Plant	Culture	Harvest Information	Comments
Cherry (*Prunus* spp.)	Standard, sweet: 3-6 bu. Standard, sour: 2-5 bu. Dwarf (genetic): up to 1 bu.	Full sun. Light, moist, well-drained soil rich in organic matter; pH 6.0-8.0. Buy 1- or 2-year-old trees. A north-facing slope protected from cold winds will help delay bloom and prevent frost damage to buds. Allow as much space between plants as their height at maturity. Sweet cherries grow in Zones 5-8; sour cherries, Zones 4-8.	Sweet cherries will fruit in 3-6 years; sours in 3-5 years. Sweet cherries ripen in early summer; sour ones ripen a little later. Harvest when cherries have full color by gently twisting stems upward off of spur; ripe sour cherries are easily pulled from pits (which remain on stem).	Cherry trees may live 30-40 years. Sour cherries are self-fertile. Sweet cherries usually require compatible cultivars with overlapping blooming periods for pollination. Dwarf trees reach 6-15 ft. Standard sweet cherries grow to 20-40 ft.; sour cherries, 15-25 ft. Sour cherries are smaller than sweet ones and used for cooking. Disease-resistant cultivars include 'Hedelfingen' (sweet), 'North Star' (sour), 'Sam' (sweet), and 'Windsor' (sweet).
Citrus (*Citrus* spp.)	Depends on fruit, tree size, and conditions. True citrus can range from 150-1,000 lbs. Kumquats: 40 lbs.	Full sun. Light, loamy, moist but well-drained soil rich in organic matter; pH 5.0-7.0. Buy 1-year-old, certified disease-free trees. Planting is best done in late winter or early spring. Choose a warm, sunny, sheltered area. Space 15-35 ft. apart. Protect young trees from sunburn and cold. Water deeply and often. Require high nitrogen. Zones 9-10.	Will fruit in 3-6 years. Harvest when fruit is fully ripened, which is indicated by its mature size, color, and taste. With shears, cut ripe fruit at point it is attached to stem. Most types will keep well on the tree, so harvest only what you can use.	Includes lime, lemon, grapefruit, orange, tangerine, and kumquat. Trees grow from 5-50 ft.; may fruit up to 100 years. Citrus trees will not grow well at temperatures below 55°F. Fruits take 7-14 months to ripen. Recommended cultivars include grapefruits 'Marsh Seedless', 'Redblush', and 'Rio Red'; blood oranges 'Moro', 'Sanguinella', and 'Tarocco'; kumquats 'Meiwa' and 'Nagami'; lemons 'Eureka' and 'Meyer'; limes 'Bearss' and 'Persian'; tangerines 'Dancy', 'Page', and 'Satsuma'; oranges 'Pineapple', 'Valencia', and 'Washington Navel'.

(continued)

SELECTING TREE FRUITS—*Continued*

Fruit	Yield per Plant	Culture	Harvest Information	Comments
Peach and Nectarine (*Prunus persica*)	Standard: 2-5 bu. Dwarf (grafted): 2-3 bu.	Full sun. Loamy or sandy soil that is moist but well drained and rich in organic matter; pH 6.0-7.0. Buy 3-5 ft., 1-year-old trees. Plant on a southern slope unless spring temperatures fluctuate widely. If so, choose a north-facing slope. Allow 15-25 ft. between trees. Zones 4-10.	Will fruit in 1-3 years. Harvest fruit in mid- to late summer when it is fairly firm and no green visible; should twist off limb without much effort.	May live 10-20 years. Standard trees grow from 8-20 ft.; dwarf trees, 6-10 ft. Both come in freestone (flesh separates easily from pit) or clingstone (flesh clings to pit) cultivars. Disease-resistant cultivars include peaches 'Clayton', 'Newhaven', and 'Redhaven'; nectarines 'Mericrest' and 'Redchief'.
Pear (*Pyrus communis*)	Standard: 5-10 bu. Dwarf (grafted): ½ to 2 bu.	Full sun to partial shade. Deep, loamy soil that is moist but well drained; pH 6.0-7.0. Buy 4-6 ft. standard, or 2½-4 ft. dwarf, 1- or 2-year-old trees. Select a site protected from harsh winds but with good air circulation. Allow 16-25 ft. between standards; 12-15 ft. between dwarfs. Zones 2-10.	Standard trees will fruit in 4-6 years; dwarfs in 2-4 years. Fruits ripen in late summer to early fall. Harvest pears when stems swell near twigs, the green skin lightens or starts to turn yellow, and they are easily separated from the twig. Fruit ripened on tree will develop brown centers and grainy texture.	Early and late-ripening cultivars available. Standard trees reach 15-25 ft.; dwarf (grafted) trees, only 8-15 ft. May live 50-75 years. Most require another cultivar for pollination; some are incompatible. Disease-resistant cultivars include 'Kieffer', 'Monterrey', 'Orient', and 'Seckel'.
Persimmon (*Diospyros virginiana, D. kaki*)	50-100 lbs.	Full sun to partial shade. Well-drained soil; pH 6.0-7.0. Buy 1- or 2-year-old trees. A southern exposure is best. Space 18-20 ft. Mulch thickly. American, Zones 4-8; Japanese, Zones 7-10.	Will fruit in 3-4 years. Fruit ripens in fall. Pick when still a bit firm, keeping stem on fruit, and let ripen in warm room. Most persimmons are astringent and can only be eaten when soft. Ripe persimmons are very sweet and can be eaten fresh, dried, or used in pastries.	May live 50 years or more. American cultivars grow to 30-60 ft.; Japanese types to 20-40 ft. Most American cultivars require a pollinator; Japanese are usually self-fertile. American persimmon has yellow-orange or purple fruit, 1-2 in. wide; Japanese are orange to bright yellow, 1½-4 in. wide. Recommended American cultivars include 'Early Golden', 'Garretson', and 'Meader'; Japanese persimmons 'Fuyu', 'Hachiya', and 'Tanenashi'.

Fruit	Yield per Plant	Culture	Harvest Information	Comments
Plum (*Prunus* spp.)	Standard: 1-3 bu. Dwarf: ½-1 bu.	Full sun. Slightly heavy, moist but well-drained soil rich in organic matter; pH 6.0-8.0. Buy 3-6 ft. standard, or 3-4 ft. dwarf, 1-year-old trees. A north-facing slope will help delay bloom and prevent bud damage from frost. Space trees 18-24 ft. apart. Japanese, Zones 4-9; European, Zones 4-8.	Japanese plums fruit in 2-4 years; European plums fruit in 3-5 years. Fruits ripen in midsummer. Harvest plums when they develop a waxy white coating ("bloom"). Pick soft for eating fresh or drying, or fairly firm for cooking.	Standard plum trees reach 15-20 ft.; dwarf trees grow 8-15 ft. Japanese plums are 2-3 in. wide and usually red or yellow; European plums, 1-2 in. wide, and usually blue or purple. Plums bear fruit 25-30 years. Cultivars may require others from the same family for successful pollination. Disease-resistant cultivars include Japanese plums 'Crimson' and 'Starking Delicious'; European plums 'Count Althann's Gage', 'Oneida', and 'President'.
Quince, orchard (*Cydonia oblonga*)	½-1 bu.	Full sun. Rich, loamy, moist but well-drained soil. Buy 2-year-old trees. Space 15-20 ft. apart. Zones 5-8.	Will fruit in 3-5 years. Ripens in late fall. Harvest when fruit is yellow turning to orange, has a strong aroma, and separates from stem easily. Rarely eaten raw, good when canned or spiced and provides interesting flavor to jellies and sauces.	This bushy tree quince is not to be confused with flowering quince, *Chaenomeles japonica* or *C. speciosa,* which are grown as ornamentals. *Cydonia oblonga* will grow to 12-24 ft. and bear fruit for 25 years or so. Slow growing and similar in requirements to pears. Flowers in late spring. Recommended cultivars are 'Orange', 'Pineapple', and 'Smyrna'.

tral leader and have wide crotch angles. These will become the scaffold branches or the main branches of the tree. Prune out all the other branches. (For information on how to train trees to establish a strong, heavy-yielding framework, see "Pruning and Training Fruit Trees" on page 276.)

Finishing Up

Here are a few final steps to settle your fruit trees into their new home.

1. Cut off any wire tags to prevent them from cutting into the tree as it grows.

2. Stake the trunks of newly planted trees. (Fruit trees grafted on dwarf rootstocks will require permanent staking.) For best support, use three stakes placed as a triangle about a foot away from the trunk. Thread a sturdy wire through an old piece of rubber hose, loop the rubber hose portion around the trunk, and attach the ends of the wire to one stake. Do the same thing for the other two stakes. (For detailed instructions on how to stake young fruit trees, see "Staking" under "Planting Trees and Shrubs" on page 328.)

3. Wrap a spiral plastic tree guard around the tree trunk to protect it from gnawing animals and winter sunscald.

4. For spring-planted trees, place a 6-inch layer of compost, straw or other organic mulch around the tree to prevent weeds and help conserve soil moisture. In the fall, move the mulch away from the trunk, as it makes a good nesting and hiding place for mice.

Pollination and Fruit Set

Blooming fruit trees are a beautiful feature of the spring landscape, but, surprisingly, plenty of flowers doesn't always mean a plentiful harvest. Before your trees' flowers can bear fruit, they need to be pollinated and have an adequate fruit set. There are a number of factors that can stand in the way. Fickle spring weather is one of them; pollen compatibility, another. Fortunately, there are some steps you can take to ensure a bountiful crop.

From Flowers to Fruits

To understand the fruiting process, you'll need to know a little basic botany. Nearly everyone can identify the petals of an apple or peach blossom. Just inside the petals are a circle of slender filaments with yellow dust on top. These are the stamens, the male flower part, topped with pollen. The stamens surround the pistil, the female part of the flower. If you pull off the petals and some of the stamens, you can see the structure of the pistil. The sticky tip of the pistil, which collects the pollen, is called the stigma. The swollen part at the bottom is the

ovary, which is connected to the stigma by a narrow stalk called the style. The ovary contains the eggs and develops into the fruit.

When a pollen grain lands on the stigma, it germinates and produces a long tube that grows down through the style into the ovary. This tube carries two sperm cells: One fuses with the egg to eventually form the seedling, the other fuses with a cell to form nutrient tissue for the seedling. Both must fuse, or no seed or fruit will form. In apples and pears, each ovary has ten eggs; ovaries of other fruit flowers have fewer eggs. Fruit size is linked to the number of seeds that mature, because developing seeds produce a hormone that signals the fleshy part of the fruit to enlarge.

Of Weather and Bugs

All of our common fruit trees need bees or other insects for pollination—to carry pollen from stamens to stigma. However, honeybees don't fly in rainy weather and are sluggish at temperatures below 65°F. Adequate pollination is a problem in wet, cold springs. Furthermore, a spring cold

snap with below-freezing temperatures can kill blossoms before bees even have a chance to pollinate them.

Even if the flower is successfully pollinated, weather still can interfere with fertilization. High temperatures can kill the ovary before the pollen tubes deliver the sperm, or cold weather (close to freezing) can delay pollen tube growth so the crucial period for fertilization is missed. In both these cases, there will be little fruit set despite a beautiful spring bloom.

Winter weather can damage fruit flowers in the bud so that they either drop before blooming or bloom but then do not set fruit. (Flower buds can be less hardy than leaf buds, so this can happen even though the tree seems otherwise undamaged.) Extreme cold can cause bud damage, but the most common cause is a winter warm spell followed by freezing temperatures. The tree loses its ability to withstand the cold during the warm spell and then is damaged in the following cold weather.

While you can't do much about the weather, you can make certain not to spray blooming trees with insecticides or other chemicals that kill or harm the all-important pollinators. Even botanical insecticides like pyrethrum and rotenone are deadly to bees; try to avoid spraying altogether or spray at dusk when bees are less active.

Pollen Compatibility

Not only must the pollen land on the stigma for pollination to occur, it often must be the *right* pollen. While the flowers of many fruit tree cultivars can be pollinated by their own pollen, some have defective pollen that either does not germinate at all or simply does not pollinate effectively. Sterile cultivars such as 'Winesap' and 'Stayman' apples require pollen from another cultivar in order to produce fruit and can't pollinate any other trees. Many fruit trees don't pollinate their own flowers effectively; for a bumper harvest, you will need a second cultivar for pollination. But some cultivars are incompatible and cannot cross-pollinate. (See "Pollination Requirements of Fruit Trees" for a guide to common cultivars and compatibility.)

Beating Blooming Problems

There are a few things you can do when you have only one tree blooming and your pollinator cultivar isn't blooming. If a neighbor or friend has a blooming pollinator cultivar, ask to

POLLINATION REQUIREMENTS OF FRUIT TREES

There are a few basic principles to keep in mind when considering pollination requirements of fruit trees. Trees can be self-unfruitful or self-sterile, meaning they can pollinate the blooms of other trees but require pollen from another cultivar to set fruit. They can be sterile, meaning they can't pollinate their own flowers or those of any other trees. Cultivars can also be incompatible, meaning they cannot pollinate each other's blooms. Some cultivars have several different forms with different names that won't pollinate each other. For example, 'Starkspur Golden Delicious' apple won't pollinate 'Golden Delicious'. Don't be fooled by dwarfing rootstocks, either; if a cultivar is self-unfruitful, a dwarf tree won't pollinate a standard tree of that cultivar.

When selecting a pollinator cultivar, you'll need to make certain that it blooms at about the same time as the tree you want to have pollinated—a late-blooming cultivar can't pollinate an early-blooming one. You'll need to plant the trees close enough for proper pollination. Your local nursery owner, cooperative extension agent, or mail-order source will have information on bloom time and compatibility of various cultivars.

Apples

Some apples are self-fertile, although most have better fruit set if pollinated by another cultivar. Trees must be no more than 80 feet apart for pollination. Crabapples can be used to pollinate apples. 'Gravenstein', 'Mutsu' (also called 'Crispin'), 'Jonagold', and 'Winesap' are sterile. 'Golden Delicious', 'Jonathan', and 'Yellow Transparent' are self-pollinating but yield more if cross-pollinated. 'Granny Smith' and 'Tydeman Red' are incompatible and are poor self-pollinators.

Apricots

Most are self-fertile. 'Early Golden', 'Chinese', and 'Moorpark' are self-fertile but will produce a better crop if cross-pollinated. A few cultivars including 'Goldrich' and 'Perfection' need cross-pollination.

Cherries

Most sweet cherry cultivars require cross-pollination for best crops; sour cherries do not require cross-pollination but set heavier crops if crossed. Trees must be no more than 40 yards apart for pollination. Sour cherries aren't good pollinators for sweet cherries because they bloom later. Sweet cherries 'Bing', 'Emperor Francis', 'Lambert', and 'Napoleon' (also called 'Royal Ann') are self-unfruitful and will not pollinate each other. 'Stella' and 'Lapins' are both self-fertile.

Peaches and Nectarines

Most cultivars are self-fertile. Peaches 'J. H. Hale', 'Erlihale', 'Indian Free', and 'White Hale' are sterile.

Pears

Common pear cultivars need cross-pollination for best fruit set. Asian pears also require cross-pollination and will cross with common pear cultivars. Trees must be no more than 150 feet apart for pollination. 'Magness' is sterile. 'Bedford', 'Bristol Cross', and 'Waite' produce little pollen. 'Max Red' is a type of 'Bartlett' and won't pollinate 'Bartlett'. 'Bartlett' and 'Seckel' are incompatible.

Plums

Many European plums (and cultivars sold as prunes) are self-fruitful, although most will produce better crops if cross-pollinated. Japanese plums need cross-pollination. Japanese and European cultivars will not cross-pollinate each other.

cut a few flowering branches. Place them in a bucket of water. Hang the bucket in the tree so that the bees will work both the flowers of the cut branches as well as those on the tree.

If there aren't many bees and you only have a few flowers, try hand-pollinating. With a paint brush, touch the stamens of the flowers to collect pollen. Then brush the pollen onto the stigma of the flower to be pollinated.

Another way to satisfy the need for different pollinating cultivars is to graft a pollinator cultivar onto the tree, creating a two-in-one tree. Many nurseries offer such specially grafted trees, making it easy to grow different cultivars of fruit on one tree. (See "Grafting Fruit Trees" on page 287 if you want to try this yourself.)

Fruit Set and Yield

Flower buds of common tree fruits form during the months of August and September of the year before blooming. If the tree lacks adequate nutrients, water, or sunlight during that critical flower development phase, there will be few flowers blooming the following spring. While it is important to provide adequate water during this time, don't feed heavily—growth won't harden adequately before cold winter weather arrives. An early spring feeding—such as a 6-inch layer of compost or well-rotted manure used as mulch—will ensure that your trees are well nourished during the summer yield and flower-development periods.

Fruit trees always produce more flowers than they can possibly ripen as fruit, and some of the developing fruit drops naturally. Generally there are two periods of fruit drop, one soon after the blooming period, and then another within the month. For many cultivars, bearing a heavy crop of fruit one year will draw nutrients away from the developing flower buds, resulting in a light crop the following year. In extreme cases, the tree will develop a pattern of bearing fruit every other year. You can even out your yield by heavily thinning the fruit in the early summer of the "on" year. (For more information see "Thinning Fruit" on page 293.)

Pruning and Training Fruit Trees

After the sometimes back-breaking work of digging planting holes and setting your trees, you may feel tempted to just lean back and watch them grow. But if your goal is healthy, early-bearing, heavy-yielding fruit trees, plan on pruning and training your trees rather than letting nature take its course.

If you think of your fruit tree as a solar collector, it is easy to see that proper spacing of the branches by training and pruning will allow more leaf surface area to face the sun. The more energy the leaves capture, the more flowers, fruit, and vegetative growth the tree will produce. In fact, sun must shine at least 30 percent of the time on fruiting branches or they won't develop flowers. Furthermore, fruits such as apples and cherries need light to develop proper color, which is why fruit borne on interior branches often isn't as highly colored as fruit on outside limbs. Proper training will encourage earlier fruit bearing.

Proper pruning helps control diseases, too. Fruit and foliage on properly spaced branches dry more quickly after rain or in humid weather, thus reducing the spread of fungal diseases that can ruin the ripening fruit as well as the tree. Thus, pruning and training can eliminate the need for expensive and time-consuming disease control.

Finally, pruning and training keep the tree small enough for easy harvests. Some fruit trees, particularly cherries, can become so large that, without proper care, much of the fruit becomes inaccessible. Fruit trees should be shaped to fit in with the scale of your landscaping.

For young trees, the only pruning tool you may need is a good pair of hand pruners. These cut small branches (up to ½-inch diameter) cleanly. As your tree grows and increases in diameter, you will need lopping shears, which make clean cuts through branches of up to 1¼ inches in diameter, and a pruning saw for larger branches.

It is important to clean your equipment by dipping it in a 10 percent bleach solution once you finish pruning a tree. Dip between cuts when trimming away diseased wood to prevent the spread of disease.

Basic Techniques

The basic principles for pruning fruit trees don't differ much from those that apply to pruning ornamental trees. Proper pruning improves and promotes the health, vigor, productivity, safety, and appearance of a tree—ornamental or fruit. (For an overview of pruning techniques, see "Pruning Trees and Shrubs" on page 346.) However, with fruit trees there are some special concerns that affect pruning and training. Fruit trees must be able to withstand the weight of heavy fruit loads. Maximum exposure to sunlight is important for fruit production and ripening.

Pruning for Strength and Yield

It's important to prune and train fruit trees so they will be able to withstand the often considerable weight of ripening fruit. Many fruit trees have branches that grow almost ver-

PARTS OF A FRUIT TREE

To understand where to prune, you need to know the parts of your fruit tree. The primary scaffold branches arise from the trunk to form the basic framework of the tree. The crotch angle is the angle formed between the primary scaffolds and the trunk. The primary scaffold branches divide into secondary scaffolds. The finer branches of a scaffold are called laterals. Water sprouts, root suckers, crossing branches, and limbs that shade or rub against one another should be pruned away annually, along with diseased and damaged limbs. Also try to remove or train branches with narrow, weak crotch angles.

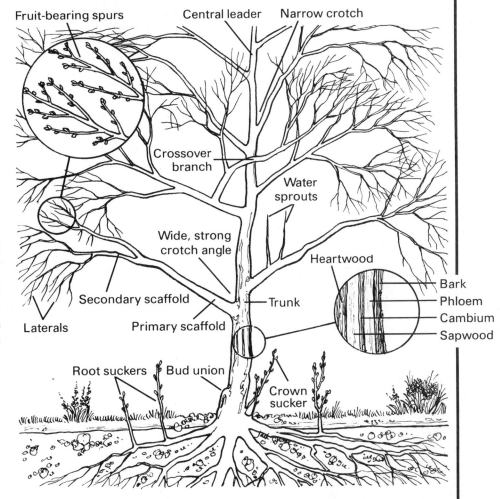

tically up from the trunk, creating narrow crotches or branch angles that are more likely to break when bearing a heavy fruit crop. These branches are also more likely to break during storms. Wide branch angles—45 to 90 degrees—are the strongest, and are the goal of all pruning and training techniques. (See "Parts of a Fruit Tree" above for more on the basic structure of a tree.)

Branch angle also affects fruit yield. Besides having a poor shape for sun-gathering, these narrow-crotched branches will be very slow to bear fruit. Branches growing at a 45- to 60-degree angle will develop more flowers and fruit.

Before you prune, it's important to know how the fruit tree bears its fruit. Many trees bear their flowers on spurs, short stubby branches that grow from the secondary scaffolds. Spurs can bear for as many as 5 to 20 years, as they do in apples, pears, European prunes, Japanese plums, and sweet cherries. Or they may bear only a few years, as in apricots and sour cherries. Try not to break off or remove spurs; the tree will have to develop new ones before fruiting again. Peaches, nectarines, apricots, Japanese plums, European prunes, and sour cherries fruit on lateral buds borne on the previous season's growth. These trees need annual pruning to ensure a constant supply of second-year wood. These plants also need pruning to keep the fruit within reach for picking and not so far out on the branches that it causes them to break under the fruit load.

Types of Cuts

There are two basic types of cuts you can make: thinning cuts and heading cuts. A thinning cut completely removes a branch, allowing sunlight to reach the center of the plant and directing energy toward the remaining branches. You can thin primary scaffold branches, which arise at the trunk, or secondary scaffold branches, which originate on the primary branches. Thinning cuts should be made at the base of the branch, but without removing the branch collar, the thickened area at the base of the branch. (See the illustration on page 278 for the proper way to make a thinning cut.)

Heading cuts are made in the middle of a branch to encourage branching and thicker, fuller growth. Cut just above a bud that points in

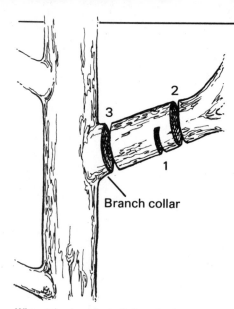

When removing a large limb, make three separate cuts so that the bark isn't stripped away below the limb as the branch is cut: (1) Make a small cut on the underside of the branch, about 6 inches from the base of the branch; (2) cut from the top of the branch until the limb can be removed; (3) once the branch has been removed, make a proper cut from the top of the bark ridge to the bottom, just outside the branch collar.

the direction you want growth to occur. Don't cut straight across the branch; instead, cut at about a 45-degree angle across the branch, sloping away from the bud. The top of the cut should be ½ inch above the top of the bud; the bottom of the cut should be at a point above and on the opposite side of the branch from the base of the bud.

Spreading

Spreading is a training technique that is very helpful for strengthening branches by increasing narrow crotch angles. Spreading is most successful when the branch is young and supple—newly sprouted or no more than one to two years old. One of the easiest methods is to clip a clothespin between the trunk and the limb so the limb is pushed into the proper position. Another method is to cut notches in a lightweight piece of wood and wedge it between the limb and trunk. Hanging a fishing weight on the young limb until it bends to the proper position is also effective. Once the limb has grown and stays naturally in the new position, remove the spreading device.

If you need to spread a limb that is older but still can be easily bent into position, tie fabric loops around the limb and then tie a light rope to each loop. Pound a stake into the ground so that when the rope is tied to the stake, the limb is bent into position. If they can be spared, it is best to remove limbs that can't be bent easily into position.

Seasonal Considerations

A tree's response to pruning depends on the season. Late winter or early spring pruning—while trees are dormant—encourages vigorous growth, because food stored for spring growth will be shared by fewer growing points. Most fruit trees need annual dormant season pruning, though in some cases it will be only to remove any dead or broken branches. It is best to wait until just before spring growth to prune most trees. This makes the tree more resistant to winter injury and eliminates the need to reprune when a late winter storm damages or kills branches. Recent research indicates that peaches, nectarines, and apricots present an exception to this rule:

Pruning them before they have finished flowering leaves them open to canker, which can invade pruning wounds. Prune these trees after they have finished flowering.

Pruning in early or midsummer results in less vigorous growth, because the stored food has already been used up by growing leaves and shoots. This is why trees trained as espaliers are often pruned in summer—to discourage vegetative growth.

Annual Pruning

To maintain healthy and fruitful trees, there are a few basic things to look for each year.

Dead or Broken Branches. The first step in pruning or training is to remove any dead or broken branches. It's easy to pick out a dead branch on a green tree, but when that same tree is dormant, live and dead wood is hard to distinguish. Dead branches are often withered or very dark when compared to living branches. An easy trick to use when dormant pruning is to start at the tip of a branch or year-old shoot, and carefully scrape a small

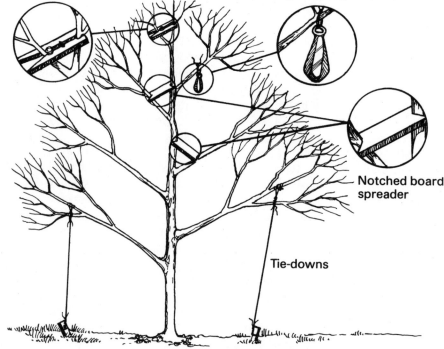

This tree illustrates several different ways to spread the crotch angles of a fruit tree.

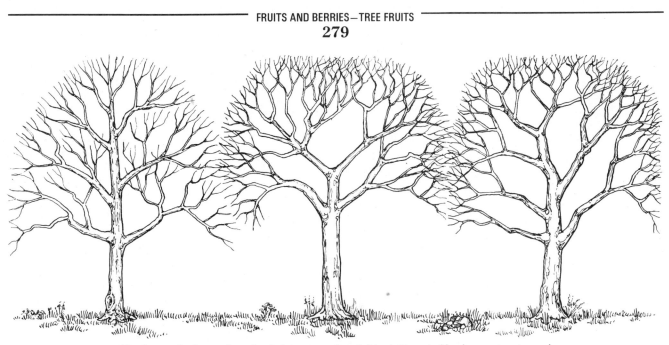

The three major forms of pruning fruit trees are, from left to right, central leader, open center, and modified central leader.

area on the surface of the branch—it should be green just under the thin bark at the tip of the shoot. If it is black, brown, or gray, that part of the branch is dead. Move closer to the trunk or back from the tip, and continue to scrape other small areas until you can determine just where the living tissue begins. Use a thinning cut to remove dead or broken branches.

Rubbing or Crossing Branches. When you prune, look for branches that cross or rub. Crossing branches can restrict sunlight and air circulation in the center of the plant; rubbing damages bark, creating entry points for disease organisms. Also look for branches that are parallel but simply too close together, so that one shades the other. In either case, remove the weaker branch.

Water Sprouts and Suckers. Water sprouts are fast-growing branches that arise on the trunk or branches and grow straight up, producing little, if any, fruit. They often appear at the site of old pruning wounds. Remove them as soon as you notice them, regardless of the time of year.

Suckers are sprouts that arise from the roots of the tree. Remove these as soon as you see them. If you have a grafted tree, the suckers will have the characteristics of the rootstock, not the cultivar you want to grow.

Training and Pruning Styles

Orchardists have developed several ways to train fruit trees, all based on obtaining maximum yield, sun exposure, and ease of care, and determined by the growth habits of the plants.

The ideal sun-gathering shape of a fruit tree is similar to that of a Christmas tree—with evenly spaced scaffold branches arising from around a single trunk. This is the basic shape of a central leader tree, the form most often used for dwarf apples, pears, cherries, plums, and prunes. To a lesser extent, this is also the basic shape of the modified central leader.

Open center trees have three or four main limbs that arise near where the central leader was removed. This form allows good light penetration and is most commonly used for peaches, nectarines, apricots, and standard-sized apple trees. Cherries, plums, and prunes may also be pruned as open center trees.

Whatever method you use, keep in mind that each tree presents its own particular pruning problem. Take time to stand back and examine the tree as you prune. Remember, you can always cut a questionable branch off later, but you can't reattach one cut by mistake!

Pruning a Central Leader Tree

It takes several seasons to properly train a central leader tree, but it's well worth the effort. For the first few years of training, the goals are to encourage vigorous growth and a sturdy branching structure.

First-Year Training. If you're starting with an unbranched whip, as soon as growth starts after planting, select the most vigorous shoot arising near the top of the trunk to serve as the central leader. If there is a trunk stub above this branch, remove it. To keep lower branches from competing with the central leader, prune away the next two shoots below the leader if they are less than 8 inches from the top of the tree. If you're starting with a branched tree, the procedure is the same: Select a central leader, remove the second and third shoot from the top if they are less than 8 inches from the top, if they have narrow crotch angles, or if they are growing vertically and crowding the central leader. Then remove any branches that are less than 20 inches from the ground.

The next objective is to choose scaffold branches that will form the framework of the tree. Often there are only two branches for scaffolds in the first summer after planting—more scaffolds will develop in the next few years. Choose vigorous branches with wide crotch angles that are spaced between 5 and 8 inches apart vertically and radiate evenly around the trunk. No two branches should be directly above one another. Use one of the spreading methods described earlier if the crotch angles are less than 45 degrees. If there are more branches than you need for scaffolds, cut them back to 4 inches from the trunk to encourage fruiting and to direct growth into the selected scaffold limbs. Pinch these branches monthly throughout the growing season, from June through August. (After a few seasons, once the primary scaffolds are bearing well, you can either remove the branches that you pinched or cut them back to a fruiting spur in the middle of the summer.)

Second-Year Training. Start second-year training by making a heading cut on the central leader to about 1½ feet above the highest scaffold branch. This will encourage new scaffold branches to form higher on the tree. Make a final selection for the lower main scaffold branches and spread these limbs so the branch angles are between 45 and 90 degrees. Head back these scaffold branches by pruning off the tips if they grew vigorously the year before; if growth was thin and weak, cut them back severely. Strive for a cone-shaped tree, leaving lower scaffold branches longer than those near the top. This will encourage development of secondary scaffolds and strengthen the primary scaffolds.

When growth starts, select the most vigorous shoot that arises from the tip of the central leader, and

PRUNING AN OPEN CENTER TREE

A mature open center tree has a short trunk with three to four strong, evenly spaced scaffold branches around it. Training starts the first season after planting.

First-Year Training

The first summer, remove any branches that are less than 18 inches from the ground. The branches that grow from the top 2 or 3 buds will have narrow, weak crotch angles; cut them back to 2 or 3 buds. Then select scaffold branches from among the lower branches. Look for branches with wide crotch angles that are spaced 3 to 5 inches apart vertically along the trunk and radiate evenly around it. Don't despair if you don't have any potential scaffold branches, or only have weak-looking ones; they will develop the first summer after the top shoots are pruned away. Use spreading techniques to increase the crotch angles of the scaffold branches you select. The angles should be between 45 and 90 degrees. About a month after pruning, check the tree and cut back any new shoots growing from the top, above the scaffold branches you've selected.

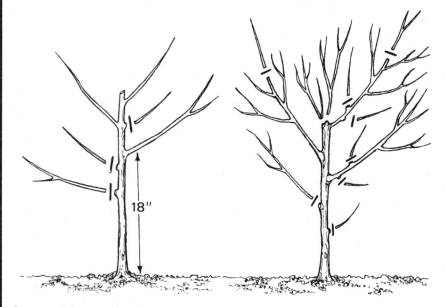

Second-Year Training

The second season, make your final selection of scaffold branches; train a third or fourth scaffold if the tree did not produce enough vigorous growth the previous season. Do this in early spring for most trees; for apricots, peaches, and nectarines, prune after flowering. For the best growth, all scaffold branches should be about equal in size. If one is much larger than the others, cut it back to a lateral branch that is growing toward the outside of the tree. Cut back the shoots that have arisen at the center of the tree—where you removed the central leader last season—to short stubs above the highest scaffold branch. These will sprout again and help keep the scaffold branches growing outward rather than vertically. Use spacing techniques to further widen the crotch angles, if necessary. Thin out lateral branches growing from the scaffolds within 6 inches of the trunk, along with any branches that arise from the trunk itself. This will open up the center of the tree and encourage growth at the tips. Remove any laterals on scaffolds that cross or touch one another, along with diseased or damaged wood. During the growing season, you'll need to head back the center shoots to 3 to 5 inches so that growth continues to be directed to the side scaffolds.

Third-Year Training

By the third year, the basic scaffold arrangement should be well established. Remove completely shoots growing from the center stubs, as the scaffold branches should have attained their permanent shape. Be sure to cut away diseased branches as well as any that cross or crowd the center of the plant.

Maintenance Pruning

The branches of peaches, nectarines, apricots, European prunes, and Japanese plums need annual heading to encourage lateral bud growth and, thus, fruit production. For apricots, use heading cuts to prune away half the length of half the new growth. For peaches and nectarines, cut back all of the previous year's growth to half its length. For plums and prunes, use both thinning and heading cuts to remove approximately one-third of the previous year's growth. Head back the new growth of sour cherries by 1 to 2 inches in June to encourage the growth of lateral leaf buds that will help the tree become more vigorous. Continue to remove crossing or diseased limbs, water sprouts, and suckers.

remove the second and third shoots that arise below it to ensure that it won't have to compete with other branches. Choose additional primary scaffold branches, using spreading techniques as needed. Head back any extra branches not needed for scaffolds to 4 inches as in the first growing season. Remove any suckers or water sprouts during the summer months. Continue pinching the small branches you pinched throughout last season.

Third-Year Training. Follow the directions for second-year training both early in the season and after growth starts. Remove any crossed or touching limbs. Continue spreading the scaffold branches—use the fabric tie-down method to spread these branches to a proper angle. Once growth begins, remove any water sprouts or suckers. If fruit is being borne on the leader, remove it if the leader begins to droop or stake to keep the central leader upright.

Maintenance Pruning. The fourth year, and every year thereafter, you'll need to prune to maintain the shape of the tree. A mature tree should have six to eight main scaffold branches. After the tree has reached its mature height, prune the central leader and the main scaffold branches back to weak lateral branches. Be sure to retain the cone shape of the tree, with lower scaffolds longer than higher ones.

Scaffolds that have fruited for several years will often droop downward because of the weight of the fruit. Don't remove all of these or you will reduce fruit production near the bottom of the tree. Drooping branches that have fruited for three or four years can be cut back to a side branch that points toward the outside of the tree.

Continue with standard annual pruning. Remove water sprouts and suckers, along with broken, diseased, or crossing branches.

Pruning a Modified Central Leader Tree

The modified central leader tree closely resembles one trained in the central leader style, and, in fact, for the first few years the training is exactly the same. After four or five main scaffold branches have been selected and trained, cut the central leader to just above the highest scaffold branch. This will open the center of the plant to sunlight. Cherries, plums, prunes, and some vigorous cultivars of apples and pears are often trained as modified central leaders.

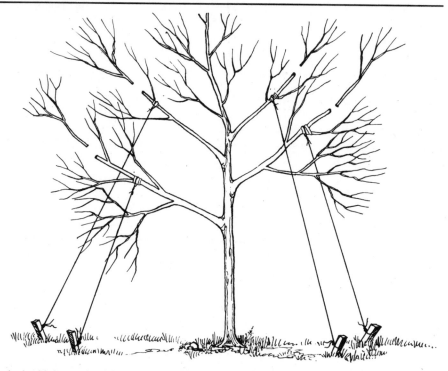

In the third year of training a central leader tree, head back the central leader and the scaffold branches, making sure that the upper branches are shorter than the lower ones. Continue spreading the scaffolds to ensure wide crotch angles.

Espalier

Having a small yard should not stop you from harvesting an orchard's worth of fruit. Dwarf fruit trees and decorative espalier training can greatly increase your yard's potential for fruit production. Espaliered trees, trained to grow flat rather than three-dimensionally, can be grown upon a trellis in shapes as simple as a single, nearly unbranched trunk with fruiting spurs along its length or as complex as a criss-crossing Belgian fence. Whatever the shape, this system of training and pruning has many advantages. Individual trees can be spaced 1½ to 2 feet apart when grown as a single cordon, or branch, making it easy to find room for a wealth of cultivars.

Why Grow Espaliered Trees?

Espaliered trees have much to offer the home gardener. Although they are small, their yield per space is quite high. An apple tree trained to a single branch, called a cordon, that is 6 to 7 feet tall can bear from 4 to 8 pounds of fruit. Peaches, nectarines, apricots, plums, and cherries trained in the shape of a 7-foot-tall fan and spaced 12 to 20 feet apart can each bear 12 to 30 pounds of fruit. Since the plants don't require as much space as conventionally grown trees, you'll have room for more cultivars. By selecting both early- and late-ripening ones, you can spread your harvests over a long season and grow just the right amount of fruit for your use. Espaliered trees begin to bear earlier than standard trees—within the third to fourth year from planting. The fruit colors and ripens well because it receives plenty of sunlight. Pruning, picking, and pest control are easy because everything is within view and reach. In cooler climates, espalier training can permit the growth of marginally hardy cultivars if the trees are planted next to a south-facing wall to take advantage of reflected heat.

While espalier training has many advantages, it takes more time and dedication to erect a sturdy trellis and carefully train and prune to achieve and maintain these tree shapes. As with most garden choices, perhaps the saying "Know thyself" is the best when determining whether this method is for you. For those of you who don't want to train trees into this shape, some nurseries offer pre-trained trees so all you need do is maintain the shape after planting.

Getting Started

While you can put espalier fruit trees anywhere you can place a trellis, there are some places that especially lend themselves to decorative trees. Driveway edges, borders of vegetable or flower gardens, and the outer edges of decks are good locations for espalier fruit trees. For instance, you might want to screen in your deck or patio area with artful panels of apples or pears grown in the latticed pattern of a Belgian fence. Espalier fruit trees also can be trained directly to a wall or fence, without a trellis. However,

The interwoven branches of Belgian fence espaliers are attractive and relatively easy to maintain.

remember that it will be almost impossible to do any maintenance on the wall once the espalier tree is growing up against it. So, do not place espaliers against wood siding, wooden door frames or windows, or a fence that will require painting. If you still would like to take advantage of reflected heat but need to maintain a wooden wall, place the trellis at least 2 feet from the wall for easy maintenance access. In climates where daytime temperatures often exceed 90°F, trees should be planted away from any walls on a free-standing trellis so that trees and fruit will not be burned by excess heat reflected from walls.

Trellis Guidelines

You can support espaliers on pipe or wooden posts strung with horizontal, vertical, or diagonal strands of heavy 14-gauge wire. (For tips on sturdy trellis construction see "Making a Rock-Steady Trellis" on page 286.) If your area has high winds, you might want to use plastic-covered wires so that the branches aren't injured as they rub up against the wire. Space wires 15 to 24 inches apart, with the first wire about 15 inches above ground level. On fences or walls, the highest wire should be at least 6 inches below the top of the structure for best appearance. If you choose to grow against a wall, fasten the branches to a system of wires that is spaced 2 to 4 inches from the wall.

Choosing Trees for Espalier Training

For best results, start with fruits that bear on long-lived short spurs, such as apples and pears. These can be trained relatively easily to many different shapes. Trees that bear mainly on lateral branches (one-year-old wood) or short-lived spurs, such as peaches, nectarines, apricots, plums, and cherries, are more difficult and less adaptable. In order to maintain fruit yield, you need to prune these plants to provide a constant source of new wood.

Choose trees with dwarfing rootstocks so that the shape of the tree will be easier to maintain. (For apples, trees grafted on M9 or M26 rootstocks work well on loam soil while more vigorous MM106 rootstock should be used on heavy or sandy soils. Pears should be grafted on Quince A or Quince C rootstocks.) Choose unbranched young trees for easiest training.

Espalier Shapes for Best Yields

The best shapes will be determined in a large part by the fruiting habit of the plants you are growing. For apples and pears, one of the easiest and highest yielding shapes is a simple cordon, simply an unbranched tree with fruiting spurs along its length that is either grown vertically or leaning at an angle. This style allows you to grow the most cultivars, and thus the widest variety of fruit, because the trees can be planted as little as 2 feet apart. Pears bear best when trained as a vertical cordon; apples, at an angle. Belgian fence is a form that uses branches growing on the diagonal and is suitable for apples

and pears. In this form, each tree has a short trunk with two branches spread at 45 degrees in a V shape. Branches of neighboring trees are woven together to form a decorative panel.

Another way to shape apples and pears is to plant a single tree and train multiple vertical arms from the trunk, making the double-U form.

Trees trained with horizontal cordons have branches growing horizontally along a trellis. These are more difficult to maintain because they work against the plant's natural tendency to grow upward. Trees trained in this manner can have two horizontal cordons or several pairs of cordons. This form offers the advantage of more fruit production in a vertical space. Depending on the length of the horizontal cordons, space these trees 8 to 20 feet apart.

Cherries, peaches, nectarines, apricots, and plums grow best when trained in a fan shape, with permanent branches radiating from the top of a short trunk. This shape allows them the extra space they need for their fruiting wood. Space trees 12 to 20 feet apart.

Pruning and Training Espaliers

Once you've selected a site, decided what trees you want to grow, and how you want to train them, it's time to plant and begin training. Plant trees just as you would any dwarf fruit tree. (See "Planting Fruit Trees" on page 267 for directions.)

Fruit trees trained with horizontal cordons, or branches, make attractive fences. They are more difficult to maintain than other espaliered styles.

TRAINING
A HORIZONTAL CORDON

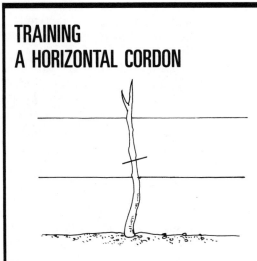

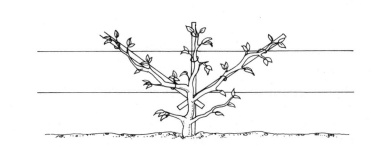

It takes at least two growing seasons to establish the basic framework for a tree trained with horizontal cordons—more, if you want several pairs of branches. With the following instructions—and a little patience—you'll be well on your way to success.

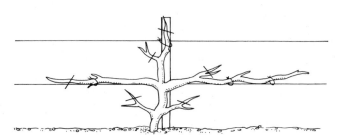

1. After planting, cut the tree back to a bud just above the lowest trellis wire. Be sure there are 3 healthy buds remaining near the top. Let the top 3 buds that sprout grow.

2. During the first summer, tie the two side shoots to two bamboo canes placed at 45 degrees. Tie the middle shoot to a third, vertical bamboo cane.

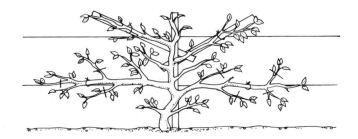

3. During the first dormant season, lower and tie the two side arms to the first horizontal wire.

4. To make the next tier of horizontal cordons, cut the center shoot back to the second wire, leaving 3 vigorous buds that will form the second tier.

5. Train the second tier the same as the first tier. In the years that follow, you can continue training until you have as many tiers as you desire.

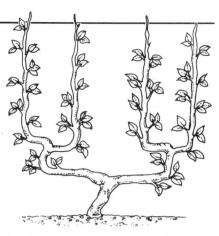

Espaliers trained in the double-U style have two pairs of vertical cordons with fruiting spurs along their lengths.

Training Basics

All of the espalier styles require slightly different training, but there are some basic techniques that apply. During early training, lash bamboo canes to the trellis wires in the direction you want a branch to grow. Then train the tips of the fruit branches to the canes. This encourages growth that is ruler-straight and precisely spaced, which is especially important for the more complex designs such as the Belgian fence. Use twine, rawhide, plant ties, cloth strips, or any material that will not constrict the branches when tying them to the trellis. As you train to establish the plant's basic framework, do not simply remove all unwanted lateral branches; treat them as described under "Controlling Growth and Increasing Yields" below, to encourage them to become fruiting spurs.

Basic directions for training several popular styles of espalier are described below. (See "Training a Horizontal Cordon" on the opposite page for step-by-step instructions for making that style of espalier.) Whatever shape you are making, do not let the tree fruit until training is finished, so that all the tree's resources are concentrated on fast vegetative growth. If the tree blooms, remove the fruit right after the blossoms fall.

Cordons. To train trees as simple, unbranched cordons that are vertical or diagonal, simply tie a bamboo cane to the horizontal wires of the trellis and then tie the stem of each tree to the cane. After the tree has grown to the top of the trellis, cut it above a bud at the desired height.

U or Double U. Although it takes a couple of growing seasons to train an espalier in a U or double-U shape, these are both attractive styles that are relatively easy to maintain. Once growth starts the first spring, cut the tree back to a bud just above the wire that will support the bottom of the U. Select the two best of the shoots that sprout, and train them to bamboo

canes set at a 45-degree angle from the main stem. As the season progresses, lower and tie the two side arms to the first horizontal wire so they form a 90-degree crotch angle. Once they have grown long enough to form the bottom of the U, allow the tips of the stems to turn upward and train them to the top of the wire.

To form a double U, train as above and then clip each side shoot just above a trellis wire. Use bamboo canes to train two more side shoots into U shapes.

Belgian Fence and Fan. The Belgian fence and fan-shaped espalier forms are similar in design. Cut the tree back to the height of the lowest wire. For the Belgian fence design, train the top two shoots to grow in opposite directions, using bamboo cane lashed at 45 degrees to the trellis wires. As the shoots grow and intersect, the branches are woven together to form a lattice design. For the fan design, allow three to seven branches to grow from the top of the trunk and train them into a fan pattern.

Controlling Growth and Increasing Yields

Once you have the basic framework established, you'll want to begin managing the tree's growth to keep it under control and maximize fruit yields. Although conventionally grown fruit trees are pruned heavily in early spring, the best way to prune espalier-trained fruit trees is to pinch or rub off unwanted growth throughout the summer as it appears. For example, buds that will produce an unwanted or misdirected branch should be rubbed off in the early spring. If the bud opens, pinch off the growth, taking care not to damage the bark. In late summer, when shoots are longer than 9 inches and the bark is starting to turn from green to brown at the base, trim the shoot back to three leaves beyond where growth began in the spring. (There will be a rosette of smaller leaves around a circular fold in the stem where growth began in the spring.) This will encourage the

development of fruit spurs at the base of the branch in the next growing season.

To encourage fruit spur formation, cut weak, year-old laterals to 4 or 5 buds during midsummer. The top buds will grow into vegetative shoots while the bottom buds are most likely to become fat fruit buds. During the next spring, before growth begins, remove the vegetative shoots, leaving only the fruit buds. When vigorous side shoots branch off the end of the cordon, control growth by bending and tying the branch into a horizontal position. If you can do this early in the season, within the first month or so of growth, fruit buds will form along the branch. Before growth begins in the next spring, cut the branch back to a fruit bud to remove the vegetative growing points and make a fruitful spur. If fruiting spurs occur unevenly along the cordon, you can often turn a dormant bud into a fruit spur by making a shallow notch $\frac{1}{8}$-inch wide and $\frac{1}{16}$-inch deep just below the bud, as soon as the tree begins to leaf out. If you place the notch above the bud, it will often turn into a vegetative branch. To prevent more vertical growth, use one of these spur-forming techniques to turn the top bud of your espalier into a fruitful spur.

On older apple and pear espalier plantings, the fruit spurs become very branched and thick with fruit buds. Thin out some of the buds so that there is space between them. For the best fruit quality, thin to one fruit per flower cluster.

Making a Rock-Steady Trellis

This trellis design provides a simple alternative to space-hungry braces and guy wires used to anchor most trellises—instead, a pair of subterranean "wings" make it rock-steady. Select the length of your lumber—6, 8, 10, or 12 feet—depending on the height of your trellis.

1. Attach one trellis wing to the bottom of the trellis post about 16 inches from the base of the post. Drive the nails in at an angle for extra strength. Repeat for the other post.

2. Attach another wing to the opposite side of the post about 4 inches from the base of the post. Drive the nails in at an angle for extra strength. Repeat for the other post.

3. Dig a 2-foot-deep, 4-foot-long trench. If there are rocks, you may need to use a pickax and metal lever bar to remove them.

4. Place one trellis post in the trench with the top wing facing inward, toward the direction of pull.

5. Backfill, tamping the soil around the post firmly. If the soil is too sandy to hold the posts securely, include rocks and stones with the backfill soil.

6. Repeat steps 3, 4, and 5 for the other post, and string the trellis with wire.

TOOLS REQUIRED

Hand or circular saw
Hammer
Shovel
Pickax and metal lever bar (if your soil is rocky)

MATERIALS

2 pcs. 4 × 4″ pressure-treated lumber (posts)
4 pcs. 1 × 4 × 4′ pressure-treated lumber (wings)
16 pcs. 3″ galvanized nails
Heavy-gauge wire

The two subterranean wings, one nailed to either side of the post, increase the below-ground surface area and provide resistance when the posts are wired together.

Dig a trench that is wide enough and deep enough to bury both wings.

Once the trench is deep enough, set the posts by backfilling and tamping the soil down firmly. In sandy soil, use rocks and stones with the backfill to increase stability.

Grafting Fruit Trees

Grafting is a technique used to join parts of two or more plants and cause them to grow together into a single plant. This may seem like a specialty with little relevance to home gardening, but grafting is much more common than one might think. In fact, most fruit trees sold today are grafted. In addition, grapes, modern roses, and many specialty trees and shrubs are also grafted.

Most dwarf and semidwarf fruit trees are a product of grafting. They are composed of a fruiting cultivar grafted onto a rootstock that affects growth rate and size at maturity. Grafting can also be used to add a pollinator to a tree that requires pollen from another cultivar in order to set fruit. In a technique called topworking, grafting can be used to change the fruit cultivars growing on an established tree or to add fruit cultivars to a tree. (A tree can be topworked with one or several cultivars.) This technique also can be used to save a tree whose branches or top have been damaged by disease or weather.

Grafting Basics

All grafted trees consist of a stock and a scion. The stock is the plant that provides the best root system for the tree. The scion is the cultivar you've chosen for its good fruiting characteristics. In some cases, a third piece is added—the interstem—if the stock and scion aren't compatible and won't graft well with each other. The interstem is compatible with both, and is grafted between them.

The actual process of grafting involves pressing the cambium—the actively growing tissue of the stem located in a thin layer just under the bark—of the stock and the scion against one another so they grow together. There are several types of grafts, but for any of them to be successful, the cambium of stock and scion must be lined up as close together as possible. Cuts on both should be clean and fresh. After positioning stock and scion, they must be held immobile so the cambium will have a chance to join. It's important to seal any cut ends with grafting wax to make sure the tissue doesn't dry out.

Most grafting is done with cultivars of a single fruit type—grafting one or more apples onto one tree, for example. Surprisingly, different fruit tree species also can be grafted on the same plant. In this case, the compatibility of the tissues from the different stocks and scions is important; incompatible plants will fail to graft together, or they will form a weak graft that breaks easily under stress. As a general rule, nearly all grafts within a single species will be successful. Many grafts within a single genus are also successful. Plums, apricots, nectarines, and peaches all belong to the genus *Prunus*. Some potential combinations among these plants include: plums grafted onto an apricot rootstock or tree; apricots grafted onto peach rootstock; nectarines or Japanese plums grafted onto European plum stock; and apricots and nectarines grafted onto Japanese plum stock. Citrus fruits can be grafted in a similar manner, with grapefruits, lemons, and oranges grafted onto an orange rootstock. When grafting apples, use cultivars with similar growth rates, because a slow-growing cultivar won't graft well with a fast-growing one.

Obtaining Scions

Whether you are planning on topworking an existing tree or are planning to graft onto a seedling that appeared in your yard, the first step is to find scion wood of a cultivar you'd like to grow. Scion wood, the fruiting cultivar, is gathered when the tree is dormant—either in the fall or before buds swell in the spring. You can cut scions from a neighbor's tree or ask a nearby orchardist for them. However, be aware that many new fruit cultivars are Plant Variety Protected (PVP), and it is illegal to propagate them or use portions of them to graft other trees. Some mail-order nurseries offer scion wood.

Scions should be cut from narrow (about pencil width), straight wood produced in the last year. Cut the scions into 6- to 12-inch-long pieces, each with 3 or 4 leaf buds. Always cut above a bud. As you gather and cut scions, bear in mind that when you graft you'll need to align the bottom of the scion with the top of the stock; the scions will die if they are inserted upside down into the stock. An easy way to keep track of which end is which is to make a slanting cut on the bottom, a straight cut on top. Tie the scion pieces in a bundle, put them in a plastic bag with moist peat or sawdust, and store them in a refrigerator.

Types of Grafts

The grafting method you use will depend upon the size of the stock. Whip and tongue grafting is generally used to graft small pieces of wood, while cleft grafting is used for 1- to 2-inch diameter stock. Bark grafting is used when the stock is 4 or more inches in diameter. If you can, always make more grafts than necessary, so there is a better chance that some will be successful.

Whip and Tongue. Whip and tongue grafting is one method used to produce commercial fruit trees and to graft pollinator branches or add cultivars to a young tree. It is usually done in early spring while the plant is still dormant and is used to join stock and scion that are nearly the same diameter, generally less than ¾-inch diameter. Whip and tongue grafting is often called tongue grafting or whip grafting.

Cut the stock back to within a few inches of the ground if you are grafting to a planted rootstock cultivar; cut back a young branch close to the trunk if you are topworking a

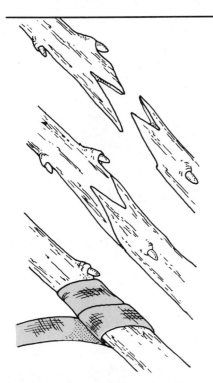

Whip and tongue grafting is used to join stocks and scions that are small and about the same diameter. Join the cuts, and then wrap them with a strip of rubber to hold them in position.

small tree. For the best results, the stock and scion need to be as close in diameter as possible.

Using a sharp grafting knife, make complementary long, diagonal cuts on the top of the stock and the bottom of the scion. The cut surface should be about 1½ inches long on both stock and scion. Make a second cut on each piece parallel to the first, about an inch below it, downward to the center of the stem. This forms the tongue-shaped piece on both parts. When the two pieces are fitted together, they form a tongue and groove joint. Line up the cambiums and wrap securely with a strip of rubber band, latex nursery tape, or plastic electricians' tape. If the two pieces aren't exactly the same diameter, don't just center one piece inside the other—line up the cambiums on at least one side of the graft. (Matching diameters with both sides lined up are preferable.) Cover all the cut surfaces with grafting wax or asphalt emulsion sealing compound. Once the scion begins to grow, remove the wrapping.

Cleft. Cleft grafting is a useful technique for topworking established fruit trees. You can cleft graft a new fruit

cultivar onto a tree that has a damaged top or is not producing well, or add extra cultivars to the tree.

Cleft grafting should be done late in the dormant season, before the buds open. In this method, two pencil-width scions are inserted in a cleft made in a fairly upright young branch.

The ends of the short scions should be cut just above a bud and have 2 to 3 buds per piece. Shave the base of each scion so that it is wedge-shaped. The edge that is on the inside of the cleft should be narrower than the edge on the outside. There should be bark on both the narrow inside edge and the wider outside edge. The end of the scion should be blunt, not tapered to a sharp point.

The limb to be grafted, called the stock, should be between 1 and 2 inches in diameter. Cut the stock straight across with a fine-toothed saw for a smooth, even surface. Then use a hammer and chisel to split the center down 4 to 6 inches to form a cleft in the trunk or branch. The depth of the cleft will be determined by the diameter of the scion, which must fit tightly in the cleft. Using a screwdriver to keep the cleft open, insert the scion so that the side with the wider piece of bark is toward the

Scions used in cleft grafting should be cut with a wedge-shaped base and should fit tightly into the stock branch.

outside of the branch. For the graft to form, you'll need to align the cambiums by pushing the scion toward the center of the cleft slightly so that the tissue just under the bark of the stock is pressing against the same tissue of the scion. Remove the screwdriver once the scion has been aligned. Wax the area and the tips of the scions as soon as the fitting is done. Wait until the following spring to cut off the weaker graft if both take.

Bark. For larger branches, bark grafting is the best technique. This can only be done in the spring, when the bark "slips," or peels easily away

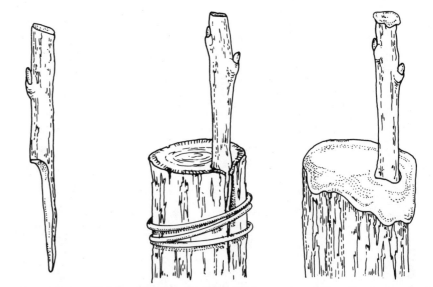

Scions for bark grafting should be cut with a long, slanting cut on one side and a short one on the other, to form a wedge-shaped point. Cut through the bark and slip it away from the cambium. Then insert the scion under the flaps, fasten in place, and wax.

from the rest of the tree. Prepare three narrow scions (more if the stock or trunk is very large) about 5 inches long. Make a 2-inch downward diagonal cut on one side of the bottom of the scion and then a slightly smaller cut on the other side, making a very thin wedge. To prepare the stock, cut away the branch to be grafted—if you're replacing a broken or diseased branch cut back to healthy wood—by making a straight cut across the wood as you would for a cleft graft. Then, starting at the top of the stock, make a 2-inch slit in the bark. The bark should slip easily away, leaving the cambium exposed. Place the scion under the bark of the stock, with the longer cut side of the scion facing the inside, against the cambium. Use a small finishing nail to fix the bark and scion in place, then wax the area and the tips of the scions to keep them from drying out.

BUDDING FRUIT TREES

Budding is a slightly different form of grafting that can be used to change or add fruit cultivars to a tree. In this case, all you need from the scion branch is a bud. The easiest technique is T-budding. Unlike grafting, T-budding is done in mid- to late summer, after the buds for next year have formed and become dormant but while the tree's bark still slips.

1. Cut a 1-foot scion from a newly grown branch. Remove the leaves, leaving the petioles (stems holding the leaf to the branch). If you can't bud right away, wrap the budstick in plastic and keep it cool. Refrigerate in a glass of water if left overnight.

2. Choose a stock branch or trunk that is pencil-sized, and make a T-shaped cut just through the bark. Using the rounded top of a budding knife (or another blunt, rounded edge such as a fingernail), gently lift the flaps of the cut, which should slip away, exposing the cambium.

3. Select a healthy bud from the middle of your budstick and make a shallow cut ½ to ¾ inch below the bud and end ½ inch above it. Slide the knife out. To release the bud, make a perpendicular cut down into the wood ½ inch above the bud. The bud is now free and looks like a little shield.

4. With the bud pointing upward just as it was on the scion, slide the shield—cut side against the wood—into the flaps of the T-cut until it is covered.

5. Press the bark over the sides of the shield and then carefully wrap the area with a strip of rubber band, leaving the bud uncovered. Rub off any buds on the stock that may compete with the grafted bud.

6. When the bud you've selected begins to grow, remove the rubber band. The following spring, after the graft has grown 2 to 3 inches, cut the stock branch above the bud, making a slanting cut back away from the bud. This will encourage bud growth. In the South, this can be done in the same growing season as budding because bud growth will start so quickly.

Controlling Pests and Diseases

Nothing will dampen your gardening enthusiasm more than the unhappy discovery that your carefully tended trees have been damaged by pests or disease, reducing yield and possibly leaving the fruit inedible. There are steps you can take to avoid this scenario without resorting to the use of poison sprays. In considering your options for fighting pests and disease, remember to weigh your effort, expense, and any possible environmental damage against the amount of harm your trees will suffer. Some insects and diseases cause mainly cosmetic damage to trees or fruits, while others can completely kill your trees.

Listed below are some general guidelines for controlling fruit tree pests and diseases without resorting to harmful pesticides. For tips on controlling the eight worst pests of fruit trees, see "Foiling Common Fruit Tree Pests". For help with other problems you find on and in your trees, consult your local nursery owner or cooperative extension agent, or see "Recommended Reading" on page 406.

Watchfulness Pays. Don't forget about your trees between planting or pruning and harvest time. Check them frequently for signs of insect or disease infestation. Telltale clues include: holes in leaves; wilting; shiny coatings on leaves; holes or cuts in fruit; yellowing or brownish areas on leaves; premature defoliation; rotten spots on leaves or fruit; distorted growth; and blistering or rupturing of bark. Pheromone or sticky traps are useful for giving early warning of the arrivals of some species of harmful insects.

Know Your Enemy. Once you identify a specific problem, learn about the life cycle of the pest involved. Many trap and barrier control measures are linked to stopping a pest at a particular point in its life cycle. For

FOILING COMMON FRUIT TREE PESTS

Apple Maggots

These pesky insects are the larvae of flies that lay eggs on fruits throughout the growing season. The larvae burrow throughout the flesh, ruining the fruit. Fortunately, it's easy to catch and kill the flies by hanging red spheres coated with an adhesive substance like Tanglefoot from the branches. The flies land on the decoys, get stuck, and die. Hang the spheres with 9 to 18 inches of open space around them. Use one trap for every 100 or so apples you expect the tree to bear.

Apple maggot

Cankerworms

Also known as inchworms, cankerworms skeletonize the leaves of apple, apricot, and other fruit trees, weakening the tree so that little fruit matures and the tree sometimes dies. Wrap heavy paper or cotton batting around tree trunks and coat it with a sticky adhesive to stop females from climbing into the tree to lay eggs. Bt (*Bacillus thuringiensis*) sprays are effective against the larvae. Tilling the soil around your trees in the fall may unearth pupae, exposing them to predators.

Codling Moths

Apple codling moth larvae, which burrow into apple, apricot, peach and pear fruit, can be controlled by spraying Bt (*Bacillus thuringiensis*) just as eggs are hatching. Spherical red sticky traps and oil sprays also help in controlling this pest. Woodpeckers will eat eggs hidden in tree bark. Attract the birds to your trees in the winter by hanging a block of suet on the trunk.

Gypsy Moths

Young gypsy moth larvae, which feed on the foliage of many fruit trees, can be controlled with Bt (*Bacillus thuringiensis*) sprays. Also trap larvae with sticky bands on tree trunks, or foot-wide burlap strips tied around the trunks, with several inches draped over the string. Older larvae feed at night and hide during the day. They will nestle under the burlap, and in the late afternoon, they can be collected and destroyed (wear gloves, as touching the larvae can cause an allergic reaction).

Leafrollers

Fruit tree leafrollers are larvae that spin webs between leaves and fruits, forming a sheltered spot where they can feed on the fruits. They will attack most fruit trees including citrus. Pheromone traps will help monitor if leafrollers are entering your area. Bt (*Bacillus thuringiensis*) or rotenone sprays provide control.

Peachtree Borers

The larvae of these pests tunnel into the trunks of apricot, cherry, peach, and plum trees, weakening and possibly killing the trees. Kill the larvae in the holes they have made by inserting a wire and jabbing it around to spear the pests. Alternatively, spraying Bt (*Bacillus thuringiensis*) into the holes will work, as long as the spray directly contacts the larvae. Borers also can be blocked from entering the tree by encircling the trunk with a piece of tin. Force it down below the surface of the ground, leaving about 2 inches between the tin and trunk. Fill the space with tobacco in late spring to make a barrier against the adult moths, which try to lay eggs near the tree base in late summer and early fall.

Pear Psylla

If your pear trees appear to be covered with soot, they have probably been attacked by pear psylla. These tiny insects secrete a sweet, sticky substance. The soot is actually a fungus that grows in the secretions. Stop pear psylla before it creates a problem by spraying with dormant oil in spring. During the growing season, psylla can be controlled by dusting dwarf trees with diatomaceous earth or ground limestone or by spraying with insecticidal soap.

Plum Curculios

These pests lay their eggs in fruits of most common backyard fruit trees, cutting out crescent-shaped holes and damaging the skin. They can be trapped by taking advantage of their natural tendency to play dead when threatened. As soon as you notice damaged fruit on a tree, spread a white dropcloth under the tree and shake the tree or limbs. The insects will drop from the branches, immobile, and you can collect and destroy them.

Plum curculio

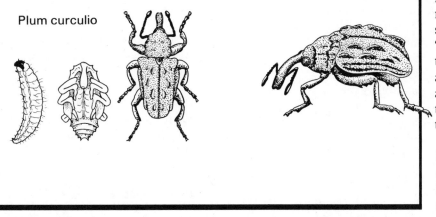

example, cankerworms, which skeletonize leaves, can be combated by tying a band of sticky material around tree trunks in fall and again in February to catch wingless adult females which would climb the trunk to lay eggs in the trees.

Encourage Pest Predators. Birds eat enormous numbers of insects and insect eggs hidden under tree bark. Encourage them to visit your yard by providing birdhouses, feeders, and birdbaths. Parasitic wasps and other beneficial insects also help control many fruit tree pests.

Harvest Thoroughly. At harvest time, remove all fruit on the tree and on the ground. Windfalls or damaged fruit left on the tree are prime targets for infestation by insects or disease. Promptly prune away any branches that show signs of disease. Burn diseased fruit and prunings.

Prune Carefully. Careless pruning can leave stubs or injured wood where diseases can get a foothold. Good pruning keeps the tree open to light and air, discouraging the many disease organisms that thrive in a wet, humid environment. Disinfect pruning tools with bleach between each cut whenever you are working on potentially diseased trees.

Plant Resistant Cultivars. This is one of the most promising ways to minimize disease problems without sprays. For example, 'Madison' and 'Harbelle' peaches and 'Mericrest' nectarine are resistant to cytospora canker, and there are many scab-resistant apple cultivars available. 'Liberty' is the most disease-resistant apple cultivar produced thus far.

Use Horticultural Oil. Oil sprays coat insects on your trees, killing them by suffocation, and break down quickly in the environment. In the past, heavier grade oils, called dormant oils, were the only option available. These should only be sprayed in winter or early spring when trees are leafless. Dormant oil also smothers insect eggs hidden in bark. The new, lighter viscosity oils, called superior oils, can be sprayed during the growing season if environmental conditions are right. These sprays will suffocate spider mites and other soft-bodied sucking insects.

Be a Good Housekeeper. Bacterial or fungal spores and dormant insects can overwinter in leaf litter under fruit trees. Clean up any plant debris around your trees. Cultivating the top inch or two of soil will expose pupae of some insects to weather and predators.

Try Interplanting. As in your vegetable garden, planting different species of trees near one another may have beneficial effects. Cherry trees may form a kind of natural barrier to prevent apple codling moths from finding all your apple trees. And a mixed planting, being more diverse, may attract more birds and beneficial insects.

Spray When Critical. If faced with the choice between spraying or losing your crop or trees, remember that Bt (*Bacillus thuringensis*) and botanical poisons are effective against many tree pests. Botanical poisons like rotenone and pyrethrum can kill honeybees—so be extra careful if spraying at bloom time. Lime sulfur, copper and bordeaux mixture are effective against many tree diseases and are considered low in environmental toxicity.

Making Apple Cider

What better way to celebrate your abundant harvest than by making fresh apple cider? It's an easy process that can be done with simple household appliances or hand tools —or if you have one, an old-fashioned apple cider press.

Apples needn't be picture-perfect to yield great tasting cider. You can use your windfalls if you pick them up promptly and store them in a cool area. Surface-blemished apples such as those with scab or hail marks are fine to use, too. Don't use any apples or parts of apples that have spoiled or have brown decay. Use only ripe apples, as green or underripe fruit produces flat-tasting cider. As with many juices, the best ciders are made from a mix of sweet, tart, and aromatic apples. If you grow only one cultivar of apple, you might want to trade some apples with another gardener whose varieties complement your own. Tart apple varieties include 'Winesap', 'MacIntosh', 'Jonathan', 'Northern Spy', and 'Wealthy', while sweet apples include 'Red Delicious', 'Golden Delicious', 'Gala', 'Cortland', 'Rome', and 'King'.

Juicing Apples

Though yields will vary between different cultivars, a bushel of apples generally will make about 3 gallons of cider. Keep in mind that fresh cider only lasts in the refrigerator for a few days. However, making hard cider and freezing fresh cider are good ways to preserve this delightful beverage.

The first step in cider-making is crushing the apples. Core the apples and crush or chop them into small pieces in a food chopper, blender, or food processor. Put the crushed apples into a clean muslin sack—an old, clean pillowcase will do—and squeeze out as much juice as possible. Pour the juice into clean glass jugs or bottles and refrigerate, or just drink right away.

If you have a cider press, its hand- or electric-powered cutting cylinder makes it easy to mince up the apples. Keep your hands and fingers away from the rotating blades. Use a large tub to hold the pulp, a smaller one to catch juice runoff, and a clean muslin sack or cheesecloth for pressing the juice out of the pulp. Once the apples are crushed, fill the muslin sack with enough pulp to fill the press. Crank the press handle until juice no longer runs. Repeat the process with the rest of the pulp. For a clearer cider, try pouring it through a paper filter such as a coffee filter. Many cider presses are designed so that apple pieces are fed into the crusher or mincer, pass through it, and fall into the cloth-lined frame, ready for pressing.

Settling and Racking-Off Cider

If you prefer a cider with a slight bite to the flavor, let it stand at room temperature for three or four days before drinking. Fill clean glass jars or clear or light-colored plastic containers to just below the brim and stopper with a cotton plug (not a regular lid or cap). The plug will pop out if fermentation causes a buildup in pressure. After the cider has settled, sediment will begin to cover the bottom of the container. To "rack-off" the cider, put one end of a rubber tube (about 3 feet in length) in the cider and suck on the other end as you would with a soda straw. As soon as you feel liquid in your mouth, pinch off this end with your fingers and put the tube into an empty container that is lower than the filled one. You've created a siphon that will draw off the clear cider. Stop the process before the sediment at the bottom of the container is disturbed.

Fermenting Cider

If you prefer a "dry" cider with more zip, allow the cider to stand longer at room temperature. To prevent the cider from turning to vinegar, it must not be stored in the open air. Close containers with an airlock or a curlicue glass "cork" sold by home-brew suppliers. Or tightly stretch three thicknesses of clean muslin over the bottle opening and secure it well with a rubber band around the neck of the bottle. For fermented cider, use heavy glass or plastic containers, such as those used for making homemade wine, that will withstand the fermentation pressure. After about ten days, the cider will begin frothing and may foam over the top. Clean off the sides of the container, replace the muslin if necessary, and let the frothing continue until fermentation subsides. Once this happens, the sugar in the cider has been turned to alcohol, making the flavor dry rather than sweet. This is often called hard cider. The longer the cider stands, the higher the alcohol content will be.

Storing Fermented Cider

You can store fermented cider in the refrigerator for four or five days. If you want to keep it longer, you'll need to pasteurize it to stop fermentation. Pasteurizing is simply heating the cider to 185°F. To be accurate, use a candy or jelly thermometer to monitor the temperature. Skim off the froth that will probably develop on the top of the cider and pour the hot cider into clean, heated plastic containers or glass jars (heat the containers so they won't crack when exposed to the hot cider). Refrigerate right away, as leaving it on the counter to cool down allows flavor to be lost.

An easy way to store fermented cider is to freeze it. If you plan to freeze it for more than six months, pasteurize it first.

Thinning Fruit

Once your trees begin to bear, you'll probably want to watch each and every fruit mature and ripen. But thinning by pulling off some of the immature fruit is one of the best things you can do to increase harvests and promote better tree health.

Why Thin?

Thinning is often the most neglected task of fruit tree growing. But fruit on an unthinned tree will be smaller and less sweet. In apples, the decrease in sweetness also means a decrease in storage life. Fruit will take longer to ripen, and in the case of cultivars that are marginally hardy, the crop may not mature before the end of the growing season.

Trees that overbear also will form fewer flowers for the following season and may revert to biennial bearing —only yielding a crop every other year. Fruit trees such as peaches that have overexpended energy in ripening fruit are more likely to suffer winter damage. Furthermore, branches heavily loaded with fruit often break, ruining the tree's form and possibly its bearing potential for years.

Thinning Guidelines

Now that you know the importance of thinning, here are a few helpful tips.

Fruit that has been properly thinned will be sweeter and of better quality than fruit produced by overburdened trees. Thinning can also reduce the weight on branches.

When thinning, use a twisting motion; don't pull. This prevents spurs from being broken or damaged.

Thin apples, pears, and plums within two months after full bloom (the time when more than half the blossoms were open).

Thin apricots within the first 38 to 41 days after full bloom.

Thin peaches and nectarines before the fruit is 1¼ inches in diameter.

Thin pears, apples, and peaches to only one fruit per cluster or spur. This keeps fruits from rubbing against one another while they are ripening.

Harvesting Tree Fruits

There's nothing better than tree-ripened fruit for fresh eating, jams, jellies, pies, or tarts. Here are some guidelines to help you decide just how and when to pick for best flavor.

When to Harvest

Ripe sweet cherries or apricots are delectable right off the tree. It's easy to tell when these fruits are ripe—just pluck and taste one when they've reached full size and have the right color. If they are sweet, they are ripe and ready for harvest. The same applies to apples, peaches, nectarines, plums, and prunes. When ripe, most of these fruits are easy to pick. Use a slight twisting motion as you lift upwards to pick the fruit without damaging the tree.

These rules don't apply to sour cherries and pears. Sour cherries are ripe when you can pull the fruit away from the pit, leaving the pit and stem on the tree. Pears need to be picked when they are full size, but not yet ripe. If pears ripen on the tree, their flesh becomes coarse or mealy in texture. The skin of ready-to-pick pears lightens from dark green to light green and the fruit easily separates from the tree when picked with a slight upward tilting motion. To ripen pears, put them in a cool place (60° to 70°F) and cover with newspaper. Some cultivars such as 'Anjou' and 'Comice' need to be stored for a couple of months at cold tempera-

tures (30° to 32°F) before ripening can occur. A trick that will ripen these cultivars soon after picking is putting the pears and a ripe banana or apple in a closed paper bag. The ripe fruit will release ethylene gas, which induces ripening.

Harvesting Tips

Don't just drop your freshly-picked fruit into a bucket—place them in gently. This will extend the storage life of fruit, particularly long-keeping apple cultivars.

To extend the storage life of sweet cherries, leave the stems attached to the fruit you pick.

On large trees, fruit on the outer limbs or at the top of the tree often ripen before fruit on the interior; plan more than one harvest.

Place buckets or boxes of harvested fruit out of the sun as soon as they are filled. This is particularly important for black cherries because the dark color absorbs heat fast, making the fruit spoil quickly.

Some fruit—plums, prunes, and apricots, for instance—continues to ripen off the tree. You can take advantage of this if your vacation is scheduled for the week these fruits will be ripening. Pick before you leave, and look forward to coming home to ripe fruit! But, peaches and nectarines soften after picking, but don't gain in sweetness—so don't pick them until the fruit is tasty.

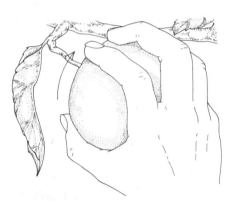

Use a slight twisting motion and lift up as you pick fruit, to pull it cleanly from the tree.

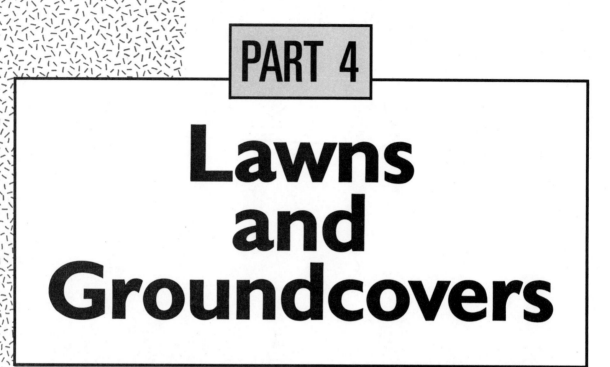

PART 4

Lawns and Groundcovers

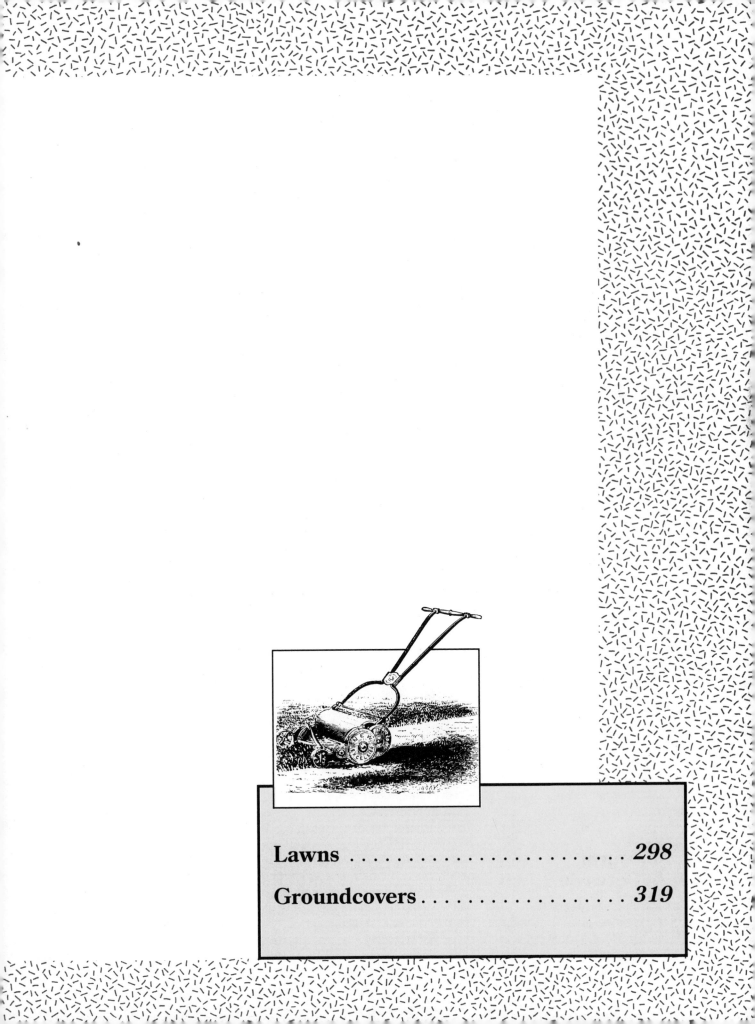

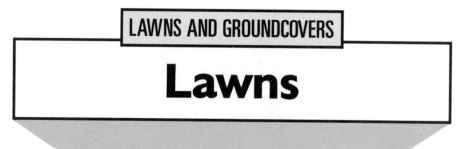

Lawns

Selecting Lawn Grasses

One of the best ways to enhance the overall beauty of your yard is to cultivate a healthy lawn. Whether your lawn is large or small, the first step toward creating a lush green carpet is to choose a lawn grass—or, better yet, a grass mixture—that fits your climate. There are many lawn grasses available today, varying in heat and drought tolerance, active growing season, shade tolerance, and general cultural conditions under which they grow best. For this reason, experts recommend different grass species for different parts of the country. Whether you're planning to sow seed or plant sod, keep in mind that a mixture of grasses rather than a single species or cultivar is best. (Both seed and sod are generally available as mixtures.) That way, you can take advantage of the best characteristics of several grasses when planting a new lawn or renovating an old one. By choosing a mixture of grasses that are adapted to your climate, soil, and site, you'll be well on your way to a healthy green carpet. (To determine which types of grasses are most suited to your garden, see the map at right.

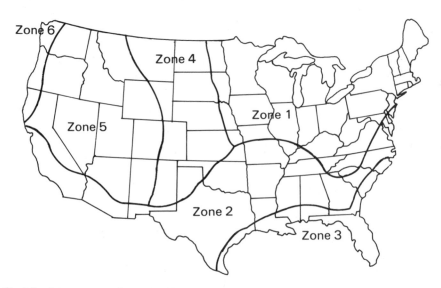

The following grasses are best suited for the regions shown above. **Zone 1.** Entire area: Kentucky bluegrass, red fescue. Southern part: tall fescue, bermudagrass, zoysiagrass. **Zone 2.** Entire area: bermudagrass, zoysiagrass. Southern part: centipedegrass, St. Augustinegrass. **Zone 3.** St. Augustinegrass, bermudagrass, zoysiagrass. **Zone 4.** Non-irrigated: crested wheatgrass, buffalograss, blue gramagrass. Irrigated: Kentucky bluegrass, red fescue. **Zone 5.** Non-irrigated: crested wheatgrass. Irrigated: Kentucky bluegrass, red fescue. **Zone 6.** Kentucky bluegrass, red fescue.

Cool, Warm, or In Between

Grass experts recognize two major groups of lawn grasses—cool season and warm season. Cool-season grasses, which grow best in the northern half of the country, include Kentucky bluegrass, perennial ryegrass, and fine fescues. The fine fescues are further divided into red or creeping fescues, Chewings fescues, and hard fescues. Cool-season grasses typically make their strongest growth in spring and fall but may remain green all winter. They tend to become brown and dormant in midsummer.

Warm-season grasses, which are suitable for the desert Southwest and Sun Belt, include low-maintenance centipedegrass, luxurious, looking zoysiagrass, shade-tolerant St. Augustinegrass, and the incredibly tough, improved cultivars of bermudagrass. These grasses are much more heat-tolerant than cool-season grasses. They are dormant in winter and do not begin to green up until early summer. All tolerate drought better than cool-season grasses.

Gardeners in the transition zone

298

Zoysiagrass

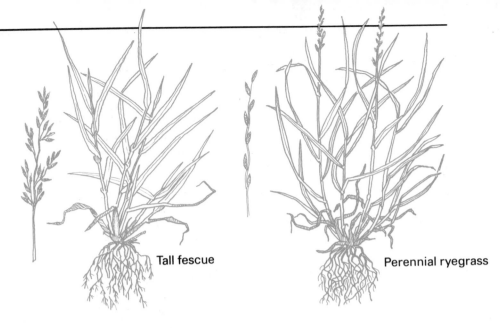

Tall fescue

Perennial ryegrass

between North and South—as well as in the West and Great Plains—can use a mixture of both cool- and warm-season grasses, commonly called transition-zone grasses. In fact, in the transitional zone, the combination of grass species found in seed or sod mixtures can become quite complex. In the East, the most important grass in the mix is often improved tall fescue, often called "turf type" tall fescue, along with small amounts of other grasses such as bluegrass and annual ryegrass. Improved tall fescues do not creep, so the other grasses in the mix help knit an otherwise tufted lawn into a smooth turf. Buffalograss and blue gramagrass, both warm-season grasses native to this country, are good choices in the western part of the transitional zone, especially in lawns that are not watered. Crested wheatgrass is probably the best choice for lawns that will not be irrigated. (For more on lawn grasses, see the chart "A Guide to Selected Lawn Grasses" on page 300.)

The overwhelming favorite among cool-season grasses is Kentucky bluegrass, a lush, sod-forming turfgrass now available in dozens of named cultivars. The best bluegrass lawns include a blend of four or five updated cultivars that have been

(continued on page 302)

CHOOSING THE BEST GRASSES

When choosing any lawn grass, always avoid "common" strains in favor of the newest improved named cultivars. For example, plain Kentucky bluegrass, Kentucky-31 tall fescue, and common bermudagrass are acceptable for roadsides and meadows, but in home lawns they grow too vigorously and become invasive. Named cultivars of lawngrasses often show superior disease resistance, cold hardiness, or shade tolerance. Although many cultivars are available as seed or sod, some of the newest ones—especially of bermudagrass and centipedegrass—are only available as sod, plugs, or sprigs.

Lawn Grasses That Resist Pests

Some grasses, such as zoysiagrass and bermudagrass, are bothered by very few insect pests. But aphids, armyworms, pillbugs, and cutworms can seriously damage succulent stems and stolons of cool-season grasses. In the last decade, scientists have found that some lawn grass cultivars, including 'Repell' perennial ryegrass and 'Rebel' tall fescue, host a type of fungi that protect them from any insect predators. Where insect populations are high, introduction of these pest-resistant cultivars can greatly enhance the health of the lawn.

In Florida and Texas, the southern chinch bug frequently injures lawns. The old St. Augustinegrass cultivar 'Bitter Blue' is extremely susceptible to this pest. Two St. Augustinegrass cultivars, 'Floratam' and 'Floralawn', show good resistance to this pest.

The following lawn grass cultivars earn high ratings for pest resistance, beauty, and adaptability.

- Kentucky bluegrass: 'America', 'Midnight', 'Baron', 'Glade', 'Challenger'
- Perennial ryegrass: 'Manhattan II', 'Repell', 'Gator', 'Citation II', 'Palmer'
- Fine fescue: 'Pennlawn', 'Ruby', 'Dawson', 'Atlanta', 'Jamestown'
- Hard fescue: 'Reliant', 'Spartan', 'Scaldis'
- Turf-type tall fescue: 'Hawk', 'Rebel', 'Mustang', 'Houndog', 'Apache'
- Bermudagrass: 'Tifway II', 'Tiflawn', 'Midiron', 'Vamont', 'Texturf 10'
- St. Augustinegrass: 'Floratam', 'Floralawn', 'Floratine'

A GUIDE TO SELECTED LAWN GRASSES

One of the best ways to develop a low-maintenance lawn is to select the right grass for your region. Cool-season grasses are best for the northern part of the country; warm-season grasses for the Southwest and Sun Belt. Transition zone gardeners should use a mixture of both warm- and cool-season grasses for best results.

Name	Description	Culture	Rate of Establishment	Nitrogen Needs
Cool Season				
Kentucky bluegrass (*Poa pratensis*)	Lush, green with fine texture. Good wear tolerance.	Moderate drought tolerance. Plants become dormant during periods of drought; require regular irrigation to stay green in summer. Fertile, nearly neutral soil with plenty of sun.	1 year from seed; 6 months from sprigs; 3 weeks from sod.	Average; fertilize in early spring and early fall.
Fine fescue (*Festuca* spp.)	Dark green color and fine texture. Blends well with Kentucky bluegrass. Very good wear tolerance.	Good drought tolerance, especially in shady spots. Grows best in fertile, slightly acid soils.	1 year from seed; 6 months from sprigs; 3 weeks from mixed-species sod.	Below average; fertilize in early spring and early fall.
Perennial ryegrass (*Lolium perenne*)	Very dark green grass with fine leaves. Somewhat clumpy unless blended with bluegrass or creeping fescue. Very good wear tolerance.	Good drought tolerance. Plant in slightly acid soil in full sun.	2 months from seed, but expect 2 years for mixed-species lawn to assume mature appearance.	Average; fertilize in early fall.
Transition				
Blue gramagrass (*Bouteloua gracilis*)	Medium-fine grass with bunching habit. Forms dense sod. Good wear tolerance.	Warm-season grass often planted in transition zone and Great Plains. Drought tolerant. Good for cool, dry regions. Alkaline soil. Turns brown in severe drought.	2 years from sod.	Below average; fertilize in late spring and early summer.
Buffalograss (*Buchloe dactyloides*)	Native American grass with fine leaves and creeping stolons. Good wear tolerance.	Warm-season grass good for Great Plains and transition zone. Excellent drought tolerance. Will grow in full sun, clayey soil, and alkaline conditions. Turns brown in midsummer and again in fall.	2 years from seed, 1-2 years from plugs.	Below average; fertilize in late spring and early summer.

Name	Description	Culture	Rate of Establishment	Nitrogen Needs
Fairway crested wheatgrass (*Agropyron cristatum*)	Vigorous bunchgrass with deep, spreading root system. Good wear tolerance.	Cool-season grass good for transition zone and Great Plains. Drought and cold tolerant.	About 1 year from seed.	Below average; fertilize in early spring and early fall.
Turf-type tall fescue (*Festuca elatior*)	Medium green grass, with coarse leaves. Noncreeping habit. Good wear tolerance.	Cool-season grass often grown in transition zone. Good drought tolerance. Will grow in many soils and tolerates a wide pH range.	3 months from seed.	Average to below average; fertilize in spring or fall.

Warm Season

Name	Description	Culture	Rate of Establishment	Nitrogen Needs
Improved bermudagrass (*Cynodon dactylon* hybrids)	Medium to dark green grass with fine, stiff leaves. Excellent wear tolerance.	Excellent drought tolerance. Plant in fertile, well-drained soil with full sun.	2-3 months from sprigs; 3 weeks from sod. Seeding not recommended.	Above average; fertilize in late spring and midsummer.
Centipedegrass (*Eremochloa ophiuroides*)	Medium green grass with somewhat coarse leaves. Thick creeping stolons. Fair to poor wear tolerance.	Excellent drought tolerance. Will grow in moderately fertile, acid soils. Plant in full sun.	1 year from sprigs; 2 years from seed.	Below average; fertilize once a year and supplement with iron sulfate improves color and vigor.
St. Augustine-grass (*Stenotaphrum secundatum*)	Dark green grass with creeping stems and broad, flexible blades. Fair wear tolerance.	Average drought tolerance. Plant in fertile, well-drained, sandy, neutral to slightly acid soil. Can grow in shade.	3 months from sprigs or plugs. Not available as seed.	Above average; fertilize in early spring and fall to improve color and vigor.
Zoysiagrass (*Zoysia* spp.)	Medium green, creeping grass with fine, stiff leaves. In the north, turns brown in winter. Very good wear tolerance if thatch is removed every few years.	Average drought tolerance. Plant in full sun with fertile, well-drained, slightly acid soil.	2 years from sprigs; 2 months from sod. Seeding not recommended.	Below average; fertilize once a year in late spring.

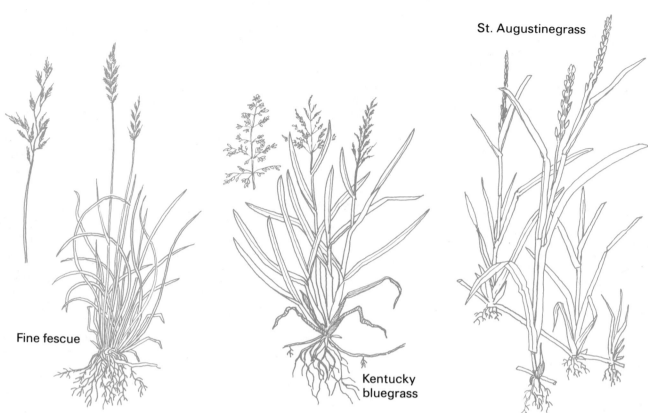

St. Augustinegrass

Fine fescue

Kentucky bluegrass

selected for such characteristics as color, drought tolerance, disease resistance, and ability to stand up to heavy wear. As the individual grass plants intertwine, the lawn benefits from the collective talents of the different cultivars in the mix.

In most mixes, the shortcomings of bluegrass—its inability to grow in heavy shade and the tendency of some cultivars to germinate slowly—are dealt with by adding other cool-season grasses to the lawn's plant population. Fine fescues are the top choices for lawns growing in shady spots in cool climates. Fast-germinating perennial ryegrass is added to bluegrass mixtures to provide short-term cover while the bluegrass becomes established.

Several older lawn grasses have lost popularity in recent years. Bentgrasses have earned a well-deserved reputation as high-maintenance, disease-prone grasses. In the South, many homeowners have become disenchanted with zoysiagrass because it requires too much care and is often invaded by winter weeds.

A few lesser-known grasses are making their way into lawns. Selected hard fescues, native to the Canadian Rockies, grow so slowly in the cool climates that they hardly need mowing. Breeders have developed perennial ryegrasses that are very dark green; a few of these new cultivars even creep a little. In warm climates, bahia grass is sometimes used near salt water since it tolerates salt spray.

Bermudagrass

HOW HIGH TO MOW

As a general rule, cut grass at the high end of the range during hot weather; lower when weather is cool or plants are growing in shade. At the end of the growing season, cut the lawn back one last time at the lowest recommended height.

Grass	Cutting Height (in.)
Annual ryegrass	2-2½
Bermudagrass	1-1½
Centipedegrass	1-1½
Fine fescue	1½-2½
Kentucky bluegrass	2½-3
Perennial ryegrass	1½-2½
St. Augustinegrass	2-3
Tall fescue	2½-3½
Zoysiagrass	1-1½

Measuring the Lawn

Whether you are planting a new lawn or rejuvenating an old one, an accurate measurement of your lawn's surface area can help you estimate how much seed, sod, or fertilizer you will need. In lawn grass lingo, materials estimates for seed or soil amendments are usually given per 1,000 square feet of surface area. Sod is sometimes sold in square yards. To measure the surface area in square yards, first determine your square footage and divide that figure by 9 for your square yard measurement.

Most houses are square or rectangular, and lawns mimic this design. To measure, divide the lawn into adjoining squares and rectangles, and measure the length and width of each. Multiply the length by the width of each unit to find the area of each section. Add these numbers together to find your lawn's total surface area.

Round or triangular-shaped sections of lawn may be measured using standard geometric formulas. To obtain the surface area of a circle, measure the distance from the center to the edge (the radius). Multiply this number by itself (for example; 10 × 10); then multiply the answer by 3.14. The result is the surface area. To find the area of a triangular section of lawn, multiply the length of the base by the length of the height;

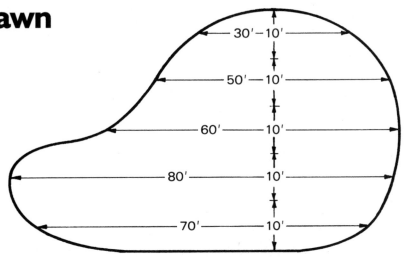

To determine the approximate area of an irregularly shaped bed, start by marking a line through the center. Mark off 10-foot sections, and then measure the width of each section. Add all the widths together and multiply by 10. In this example, the solution is (30' + 50' + 60' + 80' + 70') × 10' = 2,900 sq. ft.

then multiply the resulting number by .5.

You can calculate the surface area of irregularly shaped lawns by dividing them into their component parts—triangles, half-circles, or rectangles. Determine the area of each part; then add the figures together to find the total surface area.

How to Measure an Amoeba

To measure odd shapes with curved edges, find the approximate center of the space. Then measure a line drawn between opposite edges through the center. Divide this line into 10-foot sections. Then, at each 10-foot mark, determine the width of each 10-foot section by measuring the distance between opposite edges (perpendicular to the original axis line). To obtain the surface area, add all the widths together and multiply the total by 10. If your yard includes island beds within the lawn, use this procedure to measure the surface area of your beds, and subtract them from the total lawn area.

Sowing Grass Seed

Even the highest quality grass seed will result in a spotty, sunken lawn if it is sown into rough, unimproved soil. Preparation for seeding a lawn may be a laborious process, but is well worth the effort, for a properly planted lawn will thrive for many years.

In general, warm-season grasses are best seeded in late spring, while transitional and cool-season grasses are seeded in early spring or early fall. If you must do something with

your bare yard but the time for planting expensive seed is months away, do some preliminary leveling and sow the site lightly with annual ryegrass. The cover crop can be tilled into the soil along with other soil amendments a few weeks before planting.

Preparing the Seedbed

A raw site around a new home generally requires considerable grading

before it's ready to sow. You'll need to fill in low spots and even out high ones. Don't be in a rush to get started, for it will take several heavy rains to settle in loose dirt and reveal the true contours of your new yard. Once your yard is settled, fill in the low spots with excess topsoil from high places, or buy a load of topsoil for this purpose.

Incorporate weed-free, humus-rich organic material, like compost, well-rotted sawdust or manure, peat moss, or leaf mold, into the soil by

Add organic materials such as compost to the soil to improve the seedbed before planting.

After tilling in the soil amendments, level the seedbed, rake it smooth, and roll it twice.

For best results, be sure to distribute seed evenly.

spreading a 2- to 3-inch layer and using a rotary tiller to work it in. Organic matter will improve the drainage of heavy clay soils and the nutrient-holding capacity of sandy ones. Add organic fertilizers such as bonemeal, cottonseed meal, greensand, and ashes (see the chart "Organic Fertilizers Catalog" on page 72 for more information on these and other fertilizers). Add lime, if indicated by a pH test.

Rake out debris, and smooth out the surface once more. Do not attempt to seed lawn-quality grasses on steep slopes. Plant sod instead, or use the slope to achieve some other landscape effect. For example, you might plant the slope with low, spreading shrubs, or create a small rock garden around a stone retaining wall.

When the site of the future lawn is raked smooth, the soil should be firmed into place. You can rent a lawn roller, or you can use a large metal barrel, turned on its side. Roll over the area twice, until your feet leave only shallow prints in the seedbed.

Spreading Seed

You can use a mechanical seeder, available from rental centers, or spread seed by hand. The best way to ensure even distribution of seed is to make two applications. Take half of the seed and spread it while walking back and forth across the plot in parallel lines or strips. Make a second application with the rest of the seed by walking and sowing strips that are perpendicular to the first seeding. Rake lightly to barely cover the seed, and roll the area one last time to firm in the seeds and make sure there is good seed-soil contact. A light covering of weed-free straw (not hay, which contains weed seeds) will help retain moisture and keep the seed from washing away. If the site slopes more than a little, use burlap or cheesecloth to keep the soil and seed in place.

Aftercare

Grass seed needs good light and constant soil moisture for strong germination. Keep leaves and other debris off newly seeded lawns, and use a sprinkler to keep the soil evenly moist at all times for two to three weeks. Most grass seed germinates within two weeks, but bluegrass, buffalograss, and centipedegrass are slower to start. In bluegrass/perennial ryegrass lawns, cut the lawn for the first time about two to three weeks after sowing to help the bluegrass compete with the more vigorous perennial ryegrass.

Rolling the seedbed again after sowing ensures good contact between seed and soil, which is essential for good germination.

Planting Sod

Sod may be the perfect solution for high traffic areas, slopes, and other problem areas. Although it costs more than seed, sod is attractive from the start and becomes established quickly. In some cases, the best grass cultivars are available only as sod. Another advantage is that sod can be planted nearly any time of year, although it is sensitive to drought and must be watered faithfully until it's established. Late summer to early fall is the best time to sod cool-season grasses in the North; late spring to early summer is best for warm-season grasses.

When buying sod, look for fresh, green slabs that have been kept constantly moist. Like seed, sod is available in mixtures of cultivars suitable for different regions. Buy only from nurseries that label the mixture and certify that it is free of weeds, insects, and disease, or arrange to buy freshly dug sod from a reputable nearby sod farmer. It's important to keep the sod moist once it's been delivered to you. It's best to prepare the soil before your sod is delivered so it can be planted as quickly as possible.

To plant sod, begin by preparing the site as if you were planting seed. Level it, add soil amendments, and rake away all debris. Sod cannot be planted over an old lawn. Where grass, weeds, or any plant material is present, dig it out or till it under before planting your sod.

The day before you plan to plant, roll the prepared site and water it lightly. Firm contact between soil and sod roots is essential, so check to make sure all weeds and other debris are cleared away.

Fit strips of sod as closely together as possible. Be sure to stagger the seams between strips so that they do not line up from row to row.

Use a sharp knife to cut sod to fit around walks, edgings, or other obstacles.

Rolling sod after laying it improves contact between the roots and the underlying soil and gets the sod off to a good start.

Laying Sod

Begin laying the sod against any straight edge, such as a sidewalk or a string stretched between two pegs. Lay the sod in strips, end to end, and fit them together as tightly as you can without overlapping. To prevent erosion, stagger the seams or edges of the pieces to achieve a bricklike pattern. Trim away excess sod along curved or uneven edges with a sharp knife or shovel. You can use the pieces you cut away to fill in elsewhere or to rejuvenate dead spots in another part of your lawn.

Once the sod is in place, roll it to firm the roots into the soil. Fill crevices between sod pieces with weed-free topsoil—use a broom or the back of a wooden rake to do the spreading—and turn on the sprinklers. All types of sod should be thoroughly soaked right after planting, then twice a week for three to four weeks thereafter.

Planting Plugs and Sprigs

Some creeping grasses are planted as small pieces of sod called plugs or sprigs. Plugs are small, container-grown pieces of sod; sprigs are individual rooted grass stems made from shredded sod. Unlike conventional sodding, plugs and sprigs are spaced from 6 to 12 inches apart, with bare areas in between. This technique is most often used with warm-season grasses such as St. Augustinegrass, bermudagrass, centipedegrass, and zoysiagrass. Any type of sod can be cut into chunks and planted as plugs. For most grasses, this isn't a recommended practice for large areas because they spread less quickly than the species commonly planted in this manner.

Plugs and sprigs are best used for planting lawns that are level and in low-traffic places. When planting a lawn in this manner, keep in mind that several months may pass before the grass plants grow together completely. On slopes, heavy rains will wash away the soil between the plugs or sprigs, and the end result will be a spotty, uneven lawn. Weeds often appear in the areas between the plugs or sprigs and must be hoed out or pulled by hand.

For best results, plant plugs or sprigs in spring. Prepare the planting area as you would for seed or sod, but leave the soil loose instead of rolling it. Both plugs and sprigs dry out quickly, so keep them in a shady place and sprinkle them with water frequently until you are ready to plant them.

Plugs should be planted at their normal growing depth, 6 to 12 inches apart. With sprigs, lay the pieces in shallow furrows at an angle so that two-thirds of each sprig is buried and only a tuft of grass shows above the ground. An alternate way to plant is to drop the sprigs at intervals on the surface of the planting area, and push them into the soil with the heel of your shoe. After planting, roll the area to make sure the soil is firm and level and roots are in good contact with the soil. Then water the area thoroughly, and keep it damp for at least three weeks. Hoe out weeds as soon as they appear, and topdress with a good organic fertilizer when rapid growth commences.

Plant sprigs in 2- to 3-inch-deep furrows spaced from 6 to 12 inches apart.

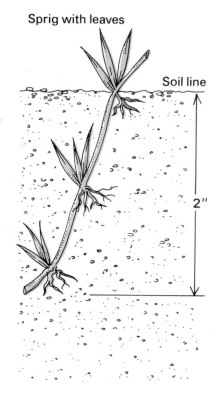

When planting sprigs, place them so that the light-colored runner is below ground but the top cluster of leaves is on the surface.

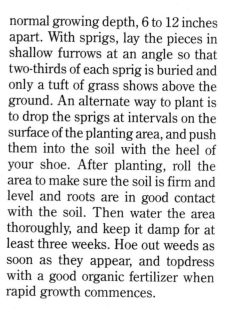

When planting a lawn from plugs, be sure to set them at the same depth they're growing in pots.

Mowing the Lawn

Each time you mow your lawn, you actually are pruning back thousands or millions of grass plants. Mowing does much more than make it possible to walk to your car in the morning without getting your feet wet. When properly done, it helps expose the crowns of the plants to sunlight and encourages the development of tillers, or creeping stems.

The rule of thumb is to remove one-third of the grass's top growth each time you mow. Mow too high and you'll need to mow again in a few days; mow too low and you may send the grass into a state of shock by exposing the crowns of the plants to sun and cutting off too much of the leaf blades, which manufacture food for the plants. Close cutting also helps create places between grass plants where weeds can become established. See the table "How High to Mow" on page 302 for recommended mowing heights for the major lawn grasses. Adjustments may be made to mowing heights, depending on the season. In midsummer, it's a good idea to mow higher than normal since long blades help insulate the plant's crowns from moisture loss. In early fall, warm-season grasses are sometimes cut very low and overseeded with annual rye for better winter color.

Always mow when the grass blades are dry. Sharpen mower blades at least yearly so that they slice off the tops of the grass cleanly instead of chewing it up. Rotary mowers (the most popular kind) are fine for most lawns. Reel-type mowers are recommended for very dense, fine-bladed grasses like zoysiagrass and hybrid bermudagrass.

Thick clumps of grass clippings may be gathered and used as mulch or added to the compost pile. Let light layers rot where they fall; they are a good source of nitrogen, and nature will take care of recycling the nutrients in the clippings.

FOOD FOR THOUGHT

Each spring, gardeners across the country rush to nurseries and garden centers to load up on fertilizers to spur their lawns into high gear so they'll green up and get growing as soon as possible. However, experts have learned that all the fertilizers recommended for a so-called healthy lawn aren't really good for the lawn at all. In fact, lawns fed frequently with high-nitrogen chemical fertilizers grow so quickly, they seem to become more open to insect and disease problems. They also need mowing more often, tend to build up thick layers of thatch, and have shallower roots.

The exact schedule of fertilizing you follow will depend on where you live, what type of grasses you have, and whether you irrigate. Cool-season grasses will grow well with as little as one application per year. Warm-season grasses need at least two. Grass clippings are a good source of nitrogen, and compost or other organic materials can provide all your lawn needs to be healthy and happy.

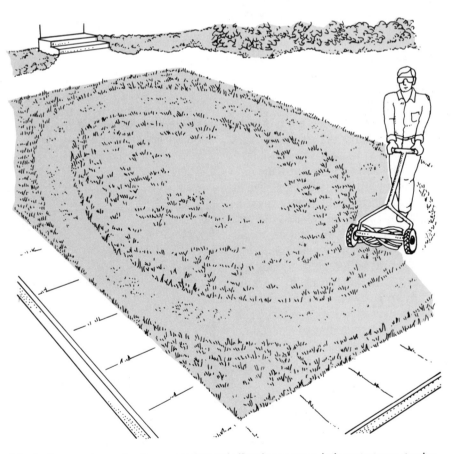

Mowing in a round or oval pattern saves time and effort, because you don't waste energy turning sharp corners.

Rejuvenating Lawns

Sooner or later, most lawns need a facelift—either of the entire lawn or of small patches that have been damaged by insects, weeds, or diseases. Many old lawns can be renovated in a weekend, though more work is in order if weeds are running rampant (in which case, it is probably best to start again from scratch) or if the soil is badly compacted as a result of heavy use.

The first step in any lawn rejuvenation project is to dig out the weeds —roots and all. For an all-over facelift, once weeds are under control, the next step is to rent a vertical mower, also called a dethatcher. Healthy lawns have about ¼ inch of thatch, the undecomposed organic matter on top of the soil, which acts as a mulch and helps conserve moisture. Heavily fertilized lawns can build up thick layers of thatch that smother the plants and create ideal conditions for insects and disease. A vertical mower cuts small slits in the turf and brings dead plant parts to the surface where they can be raked up and composted. Dethatching gives old grass new room to grow and opens little places in the turf where new grass seed can germinate.

If the soil appears hard and lifeless, some type of aeration also is in order. You can rent power aerator machines that poke holes in the turf or other machines that cut out small cores of soil. In addition, a generous topdressing with a good organic fertilizer will aerate the soil in the most natural way, by encouraging the proliferation of soil microorganisms. Fertilize after dethatching and aerating. This is also the time to apply lime, if indicated by a soil test.

Seeding or Patching

The lawn is now ready for overseeding or for patching with small pieces of sod. In bluegrass lawns, simply overseed the old, reconditioned lawn with a mixture of updated cultivars,

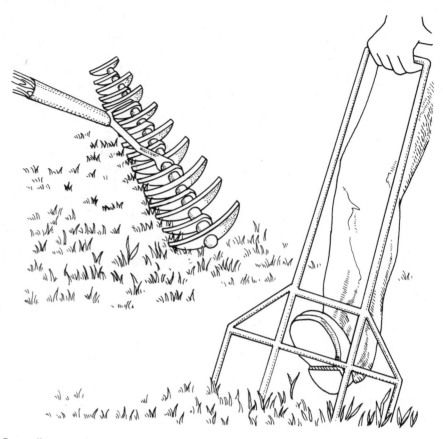

For small areas, a thatch rake (left) is an effective way to remove thatch. You can use a core cultivator (right) to manually aerate soil.

Green Thumb Tip

SPOT REPAIRS

Where weeds or lawn pests have caused damaged patches, a partial lawn renovation will usually solve the problem. Clean out weeds and dead grasses with a shovel and rake, till the soil, and amend it with an organic fertilizer. The cultivated patch of soil will compact and settle over time, so rake it into a flat-topped mound slightly higher than the surrounding turf. Plan on planting seed or sod that matches the rest of your lawn, unless you've decided on a shade- or drought-tolerant lawn grass for a particularly troublesome area. Cut pieces of sod to fit the shape you're trying to fill. After sowing or sodding, be sure to firm the soil to ensure good soil contact. Water as necessary until the new grass shows strong new growth.

and keep the area moist for three weeks. Fescues, perennial ryegrass, and other seed-sown lawns also may be overseeded in this way.

Grasses that cannot be sown from seed, such as zoysiagrass and the new hybrid bermudagrasses, often respond to reconditioning so dramatically that no further planting is necessary. However, bare spots formerly occupied by weeds should be planted with pieces of sod taken from the outer edges of the lawn.

Starting from Scratch

If you want to completely renovate your old lawn and plant a new type of grass, the entire site should be tilled up and raked clean, a major job that you may want to hire someone to do. To get rid of the old grass, you can slice it away and pull it up in strips, or till it under. (You may need to till two or three times to be sure the old grass won't come back.) In hot weather, it is sometimes possible to heat-kill areas of unwanted grass by covering them with clear plastic for several days. Decrease the chances that the grass will survive by mowing it as low as possible before tilling it under. Whatever you do, don't rush to replant; be sure the old grass is dead before proceeding. Expect to wait several weeks before the site is ready for replanting.

Use pieces of sod to repair dead or damaged spots in a lawn.

For small repairs, you can aerate the soil and work in organic matter with hand tools.

CONTROLLING LAWN PESTS

Use this guide to identify the most common insect pests of lawn grasses. You'll find the symptoms each insect causes, a description of the pest, what causes the damage, and recommended organic controls.

Insect	Symptoms	Description	Cause	Control
Armyworm	May be seen on bermudagrass. Bare patches develop in late summer or fall.	Brown, green, or black caterpillar with yellow and dark stripes. Y- or V-shaped white mark on head; 1½ in. long. Adult is night-flying, 1-1½-in. moth with gray-white mottled wings.	At night, armyworms chew the grass blades, often down to the ground.	Handpick and drop in soapy water. Trichogramma and braconid wasps parasitize the larvae. Bt (*Bacillus thuringiensis*) is an effective control.
Billbug	Most lawns attacked, especially bermudagrass, Kentucky bluegrass, and zoysiagrass. Grass is easy to pull up. Brown or yellow circular patches appear in June and July.	Adult is brown or gray weevil with large snout; ⅕-½ in. long. Larva is white, fat, and wormlike, with brown-yellow head; ⅝ in. long.	Larvae chew the stems and later feed on the roots, starting just below the thatch and moving downward. More common on dry, stressed grass.	Aerate and water deeply in spring and add organic matter to reduce stress. Remove thatch. Plant resistant cultivars. Beneficial nematodes kill both larvae and adults. Diatomaceous earth helps control adults. Milky spore disease (*Bacillus popilliae*) provides more long-lasting control. Use rotenone for severe infestations.
Black turfgrass ataenius	Brown patches on various grasses.	Adult is a shiny black beetle; ¼ in. long. Grub is curled, white, fat and wormlike with brown head; ⅟₁₆ in. long.	Grubs chew roots.	Use diatomaceous earth to control grubs. Rotenone kills adults. Pyrethrum controls both.

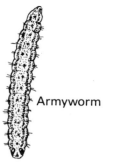

Armyworm

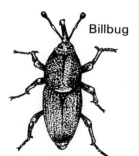

Billbug

Black turfgrass ataenius

Insect	Symptoms	Description	Cause	Control
Chinch bug	Kentucky bluegrass, fine fescue, bentgrass, St. Augustinegrass, and zoysiagrass often affected. Brown or yellow sunken circular patches appear, especially in dry weather. Offensive odor when lawn is walked on.	Adult is black with white or brown fore wings and brown legs. Malodorous when crushed; ⅕-⅙ in. long. Nymph is red with a white stripe across back or black with white spots; ⅕-¼ in. long.	Adults and nymphs feed on juices of stems and leaves. They prefer sunny, warm areas and frequent weakened or stressed grass.	Shade lawn with trees or shrubs. Reduce stress by watering. Plant resistant cultivars. Ladybugs and big-eyed bugs prey on chinch bugs. *Beauvaria bassianna* fungus helps control population. Insecticidal soap is effective.
Cutworm	Usually not a serious problem. Dead spots appear, 1-2 in. wide.	Adult is a nocturnal moth. Grayish to brown fat caterpillar, usually curled; 1-2 in. long. Overwinters in tufts of grass or debris.	Larvae chew young grass blades at base during the night.	Clean up any lawn debris and mow closely in fall, throwing away clippings. Beneficial nematodes or braconid wasps prey on cutworms. Barriers such as diatomaceous earth also control populations. Bt (*Bacillus thuringiensis*) controls some species. For severe infestations, treat lawn with pyrethrum at night.
Grasshopper	Usually not a problem unless numerous. Chewed grass or dead patches.	Adult has long body with enlarged hind legs, large hearing organs on either side of the abdomen. Various colors.	Adults chew blades, sometimes down to ground.	Handpick in morning while they are less active. Use *Nosema locustae,* a spore disease, mixed with bran, to kill young in spring.

(continued)

Chinch bug

Cutworm

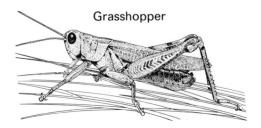
Grasshopper

CONTROLLING LAWN PESTS –*Continued*

Insect	Symptoms	Description	Cause	Control
Greenbug or aphid	Kentucky bluegrass a favorite. Rust spots or withered areas appear, especially in shaded areas. Bugs scatter as lawn is disturbed.	Tiny, light green, pear-shaped aphid.	Aphids suck plant juices. Prefer shade.	Usually not serious. Many insects such as ladybugs and green lacewings prey on aphids. Insecticidal soap helps to control populations.
Grub (White)	Kentucky and annual bluegrasses, tall and fine fescues, or bentgrass may be affected. Spongy yellow-brown patches, especially in areas lighted at night in late summer to early fall. Patches pulled are easily removed.	Larval stage of various beetles. Curled, fat, white, worm-like, ¼-¾ in. long, with yellow or brown heads.	Grubs chew roots.	Rake loose turf and expose grubs to birds. If infested, water often and lightly to reduce stress on plants caused by damaged roots. Beneficial nematodes will prey on grubs. Milky spore disease (*Bacillus popilliae*) is an effective long-term control. For serious infestations, use rotenone.
Japanese beetle	Spots of dying lawn appear in August or September.	Adult beetle is ½ in., shiny metallic green with copper wings. Grub is 1 in. long, grayish-white, fat and worm-like, with a dark brown head. Usually curled.	Roots are cut by grubs.	Keep lawn relatively dry as preventive; adults lay eggs in moist areas. Handpick beetles in morning; drop in bucket of soapy water. For long-term grub control, use milky spore disease (*Bacillus popilliae*) or beneficial nematodes. Use pyrethrum for severe infestations.

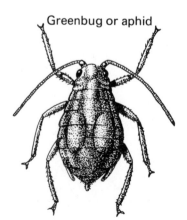

Greenbug or aphid

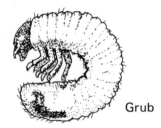

Grub

Insect	Symptoms	Description	Cause	Control
Mole cricket	Bahia grass, St. Augustinegrass, bermudagrass, or zoysiagrass may be affected. Dry soil. Brown streaks in lawn. Especially frequent near young seedlings. Pest of mainly southern areas.	Light brown cricket with large forelegs, paddle-like feet, and a large head; 1½ in. long.	Crickets' tunneling causes soil to dry out. They occasionally eat roots.	Milky spore disease (*Bacillus popilliae*), Bt (*Bacillus thuringiensis*), or beneficial nematodes are effective against these pests.
Potato leafhopper	White spots on blades, especially on new lawns. Disturbing grass will cause them to hop away.	Adult is pale green, wedge-shaped; ⅛-¼ in. long. Overwinters in garden and lawn debris.	Adults suck plant juices.	Usually not serious, unless on new lawns. Clear away debris and weeds. Treatments with insecticidal soap mixed with isopropyl alcohol (1 T. alcohol to 1 pt. soap) are effective. Use pyrethrum for severe infestations.
Scale	Various grasses may be affected, including bermudagrass, St. Augustinegrass, and centipedegrass. Withered or brown areas. Small "bumps" on blades.	Round legless insect with waxy shell. Various colors; ⅛ in. across.	Scale suck plant juices from stems or roots.	Several insects such as chalcid wasps, green lacewings, and ladybugs prey on scale. Repeated applications of insecticidal soap mix control populations. Use pyrethrum for severe infestations.

(continued)

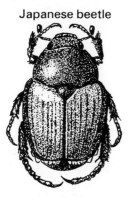

Japanese beetle

Mole cricket

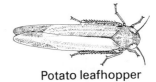

Potato leafhopper

CONTROLLING LAWN PESTS—*Continued*

Insect	Symptoms	Description	Cause	Control
Sod webworm	Kentucky bluegrass, tall and fine fescues, bentgrass, or zoysiagrass may be affected. Irregular brown spots appear, usually in July and August.	Larva of nocturnal buff-colored lawn moth that flies in a zigzag pattern. Dark brown head and spots with stiff hairs along tan body; ¾-1 in. long. Overwinters in thatch.	Larvae eat grass blades and stems at night.	Plant resistant cultivars. Remove thatch. Predatory nematodes feed on larvae. Insecticidal soap or Bt (*Bacillus thuringiensis*) also controls larvae.
Spider mite	Bermudagrass, Kentucky bluegrass, red fescue, fine fescue, or bentgrass may be affected. Yellow or thinned turf—especially during hot dry weather.	Tiny, 8-legged relative of spiders; $\frac{1}{150}$-$\frac{1}{50}$ in. long. White, green or rust-colored, several different species.	Spider mites suck plant juices. They may cause extensive damage.	Frequent light watering of soil helps limit attacks during hot, dry weather. A forceful spray of water on leaves in early morning, repeated for 3 days, deters pests. Green lacewings or ladybugs prey on these pests. Insecticidal soap is an effective control.
Wireworm	Various grasses. Irregular patterns of wilted grass.	Larva of click beetle. Brown, hard-shelled, thin, and wormlike; ½-1½ in. long. Brown or gray adult has dark spotted head; ½ in. long.	Larvae chew roots.	Usually not a serious threat. Remove any plant debris in fall. Handpick adults in spring.

Spider mite

Sod webworm

Wireworm

CONTROLLING LAWN DISEASES

Use this guide to identify the most common diseases of lawn grasses. You'll find the symptoms of each disease, a description of the conditions that encourage each particular problem, recommended organic controls, and any lawn grass cultivars that are resistant to the disease.

Disease	Symptoms	Conditions	Control	Resistant Grasses
Brown patch	Circular, dark, soaked-looking or brown patches of various sizes.	Common during hot humid weather. Highly fertilized lawns are most susceptible.	Improve drainage by top-dressing lawn with organic matter to loosen soil.	Perennial ryegrasses 'Allstar', 'Delray', 'Prelude', and 'Premier'. Tall fescues 'Brookston', 'Jaguar', 'Mustang', and 'Olympic'.
Dollar spot	Small, round, bleached spots appear that later blend together. Pale brown with red marks at blade tips.	Appears during average but dry weather, usually during summer. Dry soil and low nitrogen may encourage it.	Add nitrogen. Regular watering in early part of day. Mow infected tips and throw away clippings.	Fine fescues 'Agram', 'Checker', 'Reliant', and 'Tournament'. Kentucky bluegrasses 'Adelphi', 'Eclipse', 'Midnight', and 'Primo'. Perennial ryegrasses 'Barry', 'Dasher', 'Regal', and 'Venlona'.
***Drechslera* leaf spot (Melting out)**	Gold patches with red-brown to black edges. Then stems and roots discolor, turning into mushy spots.	Appears during cool, moist weather of spring or fall. Too much nitrogen or water or mowing too low may encourage it.	Avoid nitrogen applications in hot weather. Water deeply and only occasionally. Mow high frequently and throw away clippings. Remove thatch.	Kentucky bluegrasses 'Challenger', 'Eclipse', and 'Midnight'. Perennial ryegrasses 'Belle', 'Blazer', 'Cowboy', and 'Ranger'. Tall fescues 'Adventure', 'Brookston', 'Jaguar', and 'Mustang'.
Fairy rings	In spring, dark green rings form. Mushrooms later appear around them. These rings may crowd out grass, but as ring spreads wider, inner grass may grow back.	Common in areas where it rains frequently, or atop old, rotting tree roots. Fungi feed on dead and decaying matter in soil, competing with grass for nutrients.	Difficult to destroy. Remove thatch, which will encourage fungus to grow. If necessary, dig out turf and soil 2 feet down and about 1 foot beyond circle.	None.
***Fusarium* blight**	Tan marks beginning at tip of blade. Lawn has reddish brown circular patches turning to yellow.	Appears during hot summer temperatures, frequently on grass under stress. High nitrogen and low calcium encourage the disease.	Avoid fertilizing during later spring to early summer. Mow high and frequently and throw away clippings. Remove thatch.	Kentucky bluegrasses 'Adelphi', 'Columbia', 'Glade', and 'Parade'.
***Fusarium* patch**	Circular water-soaked spots on leaves fade from purple to white as they grow. May have pink mold.	Usually appears in cool, moist weather during fall or spring.	Do not apply a lot of nitrogen or lime in fall. Remove thatch. Increase air circulation and drainage.	Fine fescues 'Barfalla', 'Jade', 'Jamestown', and 'Scaldis'. Kentucky bluegrasses 'Adelphi', 'Bonnieblue', 'Nassau', and 'Victa'.

(continued)

Disease	Symptoms	Conditions	Control	Resistant Grasses
Necrotic ring spot	Dead spots or yellow or red leaves on vigorous lawns.	Appears spring to early fall during warm temperatures. Most common on established lawns from sod. May only affect roots first, symptoms appear when grass is stressed.	Reduce stress. Water lightly during heat. Mow high and frequently and throw away clippings. Remove thatch.	Perennial ryegrass, tall fescue.
Powdery mildew	White to gray fuzz over yellow tissue. Lawn is a dusty white; white "bloom" rubs off easily.	Appears during cool, humid weather, and in shady conditions. High nitrogen and poor air circulation encourage it.	Reduce shading, improve air circulation. Fertilize moderately. Water in morning. Mow high frequently and throw away clippings.	Fine fescues 'Dawson', 'Fortress', 'Reliant', and 'Ruby'. Kentucky bluegrasses 'Aquila', 'Mystic', 'Primo', and 'Welcome'.
***Pythium* blight (Cottony blight)**	Circular spots later join to form large, irregular, dark, wet-looking patches. Cotton-like material may be apparent.	Appears in summer during hot, humid weather. Usually attacks northern cool-season grasses. Low calcium may encourage.	Difficult to destroy. Add lime if calcium deficient. Avoid evening watering. Improve air circulation. Remove thatch.	None.
Red thread and pink patch	Red thread causes red or rusty threads at tips of blades. Pink patch shows up as pale pink gelatinous ooze on leaf blades. Overall, both appear as circular patterns of scorched leaf tips.	Related fungi occur during spring or fall, sometimes winter, in cool, wet conditions. Low nitrogen may encourage infection.	Add nitrogen. Mow infected tips and throw away clippings. Regular deep watering.	Fine fescues 'Atlanta', 'Cascade', 'Fortress', and 'Wintergreen'. Kentucky bluegrasses 'Adelphi', 'Eclipse', 'Majestic', and 'Primo'. Perennial ryegrasses 'Acclaim', 'Dasher', 'Loretta', and 'Venlona'.
Rust	Rusty bumps on leaves and stems which rub off easily. Leaves turn yellow or brown and may die.	Occurs during hot, dry weather of late spring or early fall. Stress or nitrogen deficiency may encourage infection.	Avoid stressing turf. Fertilize regularly. Water deeply and occasionally during morning. Mow high frequently and throw away clippings.	Kentucky bluegrasses 'Aquila', 'Majestic', 'Primo', and 'Windsor'.
Smut	Grass is pale green, yellow, or brown; long narrow black streaks on curled blades. Brown, thin patches on lawn.	Occurs during moderate weather during spring or fall. Dry, thatched turf is susceptible.	Mow high frequently and throw away clippings. Fertilize regularly. Water deeply and occasionally.	Kentucky bluegrasses 'Adelphi', 'Challenger', 'Eclipse', and 'Majestic'.
Summer patch	Dead patches, then brown rings around healthy grass.	Occurs in hot, humid summers. Encouraged by high nitrogen, extreme pH, and shortly cut grass.	Fertilize regularly. Improve drainage. Water lightly during heat. Mow higher.	Kentucky bluegrasses 'Adelphi', 'Eclipse', 'Georgetown', and 'Monopoly'.
***Typhula* blight**	After snow melts, large patches of white or gray mold.	Occurs in late winter and early spring after cold temperatures and slow-melting snow.	In fall, mow short, throw away clippings and avoid fertilizing. Avoid winter compaction. Melt snow early by covering with ashes or other dark material.	Perennial ryegrass cultivar 'Regal'.

Getting Rid of Moles

Lawns provide a perfect habitat for earthworms and grubs, which are the preferred foods of moles. Wherever soil is soft and damp, these subterranean pests may appear, searching for their dinner beneath your lawn. As moles tunnel through the soil in search of food, they leave behind raised ribbons of grass, often punctuated by little mounds of excavated soil.

Several strategies may be used to undo the damage done by moles. Frequently moles use a tunnel only once, while on a one-time feeding expedition. If the only signs of mole activity are a few curvy tunnels, simply press the tunnels back down by walking on them, and provide water to help the severed grass roots quickly repair the damage.

Moles frequently do create permanent tunnels, however. They use these over and over again to get from their permanent nest to new feeding areas. When these tunnels are pressed down, the mole will often reopen them within a day.

Flooding and Trapping

To get rid of resident moles, find a long, straight tunnel and press it down in a few places. If the mole reopens the passages, you have located a permanent tunnel. First, try looking for the mole early in the morning as it works on the tunnel. When you see the soil moving, sneak up and slam the tunnel and the mole beneath with the back of a shovel.

Since the mole's nest is usually located somewhere along the permanent tunnel, you may be able to flood out the mole by filling the tunnel with water. Flooding is most effective against West Coast moles, since their nests are usually located close to the molehills. Stick the garden hose into the ground close to a hill to create an underground flood. Stand ready to catch or kill the mole when it comes to the surface to escape drowning.

You can also try trapping the mole. If children play on the lawn,

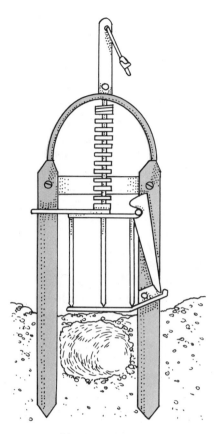

Harpoon trap

Pit trap

begin with a safe, simple trap consisting of a large can or jar buried along a permanent tunnel. Dig out a small section of the tunnel, leaving the remainder undisturbed, and bury the jar so it forms a pit in the tunnel floor. Then reconstruct the tunnel, and place a board over the trap so no sunlight can get in. When the mole comes along to repair the tunnel, it falls in the jar and is trapped.

Several commercial mole traps are available, and experts consider them effective when they are properly installed. Where moles are a recurrent nuisance, mole traps that choke, skewer, or chomp down on the mole may be the answer.

Another strategy for controlling chronic mole problems is to limit the moles' food supply by eliminating white grubs (beetle larvae). Two nontoxic methods are available. You can apply milky spore disease (*Bacillus popilliae*), a fungal disease lethal to beetle larvae and certain other pests

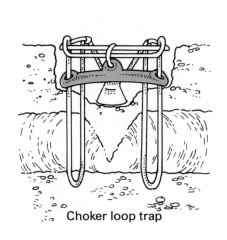

Choker loop trap

Scissor jaw trap

such as mole crickets. Or you can introduce beneficial, predatory nematodes. Both methods are slow-acting and may take two years to become effective. Remember that this is only a partial solution since moles also feed on the earthworms you are trying to encourage in your garden soil.

Finally, you can make your lawn inhospitable to foraging moles by installing rock or concrete barriers around your lawn or by using a mole fence. A fine-meshed fence with the base buried at least 18 inches underground will turn away moles, mice, and rats.

Groundcovers

Planting Groundcovers

Groundcovers are one of the most useful and care-free groups of plants you can add to your landscape. They make wonderful alternatives to conventional lawns. In fact, they're the best alternative for spots where lawn grasses just won't survive. You can also use them to provide a change of texture or color to an otherwise uninteresting corner of your yard, or to edge walks and other plantings. Perhaps best of all, they require very little care once established and can even help reduce maintenance in the garden by eliminating tasks such as trimming and edging.

The best times to plant most groundcovers are midspring and early fall. That way, they'll have time to become established before having to withstand the heat and drought of summer. It's a good idea to get the area to be planted ready before you buy your plants, so you'll be able to get them into the ground as quickly as possible. Loosen the soil in the planting site and work in moisture-holding organic soil amendments, such as leaf mold or compost. Rake up and remove weeds and grasses. When planting groundcovers in difficult places like the dry shade beneath large trees or on rocky slopes, proper site preparation is crucial.

Most groundcovers are sold in pots or packs, although you can also buy rooted cuttings of some species. Before you take the plants out of their containers, arrange them on top of the prepared soil, spacing them as evenly as possible. Space low, creeping plants such as periwinkle (*Vinca minor*) and pachysandra (*Pachysandra terminalis*) no more than 1 foot apart, but allow 3 feet or more between prostrate shrubs such as dwarf junipers.

Water the plants before removing them from their containers. Spread

Be sure to set groundcovers at or slightly above the soil line to allow for settling after planting.

tangled roots as much as possible without breaking them. Set plants in the prepared holes at about the same depth they grew in their containers. Gently firm the soil around each plant, and water thoroughly.

Rooted or unrooted cuttings of vines such as ivy may be planted 6 to 8 inches apart. Soak the cuttings in water while you make small planting holes deep enough to cover two-thirds of the cuttings when they are laid diagonally in the holes. Gently firm the soil around each plant, and then water it before you go on to the next.

When planting a bed of groundcovers that will be in full sun, it's best to plan the operation for a day when skies are overcast. If possible, plant just before several cloudy days are forecast to give the plants time to overcome transplant stress and become established before they must withstand full sun.

Preparing the Site

Level sites may be mulched with any porous organic material that will discourage weeds and help hold soil moisture. Bark chips are durable and attractive. Shredded leaves or rotted sawdust are also good choices. The first year, you may want to plant flowering annuals in the spaces between groundcover plants to improve the appearance of the site and help control weeds.

(continued on page 324)

319

A GUIDE TO SELECTED GROUNDCOVERS

There are groundcover plants for nearly every site—from full sun to shade. Some offer evergreen foliage, others produce brightly colored flowers. All are attractive and require relatively little maintenance. In addition to use as groundcovers, many can also be used as edging plants, in rock gardens, and in borders.

Groundcover	Season of Bloom	Flower Color	Description	Culture
Full Sun				
Achillea tomentosa (Woolly yarrow)	Summer	Yellow	Perennial providing a thick mat of woolly, gray-green, fernlike leaves topped with flat, 1-in.-wide flower clusters on 6-12-in. stalks.	Well-drained soil. Drought tolerant. Tolerates alkaline conditions. Propagate by division. Zones 4-10. Delicate woolly leaves are fragrant when crushed. May be mowed to maintain continuous thick carpet.
Antennaria dioica (Pussy-toes)	Early summer	White, pink	Mat-forming perennial with 1-in.-long, gray-green leaves that are white and furry underneath. Clusters of ¼-in.-wide flowers borne on 4-12-in. stalks.	Sandy, well-drained soil. Drought tolerant. Propagate by division, seeds. Zones 3-7. Good for coastal areas, exposed sites.
Dianthus gratianopolitanus (Cheddar pink)	Early summer	Rosy pink to red	Perennial forming a very dense evergreen mat. Leaves tiny and gray-green. Fragrant, ¾-in. flowers borne singly on 4-10-in. stalks.	Well-drained, slightly alkaline soil. Propagate by division, cuttings, layering, seeds. Zones 4-10. Remove flower stalks after flowering. Shear mats in fall. May need winter protection. 'Tiny Rubies' has brilliant red flowers.
Iberis sempervirens (Candytuft)	Late spring through early summer	White	Evergreen perennial forming a 6-12-in.-high mound of dark green leaves topped by myriads of tiny white flower clusters.	Any well-drained soil. Propagate by division, cuttings, seeds. Zones 4-10. Trim back hard after flowering to promote compact growth. Improved dwarf cultivars available.
***Juniperus* spp.** (Juniper)	None	None	Genus of evergreen shrubs with many mat-forming species and cultivars under 18 in. Foliage grayish green, green, blue-green.	Grows best in loamy, semi-moist soil. Propagate by cuttings, layering, seeds, grafting. Zones 2-10, depending on species. Can be planted on banks or slopes. *J. horizontalis* will grow in dry, rocky spots and will tolerate part shade; *J. conferta* in sandy soil and coastal sites.
***Potentilla* spp.** (Cinquefoil)	Spring to summer	White, yellow	Perennials or small shrubs ranging from 2-12 in. in height. Form mats or low mounds. Leaves have 3 leaflets. Small, ¼-½-in. flowers borne in loose clusters.	Sandy, well-drained, dry soil. Propagate by division, seeds. Zones 3-10. Perennial species make good cover over spring bulbs. Shrubby species very heat and drought tolerant.
***Sempervivum* spp.** (Houseleek, hen-and-chickens)	Summer	Green, yellow, or red	Succulent, rosette-forming perennial that spreads by offsets on runners surrounding central plant. Foliage green, maroon, or bicolored. Plants form dense, 2-4-in.-tall mats. Flowers are not showy.	Dry, very well-drained soil. Propagate by division. Zones 5-10, depending on species. Many cultivars with varying plant size, foliage color and/or patterns are available.

Groundcover	Season of Bloom	Flower Color	Description	Culture
Thymus spp. (Thyme)	Summer	Purple, pink	Creeping or low-growing perennials with tiny gray-green or green leaves. Height ranges from 1-10 in., depending on species. Flowers are tiny. Leaves of most species give off pleasant aroma when crushed.	Well-drained, somewhat poor soil. Drought tolerant. Propagate by division, seeds. Zones 4-10. *T. pseudolanuginosus* (woolly thyme) and *T. serpyllum* (lemon thyme) can be planted between paving stones. Flowers attractive to bees.

Full Sun to Partial Shade

Groundcover	Season of Bloom	Flower Color	Description	Culture
Arctostaphylos uva-ursi (Common bearberry)	Late spring through early summer	White, pink	Evergreen, carpet-forming shrub with tiny, ½-¾-in.-long leathery leaves. Small, bell-shaped flowers followed by attractive red berries and bronze foliage in fall. Plants 6-12 in. tall.	Sandy, acid soil. Drought tolerant. Slow-growing. Propagate by cuttings. Zones 2-4. Can be planted on banks for erosion control.
Bergenia cordifolia (Heartleaf bergenia)	Late winter or early spring	Pink	Semi-evergreen perennial that forms dense clumps. Leaves oval, leathery, and 12-18 in. long. Flowers borne in clusters above the leaves.	Will tolerate any soil, but prefers rich, humusy loam. Propagate by division. Zones 3-10. Foliage turns bronze in fall/winter.
Ceratostigma plumbaginoides (Plumbago)	Midsummer through fall	Blue	Low-growing, 9-12-in.-tall perennial that emerges in late spring. Glossy leaves turn bronze in fall. The ½-in. flowers are borne in loose clusters.	Rich, moist, well-drained soil. Best in full sun; tolerates light shade. Propagate by division, cuttings. Zones 6-10. May become invasive. Mark plantings to avoid disturbing them in spring before plants emerge. Long blooming period. Needs winter protection in the North.
Cotoneaster spp. (Cotoneaster)	Early summer	Pinkish white	Several species of deciduous to semi-evergreen shrubs with small glossy leaves, tiny flowers, and bright red berries. Plants may have creeping or arching branches and range from 1-3 ft. tall. Leaves turn dark orange-red in the fall.	Rich, well-drained soil. Drought tolerant. Prune to maintain shape desired. Propagate by cuttings, layering, seeds. Zones 4-10. Good for banks to control erosion. Species that make good groundcovers include *C. adpressus*, *C. dammeri*, and *C. horizontalis*.
Euonymus fortunei (Winter creeper)	Insignificant flowers	Pinkish	Evergreen, 1-2-ft. plant that will trail or climb. Leaves glossy green; some cultivars are variegated. Very tiny flowers followed by orange fruit clusters.	Any soil. Propagate by hardwood cuttings, layering, seeds. Zones 6-9. Good for banks to control erosion. Will grow under trees. Susceptible to euonymus scale. May become invasive; prune to maintain boundaries.
Hypericum calycinum (Aaron's beard)	Summer	Bright yellow	Evergreen subshrub that grows 1-1½ ft. tall. Leaves are oval, 3-4 in. long. Flowers are 2-3 in. wide.	Sandy, well-drained soil. Drought tolerant. Propagate by division, cuttings. Zones 6-10. May become invasive. Good for erosion control or planting under trees and shrubs. Cut back hard every few years to promote dense growth.

(continued)

Groundcover	Season of Bloom	Flower Color	Description	Culture
***Full Sun to Partial Shade*—continued**				
Liriope spp. (Lilyturf)	Midsummer to fall	Pale purple, white	Grasslike, 8-24-in. evergreen perennial with spikes of tiny flowers held above the foliage. Will spread to form thick mats.	Will grow in most soils, but prefers rich, moist loam. Propagate by division. Zones 5-10. Leaves may become tattered over winter in the North; foliage can be trimmed or mowed in spring.
Sedum spp. (Stonecrop)	Summer	Yellow, pink, white, red	A genus of succulent, creeping or mounding perennials with bright, gray- or blue-green leaves. Flowers are tiny and borne in small to large clusters. Height 2-36 in., depending on species.	Any well-drained soil. Drought tolerant. Propagate by division, cuttings. Zones 3-10. Many excellent species and cultivars available. Many spread quickly. All are very low maintenance.
Partial Shade				
Chrysogonum virginianum (Golden star)	Spring to summer	Yellow	Creeping, 3-10-in. perennial with oval leaves and attractive, small flower heads.	Semi-rich, well-drained soil. Grows best where summers are cool. Propagate by division, seeds. Zones 6-9. Good for wild gardens.
Epimedium spp. (Epimedium)	Spring	Red, pink, white	Delicate-looking perennial with light green, heart-shaped compound leaves. Plants grow 9-12 in. tall; some have leaves tinged with red. Tiny flowers borne in clusters. Leaves turn bronze in the fall and last well into winter.	Grow best in rich, moist soil, but can tolerate dry shade. Propagate by division. Zones 4-10. Many species and cultivars available.
Phlox stolonifera (Creeping phlox)	Spring	Bluish purple, pink, white	Creeping, native perennial wildflower that grows 8-10 in. high. Flowers are ¾ in. across and borne in loose clusters.	Rich, moist soil rich in organic matter. Propagate by division. Zones 4-9. Good for wildflower gardens.
Tiarella cordifolia (Foamflower)	Late spring to early summer	White	Native perennial wildflower with nearly triangular, 3-4-in. leaves with toothed margins. Tiny flowers borne in spikes held above the foliage. Leaves 6 in. tall; flower stalks 8-12 in.	Rich, moist, well-drained soil. Propagate by division, seeds. Zones 5-8. Best for wildflower gardens. Foliage may be semi-evergreen in south.
Partial Shade to Deep Shade				
Ajuga reptans (Carpet bugleweed)	Late spring to early summer	Purple, white	Low, mat-forming perennial with dark green leaves. Tiny, ¼-in. flowers borne in spikes. Leaves are ground-hugging, 1-2 in.; flower spikes 4-8 in. high.	Any well-drained garden soil. Propagate by division. Zones 4-10. Grows rapidly, can become invasive. Cultivars with variegated leaves in maroon, cream, bronze, and green are available.

Groundcover	Season of Bloom	Flower Color	Description	Culture
Asarum europaeum (European wild ginger)	Spring	Insignificant; brown	Evergreen, 4-8-in. perennial with glossy, heart-shaped, 2-3-in.-wide leaves. Flowers borne under foliage next to ground.	Rich, moist, organic soil. Spreads somewhat slowly. Propagate by division, seeds. Zones 5-9. Good for wildflower gardens, woodland areas. The tiny flowers are pollinated by slugs. Aromatic roots.
Convallaria majalis (Lily-of-the-valley)	Late spring	White, pink	Vigorous, 6-8-in. perennial with dark green leaves and spikes of tiny, fragrant, nodding, bell-shaped flowers. Forms a dense carpet.	Rich, moist soil. Propagate by division. Zones 4-9. May become invasive. Foliage may start to die down in late summer. Dig and divide if plants become crowded and stop blooming.
Hedera helix (English ivy)	Insignificant flowers	Greenish	Evergreen creeping or climbing vine with dark green or variegated leaves. Creeping plants will form a 6-10-in.-high carpet.	Rich, moist soil. Propagate by cuttings. Zones 6-10. Good for banks to control erosion. Can be planted under trees, but best to keep it from climbing. Many cultivars available, but hardiness varies.
Hosta spp. (Plantain lily)	Summer to fall	White or lavender	Genus of clump-forming perennials with broad ribbed leaves of various sizes, shapes, and colors. Tubular flowers borne in spikes usually held above the foliage. Height ranges from 6-36 in. depending on species.	Rich, moist, well-drained soil. Propagate by division. Zones 4-9. Many species and cultivars available, primarily grown for their attractive variegated leaves.
Pachysandra terminalis (Pachysandra)	Spring to summer	Off white	Evergreen, 6-10-in. perennial grown for its attractive foliage. Leaves borne in whorls. Flowers borne in spikes: not particularly showy.	Will grow in any soil; spreads fastest in moist soil rich in organic matter. Propagate by cuttings, division. Zones 6-9. Will grow under trees. Establishes readily. A cultivar with green and cream variegated leaves is available.
Vinca minor (Common periwinkle)	Early spring to early summer	Light bluish purple, white	Evergreen, mat-forming perennial with dark green leaves and small flat-faced flowers borne above foliage. Grows 4-8 in. tall.	Moderate to rich soil that is well drained. Will tolerate full sun. Propagate by division, cuttings. Zones 5-8. Good on banks for erosion control. Will grow under trees.

Before planting groundcovers on slopes, reinforce the site to keep loose soil from washing away. You can install landscape timbers, rocks, or low concrete walls if the slope is steep. If the slope is a modest one, you can rake the surface into rippled terraces, oriented perpendicularly to the slope, and set plants in the pockets of each berm. Set the plants slightly deeper than you would when planting on level ground, and mulch immediately. Small pebbles can be used in conjunction with bark or straw to hold the loose soil in place.

When naturalizing groundcovers into existing vegetation on a slope, cultivate only the soil around the planting holes rather than digging up the whole slope. When the introduced plants begin to spread, gradually remove adjoining vegetation to give the groundcover room to grow.

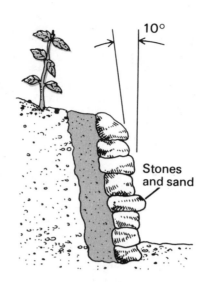
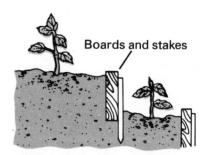

There are several ways to plant groundcovers on slopes. To prevent erosion, build 1- to 2-foot-high walls of stones backed by sand. Plant groundcovers along each wall. Have the wall slope into the hill at least 10 degrees (left). On gentler slopes, make small terraces with boards held in place by stakes (above).

PLANTS BETWEEN PAVERS

To plant creeping thyme and other compact groundcovers along the edge of a garden path or in crevices between stepping stones, begin by loosening the soil and adding sand to the pocket where the plant will grow. Compost is also a welcome soil amendment, especially when mixed with an equal amount of sand. (Excellent drainage, which sand helps provide, is important since crevices receive much more water than cultivated beds.) After planting, fill the spaces between masonry and groundcover plants with gravel or pebbles to prevent weeds and erosion. When planting groundcovers under trees—especially shallow-rooted ones—use the same soil preparation procedure.

Propagating Groundcovers

All groundcover plants, except for woody-stemmed shrubs, are easy to propagate. Most do a good job of multiplying on their own, since the best groundcovers spread naturally by underground rhizomes, runners, and stolons. There are several ways to accelerate this process to increase your supply of plants. Clumps of plants can be dug and divided and replanted elsewhere, preferably in spring or fall. Small offsets can be cut away from the parent plant and moved to a new area. And in midsummer, cuttings can be taken from vine-type ground-covers; these should develop new roots about a month after you set them in a porous planting mix.

Another way to propagate most groundcovers is by layering. This method is particularly useful for those species that develop new plants at intervals along wandering stolons or aboveground stems. The idea of layering is to provide a place where new plants will inevitably develop, and also be easy to remove for transplanting. For information on conventional layering see "Layering" on page 96. The best time to layer groundcovers varies with species, but plants tend to be most enthusiastic about spreading in early summer.

There is a simple, shortcut method for layering groundcovers that works especially well with bugleweed (*Ajuga* spp.), English ivy (*Hedera helix*), pachysandra (*Pachysandra terminalis*), periwinkle (*Vinca minor*), sedum species (*Sedum acre* and *S. album*), and winter creeper (*Euonymus fortunei*). Near the center of a healthy stand of plants, arrange two boards, 10 to 12 inches wide and 2 to 3 feet long, in a V shape, using bricks

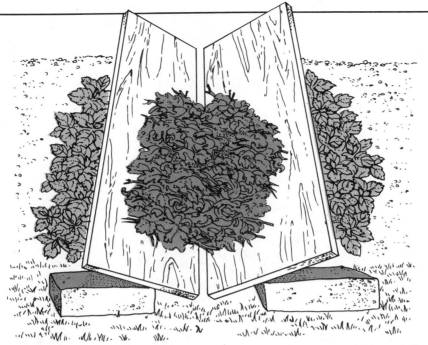

One way to increase your supply of groundcovers is to set two boards over a planting and pile mulch on the boards.

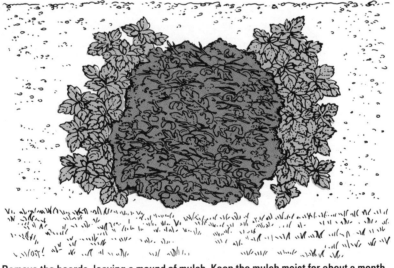

Remove the boards, leaving a mound of mulch. Keep the mulch moist for about a month.

or stones. Fill the V with shredded bark or chopped leaves. Remove the boards. The mulch should form a neat mound almost as high as the plants. Dampen the material thoroughly, and keep it damp for a month. In that time, the soft berm will become a nursery of small plants that will root in the loose organic material. The new plants may be easily dug up, snipped off, and transplanted to new sites. The mulch that was the nursery bed can be spread by hand beneath the older plants until it disappears.

New plants will form in the mulch. They can be lifted and planted permanently.

Use a bulb planter to dig holes for the new transplants.

325

PART 5
Trees and Shrubs

Growing, Planting, and Propagating

Planting Trees and Shrubs

There's no doubt about it—trees and shrubs can enhance the value of your home, both by increasing your property's monetary worth and by adding beauty and variety to your surroundings. While the cost of a well-planted property can be measured in materials, equipment, labor, and maintenance, the daily impact for most of us comes from the effects of vegetation on our physical and emotional comfort. We plant trees and shrubs because they provide welcome shade, windbreaks, privacy, and, most important, beauty. Their spring flowers, lush summer foliage, autumn color, interesting bark, and variety of forms add color, texture, and appeal to the landscape.

Design Considerations

In a design sense, trees and shrubs have a variety of uses. They can be used to screen and filter views, soften hard edges, enclose spaces, and visually connect buildings to the ground. In a good design, they also create an atmosphere that is comforting and restful.

Aesthetically, landscape plants provide visual interest, a catchall term that not only refers to flowers, fruit, fall foliage, and bark, but also to the interesting patterns, textures, and contrasts they create. And a cherished plant that might have been part of our childhood, or reminiscent of a favorite place or time, is a soul-satisfying presence.

Trees, shrubs, and other vegetation soak up noise and glare, filter atmospheric impurities, and offer shelter from winds. They also invite wildlife and bring coolness by casting shade, by transpiration, and by wind channeling. These diverse yet closely intertwined benefits should offer inspiration to gardeners to plan and plant their home landscapes with loving attention and to give them the best possible year-round care.

Let Your Site Choose the Plant

No matter how expert your planting skills, no amount of care or horticultural hocus-pocus can salvage a poor match between what a plant needs and what its site offers. The key to success with trees and shrubs is to know your site. If a designer, landscape architect, or consultant is choosing the plants for your property, make sure he or she also understands this fundamental relationship.

Soil. Begin learning about your site with a soil test. The results will tell you your soil's pH and fertility, two of the most important pieces of information that you must have when making a plant selection.

Also look at your soil's consistency and drainage characteristics. Is the soil loose or compacted? Is it clayey, sandy, or loamy? Is it rocky and shallow or chalky and poorly drained? Is it elevated, depressed, or sloping? Does water stand at any time of the year? Different plants have different tolerances for these conditions, and you're best off planting a tree or shrub that will be happy in the soil you have to offer.

Exposure. Is the planting site sunny or shady? Buildings and nearby vegetation can limit the hours of full sun that fall on a potential planting site. Be sure to check how many hours, and at what time of day, your plant will have direct sunlight.

Water. Note the amount of rainfall that you can expect your new tree or shrub to receive, and consider how you will get water to it during a dry spell. If your watering resources are limited, select plants that can tolerate occasional drought.

Other Factors. Other physical factors to watch include overhead and underground utilities (such as electric wires and water pipes); nearby buildings; actual use of the site (is it a quiet, out-of-the-way spot, or right near a path); and the size of the area, which determines the appropriate size of the plant. Recognizing these physical limitations will enable you to make better choices. If there are overhead utilities, for example, you will want to choose plants that are naturally dwarfed or slow-growing, with an ultimate height considerably lower than that of the overhead lines and equipment. Or, if your site is near a path or sidewalk, a tree with low hanging or pendant branches might pose a problem. Pavement and buildings may cause plants stress by reflecting heat, creating unnatural wind patterns, and limiting root space and water penetration. Finally, does the site have a vast, open, parklike scale or that of an intimate patio or enclosed backyard?

You'll create a more pleasing effect and minimize future headaches if you choose plants that are appropriate to the site and the prevailing conditions. Consider these "givens" to be guidelines, and work with them.

Group Plants Where Possible

Consider another strategy for success: safety in numbers.

From harsh urban streetsides to country churchyards, plants benefit greatly when arranged together in beds. Trees or shrubs sharing a bed will usually have more rooting space than if each were off in its own planting hole—especially considering the size and quality of the holes a weary gardener might dig at the end of a long day.

A group of plants also tends to create its own microclimate. Humidity in the immediate area is higher, wind is reduced, roots are shaded and cooled, perhaps a duff layer of decomposing fallen leaves is formed and begins to decompose with the mulch. Better yet, plants grouped in a bed and adequately mulched fare better at avoiding nicks, cuts, and other hardships caused by errant lawn mowers and their operators.

Since lawn mower damage is the leading cause of mechanical injury to trees, this aspect alone is reason enough to plant trees and shrubs in groups.

Grouping plants gives you more and better results from your labor. Most home gardeners will agree that preparing one good-sized bed for a group of plants is much less arduous than digging individual holes for the same number of plants, especially in a difficult soil. Maintaining, weeding, fertilizing, mulching, and especially watering a group of plants is more efficient than performing those tasks on several individual plants scattered hither and yon.

Planting Season

Planting time is determined by the nature of the species that you have selected, your climate, and the method by which your stock was transplanted. Recommendations vary based on whether a plant is bare-root, container-grown, or balled-and-burlapped (b&b). Bare-root stock should be fully dormant when received and when planted. Full dormancy is less important with container-grown and balled-and-burlapped plants, but still desirable. Your goal is to give roots a chance to become established before the demands of topgrowth become overwhelming. Some thoughtful and judicious pruning at planting time should help as well.

In areas where winter is harsh and the ground usually freezes (USDA Zone 4 and north), planting in spring as soon as the ground can be worked is the best practice. Fall planting in cold climates should be limited to those plants that establish themselves quickly. (See "Trees to Avoid Planting in Fall" for a list of trees that are slow to establish.)

In milder climates (roughly, USDA Zones 5 to 7), the opportunities for fall planting increase, although it's still best to wait until spring to plant those species that are slow to establish.

In the warmer climates (USDA Zones 8 to 10), trees and shrubs are best planted in fall and winter, as long as the ground can be worked. Spring often comes early and hot, forcing any spring-planted stock into growth that the roots may not be ready to support.

Summer planting in any but the coolest climates is rarely a good idea and should only be done in dire circumstances and with a great deal of coddling, watering, and hope.

Planting Guidelines

Try to have your planting site dug and ready before you receive your nursery stock. This may not always be practical, but if you feel a purchase coming on—dig.

Conscientious nursery operators take every measure to see that their stock is well cared for during the potentially stressful period on the sales lot. Do all that you can to plant your purchase without delay and without
(continued on page 338)

TREES TO AVOID PLANTING IN FALL

Fall planting is a wise choice for many gardeners in many climates; however, tree species that are slow in getting established should be planted in spring.

Following is a short list of plants that should not be planted in the fall.

Botanical Name	Common Name
Koelreuteria paniculata	Golden-rain tree
Liriodendron tulipifera	Tulip or yellow poplar
Quercus spp.	Most oaks
Magnolia spp.	Magnolias
Nyssa sylvatica	Black gum or tupelo
Zelkova serrata	Japanese zelkova

SELECTING TREES AND SHRUBS

Trees and shrubs are an essential part of any landscape. They provide background for flowers and other smaller plants, filter or conceal views, and can be used as borders, screens, or accents. In addition to providing shade, they also absorb pollution (including noise), control erosion, block winds, and attract wildlife. When selecting trees and shrubs, keep in mind the scale of your garden and choose plants that are an appropriate size for the use you have in mind. Also be sure to select plants that are appropriate for your climate, exposure, and soil.

Name	Height	Description	Culture
Small Trees			
Acer griseum (Paperbark maple)	25-30 ft.	Low-branching tree with cinnamon-orange bark that peels and flakes. Olive green, 2-3-in., 3-leaflet leaves turn dark orange in fall.	Full sun to partial shade. Grows best in moist, well-drained soil, but will tolerate clayey soils. Slow growing. Specimen. Zones 5-8.
Acer palmatum (Japanese maple)	20-25 ft.	Graceful, round tree with attractive lobed leaves that are reddish purple or green depending on the cultivar. Foliage turns scarlet in fall.	Full sun to partial shade. Rich, loamy or sandy, moist, acid soil. Long-lived; slow growing. Specimen. Accent plant. Shrub border. Many cultivars available. Zones 5 or 6-9, depending on the cultivar.
Amelanchier laevis (Allegheny serviceberry)	15-25 ft.	Light gray barked, multistemmed tree or large shrub with masses of white flowers in early spring. Yellow to red fall color.	Full sun to partial shade. Moist, well-drained, acid soil. Fine for naturalizing in woodlands or near ponds. Attracts birds. Zones 5-7.
Cercis canadensis (Eastern redbud)	20-30 ft.	Nearly black barked tree bearing a multitude of tiny pea-shaped flowers in spring before the heart-shaped leaves appear. Flowers are pinkish red opening to rose pink and are borne along branches and trunk.	Full sun to partial shade. Acid or alkaline, well-drained soil. Specimen. Woodland areas. Groupings. Zones 5-9.
Chionanthus virginicus (Fringe tree)	12-25 ft.	Produces fluffy white clouds of fragrant flowers in late spring; blue berries in fall. Medium to dark green leaves form as the plant is in flower. Fall foliage is yellow.	Full sun to partial shade. Loamy or sandy, moist, acid soil. Native to streambanks and edges of swampy areas. Attracts birds. Zones 4-9.
Cornus florida (Flowering dogwood)	20-30 ft.	Flowering tree bearing large white flowers with showy bracts that appear in spring. Red fall color and fruits.	Full sun. Sandy, moist but well-drained, acid soil rich in organic matter. Specimen. Shrub border. Attracts birds. Zones 5-8; select specimens grown in Zone 5 for best hardiness in the North.
Cornus kousa (Kousa dogwood)	20-30 ft.	Flowering tree with large white flowers with pointed bracts that appear in late spring, after flowering dogwoods have bloomed. Mottled ornamental bark. Red fall color. Orange fruits.	Full sun. Sandy, humusy, acid soil rich in organic matter. Specimen. Shrub border. Attracts birds. Zones 5-8.
Elaeagnus angustifolia (Russian olive)	20-25 ft.	Multi- or singletrunked tree with silvery, willowlike leaves on spiny branches.	Full sun. Any dry soil. Long-lived; medium-fast growth. Salt, drought, and pollution tolerant. Coastal area. Windbreak. Shrub border. Attracts birds. Zones 3-9.

Name	Height	Description	Culture
Lagerstroemia indica (Crape myrtle)	20-25 ft.	Multitrunked tree with attractive exfoliating bark and large, 6-8-in. clusters of summer-borne flowers in pink, white, rose, and purple.	Full sun. Moist, well-drained soil rich in organic matter. Specimen. Can be grown as a shrub. Zones 7-10.
Magnolia stellata (Star magnolia)	15-20 ft.	Dense shrub or small tree with dark green leaves and fragrant, 3-in.-wide flowers with many narrow petals borne in masses in spring.	Full sun. Moist, acid soil rich in organic matter. Specimen or accent plant. Foundation plantings. Avoid south-facing sites. Many cultivars available. Zones 4-8.
Malus spp. (Crab apple)	15-25 ft.	Large group of small trees grown for their abundant white, pink, or red flowers and showy red or yellow fruit.	Full sun. Rich, humusy, acid soil that is moist but well drained. Many cultivars available; some exhibit disease resistance. Specimen. Good street tree. Zones 3-9; hardiness varies among species and cultivars.
Syringa reticulata (Japanese tree lilac)	25-30 ft.	Multi- or singletrunked tree with attractive, cherrylike bark. Fragrant white flowers in late spring.	Full sun to partial shade. Loose, well-drained, slightly acid soil. Specimen. Good street tree. Zones 4-7.

Medium Trees

Name	Height	Description	Culture
Carpinus betulus (European hornbeam)	40-60 ft.	Attractive tree with smooth gray beechlike bark and dark green toothed leaves. Fall color is yellow to yellow-green.	Full sun to partial shade. Rich, moist, well-drained soil; will tolerate a wide range of soils. Slow growing. Screens. Hedges. Many cultivars available. Zones 4-7.
Cladrastis lutea (American yellowwood)	30-50 ft.	Fragrant white flowers borne in late spring to early summer that hang in clusters similar to wisteria. Yellow fall color. Smooth, gray, beechlike bark.	Full sun. Average, well-drained soil. Tolerates acid or alkaline pH. Prune in summer; bleeds if pruned in winter or spring. Zones 4-8.
Davidia involucrata (Dove tree)	20-40 ft.	Striking spring-blooming tree bearing showy flowers with large white bracts. Heart-shaped toothed leaves and ornamental scaly orange bark.	Partial shade, but will tolerate sun in moist soil. Rich, moist, well-drained soil. Specimen. Grow in sheltered conditions. Zones 6-9.
Halesia carolina (Silverbell tree)	30-40 ft.	Spring-blooming tree with white, bell-like flowers that hang in rows under leaves. Foliage is yellow-green; gold in fall. Gray to brown bark marked with ridges and furrows.	Full sun to partial shade. Rich, moist, well-drained acid soil. Specimen. Woodland gardens. Shrub borders. Zones 5-8.
Koelreuteria paniculata (Golden-rain tree)	30-35 ft.	Round-headed tree bearing masses of fragrant yellow flowers in summer. Attractive, papery, lantern-like fruit. Yellow fall color.	Full sun. Any well-drained soil. Drought and heat tolerant. Relatively pest-free. Good near streets. Zones 5-10.
Prunus sargentii (Sargent cherry)	40-50 ft.	Beautiful spring-blooming tree with masses of pale pink flowers. Attractive red-brown bark is shiny and smooth. Foliage is shiny and dark green, turning red or bronze in fall.	Full sun to partial shade. Rich, sandy, humusy soil that is moist but well drained. Attracts birds. Specimen. Zones. 5-9.

(continued)

Name	Height	Description	Culture
Medium Trees—continued			
Pterostyrax hispidus (Fragrant epaulette tree)	30-45 ft.	Japanese native with clusters of fragrant, creamy white flowers in dangling clusters borne in early summer.	Full sun. Rich, moist, acid soil. Small gardens. Specimen. Zones 5-9.
Pyrus calleryana 'Bradford' (Bradford pear)	30-50 ft.	Pyramid to oval-shaped tree with off white flowers in spring followed by dense glossy green foliage. Fall foliage is purple-red.	Full sun. Average to poor soil. Drought and fire blight resistant. Good street or lawn tree. Zones 4-8.
Sassafras albidum (Sassafras)	30-60 ft.	Multi- or singletrunked tree with 1-, 2- or 3-lobed leaves. Foliage bright green, turning yellow, orange, red and purple in autumn.	Full sun to partial shade. Moist but well-drained acid soil. Naturalized areas. Leaves aromatic when crushed. Zones 5-9.
Stewartia pseudocamellia (Japanese stewartia)	30-60 ft.	Summer-blooming tree bearing white flowers with a crepe-paperlike texture. Foliage is bright green, turning yellow, red to red-purple in fall. Ornamental red bark.	Full sun to partial shade. Moist, acid soil rich in organic matter. Specimen. Zones 6-9.
Large Trees			
Acer rubrum (Red maple)	92-120 ft.	Large tree bearing bright red flowers in spring before the foliage appears. Leaves are 3-lobed, medium to dark green, and turn brilliant scarlet and yellow in fall. Smooth silver-gray bark.	Full sun to partial shade. Rich to poor, moist soil; will develop chlorosis due to manganese deficiency in high pH soils. Medium-fast growth. Moist areas. Specimen. Wood may split in heavy wind, snow, or ice. Zones 3-9.
Betula nigra (River birch)	40-70 ft.	Single- or multitrunked tree with peeling cinnamon-brown bark. Medium green leaves turn brilliant yellow in fall.	Full sun to partial shade. Loamy or sandy, moist, acid soil; foliage will become chlorotic in alkaline soil. Specimen. Moist areas. Streambanks. 'Heritage' is a nearly-white barked cultivar. Zones 5-9.
Cedrus libani (Cedar-of-Lebanon)	40-60 ft.	Picturesque evergreen with clusters of attractive dark green needles and upright cones.	Full sun. Rich, loamy soil that is well drained. Specimen. Zones 6-9.
Cercidiphyllum japonicum (Katsura tree)	50-80 ft.	Multitrunked tree with heart-shaped, blue-green leaves that turn yellow to orange in fall. Foliage has a spicy scent.	Full sun to partial shade. Rich, moist, well-drained soil. Good for shade. Specimen. Can be trained to one trunk; multitrunked specimens need lots of room. Zones 5-9.
Chamaecyparis obtusa (Hinoki false cypress)	50-75 ft.	Evergreen with pyramidal habit and small fans of flattened, dark green leaflets.	Full sun. Rich, humusy, acid soil. Slow growing. Specimen. Shrub border. Dwarf cultivars available for use in rock gardens, near foundations. Zones 4-9.
Fagus sylvatica (European beech)	50-60 ft.	Spreading, gray-barked tree with branches close to the ground. Foliage is glossy and dark green, turning rust brown in autumn. Beautiful silvery, smooth bark.	Full sun to partial shade. Rich, moist but well-drained soil. Specimen for large areas. Can be pruned as hedge. Many cultivars available, including bronze-leaved and weeping. Zones 4-10.

Name	Height	Description	Culture
Metasequoia glyptostroboides (Dawn redwood)	100-110 ft.	Pyramidal deciduous conifer with light green, fernlike needles that turn golden brown before falling in autumn. Attractive reddish bark.	Full sun. Rich, humusy, moist but well-drained soil. Best in neutral to acid soils. Fast growing. Specimen. Screens. Zones 5-8.
Nyssa sylvatica (Black gum, tupelo)	50-100 ft.	Native, gray-trunked tree with dark, glossy green leaves that turn yellow, red, to red-purple in fall.	Full sun to partial shade. Rich, humusy, acid soil. Tolerates wet soil and swampy areas. Specimen. Woodland areas. Fruit attracts wildlife. Zones 5-10.
Pinus strobus (Eastern white pine)	50-80 ft.	Fast-growing evergreen with soft, blue-green needles. Pyramidal when young; picturesque and irregular when old.	Full sun. Loamy, moist but well-drained soil. Leaves will become chlorotic in very alkaline soil. Specimen. Can be pruned as a hedge. Zones 3-8.
Quercus rubra (Red oak)	60-80 ft.	Fast-growing oak with dark green leaves that turn red in autumn.	Full sun. Loamy, moist but well-drained soil that is slightly acid. Leaves can become chlorotic in alkaline soil. Specimen. Street tree. Zones 5-8.
Sophora japonica (Japanese pagoda tree)	50-75 ft.	Summer-blooming tree with small, white, somewhat fragrant, pealike flowers borne in large clusters. Foliage is medium to dark green; no autumn color of note.	Full sun. Loamy, well-drained soil. Drought resistant. Street tree. Tolerates city conditions. Specimen. Zones 5-9.
Zelkova serrata (Japanese zelkova)	60-70 ft.	Umbrella-shaped tree with dark green leaves that turn orange-red in fall. Attractive exfoliating bark.	Full sun. Deep, moist, well-drained soil. Drought and wind tolerant once established. Street tree. Specimen. Zones 5-9.

Small Shrubs

Name	Height	Description	Culture
Berberis thunbergii 'Crimson Pigmy' (Dwarf Japanese barberry)	1½-2 ft.	Thorny, deciduous shrub with maroon-red leaves and a mounded, low-growing habit.	Full sun to partial shade. Will tolerate poor, dry soil. Edgings. Shrub border. Hedge. Also sold as 'Little Gem', 'Little Pigmy', and 'Atropurpurea Nana'. Zones 4-9.
Cotoneaster horizontalis (Rock spray cotoneaster)	2-3 ft.	Low-growing, heavily branched shrub with small, glossy green leaves that are deciduous to evergreen. Tiny, white, spring-borne flowers are followed by bright red berries.	Full sun or partial shade. Moist, well-drained soil. Will tolerate acid or alkaline pH as well as dry, poor soil. Groundcover. On banks. Massed plantings. Zones 5-9.
Fothergilla gardenii (Dwarf fothergilla)	2-3 ft.	Slow-growing, spring-blooming shrub bearing clusters of fragrant white flowers. Dark green, leathery leaves turn yellow, orange, and scarlet in fall.	Full sun to partial shade. Rich, moist, acid soil. Near foundations. Shrub borders. Woodland areas. Zones 5-9.
Hypericum prolificum (Shrubby St.-John's-wort)	1-4 ft.	Summer-blooming, deciduous shrub with bright yellow flowers borne in small clusters. Glossy leaves are nearly blue-green.	Full sun to partial shade. Will tolerate any soil; good for dry, rocky sites. Shrub border. Long blooming period. Zones 5-10.

(continued)

333

Name	Height	Description	Culture
***Small Shrubs*—continued**			
Juniperus horizontalis (Creeping juniper)	1-1½ ft.	Creeping, evergreen shrub with needlelike leaves. Foliage may be gray-green or blue-green; some cultivars turn purplish in winter.	Full sun. Will tolerate sandy, dry, or clayey soil. Withstands drought and heat. Groundcover. On banks. Edgings. Foundations. Zones 3-10.
Potentilla fruticosa (Shrubby cinquefoil)	3-4 ft.	Mound-shaped deciduous shrub with yellow, buttercup-like flowers borne spring through fall. Small, light green leaves.	Full sun to partial shade. Any moist, well-drained soil, but will tolerate poor, dry soil. Shrub border. Edgings. Near foundations. Prune out ⅓ of old canes each year in late winter to maintain shape. Zones 3-9.
Medium Shrubs			
Abelia × grandiflora (Glossy abelia)	4-6 ft.	Dense, semi-evergreen shrub with shiny, dark green leaves that turn bronze in fall. Tubular, pinkish-white flowers borne summer through frost.	Full sun to partial shade. Moist, well-drained, acid soil. Specimen. Hedges. Massed plantings. On banks. Zones 6-9.
Callicarpa japonica (Japanese beautyberry)	4-6 ft.	Deciduous shrub with clusters of small pink or white flowers in summer. Brilliant purple berrylike fruit remains ornamental long after leaves fall.	Full sun to partial shade. Well-drained soil. Shrub borders. Massed plantings. Cut plants back to 4-6 in. each spring; flowers and fruit borne on new growth. Zones 5-8.
Calycanthus floridus (Carolina allspice)	8-10 ft.	Deciduous shrub with 2-in.-wide, reddish brown flowers that have a very fruity fragrance. Lance-shaped leaves turn pale yellow in fall.	Full sun to partial shade. Will adapt to many soils; rich, moist, loam soil is best. Massed plantings. Shrub border. Plant where flower fragrance can be appreciated. Zones 5-9.
Cornus alba (Tartarian dogwood)	6-10 ft.	Deciduous shrub grown for its striking, bright red branches, which are effective in winter. Bears small clusters of yellowish white flowers in spring followed by white berries.	Full sun to partial shade. Will adapt to many soils; rich, moist, loam soil is best. Tolerates wet soils. Massed plantings. Shrub border. Remove one-third of old canes each spring; younger canes are most colorful. Several cultivars available. Zones 3-10.
Deutzia gracilis (Slender deutzia)	3-6 ft.	Old-fashioned, deciduous, spring-blooming shrub with 2-4-in. clusters of abundant single white flowers.	Full sun to partial shade. Any moist, well-drained soil. Hedges. Shrub borders. Massed plantings. Prune out several older canes each spring after flowering to encourage future bloom. Zones 5-9.
Forsythia × intermedia (Border forsythia)	8-10 ft.	Popular deciduous shrub bearing many bright yellow bell-shaped flowers all along branches in early spring.	Full sun to partial shade. Will tolerate any soil. Good in masses. On banks. Hedges. Specimen. Remove some older canes immediately after flowering each spring for renewal. Several cultivars available. Zones 5-9.

Name	Height	Description	Culture
Hydrangea quercifolia (Oakleaf hydrangea)	4-6 ft.	Deciduous shrub with cinnamon-colored bark and oak-shaped leaves that turn red in fall. Bears large clusters of white flowers in spring, which turn pinkish and then dry to brown.	Full sun to deep shade. Moist, fertile, well-drained soil. Shrub border. Massed plantings. Specimen. Brittle wood. Zones 5-10, but flower buds may not be hardy in Zone 5.
Ilex crenata (Japanese holly)	4-9 ft.	Evergreen shrub with small, dark green, shiny leaves. Tiny white flowers followed by somewhat inconspicuous black fruit.	Full sun to partial shade. Loamy, moist but well-drained soil. Hedges. Foundation plantings. Massed plantings. Many cultivars available. Zones 6-10.
Ilex verticillata (Common winterberry)	9-10 ft.	Deciduous shrub or small tree that bears masses of bright red berries in fall that persist through late winter. Plant 1 male for every 2 or 3 females for berry production.	Full sun to partial shade. Moist or wet, acid soil that is rich in organic matter. Massed plantings. Shrub borders. Specimen. Waterside plantings. Zones 4-8.
Kalmia latifolia (Mountain laurel)	4-10 ft.	Evergreen shrub or small tree bearing showy clusters of small white or pink flowers marked with dark pink. Blooms appear in late spring.	Full sun to partial shade. Rich, moist, well-drained, acid soil. Specimen. Woodland areas. Effective when grown with rhododendrons. Many cultivars available. Zones 5-9.
Leucothoe fontanesiana (Drooping leucothoe)	4-6 ft.	Graceful evergreen with attractive foliage and arching branches and clusters of fragrant white flowers that resemble lily-of-the-valley. Bronze-purple winter foliage.	Partial to deep shade. Rich, moist, acid soil. Mixed borders. Woodland areas. Shady banks. Remove one-third of oldest wood in spring after flowering. Zones 5-9.
Mahonia aquifolium (Oregon grape)	3-6 ft.	Slow-growing evergreen, with spiny, holly-like leaves. Bright yellow, spring-borne flowers are followed by grapelike clusters of blue-black fruit.	Partial shade. Loamy, well-drained, acid soil rich in organic matter. Select a protected site away from sun and wind. Shrub borders. Foundation plantings. Zones 6-10.
Myrica pensylvanica (Northern bayberry)	7-10 ft.	Deciduous or semi-evergreen shrub with dark green leaves and small, waxy, gray fruits borne along the stems. Fruits and foliage have characteristic bayberry fragrance.	Full sun to partial shade. Will tolerate most soils, including very poor sand and heavy clay. Salt tolerant. Massed plantings. Shrub borders. Foundation plantings. Zones 2-6.
Pieris japonica (Japanese pieris, lily-of-the-valley bush)	8-10 ft.	Spring-blooming evergreen with dark green, lance-shaped leaves. Small, bell-shaped flowers borne in drooping clusters.	Full sun to partial shade. Moist, acid soil that is well drained and rich in organic matter. Shrub borders. Massed plantings. Specimen. Woodland areas. Many cultivars available. Zones 5-8.
Viburnum plicatum var. tomentosum (Doublefile viburnum)	8-10 ft.	Deciduous, spring-blooming shrub bearing large clusters of white flowers along the tops of its horizontal branches.	Full sun. Moist, well-drained soil rich in organic matter. Shrub borders. Massed plantings. Specimen. Foundation plantings. Several cultivars available. Zones 5-8.

(continued)

Name	Height	Description	Culture
***Medium Shrubs*—continued**			
Viburnum rhytidophyllum (Leatherleaf viburnum)	9-10 ft.	Evergreen shrub, which is semi-evergreen in the northern part of its range, with crinkled, dark green leaves. Flat clusters of off-white flowers in spring.	Partial to heavy shade. Well-drained soil rich in organic matter. Specimen. Shrub borders. Massed plantings. Select a site protected from wind and winter sun. Zones 6-9.
Weigela florida (Old-fashioned weigela)	6-9 ft.	Old-fashioned, deciduous shrub bearing masses of pink tubular flowers in late spring.	Full sun. Any well-drained soil. Mixed borders. Foundation plantings. Many cultivars available. Prune regularly to keep plant attractive. Zones 6-9.
Large Shrubs			
Aesculus parviflora (Bottlebrush buckeye)	8-15 ft.	Multistemmed, deciduous shrub that blooms in summer. Flowers borne in erect, 8-10-in.-long clusters. Individual blooms are flowers with pink, threadlike stamens.	Full sun to partial shade. Moist, well-drained soil rich in organic matter. Massed plantings. Shrub borders. Woodland or shady areas. Specimen. Spreads into wide-ranging clumps by suckers produced underground. Zones 5-9.
Buxus sempervirens (Common box, English or American box)	6-15 ft.	Slow-growing, evergreen shrub or small tree with small, densely set leaves that are glossy and dark green.	Full sun to partial shade. Moist, well-drained soil. Shallow-rooted; use mulch to protect roots. Shrub border. Hedges. Many cultivars available, including very dwarf ones. Zones 6-10; hardiness of cultivars varies.
Corylopsis spp. (Winter hazel)	6-15 ft.	Deciduous shrubs that bloom in very early spring before the leaves appear. Flowers are fragrant, pale yellow, and borne in small, pendant clusters. Dark green leaves turn yellow in fall.	Full sun to partial shade. Moist, acid soil that is well drained and rich in organic matter. Shrub border. Specimen for early bloom. Plant in sheltered location to protect bloom. Zones 5-7.
Euonymus alata (Winged spindle tree)	4-15 ft.	Spreading, graceful, deciduous shrub with small leaves that turn brilliant red in fall. Small, yellow-green flowers yield red berries attractive to birds.	Full sun to heavy shade. Will tolerate most soils, and a wide range of pH. Hedges. Shrub border. Massed plantings. Specimen. Can be pruned into a small tree. Zones 4-9.
Hibiscus syriacus (Rose-of-Sharon)	8-15 ft.	Deciduous, globe-shaped shrub or small tree that bears large, trumpet-shaped, white, red, or purple flowers from late summer to fall. Each lasts only a day.	Full sun to partial shade. Will tolerate most soils; best in rich, moist, well-drained soil. Mass plantings. Shrub borders. Screens. Zones 6-9.

Name	Height	Description	Culture
Ilex × meserveae (Blue holly)	8-15 ft.	Compact, pyramidal evergreens with spiny leaves that are blue-green. Bright red berries in fall. Plant 1 male for every 2 or 3 females for berry production.	Full sun to partial shade. Moist, well-drained acid soil rich in organic matter. Hedges. Specimens. Shrub borders. Foundation plantings. Several cultivars available. Zones 5-9; hardiness of cultivars varies.
Philadelphus coronarius (Sweet mock orange)	9-12 ft.	Deciduous, somewhat coarse-looking shrub that bears clusters of very fragrant white flowers in spring.	Full sun to partial shade. Will tolerate any soil but best in moist loam. Shrub borders. Many cultivars available. Prune after flowering to remove some old canes each year. Zones 5-9.
Pyracantha coccinea (Scarlet fire thorn)	6-15 ft.	Semi-evergreen to evergreen shrub with clusters of small white flowers in spring followed by brilliant orange berries in fall.	Full sun to partial shade. Will tolerate most well-drained soils. Best berry production in full sun. Hedge or barrier plant. Trained as espalier against walls. Many cultivars available. Zones 6-9; hardiness of cultivars varies.
Rhododendron spp. (Rhododendrons and azaleas)	2-40 ft.	Very large and diverse group, grown for spectacular clusters of flowers in white, lavender, purple, pink, red, orange, and yellow. Gardeners separate them into two major divisions: azaleas and rhododendrons. Azaleas are usually deciduous and have funnel-shaped flowers with 5 stamens; rhododendrons are evergreen, with bell-shaped flowers with 10 stamens.	Full sun to partial shade. Moist, acid soil that is well drained and rich in organic matter. Shrub borders. Massed plantings. Specimen. Many species and cultivars available. Zones 5-9; hardiness of cultivars varies.
Syringa vulgaris (Lilac)	6-15 ft.	Large deciduous shrub with extremely fragrant clusters of flowers that appear in spring. Blooms may be lilac, white, pink, purple, magenta.	Full sun to partial shade. Will tolerate most soils; neutral pH and rich organic matter content is best. Shrub borders. Hedges. Massed plantings. Prune each spring after flowering. Zones 4-7.
Taxus cuspidata (Japanese yew)	10-40 ft.	Needled evergreen with nearly black-green foliage and an attractive, densely branched, rounded habit. A shrub or small tree.	Full sun to partial shade. Moist, well-drained, somewhat sandy soil. Avoid planting in windy sites. Hedges. Shrub borders. Foundation plantings. Massed plantings. Many cultivars available, including dwarf ones. Zones 5-7.

HOLDING OVER NURSERY STOCK

While the very best strategy is to have your planting site prepared so that you can plant immediately upon receipt of the nursery stock, reality provides dozens of reasons why this might not be possible.

These guidelines will help you to successfully hold over plant material until planting time.

• Keep hold-over time to a minimum. Plants are usually stressed when their roots are out of the ground, and the sooner you plant them, the sooner they'll begin establishing themselves.

• Protect the plants from direct exposure to wind and sun. A sheltered site on the north side of a building is fine.

• Water the plants well. Don't let pots or root balls dry out or be disturbed; also make sure that drainage is not obstructed.

• Don't fertilize.

• If plants are to be held over the winter, keep their potted roots under a protective layer of

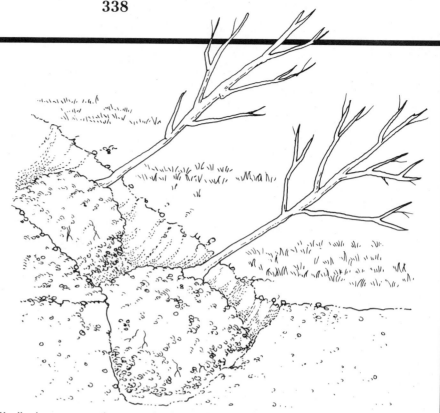

Heeling in young trees that cannot be planted immediately protects their root systems from drying out or being damaged. In a sheltered location, dig a trench with one sloped edge. Lay trees against that edge, with their roots in the trench, and fully cover the root systems with soil. Be sure to keep the soil moist, but not fully wet, until you are ready to plant.

mulch or in a trench backfilled with soil. A cold frame may also be a good choice, depending on the size and number of plants.

• Protect your stock from rodents and deer.

• Unearth your stock and plant it as soon as soil conditions permit and before active growth begins.

---

undue stress to the plants. (See "Holding Over Nursery Stock" above for tips on caring for plants that must wait for planting time.)

When preparing the planting hole, dig widely rather than deeply. Research and experience have shown repeatedly that the top 12 inches of soil—out to and beyond the anticipated dripline of the tree—is where the action is in terms of feeder roots. Dig a hole twice as wide as the root mass and just deep enough so the plant rests at a point no deeper or shallower than when dug. Remember, too, that digging should be confined to those times when the soil is nei-

ther too wet nor too dry. Dig when the soil is slightly damp and crumbly. Especially on clay soils, digging at the wrong time can worsen an already troublesome soil structure.

Rough up the sides of the hole with a spading fork or hand cultivator to reduce the possibility of glazing, a condition caused when the back of a spade or shovel smooths the walls of the hole so as to create an impenetrable "pot." Glazing effectively discourages the plant's roots from entering the surrounding soil and is especially a problem on soil with a high clay content. If possible, use a spading fork to loosen—but not turn

—the top 12 inches of the soil to a point 5 to 10 feet out from the planting hole. This will make the going easier for those important feeder roots.

Planting Nursery Stock

The proper way to plant depends on the type of nursery stock you've purchased—balled-and-burlapped, container-grown, or bare-root. Backfilling procedure is the same for all nursery stock.

Balled-and-Burlapped. Set the root ball of balled-and-burlapped stock in the hole and check for proper depth by placing a rod or straight piece of lumber across the top of the hole. The top of the root mass should be at the same level as the rod. If this is not the case, remove the tree from the hole and either backfill or dig further.

Remove all rope, twine, string, or whatever may be binding the root ball, making extra sure to remove any material binding the trunk. If the fabric used to hold the root ball is synthetic, remove it completely. Burlap can stay on the root ball, but it must be folded back and buried entirely so it will rot. Otherwise, it will create a dry root barrier by wicking moisture into the air.

Wire baskets, planting bags, and any other material should be removed. Cut away any dead or damaged roots that you can without disturbing the root ball.

Container-Grown. Regardless of the type of pot, remove it before planting. Even peat or papier-mâché pots, which will rot if buried, have the potential to wick moisture away from the roots, causing an impenetrable barrier that will limit root growth.

Once the root ball is out of the pot, check for roots that circle around the outside of the ball. These have a tendency to continue circling, even after the plant is no longer contained. You can loosen them and trim them back to encourage branching, or, if the root mass is very dense, you may want to rough up the roots by running a sharp knife down the side, across the bottom, and up the other side of the root ball. This will cut the roots and encourage branching.

Also look carefully for girdling roots, which wrap around the base of the trunk and hinder the uptake of water or completely strangle the plant. Remove girdling roots completely. Cut dead or damaged roots back to healthy tissue. Set the plant in the hole, making sure to check for appropriate depth.

Bare-Root. Remove any packing material. Check the roots and cut away any dead, dying, or diseased tissue. Soak the roots in a bucket of water for at least an hour. Prune any broken or damaged branches, any crossed branches, and any branches that emerge from the trunk at an angle of 45 degrees or less.

Make a cone of soil in the bottom of the planting hole and spread the roots over it. As you backfill, gently shake the tree so that the soil falls into all large air pockets.

Filling the Hole

Given the attention paid to this recipe and that formula for backfilling the planting holes of trees and shrubs, home gardeners may find the following advice startling: Backfill with native soil; use little or no soil amendments such as peat, purchased topsoil, or other materials. Observations and experiments at locations throughout the United States indicate that amended backfill encourages the roots to remain in the planting hole.

This keeps the tree from becoming fully established—from spreading its roots out into the surrounding soil—and makes it susceptible to waterlogging, wind throw, and disease and insect problems. Roots must be encouraged to grow beyond the

To plant a young tree, dig a hole as deep as the tree's root system and twice as wide. Then, with a digging fork, loosen the soil surrounding the hole to a distance of 5 to 10 feet from the tree trunk.

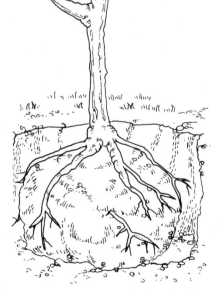

Trim any damaged or dead roots, and set the tree in the hole at the same depth as it was previously planted. Tree and root bark have different colors and textures.

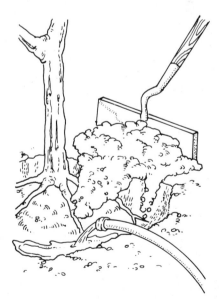

Run water from a garden hose gently into the hole as you fill it with soil, or find another method to settle the soil with water as you shovel. Shake the tree gently while you work to ensure that all air pockets around the roots are filled with soil.

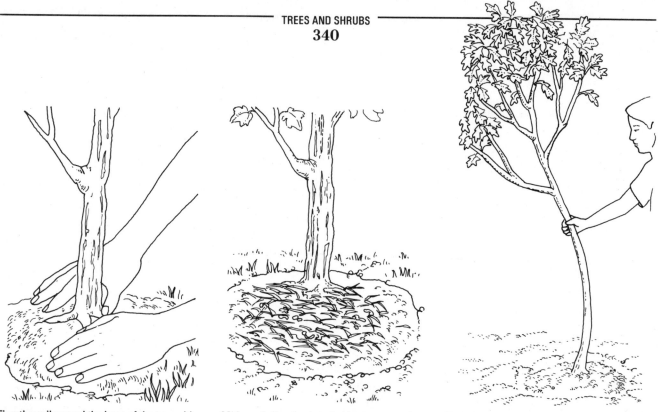

Firm the soil around the base of the tree with your hands.

Make a shallow basin to hold water around the roots, and apply a 1- to 2-inch-deep mulch layer. Your tree is ready to begin growth in its new location.

To find the right spot to attach a staking support, slide your hand up the trunk while pulling it toward you until both you and the tree are upright.

TRANSPLANTING
AN ESTABLISHED TREE OR SHRUB

Professionally grown nursery stock is usually trained for transplanting. This is accomplished in the nursery either by root-pruning the plants periodically or by container growing. An established tree or shrub, whether grown in your yard or woodlot, will need to be prepared in a similar manner. The larger the plant, the more likely that training by root-pruning will be necessary.

Transplanting frequently requires time, effort, commitment, and physical strength that might make a home gardener think twice. So think twice before you begin and make sure that the move is exactly what you want.

If the plant is a large one and you are intent on moving it, consider root-pruning at least a year before you transplant. Do this by digging a 6- to 8-inch-wide trench, 18 to 24 inches deep, around the plant. Site the trench at a distance from the plant's center that equals 24 inches for each inch of diameter of the trunk. Do your best to cut rather than tear the roots. Backfill the trench with sphagnum moss. At the same time, remove about one-third of the topgrowth by thinning, rather than heading. All of this will encourage the plant to form a more compact root system that will better survive the shock of transplanting and more quickly reestablish itself. Do not fertilize during the growing season preceding transplanting.

Whether or not you root-prune, transplant while the tree or shrub is dormant. Dig a root ball that is about 24 inches wide for each inch of trunk diameter and 12 to 18 inches deep. Keep in mind that such a root ball for a tree with only a 1-inch trunk can weigh as much as 160 pounds! Plan in advance how you'll extract the dug tree from the hole and move it to its new spot.

Do all that you can to ensure that the root ball stays in one piece during transplanting. Depending on the size of the plant and the distance of the move, you may want to wrap—or at least cradle—the root ball in burlap or some similar material.

The root ball cannot be permitted to dry out, so have the new hole ready to go and transplant without delay.

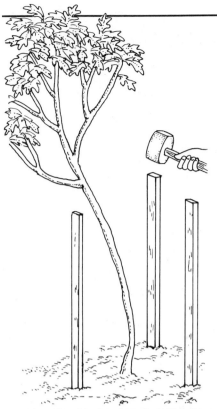

Drive three 2 × 2-inch stakes about 18 inches into the ground around the tree. Position the stakes to mark a triangle whose sides just frame the root ball. Each stake should be at least 12 inches from the trunk.

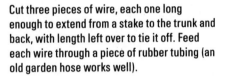

Cut three pieces of wire, each one long enough to extend from a stake to the trunk and back, with length left over to tie it off. Feed each wire through a piece of rubber tubing (an old garden hose works well).

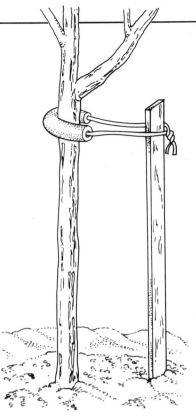

Place the covered portion of the wire around the predetermined spot. Pull the ends of the wire even on either side of one stake, twist them together, and bend the sharp ends down against the stake. Repeat, fastening one wire to each stake.

confines of the planting hole, especially in poor soils.

One exception is planting in urban or highly disturbed soils, where every trace of "native" soil has virtually disappeared. Consider checking with your local cooperative extension service or with an urban tree specialist for recommendations specific to your area and particular needs. Otherwise, backfill with the native soil, amending only the top few inches with compost if you absolutely must.

After filling the hole, firm the soil with your hands rather than your feet, making a "dish" around the edges of the hole to help hold and direct water. Water well and apply a 1- to 2-inch-deep layer of mulch.

Staking

Not every plant needs to be staked. Make your decisions based on the size of the tree: Large ones usually need the support and small ones need the protection. Trees that are listing to one side will also benefit from staking. Always leave a few inches of leeway for the tree to sway with the wind. A stronger trunk will result. Remove the stakes six months to a year after planting. For more information, see the instructions illustrated below.

Avoid wrapping the trunk with any material unless there is a clear possibility of animal damage—or of sunscald or frost cracking on trees with smooth or thin bark. Don't leave wrapping on the tree for more than a year after planting.

To encourage wide spreading root growth, water beyond the planting hole and out toward the tree's future drip line. For the first year or two, water deeply and slowly when natural rainfall is inadequate. Soaker hoses are good for this. Once the tree is established, you shouldn't need to water and you can begin to fertilize.

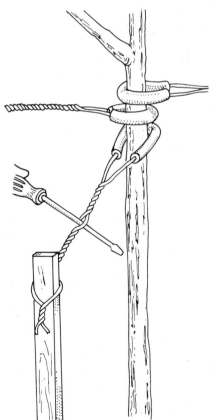

If any of the supports are slack, place a screwdriver blade between the support's two wires and rotate it to twist the wires tight.

Propagating Trees and Shrubs

Propagating trees and shrubs at home is an absolutely enjoyable aspect of gardening—a combination of science and puttering. It requires a certain amount of time, equipment, and energy, in addition to curiosity, a spirit of experimentation, and the whole-hearted appreciation of a good bargain. Home gardeners have contributed in many ways to the body of knowledge concerning the propagation of such plants. Part of experimenting with propagation at home is sharing what you have learned with other gardeners.

Layering

Layering is a form of vegetative propagation that is nicely suited for home gardeners, as it requires a minimum of equipment, virtually no greenhouse space, and few other resources. Success rates are high because the new plant is separated from the parent only after it is fully rooted. Furthermore, you can grow as few or as many new plants as you want, all for minimal cost.

Layering works well with many common landscape shrubs, including barberries (*Berberis* spp.); magnolias (*Magnolia* spp., especially the shrubby species); azaleas and rhododendrons (*Rhododendron* spp.); brambles such as blackberries and raspberries (*Rubus* spp.); lilacs (*Syringa vulgaris* and other species); and viburnums (*Viburnum* spp.).

Cuttings

Propagation by cuttings is a vegetative method by which you effectively clone, or make an exact copy, of the parent plant. Taking and rooting cuttings requires more time and resources than layering, but offers advantages—larger quantities of plants in less time, for example.

Before getting started, you'll need to obtain specific information on rooting the plant you wish to propagate. Although the general recommendations provided here will work with many species, many woody plants have exacting requirements. Consult a reference manual, your cooperative extension service, or your local arboretum, botanical garden, or plant society (i.e., American Camellia Society, Azalea Society of America, and others) for recommendations. (See "Recommended Reading" on page 406 for a list of books that contain information on propagation.)

To take and root woody cuttings at home, you will need some basic equipment.

● Pruners or a well-sharpened knife
● 6-inch plastic flowerpot or seed flat
● Plastic bags and twist ties, or a greenhouse mist bench
● Rooting medium—peat and sterile, coarse sand for a good general purpose mixture (Sand alone will often do. Check specific recommendations for the plant you are growing.)
● Rooting hormone
● A cool, bright location with indirect light and, if possible, some bottom heat
● Nursery bed and cold frame

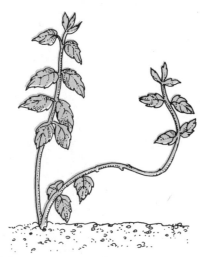

To layer, select a one-year-old stem that can be bent without breaking. Prune side stems and foliage along the section to be layered.

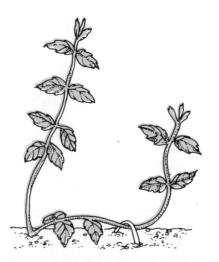

Push the stem to the ground and bend it sharply up again from the point at soil level to encourage rooting. Pin the stem down firmly with a U-shaped piece of heavy wire. Be sure the stem touches the soil.

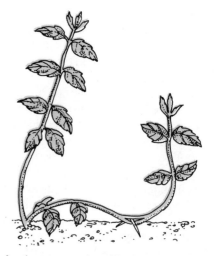

Another measure that will enhance rooting is cutting an inch-long slit in the stem's underside, propping the cut open with a toothpick.

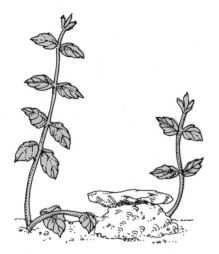

Heap 3 to 6 inches of soil over the pinned area. Top with a flat rock or mulch to preserve moisture.

After the layer has formed a good root system, cut it away from the parent plant. It can be transplanted immediately or left for another growing season.

A single stem can be staked to form more than one layer. This technique is called serpentine layering.

Types of Cuttings

The types of cuttings are named for the developmental stage of their tissues (only partially determined by the season) and the manner in which they are cut. Cuttings are usually taken from current-season, terminal growth. Some species are grown from root cuttings or, in the case of some unusual cultivars, witches'-brooms or lateral growth.

Softwood. Softwood cuttings are taken in the spring or summer from actively growing stems. This new growth, also called juvenile tissue, has the greatest potential for rooting. Take 2- to 4-inch-long cuttings, and cut at a 45-degree angle across the stem just below a node.

Semi-Hardwood or Greenwood. Semi-hardwood cuttings are taken in the spring or summer from new growth that has slowed but hasn't fully hardened off. Semi-hardwood cuttings are made by pruning off an entire shoot from the current grow-

ing season. You may be able to obtain several 4- to 6-inch-long cuttings from a single shoot. Trim the bottom of each by cutting at a 45-degree angle across the stem just below a node and pinch or cut the top just above a node.

Hardwood. Hardwood cuttings are normally taken in the fall when the current season's growth has hardened off and—if the plant is deciduous—dropped its leaves. Hardwood cuttings are 6 inches long or longer and ¼ inch in diameter. Cut straight across the stem below a bud. The top end of the cutting (the one that was farthest away from the base of the plant) is cut at a 45-degree slant above a bud. Many deciduous woody plants, plus broad and needle-leaved evergreens, are propagated by hardwood cuttings. With evergreens, heel and/or mallet hardwood cuttings, which include a small portion of older wood from the main stem, often root more readily than straight cuttings.

Tips for Success

Whatever the type of cutting, there are a few basic principles that are important to keep in mind.

● Regardless of type, take your cuttings early in the day while the cells are still turgid. Take cuttings only from plants that are healthy and not under stress.

● Make every effort to keep the cuttings from drying out.

● For all types of cuttings, remove leaves from the bottom third of the cutting before sticking it in rooting medium. Cut leaves off rather than stripping them. With a sharp knife, score or wound the base slightly and dip in a rooting hormone. Specific recommendations will vary from plant to plant.

● The rooting medium should be moist when the cuttings are stuck. Water thoroughly ahead of time and allow the container to drain. (Water-

To root cuttings of woody trees or shrubs, take semi-hardwood cuttings in the summer or hardwood cuttings in fall. Cut a 4- to 6-inch-long stem of current season growth.

Snip off leaves from the bottom third to half of the cut stem.

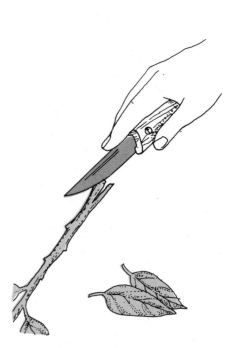

If the cutting comes from a species that is difficult to root, make a shallow, 1-inch-long wound in the stem base.

ing from the bottom will help prevent the peat from floating away.) Stick the cuttings in the medium, mist them, and cover them with plastic.

● The polarity, or top and bottom, of each cutting is important. Be sure to stick the bottom, or proximal, end of the cutting—the one that was closest to the base of the plant—in the rooting medium.

● Anything from a pot enclosed in a bag (with a pencil inserted in the rooting medium to prop the plastic away from the cuttings) to a seed flat covered with a metal-hanger-and-plastic quonset hut will do for starting cuttings. Or put cuttings in a mist bench in the greenhouse if available.

● Place the cuttings in a cool place (70°F or less), with bright, indirect light and perhaps some bottom heat (60° to 70°F). Store hardwood cuttings stuck in a container of moist sand or vermiculite in a cooler (35° to 45°F), dark location for the winter months. Then

root them as you would other types of cuttings in the spring.

● Do not disturb the cuttings or unseal the plastic unless necessary to add water or to remove rotted or diseased tissue or obvious failures.

Check the drainage holes for roots. Try not to test for rooting by tugging at the cuttings.

● With softwood cuttings, look for roots in about four weeks; hardwoods will take two to three months.

WOODY PLANTS FROM SEED

Seed propagation appeals to the experimenter and gambler inside each of us—each seed sown implies a roll of the genetic dice, and any home gardener could come up with the world's next great azalea, holly, or Japanese maple. In most cases, you will need to know the specific germination requirements for your seed. Some seeds sprout immediately; for others, the breaking of dormancy is a puzzle. You may need to stratify the seed by packing it in moist sphagnum and putting it in cold storage for the winter; you may need to scarify by nicking a hard seed coat. You may need to do both. Again, check with your cooperative extension service, local botanical garden or plant society, or see "Recommended Reading" on page 406.

Use a seed flat or plastic flowerpot with a plastic cover and follow the same general recommendations as described for cuttings. A mist bench in a greenhouse will work, too. Pay close attention to the seed's requirements for depth of sowing and light. You may or may not need bottom heat.

Once your seedlings have germinated and formed their first set of true leaves, harden them off by removing the plastic or mist for longer periods each day.

Gently lift transplants and pot them in small containers. You may find a cold frame helpful in overwintering your new plants.

Dip the cut surface in rooting hormone. Check the wound to be sure it gets covered.

Make a hole in the soil with a blunt pencil or similar object. Set cutting in the hole with the lowest leaf at soil level.

Once your cuttings are rooted, begin to harden them off by opening the plastic (or halting the mist) for longer periods each day until the cuttings are weaned from the excessive humidity they need while they are rooting.

Once they are acclimatized, gently lift them from the rooting medium and pot them up or plant them in the nursery bed. They should begin producing some top-growth by the time they're ready for transplanting.

● Depending on the time of year, your location, and the plant being propagated, a cold frame may prove helpful in wintering over your new plants. (For more information, see "Cold Frames and Hotbeds" on page 50.)

Pruning and Shaping

Pruning Trees and Shrubs

Pruning is an art and a science, but it need not be a mystery. The skillful pruner is one who combines a solid understanding of the basics with an eagerness to learn the specific needs of the plants in his or her care and the courage to make the first cut. With these skills, you can regard pruning with the same fondness ascribed to most other jobs in the garden. Moreover, pruning can be a source of learning and accomplishment.

Pruning with a Purpose

Rare is the landscape plant that wouldn't benefit from some purposeful pruning now and again; some species seem to need it more than others. The trick is to recognize and respect the natural growth habit of the particular tree or shrub and prune with a goal that honors the plant's natural inclinations.

Pruning in general improves and promotes the health, vigor, productivity, safety, and appearance of a tree or shrub. You will want to prune a young tree to give it a favorable root-to-top ratio and to promote its structural soundness and appearance as it matures. You will want to remove dead, dying, or diseased wood, along with crossing or rubbing branches. As the tree grows, you will want to

prune away water sprouts, suckers, or wood infested by insects that may appear.

If you find you want to prune a tree or shrub to force an unnatural shape, question that plant's appropriateness for the location—or the method of pruning. From flowerless, ball-shaped forsythias to dehorned sycamore trees, tragic examples everywhere prove that no amount of pruning can salvage a poor plant or site choice.

You may be tempted to prune a tree or shrub in order to keep it in bounds, a practice that should be used only on those plants—and by those gardeners—best suited for such discipline. As most plants will eventually attain the mature size appropriate for the conditions, try to make realistic choices when selecting plants. For example, if you have a small area that could be overrun by a large tree or shrub, you may want to consider the many dwarf and slow-growing landscape plants available today.

Another common but noble reason for pruning is to correct some kind of misshapenness or to rejuvenate a plant. The need for this is often created by crowding, mechanical mishaps, poor pruning in the past, or some form of neglect (benign or otherwise) usually attributed to the former resident of the property.

Another purpose for pruning is what might be called specialty pruning—things you might do after pruning has become a skill that you own completely. Topiary and espalier fall into this category.

Anatomy of a Tree

Knowing the various parts of a tree will be a great help not only when you prune but also in understanding how a tree grows. The tree on the opposite page has water sprouts, narrow crotch angles, suckers, and a broken branch that should be removed. The drooping branches near the base should also be removed. Also illustrated is the spreading root system of a well-anchored tree along with a girdling root around the base of the trunk that could eventually strangle the tree.

The phloem layer just under the bark carries food down from the leaves. Just beneath is the all-important cambium layer, a one-cell-thick layer that gives rise to all new wood. These layers, which are close to the surface, are easily damaged by girdling roots as well as lawn mowers. Inside the cambium is the sapwood, which carries water and nutrients to the foliage, and the heartwood, which is inactive sapwood that provides structural support.

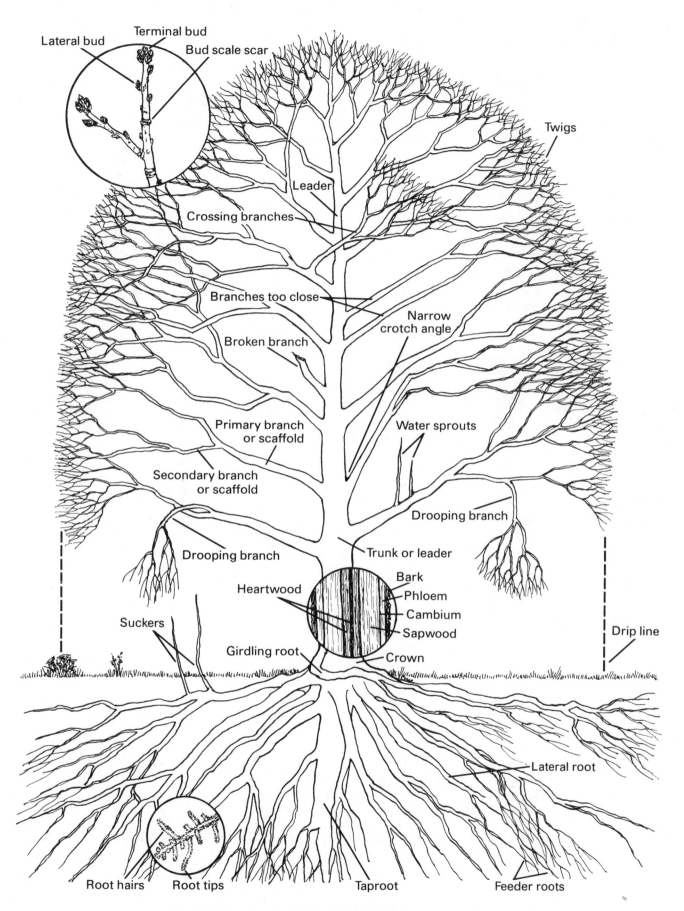

Lateral bud

Terminal bud

Bud scale scar

Twigs

Leader

Crossing branches

Branches too close

Narrow crotch angle

Broken branch

Primary branch or scaffold

Water sprouts

Secondary branch or scaffold

Drooping branch

Drooping branch

Trunk or leader

Bark

Heartwood

Phloem

Cambium

Suckers

Sapwood

Girdling root

Crown

Drip line

Lateral root

Root hairs

Root tips

Taproot

Feeder roots

It's a good idea to become familiar with the parts of a tree before you prune.

347

TEN PRUNING MYTHS

1. All pruning should be done during the dormant season.
2. A tree can bleed to death if you prune it at the wrong time.
3. A large shade tree and an overhead utility line can usually coexist peacefully.
4. All large cuts should be treated with a wound dressing.
5. Pruning will keep a tree or shrub in bounds.
6. Pruning slows growth.
7. A good pruning job should be obvious.
8. Needle evergreens can be cut back hard, just like deciduous plants.
9. Large limbs should be cut so that they are flush with the trunk.
10. Plant diseases cannot be spread through pruning tools.

Pruning Physiology

The reluctant pruner should bear in mind that pruning almost always is an invigorating process for the plant. Especially if the tree or shrub is pruned while dormant, topgrowth can be reduced while much of the plant's energy is still stored in the roots. When spring comes, the root-to-top ratio is favorable and the stored carbohydrates are more than adequate to support the rapid flush of growth on top. In fact, research has shown that young trees cut back at planting time tend to outgrow those that aren't.

In specific circumstances, pruning can be debilitating for the plant. If the tree or shrub is heavily pruned while actively growing, particularly after a rapid flush of growth, it loses tissue in which it has just invested a lot of energy, without getting any return from that foliage. Pruning can also be debilitating when it is done so late in the growing season that it brings on a flush of growth that gets damaged by the first fall frost.

Skillful pruners pay close attention to the season, the plant's condition, and its response to the weather. They are fully conscious of the annual rise and fall of sap and work according to that physiology. They avoid pruning during periods of active growth unless that's called for; they avoid spring pruning of tree species that are inclined to "bleed" sap heavily (see "Trees That Bleed Sap Profusely" on page 350).

Basic Techniques

Regardless of the type of pruning you are performing, you will be drawing from a repertoire of two basic cuts: thinning and heading.

Thinning

A thinning cut is one which follows the branch to be removed back to the branch where it originates. The cut is made at the branch collar, almost flush, but leaving the collar and never leaving a stub. A thinning cut encourages the remaining limbs to continue to grow naturally and in their normal direction. A thinning cut also opens up the plant, reducing wind, snow, or rain load, and allowing sunlight to reach the ground or the innermost branches. In the same manner, thinning can be used to open a view without removing the tree.

To remove a large limb so the bark isn't stripped away below the limb: (1) Make a small cut on the underside of the branch, about 6 inches from the base of the branch; (2) make the second cut outside the first from the top of the branch through the limb; (3) make a cut from the top of the bark ridge to the bottom, just outside the branch collar.

Heading

A heading cut, on the other hand, is one that takes the branch back to a bud or a pair of buds, rather than to the next limb. When a tree or shrub is headed back, some of the newest growth is cut away. Heading removes terminal buds, causing the buds behind the cut to break and begin to grow. Where thinning opens up the

LARGE PRUNING CUTS— TO PAINT OR NOT?

The work of Alex Shigo and other leading tree-watchers has revealed that the use of tree wound dressing is, for the most part, unnecessary. Decay of the tissues related to the cut will occur with or without treatment. The function of the tree paint as a barrier for moisture has been refuted by the discovery that there is plenty of moisture that actually needs to escape at the wound site. Thus, wound dressing serves as a barrier in a nonproductive way.

Tree wound dressing also has been shown not to be a formidable barrier to insects. When there has been mechanical injury (such as an auto or mower mishap), or if the aesthetic condition of the tree is under close scrutiny, tree wound dressing can and should be used in a cosmetic manner. It usually makes everybody feel better.

plant, heading causes it to branch and become more dense.

Shearing is a form of heading often used on hedges and in topiary culture, as well as on millions of ball-shaped shrubs in yards nationwide. Heading is often used and abused where thinning is really what's called for. The topping and dehorning of large trees are extreme, and often unnecessary, forms of heading.

When to Prune

Dead, damaged, decayed, or infested wood can be removed almost any time. If disease is involved, be sure to disinfect your pruners before you move on to the next plant. (Isopropyl alcohol is a good disinfectant and it won't corrode your pruners.) In almost every case, damaged or diseased wood is removed with a thinning cut.

Suckers, water sprouts, and crossing, rubbing, or out-of-control branches also can be removed with a thinning cut almost any time. However, the job will be easiest when the plant is dormant and the leaves have fallen away, because you can then get a good look at the tree's structure.

The timing of almost all other pruning is determined by the season of flowering. Spring-flowering shrubs, such as forsythia (*Forsythia* spp.), quince (*Chaenomeles* spp.), and most rhododendrons and azaleas (*Rhododendron* spp.), should be pruned immediately after flowering. Other spring-blooming plants include viburnum (*Viburnum* spp.), daphne (*Daphne* spp.), pieris (*Pieris* spp.), and deutzia (*Deutzia* spp.). Don't procrastinate—next year's flower buds begin to form shortly after the flowers fade, and late pruning will remove them. The only dormant-season pruning appropriate for spring-blooming plants is rejuvenation, thinning, or the removal of dead, dying, diseased, or unruly wood. Head back a spring bloomer in fall or winter and you've lost your flowers for that year.

Summer-blooming plants usually form their flower buds on the current

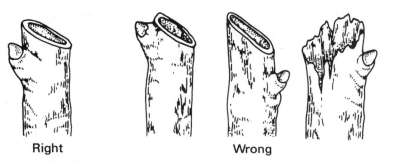

When pruning, cut stems cleanly across just above a bud. The cut should angle across the stem from a point just above the bud to a point opposite the base of the bud (left). Avoid making these mistakes: cutting too close to the bud, leaving a stub of wood above the bud, and making ragged cuts (right).

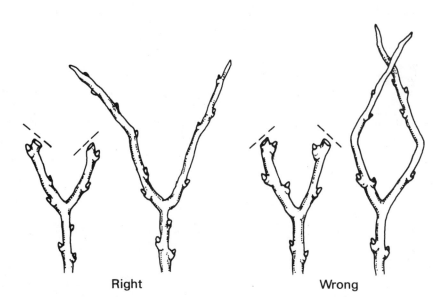

Pruning just above a bud that points toward the outside will result in branches that spread (left). Cutting to inside buds produces branches that grow toward the center of the tree and cross other branches (right).

Removing 3 or 4 buds from the end of a young branch with a heading cut allows the other lateral buds to develop, creating a well-branched limb.

PRUNING AZALEAS

Each year, during the dormant season, remove any dead, dying, crossing, or rubbing branches. Also remove—at the base—any overgrown or out of proportion branches. Use thinning cuts for this.

After flowering, make any heading cuts that are necessary to maintain the desired shape of the plant. Shearing may be necessary depending on your gardening style, but not usually. Do not delay, because next year's flower buds form soon after blooming time.

Pinch off any seed heads that might be forming. This directs the plant's energy toward next year's flowers.

season's wood. Therefore, plants such as crape myrtle (*Lagerstroemia indica*), hibiscus (*Hibiscus* spp.), and abelia (*Abelia* spp.) can, and should, be pruned in the winter. Also included in this list are chaste-tree (*Vitex* spp.), butterfly bush (*Buddleia* spp.), bluebeard (*Caryopteris* spp.), hydrangea (*Hydrangea* spp.), and some species of rhododendron such as the late-blooming native azaleas *Rhododendron prunifolium* and *R. arborescens*.

Winter-bloomers such as some daphne species, winter jasmine (*Jasminum nudiflorum*), and winter honeysuckle (*Lonicera fragrantissima*) can be treated essentially as spring-bloomers, and pruned after blooming.

Special recommendations for pruning young and mature shade trees, evergreens, shrubs, and hedges are given in the sections that follow.

TREES THAT BLEED SAP PROFUSELY

When pruned heavily in spring, some trees will often bleed sap in a rather alarming manner. Such a loss of sap is not usually harmful, but it may invite secondary insect and disease problems. It is best to prune these trees in late spring or summer, after the leaves have matured. Beech (*Fagus* spp.), maples (*Acer* spp.), birches (*Betula* spp.), dogwoods (*Cornus* spp.), elms (*Ulmus* spp.), flowering plums and cherries (*Prunus* spp.), American yellowwood (*Cladrastis lutea*), and willows (*Salix* spp.) all bleed if pruned in spring.

Pruning and Training Young Trees

Get any young tree off to a good start with some judicious pruning at planting time. Use thinning cuts to eliminate dead, diseased, crossing, or rubbing branches, along with suckers, water sprouts, and branches with narrow crotch angles. Once these basic concerns are attended to, give some thought to the tree's intended purpose and devise a strategy to attain that goal. Will the tree be used for shade, to screen an unsightly view, or to frame or filter a pleasing one? Will it be expected to hold up one end of a hammock? Plan to prune accordingly.

The first five to seven years of a young tree's life will be its training period for a future as either an asset or a liability. Assuming that you removed all troublesome growth at planting time, make an appointment with the tree each winter to look for more of those same signs of trouble.

If the tree is to be walked under,

consider removing the lowest limb or two after about the third or fourth year. Continue this annually until the lowest branches are at an appropriate height. This technique is called limbing up and, on a young tree, should be done gradually over several years. This is part of your tree's training; by leaving limbs and removing them gradually you allow them to contribute to the girth and taper of the trunk.

During this time, also give some attention to the scaffold branches, those growing directly from the trunk. Thin them to ensure that they are evenly spaced and not crowding one another. Also watch for narrow crotch angles and thin in favor of wider ones, which are structurally stronger. Feel free to remove the errant branch that heads for the roof of your house or threatens to ruin the natural silhouette of the tree. Also watch the central leader of your young tree and

thin out any branches that compete directly with it.

After about the fifth year, consider thinning the crown to reduce loads from wind, snow, ice, or rain. If the plant is destined to become a large shade tree, you will eventually need to hire an arborist for this job. Remove no more than about one-third of the crown at a time.

If your tree has been planted to screen an unsightly view, retain its lower branches and prune it for fullness. To do this, use thinning cuts to attain a sound structural framework, and follow with judicious heading cuts to promote branching. The earlier you begin with this sort of training, the better the eventual results.

If you wish to have your tree filter rather than screen a view, thin it regularly without heading back the branches.

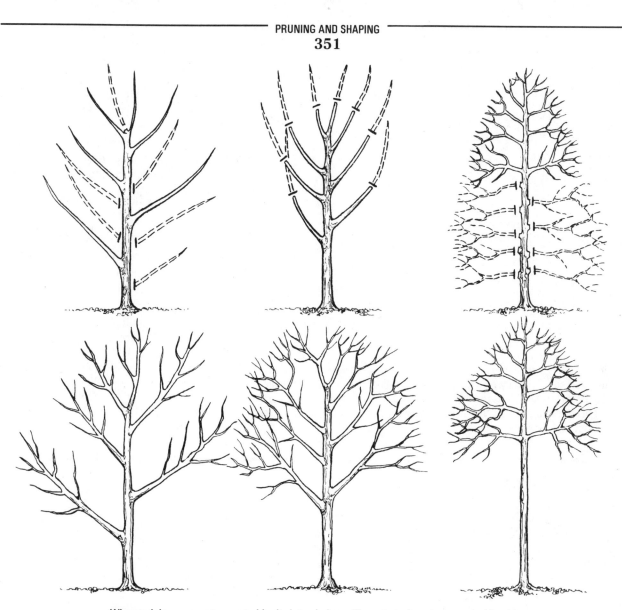

When training a young tree, consider its intended use. These trees have been pruned for three different purposes. *Left (top and bottom),* the tree has been thinned to filter sunlight or expose an attractive view; *center (top and bottom),* the branches of the tree have been headed back to promote branching and thick growth to screen a view; *right (top and bottom),* the tree has been limbed up so that its branches can be walked under, a process done gradually over several years.

Pruning a Mature Tree

The ongoing training you provide your trees will determine their form and strength as they mature; at maturity, the form and structural strength of a tree, which is maintained by proper pruning, can be a life-and-death matter. Training a young sapling is serious business—just ask any nursery operator. Nursery owners know that uniformity and pre-dictability are important factors in mass production and sales.

When to Use an Arborist

In caring for a mature tree, it is critical to recognize your limitations and know when and how to hire an arborist. Without appropriate climb-ing, safety, and technical skills, removing even one errant branch can be risky business for a home gardener. Entrust your mature trees to a professional arborist.

Following are some of the services provided by professional, accredited arborists.

● **Plant management.** A management program will ensure that

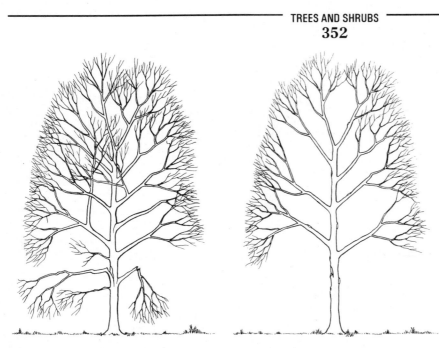

Pruning a large tree is generally a job for a professional who has the equipment and experience to do the job safely and effectively. A good pruning job is difficult to detect. *Left,* the tree has broken and crossing branches, water sprouts, and branches that are too close together; *right,* after pruning, it exhibits a strong scaffold that is open and attractively shaped. It has also been limbed up so that it can be walked under.

your trees will be examined, and corrected or treated if necessary, on a regular basis. Fertilizing, soil aeration, and pest control are other routine services that might be provided under a management program.

● **Regular pruning.** Structural correction and thinning are regular pruning services offered by arborists.

● **Storm-proofing.** This includes thinning to reduce snow, rain, or wind load; removal of weak branches; and balancing the crown so that, should it fall, it would cause the least human hazard or property damage.

● **Grounding.** For old and valuable trees, especially on a high spot, cables can be installed that will minimize the damage of a lightning strike.

PRUNING CONIFERS

Whether tree or shrub, a conifer requires an approach slightly different than those mentioned for deciduous plants and broadleaved evergreens. The outstanding difference is that broadleaved plants have buds all along entire branches that will usually grow when stimulated. Most needle evergreens grow solely from the branch tip. So any heading cut made behind the actively growing tip will yield a stub that will probably not grow back.

Approach the early training of an evergreen as you would any other tree. Pay attention to structural stability, narrow crotch angles, crossed branches, and other errant growth. Also decide whether you want the lower branches limbed up or sweeping the ground. Make every cut a thinning cut.

If you want to encourage denseness or limit size, carefully head back or shear the newest

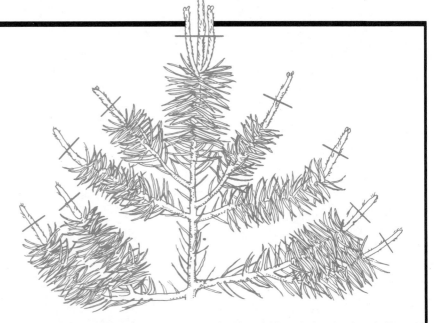

Trim back the candles, or new growth, on red, white, and Scotch pines by about half to encourage dense growth and control the size of these trees.

growth during the growing season. On pines, pinch off about half of each candle after it has elongated. On other evergreens, you can reduce size and encourage denseness by making a series of thinning cuts, taking a branch back to a side shoot. (Don't do this on the central leader for it will destroy the tree's shape.) If you absolutely must shear, do it once or twice during the growing season, making sure that your tool is very sharp and your "bite" goes only into new growth.

● **Cabling and bracing.** This is for trees that are structurally weakened in some way. Like grounding, cabling and bracing is worth considering for mature trees considered to be extremely valuable.

● **Topping.** Consider replacing either your arborist or your tree if this is recommended. Topping is the removal of most of the crown of the tree and usually results in horrible disfigurement. It is considered a necessary evil, especially where mature trees and overhead utility lines coexist. Still, few trees are worth having once topping has been done; consider replacing the tree with something more compatible with the reality of the site.

● **Removal.** The ultimate pruning job. If the task calls for equipment that you don't already have or don't have the training for, such as a chain saw, consider hiring an arborist.

Choosing an Arborist

When shopping for an arborist, look around your own neighborhood, or a neighborhood with mature trees in it. You should be able to identify good work and sloppy work after some looking: The good work is practically invisible. Ferret out happy customers and ask for a referral.

If scouting around isn't for you, look up your nearest chapter of the International Society of Arboriculture in the telephone directory, and ask for a list of accredited arborists. Your nearest arboretum or botanical garden may also have such a list.

Be sure that your arborist is bonded or insured in some fashion. Don't be fooled by an impressive assortment of chain saws and a truck with a chipper. Ask for accreditation, insurance, and a look at some of the individual's previous work. A professional will be happy to show you those things. Your investment of time and effort will be well worth it.

Pruning Shrubs

As with trees, your first concern when pruning shrubs should be to preserve structural stability and health. This includes removing crossed or rubbing branches, water sprouts, and suckers, along with dying, diseased, or infested wood. Such pruning can be done during any month of the year. A thinning cut is the cut to use.

The rest of the pruning work is done according to the season and the plant's physiology and bloom time. Most spring-blooming shrubs are pruned soon after they bloom, before they set flower buds for the following year. Winter-bloomers are handled in the same manner. Shrubs that bloom in summer usually can be pruned in the winter while they are dormant. (See "When to Prune" on page 349 for some examples.)

Pruning Objectives

There are several other reasons to prune shrubs beyond the basic structural concerns. Shrubs are pruned to reduce or limit their size, to keep them vigorous and flowering, and to

Shrubs with long, loose branches should be headed back until the shrub is fairly upright and compact. Cut just above a bud to encourage branching and thicker growth.

thin them so that sunlight can penetrate the interior of the plant. For seriously overgrown plants, all of these processes are combined into one technique called rejuvenation.

Limiting Size

One of the best ways to reduce or limit the size of a shrub is to use thinning cuts to prune away branches to the next side shoot, allowing the shoot to camouflage the cut. In this case, thinning will allow light to reach the interior of the plant and encourage new growth near the interior of the plant. Thinning works much better in the long run than shearing or heading back with pruners. Heading back new growth causes the shrub to have lots of dense growth around the tips, which shades the interior of the plant and makes it hollow. Many are the azaleas and forsythias that have been shorn rather than thinned and languish as round balls, hollow shells of their former selves. Prune with the understanding of how the plant would like to look.

Opening Up

Many shrub species respond well to being opened up on a regular basis. This is a form of rejuvenation done while the plant is dormant. With this method, you remove two or three of the oldest (and usually least healthy) branches each year. Lilacs (*Syringa* spp.), forsythia (*Forsythia* spp.), abelia (*Abelia* spp.), heavenly bamboo (*Nandina domestica*), and Oregon grape (*Mahonia* spp.) do well with this approach. In addition to effectively reducing the height of the plant, keeping it in bounds, opening up also keeps the shrub well supplied with new wood. By rotating out old branches by cutting them back to the ground, you expose the innermost sections of the plant to sunlight, thus stimulating new, vigorous growth.

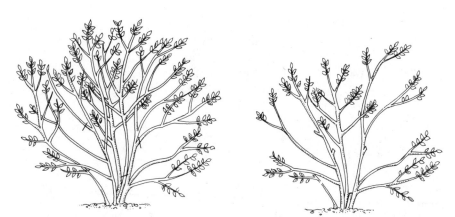

Rejuvenation is a technique used to give new life to overgrown shrubs whose dense branches prevent sunlight from reaching the center of the plant. Remove up to three of the oldest branches, and thin—don't head back—crowded or crossing branches to a main stem.

Rejuvenation

Frequently, new homeowners are faced with assortments of neglected, overgrown shrubs; occasionally, longtime homeowners are faced with a shrubby jungle if they don't stay on top of maintenance. Rejuvenation by thinning is effective on many such overgrown shrubs.

The first step is to decide whether the specimen is worth keeping, as your rejuvenation effort will require considerable commitment of time and energy. If a plant is horribly misshapen from competition with other plants, crowding, or mechanical mishaps, think twice and perhaps opt to remove it. If it's just an overgrown shrub with plenty of room and lots of appeal, determine if it can be rejuvenated and have at it.

As with the shrub where you removed old growth on a rotational basis, begin the first winter by removing—to the ground—two or three of the oldest limbs. Then come back the next year and do the same, being careful not to remove too much at one time, since full sun can be quite a shock to the innermost reaches of a plant. This process must be gradual. Eventually, the removal of the old growth will stimulate and make room for new growth and the plant will assume a new life.

Another form of rejuvenation involves the complete removal of the top of the plant during the dormant season. Although this can be done

on some overgrown plants, the best results are with young, vigorous, annually-renewed specimens that bloom in the summer on new growth. Dwarf crape myrtles (*Lagerstroemia indica*), bluebeard (*Caryopteris* spp.), and abelia (*Abelia* spp.) are good candidates for this rather radical act of faith. Spring bloomers such as forsythia (*Forsythia* spp.) also can be rejuvenated this way, but, because the buds are already set, you will lose the spring bloom. Sometimes the sacrifice is worth getting the plant back under control.

One final method of rejuvenation pruning is a thinning process in which you transform an overgrown

shrub into a comparably sized—but tamer—tree. Remove water sprouts and suckers; then begin limbing up and thinning back to a single or multiple trunk, selecting your scaffold branches as you go. This method works well for crape myrtle (*Lagerstroemia indica*), some viburnums (*Viburnum* spp.), and red buckeye (*Aesculus pavia*).

Pruning Hedges

Hedges can be short or tall, narrow or wide, formal or informal, depending on the plants you have chosen or inherited, the care required, and their natural growth habit.

REJUVENATE A LILAC

Many an overgrown lilac (*Syringa* spp.) has limped through its final days, blooming sporadically, while its owner stood helplessly by not knowing that his plant could be rejuvenated in a few simple steps. Most lilacs practically beg for rejuvenation!

The solution is a two to four year process that makes up for its length by its ease and chance for success. The job calls for a certain amount of commitment and patience, but only minimal time and talent.

Begin in the winter by identifying the oldest and most overgrown branches. Remove two or three of them as close to the ground as your pruning saw and the surrounding wood will permit, trying not to nick or cut adjacent wood. Then repeat the same procedure in the following year or two until the plant is "lowered" and new growth is beginning to appear at the base of the plant where light is now reaching.

With a new hedge, follow the same general strategy at planting time as described for other shrubs. The only pruning needed initially will be thinning to remove dead, diseased, or damaged branches.

Once the planting becomes established, pruning time and strategy will be determined by the hedge's level of formality. Prune an informal flowering hedge according to its flowering time—for example, prune forsythia for shape, if necessary—after flowering. (See "When to Prune" on page 349 for other examples.) Thin informal hedges to rejuvenate them during the dormant season. This helps keep the growth thick and lush and opens up the interior of the plant to encourage a steady supply of new shoots. Never shear an informal hedge.

Glossy abelia (*Abelia × grandiflora*), barberry (*Berberis* spp.), forsythia (*Forsythia* spp.), Chinese holly (*Ilex cornuta*), winter honeysuckle (*Lonicera fragrantissima*), and shrub roses (*Rosa* spp.) are all fine prospects for informal hedges. For a large informal hedge, consider hedge maple (*Acer campestre*) or Canada hemlock (*Tsuga canadensis*).

Treat a formal hedge much like a lawn, and trim or shear frequently throughout the growing season. As with grass, the best strategy is to cut as often as you can stand it, removing only a small bit of growth at a time. This frequent shearing is a form of heading back and encourages dense growth and the filling-in of holes. Among the plants that lend themselves to formal hedges are Japanese

holly (*Ilex crenata*), yews (*Taxus* spp.), privet (*Ligustrum* spp.), and arborvitae (*Thuja* spp.).

Whether formal or informal, hedges should always be shaped so they are wider at the bottom than at the top, if only slightly. Failure to do this results in a hedge with bare ankles, then calves, knees, and so forth, because the top quickly shades the bottom and the plants become leggy. This is especially a problem with formal hedges. By making the top slightly narrower than the bottom, you allow sunlight to reach the bottom of your hedge and you are likely to have an enviable hedge . . . full to the ground.

Hedges should be slightly wider on the bottom than on the top to ensure that sunlight will reach all sides of the shrub. *Left,* the four shrubs with rounded or pointed tops will show best overall growth; *right,* these three shrubs will gradually lose their lower leaves.

PART 6

Houseplants and Container Gardens

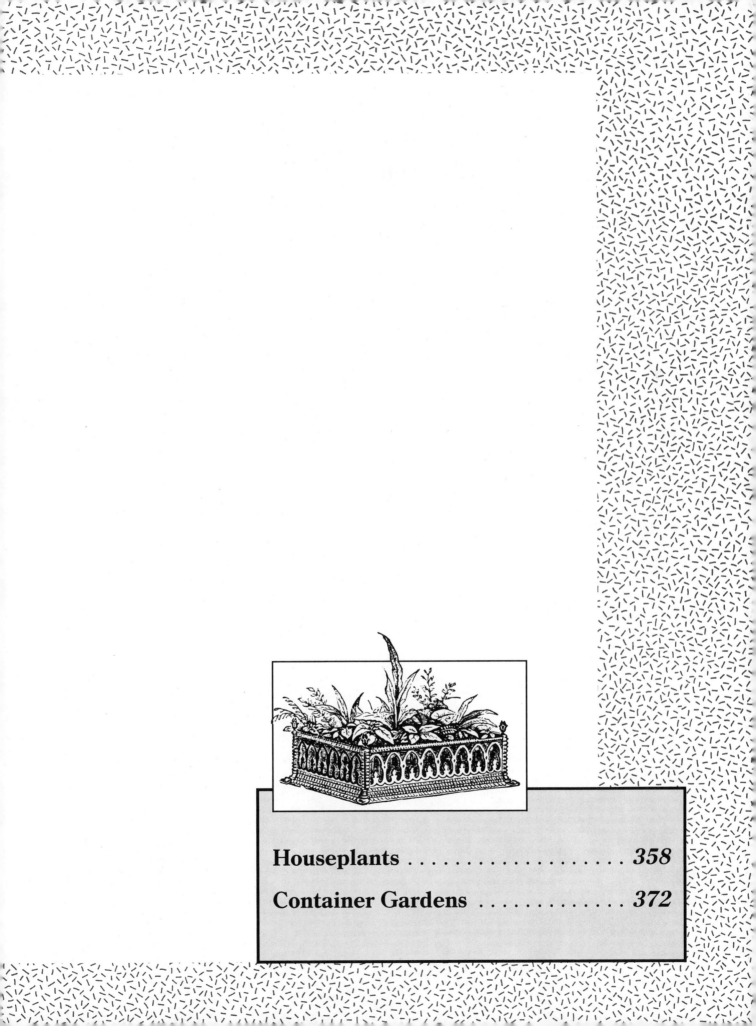

Houseplants

Potting and Repotting Houseplants

Raising houseplants provides year-round gardening pleasure. Foliage and flowering indoor plants are generally easy to care for, and species can be found that will grow well in almost any part of your home. Houseplants are a great medium for experimenting with propagation techniques and satisfying the urge to garden, no matter what the weather.

Your first task in caring for a houseplant fresh from the greenhouse or plant store may be to repot it in a larger or more decorative container. Many gardeners assume that a plant should subsequently be repotted every few months. Actually, a plant should be repotted only if its roots fill its container, or if you prefer a different pot or type of soil mix for the plant. Spring is usually the best season to repot a houseplant. Wait until a plant finishes blooming before changing its container. Before repotting a plant, always check to see if its roots have run out of growing space.

To check the condition of a houseplant's roots, water the plant well and wait a few minutes for the moisture to soak in. Then turn the plant upside down, holding your palm flat against the soil with the stem between your fingers. Tap the edge of the pot lightly against the hard edge of a counter or workbench. The root ball should fall free of the container. If the plant will not come loose, run a kitchen knife around the inside edge of the container and then tap it again.

Rootbound plants have a mass of tangled white roots which fill the pot and may even protrude through the pot's drainage holes (if your plant is not rootbound, you can simply set it back into its pot). Healthy roots are

TYPES OF CONTAINERS

Selecting interesting or unusual containers for your houseplants can be fun, but keep your plants' growing needs in mind when you choose pots. Plastic and clay are the most common materials for houseplant containers. Clay works well in a humid home. Use clay pots if you tend to water generously. Certain plants such as cacti, begonias, and orchids prefer clay pots.

Plastic is preferable if you have a normal or dry atmosphere in your home and tend to water sparingly. Many gardeners find that plants in plastic containers require less care and attention than plants in clay.

Both plastic and clay pots commonly come in two styles, "standard" and "azalea." Standard pots are as deep as they are wide—a standard 6-inch pot will be 6 inches deep and 6 inches wide. Standard pots work well for plants that have roots that plunge down, such as coleus and hibiscus. Azalea pots are shallower than they are wide. Plants that have surface roots or roots that grow horizontally grow best in azalea pots. Hanging plants, ground-covering plants, begonias, and most bulbous plants are best grown in azalea pots. You can set either plastic or clay pots inside a decorative container or basket.

A layer of broken crockery at the bottom of the pot will encourage drainage and also keep the soil from sifting out of the container. Just be sure not to block the drainage hole. In this illustration, a pot shard is blocking the hole and will impede drainage.

usually creamy white and plump. Dead roots are brown or black and shriveled. Remove any dead roots before putting the plant in a new container.

How to Repot

Repot a houseplant in a container one size larger than its present pot. For example, if your plant is growing in a 6-inch pot, move it into an 8-inch container. Soak empty clay pots in water for several hours before placing a plant in them. Make sure that the plant's soil is thoroughly moist before transplanting.

You can fill the bottom of a new pot with a shallow layer of broken crockery to encourage good drainage.

Next, put in a layer of fresh soil, and insert the root ball so the old soil line is just below the new soil level. Make sure that the stem sits symmetrically in the middle of the pot. Fill in the edges with soil medium and compact it with your fingers or a pencil. Water the plant generously after repotting and keep it in a shady spot for several days.

Soil Mixes for Houseplants

Whether you mix your own potting soil or buy one of the many formulations offered in plant stores and garden centers, there are a few things all potting soils have in common. Although certain plants are grown in pots filled with a single ingredient—some orchids can be grown in fir bark, and bromeliads are often grown in sphagnum moss, for example—most plants grow best in a medium that combines several ingredients. Some of the ingredients in potting soil provide nutrition; others improve texture, enhance drainage, or aid water retention. For example, peat moss soaks up water, and sand ensures that the soil doesn't remain soggy; compost and other organic matter add texture and provide nutrition.

For handsome and healthy houseplants, you'll need to match the conditions a particular plant prefers with the right soil mix. For example, while all potting soils retain water for the plant, some plants require more soil moisture than others. Most cacti are grown in mixtures that drain quickly and retain little moisture; most ferns, on the other hand, grow best in a mixture that remains moist but not soggy. (See "Houseplants for Four Exposures" on page 360 and the recipes that follow for recommendations of mixes for a variety of houseplants.)

Soil pH affects how plant roots absorb both water and nutrients. The pH scale runs from 0 to 14, with the lower numbers reflecting acid conditions and the higher numbers, alkaline conditions. Most houseplants prefer to grow in a neutral to slightly acid soil with pH between 6.2 and 6.8. There are a few exceptions—gardenias (*Gardenia* spp.), hydrangeas (*Hydrangea* spp.), and acacias (*Acacia* spp.) are popular houseplants that will not thrive unless they are grown in an acid soil mix. Adding iron chelate to the soil will effectively acidify the medium. Store-bought mixes are usually carefully balanced to provide plants with a neutral pH. If you are making your own soil mix, be sure to check its pH. (See "Understanding pH" on page 12 for more on pH and pH testing.)

Ingredients

A good potting soil should start with soil and/or compost. Whatever you use, it's important that it be free of fungi, soilborne diseases, insects, and weed seeds. Also, it should be well drained. Don't use plain garden soil—it is usually much too heavy when used in containers and tends to pack and crust. Also, unsterilized garden soil harbors fungi and insects. You can start with good garden loam or purchased topsoil, then sift it through a screen to remove rocks and large clods and sterilize it at temperatures of 150° to 180°F for 30 minutes. Sift and sterilize compost or composted manure before you use it, as well.

Sharp sand, also known as builder's sand, is another basic ingredient. It increases drainage, allowing soil aeration around the roots. Perlite and vermiculite are common ingredients that add no nutritional value but increase the air- and water-holding capacity of the mix. Peat moss is a good source of organic matter to hold moisture in the soil. Leaf mold is another common ingredient that offers nutrients and water-holding capacity and contributes to the structure of a mix. Leaf mold is not generally commercially available, but it can easily be homemade by composting autumn leaves. (See "Ingredients" on page 29 for information on some of the common materials used in potting soils and the properties they offer.)

To these main ingredients, you can add soil amendments such as lime, which neutralizes soil pH and provides calcium. Bonemeal is an excellent source of phosphorus and nitrogen. Wood ash is a source of potassium, but should be used sparingly as it has a potent effect on soil pH.

Commercial Potting Soils

Commercial potting mixes have a variety of ingredients, and not all manufacturers list the contents of their mixes. Choose a mix that specifies its contents on the package. Try to find a mixture that closely matches

(continued on page 366)

HOUSEPLANTS FOR FOUR EXPOSURES

Keep your houseplants healthy and happy by giving them the amount of light they need for best growth. This chart will help you match your choice of houseplants to the exposure of your windows. With the right place to grow and good basic care, your plants should flourish.

Plants for the north window grow well in bright indirect light and do not require direct sun. An unobstructed north or northeast window will suit them fine. If the window is shaded by curtains or trees, give your plants supplemental lighting.

An east or west window is good for houseplants that like bright light and can withstand some sun. West windows receive more afternoon sun and tend to be hotter than east windows, so you may need to water them more often. A south window is best for houseplants that like several hours of direct sun daily.

Remember, if your window is shaded, you can give your plant supplemental lighting—or choose a resident with lower light requirements.

Name	Description	Culture	Comments
Plants for North Windows			
Aglaonema commutatum (Aglaonema)	Foliage plant with leathery, dark green leaves marked with silver, cream, or white. Plants reach 1-2 ft.	Pot in all-purpose houseplant mix. Allow soil to dry slightly between waterings. Propagate by division.	Many cultivars with different foliage patterns available. Specimens with all-green leaves tolerate lowest light levels.
Aspidistra elatior (Cast-iron plant)	Dark green leaves are 15-30 in. long, 3-5 in. wide. Some cultivars have leaves variegated with white or cream. Plants reach 2½-3 ft.	Good for north, east, or west window. Pot in all-purpose houseplant mixture. Keep soil barely moist at all times. Will tolerate low humidity. Propagate by division.	Survives cold, heat, drought, and neglect, but will be most attractive in ideal conditions. Variegated plants need more light than all-green ones.
Asplenium nidus (Bird's-nest fern)	Fern with wavy-edged, pale green fronds surrounding a central growing point—the "nest." Plant normally 1-1½ ft., but can reach 3 ft.	Pot in rich houseplant mixture with lots of humus or other organic matter. Keep soil evenly moist. Grows best in high humidity. Propagate by spores.	Trim off yellowed fronds, which can be caused by too low humidity or too much sun.
Cryptanthus spp. (Earth-star)	Low-growing, star-shaped plants grown for their colorful foliage. Leaves are green-brown or green and striped with pink, red-brown, or white.	Pot in rich houseplant mix. Allow soil to dry slightly between waterings. Grows best in high humidity. Propagate from offsets produced at base of plant.	Grown primarily for foliage, but will produce tiny flowers in summer.
Cycas revoluta (Sago palm)	Attractive, palmlike plant with thick, fernlike leaves that feel nearly plastic in texture.	Pot in 2 parts all-purpose houseplant mix, 1 part sharp sand. Allow soil to dry out slightly between waterings. Will tolerate low humidity. Propagate by suckers.	A slow-growing plant that resents repotting. Roots adhere to sides of pot; repot only if absolutely necessary.
Cyrtomium falcatum (Holly fern)	Fern with leathery, glossy, dark green leaflets with 3-5 sharp points like holly leaves. Plants can reach 1-2 ft.	Pot in epiphyte mix. Keep soil evenly moist. Will withstand low humidity. Propagate by division.	Repot only when necessary. Roots adhere to sides of pot; dislodge them gently.
Davallia trichomanoides (Squirrel-foot fern)	Fern with lacy, much-divided leaves and creeping rhizomes covered with whitish or tan furlike scales.	Pot in epiphyte mix. Keep soil evenly moist. Grows best in high humidity. Can be propagated by division or by rooting cut pieces of rhizome.	Rhizomes creep along soil, so plants don't need deep pots.
Dieffenbachia spp. (Dumb cane)	Large-leaved plants grown for their foliage, which can be variegated with green, cream, and white. Plants reach 5-6 ft. Leaves 12-18 in. long, 4-6 in. wide.	Pot in all-purpose houseplant mix. Allow soil to dry out between waterings. Propagate by stem cuttings or layering.	Plants grow best when potbound; repot only if necessary. Specimens with all-green leaves will tolerate lowest light levels.

Name	Description	Culture	Comments
Ficus pumila (Creeping fig)	Creeping vine with light green, 1-in.-long leaves. Plants under 2 in. unless trained on a trellis or other support. Cultivars with variegated leaves are available.	Pot in all-purpose houseplant mix. Keep soil evenly moist. Grows best with high humidity. Propagate by rooting cuttings or digging and potting rooted stem sections.	Use as a creeping groundcover under large houseplants. Plants can be allowed to trail, or can climb a trellis with clinging roots.
Fittonia verschaffeltii (Nerve plant)	Creeping plant with oval, 2-4-in. leaves that have prominent pink or white veins.	Pot in all-purpose houseplant mix. Keep soil evenly moist. Grows best with high humidity. Propagate by cuttings.	Plants can become scraggly; pinch regularly to encourage bushiness.
Maranta leuconeura (Prayer plant)	Colorful leaves fold up in darkness. Foliage marked with light green, dark green, and purple. Plants reach 10-12 in.	Pot in all-purpose houseplant mix. Keep soil evenly moist, but allow to dry slightly between waterings in winter. Will grow in average humidity. Propagate by division.	Exposure to direct sun will fade foliage color. Grows best when pot-bound, so avoid repotting.
Phalaenopsis spp. (Moth orchid)	Low-growing orchids with 5 or 6 fleshy, 6-12-in. leaves. Pink, white, yellow, or purple flowers are 3-4 in. across, borne on 2-4-foot stalks; many flowers per plant.	Pot in commercial orchid mix. Keep potting medium evenly moist. Grows best in high humidity. Propagate by cuttings.	For best growth, feed monthly with fish emulsion or other dilute organic fertilizer.
Philodendron spp. (Philodendron)	Large genus of climbing or clump-forming plants grown for ornamental foliage. Leaves dark green, burgundy, or variegated with white. Plants climb several feet if supported; leaves are 3 in.-3 ft. long.	Pot in all-purpose houseplant mix. Allow soil to dry slightly between waterings. Propagate by tip cuttings.	Provide a trellis or other support for climbing types, or allow them to trail.
Spathiphyllum spp. (Spathe flower)	Attractive 8-10-in.-long leaves are dark green and shiny. Plants reach 2 ft.; flower stalks 1½-2 ft. Flowers last 1 month and are white fading to green.	Pot in all-purpose houseplant mix. Keep evenly moist. Will grow in average humidity. Propagate by division.	Several cultivars are available, including dwarf ones.
Zebrina pendula (Wandering Jew)	Trailing plant grown for its colorful foliage. Leaves usually marked deep green and silver on top, purple on underside.	Pot in all-purpose houseplant mix. Allow soil to dry slightly between waterings. Pinch ends of vines regularly to keep plant bushy and compact. Propagate by rooting tip cuttings.	Foliage color best in bright light. Cultivars with dark red-green leaves or ones striped with green, pink, and white are available.

Plants for East or West Windows

Name	Description	Culture	Comments
Aechmea fasciata (Urn plant)	Bromeliad with leathery, 8-10-in. leaves forming a central urn or water-holding cup. Showy pink flower spike rises 12-15 in. and lasts for 4-5 weeks.	Pot in epiphyte mix. Allow soil to dry slightly between waterings, but keep urn or cup full of water. Propagate from offsets produced after bloom fades.	Change the water in the central urn occasionally, replacing with fresh water.
Araucaria heterophylla (Norfolk Island pine)	Pyramid-shaped tree with needlelike leaves. Symmetrical flat branches borne in tiers. Trees can reach 6 ft.	Pot in all-purpose houseplant mix or 1 part houseplant mix, 1 part peat. Keep soil evenly moist but not wet. Trimming will result in asymmetrical growth. Propagate by seed.	Slow-growing plant. Repot specimens only every 3-4 years.

(continued)

HOUSEPLANTS FOR FOUR EXPOSURES—*Continued*

Name	Description	Culture	Comments
***Plants for East or West Windows*—continued**			
Begonia spp. (Begonia)	Large genus grown for ornamental foliage and/or flowers. Leaves solid green or marked with gray, maroon, white, cream, or pink. Flowers are pink, coral, or white; borne in clusters. Height ranges from 8 in.-4 ft.	Pot in 1 part potting soil, 1 part peat moss. Let soil dry slightly between waterings. Grows best with high humidity. Pinch stem tips to keep plants compact. Propagate by cuttings of stems or rhizomes.	Tall, canelike species, may need staking. Plants grown for flowers require some direct sun; ones grown for foliage need bright indirect light.
Carissa grandiflora (Natal plum)	Medium-size tropical shrub grown for its leathery, 1-in.-long oval leaves, fragrant white flowers, and edible plumlike fruit.	Pot in all-purpose houseplant mix. Keep soil evenly moist, although plants will withstand some drought. Propagate by cuttings.	An excellent plant for indoor bonsai. Prune plants to keep them compact.
Ceropegia woodii (String-of-hearts)	Creeping or trailing plant with stringlike stems and heart-shaped, 1-in. leaves that are dark green marbled with silver or white.	Pot in all-purpose houseplant mix. Allow soil to dry out slightly between waterings in spring and summer; keep plant drier in winter. Propagate from tubers produced on stems.	Best when grown in a hanging basket or pot.
Chamaedorea elegans (Parlor palm)	A palm native to tropical rain forest. Plants normally 1-3 ft. when pot grown; occasionally to 6 ft.	Pot in all-purpose houseplant mix. Keep soil evenly moist but not wet. Grows best with high humidity. Propagate by seeds.	Repot only when plants are very pot bound; roots very brittle, handle with care.
Cissus rhombifolia (Grape ivy)	Trailing or vining foliage plant with deep green, 3-part leaves with rust-colored hairlike scales on undersides.	Pot in all-purpose houseplant mix. Let soil dry slightly between waterings. Pinch tips of stems to keep plant bushy. Propagate by stem cuttings.	Plants will tolerate very low light.
Clivia miniata (Kaffir lily)	Large, clump-forming plant grown for dark green, strap-shaped leaves and clusters of 10-20 brilliant orange flowers. Foliage reaches 2 ft.	Pot in all-purpose houseplant mix. Keep plants evenly moist spring through fall. Propagate by division.	To encourage flowering, let soil dry out thoroughly between waterings and keep in a cool (50°F) room in winter. Resume watering when flower stalk emerges.
Columnea spp. (Columnea)	Tropical, trailing plants related to African violets. Flowers somewhat resemble goldfish and come in orange, red, or yellow. Stems can trail several feet.	Pot in rich houseplant mix. Keep soil evenly moist. Grows best with high humidity. Propagate by stem cuttings.	Prune plants after flowering to encourage branching. Good for hanging baskets.
Episcia spp. (Flame violet)	Trailing African violet relatives grown for colorful, 2-3-in. leaves and trumpet-shaped lavender, white, pink, yellow, or red flowers. Leaves can be green or marked with bronze, white, pink, or maroon.	Pot in rich houseplant mix. Keep soil evenly moist. Grows best with high humidity. Propagate by stem cuttings.	Pinch plants regularly to encourage branching. Good for hanging baskets. Water sprinkled on foliage can cause unsightly spots.
Eucharis grandiflora (Amazon lily)	Bulbous plant grown for its large glossy leaves and clusters of fragrant, white, daffodil-like flowers. Plants reach 1½-2 ft. Flowers on 2-2½-ft. stems.	Pot in all-purpose houseplant mix. Let soil dry slightly between waterings. Propagate by division.	Flowers appear in spring and summer. Transplant only when plants become overcrowded. They resent transplanting and bloom best when potbound.

Name	Description	Culture	Comments
Ficus benjamina (Weeping fig)	Large tropical tree grown potted as a 2-20-ft. shrub or tree. Leaves are leathery and 1-1½ in. long. Leaves, stems bleed milky sap when cut.	Pot in all-purpose houseplant mix. Allow soil to dry out slightly between waterings. Wash foliage with a sponge or gentle spray in the shower or outdoors. Prune roots and tops if plants get too large. Propagate by air layering.	Sudden temperature or lighting changes can cause plants to drop leaves. Cultivars with white and green variegated leaves available.
Ficus elastica (Rubber plant)	Large tropical tree grown potted as a 2-20-ft. shrub or tree. Leaves are oval, leathery, and 10-15 in. long.	Pot in all-purpose houseplant mix. Keep soil evenly moist. Wash foliage with a sponge or gentle spray in the shower or outdoors. Cut plants back to encourage branching. Propagate by air layering.	Many cultivars are available including variegated ones with cream, yellow, or white patches.
Monstera deliciosa (Swiss-cheese plant)	Climbing tropical plant with cut or deeply lobed 8-12-in.-long leaves. Foliage is dark green. Plants can climb to 6 ft. or more.	Pot in all-purpose houseplant mix. Keep soil evenly moist. Wash foliage with a sponge or gentle spray in the shower or outdoors. Propagate by cuttings.	Foliage of plants grown in insufficient light will not form cuts or holes.
Neomarica spp. (Walking iris)	Clump-forming plants with narrow, arching, sword-shaped leaves arranged in a fan. Leaves 1½-2 ft. long.	Pot in all-purpose houseplant mix. Let soil dry out nearly completely between waterings. Propagate by offsets produced at tips of flowering stems or by division.	Irislike flower open for only a day.
Nephrolepis exaltata (Boston fern)	Fern with graceful, drooping fronds that reach 3 ft. Many cultivars available; leaflets may have smooth or ruffled edges.	Pot in all-purpose houseplant mix. Keep soil evenly moist. Fronds can burn in direct sun. Propagate by division.	Prune plants regularly by removing yellowed or damaged fronds all the way to the base of the plant.
Oxalis spp. (Shamrock)	Low-growing, 6-10-in. plants with cloverlike leaves and clusters of white, pink, or yellow flowers. Leaves green or marked with maroon.	Pot in all-purpose houseplant mix. Keep plants evenly moist. Grow best with cool (50°-60°F) nights. Propagate by division.	Some species have dormant season in fall or winter; keep soil barely moist once foliage begins to fade, then resume watering in early spring.
Polypodium aureum (Rabbit's-foot fern)	Fern with large, leathery leaves with wavy, lobed edges. Spreads by creeping rhizomes covered with whitish or tan furlike scales. Some forms have blue-green foliage.	Pot in epiphyte mix. Keep soil barely moist at all times. Can be propagated by division or by rooting cut pieces of rhizome.	Rhizomes creep along soil, so plants don't need deep pots.
Rhapis excelsa (Bamboo palm)	Clump-forming palm with fronds made of 3-10 leaflets. Plants reach 5 ft.	Pot in all-purpose houseplant mix. Keep soil evenly moist. Propagate by division.	Cultivars with variegated leaves are available.
Rhoeo spathacea (Moses-in-the-cradle)	Foliage plant with deep green, sword-shaped leaves that are purple underneath. Tiny white flowers borne in clusters surrounded by boat-shaped bracts. Plants 10-15 in. tall.	Pot in all-purpose houseplant mix. Keep plants evenly moist but not wet. Will grow well with cool (50°F) nights. Propagate by division.	A variegated cultivar with leaves striped in yellow is available.

(continued)

HOUSEPLANTS FOR FOUR EXPOSURES – *Continued*

Name	Description	Culture	Comments
Plants for East or West Windows—continued			
***Santpaulia* spp.** (African violet)	Popular plants grown for abundant, 1-2-in. flowers that may be single or double. Foliage and flowers can have ruffled edges. Foliage hairy and solid green or variegated.	Pot in rich houseplant mix. Keep soil evenly moist. Grows best with high humidity. Propagate by leaf cuttings.	Miniature cultivars, as well as trailing cultivars for hanging baskets, are available. Water sprinkled on foliage can cause unsightly spots.
Sansevieria trifasciata (Snake plant)	Tough plant with narrow, leathery leaves that are 2-3 in. wide and 2-3 ft. tall. Foliage upright and dark green mottled with silver. Yellow-edged cultivars are available.	Pot in all-purpose houseplant mix. Allow soil to dry nearly completely between waterings from spring through fall; in winter water only enough to keep the foliage from shriveling. Propagate by division or leaf cuttings.	Low-growing (6-8 in.) cultivars are available.
***Streptocarpus* spp.** (Cape primrose)	African violet relatives with trumpet-shaped, 1-3-in.-long, pink, white, or lavender flowers. Leaves are ground-hugging, strap-shaped, and hairy; 8-12 in. long.	Pot in rich houseplant mix. Keep plants evenly moist but not wet. Use shallow pots; transplant only when plants become crowded. Propagate by division, cuttings, seeds.	Plants need bright light but no direct sun to bloom. Grown much the same as African violets.
Syngonium podophyllum (Nephthytis)	Climbing plant related to philodendrons. Leaves are arrowhead-shaped and can be solid green or variegated with white and/or silver.	Pot in all-purpose houseplant mix. Keep soil barely but evenly moist. Propagate by cuttings or division. Pinch branches to encourage compact growth.	Can be grown in hanging baskets or trained to climb a trellis or bark slab.
Plants for South Windows			
Aloe barbadensis (Medicinal aloe)	Succulent plant with tough, fleshy leaves that can reach 2 ft. Leaves are round on bottom, have toothed edges, and are gray-green marked with white.	Pot in a mixture of 1 part all-purpose houseplant mix, 1 part sharp sand. Allow soil to dry nearly completely between waterings. Propagate by potting shoots or suckers that are borne at base of plant.	Source of medicinal aloe; juice from cut leaves can be used to treat burns.
Beaucarnea recurvata (Ponytail)	Palmlike plant also called elephant-foot tree for the swollen base of the trunk. Narrow, ribbonlike foliage borne in a tuft at top of plant. Height 1-4 ft. or taller.	Pot in all-purpose houseplant mix. Allow soil to dry nearly completely between waterings.	Will withstand small containers. Swollen trunk base provides water storage for plant.
Brassaia actinophylla (Shefflera)	Tropical tree and shrub grown as a medium to large (2½-6 ft.) pot plant. Foliage is leathery and dark green. Leaves divided into from 3 to as many as 16 leaflets.	Pot in all-purpose houseplant mix. Allow soil to dry slightly between waterings. Prune plants to encourage branching by cutting stems above a leaf. Propagate by cuttings, air layering, seeds.	Wash foliage regularly with a sponge or spray from hose. Plants will withstand low light levels, but will become spindly.
Citrofortunella mitis (Calamondin)	Tropical citrus tree grown as a medium to large (2½-6 ft.) pot plant. It bears fragrant white flowers and tiny, bright-orange, 1-1½-in. fruit.	Pot in all-purpose houseplant mix. Allow soil to dry slightly between waterings. Prune plants regularly to encourage compact growth. Propagate from cuttings taken in late summer or fall.	Flowers must be cross-pollinated to form fruit. Summer plant outdoors so bees will visit flowers, or hand pollinate with a small brush.

Name	Description	Culture	Comments
Crassula argentea (Jade plant)	Succulent plant with fleshy stems and foliage. Leaves are oval, dark green, and 1-2 in. long. Plants can range from 1-3 ft. or more tall.	Pot in a mixture of 1 part all-purpose houseplant mix, 1 part sharp sand. Allow soil to dry nearly completely between waterings. Propagate by leaf or stem cuttings.	Plants can be pruned to keep growth compact; or pinch out newest set of leaves to encourage branching.
Echeveria spp. (Echeveria)	Low-growing, fleshy-leaved plants that form 2-4-in.-wide rosettes of blue-green leaves. Foliage generally 2-3 in. tall; blooming plants reach 1-1½ ft. Tiny flowers are yellow, red, pink, or orange.	Pot in a mixture of 1 part all-purpose houseplant mix, 1 part sharp sand. Allow soil to dry nearly completely between waterings. Propagate by leaf or stem cuttings or potting offsets that appear at base of plant.	Many different foliage colors and forms are available. Will grow in shallow pots.
Grevillea robusta (Silk oak)	Tropical tree grown as a medium to large pot plant. Lacy, fernlike leaves range from 6-18 in. long and are gray-green in color.	Pot in all-purpose houseplant mix. Allow soil to dry slightly between waterings. Prune plants to encourage branching by cutting stems above a leaf.	Can be grown from seeds. Attractive plant, can also be grown in greenhouse, and as shrub or tree in Zones 9-10. Valued for its timber.
Hedera helix (English ivy)	Trailing or climbing vine with dark green or variegated leaves ranging from 1-4 in. long. Leaves may be heart shaped, deeply lobed, or nearly round; edges may be ruffled or serrated.	Pot in all-purpose houseplant mix. Keep soil barely moist at all times. Pinch plants to encourage bushy growth, or train on trellis or other support. Propagate by rooting shoot cuttings.	Many cultivars are available. The species, hardy in Zones 6-10, and its cultivars can be grown outdoors; hardiness of cultivars varies.
Pelargonium spp. (Geranium)	Popular plants grown for showy flowers and/or foliage. Bedding or zonal geraniums grown for their 3-5-in.-wide flower clusters and large, rounded leaves. Other species are grown for their scented foliage.	Pot in all-purpose houseplant mix. Allow soil to dry slightly between waterings. Prune plants to encourage branching by cutting stems above a leaf. Propagate by rooting stem cuttings.	Many cultivars available. Flowers may be red, pink, white, salmon. Foliage may be variegated with white or cream or marked with dark green. Dwarf cultivars and many scented geraniums are available.
Punica granatum 'Nana' (Dwarf pomegranate)	A dwarf cultivar of pomegranate that has tiny narrow leaves and reaches 1½-2 ft. in height. Flowers are 1 in. long and bright orange. Blooms that are pollinated will produce red, 2-in.-wide fruit.	Pot in all-purpose houseplant mix. Keep soil evenly moist at all times. Pinch stem tips regularly to encourage branching. Propagate by seed or stem cuttings.	Long flowering season. May need shelter in colder months if grown in outside container.
Saxifraga stolonifera (Strawberry geranium)	Low-growing, rosette-forming plant with dark green, nearly round leaves. Panicles of tiny white flowers borne atop 10-12-in. stalks. Plants spread by producing small plants at the ends of trailing runners.	Pot in all-purpose houseplant mix. Allow soil to dry slightly between waterings. Propagate by potting plants produced at the ends of runners.	A variegated cultivar with leaves marked with white and pink is available. Good for hanging baskets. The species is hardy to Zone 6 and can be grown outdoors.
Sedum morganianum (Burro's-tail)	A trailing plant with succulent, blue-green leaves tightly clustered along drooping stems. The 1-in.-long leaves completely conceal the stems.	Pot in mixture of 1 part all-purpose houseplant mix, 1 part sharp sand. Allow soil to dry nearly completely between waterings. Propagate by potting individual leaves or stem tips.	Good for hanging baskets. Leaves and stems are brittle and can be broken easily; keep plants where they can remain undisturbed if possible.

the components in the recommended homemade mixes below. Avoid mixes that contain chemical fertilizers.

Recipes for Potting Mixes

Potting mixes can be as simple or as complex as you wish. Here are a few that are suitable for a wide range of houseplants.

All-Purpose Houseplant Mixes

● One part peat moss, compost, or leaf mold; 1 part sterilized garden loam or purchased potting soil; and 1 part sharp sand or perlite.

● One part peat moss; 1 part sterilized garden loam or purchased potting soil and sterilized, composted manure mixed half-and-half; and 1 part sharp sand.

● Two parts sterilized garden loam or purchased potting soil; 1 part peat moss, compost, or leaf mold; and 1 part sharp sand or perlite.

Rich Houseplant Mix

Humus-loving plants grow better in a somewhat richer mixture.

● One part sterilized garden loam or purchased potting soil; 2 parts compost or leaf mold; and 1 part sharp sand or perlite.

Epiphyte Mix

Epiphytes are plants that grow on other plants—such as in the crotches of trees—without parasitizing them. They grow in leaf litter and other organic matter that collects around them. Several common houseplants, including some ferns, orchids, and bromeliads, fall into this category.

● One part sterilized garden loam or purchased potting soil; 2 parts leaf mold, peat moss, osmunda fiber, or shredded fir bark, or a mixture of all these ingredients; 1 part sharp sand or perlite; and ½ part crushed clay pot, brick, or gravel.

To each peck (roughly 2 gallons) of the above recipes, add ½ cup of bonemeal and ½ cup of lime.

SOILLESS MIXES

Soilless mixes are light soils composed of peat moss, sand, and perlite or vermiculite. The fact that they are so light in weight explains their great popularity among professional growers— light soils save shipping costs. But, as the name infers, soilless mixes have no nutrients to offer a growing plant. Plants grown in soilless mixes look beautiful when they receive constant feeding. However, when amateur indoor gardeners buy houseplants potted in soilless mix, they often have difficulty keeping the plants properly fed. Remember to fertilize plants growing in soilless mix regularly. For best results, give them diluted fertilizer such as manure tea every time you water.

Dividing Houseplants

Houseplants can be propagated in many different ways. Division is one of the easiest ways to produce new plants. The method varies slightly depending on the type of plant you are propagating. (For information on propagation by seeds, cuttings, and layering, see "Starting Seeds" on page 29 and "Plant Propagation" on page 91.

Propagating with Offsets and Suckers

The easiest and most successful method for propagating houseplants

is to divide off runners or offsets. Any plant that multiplies by producing "pups" can be divided. Episcias (*Episcia* spp.), African violets (*Saintpaulia* spp.), aloes (*Aloe* spp.), and mints (*Mentha* spp.), along with ferns, bromeliads, and many succulents, are among the many popular plants that can be successfully propagated by this method.

Separating a side shoot from its parent is as simple as it sounds. First, turn the plant out of its pot and examine the roots. For this method to succeed, all the separate divisions must have individual root systems. You'll probably find that each offset

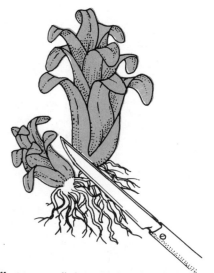

Offsets are small plants produced at the base of the parent plant. Use a knife to cut them apart, then gently work the roots loose and pot them up.

has vigorous roots which are intertwined with the parental root system.

Take the base of each crown in your hand and tease the roots free by pulling them slowly apart. Try not to damage any roots, and never pull at the foliage. When they're completely untangled, pot each plant separately, providing fresh soil for both the parent and its progeny. Keep the newly potted plants in a cool, shady spot for several days.

Some plants such as African violets, saxifrages (*Saxifraga* spp.), and episcias send out aerial runners with new plantlets dangling from the tips. Those plantlets won't send down roots until they can sink their feet into soil. To encourage root development, take a U-shaped hairpin and secure the plantlet firmly on top of a pot filled with loose, humusy soil (rich houseplant mix is fine). Leave the plantlet attached to its parent and keep the soil moist for two to three weeks while it develops roots. Then cut the runner. The dangling offsets of spider plants (*Chlorophytum* spp.) will even begin to initiate roots while hanging in the air. These can be removed from the parent plant and rooted in water or rich houseplant mix.

Dividing Rhizomatous Plants

Many common houseplants spread by underground rhizomes, which will send up new plantlets that can be cut and potted up. Rhizomatous begonias (*Begonia* spp.), snake plants (*Sansevieria* spp.), and many gesneriads form underground rhizomes that send up new plantlets. If left undivided, the plant will form an expanding cluster of growth, eventually choking itself into starvation. One solution is to keep repotting the growing plant. Another remedy is to divide

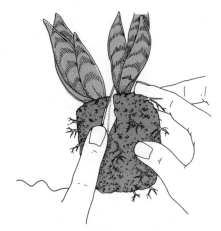

Many houseplants can be propagated by cutting apart the fleshy rhizomes. Use a sharp knife to slice through the roots, and pot the new plants up as soon as possible.

the plant into two or more smaller specimens.

Turn the root ball out of the pot and use a sharp knife to cut the rhizome and its accompanying section of roots. The easiest method is simply to cut the root ball in half. You can divide it into small sections if you have many rhizomes sending up growing shoots. Repot all the divisions in separate containers, adding new soil around the sliced root systems. Put the plants in a shady spot and water them generously while they recover.

Dividing Bulbs, Corms, Tubers, and Tuberous Roots

Tuberous begonias (*Begonia* × *tuberhybrida*), oxalis (*Oxalis* spp.), achimenes (*Achimenes* spp.), dahlias (*Dahlia* spp.), and caladiums (*Caladium* spp.) are among the many popular houseplants that sprout from bulbs, tubers, or corms. Although each of these underground structures is different, they all store food during growth in preparation for dormant periods. And they usually produce new bulbs, corms, or tubers during their growing cycle, which can be divided when the plants go dormant.

To divide these plants, wait until the foliage dies back completely, and withhold water until the soil is dry. Turn the plant out of its pot and remove excess bulbs. They can be potted up right away or stored in a cool, dark, dry place until their growing season arrives. When stored bulbs begin to grow, pot them with growing ends up and begin supplying sun and water.

Increasing Humidity

Low humidity is one of the greatest problems encountered by indoor gardeners. During the winter, when furnaces and woodstoves are pouring out dry heat, indoor humidity is especially low. In extreme cases, homes can have as little as 10 percent humidity during the heating season.

If you suffer from chapped lips, dry skin, and clogged sinuses in the winter, you can imagine how uncomfortable your tropical plants must feel. Most tropical species require 40 to 60 percent humidity to thrive. When the air is dry, indoor plants lose water continuously through their leaf pores. The leaves look dehydrated, leaf edges turn brown, and leaves fall.

The easiest method of increasing humidity is to purchase a humidifier or vaporizer. However, there are less expensive methods of raising humidity for plants. When you group plants together, especially in a recessed bay window or window greenhouse, leaf transpiration increases the moisture in their immediate area. Setting pots on pebble trays filled with an inch of pebbles and ½ inch of water (remember to refill the tray as the water evaporates) also raises humidity for clustered plants. Simply putting a pan of water near a radiator, heat register, baseboard heater or on a woodstove can help increase the humidity in a room.

Misting plants is not an efficient way to combat a humidity deficit. Misting may raise humidity for a few moments, but only continual misting significantly increases moisture in the air around your plants. And, constantly moist leaves can develop fungal problems.

A saucer or tray filled with pebbles and water will provide much-needed humidity for houseplants.

HOUSEPLANTS THAT LOVE HIGH HUMIDITY

Although nearly all houseplants benefit from increased humidity, the following require high humidity for best performance.

Allamanda spp. (common allamanda)

Begonia spp. (begonia, especially rex)

Bougainvillea spp. (bougainvillea)

Calathea spp. (calathea)

Gardenia spp. (gardenia)

Mandevilla (mandevilla)

Maranta spp. (maranta, including prayer plant)

Gesneriad-family members such as African violets (*Saintpaulia* spp.), columnea (*Columnea* spp.), episcia (*Episcia* spp.), lipstick plant (*Aeschynanthus* spp.), gloxinia (*Gloxinia* spp.), and many ferns also thrive in high humidity.

Pruning and Training Houseplants

If left to their own devices, most plants send a single stem shooting straight upward. A skillful gardener counteracts that tendency and coaxes the plant to bush into a handsome, shapely specimen. The secret is pruning.

Actually, although the scale is quite different, the principles of pruning houseplants differ little from those used for pruning trees. Early pruning can be used to shape and train a plant into an attractive shape. Heading cuts can be used to encourage bushy growth; thinning to remove unsightly branches and open up the center of the plant. (For more information, see "Pruning with a Purpose" on page 346.)

Pruning techniques vary depending on how severely you plan to prune. If your plant is young and has only a few sets of mature leaves, merely pinch the growing bud. Pinching is a type of heading cut that doesn't require knives or shears. Simply grasp the growing stem and snip off the terminal bud, with or without the top pair of leaves, using your thumb and forefinger. After pinching, the stem is not noticeably shorter, but the side shoots receive a "growth message" and immediately begin to develop. Regular pinching encourages branching and dense growth.

If your plant is too tall, use a pair of sharp pruning shears and cut the growth to the desired height. Cut to either softwood or hardwood, and always cut just above a bud or a set of leaves. When judging the target height, remember that the plant will probably branch out just below the

WHEN NOT TO PRUNE

In some cases, pruning at the wrong time of year can forfeit that season's floral display. Although it's safe to prune ever-blooming plants at any time of year, think twice before pruning seasonal bloomers. Allow at least two months of unpruned growth before a plant's flowering period. If the plant produces blossoms only on terminal buds, do not prune for three to four months before flowering.

Some plants blossom only on old, unpruned growth. In the houseplant realm, members of the Bignonia family, such as *Tecomanthe venusta* and *Clytostoma callistegioides,* are the most noteworthy examples. These plants must be left unpruned if you hope to have flowers in the coming year.

Pinching is a form of pruning that will encourage branching and bushy growth.

KEEPING HOUSEPLANTS HEALTHY

Symptom	Cause	Treatment
Brown circles on leaves	Fungal infection	Keep leaves dry. Water in the morning so foliage can dry before evening. Remove and discard infected foliage if possible.
Brown leaf tips	Bacterial infections	Do not splash water on leaves. Remove and destroy infected foliage.
	Humidity too low	Increase humidity with humidifier, pebble tray, or clustered plants.
	Soil too wet	Avoid overwatering; use well-drained soil mix. Check soil moisture with finger before watering. Few plants will tolerate constantly soggy soil.
	Too much fertilizer	Feed less or at longer intervals; flush roots with water and repot if fertilizer burn is suspected.
Brown or cream-colored scabs on leaves or stem	Scale	Wash or spray foliage with insecticidal soap. Remove scales with cotton swab dipped in alcohol.
Chewed holes in or slimy trails on leaves	Slugs or snails	Repot, discarding soil. Check for slugs, snails, or eggs before repotting; remove any that are found.
Cottony masses on rootball	Root mealybugs	Try repotting in fresh soil; if this fails, discard plant.
Curled leaves at growing tips	Aphids	Spray or wash foliage with water or insecticidal soap.
Curled leaves	Cold damage	Keep nighttime temperatures above 65°F. Keep foliage away from cold windows.
	Fluorescent light damage	Move plant farther from lights.
	Soil too wet	Allow soil to dry out between waterings. Avoid overwatering; use well-drained soil mix. Check soil moisture with finger before watering.
	Too much fertilizer	Feed less or at longer intervals; flush roots with water and repot if fertilizer burn is suspected.
Desiccated leaves	Humidity too low	Increase humidity with humidifier, pebble tray, or clustered plants.
Failure to bloom	Insufficient light	Move to brighter location. (Move gradually to avoid sunburned foliage.)
	Short-day bloomer exposed to too much light	Three months before blooming period, put Christmas cacti, kalanchoes, or poinsettias in a closet or a room that receives no artificial light during hours of darkness for 14 hours daily.
	Too large a pot	Repot into smaller container.
	Too much fertilizer	Feed less or at longer intervals. Flush soil with water; repot if fertilizer burn is suspected.

(continued)

Many older houseplants benefit from being cut back severely. When pruning, be sure to cut just above a bud or pair of leaves.

cut. Many older houseplants can be completely rejuvenated with a stern hardwood pruning. Use sharp, heavy-duty pruning shears to cut the stems back close to the base. New, fresh growth will shoot out within a few weeks.

Root Pruning

If a plant is potbound, repot when you prune to provide nourishment for the new growth. This is especially important when pruning hardwood plants. If you don't want to move the plant to a larger container, prune the roots as well and pot the plant back into the same container.

To root prune, turn out the roots and, with a sharp knife, carve off an inch (or more for large plants) around the entire surface of the root ball. Work quickly, and cut the roots cleanly. Put the roots back in the pot, and add fresh soil. Keep the plant in the shade and water frequently until new roots grow.

Symptom	Cause	Treatment
Leaf drop, slow	Humidity too low	Increase humidity with humidifier, pebble tray, or clustered plants.
	Insufficient light	Some plants will lose foliage if they don't get enough light.
	Soil too dry	Water more frequently. Water should thoroughly moisten soil and run through the pot each time.
	Soil too wet	Avoid overwatering; use well-drained soil mix. Check soil moisture with finger before watering. Few plants will tolerate constantly soggy soil.
	Too much fertilizer	Feed less or at longer intervals; flush roots with water and repot if fertilizer burn is suspected.
Leaf drop, sudden	Indoor pollution, especially from gas utilities	Check appliances for leaks; move plant away from source of gas.
	Soil too wet	Water less frequently. Use well-drained soil mix. Check soil moisture with finger before watering.
	Sudden change of location or temperature	When moving plants from one spot to another, make change as gradual as possible.
	Too much fertilizer	Feed less or at longer intervals; flush roots with water and repot if fertilizer burn is suspected.
Leggy growth	Crowded plants	Leave space between plants to reduce competition for light and air.
	Improper or insufficient pruning	Prune plant.
	Insufficient light	Move to brighter location. (Move gradually to avoid sunburned foliage.)
	Too much heat	Reduce nighttime temperature to 60°F.
Rust-colored spots on leaves	Fungal or bacterial infection	Increase air circulation. Do not wet leaves when watering. Separate plants from other houseplants. Remove infected foliage and destroy.
Seedlings or young plants collapse at soil level	Fungal infection (damping-off)	Increase air circulation; thin out seedlings in pot. Use pasteurized potting mix.
Spotted foliage	Fungal infection	Keep leaves dry when watering. Water in the morning so foliage can dry before evening.
Stunted plant	Insufficient nutrients, pot-bound plant	Repot plant in fresh soil and/or fertilize more frequently.
Sudden blackening of new growth	Frost injury	Move plants from frosty windowpanes.
	Hot drafts	Move plant away from heating unit, especially hot-air unit.
	Sunburn	Use shades on sunny, hot days. Move plant away from windowpanes.

Symptom	Cause	Treatment
Tiny white insects flying from leaves	Whitefly	Use a pyrethrum or rotenone spray.
White cottony mass on leaf underside and nodes	Foliar mealybugs	Use cotton swabs, dipped in alcohol, and apply to insects.
White, crusty buildup on soil surface	Fertilizer salts or calcium built up from hard water.	Use softened water. Remove crusty surface and flush out salts with softened water.
White powdery spots on leaves	Botrytis	Keep foliage dry when watering. Water in the morning so foliage can dry before evening.
	Powdery mildew	Increase air circulation. Do not water in damp weather and keep leaves dry when watering.
Wilted foliage	Cold damage	Grow in warmer environment. Protect plants from cold drafts.
	Dormancy	Water sparingly and wait for growing season.
	Insufficient soil moisture	Water more frequently. Water should thoroughly moisten soil and run through the pot each time.
	Root rot (stems collapse at soil line)	Use carefully sterilized tools, pots, and soil. Root tips of stems, if healthy, to start new plant.
	Soil too wet	Water less frequently. Use well-drained soil mix. Check soil moisture with finger before watering. Few plants will tolerate constantly soggy soil.
Wilted foliage even after plant is watered	Root-knot nematodes	No practical control method; discard plant. Do not increase water to counteract wilting.
	Roots crowded; soil depleted	Repot into larger container.
Yellow leaves	Acid-loving plant (such as azalea) grown in alkaline soil	Repot into peat-rich soil medium, or use vinegar water to increase soil acidity.
	Insufficient light	Move plant to brighter spot. (Move gradually to avoid sunburned foliage.)
	Insufficient nitrogen	Apply fertilizer more often and/or repot the plant.
	Sunburn	Move to shadier location or farther from window. Shade window with lightweight curtains.
Yellow speckled leaves with tiny webs; cupped or curled leaves	Spider mites	Spray or wash foliage with cold water. Spray with insecticidal soap.

Container Gardens

Growing Vegetables in Containers

Container gardening is more popular today than ever—and for good reason. It is a boon for apartment dwellers, a necessity for rooftop gardeners, and just plain fun even for those of us blessed with ample garden space. Raising flowering plants in containers has long been a favorite activity, and more and more gardeners are discovering the challenges and rewards of container vegetable gardening.

Vegetables and flowers can readily be grown in tubs, crocks, pots, barrels, sacks, baskets—nearly any vessel that is nontoxic and large enough to accommodate the plants and allow sufficient drainage. Containers may be decorative—half-barrels and wood planting tubs are both popular—or strictly practical. Some containers are especially designed for vegetable growing.

You can make a simple container by slitting plastic bags of soil mix and setting transplants directly into the bag. Or consider recycling baby bathtubs, leaky buckets, plastic milk jugs, and other containers that otherwise would help to clog a landfill. Whatever you choose, be sure there are holes in the bottom so that excess water drains away. Otherwise, your plants can easily become waterlogged and drown. Drainage holes also are important for flushing water through the soil to dissolve accumulated salts.

Almost any vegetable can be grown in containers, but the most popular are the salad vegetables, including lettuce, radishes, onions, cucumbers, and peppers. Carrots, beets, and other root crops will do well in containers as long as you provide sufficient rooting space. Cucumbers are particularly suited to hanging baskets; peppers and eggplant can be interplanted with flowering annuals. In response to the increasing popularity of container gardening, breeders have developed dwarf or compact cultivars of most common vegetables. Even watermelons can now be raised in 5-gallon containers.

Herbs grow well in smaller containers. Parsley and thyme are well suited for hanging baskets, where they may be interplanted with flowering annuals. Two-gallon tubs or baskets are large enough to support vigorously growing perennial herbs such as mint

Even a tiny backyard or deck can be a productive vegetable garden with imaginative container plantings. Herbs, root vegetables, celery, and cucumbers grow well in containers as long as they have sufficient light and rooting space and are watered and fed frequently.

and rosemary. Eight- to 12-inch pots are sufficient for basil and lavender. And even 4- to 6-inch pots will support chives, dill, parsley, and thyme. A box planter under the kitchen window is a convenient place to grow chives, parsley, and other low-growing herbs so you can to snip quickly while cooking.

A word to the wise: Be sure to pick a container that will be large enough to handle the mature plant. Transplanting can stress a plant, which will affect your harvest. Again, be sure that your containers have drainage holes.

Keys to Success

The keys to successful container vegetable growing are a good soil mix, adequate soil moisture, and a steady nutrient supply, along with some good basic gardening practices.

Soil

The soil mix should be light, airy, capable of holding moisture and nutrients, yet quick to drain. A common mixture is 1 part potting soil, 1 part compost, and 1 part sharp sand, with a little added bonemeal. A more expensive variation of this mix substitutes vermiculite for the sand, producing a mix that weighs less but holds more moisture. (For other recipes, see "Soil Mixes for House-plants" on page 359.)

Water

Adequate soil moisture is critical. Summer heat dries soil mix in containers rapidly. Soil in wood and unglazed clay containers dries out more quickly than that in plastic or other nonporous containers. If your area has intensely hot summers, don't use dark-colored containers, which absorb heat more readily than those made of light-colored materials. Wooden containers have an insulating effect and may help to keep roots cooler.

In general, you'll need to water all container plants daily in hot weather, not only to keep roots moist, but to help cool your plants and wash away accumulated salts.

Food

Vegetables in containers need more frequent feeding than those grown in the open garden. The most popular fertilizer is ordinary fish emulsion, although liquid seaweed is also suitable. Mix according to label directions and apply once a week. You can also feed container vegetables with homemade manure tea.

Training Standards

Visitors to formal gardens are often impressed upon seeing container-grown roses, geraniums, lantanas (*Lantana* spp.), and other woody shrubs that have been specially trained into treelike forms called standards. You can train standards for your own garden and enjoy them indoors or out, all year around, depending on your climate. The training takes patience and care, but is by no means a task for experts only.

The perfect candidate to be trained as a standard is a fast-growing woody shrub that produces many small-sized leaves. If the shrub blooms freely, so much the better. Geraniums, roses, and lantanas are often trained into standards. But there are many other candidates—figs (*Ficus* spp.), fuchsias (*Fuchsia* spp.), citrus trees (*Citrus* spp.)—nearly any woody shrub that appeals to you. Even woody herbs such as lavender (*Lavandula* spp.) sweet bay (*Laurus nobilis*), and rosemary (*Rosmarinus officinalis*) may be trained to tree form. Plants with small leaves are best because when the standard has grown to 3 to 4 feet in height, the crown of small leaves atop the single "trunk" helps to create the impression of a real tree in miniature.

Standards can be grown in garden beds, but container growing is preferred because the plants can then be moved indoors or outside, depending on the season, the weather, and the hardiness of the plant. Some standards are produced by grafting compatible plants—a favorite tea rose scion grafted or budded onto a *Rosa multiflora* rootstock, for example. The following directions are for turning an ordinary shrub into a miniature tree, without grafting.

The first steps in training a standard are to prune the plant to a single, straight shoot and then stake it to keep it growing perfectly upright.

Steps for Training

1. Start your standard with a small, rooted cutting, but choose a strong and straight one. You may also use a small plant if it has a single, strong leader that is growing upward. Plant it into a 3-inch pot and begin the training immediately.

2. Insert a 10-inch stake next to the plant to train the leader to grow perfectly vertical. Tie the main stem to the stake using soft cord, and remove any side shoots that appear.

3. As the leader grows, continue to tie it every 2 to 3 inches—or even more closely if it threatens to stray. Continue removing any side shoots that appear. Leaves that grow directly from the leader may be kept temporarily, since they help to manufacture food for the plant's growth. They will be removed after the tree is trained.

4. When the plant reaches about 12 inches in height, transplant it to a larger pot, if necessary, and insert a new stake that will be nearly as tall as the eventual height of the standard. Continue to grow the plant in this manner, repotting as necessary when the plant becomes rootbound, until it reaches the desired height.

5. When it has grown as tall as you wish, stop the plant's vertical growth by pinching the terminal bud. This will force the growth of lateral branches. Allow these to grow for about an inch, then pinch these back, also, to encourage still more lateral branches to form. By encouraging lateral branching and removing side shoots from the trunk, you are forcing the plant to form a globular head or top.

6. To maintain the standard at the desired height and shape, you'll need to pinch and prune it regularly. In several years, the main trunk or stem will become thick and sturdy enough so that the supporting stake can be removed.

7. For continued health, be sure to meet all the other requirements—light, humidity, temperature, seasonal rest—of the species you have chosen.

As your standard grows, continue tying and pruning off side shoots.

Pinch the plant's terminal bud when it has grown to the desired height. This will promote side branching.

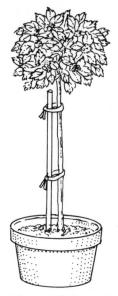

Continued pruning and pinching will result in a beautiful standard. When the trunk becomes sturdy (usually after several years' growth), you will be able to remove the stake.

Creating a Tub Garden

If a full-sized lily pond is not in your immediate gardening future, you can at least experience a bit of the aquatic gardening world with a tub garden of your very own. Lily ponds are certainly lovely, but tub gardens also have advantages. They're easy to set up and maintain, may be moved about if necessary, and can be used on porches, patios, decks, and terraces.

Be sure to pick a site in full sun—at least five hours of direct sun daily—for best bloom of water lilies.

Getting Started

Almost any large container at least 20 inches deep and 12 inches wide may be used for a tub garden, as long as it is watertight. If you have an attractive container that is not watertight, then look for a suitable plastic liner. Wooden half-barrels are commonly used for tub gardens, as are large ceramic tubs. If you choose to sink the container into the ground, then, of course, outward appearance is not important. Be sure that there are no residues of toxic substances in the container you choose. Wooden

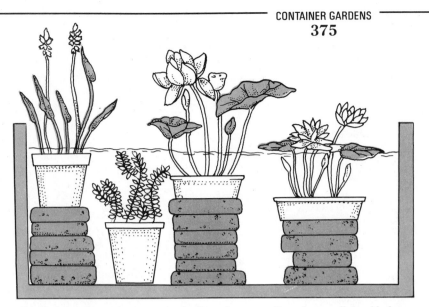

Tub gardens add novelty to your gardening and are versatile and generally trouble-free.

half-barrels used for aging whiskey can be toxic to fish. Fresh barrels will smell of whisky. Age them several months until they no longer smell before you try adding fish or plants.

Selecting Plants for Tub Gardens

Water lilies (*Nymphaea* spp.) are the most popular plants for tub gardens. Since water lilies need ample growing space, most tubs are capable of handling no more than one full-sized plant. Your best bet is one of the dwarf water lilies; that way, you'll have room for one or more of the fascinating bog plants available. For visual interest, consider adding a plant that will provide a vertical accent. For the latter, consider pickerel weed (*Pontederia cordata*), bog rush (*Juncus effusus*), elephant's-ear (*Colocasia* spp.), or arrowhead (*Sagittaria* spp.). Water poppy (*Hydrocleys nymphoides*) is a floating-leaved plant with showy yellow flowers. European water clover (*Marsilea quadrifolia*) has bright green, floating leaves shaped like four-leaf clovers. Other aquatic plants may be found in mail-order water garden catalogs. (See "Sources" on page 401 for suppliers.)

To provide clear water and a proper habitat for fish, each tub should have at least one pot of submerged oxygenating plants, such as elodea (*Elodea* spp.) or hornwort (*Ceratophyllum demersum*).

Potting Plants

Once you've selected the container for your tub garden and chosen a site in full sun, you're ready to pot up your plants. It's best to pot the plants and set them in place before filling the tub with water. Wait a week or two for the plants to become established before introducing fish.

Each plant should be grown in its own pot. In this case, it's not necessary to use pots with holes in the bottom; plastic dish tubs are ideal. The best soil for tub plants is ordinary garden loam that has been sieved to remove rocks, pieces of roots, and other organic matter. Manure, compost, peat moss, and raw organic matter such as roots or leaves will foul the water.

Position the roots and fill the containers. Leave enough room at the top of the pot for a 2-inch layer of pea gravel on the surface of the soil. This will help keep the water clear and discourage fish from digging in the soil and muddying the water. (See

"Creating a Water Garden" on page 181 for more information on planting water lilies.)

Filling the Tub

Set the plants in place in the tub. The amount of water that should cover the pots varies from plant to plant. Pots of oxygenating plants rest on the bottom. Full-sized water lilies can rest on the bottom, generally. Miniatures or bog plants must be positioned closer to the surface. Use bricks under pots to adjust them to the proper depth. Then fill the tub slowly by trickling in water.

It will take a few weeks for your tub to become balanced. Once the soil has settled to the bottom and the plants begin to grow, the water should clear. If the water turns very green before the plants have had a chance to grow, empty the tub and refill it. Once the leaves of water lilies and other floating-leaved plants appear, they will shade the water. This will not only keep it cool during the hot summer months, but will also help reduce free-swimming algae in the water. Plants and fish prefer water temperatures in the 65° to 75°F range. When you are ready to introduce fish, float them on the surface of the water in a water-filled plastic bag for an hour to equalize the temperature, before opening the bag and releasing them. (Remove fish immediately if they begin gulping air at the surface.)

In the fall, unless you live in an area where temperatures do not fall below freezing, you'll need to drain and clean the tub. Fish can be moved indoors into an aquarium or other container; goldfish can be kept through the winter at temperatures between 40° and 45°F. Tropical lilies grown in temperate climates are best discarded at this time. Hardy lily tubers may be stored in moist sand over winter and replanted the following spring.

SELECTING PLANTS FOR CONTAINER GARDENS

Container gardening is a great way to brighten up a deck or patio—or just a corner of your backyard where you're tight on space. Any of the following plants will thrive in containers such as tubs, old wheelbarrows, pots, urns, troughs, sinks, or hanging baskets—just make sure there are holes for adequate drainage. Position your container before you fill it—it may be too heavy to move later.

It is very important to feed and water plants regularly. After a couple of months in their containers, plants will need about a pint of liquid fertilizer, like manure tea or fish emulsion, every two weeks during the summer.

Name	Height	Description	Culture
Achimenes spp. (Achimenes)	8-12 in.	Flowering African violet relatives with scaly rhizomes and flat-faced, tubular flowers in pink, blue, purple, red, orange, yellow, or white. Blooms spring to frost.	Tender perennial usually grown as an annual from scaly rhizomes. Partial to deep shade. Light, well-drained soil rich in organic matter. Water and feed heavily. Propagate by division, cuttings, seeds. Rhizomes can be dried and overwintered indoors.
Begonia × *semperflorens-cultorum* hybrids (Wax begonia)	6-12 in.	Compact, fleshy plants with waxy single or double flowers that are pink, red, or white. Foliage is fleshy and green, maroon, or bronze. Blooms spring to frost.	Tender perennial usually grown as an annual. Full sun to partial shade. Moist, well-drained soil rich in organic matter. Best propagated by cuttings. Or sow seed indoors 12-14 weeks before last frost. Almost continuous bloom. Can be brought indoors in fall and overwintered as a houseplant.
Browallia speciosa (Browallia)	12-15 in.	Attractive plant with bell-shaped flowers in blue or white. Leaves are narrow and dark green. Blooms spring to frost.	Tender perennial usually grown as an annual. Full sun to partial shade. Moist, well-drained soil rich in organic matter. Propagate by cuttings or sow seed indoors 6-8 weeks before last frost. Can be brought indoors in fall and overwintered as a houseplant. Attractive when combined with other annuals.
Caladium spp. (Caladium)	9-30 in.	Genus grown for its showy, many-colored leaves marked and patterned in combinations of white, pink, red, or green.	Tender perennial grown as summer-flowering bulb from tuber-corms. Partial to deep shade. Moist, well-drained soil rich in organic matter. Remove flowers as they appear. Propagate by division. Hardy only in Zone 10; dig tuber-corms and store in a cool, dry spot over winter. Many cultivars available.
Calendula officinalis (Pot marigold)	6-24 in.	Daisy-family member with yellow, cream, white, or orange daisylike flowers and bright green leaves. Blooms spring to frost.	Annual. Full sun to partial shade. Rich moist soil. Sow seeds in the containers where the plants are to grow. Excellent cut flower. Best where summers are cool.

Name	Height	Description	Culture
Catharanthus roseus (Rose periwinkle)	18-24 in.	Low-growing, summer-blooming plant with showy, flat-faced flowers in white, rose, pink, or mauve. Leaves are glossy green. Sometimes sold as *Vinca rosea*.	Tender perennial usually grown as an annual. Full sun to partial shade. Will tolerate most soils, including dry ones. Hardy in Zone 10. Prefers warm temperatures.
Celosia cristata (Cockscomb)	6-36 in.	Unique-looking, summer-flowering annual with crested or plumed flower heads in yellow, orange, red, and purple.	Annual. Full sun. Sandy, well-drained soil rich in organic matter. Sow seeds indoors 4-6 weeks before last frost, or sow outdoors. Good cut flower. Blooms can also be dried. Attractive when combined with other annuals.
Chrysanthemum × *morifolium* (Hardy chrysanthemum)	12-48 in.	Popular, fall-blooming perennial with yellow, purple, scarlet, orange, pink, or white daisylike flowers that may be single or double.	Hardy perennial. Full sun to partial shade. Rich to average, moist, well-drained soil. Pinch back stems in early part of season to encourage branching. Zones 3-10; often grown as annual. Good cut flower. Many reclassified as *Tanacetum* or *Leucanthemum*.
Coleus × *hybridus* (Coleus, flame nettle)	6-36 in.	Shrubby plant grown for its ornamental foliage, which is variegated in combinations of chartreuse, white, bronze, gold, copper, yellow, pink, red, purple or green.	Tender perennial usually grown as an annual. Full sun to partial shade. Moist, well-drained soil rich in organic matter. Propagate by cuttings, seeds. Pinch off flowers as they form. Can be brought indoors in fall and overwintered as a houseplant. Excellent plant to add color to a shady spot.
Crocus spp. (Crocus)	3-6 in.	Early spring-blooming plants with purple, lilac, blue, cream, yellow, white, or orange chalice-shaped flowers and grassy leaves.	Hardy perennial grown from a corm. Full sun to partial shade. Sandy or gritty, well-drained soil. Propagate by cormels, seeds. Zones 3-8. Useful for adding spring color to large containers that remain unplanted during winter.
Hemerocallis hybrids (Daylily)	12-48 in.	Summer-blooming, clump-forming plants with sword-shaped leaves and trumpet-shaped flowers in yellow, orange, red, pink, or lavender. Each bloom opens for only a day.	Hardy perennial. Full sun to partial shade. Moist, well-drained soil rich in organic matter. Propagate by division. Zones 3-8. Many cultivars available; miniature selections are especially effective in containers.
Hosta spp. (Plantain lily)	6-36 in.	Sturdy, clump-forming perennials grown for their attractive foliage, which may be blue-green, green, or patterned with yellow and/or white. Spikes of violet or white, bell-shaped flowers produced in summer or fall.	Hardy perennial. Partial to deep shade. Moist, well-drained soil rich in organic matter. Propagate by division. Zones 4-9. Many cultivars available. Underplant with crocuses or daffodils for spring color.

(continued)

SELECTING PLANTS FOR CONTAINER GARDENS – *Continued*

Name	Height	Description	Culture
Impatiens wallerana (Busy Lizzy, patient Lucy)	6-30 in.	Mound-shaped, fleshy plant covered with single or double flowers of white, pink, orange, salmon, red, or lavender. Flowers may be a solid color or bicolor. Blooms appear spring to frost.	Tender perennial usually grown as an annual. Partial to dense shade. Moist, well-drained soil rich in organic matter. Prefers warm weather. Can be brought indoors in fall and overwintered as a houseplant.
Lantana camara (Yellow sage)	12-36 in.	Shrubby plant with many clusters of tiny flowers that are usually yellow or pink on opening and change to red, orange, or lavender. Blooms appear spring to frost.	Tender shrub usually grown as an annual. Full sun. Rich, loamy, well-drained soil. Propagate by softwood cuttings. Seed takes 8 weeks to germinate; sow indoors 12-14 weeks before last frost. Zones 8-10; has become a weed in areas where it is hardy. Can be brought indoors in fall and over-wintered as a houseplant.
Lobelia erinus (Edging lobelia)	4-8 in.	Trailing, summer-blooming annual with many small fan-shaped flowers in deep blue, pale blue, red, or white.	Annual. Full sun to partial shade. Rich, sandy, moist soil. Sow seed indoors 10-12 weeks before last frost; do not cover, seed requires light for germination. Pinch plants to promote bushiness. Attractive when combined with other annuals.
Lobularia maritima (Sweet alyssum)	6-12 in.	Ground-hugging, spring- to summer-blooming plant with abundant clusters of fragrant white, pink, or purple flowers.	Perennial usually grown as an annual. Full sun. Average well-drained soil. Shear back plants occasionally to encourage repeat bloom. Can be brought indoors in winter for further bloom. Attractive when combined with other annuals.
***Muscari* spp.** (Grape hyacinth)	8-12 in.	Low-growing, spring-blooming bulbs with dense grapelike clusters of bluish purple or white, bell-shaped flowers. Grasslike leaves.	Hardy bulb. Full sun to partial shade. Sandy, well-drained soil rich in organic matter. Zones 5-8. Edging plant. Useful for adding spring color to large containers that remain unplanted during winter.
Myosotis sylvatica (Garden forget-me-not)	6-18 in.	Spring-blooming annual with tiny blue, pink, or white flowers.	Reseeding annual. Partial shade. Moist, well-drained soil rich in organic matter. Tolerates wet conditions. Sow seeds in the containers where the plants are to grow. Best where summers are cool.
***Narcissus* spp.** (Daffodil, narcissus, jonquil)	6-15 in.	Popular, spring-blooming bulbs with showy, cup-shaped flowers with 6 surrounding petal-like segments. Blooms are yellow, orange, orange-red, white, or pink. Leaves are narrow and strap-shaped.	Hardy bulb. Full sun to partial shade. Moist, well-drained soil. Propagate by offsets. Zones 5-8. Good for cutting. Many cultivars available. Useful for adding spring color to large containers that remain unplanted during winter.
Nicotiana alata (Flowering tobacco)	18-30 in.	Summer-flowering plant with white, lime, lavender, pink, or red, trumpet-shaped flowers that are very fragrant at night.	Full sun to partial shade. Moist, well-drained soil rich in organic matter. Sow seed indoors 6-8 weeks before last frost.

Name	Height	Description	Culture
Pelargonium spp. (Geranium)	12-36 in.	Large genus grown for ornamental flowers and/or foliage. Bedding or zonal geraniums grown for their 3-5-in.-wide flower clusters in pink, salmon, red, or white. Other species grown for their scented foliage. Blooms appear spring to frost.	Tender, shrubby perennial usually grown as annual. Full sun. Loamy to sandy, well-drained soil rich in organic matter. Propagate by cuttings. Remove flowers as they fade. Hardy in Zone 10; can be brought indoors in fall and over-wintered as a houseplant. Many cultivars available.
Petunia spp. (Petunia)	10-18 in.	Popular, sprawling annuals with trumpet-shaped blooms in many forms and colors. Blooms may be violet, pink, salmon, rose, red, yellow, or white, either solid colors or bicolors. Blooms may be single or double and appear spring to frost.	Full sun. Rich, light, sandy soil with very good drainage. Pinch branch tips after first flush of bloom to encourage branching. Attractive when combined with other annuals.
Portulaca grandiflora (Rose moss)	4-8 in.	Fleshy, mat-forming plant with red, gold, yellow, cream, rose, white, or salmon flowers that open in sunny weather. Blooms appear spring to frost.	Annual. Full sun. Sandy, dry, well-drained soil. Withstands heat, drought. Attractive when combined with other annuals.
Thunbergia alata (Black-eyed Susan vine)	48-120 in.	Vining plant with orange, buff, or apricot flowers that have a purple or black throat and dense, dark green leaves. Blooms appear spring to frost.	Tender perennial usually grown as an annual. Full sun to partial shade. Light, rich, moist, well-drained soil. Provide a trellis or allow to trail over edges of pot or hanging basket. Sow seed indoors 6-8 weeks before last frost.
Tulipa spp. (Tulip)	6-30 in.	Popular spring-blooming plants with cup-shaped blooms in many colors including red, yellow, pink, white, maroon, and orange.	Hardy bulb. Full sun. Sandy, well-drained soil rich in organic matter. Propagate by offsets. Zones 2-9. Can be grown as an annual, or, when leaves yellow, lift and store bulbs in a cool, dry spot and replant outdoors in fall. Useful for adding spring color to large containers that remain unplanted during winter.
Viola spp. (Violet, pansy)	4-6 in.	Attractive, spring-to-summer blooming plants with purple, blue, red, yellow, white, or ivory flowers. Many are bicolored with large, facelike patches.	Annual and perennial species. Full sun to partial shade. Moist, rich soil. Best in areas with cool summers. Pinch back plants in midsummer to encourage further bloom. Mulch in summer to keep soil moist and cool. Good for adding early spring color to containers left outdoors; attractive when combined with other annuals.

Building a Planter

This 8-cubic-foot planter is versatile, durable, portable, and protective for both ornamentals and container food crops. It can be used to grow a tree rose, a dwarf fruit tree, or a mixture of vegetables and flowering annuals on porch, patio, balcony, or deck. Fitted with casters, it can easily be rolled indoors in the fall to grow by a bright kitchen window or in a greenhouse over the winter, and then rolled back outdoors in the spring. It will last for many years.

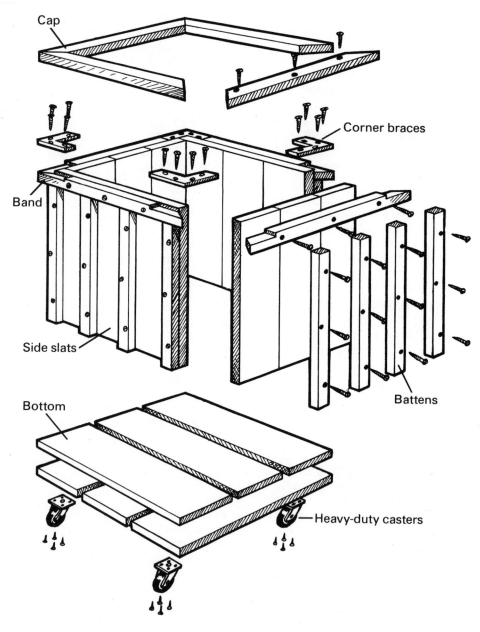

This three-dimensional view of the structure of an 8-cubic-foot redwood planter shows the double layer construction of the base, the braces that strengthen the planter sides, and the bottom-mounted casters, which allow for easy moving.

TOOLS REQUIRED

Screwdriver
Electric drill
Miter box and saw
Saw (crosscut or electric)
Paintbrush

MATERIALS

LUMBER – CUT LIST

Use redwood, cedar, or pressure-treated wood.

6 pcs. ¾ × 7¼ × 21¾" (base)

12 pcs. ¾ × 7¾ × 23¾" (side slats)

4 pcs. ¾ × 1½ × 25¾" (band)

4 pcs. ¾ × 2 × 26¾" (cap)

16 pcs. ¾ × 1½ × 22¼" (battens)

HARDWARE

#6 × 1¼" galvanized wood screws

12 to 16 pcs. #6 × 1⅝" galvanized wood screws (for side corners only)

4 pcs. 3½" corner braces

4 heavy-duty casters

Clear wood finish for exterior wood or other ultraviolet inhibitor

1. **Base.** The 22¾-inch-square base consists of two layers, with three boards per layer, running in opposite directions. The ½-inch gap between each board allows for drainage; four drainage holes are created in the center of the planter, as well as a hole near each of the four corners. To assemble the base, screw the two layers together, drilling from the bottom layer of boards into the top layer. Attach the casters

380

to the base. Throughout the construction, predrill all holes.

2. Sides. Screw individual side slats into the base, allowing the sides to completely cover and extend about ½ inch below the base, depending on the size of the casters. The sides of the planter should be 1¼ inches above the ground. For added strength, use three or four #6 1⅝-inch screws on each side corner.

3. Band. Use the miter box to cut the ends of the four band pieces to join at corners. Notch corners of the four pieces ⅟₁₆ × 3½ inches to accept

corner braces. Screw the bands into the sides. Attach the corner braces to band corners at top.

4. Cap. Use the miter box to cut the ends of the four cap pieces. Screw the cap pieces into the top of the planter so the cap covers the top edges of the side slats and braced band. The inside edge of the cap is flush with the inside of the planter. The outside edge of the cap extends slightly beyond the band. Predrill all holes.

5. Battens. Screw the battens into the sides, four battens per side,

so the side slat seams are covered. The corner battens are flush with the side edges. Stagger the screw holes on either side of the seams.

6. Finish. If you've used redwood or cedar, paint the outside of the planter with a clear finish. It is not necessary to paint the inside of the planter. Add 1 inch of gravel to the inside bottom of the planter for additional drainage. Indoors or on a wooden deck, be sure to use a drip tray beneath the planter.

Your finished planter will hold tomatoes, a dwarf fruit tree, or an ornamental shrub trained as a standard.

Making Window Boxes

Window boxes can bring the vivid colors and forms of the outdoor garden into virtually any room of your house. For apartment dwellers, they may be the only form of outdoor gardening available. Window boxes are easy to build and maintain. They can be designed for installation on or below a window sill.

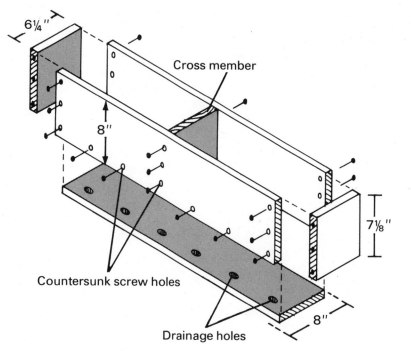

6¼"

Cross member

8"

7⅛"

Countersunk screw holes

Drainage holes

8"

This diagram shows location of cross-member and bottom drainage holes in the window box.

1. Screw the front and back to the ends and divider.

2. Drill two rows of ½-inch drainage holes in the bottom of the window box. Space holes 6 inches apart in the row. Position the center of the holes at least 1¼ inches from the edge of the bottom.

3. Screw the bottom to the assembled front, back, and ends.

4. Mount the box. For on-sill mounting, use long-arm hooks and eyes. Attach the arm to the window frame and the eye to the window box. Hook the arm to the eye to attach the box. For below-sill mounting, screw brackets to the box and house, as shown in the drawings.

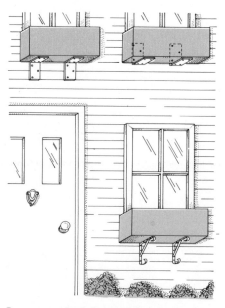

Proper mounting is important to prevent your window boxes from falling. There are several types of brackets to use for below-sill mounting.

TOOLS REQUIRED
Screwdriver
Electric drill
Router (for sill mounting)
Saw (circular or hand)

MATERIALS
The dimensions below will vary for window boxes of different lengths.

Adjust dimensions to fit your windowsill. Measure the sill from end to end if you plan to mount your box below the sill. For mounting on the sill, measure between the window moldings and subtract ⅛ inch for clearance.

To avoid splitting the wood, predrill all holes for the screws. Hardware stores sell an inexpensive combination bit that drills pilot and clearance holes for the screws and countersinks for the screw head at the same time.

LUMBER – CUT LIST
1 pc. ¾ × 7¼ × 30½" cedar (bottom)
1 pc. ¾ × 7¼ × 30½" cedar (front)
1 pc. ¾ × 7¼ × 30½" cedar (back)
2 pcs. ¾ × 7¼ × 5¾" cedar (ends)
1 pc. ¾ × 7¼ × 5¾" cedar (middle divider)

HARDWARE
#6 × 1¼" galvanized wood screws
Long-arm hook and eye or metal brackets

WINDOW BOX GARDENING

If your mental image of a window box is just a boxful of geraniums (*Pelargonium* spp.) or petunias (*Petunia* × *hybrida*), open your eyes and think again. Nearly any outdoor plant that grows less than 18 inches tall is suited to window box growing. The plants you choose will be limited only by your imagination and by the growing conditions at the box's location.

Consider moving some spring-flowering bulb shoots to the window box just as the bulb shoots emerge from the ground. Some smaller summer-flowering bulbs also are suited to window box growing. Cascading roses (*Rosa* spp.) can trail over the box along with the traditional vining vinca (*Vinca* spp.). And don't forget that salad vegetables can be decorative as well as practical additions to the box garden. A window box of 'Patio' tomatoes, chives, and scallions is perfect for growing under the kitchen window.

Also consider giving some of your houseplants a summer vacation in the window box. But remember, they'll need proper protection from strong sun and wind. Try a site on the north side of your house, or a shaded window away from prevailing winds.

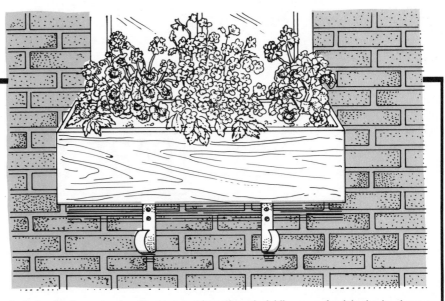

A window box in a sunny location is a great home for colorful flowers or fresh herbs. In winter, a box filled with berry-laden tree or shrub boughs may attract a variety of birds.

Houseplants can be set into the window box right in their pots and easily moved back indoors at a moment's notice.

Location is important when choosing plants for boxes. In a hot location, such as under a south-facing window, choose heat-resistant plants—marigolds (*Tagetes* spp.), zinnias (*Zinnia* spp.), petunias (*Petunia* × *hybrida*), and salvia (*Salvia* spp.), or heat-loving vegetables. Below a shady north-facing window, consider wax begonias (*Begonia* × *semperflorens-cultorum*), impatiens (*Impatiens* spp.), nemesia (*Nemesia strumosa*), fuchsia (*Fuchsia* spp.), coleus (*Coleus* × *hybridus*), and rock garden plants. In northern areas in the fall, use low-growing chrysanthemums (*Chrysanthemum* spp.) to flood a window

box with color. When winter approaches, remove the mums and fill the box with evergreen boughs and holly (*Ilex* spp.).

For best results, line the bottom of the window box with gravel for drainage and use a rich growing medium—the same as you would use for houseplants. (See "Soil Mixes for Houseplants" on page 359 for some recipes.) A good general mix is 1 part peat moss, 1 part potting soil, and 1 part sharp sand or vermiculite, with ½ cup of bonemeal and ½ cup of lime added to each peck (roughly 2 gallons) of mix. During the growing season, fertilize weekly with fish emulsion or manure tea. Watch soil moisture carefully, especially during hot weather when the box might have to be watered daily.

PART 7
Tools

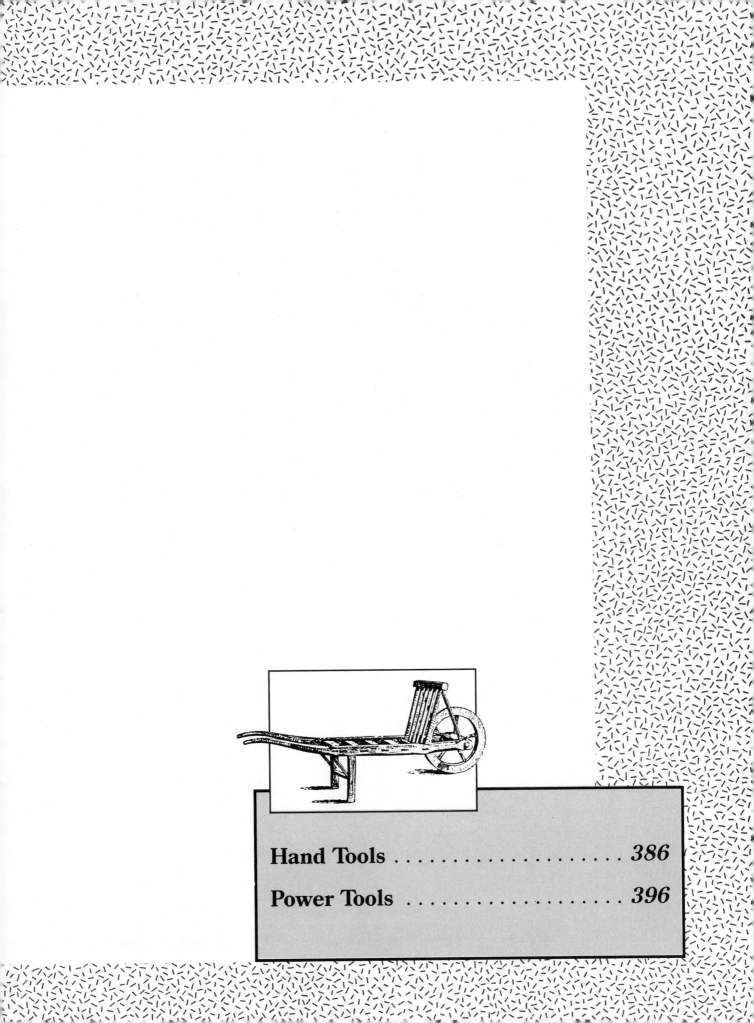

Hand Tools

The Basics

The range of garden tools offered today is bewildering, even for experienced gardeners, and a trip to the tool section of the hardware store or garden center may completely confuse the beginner. The wise gardener will start small, beginning with the basic hand tools and adding more only after learning the full use of the tools he or she already has.

You can probably get by with a few basic tools—a fork or spade for digging, a garden rake for smoothing the soil and preparing beds, a hoe for cultivating and weeding, and a trowel for working closely around plants.

The first rule of tool buying is to avoid cheap tools at all costs. The $1 trowel at the discount store is stamped out of cheap sheet metal, poorly designed, and even more poorly constructed. Not only will it break in a short time, but it will annoy you while you use it because it won't do the job well. Do not buy cheap tools for children, either. Even children should have good tools, because they'll never learn to love gardening if the first tools they use do not work well.

The best wood for a shovel handle, as for all long-handled garden tools, is North American white ash, which is strong, light, and resilient. Hickory is stronger and is ideal for hammers and other short-handled tools. It is sometimes used for spades and forks, but is too heavy and inflexible to use for shovels and

rakes. Examine the lines (rings) in the wood; they should run straight down the entire length of the handle, with no knots. Avoid painted handles, which often hide cheap wood. Also watch out for handles that are painted to look like straight-grain ash.

The attachment of the metal part of the tool to its handle is important to durability, especially for shovels.

Avoid shovels of open-socket construction. The scoops are die-cut from sheet metal, then wrapped around the handle and riveted, leaving a seam. Instead, buy a shovel with solid-socket or solid-strapped construction. These are forged from a single bar of steel and completely envelop the handle, thus protecting it and greatly adding strength.

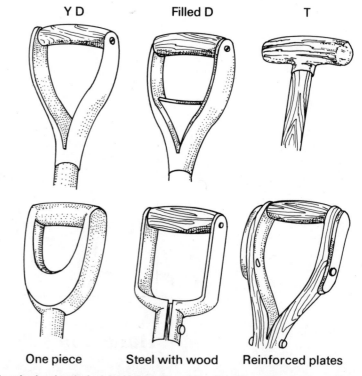

Y D   Filled D   T

One piece   Steel with wood   Reinforced plates

When choosing hand tools, look for high quality ash handles. The grips come in a variety of shapes; choose one that feels comfortable and fits your hand. The reinforced plate handle is exceptionally strong. The handle is split-sawn and bent, the sides reinforced, and a wooden cob, or handle, is fastened in place. Avoid tools with grips that are not visibly fastened to the handle.

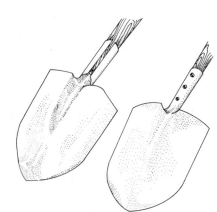

Left, open socket construction leaves the base of the wooden handle exposed to contact with water and mud, which can cause wood rot; *right,* solid socket and solid strapped tools fully enclose the handle, protecting it and increasing the overall strength of the tool.

Keeping Tools in Shape

After making a considerable investment in good quality hand tools, it is wise to spend some time to keep them in good shape.

Routine Care

At the end of each day of gardening, clean, dry, and put away all the hand tools you used. Keep a large plastic kitchen spoon handy to knock dirt off metal blades. Do not use a trowel or other metal tool, as you could damage the blades of both tools. A 5-gallon bucket of sharp builder's sand in the tool shed or garage is useful for cleaning tools. Dip the metal blade of each tool into the sand and plunge it up and down a few times to work off any clinging soil. Use a wire brush to remove any rust that may have formed.

Caring for Handles

Wooden handles and shafts of hand tools should be kept varnished and sanded to keep them resilient and good-looking. If you buy a good-quality tool secondhand, and it has a weather-beaten handle, refresh it with several coats of varnish, sanding between each coat.

You can repair split handles temporarily with tape and glue, but replace broken handles as soon as possible.

Sharpening

Sharp-bladed hand tools will perform efficiently and with ease only if they are kept sharp. Take the time to study the angle of the bevels on all your tools, then sharpen each as needed to keep the proper bevel. And, for tools that are especially difficult to sharpen, don't hesitate to take them to a known and trusted professional.

The edge of a hoe can regain its sharpness if you run it across a grinding wheel several times. Bevel the side of the blade opposite the handle, holding the hoe at a 35- to 40-degree angle to the wheel.

The edge of a shovel need not be especially sharp, but it should be kept smooth so that dirt will readily slide off the blade. Hammer out any curls with a ball-peen hammer, and smooth out nicks with a fairly fine metal-cutting file.

On pruners, the outside of the cutting blade should be kept as sharp as possible, maintaining a fairly steep angle (10 to 15 degrees) of file to edge. The cutting edge of loppers should be filed at a similar angle.

At the end of the season, polish all the metal parts of your hand tools with steel wool, oil them to prevent rust, and store them in a dry place. Lubricate all tools that have moving parts. This is also a good time to take tools to the sharpening shop, particularly those that are tricky to sharpen at home.

Hoes

There are probably more different kinds of hoes than any other garden tool. Avid gardeners become as attached to favorite hoes as golfers do to putters, probably because their hoe is the tool they use most frequently. With a hoe, you can lay out rows, dig furrows, cultivate around plants to loosen the soil and kill weeds, create hills and raised beds, break up clods, and prepare bare spots in lawns for reseeding.

Types of Hoes

The standard American pattern hoe is a long-handled tool that allows you to work without too much bending. It has a broad and straight blade, a little larger than 6-by-4 inches. However, many gardeners prefer a nursery hoe, which has a shallower (2- to 3-inch) blade and is lighter to work with.

In many Third World countries, the eye hoe, with its large, heavy, and deep blade, is the standard tool for breaking new ground and digging holes and trenches, as well as for cultivating.

The oscillating hoe is a modern version of the Dutch hoe, both of which were designed to slice weeds

The American pattern hoe works well for heavy weeding and digging garden beds.

The oscillating hoe swivels as you move the handle, cutting weeds in both directions.

The swan-neck hoe's curved neck makes it easy to do light weeding without having to stoop.

The grub hoe is similar to an American pattern hoe, but has a thinner and longer blade.

just below the soil surface. It cuts both as it is being pushed and pulled along the ground. In modern variations, often called the "hula" or action hoe, the slicing blade moves back and forth slightly to position itself for cutting while being pulled or pushed.

An onion hoe has a thin blade 1½ inches high and 7 inches wide, and can be pulled easily along the row to cut weeds well below the soil surface. Some are short handled, for use while kneeling. The blade of the grub hoe is narrower and taller than that of the standard American pattern hoe, enabling it to work deeply in tight rows.

Very different is the Warren hoe, which has a pointed, arrowhead-like blade used to make planting furrows quickly. It is also handy for digging down to bring up stubborn weeds. The scuffle or slicing hoe is used for easy weeding in beds and borders. Its blade may be pointed or flat. A variation is the swan-neck hoe, named

for the curve of the neck going into the blade. Its configuration allows the user to maintain a straight back and good balance while working. It is good for weeding in tight spaces, since the handle is held close to the body. There is also a pinpoint weeder, which has a narrow loop on the end to take up single weeds in very tight spaces.

The Canterbury hoe has three tines instead of a solid blade, and is perfect for breaking up soil, gathering up weeds and brush, and for aerating the top 4 to 6 inches of soil in rows and around plants. The double hoe has a blade on one side, tines on the other.

The grape hoe, sometimes called a hazel or adze hoe, is a large, strong tool used for weeding and general cultivation in vineyards.

Selecting and Using Hoes

When choosing a hoe, remember that narrower blades transmit your arm power more efficiently to the tool head

than wider blades. Unless you need the depth of the standard hoe blade, you will probably be better off using an onion hoe, which is lighter and easier to use. The hoe handle should be at least 54 inches long (the traditional Dutch hoe is 64 inches) so you can work without bending over and straining your lower back muscles. In general, when working with hoes, try to remain standing upright. Run the hoe blade below and parallel to the soil surface to loosen the soil or to cut the roots of weeds. Remember to sharpen your hoe so that it will cut through weeds, which is easier than using the tool to yank the weeds out of the soil.

The blade, shank, and handle socket should be made of one-piece forged steel, attached to the handle by solid-socket construction. The handle will then be relatively easy to replace in case it breaks.

Spades, Shovels, and Forks

The standard American long-handled shovel has many uses around the home grounds, but some experienced gardeners seldom use it in actual garden work. For while a shovel is the best tool for digging rounded planting holes, most digging jobs are best accomplished with a four-tine garden fork or a spade.

Spades

A short-handled, square-end spade is one of the most valuable and versatile garden tools you will ever own. A spade has a flat, rather than scooped blade, with squared edges. The handle is generally shorter than a shovel handle, usually ranging from 28 to 32 inches. The angle between shaft and blade is shallow, and the handle usually has a D-shaped grip for fine control.

On a good quality spade, the grip is made of wood or metal-reinforced wood that is firmly attached to or part of the handle. A spade should also have a turned edge or footrest along the shoulders of the blade to protect your feet when you step on the tool.

With a spade, you can cut easily through sod and create straight edges in soil. Spades are used for digging planting holes, prying up rocks, digging up strong roots, dividing perennial clumps, cutting unwanted tree and shrub roots, tamping sod, hammering stakes, cutting cord, digging trenches, and moving perennials.

There are several spades designed for special purposes. One is the drain-tile spade, a narrow-bladed spade used for digging small trenches. It's also good for digging postholes and for transplanting in close quarters. A border spade has a short handle and a narrow blade and may be more comfortable for short people to use. The nurseryman's spade has a small, slightly curved blade especially designed for transplanting.

Shovels

Shovels are good for mixing cement, and for moving soil, gravel, and sand. In a pinch, you can use a shovel as a scuffle hoe to cut weeds just below the soil surface, as a garden edger, and as a posthole digger. It's a good tool for prying rocks and root clumps from the soil, although be careful not to strain the handle to the breaking point.

The standard American shovel has a handle about 48 inches long. The shovel handle should come to shoulder height or higher, to enable you to work most efficiently. Shovels should also have a turned edge or footrest along the shoulders of the blade to protect your feet when you step on the tool.

If you want to buy a shovel that will last a lifetime, ask a local building contractor for the most reliable source.

Forks

A spading fork can cut into soil like a shovel or a spade, but usually does it more easily than solid-bladed tools can. A spading fork is handy for mixing materials into the soil, and for harvesting potatoes, carrots, and other

Left, the garden spade is generally rectangular, with straight sides and squared corners; a shovel may be round-pointed, *center,* or square-mouthed, *right.* Shorter-handled spades and shovels often have a D-grip at the top.

USING SPADES AND SHOVELS SAFELY

When digging or lifting materials with either a spade or shovel, remember these guidelines to avoid unnecessary stress on your back.

• Push the blade vertically into the soil with your foot, using your body weight to force the blade down—don't jump onto the tool to force it into the earth.

• The angle between the blade and the handle is a design feature that helps the digging process. After you push the blade down, remain upright, and pull the handle (which will be tilting away from you) back, close to your body. This action will loosen the shovelful of soil, making it easier to lift.

• Use your arms to lift the tool, and if possible, support the weight of the full blade with your thigh.

• Move your feet and turn your entire body to face the spot where you will be depositing the soil, rather than twisting from the hips to move the tool.

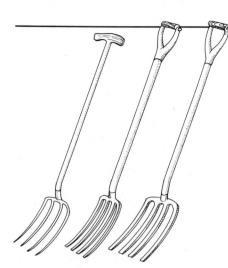

Left, the manure fork has rounded tines; *center,* cultivating forks have square tines; *right,* spading forks have broad, flat tines.

root crops. The tines of the standard spading fork are broad and flat. Those of the English cultivating fork are thinner and square. The English version is better for cultivating and aerating soil. Remember that forks are used to loosen soil, not to lift it.

The standard handle length for a spading fork is 28 inches. Very tall gardeners may prefer a 32-inch handle (it will be more expensive, but well worth it). Short gardeners, including children, should use a border fork, which is smaller in both handle and tine lengths. Border forks, like bor-

der spades, are also ideal for transplanting in tight spaces.

A pitchfork (three tines) and a straw fork (five or six tines) are used for picking up, turning, and scattering hay mulch, leaf mold, and light compost materials. They are also useful for spreading mulch and for cleaning up garden beds in spring.

Trowels and Cultivators

When working on hands and knees, your best friend is your garden trowel, actually a miniature version of a shovel. Use it for digging planting holes for small plants and bulbs, for transplanting seedlings, for leveling the ground, and even for digging up weeds in thickly planted beds and borders.

A well-designed trowel is efficient and comfortable to use, and does not bend or break when you exert pressure on it. Some trowels are made from forged steel and fitted with hard-

wood handles, but good ones are also available in unbreakable one-piece cast aluminum. When buying an aluminum trowel, look for one that includes a plastic sleeve over the handle. This will prevent your hands from blackening from contact with the aluminum.

Trowels come in a variety of blade widths and lengths. Choose one that feels comfortable in your hand. You can use a narrow-bladed trowel for planting fine seed. First use the trowel to open a small furrow, and then put

seed in the trowel and let it slowly trickle out into the furrow.

A few other small tools are more suitable than a trowel for particular tasks. A hand fork is good for loosening the soil around plants and for preparing small areas for planting. A hand cultivator works well to cultivate shallowly around plants. And a daisy grubber, also called an asparagus fork, has a long shaft and forked blade which make it ideal for jabbing deep into the soil to rout out long-rooted weeds.

Garden trowels are handy for digging planting holes, sowing seed, pulling out stubborn weeds, and getting compost or mulch to hard-to-reach spots.

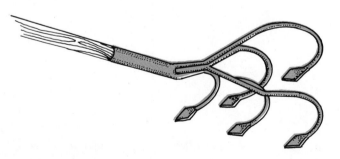

Short-handled hand cultivators help with weeding and loosening soil around plantings. Similar cultivators with long handles are also very useful.

Rakes

The traditional metal bow garden rake is so named because its head is attached to the handle with two bows, providing spring action. Popular alternatives to the bow rake include the level-head or square-back rake, which is generally narrower with shorter teeth and a shorter handle, and the landscaper's rake, which is very wide and designed specifically to level out broad areas.

These rakes are essential tools for leveling ground, creating raised beds, killing emerging weeds, gathering up debris from rows, covering furrows, thinning seedlings, working materials shallowly into the soil, erasing footprints, and pushing around mulch. Bow rakes come in many widths, with long or short teeth that are widely or closely spaced. The handle should be long, 54 to 60 inches, and the head should be heavy enough to bite into the soil easily. Wide-spaced teeth are recommended for working in rocky soil.

Lawn or Leaf Rakes

Also called fan rakes, these are good for gathering up leaves, grass, weeds, and other debris, and for dislodging thatch from the lawn. They come in different sizes; a 19-inch head seems to be close to standard.

Metal lawn rakes last longest and are the springiest, although many gardeners prefer the action and feel of bamboo tines, and some prefer plastic or rubber. Some lawn rakes have adjustable heads that can be made narrower for raking in tight spaces such as under shrubs or in garden beds.

The square-back rake is used for working materials into the soil, covering furrows, and other surface soil work.

A lawn or fan rake is the best tool for moving leaves, grass, and other light materials.

Scythes and Sickles

A scythe is a traditional hand tool used for mowing grain crops or tall grass and weeds. The tool consists of a long curving blade attached at an angle to a curved handle called a snath. Two short grips, called nibs, project from the snath. A sickle has a shorter blade and handle than a scythe and is used primarily for cutting back tall weeds in hard-to-reach areas.

The mechanical reaper invented in 1831 and subsequent modern machinery have made the scythe nearly obsolete. However, gardeners may still find the scythe useful for mowing grass on very steep slopes or in rocky areas. Scythes, mostly Austrian-made, are still found in many hardware stores, especially in rural areas.

A cross between the scythe and sickle is the grass hook (common names for these tools often overlap), a modern instrument with a slightly curved detachable blade that can be fastened to either a long or a short shaft. Used with two hands, it is much lighter and easier to handle than a scythe, yet has a cutting blade longer than that of a sickle.

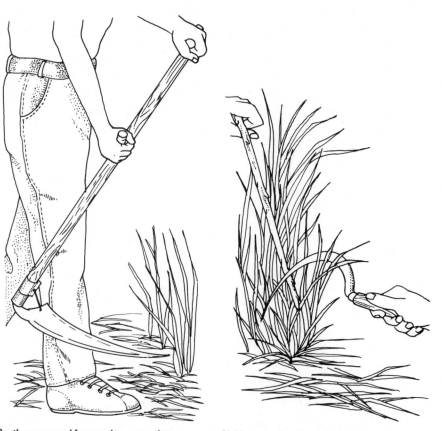

Scythes are used for mowing areas that cannot be cut with power equipment—including very steep slopes or rocky meadows.

Sickles can slice through clumps of tall weeds along fencerows or around tree bases.

Using a Scythe

Using a scythe is a tricky process that requires some strength and endurance. To mow with a scythe, stand with your feet spread moderately apart, and hold one nib of the scythe in each hand. Sweep the tool in an arc from right to left in front of you, with the blade parallel to the ground, to cut a swath. Swing the tool back from left to right to prepare to cut the next swath. Allow your feet to take small steps as you work, in natural rhythm with the swinging blade.

Scythe blades must be sharpened frequently with a whetstone or grinding stone to work efficiently. (See "Keeping Tools in Shape" on page 387 for sharpening guidelines.) Grass or weeds may be easier to mow when they are green and wet than if they are dry or dead.

Using a Sickle

A sickle is useful wherever tall weeds must be chopped down—along fence rows, up against buildings, around trees, wherever other tools cannot reach. The curved steel blade, typi-cally 18 to 26 inches long, is attached to a hardwood, steel, or aluminum alloy handle.

Cut weeds with a scythe by slicing with one hand in a sideways motion. Use a stick held in your other hand to hold back overhanging grass so that you can cut growth near the stem bases. If the grass is wet, you may want to hold the stick upright with one end touching the ground as a barrier between the sickle and your body, in case the sickle slips on the wet grass as you swing. As with the scythe, keep your sickle sharp at all times.

Pruning Tools

Any garden that has trees, shrubs, and hedges needs frequent snipping, trimming, cutting, chopping, and pruning. While these jobs can be arduous with the wrong tools, they are a pleasure when using proper tools that are in good condition.

Pruning Shears

A pair of good quality pruning shears is essential for cutting small branches, shaping shrubs, deadheading plants, harvesting grapes, removing raspberry canes, and cutting back tree roots. Most models will cut hardwood branches of up to ½ inch in diameter.

There are two basic types of pruners: the anvil type, in which a straight, sharp blade closes down onto an anvil or plate; and the bypass type, in which a curved cutting blade passes by a so-called hook blade, acting like household scissors. Anvil pruners are often easier to use, requiring less hand pressure to make the cut. Bypass shears make a cleaner cut, can work in tighter spaces, and can cut flush against a tree trunk or branch instead of leaving a short stump as anvil pruners do.

Many models of both anvil and bypass pruners are available, including some that have narrow blades for light trimming and working with flowers. The Japanese ikebana-style clippers have small bypass blades and large loops to fit the hand and are popular for working with flowers.

Whatever type you select, it's easiest to make pruning cuts if you work with the tool's design to get the greatest possible leverage. Position a branch between the blades as close as possible to the pivot point (the place where the two blades are attached to one another) before starting to cut, for greatest efficiency.

Other Pruners

There are other types of pruners that will make your gardening chores easier.

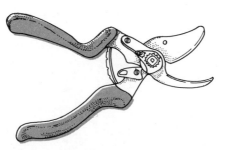

Bypass pruning shears have two blades which cross when making a cut.

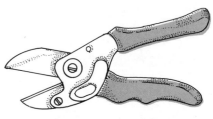

Anvil pruning shears have a single sharp blade that makes contact with a flat anvil during a cut.

Use a long-handled pole pruner to prune small branches that are beyond arms' reach.

Pole Pruners. These are useful for reaching high tree branches or getting into the base of a thickly grown shrub. Most pole pruners operate with a lever handle or a pulley and rope mechanism.

Lopping Shears. Also called loppers, these are heavy-duty pruners with wood or metal handles 25 to 30 inches in length. Made of either anvil or bypass construction, most can cut branches up to 2 inches in diameter. Some include ratchets or gears to increase leverage, or use several pivot points like a bolt cutter.

Hedge Shears. These tools have long blades and relatively short hardwood handles. They can cut branches up to ¼ inch thick. Most good quality shears have ash or hickory handles, although some are of metal or fiberglass. Most also have a shock absorber near the pivot point to reduce stress to the user's arm joints and to prevent knuckles from banging together. They are designed for cutting the tender new growth of hedges, and are also useful for trimming tall, coarse grass.

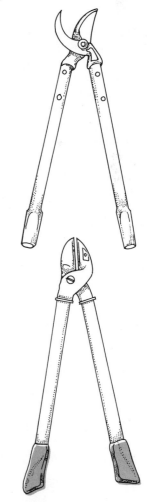

Bypass loppers are commonly used for pruning small-diameter woody branches, *top.* Loppers are also made with anvil blades, *bottom.*

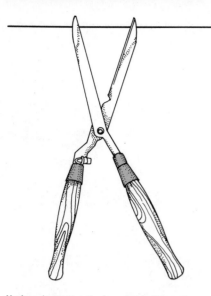

Hedge shears are designed only for cutting tender, nonwoody growth on shrubs.

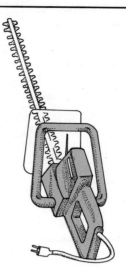

Electric hedge trimmers have a scissor-like action and can cut small twigs and shoots.

Electric Clippers. Power hedge clippers make short work of many trimming jobs. Some models are cordless, operating more than a half hour with a single battery recharge, and some even have small gasoline engines. The clipper blades range from 16 to 30 inches long. The shorter ones are easier to handle, the longer ones capable of doing more work.

Electric clippers seldom if ever need sharpening, since the scissor-like action of the blades keeps them sharp through use. Moderately priced clippers are dependable for cutting branches up to ¼ inch thick and will last for many years with little attention.

Saws

Pruning saws can cut through most branches that are too thick for pruning or lopping shears. The standard seven-point (seven teeth to the inch) model has a hardwood handle and a removable curved blade 9 to 15 inches long. It can fine-cut branches up to 3 inches in diameter. For larger limbs, use a four-point saw, curved or straight-edge, with a D-grip and both cutting and raker teeth (the latter to remove sawdust as cutting takes place).

Pole saws are useful for high limbs. Some are made in combination with pole pruners. Because of their thin blades, bow saws can cut through

wood very quickly. They are difficult to use when you don't have a lot of space in which to maneuver. Double-edge saws can cut both coarsely and finely, but sometimes damage other limbs when used in close quarters.

What to Look For

The difference between an inferior and a good quality saw is often in the arrangement and beveling of the teeth. The teeth should be set—bent alternately to left and right—so that the cut is slightly wider than the saw blade. This will keep the blade from getting stuck. Cheaper saws have teeth arranged like those of a rip saw and are cross-filed, making the top of each tooth flat like a chisel. Good quality saws are bevel-filed, a more expensive process than cross-filing but one that produces sharper teeth.

The blade of a swivel-blade pruning saw can be rotated to horizontal or even upside down to adapt the tool to cutting in different positions.

The standard curved pruning saw is easier to use in tight quarters than a double-bladed or swivel saw.

Use a pole saw to cut larger limbs that are too high to reach with a standard pruning saw.

Wheelbarrows and Garden Carts

A wheelbarrow or garden cart can be a lifesaver if you're faced with transporting various and sundry plants, tools, flats, hay bales, compost, and other materials. Each type of garden conveyance has advantages and disadvantages; be sure to select one that meets your specific gardening needs.

The traditional garden wheelbarrow differs from a contractor's model, which is specifically designed for transporting cement. A garden wheelbarrow is made of wood and has removable straight sides, not the sloping metal sides of the contractor's wheelbarrow. Many variations of the garden wheelbarrow have appeared over the years, including some with double wheels. Still, the basic design has been retained, and therein lies the major disadvantage of the wheelbarrow for garden work: the distribution of weight. Since the load lies well behind the axle and wheel, the user must share much of the load with arms, shoulders, and back.

The garden cart, on the other hand, is a large, spoke-wheeled cart that places the load directly above the axles and wheels, enabling you to move heavy loads with comparatively little effort. The large diameter bicycle-type wheels also contribute to ease of transport. They ride easily over rocks and ruts, and yet their thin tires create little friction for easy movement.

The garden cart's two wheels, placed on either side of the load, also stabilize the cart so you don't have to work to keep the load balanced and steady, as is necessary when pushing a wheelbarrow.

Another advantage of the garden cart is its large capacity. Your transplanting job will be much easier if you can load your tools, compost, and other supplies all on the flat bed of the garden cart, and wheel it easily in one trip from the tool shed to the vegetable garden.

The wheelbarrow, on the other

The contractor's wheelbarrow is designed for mixing and moving cement.

The traditional garden wheelbarrow has straight, removable sides.

Garden carts carry the main load directly over the large, bicycle-type wheels. Some models have a removable front panel for easier dumping.

Garden carts can be tipped upright for loading heavy materials such as large rocks.

hand, can maneuver into tight spaces where a large garden cart cannot go. It can be pushed between two rows of corn, or down a narrow path to the woodpile. But pushing most loaded wheelbarrows through soft earth is virtually impossible.

Two-wheel garden carts are better for most garden uses, but there are still times when a wheelbarrow is the right tool for the job. Many gardeners own both.

The classic garden cart, which comes in several sizes, has a metal-reinforced plywood body. The standard model has a nonremovable front panel, but many gardeners prefer a model with a removable front panel for easier dumping.

It is difficult to find a traditional wood garden wheelbarrow today, although they are still being made (see "Sources" on page 401). If you buy a contractor's wheelbarrow, be sure to buy one of professional or industrial grade, not "homeowner's" or "promotional" grade. Many cheap wheelbarrows and garden carts are sold at discount and department stores every year, but most of these are little more than toys that will not stand up to serious garden work.

Power Tools

Tillers

Rotary tillers can make short work of turning and churning garden soil, breaking new ground, cultivating, aerating, weeding, and mixing materials into the soil. The rotary tiller is a gasoline-powered machine equipped with steel blades that rotate on a central spindle. The two basic types are front-bladed and rear-bladed, terms that refer to the placement of the blades in relation to the engine. Front-bladed tillers are less expensive. The least expensive of these have have no wheels at all, letting the tines themselves power the machine forward. The heaviest and most expensive tillers have rear tines and power-driven wheels, and are more comfortable to operate. Sizes range from 20-pound machines, used for cultivating in flower and vegetable beds, to the 375-pound giants designed for heavy ground moving.

Most tillers depend on four-cycle engines, running from 2 to 8 horsepower, and drive mechanisms in the form of gears, chains, or belts —all of which are about equally dependable.

If you plan to buy a tiller, learn about various models by actually using them in your garden. Borrow or rent before choosing a tiller to purchase. Remember that wheeled tillers are always easier to operate than those without wheels. Large wheels provide more maneuverability than small ones. Look for heavy, heat-treated carbon steel blades.

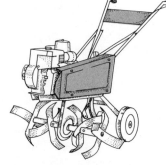

The tines of a front-mounted tiller pull the machine forward as they till.

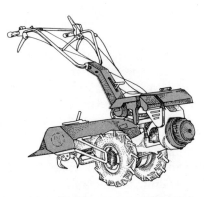

Rear-mounted tillers are pushed forward by the action of the tines. Some also have power-driven wheels for easier operation.

Some models offer optional attachments, including snow blades and throwers, log splitters, generators, shredders, blowers, sprayers, various cultivators, and even chain saws. The quality of these attachments varies widely. Garden tractors also offer tiller attachments.

Care and Maintenance

How you operate and care for your tiller will go far in determining how long it will last and how well it will perform. The first rule is, Never try to make a tiller do more than it was designed to do. It cannot clear a meadow of rocks, turn under a field of cornstalks, or uproot a tree. When you are incorporating organic matter into the soil, work in several thin layers, one at a time, so that the tiller (and you) can work with ease. When you till new soil, don't expect to reach 8 or 9 inches in depth with a single pass. Learn the limits of your tiller, and work with it—not against it.

Tiller maintenance is similar to caring for a four-cycle lawn mower. Keep the air filter clean, and change the oil every 25 hours or once a season, whichever comes first. Also check the seals of the drive system regularly, and keep debris out of the fins on the cylinder (which are meant to help cool the engine) and the grass screen over the fan. Never use gasoline that is more than two months old.

Clean your tiller thoroughly before winter. Knock out any carbon that might be plugging the portholes in the exhaust system, change the oil and filter, drain the gasoline, run the engine until all the gasoline has left the carburetor, and remove the spark plug. Then roll it into a corner and throw a blanket over the machine until spring.

Shredders and Chippers

One of the favorite large power tools of organic gardeners is often a shredder or chipper. This machine, powered with gasoline or electricity, can reduce all those leaves, pruned branches, and plant debris to beautiful mulch or compost material. Some machines are designed specifically for shredding soft plant material, others for chipping thick branches, and some have separate chutes for both functions built into the same machine.

Shredders usually operate with a spinning drum fitted with fixed hammers or swinging flails that pulverize materials. Chippers typically slice branches with one or two knife blades mounted on a metal flywheel. Shredders are better at handling weeds and other soft plant material; chippers will handle heavier, woody materials. Large 5-horsepower models can chip branches up to 3 inches in diameter. Small chippers (around 2 horsepower) can take branches up to about 1 inch.

Many of these machines have

Power shredders can transform leaves and brush into valuable mulching materials. Shredding will also speed decomposition in the compost pile.

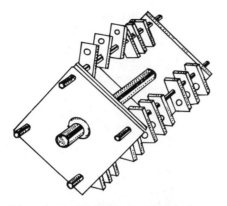

The swinging rectangular steel bars in the spinning drum of a shredder whirl at high speeds to pulverize organic materials.

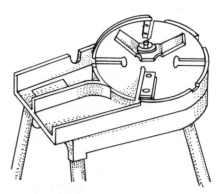

Chippers usually have knife blades mounted on a high-speed cutter disc.

trouble handling leaves. It is difficult to feed dry leaves into the machine chute quickly enough to attain any degree of efficiency—and wet leaves often clog the machine. Plus, the leaves must be collected before they are fed into the shredder. There are now string-trimmer shredders made especially for leaves, but many gardeners still find it simpler and quicker to collect leaves using a rotary mower with a bagger attached.

Electric shredder/chippers are gaining quick acceptance among gardeners. Compared with gasoline-engine models, the electrics are smaller, easier to start, quieter, and require less maintenance. However, they must be operated where there is a power source, and there is a drop in voltage when long extension cords are used.

For small amounts of garden debris, a 1- to 3-horsepower model should suffice. For a large suburban or country lot, a 5- to 8-horsepower model will both shred and chip all the waste you can produce. Some-

times neighbors will pool their resources and buy a large machine to be used by all.

Care and Maintenance

Safety is a prime concern when using these machines. Ear pads and safety goggles are mandatory, as is common sense in feeding in materials and removing clogs. Never put your hand inside a chipper/shredder without first—*every time*—unplugging it or removing the spark plug. Follow all the safety precautions of the manufacturer.

Electric shredder/chippers are virtually maintenance-free. Gasoline-powered machines must have oil and filter changes according to the manufacturer's instructions. You may use this machine year-round, but if you plan to store it for the winter, drain the gasoline as you would for a tiller. For both electric and gasoline-powered machines, be sure the hopper and discharge chute are cleared of all plant debris after each use.

Mowers

Until the end of World War II, the only lawn mower common in the United States was the push reel type, in which several revolving blades move against a single fixed blade, producing a neat trim. It did a fine job on small lawns, cutting evenly and quietly. For those with small, level lawns, the push reel is probably still the ideal lawn-cutting instrument. It is inexpensive, not difficult to push, nonpolluting, still produces a neat-looking lawn—and its gentle sound of metal kissing metal is music to the ears.

The popularity of the gasoline-powered rotary mower grew with the spread of large suburban lots in the postwar period. Lawns often were too large to be cut by hand. Power reel models were in favor for a while, but gradually lost out to the standard rotary mower, whose single blade revolves at a high rate of speed, literally ripping the tops off grass plants. It can easily handle rough terrain and knock down high weeds, while a reel mower cannot.

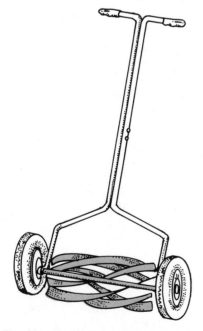

The old-fashioned push reel mower trims level grassy areas nicely, but requires lots of user energy.

MOWER SAFETY

According to the U.S. Consumer Products Safety Commission, power mowers cause more than 60,000 accidents each year. The whirling blades of a rotary mower can easily slice and crush human limbs. They can also propel rocks and other objects with awesome force. Following the manufacturer's safety precautions, and using old-fashioned common sense, will help to prevent most accidents.

Always wear safety goggles, long trousers, and heavy-duty work shoes or boots with nonslip soles when mowing. If using a gasoline-powered mower, wear ear plugs to prevent hearing loss. Never let anyone—children or adults—mow with their feet bare or while wearing shorts. Never pull a walk-behind mower toward you.

While the engine is running, never do anything but mow grass. If you pause to clean out the chute, empty the bag, or adjust the mowing height, always stop the engine first. If you ever have cause to look or reach under the housing, stop the engine *and* disconnect the spark plug, or unplug an electric model.

Never tamper with or disconnect the manufacturer's safety devices, even if it might save a few moments for you in the mowing process.

Before mowing, walk over the area to be mowed and remove any objects that could be kicked up by or damage the mower blade. Then keep a close eye on the area just in front of the mower as you work. With a walk-behind mower, always mow across an incline. But with a riding mower, ride up and down the incline.

A power mower is a common tool, easy to take for granted—but it is also a powerful machine capable of doing great harm if not used properly and with respect. Follow the rules, and insist that everyone in the family does the same.

Rotary mowers have cutting widths ranging from 18 to 24 inches and can be adjusted to cut grass at different heights. Some are self-propelled, a valuable feature if your lawn is large or sloping. Electric starters are appreciated by people with physical limitations that might preclude yanking on a cord. (Newer models use an overhead valve system—OHV—which virtually guarantees starting on the first or second pull.) A bagger is a valuable option, since it can be used to collect leaves in the fall. However, if you cut your lawn frequently and depend on grass clippings for nitrogen to feed your lawn, it's best to leave clippings on the lawn, where they'll decompose and return nutrients to the soil. A mulching mower has a blade that blows finely cut pieces of grass back onto the lawn, thus building up the lawn's organic matter while obviating any raking or bagging of clippings.

Electric rotary mowers are quiet and easy to maintain, but working around the cord which supplies power to the mower is a constant annoyance. Still, many urban homeowners with small lawns prefer them over noisy and fumy gasoline-powered machines.

Gasoline-powered motors are either two or four cycle. The former, which is less common, is more efficient and likely to last longer than the latter. You must mix gas and oil each time you refuel a two-cycle engine. A four-cycle engine has a separate crankcase; you must check the

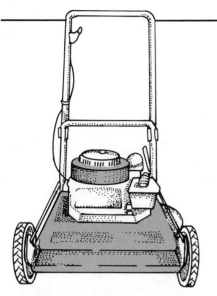

The gasoline-powered rotary mower is a standard for many homeowners.

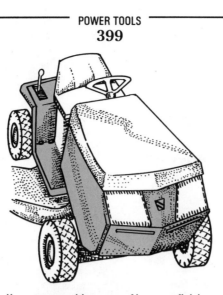

Homeowners with an acre of lawn can finish their mowing job in one hour using a riding mower with a 7-horsepower engine.

blades or shaft. And be sure to disconnect the spark plug or pull the electric plug before you work under the housing—every time.

Keep the air filter clean during the mowing season, following the manual directions. Clean the spark plug several times during the season, carefully scraping the tip clean and adjusting the gap to manual specifications. A plug should last two or three years and should be discarded when it becomes corroded or deformed.

Before putting the mower away for the winter, remove both gas and oil, clean it thoroughly, and sharpen the blade.

oil level regularly and change the oil at least once a season. Insufficient oil is the number one cause of lawn mower trouble.

A 7-horsepower riding mower with a 25-inch deck can mow an acre of lawn in an hour. An 8-horsepower model with a 32-inch deck can mow 1½ acres of grass in the same amount of time. But if your lawn is larger than 1½ acres, consider acquiring a small lawn or garden tractor, which would also be useful for many other jobs around your property. These have engines in the 15 to 25 horsepower range and power take-off (PTO) capability to drive a number of optional attachments such as a log splitter, chipper, snow blower, or generator.

Care and Maintenance

Routine care of your rotary mower will greatly improve both its performance and its life. Use the oil recommended by the manufacturer and change it according to schedule. Use fresh gasoline—never more than two months old—and be sure to get the kind recommended in the owner's manual. Generally, it's unleaded for four-cycle engines, leaded for two-cycle.

After every second or third use, clean out any debris that has lodged under the housing. Cut away any string that may have wrapped itself around

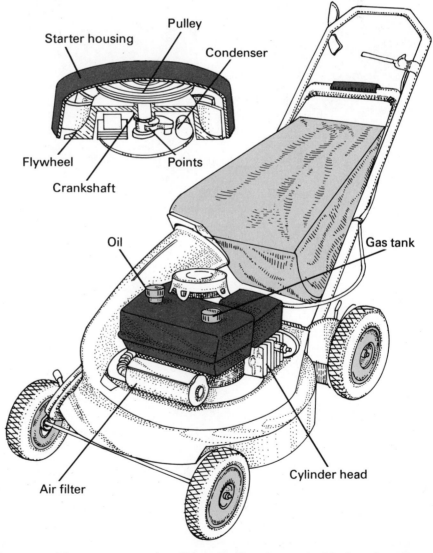

Proper care of the rotary mower engine will extend its life and ensure that it is always in working order. Read the owner's manual and familiarize yourself with the various parts of your mower.

USDA Hardiness Zone Map

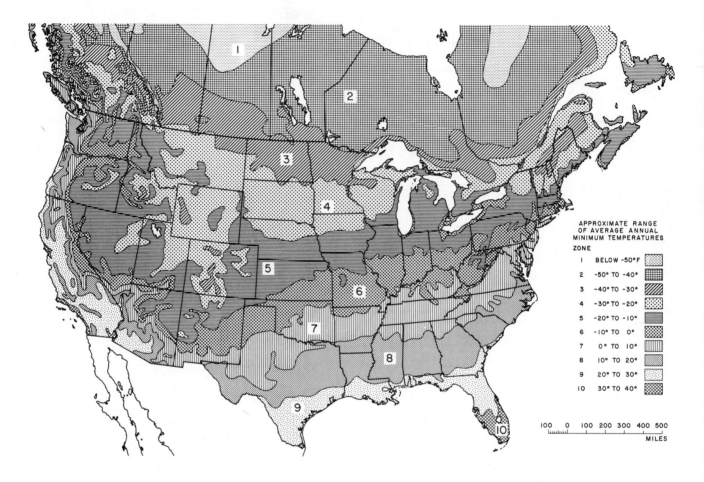

APPROXIMATE RANGE
OF AVERAGE ANNUAL
MINIMUM TEMPERATURES

ZONE		
1	BELOW -50°F	
2	-50° TO -40°	
3	-40° TO -30°	
4	-30° TO -20°	
5	-20° TO -10°	
6	-10° TO 0°	
7	0° TO 10°	
8	10° TO 20°	
9	20° TO 30°	
10	30° TO 40°	

100 0 100 200 300 400 500

MILES

Sources

General Gardening Equipment and Supplies

The following companies offer merchandise such as organic fertilizers, composting equipment, animal repellents and traps, beneficial insects and microbes, shredders, sprayers, tillers, row covers and shading materials, irrigation equipment, hand tools, and carts.

Amerind-MacKissic Co.
P.O. Box 111
Parker Ford, PA 19457

Bountiful Gardens
19550 Walker Rd.
Willits, CA 95490
Also offers organically grown herb and
vegetable seed.

Brookstone Co.
127 Vose Farm Rd.
Peterborough, NH 03458

Charley's Greenhouse Supply
1569 Memorial Hwy.
Mt. Vernon, WA 98273
Also offers hobby greenhouses and
supplies, indoor gardening aids, and
books.

The Clapper Co.
1121 Washington St.
W. Newton, MA 02165
Also offers garden ornaments, furniture,
and books.

Cumberland General Store
Rt. 3, Box 81
Crossville, TN 38555
Also offers equipment such as fruit
presses, corn grinders, shellers, and
beekeeping supplies.

Florist Products, Inc.
2242 N. Palmer Dr.
Schaumburg, IL 60173

Gardener's Supply Co.
128 Intervale Rd.
Burlington, VT 05401

Green Earth Organics
9422 144th St. E.
Puyallup, WA 98373

Harmony Farm Supply
P.O. Box 451
Graton, CA 95444
Also offers food dehydrators and other
food preservation equipment.

The Kinsman Co., Inc.
River Rd.
Point Pleasant, PA 18950
Also offers garden ornaments and equip-
ment such as apple grinders and fruit
presses.

Lehman's Hardware & Appliances
P.O. Box 41
Kidron, OH 44636
Also offers a large variety of kitchen
and canning tools, garden ornaments,
and lawn care equipment.

A. M. Leonard, Inc.
P.O. Box 816
Piqua, OH 45356

Mantis Mfg. Corp.
1458 County Line Rd.
Huntington Valley, PA 19006

The Natural Gardening Co.
217 San Anselmo Ave.
San Anselmo, CA 94960

Necessary Trading Co.
703 Salem Ave.
New Castle, VA 24127

Ohio Earth Food
13737 Duquette Ave. N.E.
Hartville, OH 44632

Organic Pest Management
P.O. Box 55267
Seattle, WA 98155

Peaceful Valley Farm Supply Co.
P.O. Box 2209
Grass Valley, CA 95945

The Plow and Hearth
301 Madison Rd.
Orange, VA 22960
Also offers garden ornaments and
furniture.

Ringer Corp.
9959 Valley View Rd.
Eden Prairie, MN 55344

Smith & Hawken
25 Corte Madera
Mill Valley, CA 94941
Also offers flower-arranging supplies,
garden ornaments, and furniture.

The Urban Farmer Store
2833 Vicente St.
San Francisco, CA 94116
Offers water-conserving irrigation systems and other supplies.

General Seed and Nursery Catalogs

The following companies offer a wide range of seeds, including vegetables, flowers, and herbs. Many also offer plants and some gardening supplies.

Abundant Life Seed Foundation
P.O. Box 772
Port Townsend, WA 98368
Offers naturally grown seeds of old-fashioned vegetables and flowers, as well as native plants.

Burgess Seed and Plant Co.
Dept. 91
905 Four Seasons Rd.
Bloomington, IL 61701
Offers primarily vegetable seeds.

W. Atlee Burpee & Co.
300 Park Ave.
Warminster, PA 18991

Farmer Seed and Nursery Co.
Faribault, MN 55021

Gurney Seed and Nursery Co.
Second & Capitol Streets
Yankton, SD 57078

Harris Seeds
P.O. Box 22960
Rochester, NY 14692

Hastings
1036 White St. S.W.
P.O. Box 115535
Atlanta, GA 30310
Specializes in plants for southern climates.

J.L. Hudson, Seedsman
P.O. Box 1058
Redwood City, CA 94064

Johnny's Selected Seeds
RFD 1, Box 2580
Foss Hill Rd.
Albion, ME 04910
Offers primarily vegetable seeds, specializing in short-season types.

J. W. Jung Seeds & Nursery
335 S. High St.
Randolph, WI 53957

Orol Ledden & Sons
Center & Atlantic Aves.
P.O. Box 7
Sewell, NJ 08080

Earl May Seed & Nursery
208 N. Elm St.
Shenandoah, IA 51603

Mellinger's, Inc.
2310 W. South Range Rd.
North Lima, OH 44452
Also offers a large selection of trees and shrubs.

Park Seed Co.
Cokesbury Rd.
Greenwood, SC 29647

Stokes Seeds, Inc.
P.O. Box 548
Buffalo, NY 14240

Thompson & Morgan
P.O. Box 1308
Jackson, NJ 08527

General Flower and Plant Catalogs

The following companies offer a wide selection of perennials. Many also offer herbs, ornamental grasses, rock garden plants, and other ornamentals.

Kurt Bluemel, Inc.
2740 Greene Ln.
Baldwin, MD 21013
Specializes in ornamental grasses.

Bluestone Perennials
7211 Middle Ridge Rd.
Madison, OH 44057

W. Atlee Burpee & Co.
300 Park Ave.
Warminster, PA 18991

Busse Gardens
Rt. 2, Box 238
Cokato, MN 55321

Carroll Gardens
P.O. Box 310
Westminster, MD 21157

The Crownsville Nursery
P.O. Box 797
Crownsville, MD 21032
Offers many rare and unusual cultivars.

Emlong Nurseries, Inc.
P.O. Box 236
Stevensville, MI 49127

Henry Field Seed & Nursery Co.
Shenandoah, IA 51602
Fruits and ornamentals.

Heritage Gardens
1 Meadow Ridge Rd.
Shenandoah, IA 51601

Inter-State Nurseries
P.O. Box 208
Hamburg, IA 51640

Kelly Nurseries
P.O. Box 800
Dansville, NY 14437
Fruits and ornamentals.

Klehm Nursery
Rt. 5, Box 197
Penny Rd.
South Barrington, IL 60010

Park Seed Co.
Cokesbury Rd.
Greenwood, SC 29647

Spring Hill Nurseries
6523 N. Galena Rd.
P.O. Box 1758
Peoria, IL 61632

Andre Viette Farm and Nursery
Rt. 1, Box 16
Fishersville, VA 22939

Wayside Gardens
1 Garden Ln.
Hodges, SC 29695

We-Du Nurseries
Rt. 5, Box 724
Marion, NC 28752

White Flower Farm
Litchfield, CT 06759

Bulbs

The following companies offer a variety of spring- and summer-blooming bulbs.

Breck's
6523 N. Galena Rd.
P.O. Box 1758
Peoria, IL 61632

W. Atlee Burpee & Co.
300 Park Ave.
Warminster, PA 18991

Dutch Gardens
P.O. Box 200
Adelphia, NJ 07710

McClure & Zimmerman
108 W. Winnebago St.
P.O. Box 368
Friesland, WI 53935

Park Seed Co.
Cokesbury Rd.
Greenwood, SC 29647

John Scheepers, Inc.
R.D. 6
Phillipsburg Rd.
Middletown, NY 10940

Smith & Hawken
25 Corte Madera
Mill Valley, CA 94941

Van Bourgondien Bros.
P.O. Box A
Babylon, NY 11702

Wildflowers

For a list of nurseries that offer only propagated, not wild-collected, plants send a self-addressed, stamped envelope to the New England Wild Flower Society, Inc., Garden in the Woods, Hemenway Rd., Framingham, MA 01701. Request current information on their publication *Nursery Sources: Native Plants and Wildflowers.*

Herbs and Flower Crafts

In addition to the General Flower and Plant Catalogs, many of which list herbs, the following companies also offer plants, seeds, and products for herbs, herb crafts, and flower crafts.

Caprilands Herb Farm
534 Silver St.
Coventry, CT 06238
Over 300 herb plants and seeds.

Fox Hill Farms
440 W. Michigan Ave.
Box 9
Parma, MI 49269
Large selection of herb plants.

Golden Meadows Herbal Emporium
431 S. St. Augustine
Dallas, TX 75217
Over 900 dried herbs and spices.

Goodwin Creek Secret Garden
P.O. Box 83
Williams, OR 97544
Plants and seeds for dried flowers and
    native American herbs.

Herb Gathering, Inc.
5742 Kenwood Ave.
Kansas City, MO 64110
Culinary herb and French gourmet veg-
    etable seeds as well as seeds for
    everlastings and herb crafts.

Meadowbrook Herb Garden
Rt. 138
Wyoming, RI 02898
Organically grown herbs, seeds, garden
    and pet supplies, and cosmetics.

Nichols Garden Nursery
1190 N. Pacific Hwy.
Albany, OR 97321
Offers herb seeds and plants, as well as
    many other unusual vegetables,
    ornamentals, everlastings, and wild-
    flowers. Also has spices, potpourri,
    and teas.

Sandy Mush Herb Nursery
Rt. 2
Surrett Cove Rd.
Leicester, NC 28748
Over 600 herb plants, scented geraniums,
    dye plants, and gourmet vegetables.

Tom Thumb Workshops
Rt. 13
P.O. Box 357
Mappsville, VA 23407
Offers herbs, spices, potpourri and fra-
    grance supplies, books, wreath kits,
    gifts, and everlastings.

Wrenwood
Rt. 4, Box 361
Berkeley Springs, WV 25411
Large selection of herbs and perennials,
    and rock garden plants.

Roses

Antique Rose Emporium
Rt. 5
Box 143
Brenham, TX 77833

Historical Roses
1657 W. Jackson St.
Painesville, OH 44077

Jackson & Perkins Co.
1 Rose Ln.
Medford, OR 97501

Krider Nurseries
303 W. Bristol
P.O. Box 29
Middlebury, IN 46540

Nor'East Miniature Roses, Inc.
58 Hammond St.
Rowley, MA 01969

Roses of Yesterday & Today
802 Brown's Valley Rd.
Watsonville, CA 95076
Offers old, rare, and unusual roses.

Water Gardens

Lilypons Water Gardens
6800 Lilypons Rd.
P.O. Box 10
Lilypons, MD 21717

Slocum Water Gardens
1101 Cypress Gardens Blvd.
Winter Haven, FL 33880

William Tricker, Inc.
7125 Tanglewood Dr.
Independence, OH 44131

Paradise Water Gardens
14 May St.
Whitman, MA 02382

Van Ness Water Gardens
2460 N. Euclid Ave.
Upland, CA 91786

Rock Garden Plants

Many of the companies listed under General Flower and Plant Catalogs offer plants appropriate for a rock garden. The following companies specialize in alpines, perennials, and dwarf shrubs for rock gardens.

Alpine Plants
P.O. Box 245
Tahoe Vista, CA 95732

Rice Creek Gardens, Inc.
1315 66th Ave. N.E.
Minneapolis, MN 55432

We-Du Nurseries
Rt. 5, Box 724
Marion, NC 28752

Daystar
Rt. 2, Box 250
Litchfield, ME 04350

Rocknoll Nursery
9210 U.S. 50
Hillsboro, OH 45133

Montrose Nursery
P.O. Box 957
Hillsborough, NC 27278

Siskiyou Rare Plant Nursery
2825 Cummings Rd.
Medford, OR 97501

Fruits and Berries

Most General Seed and Nursery Catalog companies offer tree fruits, such as apples, and small fruits, such as brambles. The following companies are specialists in these areas.

Adams County Nursery, Inc.
Nursery Rd.
P.O. Box 108
Aspers, PA 17304
Fruit trees.

Applesource
Tom Vorbeck
Rt. 1
Chapin, IL 62628
Rare apple cultivars; offers sample
    apples for tasting.

Country Heritage Nursery
P.O. Box 536
Hartford, MI 49057
Mainly small fruits, some trees.

Ahrens Nursery
R.R. 1
Huntingburg, IN 47542
Mainly small fruits, some fruit trees,
    evergreens, garden supplies.

Bear Creek Nursery
P.O. Box 411
Northport, WA 99157
Fruit trees; scionwood, summer budwood,
    bench grafts, budded trees, rootstocks.

Cumberland Valley Nurseries, Inc.
P.O. Box 471
McMinnville, TN 37110
Fruit trees.

Allen Co.
P.O. Box 310
Fruitland, MD 21826
Small fruits.

C & O Nursery Co.
P.O. Box 116
Wenatchee, WA 98807
Fruit trees.

Henry Leuthardt Nurseries, Inc.
P.O. Box 666
E. Moriches, NY 11940
Offers old and new cultivars of fruit
    trees, including espaliered specimens,
    along with small fruits.

Makielski Berry Nursery
7130 Platt Rd.
Ypsilanti, MI 48197
Small fruits.

J. E. Miller Nurseries, Inc.
5060 W. Lake Rd.
Canandaigua, NY 14424
Mainly fruits and ornamentals.

New York State Fruit Testing
    Cooperative Association, Inc.
P.O. Box 462
Geneva, NY 14456
Also offers scionwood.

Northwoods Nursery
28696 S. Cramer Rd.
Molalla, OR 97038
Mainly fruits; also trees and shrubs.

Rayner Bros., Inc.
P.O. Box 1617
Salisbury, MD 21801
Mainly small fruits, some fruit trees and
    evergreens.

St. Lawrence Nurseries
R.D. 2
Potsdam, NY 13676
Mainly fruits and nuts; grown organically.

Southmeadow Fruit Gardens
Lakeside, MI 49116
Choice and unusual fruit varieties.

Stark Bro's Nurseries & Orchards Co.
Louisiana, Missouri 63353
Fruits and ornamental trees and shrubs.

Waynesboro Nurseries, Inc.
Waynesboro, VA 22980
Fruits, nuts, and ornamentals.

Trees and Shrubs

Many of the companies listed under General Seed and Nursery Catalogs and Fruits and Berries offer ornamental trees and shrubs. The following companies offer seed, seedlings, or transplants of such plants.

Appalachian Gardens
P.O. Box 82
Waynesboro, PA 17268

Cascade Forestry Service
Rt. 1
Cascade, IA 52033

The Cummins Garden
22 Robertsville Rd.
Marlboro, NJ 07746
Specializes in rhododendrons and azaleas.

Forestfarm
990 Tetherow Rd.
Williams, OR 97544

Foxborough Nursery, Inc.
3611 Miller Rd.
Street, MD 21154
Very extensive selection.

Girard Nurseries
P.O. Box 428
Geneva, OH 44041

Greer Gardens
1280 Goodpasture Island Rd.
Eugene, OR 97401
Large selection of rhododendrons and
    azaleas; also trees and shrubs.

Louisiana Nursery
Rt. 7, Box 43
Opelousas, LA 70570
Large selection of magnolias along with
    trees, shrubs, perennials, and exotics.

Musser Forests, Inc.
Rt. 119 North
P.O. Box 340
Indiana, PA 15701

Weston Nurseries
East Main St.
Rt. 135
P.O. Box 186
Hopkinton, MA 01748

Woodlanders, Inc.
1128 Colleton Ave.
Aiken, SC 29801
Large selection of native trees and
    shrubs along with hard-to-find exotic
    species and cultivars.

Houseplants and Container Gardens

Davidson-Wilson Greenhouses
Rt. 2, Box 168
Crawfordsville, IN 47933
Specializes in geraniums and African
    violets.

Indoor Gardening Supplies
Box 40567
Detroit, MI 48240
Plant stands, seed starters, light fixtures,
    accessories, and lamps.

K & L Cactus Nursery
12712 Stockton Blvd.
Galt, CA 95632
Offers cacti and succulents.

Kartuz Greenhouses
1408 Sunset Dr.
Vista, CA 92083
Specializes in gesneriads, begonias, and
    terrarium plants.

Logee's Greenhouses
141 North St.
Danielson, CT 06239
Exotic flowering plants, rare jasmines,
    begonias, orchids, geraniums, herbs,
    and vines.

Merry Gardens
P.O. Box 595
Camden, ME 04843

Recommended Reading

The Basics

Bristow, Alec. *The Practical Guide to Successful Gardening.* Salem, N.H.: Salem House, 1985.

Bubel, Nancy. *The New Seed-Starter's Handbook.* Emmaus, Pa.: Rodale Press, 1988.

Bush-Brown, James and Louise. *America's Garden Book.* rev. ed. New York: Charles Scribner's Sons, 1980.

Calkins, Carroll C., ed. *Reader's Digest Illustrated Guide to Gardening.* Pleasantville, N.Y.: The Reader's Digest Association, 1978.

Carr, Anna. *Rodale's Color Handbook of Garden Insects.* Emmaus, Pa.: Rodale Press, 1979.

Damrosch, Barbara. *The Garden Primer.* New York: Workman Publishing, 1988.

Hartmann, Hudson T., and Dale E. Kester. *Plant Propagation: Principles and Practices.* 4th ed. Englewood Cliffs, N.J.: Prentice-Hall, 1983.

Reilly, Ann. *Park's Success with Seeds.* Greenwood, S.C.: Geo. W. Park Seed Co., 1978.

Seddon, George, and Andrew Bicknell. *Plants Plus: A Comprehensive Guide to Successful Propagation of House and Garden Plants.* Emmaus, Pa.: Rodale Press, 1987.

Smith, Miranda, and Anna Carr. *Rodale's Garden Insect, Disease and Weed Identification Guide.* Emmaus, Pa.: Rodale Press, 1988.

Stein, Deni W. *Ortho's Complete Guide to Successful Gardening.* San Francisco: Ortho Books, Chevron Chemical Co., 1983.

Westcott, Cynthia. *The Gardener's Bug Book.* Garden City, N.Y.: Doubleday & Co., 1973.

———. *The Plant Disease Handbook.* 3d ed. New York: Van Nostrand Reinhold Co., 1971.

Wirth, Thomas. *The Victory Garden Landscape Guide.* Boston: Little, Brown & Co., 1984.

Wyman, Donald. *Wyman's Gardening Encyclopedia.* 2d ed. New York: Macmillan Co., 1986.

Yepsen, Roger B., Jr., ed. *The Encyclopedia of Natural Insect and Disease Control.* Emmaus, Pa.: Rodale Press, 1984.

Flowers

Austin, Richard L. *Wild Gardening: Strategies and Procedures Using Native Plantings.* New York: Simon and Schuster, 1986.

Ball, Jeff, and Charles O. Cresson. *The 60-Minute Flower Garden.* Emmaus, Pa.: Rodale Press, 1987.

Ball, Jeff and Liz. *Rodale's Flower Garden Problem Solver.* Emmaus, Pa.: Rodale Press, 1990.

Brookes, John. *The Garden Book.* New York: Crown Publishers, 1984.

———. *The Small Garden Book.* New York: Crown Publishers, 1984.

Carr, Anna, et al. *Rodale's Illustrated Encyclopedia of Herbs.* Emmaus, Pa.: Rodale Press, 1987.

Cox, Jeff and Marilyn. *The Perennial Garden: Color Harmonies through the Seasons.* Emmaus, Pa.: Rodale Press, 1985.

Fell, Derek, et al. *The Complete Garden Planning Manual.* Los Angeles: HP Books, 1989.

Hobhouse, Penelope. *Color in Your Garden.* Boston: Little, Brown & Co., 1985.

Leighton, Phebe, and Calvin Simonds. *The New American Landscape Gardener.* Emmaus, Pa.: Rodale Press, 1987.

Loewer, Peter. *The Annual Garden.* Emmaus, Pa.: Rodale Press, 1988.

———. *Gardens by Design: Step-by-Step Plans for 12 Imaginative Gardens.* Emmaus, Pa.: Rodale Press, 1986.

———. *A Year of Flowers.* Emmaus, Pa.: Rodale Press, 1989.

Martin, Laura C. *The Wildflower Meadow Book.* Charlotte, N.C.: East Wood Press, 1986.

Oster, Maggie. *Gifts and Crafts from the Garden: Over 100 Easy-to-Make Projects.* Emmaus, Pa.: Rodale Press, 1988.

Rogers, Barbara Radcliffe. *The Encyclopedia of Everlastings.* New York: Weidenfeld & Nicolson, 1988.

Squire, David, and Jane Newdick. *The Scented Garden.* Emmaus, Pa.: Rodale Press, 1988.

Taylor's Guide to Garden Design. Boston: Houghton Mifflin Co., 1988.

Taylor, Norman. *Taylor's Guide to Annuals.* rev. ed. Boston: Houghton Mifflin Co., 1986.

———. *Taylor's Guide to Bulbs.* rev. ed. Boston: Houghton Mifflin Co., 1986.

———. *Taylor's Guide to Perennials.* rev. ed. Boston: Houghton Mifflin Co., 1986.

Thorpe, Patricia. *Everlastings: The Complete Book of Dried Flowers.* New York: Facts on File, 1985.

Westland, Pamela. *Decorating with Wild Flowers.* Emmaus, Pa.: Rodale Press, 1976.

The Food Garden

Ball, Jeff. *Jeff Ball's 60-Minute Garden.* Emmaus, Pa.: Rodale Press, 1985.

———. *Rodale's Garden Problem Solver: Vegetables, Fruits, and Herbs.* Emmaus, Pa.: Rodale Press, 1988.

Bartholomew, Mel. *Square Foot Gardening.* Emmaus, Pa.: Rodale Press, 1981.

Bilderback, Diane E., and Dorothy Hinshaw Patent. *Backyard Fruits & Berries.* Emmaus, Pa.: Rodale Press, 1984.

Coleman, Eliot. *The New Organic Grower: A Master's Manual of Tools and Techniques for the Home and Market Gardener.* Chelsea, Vt.: Chelsea Green Publishing Co., 1989.

Cox, Jeff, and the Editors of *Rodale's Organic Gardening* magazine. *How to Grow Vegetables Organically.* Emmaus, Pa.: Rodale Press, 1988.

Creasy, Rosalind. *The Complete Book of Edible Landscaping.* San Francisco: Sierra Club Books, 1982.

———. *The Gardener's Handbook of Edible Plants.* San Francisco: Sierra Club Books, 1986.

DeWolf, Gordon P., Jr. *Taylor's Guide to Vegetables and Herbs.* Boston: Houghton Mifflin Co., 1987.

Gesshert, Kate Rogers. *The Beautiful Food Garden: Creative Landscaping with Vegetables, Herbs, Fruits, and Flowers.* Pownal, Vt.: Storey Communications, 1987.

Hill, Lewis. *Fruits and Berries for the Home Garden.* Pownal, Vt.: Storey Communications, 1980.

Hunt, Marjorie B., and Brenda Bortz. *High-Yield Gardening.* Emmaus, Pa.: Rodale Press, 1986.

National Gardening Association Staff. *Gardening: The Complete Guide to Growing America's Favorite Fruits and Vegetables.* Reading, Mass.: Addison-Wesley Publishing Co., 1986.

Newcomb, Duane. *The Backyard Vegetable Factory: Super Yields from Small Spaces.* Emmaus, Pa.: Rodale Press, 1988.

Rodale Press Editors. *The Organic Gardener's Complete Guide to Vegetables and Fruits.* Emmaus, Pa.: Rodale Press, 1982.

Thomson, Bob. *The New Victory Garden.* Boston: Little, Brown & Co., 1987.

Whealy, Kent, ed. *Fruit, Berry and Nut Inventory.* Decorah, Iowa: Seed Saver Publications, 1989.

Winkler, A. J., et. al. *General Viticulture.* 2nd ed., rev. Richmond, Calif.: University of California Press, 1974.

Lawns and Groundcovers

Franklin, Stuart. *Building a Healthy Lawn: A Safe and Natural Approach.* Pownal, Vt.: Storey Communications, 1988.

MacCaskey, Michael. *Lawns and Ground Covers: How to Select, Grow and Enjoy.* Tucson, Ariz.: HP Books, 1982.

Schultz, Warren. *The Chemical-Free Lawn: The Newest Varieties and Techniques to Grow Lush, Hardy Grass.* Emmaus, Pa.: Rodale Press, 1989.

Taylor's Guide Staff. *Taylor's Guide to Ground Covers, Vines and Grasses.* Boston: Houghton Mifflin Co., 1987.

Trees and Shrubs

Baumgardt, John Philip. *How to Prune Almost Everything.* New York: William Morrow & Co., 1968.

Brickell, Christopher. *Pruning.* New York: Simon & Schuster, 1988.

Davis, Brian. *The Gardener's Illustrated Encyclopedia of Trees and Shrubs.* Emmaus, Pa.: Rodale Press, 1987.

Dirr, Michael A. *Manual of Woody Landscape Plants.* 3rd ed. Champaign, Ill.: Stipes Publishing Co., 1983.

Elias, Thomas S. *The Complete Trees of North America Field Guide and Natural History.* New York: Crown Publishers, 1987.

Fell, Derek. *Trees and Shrubs.* Tucson, Ariz.: HP Books, 1986.

Hill, Lewis. *Pruning Simplified.* updated ed. Pownal, Vt.: Storey Communications, 1986.

The Horticultural Committee of the Garden Club of America. *Plants That Merit Attention: Trees.* Portland, Oreg.: Timber Press, 1984.

Johnson, Hugh. *Hugh Johnson's Encyclopedia of Trees.* 2d ed. New York: Gallery Books, 1984.

Schopmeyer, C.S., Technical Coordinator. *Seeds of Woody Plants in the United States.* Washington, D.C.: Forest Service, U.S. Department of Agriculture, Handbook No. 450, 1948.

Shigo, Alex L. *A New Tree Biology: Facts, Photos, and Philosophies on Trees and Their Problems and Proper Care.* 2d ed. Durham, N.H.: Shigo & Trees Associates, 1989.

————. *A New Tree Biology Dictionary: Terms, Topics and Treatments for Trees and Their Problems and Proper Care.* 2d ed. Durham, N.H.: Shigo & Trees Associates, 1989.

Stebbins, Robert L., and Michael MacCasky. *Pruning: How to Guide for Gardeners.* Tucson, Ariz.: HP Books, 1983.

Taylor's Guide Staff. *Taylor's Guide to Shrubs.* Boston: Houghton Mifflin Co., 1987.

Taylor's Guide to Trees. Boston: Houghton Mifflin Co., 1988.

Wyman, Donald. *Shrubs and Vines for American Gardens.* enl. rev. ed. New York: Macmillan Co., 1969.

Houseplants and Container Gardens

Beckett, Kenneth A. *The RHS Encyclopedia of House Plants Including Greenhouse Plants.* Topsfield, Mass.: Salem House Publishers, 1987.

Brookes, John. *The Indoor Garden Book.* New York: Crown Publishers, 1986.

DeWolf, Gordon P., Jr. *Taylor's Guide to Houseplants.* Boston: Houghton Mifflin Co., 1987.

Halpin, Anne M. *Rodale's Encyclopedia of Indoor Gardening.* Emmaus, Pa.: Rodale Press, 1980.

Herwig, Rob. *The Good Housekeeping Encyclopedia of House Plants.* New York: Hearst Books, 1984.

Powell, Charles C., and Donald M. Vining. *Ortho's Complete Guide to Successful Houseplants.* San Francisco: Ortho Books, Chevron Chemical Company, 1984.

Reader's Digest Editors. *Reader's Digest Success with House Plants.* Pleasantville, N.Y.: The Reader's Digest Association, 1979.

Seddon, George, Andrew Bicknell, and Elizabeth Dickson. *The Essential Guide to Perfect Houseplants.* New York: Summit Books, 1984.

Squire, David, and Peter McHoy. *The Book of Houseplants.* London: Octopus Books, 1978.

Tools

Branch, Diana S., ed. *Tools for Homesteaders, Gardeners, and Small-Scale Farmers.* Emmaus, Pa.: Rodale Press, 1978.

Hall, Walter. *Barnacle Parp's Guide to Garden and Yard Power Tools: Selection, Maintenance and Repair.* Emmaus, Pa.: Rodale Press, 1983.

Index

Page references in *italic* indicate illustrations.

Rodale Press, Inc., publishes RODALE'S ORGANIC GARDENING,
the all-time favorite gardening magazine.
For information on how to order your subscription,
write to RODALE'S ORGANIC GARDENING, Emmaus, PA 18098.